New Perspectives on

Microsoft® Office PowerPoint® 2007

Comprehensive

What is the Microsoft Business Certification Program?

The Microsoft Business Certification Program enables candidates to show that they have something exceptional to offer – proven expertise in Microsoft Office programs. The two certification tracks allow candidates to choose how they want to exhibit their skills, either through validating skills within a specific Microsoft product or taking their knowledge to the next level and combining Microsoft programs to show that they can apply multiple skill sets to complete more complex office tasks. Recognized by businesses and schools around the world, over 3 million certifications have been obtained in over 100 different countries. The Microsoft Business Certification Program is the only Microsoft-approved certification program of its kind.

What is the Microsoft Certified Application Specialist Certification?

The Microsoft Certified Application Specialist Certification exams focus on validating specific skill sets within each of the Microsoft® Office system programs. The candidate can choose which exam(s) they want to take according to which skills they want to validate. The available Application Specialist exams include:
- Using Windows Vista™
- Using Microsoft® Office Word 2007
- Using Microsoft® Office Excel® 2007
- Using Microsoft® Office PowerPoint® 2007
- Using Microsoft® Office Access 2007
- Using Microsoft® Office Outlook® 2007

What is the Microsoft Certified Application Professional Certification?

The Microsoft Certified Application Professional Certification exams focus on a candidate's ability to use the 2007 Microsoft® Office system to accomplish industry-agnostic functions, for example Budget Analysis and Forecasting, or Content Management and Collaboration. The available Application Professional exams currently include:
- Organizational Support
- Creating and Managing Presentations
- Content Management and Collaboration
- Budget Analysis and Forecasting

What do the Microsoft Business Certification Vendor of Approved Courseware logos represent?

The logos validate that the courseware has been approved by the Microsoft® Business Certification Vendor program and that these courses cover objectives that will be included in the relevant exam. It also means that after utilizing this courseware, you may be prepared to pass the exams required to become a Microsoft Certified Application Specialist or Microsoft Certified Application Professional.

For more information:

To learn more about Microsoft Certified Application Specialist or Professional exams, visit
www.microsoft.com/learning/msbc.
To learn about other Microsoft Certified Application Specialist approved courseware from Course Technology, visit
www.course.com.
*The availability of Microsoft Certified Application exams varies by Microsoft Office program, program version and language.
Visit www.microsoft.com/learning for exam availability.
Microsoft, the Office Logo, Outlook, and PowerPoint are either registered trademarks or trademarks of Microsoft Corporation in the United States and/or other countries. The Microsoft Certified Application Specialist and Microsoft Certified Application Professional Logos are used under license from Microsoft Corporation.

New Perspectives on

Microsoft® Office PowerPoint® 2007

Comprehensive

Beverly B. Zimmerman
Brigham Young University

S. Scott Zimmerman
Brigham Young University

COURSE TECHNOLOGY
CENGAGE Learning™

Australia • Brazil • Japan • Korea • Mexico • Singapore • Spain • United Kingdom • United States

New Perspectives on Microsoft Office PowerPoint 2007—Comprehensive

Acquisitions Editor: Kristina Matthews

Senior Product Manager: Kathy Finnegan

Product Manager: Erik Herman

Associate Product Manager: Brandi Henson

Editorial Assistant: Leigh Robbins

Senior Marketing Manager: Joy Stark

Marketing Coordinator: Jennifer Hankin

Developmental Editor: Katherine T. Pinard

Senior Content Project Manager: Jennifer Goguen McGrail

Composition: GEX Publishing Services

Text Designer: Steve Deschene

Cover Designer: Elizabeth Paquin

Cover Art: Bill Brown

For product information and technology assistance, contact us at
Cengage Learning Academic Resource Center, 1-800-423-0563

For permission to use material from this text or product, submit all requests online at **www.cengage.com/permissions**
Further permissions questions can be emailed to
permissionrequest@cengage.com

ISBN-13: 978-1-4239-0593-6
ISBN-10: 1-4239-0593-8

Course Technology Cengage Learning
25 Thomson Place
Boston, MA, 02210
USA

Cengage Learning products are represented in Canada by Nelson Education, Ltd.

For your lifelong learning solutions, visit **course.cengage.com**

Visit our corporate website at **www.cengage.com**

Printed in the United States of America
2 3 4 5 6 7 8 9 RRD-WI 11 10 09 08 07

Preface

The New Perspectives Series' critical-thinking, problem-solving approach is the ideal way to prepare students to transcend point-and-click skills and take advantage of all that Microsoft Office 2007 has to offer.

In developing the New Perspectives Series for Microsoft Office 2007, our goal was to create books that give students the software concepts and practical skills they need to succeed beyond the classroom. We've updated our proven case-based pedagogy with more practical content to make learning skills more meaningful to students.

With the New Perspectives Series, students understand *why* they are learning *what* they are learning, and are fully prepared to apply their skills to real-life situations.

"I really love the Margin Tips, which add 'tricks of the trade' to students' skills package. In addition, the Reality Check exercises provide for practical application of students' knowledge. I can't wait to use them in the classroom when we adopt Office 2007."

—Terry Morse Colucci
Institute of Technology, Inc.

About This Book

This book provides comprehensive coverage of the new Microsoft Office PowerPoint 2007 software, and includes the following:

- A new "Getting Started with Microsoft Office 2007" tutorial that familiarizes students with the new Office 2007 features and user interface
- Coverage of the most important basic PowerPoint skills—planning and creating a presentation, inserting and modifying text, applying and using graphics, and creating and editing tables, diagrams, and shapes—as well as the exciting new features of PowerPoint 2007, including design themes, Live Preview, and SmartArt
- Instruction on customizing presentations, including creating custom design themes, applying graphics and sounds, using SmartArt to create and animate diagrams, adding slide transitions, and adding custom animations
- Guidance in how to integrate PowerPoint with other programs, share presentations, and save presentations in other formats such as PDF files and encrypted files
- Two Presentation Concepts tutorials that provide detailed information on planning, developing, and giving a presentation
- New business case scenarios throughout, which provide a rich and realistic context for students to apply the concepts and skills presented
- Certification requirements for the Microsoft Certified Application Specialist exam, "Using Microsoft® Office PowerPoint® 2007"

System Requirements

This book assumes a typical installation of Microsoft Office PowerPoint 2007 and Microsoft Windows Vista Ultimate with the Aero feature turned off (or Windows Vista Home Premium or Business edition). Note that you can also complete the tutorials in this book using Windows XP; you will notice only minor differences if you are using Windows XP. Refer to the tutorial "Getting Started with Microsoft Office 2007" for Tips noting these differences. The browser used in this book for any steps that require a browser is Internet Explorer 7.

The New Perspectives Approach

Context

Each tutorial begins with a problem presented in a "real-world" case that is meaningful to students. The case sets the scene to help students understand what they will do in the tutorial.

Hands-on Approach

Each tutorial is divided into manageable sessions that combine reading and hands-on, step-by-step work. Colorful screenshots help guide students through the steps. **Trouble?** tips anticipate common mistakes or problems to help students stay on track and continue with the tutorial.

InSight

InSight Boxes

New for Office 2007! InSight boxes offer expert advice and best practices to help students better understand how to work with the software. With the information provided in the InSight boxes, students achieve a deeper understanding of the concepts behind the software features and skills.

Tip

Margin Tips

New for Office 2007! Margin Tips provide helpful hints and shortcuts for more efficient use of the software. The Tips appear in the margin at key points throughout each tutorial, giving students extra information when and where they need it.

Reality Check

Reality Checks

New for Office 2007! Comprehensive, open-ended Reality Check exercises give students the opportunity to practice skills by creating practical, real-world documents, such as resumes and budgets, which they are likely to use in their everyday lives at school, home, or work.

Review

In New Perspectives, retention is a key component to learning. At the end of each session, a series of Quick Check questions helps students test their understanding of the concepts before moving on. Each tutorial also contains an end-of-tutorial summary and a list of key terms for further reinforcement.

Apply

Assessment

Engaging and challenging Review Assignments and Case Problems have always been a hallmark feature of the New Perspectives Series. Colorful icons and brief descriptions accompany the exercises, making it easy to understand, at a glance, both the goal and level of challenge a particular assignment holds.

Reference Window
Task Reference

Reference

While contextual learning is excellent for retention, there are times when students will want a high-level understanding of how to accomplish a task. Within each tutorial, Reference Windows appear before a set of steps to provide a succinct summary and preview of how to perform a task. In addition, a complete Task Reference at the back of the book provides quick access to information on how to carry out common tasks. Finally, each book includes a combination Glossary/Index to promote easy reference of material.

Our Complete System of Instruction

Coverage To Meet Your Needs

Whether you're looking for just a small amount of coverage or enough to fill a semester-long class, we can provide you with a textbook that meets your needs.

- Brief books typically cover the essential skills in just 2 to 4 tutorials.
- Introductory books build and expand on those skills and contain an average of 5 to 8 tutorials.
- Comprehensive books are great for a full-semester class, and contain 9 to 12+ tutorials.

So if the book you're holding does not provide the right amount of coverage for you, there's probably another offering available. Go to our Web site or contact your Course Technology sales representative to find out what else we offer.

Student Online Companion

This book has an accompanying online companion Web site designed to enhance learning. This Web site includes:

- Internet Assignments for selected tutorials
- Student Data Files
- PowerPoint presentations

CourseCasts – Learning on the Go. Always available…always relevant.

Want to keep up with the latest technology trends relevant to you? Visit our site to find a library of podcasts, CourseCasts, featuring a "CourseCast of the Week," and download them to your mp3 player at http://coursecasts.course.com.

Our fast-paced world is driven by technology. You know because you're an active participant—always on the go, always keeping up with technological trends, and always learning new ways to embrace technology to power your life.

Ken Baldauf, host of CourseCasts, is a faculty member of the Florida State University Computer Science Department where he is responsible for teaching technology classes to thousands of FSU students each year. Ken is an expert in the latest technology trends; he gathers and sorts through the most pertinent news and information for CourseCasts so your students can spend their time enjoying technology, rather than trying to figure it out. Open or close your lecture with a discussion based on the latest CourseCast.

Visit us at http://coursecasts.course.com to learn on the go!

Instructor Resources

We offer more than just a book. We have all the tools you need to enhance your lectures, check students' work, and generate exams in a new, easier-to-use and completely revised package. This book's Instructor's Manual, ExamView testbank, PowerPoint presentations, data files, solution files, figure files, and a sample syllabus are all available on a single CD-ROM or for downloading at www.course.com.

Skills Assessment and Training

SAM 2007 helps bridge the gap between the classroom and the real world by allowing students to train and test on important computer skills in an active, hands-on environment.

SAM 2007's easy-to-use system includes powerful interactive exams, training or projects on critical applications such as Word, Excel, Access, PowerPoint, Outlook, Windows, the Internet, and much more. SAM simulates the application environment, allowing students to demonstrate their knowledge and think through the skills by performing real-world tasks.

Designed to be used with the New Perspectives Series, SAM 2007 includes built-in page references so students can print helpful study guides that match the New Perspectives textbooks used in class. Powerful administrative options allow instructors to schedule exams and assignments, secure tests, and run reports with almost limitless flexibility.

Blackboard

Online Content

Blackboard is the leading distance learning solution provider and class-management platform today. Course Technology has partnered with Blackboard to bring you premium online content. Content for use with *New Perspectives on Microsoft Office PowerPoint 2007, Comprehensive* is available in a Blackboard Course Cartridge and may include topic reviews, case projects, review questions, test banks, practice tests, custom syllabi, and more.

Course Technology also has solutions for several other learning management systems. Please visit http://www.course.com today to see what's available for this title.

Acknowledgments

The authors would like to thank the following reviewers for their valuable feedback on this book: Candice Spangler, Columbus State Community College, and Barbara Tollinger, Sinclair Community College. We also thank the competent and conscientious team at Course Technology: Kristina Matthews, Acquisitions Editor; Brandi Henson, Associate Product Manager; Leigh Robbins, Editorial Assistant; Jennifer Goguen McGrail, Senior Content Project Manager; Christian Kunciw, Manuscript Quality Assurance Project Leader; and John Freitas, Serge Palladino, Danielle Shaw, Teresa Storch, and Susan Whalen, MQA Testers. They are a joy to work with and an example of what faithful dedication can accomplish. We give special thanks to Kathy Finnegan, Senior Product Manager, for her vision, guidance, and patience. Finally, we express deep gratitude to our Developmental Editor and dear friend, Katherine T. Pinard, with whom we have worked for 15 years. She has guided our work, given us valuable feedback, provided encouragement, kept us on task, and gone the extra mile in helping us meet deadlines and improve the quality of our books.

–Beverly B. Zimmerman
–S. Scott Zimmerman

Brief Contents

Table of Contents

Presentation Concepts Tutorials

Tutorial 1 Planning and Developing Your Presentation

Planning a Presentation for Faculty-Student Mentoring Projects . . . . .PRES 1

PowerPoint Level I Tutorials

Tutorial 1 Creating a Presentation

Tutorial 2 Applying and Modifying Text and Graphic Objects

PowerPoint Level II Tutorials

Tutorial 3 Adding Special Effects to a Presentation

Tutorial 4 Integrating PowerPoint with Other Programs and Collaborating with Workgroups

PowerPoint Level III Tutorials

Tutorial 5 Applying Advanced Special Effects in Presentations

*Adding Complex Sound, Animation, and Graphics
to a Presentation* . . . . .PPT 217

Tutorial 6 Creating Special Types of Presentations

*Using PowerPoint to Prepare Transparencies,
Photo Albums, Posters, and Banners* . . . . .PPT 273

Planning and Developing Your Presentation

Planning a Presentation for Faculty-Student Mentoring Projects

Case | Maclay University

As a student at Maclay University in Tallahassee, Florida, you've worked several semesters for the Office of Faculty-Student Mentoring Programs. The mission of the Office of Faculty-Student Mentoring Programs is to foster formal mentoring opportunities in which faculty, staff, and students can participate.

Sela Topeni, Director of the Office of Faculty-Student Mentoring Programs, wants you to make several oral presentations as part of your job. Some of these presentations will be brief and informal, such as communicating pertinent information to the Office staff. Other presentations will be lengthy and formal, such as encouraging faculty and students to enroll in mentoring programs or requesting funds from the Student Senate. Sometimes you'll need to convey your entire message in an oral format; other times your presentation might supplement a written document, such as a financial statement or a wrap-up report on a successful mentoring project. Sometimes you'll give your presentation as part of a group or team; other times you'll give your presentation alone. The success of your job—and of many of the mentoring programs—will depend upon the quality of your presentations.

In this tutorial, you'll plan your presentation by determining the purpose and outcome of your presentation and analyzing the needs and expectations of your audience. You'll assess the situation for giving your presentation and select appropriate media. Next, you'll determine a focus for your presentation, identify your main ideas, and decide how you will persuade your audience. Finally, you'll organize your presentation and develop an introduction, body, and conclusion for your presentation.

Starting Data Files

There are no starting Data Files needed for this tutorial.

Session 1.1

Planning Your Presentation

You should plan an oral presentation the same way you would plan a written document—by considering your purpose, audience, and situation. Oral presentations, however, differ from written documents in the demands placed upon your audience, so you'll need to apply special techniques to ensure a successful presentation.

Planning a presentation in advance will improve the quality of your presentation, make it more effective and enjoyable, and, in the long run, save you time and effort. As you plan your presentation, you should determine why you're giving the presentation, who will be listening to the presentation, and where the presentation will take place.

Figure 1-1	Planning saves time

You should ask yourself the following questions about the presentation:

- What is the purpose of this presentation?
- What type of presentation do I need to give?
- Who is the audience for my presentation, and what do they need and expect?
- What is the situation (location and setting) for my presentation?
- What is the most appropriate media for my presentation?

Answering these questions will help you create a more effective presentation, and will enable you to feel confident in presenting your ideas. The following sections will help you answer these questions.

Determining the Purpose of Your Presentation

Your purpose in giving a presentation will vary according to each particular situation, so the best way to determine your purpose is to ask yourself why you're giving this presentation and what you expect to accomplish. Common purposes for giving presentations include the following: to present information, to persuade your audience to change beliefs and behaviors, and to demonstrate or train.

Giving Informative Presentations

Informative presentations provide your audience with background information, knowledge, and specific details about a topic that will enable them to gain understanding, make informed decisions, or increase their expertise on a topic.

Examples of informative presentations include:

- Academic or professional conference presentations
- Briefings on the status of projects
- Reviews or evaluations of products and services
- Reports at company meetings
- Luncheon or dinner speeches
- Informal symposia

Giving informative presentations   Figure 1-2

Informative presentations can address a wide range of topics and are given to a wide range of audiences. For example, you might want to educate faculty at Maclay University about the goals and activities of the Office of Faculty-Student Mentoring Programs, or you might want to inform Office staff members about plans for next month's mentoring activity. Your main purpose in these presentations is to provide useful and relevant information to your intended audience.

Giving Persuasive Presentations

Although every presentation involves convincing an audience to listen and be interested in a specific topic, some presentations are more persuasive than others. **Persuasive presentations** have the specific purpose of influencing how an audience feels or acts regarding a particular position or plan.

Examples of persuasive presentations include:

- Recommendations
- Sales presentations
- Action plans and strategy sessions
- Motivational presentations

Figure 1-3 | **Giving persuasive presentations**

Persuasive presentations cover a wide range of topics and are given to a wide range of audiences. In addition, persuasive presentations are usually designed as balanced arguments involving logical as well as emotional reasons for supporting an action or viewpoint. For example, you might want to persuade students at Maclay University to sign up to be a mentor, or you might want to recommend that the Student Senate create a formal partnership with the Office of Faculty-Student Mentoring Programs. Your main purpose in these persuasive presentations is to convince your audience to accept a particular plan or point of view.

Giving Demonstrations or Training Presentations

Demonstrations are a specific type of presentation that shows an audience how something works or helps them to understand a process or procedure. Examples of demonstration presentations include:

- Overviews of products and services
- Software demonstrations
- Process explanations

For example, you might need to show students how to fill out a Request for a Mentor form. In another situation, you might want to demonstrate to staff how to match students and faculty who enroll in the university's mentored learning programs. In these presentations, your main purpose is to show how something works so your audience understands the process.

Training presentations provide audiences with an opportunity to learn new skills, or to be educated on how to perform a task, such as how to operate a piece of equipment. Training presentations usually differ from demonstrations by providing listeners with hands-on experience, practice, and feedback, so they can correct their mistakes and improve their performances.

Examples of training presentations include:

- Employee orientation (completing job tasks such as running the copy machine)
- Seminars and workshops
- Educational classes and courses

Giving demos or training **Figure 1-4**

For example, you might want to train students from Maclay University on how to work as a research assistant, or you might want to teach the Office staff how to prepare exhibits for the Mentored Research Fair. In these presentations, your main purpose is to assist your audience in learning and practicing new abilities and skills.

Sometimes you may have more than one purpose for your presentation. For instance, you might need to inform the staff of a newly revised policy on evaluating Mentored Learning Grants. In addition to explaining the new policy, you might need to persuade your co-workers of the importance of following the new guidelines. You might also need to answer any questions they have about how to implement certain aspects of the policy.

Having too many purposes can complicate your presentation and keep you from focusing on the needs of your audience. For that reason, you should try to limit your presentation to one main purpose, and one or two secondary purposes, as explained in Figure 1-5.

Figure 1-5 ▶ Purposes for giving presentations

Type of Presentation	Goal of Presentation	Examples
Informative	Present facts and details	Academic or professional conferences, status reports, briefings, reviews of products and services, luncheon or dinner speeches, informal symposia
Persuasive	Influence feelings or actions	Recommendation reports, sales presentations, action plans and strategy sessions, motivational presentations
Demonstrations or Training	Show how something works; provide practice and feedback	Overviews of products and services, software demos, process explanations, employee orientation, seminars and workshops, educational courses

In addition to determining your purpose for a presentation, you should also consider the needs of your audience. Effective presentations are those that enable listeners to achieve their goals. We will now consider how to determine what the audience should gain or learn from your presentation.

Determining the Outcome of Your Presentation

Your goal in giving a presentation should be to help your listeners understand, retain, and use the information you present. That means you need to determine the desired **outcomes** of your presentation. Focusing on the outcomes of your presentation—what you want your listeners to think or do after listening to your message—forces you to make your presentation more audience-oriented. By addressing the needs of your listeners, you'll worry less about yourself and more about how to make your presentation effective for your audience.

Writing Purpose and Outcome Statements

Writing down the purpose and desired outcomes of your presentation helps you to analyze what the presentation will involve, and enables you to create a more effective presentation. When you write down the purpose and desired outcomes of your presentation, you should use just two or three sentences. A good statement of your purpose and desired outcomes helps you later as you write the introduction and conclusion for your presentation.

Consider the following examples of purpose statements and outcomes:

- Purpose: To inform faculty at Maclay University about the goals and programs of the Office of Faculty-Student Mentoring Programs. Outcomes: Faculty will want to obtain funds for formal mentored-research activities. Faculty will know the eligibility criteria for participation, and how to apply for funds from our organization.
- Purpose: To demonstrate to the staff the newly purchased projector that can be used for giving presentations to small groups of students and faculty. Outcomes: Staff members will understand how to use the new equipment. Staff members will want to use the new equipment at next month's Mentored Research Fair.

In both of these examples, the presenter stated a specific purpose with specific outcomes.

- Why am I giving this presentation?
- What is the primary purpose of this presentation?
- What are the secondary purposes of this presentation?
- What should the audience know or do as a result of this presentation?

Your supervisor, Sela, asks you to give a presentation about mentoring to faculty at Maclay. Your written purpose might be: To inform faculty of the goals and programs of the Office of Faculty-Student Mentoring Programs. Your written outcome might be: Faculty will want to participate in the mentored-research programs.

Figure 1-6 provides a basic worksheet for helping you determine the purpose and outcomes of this and other presentations.

Purpose and Outcomes worksheet | Figure 1-6

Purpose and Outcomes
Worksheet

Why are you giving this presentation?

What is the primary purpose of your presentation? Check one and explain it:

☐ Provide useful and relevant facts and details:

☐ Persuade or influence how audience feels or acts:

☐ Show how something works or demonstrate a procedure:

☐ Provide hands-on experience, practices, and feedback:

What are the secondary purposes for your presentation? Check and explain all that apply:

☐ Provide useful and relevant facts and details:

☐ Persuade or influence how audience feels or acts:

☐ Show how something works or demonstrate a procedure:

☐ Provide hands-on experience, practices, and feedback:

☐ Other:

What should the audience know, feel, or do as a result of your presentation?

What other outcomes are there for your presentation?

Next you'll analyze what your audience will need and expect from your presentation.

Analyzing Your Audience's Needs and Expectations

The more you know about your listeners, the more you'll be able to adapt your presentation to their needs. By putting yourself in your listeners' shoes, you'll be able to visualize your audience as more than just a group of passive listeners, and you can anticipate what they need and expect from your presentation. Anticipating the needs of your audience will also increase the chances that your audience will react favorably to your presentation.

When you give your presentation to student leaders at Maclay University, your audience will consist of decision makers. Such audiences typically want to know what would be the best solution in terms of time and resources. They will expect to learn what a partnership between the Student Senate and the Office of Faculty-Student Mentoring Programs would entail, what the costs of such a partnership would be, and how many students would benefit from such a partnership.

When you give your presentation to the faculty, your audience will consist of your superiors. Such audiences typically want to know how your desired outcomes will affect their workload and fulfill their goals and objectives. They will expect to learn what the benefits of mentored research are for faculty and students, what the constraints of mentored research are for faculty, and how to obtain mentored research funding.

When you give your presentation to the student staff of the Office of Faculty-Student Mentoring Programs, your audience will consist of peers who know less than you do. Such audiences want to know how to perform their tasks more efficiently and effectively. They will expect to know how the new policies pertain to them and what their responsibilities are in the various mentoring programs. In addition, your coworkers usually will want a less formal presentation than audiences outside your organization.

Other characteristics of your audience that you'll want to consider include their **demographic characteristics**; that is, features such as age, gender, educational level, expertise with your topic and cultural background.

Examples of how demographic characteristics can affect your presentations include:

- **Age:** People of different age groups may vary in terms of attention span and the way they relate to examples. A presentation on the educational impact of student involvement in mentoring programs would be appropriate for college students, but not for elementary-school students. Moreover, young children have shorter attention spans and generally can't sit for as long as adults. Presentations to young children should be divided into short sessions interspersed with physical activity.
- **Gender:** It's important to fairly represent both genders by avoiding male pronouns (he, his) to represent both sexes, and by using examples that show both men and women performing all jobs at work and at home.
- **Education:** Audiences with specialized training expect examples that use terms and concepts from their field. Audiences with more education expect a higher level of technicality than audiences with less education.
- **Expertise with the topic:** Audiences familiar with your topic won't need as many definitions and explanations as audiences not familiar with your topic.
- **Cultural background:** Each culture has its own expectations for how to write, speak, and communicate, including the nonverbal conventions such as gestures and body movement.

Understanding the Needs of an International Audience

With the continually expanding world-wide community, it is important to understand the different cultural expectations that international audiences may have for your presentation (including expectations for non-verbal communication). These cultural expectations are subtle but powerful, and you can immediately create a negative impression if you don't understand them. For example, audiences from cultures outside the United States may expect you to speak and dress more formally than you are used to in the United States. In addition, some cultures are hesitant to debate an issue or present disagreement towards popular views.

There are no universal guidelines that would enable you to characterize the needs of all international audiences; however, there are some commonsense recommendations. You should analyze the hand gestures and symbols you use routinely to see if they have different meaning for other cultures. Be cautious about using humor because it is easy to misinterpret. Although it is impossible to completely understand another culture unless you have lived in it, special care should be taken to avoid using cultural stereotypes as well as using racist, sexist, or culturally derogatory terms or stories.

Consider How Your Audience Will Use Your Presentation

In addition to analyzing general features and characteristics of your audience, you should also consider how your audience will use the information that you present. For example, administrators attending a presentation on potential fundraising activities for mentoring programs need to know how much money is to be raised, and how much the fundraising activity itself would cost, in order to estimate net profits.

Understanding the needs and expectations of your audience helps you adapt the content of your presentation to a particular audience, and enables you to address their concerns. By anticipating questions your listeners might ask about your topic, you can plan to address those questions and concerns in your presentation. Finally, understanding the needs and concerns of your audience assures that your presentation is useful, interesting, and relevant.

Questions for Analyzing Your Audience | Reference Window

- Who will be listening to my presentation (peers, superiors, subordinates, visitors)?
- What does the audience expect me to talk about?
- What general characteristics or demographics do I know about the audience (age, gender, education level, knowledge of the topic, cultural expectations)?
- What does the audience need to know about the topic of the presentation (general background or overview, details, cost estimates)?
- How will listeners use this information (make decisions, perform a task)?
- What are the major concerns or objections to my point of view (too expensive, too difficult, takes too much time)?
- What do I want the audience to think, know, or do as a result of this presentation?

In your presentations about faculty-student mentoring programs, you realize that your audience will be both your peers and your superiors. Although they will vary in their experience with your topic of mentored research, most audiences will be somewhat familiar with the concept of mentoring. You realize that a big concern of both students and faculty is that their commitment to formal mentoring activities might be time-consuming. So you'll need to address that concern in your presentation.

Figure 1-7 provides a basic worksheet for helping you analyze the needs and expectations of your audience for this and other presentations.

Figure 1-7   Audience Analysis worksheet

Audience Analysis
Worksheet

Who will be listening to your presentation? Check all that apply:

☐ Peers:

☐ Superiors:

☐ Subordinates:

☐ Strangers:

What do they expect you to talk about?

What general characteristics do you know about the audience?

☐ Age

☐ Gender

☐ Education

☐ Expertise with topic

☐ International audience

☐ Other

What does your audience need to know about the topic? Check and explain all that apply:

☐ General background or overview:

☐ Details:

☐ Cost estimates:

☐ Other:

How will your listeners use this information? Check and explain all that apply:

☐ Make decisions:

☐ Perform a task:

☐ Form an opinion:

☐ Increase understanding:

☐ Follow a process:

☐ Other:

What are your audience's biggest concerns or objections? Check and explain all that apply:

☐ Too expensive:

☐ Too difficult:

☐ Too much time:

☐ Other:

What do you want your audience to think, know, or do as a result of this presentation?

Assessing the Situation or Context for Your Presentation

Many of your presentations will involve speaking on the same subject to different audiences and in different settings. Planning an effective presentation will be a matter of learning to adapt your content to your **situation** or context, the unique setting, time frame, or circumstances (such as the size of your audience) for your presentation. The more you know about the context of your presentation, the better you can adapt your presentation to different audiences.

Probably the most important aspects to consider are how much time you'll have, and whether someone else will speak before or after you. Giving a presentation along with others means you'll have to watch the clock closely so you don't infringe on someone else's time. It can also mean that you'll have to cut your presentation short if someone uses part of your time. Even if you're the sole speaker, it's wise to make back-up plans in case your time limit changes just before you speak.

Setting and location affect expectations   Figure 1-8

The setting for a presentation can affect audience expectations and, therefore, will dictate the appropriate level of formality. That's why it's important to know where your presentation will occur, including the size and shape of the room, and the seating arrangement. The small conference room with a round table and moveable chairs in the Office of Faculty-Student Mentoring Programs would call for a much more informal presentation than the large rectangular lecture hall with fixed seating in the Maclay Student Union Building where the Student Senate meets.

You'll also need to adapt your presentation according to the size of your audience. Four or five co-workers at the Office of Faculty-Student Mentoring Programs would probably expect to be able to interrupt your presentation and ask questions or express their own views, whereas the large audience in the Maclay Student Union Building would not. The setting for your presentation and the size of your audience will also influence the method and equipment you use to give your presentation, and the size of your visuals. Students in large rooms often sit toward the back, far away from your visuals. So you will need to increase the size of your visuals in your presentation in the Maclay Student Union Building, or use an overhead, slide, or computer projection system. On the other hand, if your audience at the Office of Faculty-Student Mentoring Programs is fewer than ten people, you might be able to use a laptop computer screen for your visuals.

Questions for Analyzing the Situation for Your Presentation

- How much time will I have for my presentation?
- Will I be speaking alone or with other people?
- How large will the audience be?
- How formal or informal will the setting be?
- What will the room be like, and how will it be arranged?
- What equipment will be available for my presentation (chalkboard, overhead projector, slide projector, computer projection system)?
- Do I have the skills to operate available equipment?
- Who will be available to assist me in case of an equipment failure?
- How much time will I have to set up for my presentation?
- What other aspects must I consider (temperature, extraneous noises)?
- Who will be available to assist me with room temperature, lights, or extraneous noise problems?

Now you need to decide what kind of presentation methods you'll use in your presentation.

Selecting Appropriate Media

As you plan your presentation, you'll need to select the **media**, or presentation methods, you'll use to support and clarify your presentation. Media commonly used for oral presentations include:

- Chalkboard
- Whiteboard
- Notepad and easel
- Flip chart
- Posters
- Black-and-white or color overheads
- Handouts
- 35mm slides
- Computer-projected visuals, such as PowerPoint slides
- Websites or broadband media including videoconferencing

In selecting appropriate media for your presentation, it's important to fit the media to your particular purpose, audience, and situation. Every medium allows you to provide support for the points you'll make in your presentation, and help your audience see and hear your ideas. Each medium, however, has its own strengths and limitations.

Using a Chalkboard, Whiteboard, or Notepad

Chalkboards, whiteboards, or large paper notepads work well for small meetings and informal discussions, and are especially helpful in stressing important points from your presentation or in recording comments from the audience. These media usually require little advance preparation, other than bringing along a piece of chalk or a marker, and they come in portable forms.

Chalkboards emphasize main points ◄ Figure 1-9

On the other hand, these media have disadvantages, including the difficulty of speaking to your audience while you write or draw. If your handwriting is difficult to read, it can detract from your presentation, as can poor spelling. In addition, these media are only effective for writing a few words or short phrases, or making simple drawings.

Using a Flip Chart

Flip charts, previously prepared pictures and visuals that are bound together and shown one at a time, can be used in both formal and informal settings. Using a flip chart allows you to highlight the main points of your presentation, and present information in an appropriate sequence. Flip charts work best when used in a small, well-lighted room.

Figure 1-10 ▶ **Flip charts show sequence**

The disadvantages of flip charts are that they are too small to be seen in large rooms or by large audiences, they require significant advance preparation, and they are cumbersome.

Using Posters

Posters, written summaries of your presentation that can be displayed on stationary blackboards or attached to the walls of a room, are effective for letting audiences refer to your presentation before or after the event. Posters are especially prevalent at academic or professional conferences, and presenters often stand by their posters to answer questions from the audience.

Posters provide visual summaries | Figure 1-11

Because posters usually contain professional lettering, as well as technical graphics and illustrations, they can't be easily revised, and they do require advance preparation.

Using Black-And-White or Color Overheads

Overheads, transparent sheets that enable text and visuals to be projected onto a screen, are used frequently, but equipment for showing them must be available. Creating overheads can be as simple as copying your presentation notes onto the overhead transparencies. Overheads do require some advance preparation, and they can look amateurish or uninteresting. In addition, overheads are ineffective if the lettering is too small or too dense.

Tip

Photocopiers, laser printers, and inkjet printers all use different kinds of transparency masters, so make sure you buy the right kind and that you print on the correct side.

Figure 1-12 | **Overheads focus attention**

Overheads allow for flexibility in your presentation as they can quickly be reorganized or adjusted, as necessary. You can also draw on overheads using a transparency marker during your presentation.

Using Handouts

Handouts, sheets of paper summarizing key points of your presentation or numerical data, give your listeners something to take with them following your presentation. Handouts can assist your listeners in understanding difficult concepts, and can also alleviate the difficulties of taking notes.

Tip

If you put too much text on your handout, your audience might not take the time to read it. If you put too little text, your audience might not take the handout seriously.

Handouts alleviate note taking　　Figure 1-13

Although handouts are helpful, they require advance preparation to look professional. Also, be careful that your handouts don't detract from your presentation by enticing your audience to pay more attention to them than your presentation.

Using 35mm Slides

Using **35mm slides**, photographic transparencies that are projected onto a screen, requires advance preparation, so you must allow enough time to take pictures and have them developed into professional-looking slides. Slides are especially good for presentations in a formal setting, in large rooms, or with large audiences. Slides require that you turn the lights down, however, which makes it difficult for you to see your presentation notes, for the audience to take notes, and for some people to stay awake. In addition, using slides forces you to choose between facing your audience and standing at a distance from the slide projector, or standing behind the slide projector and talking to the backs of your audience.

Figure 1-14 **Slides require advance preparation**

You can increase the effectiveness of your slide presentation by using a hand-held remote to advance your slides, and a laser pointer to draw attention to important aspects of the slides. Or, you could give the presentation in tandem with someone else—you as the presenter and the other person as the operator of the equipment.

Using Computer-Projected Presentations

Computer-projected presentations (electronic on-screen presentations created with Microsoft PowerPoint, Corel Presentations, or other presentation software and projected onto a screen) allow you to create professional-looking presentations with a consistent visual design. They also enable you to incorporate other media into your presentations, such as photographs, sound, animation, and video clips. Computer-projected presentations are also easy to update or revise on the spot, and can easily be converted into other media, such as overheads, posters, or 35mm slides.

Computer-projected presentations require special equipment such as a computer projection system that may not always be available. And, sometimes you must present your computer presentation in a darkened room, making it difficult for you to see your notes and for your listeners to take notes. You can reduce the difficulty by asking someone else to operate the computer equipment for you.

In addition, computer-projected presentations require advance preparation and set up to ensure compatibility of the computer, the projection system, and the disk containing your presentation files. Moreover, many presenters create on-screen presentations that are too elaborate, rather than being simple and straightforward.

Using Web Sites and Videoconferencing

Using **Web sites** (accessing information and images from the Internet) allows you to provide current information with visual appeal for your audiences. Web sites are valuable for presenting interactive and entertaining aspects of a topic. In addition, **videoconferences** (also known as videoteleconferences) enable audiences from various locations to participate "face-to-face" via telephone wires, satellite technology or ground wires.

Figure 1-16 **Video conferencing allows distance participation**

Although Web sites and videoconferencing are becoming more common, they still require high-speed Internet access and/or special telephone equipment that may not always be available. Both web-based presentations and videoconferences can be expensive if the presentation needs to be projected to a large screen. Convention centers and hotels usually charge hefty fees for using their sophisticated equipment and technical support staff.

In addition, you may have difficulty accessing the specific Web page or information you need because the Web site may change or the information may no longer exist as you originally found it. Technical difficulties such as loss of the video stream or buffering problems can also detract from your presentation.

Figure 1-17 summarizes the strengths and weaknesses of different presentation media.

Strengths and weaknesses of presentation media **Figure 1-17**

Type of Medium	Strengths	Weaknesses	Audience Size	Advance Preparation	Formality
Chalkboard, Whiteboard or Notepad	Enables audience input; good for summarizing; adaptable	Must write and talk simultaneously requires good handwriting and spelling	Small	None required	Informal
Flip chart	Can highlight main points and sequence information	Too small to be seen in large room	Small	Required	Formal and Informal
Posters	Can be referred to following your presentation; good for displaying other materials	Can't be easily revised; needs explanation	Medium, Large	Required	Formal and Informal
Overheads	Equipment readily available; adaptable; can draw on	Often boring, uninteresting, or ineffective	Medium, Large	Required	Formal and Informal
Handouts	Alleviate taking notes; can be referred to later	Can distract from your presentation	Small, Medium, Large	Required	Formal and Informal
35mm slides	Good for formal presentations in large rooms	Difficult to see your notes and to advance slides; require special equipment	Large	Extensive preparation	Formal
Electronic on-screen slides	Incorporate media; good for formal presentations in large rooms	May be too elaborate or distracting; require special equipment	Small, Large	Extensive preparation	Formal
Web-based media and video-conferencing	Provide current information; allow people in multiple locations to participate	May be difficult to access; require expensive equipment and technical support staff	Small, Large	Extensive preparation	Informal; Formal

Every medium has its strengths and weaknesses. No matter what media you use, your goal should be to keep your presentation simple and to adapt it to the purpose and audience of each unique situation.

At the Maclay Student Union, you'll give your presentation in a room that isn't equipped with a computer projection system, but does have a large screen and overhead projector. So you might want to create a poster displaying photographs of activities sponsored by the Office of Faculty-Student Mentoring Programs, show an overhead transparency explaining how a partnership between the Office and the Student Senate would work, and prepare a handout containing information on Faculty-Student Mentored-Research projects.

Transporting Presentation Files | InSight

You might have to give a presentation at a location where you can't use your own computer, in which case you will have to transport your presentation files to the site of your presentation in a compatible medium. Here are some tips to help you decide how to transport your presentation files:

- Check with your host or the presentation organizer to make sure you know the type of equipment in the presentation room.
- The most common medium for transporting presentation files is a USB flash drive (also called a thumb drive). Most computers have USB ports and accept flash drives.
- Experienced airplane travelers carry a copy of their presentations in their carry-on bags and another copy in their check-in bags.
- If you plan to give a computer presentation, you might want to also carry a backup copy of your presentation as paper handouts or as overhead transparencies, just in case you encounter computer problems at the site of your presentation.

Figure 1-18 provides a basic worksheet for helping you assess the situation and media for this and other presentations.

Figure 1-18   **Situation and Media Assessment worksheet**

Situation and Media Assessment *Worksheet*

How much time will you have for your presentation and the setup?

How large will your audience be?

How formal will the setting be?

What will the room be like and how will it be arranged?

What equipment will be available for your presentation?

- ☐ Chalkboard
- ☐ Whiteboard
- ☐ Notepad and easel
- ☐ Stationary posterboard
- ☐ Overhead projector
- ☐ Slide projector
- ☐ Computer projection system
- ☐ High speed Internet connection
- ☐ Telephone, land, or satellite equipment for videoconferencing

What other aspects must you consider for your presentation?

- ☐ Temperature
- ☐ Lighting
- ☐ Noise and distractions
- ☐ Other:

Who will assist you with the equipment and other situational aspects?

- ☐ Friend or colleague
- ☐ Technical support staff
- ☐ Custodial staff
- ☐ Room monitor:
- ☐ Other:

What media will be appropriate for your presentation? Check all appropriate media and explain:

- ☐ Chalkboard:
- ☐ Whiteboard:
- ☐ Notepad and easel:
- ☐ Flip chart:
- ☐ Poster:
- ☐ Black-and-white or other overheads:
- ☐ Handouts:
- ☐ 35mm slides:
- ☐ Computer projection system and electronic slides:
- ☐ Internet media:
- ☐ Teleconference:

How will you introduce yourself and your qualifications?

Review | Session 1.1 Quick Check

1. Define and give examples for the following types of presentations:
   a. Informative presentation
   b. Persuasive presentation
   c. Demonstration or training session

2. In two or three sentences, describe how knowing the educational level of an audience would affect a presentation on Mentoring Undergraduate Researchers to be given to Maclay University faculty.

3. List at least two important questions you should ask as part of assessing the presentation situation.

4. Consider the following presentations. In each instance, list two media that would be effective for that presentation, and explain why they would be effective.
   a. A presentation at the local floral shop to 8–10 floral designers on how to successfully create a spring floral arrangement

    b. A presentation at a hotel ballroom to 40–50 convention planners on why they should hold their next convention in New Orleans, Louisiana

    c. A presentation to two or three administrative staff at a local business on how to conduct a successful Web conference

5. List two media that are useful for recording comments from the audience.

6. If you want to use sound and animation in your presentation, which media would be appropriate?

Session 1.2

Focusing Your Presentation

Once you determine your purpose, analyze your audience's needs and expectations, and assess the particular situation in which you'll give your presentation, you need to plan the content of your presentation. You should begin by identifying the major points or main ideas that are directly relevant to your listeners' needs and interests, and then focus on those.

One of the biggest problems every presenter faces is how to provide **focus** (a narrowed aspect of the topic) to make the presentation manageable. Your tendency will be to want to include every aspect of a topic, but trying to cover everything usually means that you'll give your audience irrelevant information and lose their interest. Focusing on one aspect of a topic is like bringing a picture into focus with your camera—it clarifies your subject and allows you to emphasize interesting details. Failing to focus in presentations, as in photography, always brings disappointment to you and your audience.

How you provide focus for your topic will depend upon the purpose, audience, and situation for your presentation. Remember, the narrower the topic, the more specific and interesting the information will be. Strategies for focusing or limiting your presentation topic are the same as those you would use to limit the scope of any written document—focus on a particular time or chronology, geography or region, category, component or element, segment or portion of a procedure, or point of view.

- **Time or chronology:** Limiting a topic by time means you focus on a few years, rather than trying to cover the entire history of a topic. Unfocused: The history of Egypt from 640 to 2000. Focused: The history of Egypt during the Nasser years (1952–1970).
- **Geography or region:** Limiting a topic by geography or region means you look at a topic as it relates to a specific location. Unfocused: Fly fishing. Focused: Fly fishing in western Colorado.
- **Category or classification:** Limiting a topic by category means you focus on one member of a group or on a limited function. Unfocused: Thermometers. Focused: Using bimetallic-coil thermometers to control bacteria in restaurant-prepared foods.
- **Component or element:** Limiting a topic by component or element means you focus on one small aspect or part of an organization or problem. Unfocused: Business trends. Focused: Blending accounting practices and legal services, a converging trend in large businesses.
- **Segment or portion:** Limiting a topic by segment or portion means you focus on one part of a process or procedure. Unfocused: Designing, manufacturing, characterizing, handling, storing, packaging, and transporting of optical filters. Focused: Acceptance testing of optical filters.
- **Point of view:** Limiting a topic by point of view means you look at a topic from the perspective of a single group. Unfocused: Employee benefits. Focused: How school districts can retain their teachers by providing child-care assistance and other nontraditional benefits.

Reference Window | **Ways to Limit Your Topic**

- Time or chronology
- Geography or region
- Category or classification
- Component or element
- Segment or portion of a process or procedure
- Point of view or perspective

In your presentation to faculty on the mentored-research programs at Maclay University, you'll need to limit your topic. You decide to discuss only current mentoring programs, not past or proposed programs. You'll also limit your presentation to mentoring opportunities at the Tallahassee campus, and not include mentoring opportunities at the Maclay satellite campuses. In addition, you'll only present information on formal programs for involving undergraduate students in faculty-sponsored research, not programs for advising students on graduation requirements or helping students obtain employment. Finally, you'll approach your topic from a student's perspective.

Identifying Your Main Ideas

As you identify your **main ideas**, or key points of your presentation, you should phrase them as conclusions you want your audience to draw from your presentation. This helps you to continue to design your presentation with the listener in mind.

Your main ideas for your presentation about mentored-research opportunities for faculty at Maclay University include:

1. University faculty and students benefit when students are involved in mentored-research projects.
2. Students can apply what they learn in the classroom to help faculty complete academic research.
3. Using undergraduate students in academic research saves faculty time and money.
4. Faculty can apply for funds to create a mentored-research opportunity for undergraduates using their current research projects.

You're now prepared to consider the content and organization of your presentation. In the sections that follow, you'll formulate the general organization of your presentation.

Persuading Your Audience

If your goal is to persuade your audience to change their beliefs or behavior, you must consider how you will establish a convincing argument. Persuading an audience should be approached in the following ways: establishing your credibility, building a rapport or emotional connection with the audience, and presenting arguments that lead to a logical conclusion.

Establishing Your Credibility

When you establish your credibility with an audience, it means that you inspire trust in what you have to say. You can help your audience accept you as a credible speaker by showing that you are knowledgeable about your topic; by presenting accurate, reliable, and pertinent information; and by referring to authorities who agree with you.

Tip

Don't try to establish your credibility by boasting about your accomplishments. If possible, let the person who introduces you present your qualifications.

For example, in your presentation to the Maclay Student Senate, you might provide an overview of the goals and benefits of current mentoring programs, quote the president of Maclay University who stated that every student at Maclay University deserves the benefits of mentored learning, and explain that you have participated in mentored-research activities for the past two semesters.

Establishing a Common Ground with Your Audience

In order to be believable as a speaker, you must show that you and your audience have similar needs, values, and goals. Establishing a common ground with your audience, means taking a "we're all in this together" attitude that demonstrates that you and your ideas are approachable. It also shows that you care about your audience and their needs.

For example, in your presentation to the Maclay Student Senate you might state, "None of us needs reminding of the fierce competition to get into a prestigious graduate school. Participating in mentored research can help Maclay students set themselves apart from students at other universities." Or you might state, "Most of us probably realize that having a good mentor is critical to career success. That makes it imperative that we consider ways to give every student at Maclay a valuable mentoring experience."

Taking a Logical, Even-Handed Approach

You will have a better chance of persuading your audience if you take a reasoned, logical approach to the topic and consider both sides of an issue even-handedly and fairly. You should explain the reasoning behind your arguments, provide support for your claims, present sensible recommendations, and anticipate other people's objections to your conclusions. Supporting your claims means going beyond your personal experience and doing in-depth research to provide verifiable facts, statistics, and expert testimony. If your audience is confident that you are taking a logical approach, they will feel sure you are suggesting the best alternative, not the most comfortable or convenient one.

For example in your presentation to the faculty at Maclay University, you might explain that although faculty are concerned about the time involved in doing mentored research, 98% percent of the faculty who participated in the program last semester are participating again this semester. Or you might point out that with current applications for government research funding, granting agencies now ask if undergraduates will be participating in the research.

Organizing Your Presentation

Once you've finished planning your presentation, you'll need to assemble the content or ideas of your presentation, and organize them in a logical manner. There are many different ways to organize or arrange your presentation, depending upon your purpose, the needs of your audience, and the particular speaking situation. In general, all good presentations start with an effective introduction, continue with a well-organized body, and end with a strong conclusion. See Figure 1-19.

Figure 1-19 ▶ **Introduction, body, and conclusion**

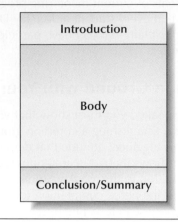

The **introduction**, or opening statements of a presentation, enables you to gain your listeners' attention, establish a relationship with your audience, and preview your main ideas. The **body** of your presentation is where you'll present pertinent information, solid evidence, and important details. The **conclusion** allows you to restate your main points, suggest appropriate actions, and recommend further resources.

Reference Window | **General Organization of Presentations**

- Introduction
  - Gains and keeps attention of audience
  - Creates favorable impression
  - Establishes credibility
  - Provides overview of presentation
- Body
  - Follows main point of presentation
  - Provides evidence and support for main points
  - Presents research in adequate detail
  - Shows relevance of data
- Conclusion
  - Restates main point of presentation
  - Suggests appropriate action
  - Recommends ways of finding additional data

In the next section, you'll learn how to develop the introduction to your presentation.

Developing an Introduction

Your introduction is the most important part of your entire presentation because it provides your listeners' first impression of you and your presentation, and sets the tone for the rest of your presentation. An effective introduction enables you to gain your listeners' attention, establish a rapport with your audience, and provide your listeners with an organizational overview or preview of your presentation.

Gaining Your Audience's Attention

Your first task in giving an effective presentation is to gain and keep your audience's attention. Even if your audience is interested in your topic, they can be easily distracted, so it's important to create an effective introduction that will immediately grab their attention. Here are some ways to gain your audience's attention:

- Anecdotes, stories, or personal experiences
- Surprising statistics or relevant data
- A quotation, familiar phrase, or definition
- Rhetorical questions
- Unresolved issues and current problems
- Comments about the audience or occasion
- Audience participation
- Statement of your topic

Using Anecdotes

Think back to a presentation you attended recently. What do you remember most about it? Isn't it a story or experience that sticks out most in your mind? **Anecdotes** (short stories or person experiences that demonstrate a specific point) help you to gain your listeners' attention because they draw the listener into your topic and make the topic more personal. Sharing a personal experience helps your audience relate to you as a real person and makes your topic more relevant.

You could begin your presentation to faculty at Maclay University by relating your personal experience in working with Professor Suzanne Hansen, a Psychology professor:

"Last year, I became involved in Dr. Hansen's mentored research program, studying how the siblings of disabled children are affected by disability in a family. I was particularly interested in this research because my brother suffers from autism. Under Dr. Hansen's mentoring, I conducted interviews of 10 children whose siblings had autism. I also learned how what I'm studying in my psychology classes can be applied in the real world."

Using Statistics and Quantitative Data

Interesting statistics and quantitative data relating to the needs of your audience can increase the listeners' interest in knowing more about your topic. Make sure, however, that the statistics and data you use are current, accurate, and easily understood.

In your presentation at Maclay you could refer to interesting and related data as follows: "Last year, nearly 200 students at Maclay University participated in the Faculty-Student Mentored-Research Program. Nearly half of them have been accepted to graduate school at other universities."

Using Quotations, Familiar Phrases, and Definitions

Short quotes, familiar phrases, or definitions can effectively gain your audience's attention because they lead into the rest of your talk. You could use use a quotation as shown here to introduce your presentation to faculty at Maclay University:

"'Mentoring is not about telling the caterpillar how to fly; it's about helping the caterpillar see the possibility of flight.' That simple adage could describe Maclay faculty who currently participate in programs sponsored by the Office of Faculty-Student Mentoring Programs."

Using Questions

Asking questions to introduce your topic can be effective if the questions are thought-provoking and the issues are important. **Rhetorical questions** (questions you don't expect the audience to answer) are especially effective. You should exercise caution, however, and not use too many questions. You should also be aware that someone in the audience might call out humorous or otherwise unwanted answers to your questions, detracting from the effectiveness of your introduction, and putting you in an awkward position.

Some examples of rhetorical questions you could use in your presentation to faculty at Maclay University include:

- "Why have colleges and universities across the country begun to establish formal mentored-research opportunities for undergraduate students?"
- "What are the benefits to faculty for using undergraduates in their academic research?"
- "How can the Office of Faculty-Student Mentoring Programs help you in your current research?"

Raising a Current Problem or Unresolved Issue

Raising a current problem or unresolved issue provides you with an opportunity to suggest a change or a solution to the problem. By defining a problem for your audience, you develop a common ground upon which you can provide insight, examine alternatives and make recommendations.

In your presentation to the Student Senate, you could raise current problems such as the following:

- "Currently there are 25 mentored research projects without adequate funding."
- "Although 200 students at Maclay University are currently participating in mentored research, that represents less than one percent of the student body and less than 10 percent of the graduating seniors."

Commenting About the Audience or Occasion

Comments about the audience or occasion enable you to show your enthusiasm about the group you're addressing, as well as about your topic. Remember, however, that your comments should be brief and sincere. Referring to the occasion can be as simple as:

- "I'm happy that, as we're nearing the end of another academic year, you've given me an opportunity to relate my experiences as part of the mentored-research program."
- "As you know, Skylar de Paula, our student-body president, has invited me to explain how you could help more students participate in formal mentored research."
- "As student leaders at Maclay University, you're probably interested in the growing movement in higher education to give undergraduate students experience in doing research under the direction of a mentoring professor."

Using Audience Participation

Audience participation (allowing your audience to be actively involved in your presentation) encourages the audience to add their ideas to your presentation, rather than to simply sit and listen. Audience participation is especially effective in small group settings or situations where you're attempting to find new ways to approach ideas. Audience participation can also consist of asking for volunteers from the audience to help with your demonstration, or asking audience members to give tentative answers to an informal quiz or questionnaire, and then adjusting your presentation to accommodate their responses.

Using Audience Participation | InSight

Allowing your audience to participate requires that you take extra precautions to avoid losing control of your presentation. Here are some tips to help you handle audience participation:

- State a limit on the length of each response (such as 30 seconds) or the number of responses.
- Be prepared with tactful ways to interrupt a participant who monopolizes the time. If necessary, you can simply state, "I'm sorry. We must move on," and then continue with your presentation.
- If you are inexperienced with handling audience participation, consider allowing for audience participation only at the end of your presentation, rather than at the beginning. Conference organizers often leave time at the end of a presentation for the audience to ask questions. If not, conclude your presentation early and allow time for questions.

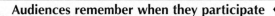

Audiences remember when they participate | Figure 1-20

In your presentation to faculty at Maclay University, you might ask a few members of the audience to relate their past mentoring experiences.

Giving Your Purpose Statement

Simply announcing your purpose works well as an introduction if your audience is already interested in your topic, or your time is limited. Most audiences, however, will appreciate a more creative approach than simply stating, "I'm going to try to persuade you to participate in a mentored-research project sponsored by the Office of Faculty-Student Mentoring Programs." Instead, you might say something like, "My purpose is to discuss a situation that affects every faculty member at Maclay University."

Be on the lookout for ideas for effective introductions. You might want to keep a presentations file for collecting interesting stories and quotations that you can use in preparing future presentations. Figure 1-21 summarizes some ways to gain your audience's attention.

Figure 1-21 ▶ **Ways to gain your audience's attention**

Method for Gaining Attention	Strength of Method
Anecdote or personal experience	Helps audience relate to you as a real person
Surprising statistic or relevant data	Increases audience interest in topic
Quotation, familiar phrase or definition	Leads in well to remainder of presentation
Rhetorical question	Gets audience thinking about topic
Statement of problem or issue	Prepares audience to consider solutions or recommendations for change
Comment about the audience or occasion	Enables you to show your enthusiasm
Audience participation	Encourages audience to add their own ideas
Statement of the topic	Works well if audience is already interested

Establishing a Rapport with Your Audience

Tip

Don't try to impress your audience with insincere comments, exaggerated information about yourself, patronizing attitude, flowery speech, or unnatural tone of voice. Be yourself—natural and sincere.

How an audience perceives a speaker can be more important than what the speaker says; therefore, it is important to establish a **rapport**, or connection, with your audience. The methods you use to gain your audience's attention will determine how the audience responds to you and to your presentation. It's important, then, that whatever you do in your introduction creates a favorable impression.

If your audience is unfamiliar with you or no one formally introduces you, you should introduce yourself and provide your credentials. Be careful not to spend much time on this, however, or to distance yourself from your audience by over-emphasizing your accomplishments.

In your presentation to the Student Senate at Maclay University, you might start out by simply saying, "Hi. I'm _____ , a senior at Maclay U. and a psychology major."

Providing an Overview of Your Presentation

One of the most important aspects of an introduction is to provide your audience with an overview of your presentation. Research indicates that **overviews**, sometimes called advance organizers or previews, prepare your audience for each point that will follow, and provide them with a way to structure your main points. Overviews help your audience remember your presentation by providing a verbal road map of how your presentation is organized.

Overviews should be brief and simple, stating what you plan to do and in what order. After you've given your audience an overview of your presentation, it's important that you follow that same order.

Avoiding Common Mistakes in an Introduction

An inadequate introduction can ruin the rest of your presentation no matter how well you've prepared. So you should allow yourself plenty of time to carefully plan your introductions. In addition, you should consider these guidelines to avoid common mistakes:

- Don't begin by apologizing about any aspect of your presentation, such as how nervous you are, or your lack of preparation. Apologies destroy your credibility and guarantee that your audience will react negatively to what you present.
- Check the accuracy and currency of your stories, examples, and data. Audiences don't appreciate being misled, misinformed, or manipulated.

- Steer clear of anything potentially vulgar, ridiculing, or sexist. You won't be respected or listened to once you offend your audience.
- Don't use gimmicks to begin your presentation, such as making a funny face, singing a song, or ringing a bell. Members of your audience won't know how to respond and will feel uncomfortable.
- Avoid trite, flattering, or phony statements, such as, "Ladies and gentlemen, it is an unfathomable honor to be in your presence." Gaining respect requires treating your audience as your equal.
- Don't coerce people into participating. Always ask for volunteers. Putting reluctant members of your audience on the spot embarrasses everyone.
- Be cautious when using humor. It's difficult to predict how audiences will respond to jokes and other forms of humor; therefore, you should avoid using humor unless you know your audience well.

Once you've introduced your topic, you're ready to develop the body of your presentation.

Developing the Body of Your Presentation

To develop the body, the major points and details of your presentation, you'll need to gather information on your topic, determine the organizational approach, add supporting details and other pertinent information, and provide transitions from one point to the next.

Gathering Information

Most of the time, you'll give presentations on topics about which you're knowledgeable and comfortable. Other times, you might have to give presentations on topics that are new to you. In either case, you'll probably need to do sufficient research to provide additional information that is effective, pertinent, and up-to-date.

You can find additional materials on your topic by consulting the following:

- Popular press items from newspapers, radio, TV, and magazines. This information, geared for general audiences, provides large-scale details and personal opinions that may need to be supplemented by additional research.

Figure 1-22   Using newspapers and magazines

- Library resources such as books, specialized encyclopedias, academic journals, government publications, and other reference materials. You can access these materials using the library's computerized catalog, card catalog, indexes, and professional database services.

Figure 1-23   Using information in libraries

- Corporate documents and office correspondence. Since using these materials might violate your company's nondisclosure policy, you might need to obtain your company's permission, or get legal clearance beforehand.

Using corporate documents ◄ **Figure 1-24**

- Experts and authorities in the field, or other members of your organization. Talking to other people who are knowledgeable about your topic will give you additional insight.

Talking to experts and authorities ◄ **Figure 1-25**

- Interviews, surveys, and observations. If you do your own interviews, surveys, and observations, be prepared with a list of specific questions, and always be respectful of other people's time.

Figure 1-26 **Interviewing and surveying**

- Internet sources. The Internet is an excellent place to find information on any topic. Be sure, however, to evaluate the credibility of anything you obtain from online sources.

Using the Internet ◀ **Figure 1-27**

Evaluating and Interpreting the Information You've Gathered

Not all of the information you gather will be of equal value. You still must evaluate the information you gather by asking whether it is accurate, up-to-date, and reputable. In evaluating Internet sources in particular, it's important that you consider the site's domain type (.com = business, .edu = educational institution, .gov = government organization, .net = any group or individual, and .org = nonprofit organization) and sponsor. Web sites may contain a bias or viewpoint that influences the information, such as a sales pitch. Knowing about the sponsor of a site can help you determine the credibility of the information you obtain. Information is considered biased when the authors overstate their claims, omit vital facts, or frame their statements to obscure the real issues.

> **Tip**
>
> Some sources have the look and feel of authoritative, research-based information, but are skewed by politics, profits, or personal opinions. When in doubt, check with an accepted authority in the field on the authenticity and reliability of your sources.

You should also evaluate whether the information is pertinent to your particular topic. For your presentation to the faculty at Maclay University, you located the following additional information: an article from the Tallahassee Times entitled, "Mentoring Helps Faculty Member Prepare for Tenure;" a book from the Maclay University library entitled, *A Guidebook for Providing Opportunities for Mentored Research for Graduate Students in Higher Education*; the latest annual report from the Office of Faculty-Student Mentoring Programs; an informal survey of 25 business people enrolled in a mentoring program for new businesses; and printouts of the Office of Faculty-Student Mentoring Programs Web page describing the organization's goals, funding sources, and current activities. Although all of the information is accurate, current, and interesting, the information on mentoring of graduate students and mentoring by business owners is not pertinent to the topic you will be addressing.

After you have fully researched your topic and evaluated the information you've gathered, you're ready to organize the information in an understandable and logical manner so that your listeners can easily follow your ideas.

Organizing Your Information

You should choose an organizational approach for your information based upon the purpose, audience, and situation of each specific presentation. Sometimes your company or supervisor might ask you to follow a specific organizational pattern or **format** in giving your presentations. Other times you might be able to choose your own organizational approach. Some common organizational options include: inductive, deductive, chronological, spatial, and problem-solution.

Organizing Information Inductively

When you begin with the individual facts and save your conclusions until the end of your presentation, you are using **inductive organization**. See Figure 1-28. Inductively organized presentations usually are more difficult to follow because the most important information may come at the end of the presentation. Inductive organization can be useful, however, when your purpose is to persuade your audience to follow an unusual plan of action, or you feel your audience might resist your conclusions.

| Figure 1-28 | Inductive organization |

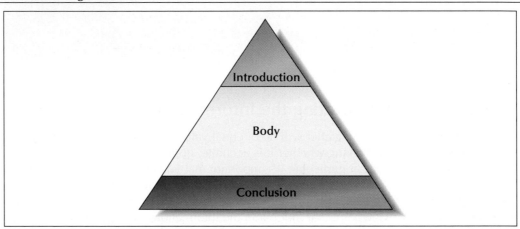

If you thought Student Senate leaders at Maclay University would resist your recommendation (that $60,000 from student fees be allocated to the operating budget of the Office of Faculty-Student Mentoring Programs to fund mentored-research grants involving undergraduate students), you would probably want to first present your reasons for making that recommendation.

Organizing Information Deductively

Deductive organization means that you present your conclusions or solutions first, and then explain the information that led you to reach your conclusions. See Figure 1-29. Deductive organization is the most common pattern used in business because it presents the most important or bottom-line information first.

Deductive organization   Figure 1-29

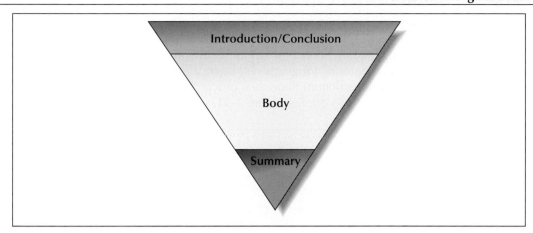

Deductive organization works well for informative presentations because it allows your audience to know your recommendations at the beginning of the presentation when their attention level is highest. Organizing your presentation to the Student Senate at Maclay University in a deductive manner would mean that you would begin by stating your opinion that student leaders should support an official partnership between the Student Senate and the Office of Faculty-Student Mentoring Programs. Then you would go on to support your opinion with further information about the value of that partnership.

Organizing Information Chronologically

When you use **chronological organization**, you organize information according to a time sequence. See Figure 1-30. Chronological organization works best when you must present information in a step-by-step fashion, such as demonstrating a procedure, or training someone to use a piece of equipment. Failing to present sequential information in the proper order (such as how to bake a cake, or conduct a soil analysis) can leave your listeners confused, and might result in wasting time and resources.

Chronological organization   Figure 1-30

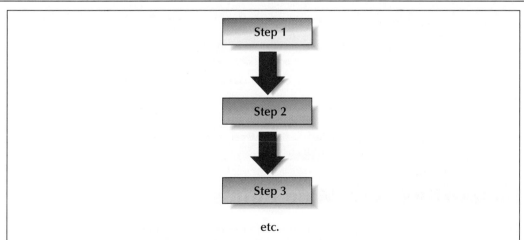

If you were explaining to faculty how to apply for funds for mentored-research activities, you would need to explain how to complete the process in a specified sequence.

Organizing Information Spatially

Spatial organization is used to provide a logical and effective order for describing the physical layout of an item or system.

If you were describing the blueprints or plans for a new office building in which the Office of Faculty-Student Mentoring Programs will be located, you would begin by describing all the rooms on the bottom floor, then proceed to the next floor and describe all the rooms on that floor, and so on. See Figure 1-31.

Figure 1-31 ▶ **Spatial organization**

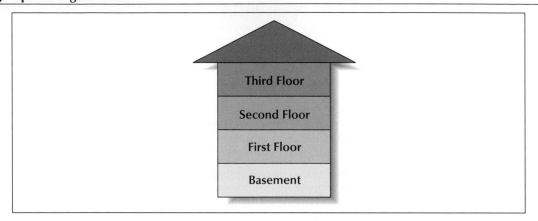

Organizing Information by Problem and Solutions

Problem-solution organization consists of presenting a problem, outlining various solutions to the problem, and then explaining the solution you recommend. Problem-solution presentations work best for recommending a specific action or solution.

Figure 1-32 summarizes the five main ways to organize a presentation.

Figure 1-32 ▶ **Ways to organize your presentation**

Organizational Pattern	Explanation of Pattern	Type of Presentation
Deductive	Present conclusions or solutions first	Informative presentations
Inductive	Present conclusions or solutions last	Persuasive presentations
Chronological	Order by time sequence	Demonstrations and training
Spatial	Order by space or position	Physical layouts
Problem/Solution	Present problem and various solutions, then recommend solution	Persuasive presentations

Supporting Your Main Points

In every presentation, it's important to keep the information simple and relevant. Research has shown that short-term memory limits what people can recall to a maximum of seven chunks of information, and that people remember specific, concrete details long after they remember generalities or unrelated pieces of information.

You should, therefore, support the main points of your presentation with evidence in the form of specific reasons, explanations, examples, data, or agreement of experts. Remember to give full credit to the authors of information you have obtained in your research. In addition, you should try to intersperse difficult concepts with easier-to-understand material, and try to move from what your audience already understands to new information.

Providing Transitions

In any presentation, you need to provide **transitions**, organizational signposts that indicate the organization and structure of your presentation. Transitions enable your listeners to realize that you're shifting gears or moving to a new topic. Effective transitions help your audience mentally summarize what you have discussed previously and prepare themselves for what you'll discuss next. Transitions also enable you to pause briefly to check your notes or to reestablish eye contact with your audience.

Appropriate transitions include words that indicate you will provide examples, make additional points, compare similar concepts, discuss results, or make recommendations. Figure 1-33 describes some useful transitions.

Using transitions | **Figure 1-33**

Purpose	Word or Phrase
Provide examples	For example, For instance, To illustrate
Make additional points	In addition, Furthermore, Next, Now I will discuss
Establish order	First, Second, Third
Compare	Likewise, In the same manner, Let's consider another
Discuss results	Consequently, Therefore, Thus
Summarize	In brief, To conclude, To move to my last point, Finally
Recommend	I'd like to suggest, What do we do now?

Now that you've developed an effective body for your presentation by supporting your main points with adequate details and creating effective transitions, you're ready to develop a conclusion or summary.

Developing Your Summary or Conclusion

The ending or final part of your presentation should take the form of a summary or conclusion. Summaries and conclusions are valuable because they help your listeners remember important information from your presentation and allow you to reemphasize your main points. Your conclusion leaves your audience with a final impression of you and your presentation, so you don't want to leave your conclusion to chance. Plan to spend as much time on the conclusion as you did on your introduction.

The following suggestions will help you create an effective summary or conclusion:

- Use a clear transition to move into your conclusion. This will signal your audience that you're moving from the body of your presentation to the closing statements.
- Recap or restate the key ideas of your presentation. Repeating the main points of your presentation will help your audience remember what you covered.
- Review the relevance or importance of what you said. Don't introduce new ideas; simply remind your audience why they should care about your topic.

- If possible, suggest where your audience can find additional resources by providing important phone numbers, addresses, e-mail addresses, or Web addresses.
- Relate your conclusion to your introduction. Some experts suggest writing your conclusion at the same time you write your introduction to assure that they both provide the same focus. Whenever you write your conclusion, compare it to your introduction to make sure they are complementary.

In your presentation to the Student Senate, you could conclude your presentation by stating, "Now that you've seen how a formal partnership between the Student Senate and the Office of Faculty-Student Mentoring Programs would work, I'd like to briefly summarize the main points I've made today. First, university students benefit when they are involved in mentored research. Second, more funds are needed to sponsor additional mentored-research experiences. Third, by forming a partnership with the Office of Faculty-Student Mentoring Programs, the Student Senate could support more mentored-research programs; programs that would directly benefit students at Maclay University."

Encouraging Action or Future Plans

If appropriate, your conclusion should suggest a clear plan of action. If your purpose was to persuade your audience to take a specific action, you should use your conclusion to suggest what the audience should do now.

For example, you could end your presentation to the faculty by stating: "Finally, it's important to understand how to apply for research funding from the Office of Faculty-Student Mentoring Programs so that you can turn your current research projects into a formal mentoring-research program. By simply submitting a Mentored-Research Grant Proposal you can receive up to $10,000 to provide undergraduate students with an opportunity to participate in your research."

Avoiding Common Mistakes in Your Conclusion

An inadequate conclusion can ruin an otherwise fine presentation. Therefore, it's important to allow yourself plenty of time to plan an effective conclusion. In preparing your conclusion, you should consider these guidelines to avoid common mistakes:

- Don't end by apologizing about any aspect of your presentation, such as how nervous you were, or your lack of time. As in an introduction, apologies in a conclusion will destroy your credibility and guarantee that your audience will react negatively to what you have presented.
- Make sure the conclusion contains only the central points or essential message of your presentation. Audiences won't appreciate a rehash of your entire presentation.
- Don't add new information to your conclusion. Your audience won't be anticipating new details and won't be prepared for it.
- Avoid ending with a trite statement like "I see my time is up, so I'll quit." When you're finished, say "Thank you," and sit down.
- Keep your conclusion short and simple. Audiences appreciate speakers who keep their presentations within the allotted time limit.

Figure 1-34 provides a basic worksheet for helping you determine the focus and organization for this and other presentations.

Focus and Organization worksheet   **Figure 1-34**

Focus and Organization
Worksheet

How will you focus your presentation?

☐ Time or chronology

☐ Geography or region

☐ Category or classification

☐ Component or element

☐ Segment or portion

☐ Point of view

What are your main ideas for your presentation?

How will you gain your audience's attention?

☐ Anecdote, story, or personal experience

☐ Statistic or relevant data

☐ Quotation, familiar phrase, or definition

☐ Rhetorical question

☐ Issue, or problem

☐ Comment about audience or situation

☐ Audience participation

☐ Statement of topic

How will you establish a rapport with your audience?

Where can you find additional information about your presentation?

☐ Newspapers or magazines

☐ Library resources

☐ Corporate documents

☐ Experts and authorities

☐ Interviews and surveys

☐ Internet sources

How will you organize your information? Check one and then explain it:

☐ Inductively:

☐ Deductively:

☐ Chronologically:

☐ Spatially:

☐ Problem/Solution:

How will you support your main points?

What transitions will you use?

How will you conclude or summarize your presentation?

Session 1.2 Quick Check | Review

1. List three methods for focusing your topic.
2. Determine which methods have been used to focus the following topics: (a) Creating Web-based Advertising Campaigns for Small Business Owners (b) How to Submit a Proposal for Doing Research with Human Subjects: Obtaining University Clearance.
3. Why should you phrase the main ideas of your presentation as conclusions you want your audience to draw?
4. What are the three basic parts of every presentation, and what is the purpose of each part?
5. List one advantage for each of the following ways to gain your audience's attention: (a) personal experiences (b) statistics or data (c) rhetorical questions.
6. List four places to find additional materials on a topic.
7. What is the difference between organizing your presentation deductively and inductively, and when would you use each of these organizational patterns?
8. Give an example of a transitional phrase you could use to indicate that you're moving to your next main point.

Review | **Tutorial Summary**

In this tutorial, you learned how to plan your presentation by determining the purpose and outcome of your presentation and how to analyze the needs and expectations of your audience. You learned how to assess the situation for giving your presentation and how to select appropriate media. In addition, you learned how to focus your presentation, identify your main ideas and persuade your audience. Finally, you learned how to organize your presentation and how to develop an effective introduction, body, and conclusion for your presentation.

Key Terms

35mm slides
anecdote
audience participation
body
chronological organization
computer-projected
    presentations
conclusion
deductive organization
demographic characteristics
demonstration
electronic on-screen
    presentation

flip chart
focus
format
handouts
inductive organization
informative presentation
introduction
main ideas
media
outcome
overheads
overview

persuasive presentation
posters
problem-solution
    organization
rapport
rhetorical question
situation
spatial organization
training presentation
transition
videoconference
Web sites

Practice	**Review Assignments**

While you're preparing your presentation to Student Senate leaders at Maclay University, your supervisor, Sela Topeni, decides to have you give three presentations on mentoring.

The first presentation will be a 30-minute, informative presentation on the value of participating in mentored-research programs. You'll give this presentation, as part of Freshman Orientation, to over 200 students in a large, computer-equipped auditorium with fixed seating.

The second presentation will be a 15-minute, persuasive presentation to faculty on mentoring students in their academic research. You'll give this presentation as part of a faculty in-service meeting, to approximately 15 teachers in a faculty lounge with small tables and movable chairs.

The third presentation will be a 5-minute presentation for university donors on why they should contribute to Maclay University's mentoring programs. You'll give this presentation, as part of a donor dinner, to about 50 potential donors in a medium-sized dining area with circular tables. Complete the following steps (note that your instructor may provide you with files containing the different worksheets you need to complete):

1. Complete a Purpose and Outcomes Worksheet for each of the three types of presentations.
2. Determine differences and similarities between the three groups in terms of the following demographic features: age, gender, and level of education. Then complete an Audience Analysis Worksheet for each of the three types of presentations.
3. Determine how the settings for these presentations will affect your audience's expectations and the appropriate level of formality. Also, determine appropriate and inappropriate media for each of the three presentations. Then complete a Situation and Media Assessment Worksheet for each of the three types of presentations.
4. Determine how you could focus the topic for the first presentation by limiting it by geography or region.
5. Determine how you could focus the second presentation by limiting it by point of view.
6. Determine how you could focus the third presentation by limiting it by category or classification.
7. Prepare an introduction for the first presentation using a story or anecdote. (You may create a fictional anecdote.)
8. Prepare an introduction for the second presentation using rhetorical questions.
9. Prepare an introduction for the third presentation using some kind of audience participation.
10. List two places to find additional information on the topics of each of these presentations.
11. Determine an appropriate organizational pattern for each of the three presentations.
12. Complete a Focus and Organization Worksheet for each of the three presentations.

Apply | **Case Problem 1**

Apply information you learned in the tutorial to prepare a presentation for an automated lighting-control company.

SystemsAide   Zoe Gallagher is director of marketing for SystemsAide, a company marketing controls to automatically control lighting, temperature, and audio/visual components in custom-built homes. Zoe asks you to help prepare presentations for her company. Complete the following steps (note that your instructor may provide you with files containing the different worksheets you need to complete):

1. Complete a Purpose and Outcomes Worksheet for each of these audiences: (a) sales personnel (b) potential clients (c) electricians and technicians who will be installing the SystemsAide controls in new homes.
2. Determine the differences and similarities between the above three groups in terms of the following demographic features: age, level of education, and familiarity with the subject. Complete an Audience Analysis Worksheet for each of the three presentations.
3. Determine the likely settings for each of these presentations and how these will affect your audience's expectations and dictate the appropriate level of formality.
4. Determine appropriate and inappropriate media for each of the three presentations.
5. Complete a Situation and Media Assessment Worksheet for each of the three presentations.
6. Determine how to focus or limit each presentation.
7. Identify three main ideas for each presentation.
8. Prepare an appropriate introduction for each presentation. (Some of your introductory information may be fictional.)
9. Determine how to establish a rapport with each audience.
10. List two places to find additional information on the topics for each of these presentations.
11. Determine an appropriate organizational pattern for each of the three presentations.
12. Write an effective conclusion for each of the three presentations.
13. Complete a Focus and Organization Worksheet for each of the three presentations.

Research | **Case Problem 2**

Use the Internet to collect information for a presentation about a nonprofit organization.

Asthma and Allergy Foundation of America   The Asthma and Allergy Foundation of America (AAFA) is a well-known nonprofit organization providing information on common allergies. Working with another member of the class, create a team presentation to inform your classmates about the goals and programs of the Asthma and Allergy Foundation of America. Obtain information about the organization by searching the Internet. Complete the following steps (note that your instructor may provide you with files containing the different worksheets you need to complete):

1. Decide on a type of presentation.
2. Complete a Purpose and Outcomes Worksheet.
3. Define your audience according to their general demographic features of age, gender, level of education, familiarity with your topic, and cultural expectations. Determine how the demographic characteristics of your audience will affect your presentation.
4. Complete an Audience Analysis Worksheet.
5. Determine the setting for your presentation and the size of your audience. Select appropriate media for your presentation and explain why they are appropriate. Explain why other media would be inappropriate.
6. Complete a Situation and Media Assessment Worksheet.

7. Determine two ways to focus your presentation and limit the scope of your topic.

8. Each of you should select a method for gaining your audience's attention, and write an introduction using that method. Discuss the strengths of each method for your particular audience.

9. Create an advance organizer, or overview.

10. Identify at least two sources for information on your topic and consult those sources. For one of your sources, connect to the Internet, and go the Asthma and Allergy Foundation of America's web site at *www.aafa.org*. To find a second source, use a search engine and try searching for information on "Common Allergies." Print out at least one page of information that supports the main points of your presentation.

11. Select an appropriate organizational pattern for your presentation. Explain why that pattern would be appropriate.

12. Identify four transitional phrases that you'll use.

13. Write a summary for your presentation recapping the key ideas.

14. Complete a Focus and Organization Worksheet.

Apply	**Case Problem 3**

Apply information you learned in the tutorial to prepare a presentation about an online company.

PersonaLine   PersonaLine, a customer support center in Westport, Indiana, assists customers in selecting and purchasing products and services from online vendors. Vendors who list their products with PersonaLine qualify for points that can be used for gift certificates for their employees. Rasmi Youssef, marketing director for PersonaLine, asks you to prepare several presentations about PersonaLine. Complete the following steps (note that your instructor may provide you with files containing the different worksheets you need to complete):

1. Think of the most recent purchase you have made online (such as concert tickets, some electronic equipment, or a birthday gift). Complete a Purpose and Outcomes Worksheet for a presentation to online shoppers, trying to convince them that they should make future online purchases using PersonaLine.

2. Complete a Purpose and Outcomes Worksheet for a presentation to online vendors, explaining how they can provide information to PersonaLine regarding their products and services.

3. Complete a Purpose and Outcomes Worksheet for a presentation to customer-support representatives explaining how to help customers who are interested in buying a product or service online.

4. Rasmi asks you to present information about PersonaLine's gift certificate programs at a retailers' convention. You'll give your 15-minute presentation in the ballroom of a hotel to over 300 conference attendees. Describe how your presentation will be influenced by this situation. Complete an Audience Analysis Worksheet.

5. Determine what would be appropriate media for the convention presentation if no on-screen technology is available.

6. Complete a Situation and Media Assessment Worksheet.

7. Determine how to focus your topic for this particular audience.

8. Create an appropriate attention-getting introduction for your presentation. Explain why other attention-getters might be inappropriate.

9. Determine an appropriate organizational pattern.

10. Complete a Focus and Organization Worksheet.

| Apply | | Case Problem 4 |

Use a presentation to analyze another presentation.

Analyzing an Oral Presentation   Attend or read a presentation, lecture, or speech and, if possible, obtain a transcript of the presentation. For example, you might hear a political speech or attend an academic presentation. Make copies of your notes or the complete transcript of the presentation for your teacher. Complete the following steps (note that your instructor may provide you with files containing the different worksheets you need to complete):

1. Complete a Purpose and Outcomes Worksheet.
2. Determine the audience for the presentation, including any general demographic information that you can determine. Complete an Audience Analysis Worksheet.
3. Determine where the presentation was given, including the setting and the number of people who were attending the presentation. Determine the media the speaker used for the presentation. Decide whether or not you feel the media used were appropriate, and whether other media would have been more effective. (For example, if overheads were used, would it have been more effective to use an online electronic presentation?)
4. Complete a Situation and Media Assessment Worksheet.
5. Determine how the speaker established a rapport with the audience.
6. Determine whether the speaker apologized to the audience or failed to consider the needs of the audience. How could these mistakes have been prevented?
7. Determine the structure of the presentation. If you have a written copy of the presentation, mark the introduction, the body, and the conclusion on the copy.
8. Determine how the speaker gained the audience's attention.
9. Determine whether the speaker provided an overview, or preview, of the presentation. If you have a written copy of the presentation, underline any overviews or previews.
10. Identify the major points in the presentation. If you have a written copy of the presentation, underline the details the presenter used to support these major points.
11. Identify the organizational pattern used in the presentation. Determine whether or not you think that the organizational pattern was effective, or if another organizational pattern might have been better.
12. Identify any transitional phrases the speaker used.
13. Determine how the speaker ended the presentation. Explain whether or not you feel the ending was effective.
14. Complete a Focus and Organization Worksheet.
15. Interview a professional in your field and ask about the types of presentations he or she gives. Organize these into the types of presentations given above. Explain your findings.

Review | **Quick Check Answers**

Session 1.1

1. a. Explains background information, knowledge, and details about a topic; academic and professional conference presentations, briefings, reviews, reports, meetings, luncheon or dinner speeches, informal symposia.
    b. Convinces audience to feel or act a certain way; recommendations, sales, action plans, strategy sessions, motivational speeches.
    c. Demonstrations: show how something works; product and services overviews, computer software demonstrations. Training sessions: give hands-on practice and feedback on performance; employee orientation, seminars, workshops, classes, courses.

2. Audiences with specialized education, such as university faculty, would expect you to use specialized terms. Audiences with less education would need more explanations and definitions.

3. How much time will I have? Will I be speaking alone? How large of an audience? How formal or informal is the setting? What will the room be like? How will the room be arranged? What equipment will be available? How much time will I have to set up? What other aspects must I consider? Will I need to introduce myself?

4. a. Effective: flip chart, poster, handout; they work with small informal groups and don't require additional equipment.
    b. Effective: posters, black-and-white or color overheads, 35mm slides, computer-projected visuals; they're better for large groups where visuals need to be enlarged, and for formal presentations.
    c. Effective: chalkboard, whiteboard, notepad, handout; they're best for small groups where audience involvement is important.

5. chalkboard, whiteboard, notepad

6. computer-projected presentations such as those created with Microsoft PowerPoint or other presentation software, Web-based media

Session 1.2

1. by time or chronology, geography or region, category or classification, component or element, segment or portion, point of view

2. (a) category, component, point of view (b) category, component, segment

3. You should phrase the main ideas of your presentation as conclusions you want your audience to draw so that you design your presentation with the listener in mind.

4. introduction (to gain and keep attention, create favorable impression, establish credibility, present overview), body (provide evidence and support for main points, present research, show relevance), conclusion (restate main points, suggest action, recommend additional sources)

5. (a) draw audience into the topic, makes topic more personal and relevant, helps audience relate to you as a person (b) increase interest in topic (c) address thought-provoking and important issues

6. popular press, library resources, corporate documents, experts, interviews, surveys, observations, Internet

7. deductive: presents conclusions first and reasoning second; informative presentations. inductive: presents reasons first, conclusions last; persuasive presentations, or when audience will resist conclusions

8. in addition, furthermore, next, now I will discuss

Ending Data Files

There are no ending Data Files needed for this tutorial.

Objectives

Session 2.1
- Select and create appropriate and effective visuals
- Present your visuals effectively

Session 2.2
- Choose an appropriate delivery method
- Prepare for questions from the audience
- Overcome your nervousness and control your speaking anxiety
- Improve your delivery
- Analyze your nonverbal communication
- Give a collaborative presentation
- Set up for your presentation

Giving Your Presentation

Selecting Visuals and Practicing Your Presentation

Case | Maclay University

Sela Topeni invites you to speak to members of the faculty at Maclay University to discuss the mentored-research programs funded by the Office of Faculty-Student Mentoring Programs. You planned and organized your presentation; now you'll prepare to give it.

In this tutorial, you'll learn the benefits of using visuals in your presentations, and how to select and create appropriate visuals. You'll also choose an appropriate method for delivering your presentation, and learn ways to improve your delivery. In addition, you'll learn how to give collaborative or team presentations, set up for your presentation, and use a facilities checklist. Finally, you'll learn how to evaluate your performance after your presentation is over.

Starting Data Files

There are no starting Data Files needed for this tutorial.

Session 2.1

Understanding the Benefits of Using Visuals in Your Presentation

It's much more difficult for people to understand and remember what they hear versus what they see. You can help your listeners comprehend and retain the ideas from your presentation by supplementing your presentation with effective **visuals**, including tables, charts, graphs and illustrations. The old adage, "A picture is worth a thousand words" especially applies to presentations because listeners understand ideas faster when they can see and hear what you're talking about. Using visual aids to supplement your presentation does the following:

- **Increases your audience's understanding.** Visuals are especially helpful in explaining a difficult concept, displaying data, and illustrating the steps in a process.
- **Helps listeners remember information.** Audiences will remember information longer when you use visuals to highlight or exemplify your main points, review your conclusions, and explain your recommendations.
- **Highlights your organization.** Visuals can serve the same purpose as headings in a printed manuscript by allowing your audience to see how all the parts of your presentation fit together. Visuals can also help you preview and review main points, and differentiate between the main points and the sub-points.
- **Adds credibility to your presentation.** Speakers who use visuals in their presentation are judged by their audiences as more professional and better prepared, as well as more interesting.
- **Stimulates and maintains your listeners' attention.** It's much more interesting to see how something functions, rather than just hear about it. Giving your listeners somewhere to focus their attention keeps them from being distracted or bored.
- **Varies the pace of your presentation.** Visuals enable you to provide sensory variety in your presentation, and keep your presentation from becoming monotonous.
- **Keeps you on track.** Visuals not only benefit your audience, but also help you by providing a means for remembering what you want to say, and for staying on track.

In your presentation at Maclay University, if you want to present information showing how the number of students involved in mentored research has dramatically increased in the last few years, you could simply read a summary of the numbers, as shown in Figure 2-1.

Written summary ◀ **Figure 2-1**

Mentored Research Data Presented in Verbal Format

"In fall semester of 1997, the number of students at Maclay University who were involved in mentored research was 40. Then for the next three years, it fell almost steadily, dropping to 30 in 1998 and 20 in 1999. There was a slight upsurge in 2000 to 50, then another little drop in 2001 to 45. Then in 2002, the Office of Faculty-Student Mentoring Projects was organized and the tide seemed to turn. In the five years from 2002 to 2007, the number of students involved in mentored research more than doubled, as the number grew from 100 in 2002 to 150 in 2003, 180 in 2004, 200 in 2005, and 220 in 2006 and 240 in 2007. The numbers increased to 260 in 2008, 280 in 2009 and 300 in 2010. During the eight years of its existence, the Office of Faculty-Student Mentoring Programs has increased by five fold the number of undergraduate students doing research with a mentoring professor."

But reading a long series of numbers would be difficult for your audience to understand, and it would be boring. By using visuals, you can present the same data in a format that's easier to understand, and more interesting. You could present the data in tabular format, as shown in Figure 2-2.

Tabular summary ◀ **Figure 2-2**

Mentored Research Data Presented in Visual Format	
Year	**Number of Students**
1997	40
1998	30
1999	20
2000	50
2001	45
2002	100
2003	150
2004	180
2005	200
2006	220
2007	240
2008	260
2009	280
2010	300

Or, you might want to create a graph instead, as shown in Figure 2-3.

Figure 2-3 ▸ **Graphical summary**

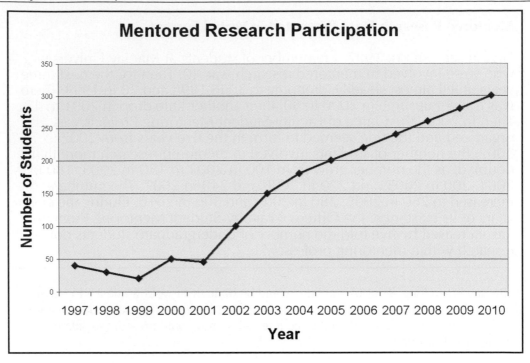

Using visuals improves the quality of your presentation and enables your audience to better understand your presentation. Visuals add information, clarification, emphasis, variety, and even pizzazz to your presentation.

You can choose from many types of visuals for your presentations: tables (text and numerical), graphs (bar and line), charts (pie, organizational, flow), and illustrations (drawings, diagrams, maps, and photographs). In the past, creating visuals was expensive, but the recent development of inexpensive computer software allows you to quickly and inexpensively create tables and graphs, scan photographs, resize drawings, and download visuals from the Internet for your presentation.

To use visuals effectively in your presentations, you'll need to ask yourself which visuals are best for your particular purpose, audience, and situation. You should also ask yourself which visuals you can create effectively.

Reference Window | Selecting Appropriate Visuals

- Which visuals are suitable for my purpose and desired outcomes?
- Which visuals would my audience understand?
- Which visuals work best for the situation in which I'll give my presentation?
- Which visuals can I create effectively?

Answering these questions to the best of your ability will increase the chances that your visuals will be effective.

Selecting Appropriate Visuals for Your Purpose

The following sections provide suggestions to help you select appropriate visuals—tables, graphs, charts, or illustrations—for your particular purpose.

Using Tables

Tables are a visual method of organizing words and numerical data in horizontal rows and vertical columns. Tables are especially useful in informative presentations where your purpose is to provide your audience with specific information in a systematic and economical manner. Tables are also effective in:

- Making facts and details accessible
- Organizing data by categories
- Summarizing results and recommendations
- Comparing sets of data
- Facilitating decisions

In your presentation at Maclay, you might want to explain the many benefits that faculty receive as a result of doing mentored research. You could use a table to summarize and emphasize the broad benefits as well as the specific benefits within each main category. See Figure 2-4.

Textual table — Figure 2-4

Benefits to Faculty From Mentored Research Projects	
Category	**Specific Benefits**
Research	Training provided for undergraduates research assistants Salaries for undergraduates provided by university Travel to conferences provided by the university
Teaching	Increased involvement with students outside classroom Mentoring research counts toward teaching load Annual Outstanding Mentoring Professor award
Citizenship	Mentored research projects considered university service Mentored research valued by other universities

Or, perhaps you want to show the number of students who participated in mentored research during a specific year. You could use a table to make those numbers more accessible to your audience. Using a table allows you to organize the number of undergraduate students involved in mentored research according to semester, and the student's year in school. See Figure 2-5.

Numerical table — Figure 2-5

Number of Maclay Undergraduate Students Participating in Mentored Research During 2008–2009 (by Semester)				
	Fall	**Winter**	**Summer**	**Total**
Freshman	0	2	2	4
Sophomore	4	8	15	27
Junior	30	38	28	96
Senior	45	57	31	133
Total	79	105	76	260

In both instances, using a table (Figures 2-4 and 2-5) allows you to organize the information so that your audience can quickly see and understand your presentation.

Using the Table feature of your word processor, you can create professional-looking tables. Remember to follow these suggestions to make your tables more effective:

- Keep the table simple. Limit the amount of text and numerical data you use. Dense text is difficult to read, and complex numbers are difficult to understand.
- Use a descriptive title and informative headings. Use a title that explains what you're summarizing or comparing, and label rows and columns so your readers know what they're looking at.
- Remove excess horizontal and vertical lines. To simplify your table, use as few vertical lines and horizontal lines as possible.
- Use shading and emphasis sparingly. Shading and textual features, such as bolding, italics, and underlining, can be distracting. Don't use heavy shading, and keep textual variety to the main headings.
- Align numbers by place value.
- Keep all numbers consistent in value and number of significant digits.

Whether or not you use a table in your presentation will depend on your purpose. Although tables are good for showing exact numbers (such as, how many seniors participated in mentored research during fall semester), they're not as good for showing trends (for instance, the increase or decrease over the past five years in the number of students participating in mentored research).

Using Graphs

Graphs show the relationship between two variables along two axes or reference lines: the independent variable on the horizontal axis, and the dependent variable on the vertical axis. Like tables, graphs can show a lot of information concisely. Graphs are especially useful in informative presentations, when you're showing measurable quantities; or, in persuasive presentations when you're comparing similar options using factors such as cost. Graphs are also effective for:

- Comparing one quantity to another
- Showing changes over time
- Indicating patterns or trends

Common graphs include bar graphs and line graphs. **Column** and **bar graphs** (graphs that use horizontal or vertical bars to represent specific values) are useful in comparing the value of one item to another over a period of time, or a range of dates or costs. In your presentation to Maclay University faculty, suppose you want to show the difference between the number of men and women participating in mentored research over the past few years. By using a column or bar graph, you could easily compare the differences between students. See Figure 2-6.

Column graph | Figure 2-6

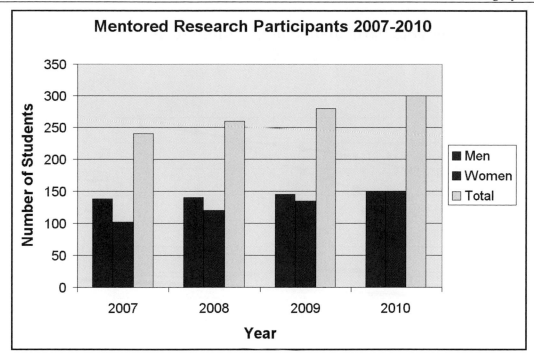

Line graphs (graphs that use points to represent the specific values and then join the points by a line) are especially effective for illustrating trends. You should use them instead of bar graphs when you have large amounts of information, and exact quantities don't require emphasis. Suppose you want to show the number of students participating in mentored research as sophomores, juniors, and seniors during the last six years (2005–2010). Using a column or bar graph would require 18 columns or bars. A more effective way to show the data would be a line graph, as shown in Figure 2-7. Your audience would immediately recognize that, while the number of sophomores has remained constant, the number of juniors participating in mentored research has increased greatly over the past six years.

Figure 2-7   Line graph

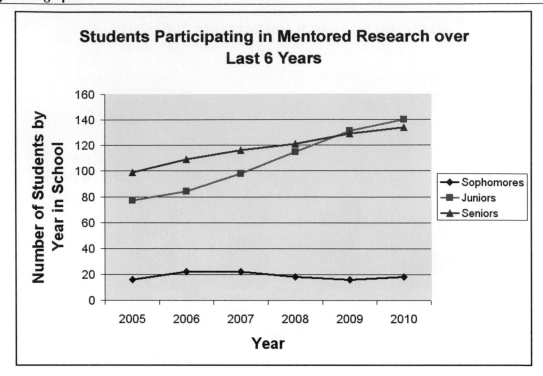

Whether or not you use a graph in your presentation will depend on your purpose. If you choose to use a graph, follow these guidelines:

• Keep graphs simple, clear, and easy to read. Limit the number of comparisons to no more than five.
• Compare values that are noticeably different. Comparing values that are similar means that all the bars will appear to be the same, and all the lines will overlap.
• Make each bar or line visually distinct. Use a different pattern, shade, or color for each line or bar in a group, and keep bars the same width.
• Label each line and bar. Remember that you're trying to help your listeners understand and use the information.
• Label both axes.

You can create simple bar graphs and line graphs by using the graphing feature of your spreadsheet or database program, or the chart feature of your word-processing or presentation program.

Using Charts

The terms chart and graph often are used interchangeably; however, they are in fact distinct. **Charts** are visuals that use lines, arrows, and boxes or other shapes to show parts, steps, or processes. While charts show relationships, they don't use a coordinate system as do graphs. Charts are especially helpful in presentations where your goal is to help your listener understand the relationships between the parts and the whole. Common charts include pie charts, organizational charts, and flowcharts.

Pie charts (charts that are shaped like a circle or pie) are best for showing percentages or proportions of the parts that make up a whole. Pie charts allow your listeners to compare the sections to each other, as well as to the whole. Pie charts can be created to display either the percentage relationship or the amount relationship.

Whether or not you use a pie chart in your presentation will depend on your purpose. In your presentation at Maclay University, you want to explain how mentored research projects benefit the university faculty as well as students. You could do that by using a pie chart to show the amounts spent on each aspect of mentored research programs. See Figure 2-8. Or, you could create the pie chart to show what percent of the Office of Faculty-Student Mentoring Programs budget is allotted to various grants to faculty, including training and travel benefits for undergraduate research assistants.

Pie chart Figure 2-8

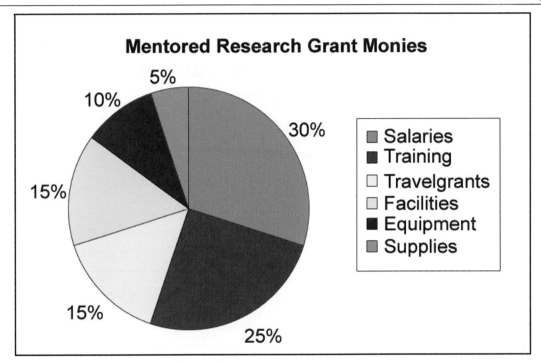

General suggestions for creating effective pie charts include:

- Keep slices of the pie relatively large. Comparisons of more than eight sections are difficult to see and differentiate. If necessary, combine several small sections into a section titled, "Other."
- Use a descriptive title for the whole and label each segment. Help your audience understand what you're comparing in terms of the whole, as well as each section of the pie. Keep all labels horizontal so they can be read easily.
- Make sure the parts add up to 100 percent.
- Begin the largest section at the top of the pie. The largest section should begin at the 12 o'clock position. The other sections should get smaller as they move around the pie clockwise, except for the "Other" section, which is usually the last section.
- Use a normal flat pie chart, unless it has fewer than five slices. In other words, you should not display the pie chart with 3D perspective, pulled-out pie slices, or in donut format. These effects can detract from seeing the pie as a whole, and can make the chart difficult to read.

You can create simple pie charts by entering your data into a spreadsheet program and then using the graphing feature of that program, or you can use a program such as Microsoft Chart directly in Word, PowerPoint, or other applications software.

Organizational charts (charts that show relationships using boxes and lines in a horizontal and vertical pattern) are effective for showing a hierarchy, such as the structure of a company or other organization, or for illustrating the relationship between departments. In your presentation at Maclay University, you could show the structure of the Office of Faculty-Student Mentoring Programs by creating an organizational chart, as shown in Figure 2-9.

| Figure 2-9 | **Organizational chart** |

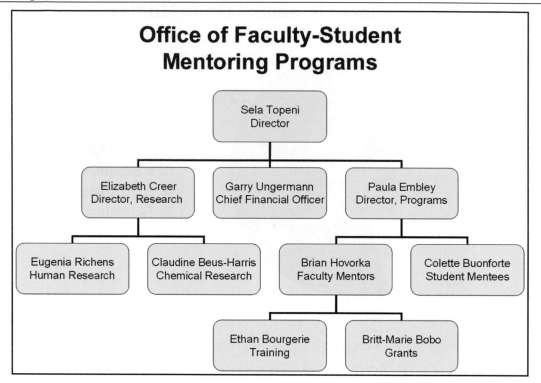

You can create organizational charts using the Organization Chart feature in Microsoft applications. There are also a number of software applications designed specifically for creating charts.

Flowcharts (charts that use lines, arrows, and boxes or other shapes to show sequence) are useful for describing the steps in a procedure or stages in a decision-making process. Flowcharts are especially effective in demonstrations and training presentations because they can visually supplement verbal instructions, and show the results of alternative decisions. In your presentation, you could present a flow chart showing the process faculty should go through in applying for a mentored research grant. See Figure 2-10.

Flowchart ◄ Figure 2-10

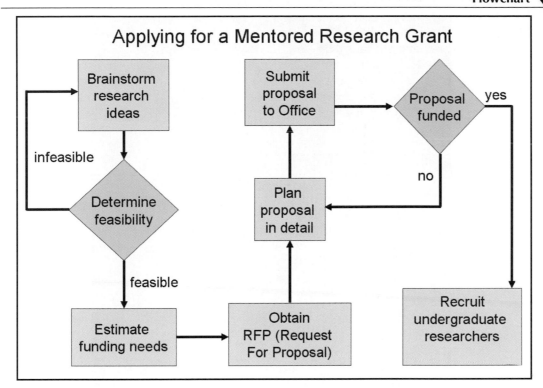

Applying for a Mentored Research Grant

Using Illustrations

Illustrations (pictorial ways to represent parts and processes) consist of diagrams, drawings, maps, photographs, and clip art. Illustrations are especially helpful in showing relationships that aren't numerical. **Diagrams** and **line drawings** are simple illustrations using lines and shapes to represent parts, objects and processes, and can be used to show how to assemble a piece of equipment, or how the parts of an item or process are related to each other. **Maps** show spatial relationships (position and location) in a geographic area. **Photographs** show what something looks like. In the past, it was difficult to obtain and use photographs in presentation visuals, but now it is relatively easy because of digital cameras and scanners. Moreover, you can improve the quality of your photographs by removing blemishes, enhancing the colors and contrast, cropping, and making other modifications with photo-editing software.

In your presentation at Maclay University, you could scan a picture (or take one with a digital camera) of students reviewing data from their research. You could then use photo-editing software to enhance the picture, enlarge it, and use it on a poster. See Figure 2-11.

Figure 2-11 ▸ **Photograph**

Clip art consists of collections of easy-to-use images that have been bundled with computer programs or purchased separately. Although clip art is readily available, not all clip art images are of the same quality. Whenever you use clip art, you should make sure the image is professional-looking and appropriate for your presentation. There are also many Web sites that offer free still and animated clips, as well as sound clips.

General guidelines for using illustrations in your presentations include:

- Use illustrations to supplement your main points. You should use illustrations, especially photographs, in a presentation because they convey meaning, not because they look pretty.
- Make diagrams and drawings accurate. New computer technology enables you to retrieve, edit, and even alter an image. Distorting the image can make it harder for your listeners to recognize and accurately interpret the illustration.
- Provide scale and focus. Crop or trim photographs to emphasize what is important and eliminate unnecessary details.
- Abide by all copyright laws. Illustrations, including photographs and clip art, retrieved from the Internet are subject to copyright laws. Make sure you understand and abide by copyright laws.

Tip

Copyright laws include the principle of Fair Use, which allows you to use portions of copyrighted materials for the purpose of education, commentary, and criticism. Feel free to use the information in copyrighted materials and to quote from them, but make sure the quotations are short and properly referenced.

- Avoid plagiarism. If you use someone else's chart, diagram, illustration, or photograph, give proper credit. If you use someone else's data to create your own visuals, you must give proper credit as well.

In summary, selecting an appropriate visual for your purpose is a matter of knowing the strengths and weaknesses of each type of visual. If you want your audience to know facts and figures, a table might be sufficient; however, if you want your audience to make a particular judgment about the data, a bar graph, line graph, or pie chart might be better. If you want to show processes and procedures, diagrams are better than photographs.

Figure 2-12 summarizes the strengths of each type of visual for the particular purposes you may have in your presentations. Use this summary to help you decide which visual is appropriate for a particular type of information and purpose.

Selecting appropriate visuals for your purpose — Figure 2-12

Purpose	Types of Visuals								
	Table	Bar graph	Line graph	Pie chart	Flow-chart	Org chart	Drawing	Photo	Map
Summarize costs	X	X	X	X					
Relate parts to whole	X				X	X		X	X
Illustrate trends		X	X	X					
Demonstrate cause and effect		X	X						
Compare alternatives	X	X	X	X				X	
Summarize advantages/ disadvantages	X								
Provide chronology	X	X	X		X		X		
Follow procedure/work flow					X				
See parts and apparatus	X						X	X	
Explain organization	X					X			
Show spatial relationship							X		X

Selecting Appropriate Visuals for Your Audience

Now that you know the purpose of each type of visual, you also need to understand how to choose a visual based on your audience. In analyzing whether a visual is appropriate for a particular audience, a general guideline to follow is that audiences familiar with the topic prefer visuals they can interpret themselves, such as flowcharts, graphs, and diagrams. On the other hand, audiences unfamiliar with the topic need help interpreting the information. Visuals for these audiences should consist of basic tables, graphs, and simple diagrams.

In addition, non-expert audiences generally have a harder time interpreting numerical data than words, so try to avoid numerical visuals. On the other hand, if you can't avoid numerical data, plan to devote extra time during your presentation to explain the numerical data. Likewise, non-expert audiences unfamiliar with certain types of images need additional help interpreting those images. For example, if you show an apparatus, equipment, or machine to non-experts, you must explain in detail what they are seeing and why it's important.

Selecting Appropriate Visuals for Your Situation

You not only have to select different visuals for different purposes and audiences, you also have to select visuals based on your situation. Selecting visuals that are appropriate for your situation involves determining which visuals work best for the medium, equipment, and room setup where you'll give your presentation. If the room doesn't have a slide projector or overhead transparency projector, you might find it difficult to use photographs. If you're limited to using a chalkboard, white board, or notepad, you might not have time to create a complex table. In such cases, you might have to provide the complex tables or graphs in posters or handouts. Flowcharts may be effective on a flip chart in a small, well-lit room; however, flip charts aren't effective in a large room, or with large audiences. Maps also are difficult to use in presentations unless they are enlarged or projected, and then they usually need a lot of explanation for the audience to understand them.

No matter which visual you select, be sure everyone in your audience can see, and make sure the medium you use to display the visual enables your audience to understand and correctly interpret your visual.

Now that you've determined which visuals are appropriate for your presentation, you'll need to determine whether you can create them yourself or need to have someone else create them for you.

Creating Effective Visuals

Even though computer programs now make it easier for you to create visuals, such as graphs and illustrations, they don't guarantee that the visuals you make will be effective. It's important to learn good design principles to make your visuals effective, especially two of the most common visuals—handouts and PowerPoint slides.

Creating Effective Handouts

Handouts are effective when the information they contain supplements, rather than competes with, the information contained in your presentation. For that reason, it's important to keep your handouts simple and easy to read. Begin by considering the overall design or shape of the page. Your audience is more apt to read your handout if it looks uncluttered and approachable. You can do this by providing ample margins, creating adequate white space, and using prominent headings.

Once you have chosen the overall design of your handout, make typographic choices that will keep the text of your handout easy to read. That means choosing an appropriate font and standard type size. Audiences in the United States typically find serif fonts (fonts with tiny lines that extend horizontally beyond the main stroke of a letter) easier to read than fonts without serifs. Sentences or long paragraphs in full capital letters, italics, boldface, or centered on the line are also more difficult to read, so these methods of emphasizing text should be reserved for headings.

Help your readers distinguish what is important in your handout by keeping related ideas together and by emphasizing key points. You can keep your handouts interesting by incorporating other visuals such as tables, graphs, and charts into the handout.

Creating Effective PowerPoint Slides

PowerPoint slides are becoming commonplace in both business presentations and classrooms. As a student, you may have objected when a teacher used PowerPoint slides to oversimplify a complex topic or created monotony by showing one bulleted list after another. Visuals are valuable because they help audiences visualize difficult concepts and to see relationships between various data, and bulleted lists are usually the least effective method for doing this.

Some suggestions for improving your PowerPoint slides include the following:

- Vary the design of your slides to keep your presentation from becoming monotonous and your audience from being bored.
- Incorporate tables, graphs, charts, and illustrations into your slides in addition to using the automatic listing function.
- Use brief overview and summary statements to help your listeners understand complex relationships and to draw conclusions.
- Don't get caught up with the "bells and whistles" of PowerPoint, thinking they will make your presentation seem more polished than it actually is. Instead, focus on making your slides coherent and your presentation well organized.

Determining Whether to Create Your Own Visuals

Even if you have access to computer programs for creating visuals, you may still need to hire a technical illustrator or graphic artist to create specialized diagrams and drawings. In analyzing whether to create visuals yourself or obtain the help of a professional, you should consider what your audience will expect, how much time you have to prepare your visuals, whether you have the expertise and equipment necessary to create the visuals, and whether you have the budget to hire an illustrator or artist.

Determining Whether You Can Create Visuals | Reference Window

- What are the expectations for my visuals?
- How much time will I have to prepare the visuals?
- Do I have adequate knowledge or expertise to create the visuals?
- What computer equipment and other production resources do I have available for creating my own visuals?
- How much money is budgeted to hire a technical illustrator or graphic artist?

If you decide to create your own visuals, be aware of the difficulties involved. Make sure you apply the best practices possible in making your visuals effective.

Creating Effective Visuals | InSight

- Keep your visuals simple. Remember that "less is more" when it comes to creating effective visuals.
- Make your visuals professional-looking. Shabby-looking or amateurish visuals will detract from your presentation and from your credibility.
- Keep your visuals consistent. Keep titles in all of your visuals consistent in size and color, so your audience can quickly recognize what your visuals are about.
- Use color sparingly and purposefully. Use the brightest color for the most important information, or to indicate patterns. Don't add color just to make things "look good," or you may end up with something garish.

Tip

A great source of visuals is the Microsoft Office Online website (*http://office. microsoft.com*). The site includes thousands of clip-art images, photographs, animations (movies), and even sound effects and music.

Of course, one alternative to preparing visuals yourself, or hiring someone to prepare them for you, is to purchase CDs of photographs and clip art, or download images from the Internet. But be aware of copyright laws. As a student, you fall under copyright "fair use" rules, meaning that you can, for educational purposes only, use copyrighted material on a one-time basis without getting permission from the copyright holder. On the other hand, if you work for a not-for-profit or for-profit company, much stricter copyright laws apply. Learn the copyright laws and abide by them.

Once you've created your visuals or obtained them from some other source, you'll need to plan how to manage and present your visuals during your presentation. The following section will help you understand how to use your visuals.

Making the Most of Your Visuals

Effective visuals can become ineffective if they aren't presented successfully. You'll need to prepare everything beforehand, and then plan how you'll integrate your visuals into your presentation. Perhaps the easiest way to figure out how to present visuals in your presentation is to create a simple storyboard showing the points you want to discuss, and the visual you want to accompany each point.

Using a Storyboard

A **storyboard** is a table or map of instructions and visuals that explains how to complete a process or describe a series of events. Storyboards are used in the motion picture industry to map the narrative of a movie with the particular camera shots and special effects that are to accompany that narrative. You can adapt the same storyboarding technique in planning your presentation. Simply take a piece of paper and fold it in half lengthwise. On the left side of the page, briefly describe your presentation point, or write down a heading from your outline. Then on the right side of the page, list or sketch the visual or visuals that you want to accompany that point. You can also include any physical movements or gestures that you want to make, such as pointing to a particular part of a slide or overhead. Figure 2-13 shows a sample storyboard for your presentation at Maclay University.

Figure 2-13	Storyboard

Benefits to Faculty From Mentored Research Projects

The first benefit to faculty is in the area of research. Currently, the Office of Faculty-Student Mentoring Programs provides 55% of its mentored research grant monies on training and salaries for undergraduate research assistants.

Show pie chart illustrating mentored research grant monies.

The second benefit to faculty is in the area of teaching. Mentored research increases your involvement with students in your research field outside the classroom.

Show photo of students reviewing their research data.

The third category of benefits to faculty is service. Mentored research projects are considered a university service because they help students get into graduate school.

Show graph illustrating increase in students getting into graduate school

A storyboard like the one in Figure 2-13 can help you choose and use the best possible visuals for your presentation.

Effectively Presenting Visuals

Follow these simple guidelines for effectively presenting your visuals:

- Use visuals to support your ideas, not just as attention getters or gimmicks. Most visuals work best when they supplement your ideas, rather than being tacked on at the beginning or end of your presentation. However, in a formal setting, you should begin your presentation with a slide or overhead showing your name, the title of your presentation, and your company logo.
- Display the visual as you discuss it. Use your storyboard to indicate when you want to display the visual; then, remove the visual after you're through discussing it. Don't let your visuals get ahead of or behind your verbal presentation.
- Stand to the side, not in front, of the visual. Avoid turning your back on your audience as you refer to a visual. Talk directly to your audience, rather than turning toward or talking at the visual.
- Introduce and interpret the visual. Explain to your audience what they should be looking at in the visual and point to what is important. But don't get sidetracked and spend all your time explaining the visual.
- Avoid using too many visuals. Present your material in simple, digestible amounts rather than overwhelming your audience with too much information.
- Turn off the equipment when you're finished.

Figure 2-14 provides a basic worksheet for helping you select appropriate visuals and determining whether you can create them.

Presentation Visuals worksheet ◀ **Figure 2-14**

Presentation Visuals
Worksheet

Which visuals are suitable for your purpose and desired outcomes?
- ☐ Text table
- ☐ Numerical table
- ☐ Bar graph
- ☐ Line graph
- ☐ Pie chart
- ☐ Organizational chart
- ☐ Flowchart
- ☐ Diagram
- ☐ Illustration

Which visuals would your audience expect and understand?
- ☐ Text table
- ☐ Numerical table
- ☐ Bar graph
- ☐ Line graph
- ☐ Pie chart
- ☐ Organizational chart
- ☐ Flowchart
- ☐ Diagram
- ☐ Illustration

Which of the visuals you checked above could you create effectively?

How much time will you have to prepare the visuals?

What computer equipment and other production resources are available for creating these visuals?

How much money has been budgeted to hire help in creating these visuals?

Tip

Be consistent in your choice of visuals in a particular presentation. For example, if you use professional photographs in one part of your presentation, you probably don't want to use cartoon-like clip art in another part. If you use a line graph on one visual to show a trend, don't use a bar graph on another visual to show a similar type of information.

Now that you've determined which visuals would be appropriate for your presentation and how to integrate them into your presentation, you're prepared to plan how to deliver your presentation.

| Review | **Session 2.1 Quick Check** |

1. Define the purpose for each of the following visuals:
   a. table
   b. graph
   c. chart
   d. illustration
2. Describe a strength and weakness of each of the following visuals:
   a. table
   b. graph
   c. chart
   d. illustrations
3. If you want to show how the number of students in your major has increased in the last five years, which of the following visuals would be appropriate? (a) table, (b) bar graph, (c) line graph, (d) pie chart
4. If you want to show the percentage of your monthly budget that goes to housing, which of the following visuals would be appropriate? (a) table, (b) bar graph, (c) line graph, (d) pie chart
5. If you want to show the managerial structure of your company, which of the following visuals would be appropriate? (a) table, (b) pie chart, (c) organization chart, (d) flowchart
6. If you want to show the procedure for getting money from an ATM, which of the following visuals would be appropriate? (a) organization chart, (b) flowchart, (c) map, (d) photograph
7. If you want to show where the Student Senate meets, which of the following visuals would be appropriate? (a) flowchart, (b) map, (c) drawing, (d) photograph
8. What is a storyboard and how would you use it to make your presentation more effective?

Session 2.2

Choosing an Appropriate Delivery Method

The **delivery method** is the approach you use to give your presentation. For example, you might write out your presentation and read it word for word. You might prefer to refer to a simple outline or notes, or you might prefer to work without notes, giving an off-the-cuff presentation. Questions you should ask yourself in choosing a delivery method include those that would enable you to determine the most appropriate method for your purpose, audience, and situation.

Determining an Appropriate Delivery Method

- What delivery method is the most appropriate for my purpose?
- What delivery method will my audience expect?
- What delivery method is the most appropriate for this setting and situation?

You could present the information you prepared in several different ways. Common delivery methods include:

- Written or memorized delivery, reading your entire presentation or repeating it from memory
- Extemporaneous delivery, giving your presentation from brief notes or an outline
- Impromptu delivery, speaking without notes and without rehearsal

Each type of presentation has its own advantages and disadvantages. You should select the delivery method that is appropriate for your purpose, audience, and situation. The following sections will help you determine which type of presentation is best.

Giving a Written or Memorized Presentation

Giving a **written** or **memorized presentation** involves completely writing out your presentation and then reading it word for word, or memorizing it in advance.

Written presentation ◄ Figure 2-15

Written or memorized presentations are especially effective when you are:

- Unfamiliar with the topic or have a highly complex topic
- Interested in using specific words for persuading or informing your audience
- Addressing a large, unfamiliar, or formal audience
- Speaking with a group, or under a strict time limit
- Extremely nervous or anxious
- Inexperienced in public speaking

Tip

A memorized or written presentation can be inappropriate when you are giving a presentation as part of a job application. This type of presentation might give interviewers the impression that you don't have confidence in your ability to explain things naturally and spontaneously.

Written or memorized presentations don't leave a lot to chance, so they work well in formal settings when you must stick to a topic and stay on time. They're also helpful if you think you'll forget what you prepared, or become nervous and tongue-tied as a result of your inexperience with the topic, or with giving presentations. Written or memorized presentations often are given on certain occasions, such as formal paper sessions at academic or professional conferences.

On the other hand, written or memorized presentations take a long time to prepare, and once you've memorized your presentation, it's not easy to alter it in response to changes in time limits or audience questions. Perhaps the biggest drawback to written or memorized presentations is that it's difficult to sound natural while reading your presentation or reciting it from memory. So your listeners may lose interest.

For your presentation to the Maclay University faculty, you're one of several speakers presenting your ideas during the faculty in-service meeting. You also have a strict time limit of 15 minutes. In this instance, you want to give a written or memorized presentation so that you can cover everything you want to say in the fewest possible words.

Giving an Extemporaneous Presentation

Extemporaneous presentations involve speaking from a few notes or an outline. Extemporaneous presentations are more flexible than written or memorized presentations, and are ideal for a more informal setting.

Figure 2-16 ▶ **Extemporaneous presentation**

Extemporaneous presentations are ideal when you are:

• Familiar with the topic or audience
• Presenting to a medium-sized group, or in an informal setting
• Giving a shorter presentation, or have a flexible time limit
• Seeking audience participation or questions
• Experienced in public speaking

Speaking extemporaneously works well when you're using media requiring no advance preparation, such as chalkboards, white boards, and notepads. An extemporaneous delivery also allows you to have a more natural-sounding presentation, or to adapt your presentation for audience questions or participation.

On the other hand, when you give an extemporaneous presentation, you may have a tendency to go over your time limit, leave out crucial information, or lack precision in explaining your ideas to your listeners. In addition, speaking extemporaneously can make you appear less credible if you have a tendency toward nervousness or anxiety.

Suppose that you're asked to speak for 25–30 minutes before a subcommittee of the Student Senate. In that instance, you would probably want to use an extemporaneous delivery so you could speak more naturally and allow members of the subcommittee to ask questions.

Giving an Impromptu Presentation

Impromptu presentations involve speaking without notes, an outline, or memorized text. Impromptu presentations are more flexible than written, memorized, or extemporaneous presentations; however, they're also more difficult to deliver effectively.

> ### Tip
> You can mix memorized and extemporaneous parts in a presentation. Sometimes your best approach is to speak extemporaneously for most of your presentation, but to read or recite memorized text when giving key information, explaining difficult concepts, or making an important summary.

Impromptu presentation ◀ **Figure 2-17**

Impromptu presentations work best when you're in the following situations:

- Very familiar with your topic and audience
- Speaking to a small, intimate group, or in an in-house setting
- Asked to speak at the spur of the moment
- More interested in getting the views of your audience than in persuading them

Generally, you should be wary of impromptu presentations because they leave too much to chance. Speaking without notes may result in taking too much time, saying something that offends your audience, or appearing unorganized. If you think you might be asked to speak impromptu, jot down some notes beforehand so you'll be prepared.

Figure 2-18 summarizes the three delivery methods.

| Figure 2-18 | Three delivery methods |

Method	Preparation	Audience	Situation	Strengths
Written or memorized	Much advance preparation	Large	Formal setting; complex or unfamiliar topic; unfamiliar with audience; definite time limit; inexperienced presenter	Effective when exact wording is important; helps overcome nervousness
Extemporaneous	Some advance preparation	Medium, small	Informal setting; familiar with topic and audience; flexible time limit; experienced presenter	Allows more natural presentation; enables audience participation
Impromptu	Little advance preparation, but difficult to give	Small	Informal setting; very familiar with topic and audience; shorter time limits; experienced presenter	Allows flexibility; enables audience participation; spur of the moment

Sela Topeni, your supervisor, will probably ask you to take 2–3 minutes during the next staff meeting of the Office of Faculty-Student Mentoring Programs to discuss your presentation to the Maclay University faculty. You'll want to write down a few notes so you'll be more focused, but you don't need to do extensive planning.

No matter which method of delivery you choose, you'll need to decide whether you want your audience to have an opportunity to ask questions. Preparing for questions from the audience is an important part of giving an effective presentation.

Preparing for Questions from the Audience

Some professional speakers suggest that you should savor the idea of questions from the audience, rather than trying to avoid them. The absence of questions, they argue, may actually indicate that your audience had no interest in what you said, or that you spoke too long. Adopting the attitude that interested listeners will have questions enables you to anticipate and prepare for the questions your audience will ask.

Interested listeners have questions ◀ **Figure 2-19**

Things you should consider in preparing for questions include:

- Announce a specific time limit for questions and stick to it. When you want to end, simply state, "We have time for one more question."
- Realize that your audience will ask questions about the information in your presentation that is new, controversial, or unexpected.
- Listen carefully to every question. If you don't understand the question, ask to have it rephrased.
- Repeat the question to make sure everyone in the audience heard it.
- Keep your answers brief. If you need additional time, arrange for it after your presentation.
- If you can't answer a question, admit it, and move on.
- Don't be defensive about hostile questions. Treat every person's question as important, and respond courteously.

In your presentation to the Maclay University faculty, you anticipate that your audience will have questions, such as the following: "What other schools provide opportunities for undergraduate students to do mentored research?" "How would I obtain funding for mentoring students in my research? How do I locate students who would like to be involved in mentored research?" Assuming that you'll be asked these questions, you can begin to plan answers to them immediately.

Now that you've determined which type of presentation you want to give, and you're prepared to answer questions from your audience, it's time to think about an almost universal problem—overcoming nervousness.

Overcoming Nervousness

Just thinking about speaking in front of other people may cause your heart to beat faster, and your palms to sweat. You aren't alone. Feeling nervous about giving a presentation is a natural reaction. But you don't need to let your nervousness interfere with you giving a successful presentation. Being nervous is not all bad, because it means your adrenalin is flowing, and you'll have more energy and vitality for your presentation. In most instances, your nervousness will pass once you begin speaking.

Sometimes, however, nervousness arises from feelings of inadequacy or from worrying about problems that could occur during a presentation. The best way to overcome these concerns is to carefully plan and prepare your presentation, and then practice it so you can relax and not worry.

Figure 2-20 | **Plan, prepare, and practice**

Overcoming Nervousness | InSight

Experienced public speakers have learned several ways of overcoming nervousness:

- Focus your presentation on your listeners' needs, not on yourself. When you focus your mind on meeting the needs of your audience, you begin to forget about yourself and how the audience might respond to you.
- Think positively about your presentation. Be optimistic and enthusiastic about your opportunity to gain experience. Visualize yourself as calm and confident.
- Work with your nervousness. Realize that some nervousness is normal and will help make your presentation better. Remember, your audience isn't nearly as concerned about your nervousness as you are.
- Give yourself plenty of time before your presentation. Arrive early to avoid rushing around before your presentation. Devote a few minutes beforehand to relax and review your presentation notes.
- Talk to people beforehand. It's easier to talk to people you know than to complete strangers. If you will think of your audience as friends who want you to succeed, you'll gain new confidence in presenting your ideas to them.
- When you first stand up, look at your audience and smile. Then take a few slow breaths to calm yourself before you begin to speak.
- Don't expect everything to be perfect. Have backup plans in case something goes wrong, but handle problems with grace and a sense of humor.
- Observe other presenters. Make a list of the things they do that you like, and try to implement them into your own presentations.

In preparation for your presentation to the Maclay faculty, you decide to talk to a few teachers beforehand. After meeting with several faculty members, you realize that they're concerned with many of the same questions, such as how to submit a proposal for funding their research. You realize that they're interested in obtaining helpful information about what the Office of Faculty-Student Mentoring Programs is looking for in a grant proposal. You decide to add some information about grant applications in your presentation.

Practicing Your Presentation

The most effective way to overcome your nervousness and deliver a smooth presentation is to practice, practice, and practice. Begin by simply rehearsing the key points of your presentation in your mind. Then rehearse your presentation in front of a few close friends. Ask your friends what you can do to improve your presentation. Pay special attention to what they say about key aspects of your presentation, such as your introduction, main points, and conclusion. Then rehearse your presentation again.

Tip

If you ask someone to critique your presentation, be prepared to take criticism. Even if you think the criticism is unjustified, make a note of it and ask yourself, "How can I use this criticism to improve my presentation?"

Figure 2-21 | **Practicing gives you confidence**

As you rehearse, use your visual aids and try to speak at the same pace you'll use when giving your presentation. Ask someone to time your presentation. By practicing your presentation until you're comfortable with every aspect of it, you'll go a long way toward reducing the apprehension that comes with feeling unprepared. Practicing your presentation will help you feel more confident as a speaker.

Practicing Your Presentation | Reference Window

- Practice in front of a few friends and a sample of your presentation audience.
- Ask your friends to give you suggestions on how to improve your presentation.
- Time your presentation using the speaking pace you'll use during your presentation.
- Practice with your visual aids.
- Pay particular attention to your introduction, main points, and conclusion.

In an effort to prepare for your presentation to the Student Senate, you ask another intern to listen to what you prepared. She says she's not clear on how working as a mentored research assistant helps develop problem-solving skills for graduate school. You make a note to add another example to support that point.

The next sections will help you learn how to improve your delivery by establishing eye contact and using a pleasant, natural speaking voice.

Improving Your Delivery

No matter how well you prepare your presentation, you won't be successful if your delivery is ineffective. No one enjoys a presentation when the speaker refuses to look up, or drones on endlessly in a monotone voice. The best presentations are those where the presenter appears confident and speaks naturally in a conversational manner.

As you practice your presentation, remember to project yourself as a confident and qualified speaker. Two ways that help you appear confident are establishing eye contact with your listeners and speaking in a natural voice.

Establishing Eye Contact

One of the most common mistakes beginners make is failing to establish eye contact with their audience. Speakers who keep their eyes on their notes, stare at their visuals, or look out over the heads of their audience create an emotional distance between themselves and their listeners.

A better method is to look directly at your listeners, even if you have to pause to look up. To establish eye contact, you should look at individuals, not just scan the audience. Focus on a particular member of the audience for just a second or two, then move on to someone else until you eventually get to most of the people in the audience or, if the audience is large, to most parts of the presentation room. You can usually judge how the presentation is going by your audience's reaction, and make adjustments accordingly.

Figure 2-22 ▶ **Establish eye contact**

Reference Window | **Establishing Eye Contact**

- Look directly at your listeners.
- Look at individuals; don't just scan the audience.
- Focus on a particular person, and then move on to someone else.
- Eventually look at most of the people or most areas of the audience.

As part of your presentation to the faculty, you'll want to look directly at each faculty member. Doing so will enable you to create a personal connection with your audience, and see how they're responding to your presentation.

Using a Pleasant, Natural Voice

Most successful presenters aren't blessed with the deep voice of a professional news broadcaster or the rich, full voice of an opera singer; however, they use a pleasant, natural voice to make their presentations more interesting.

Consider these suggestions for making your voice more pleasant and appealing:

- Use your natural speaking voice and a conversational manner. Think of talking to your audience as you would to a friend or teacher. This will allow you to use a voice that is more natural and easy to listen to.
- Vary the pitch, rate, and volume of your voice. Overcome monotony by emphasizing important words, pausing at the end of lengthy sentences, and slowing down during transitions. However, don't let the volume of your voice drop at the end of sentences.
- Stand up straight. Improving your posture allows you to project your voice by putting your full strength behind it.

- Learn to relax. Relaxing will improve the quality of your voice by keeping your muscles loose and your voice more natural.
- Practice breathing deeply, which gives you adequate air to speak properly.

Use your natural voice | **Figure 2-23**

Using Proper Grammar and Pronunciation

One of the best ways to be seen as a credible speaker is to use proper grammar and pronunciation. To assure you're pronouncing a word correctly, check its pronunciation in a dictionary.

Avoiding Common Problems in Pronunciation | InSight

Here are some common pronunciation problems:

- Mispronunciations caused by dropping a letter, such as "liberry" instead of "library," or "satistics" instead of "statistics"
- Mispronunciations caused by adding a letter or inserting the wrong letter, such as "acrost" instead of "across," "learnt" instead of "learned," or "stadistics" instead of "statistics"
- Colloquial expressions, such as "crick" instead of "creek," or "ain't" instead of "isn't" or "aren't"
- Lazy pronunciation caused by dropping the final letters, such as "speakin" rather than "speaking"

As part of your presentation to the Maclay faculty, you wonder how to pronounce the word "data." You look it up in your dictionary and find that the preferred pronunciation is "dāta," not "dăta."

Using Non-Verbal Communication

Nonverbal communication is the way you convey a message without saying a word. Most nonverbal communication deals with how you use your body to communicate—how you look, stand, and move.

Checking Your Appearance and Posture

Your appearance creates your audience's first impression of you, so make sure your dress and grooming contribute to the total impression you want to convey to your audience. Dress appropriately for the situation, and in a manner that doesn't detract from your presentation.

For your presentation to the Maclay faculty, you should wear nicer clothing than you wear to class. This might mean dress slacks and shirt for a man, and a skirt and blouse or dress for a woman. For a formal presentation, you should wear business attire, such as a suit and tie for a man and a suit or tailored dress for a woman.

Figure 2-24 ▶ **Dress appropriately**

An important part of how you communicate is your posture. Refrain from slouching, as your audience may interpret this to mean that you don't care or you're insecure. Stand tall and keep your hands at your side, except to change overheads. Don't bend over or stretch up to speak into the microphone; adjust the microphone for your height.

Using Natural Gestures and Movement

The gestures or movements you make with your hands and arms will depend on your personality and your delivery method. It's important to choose gestures that are natural for you, so ask someone else whether your gestures are distracting. Informal presentations lend themselves to more gestures and movement than do formal presentations where you're standing in front of a microphone on a podium. But giving a formal presentation doesn't mean you should hide behind the lectern, or behave like a robot. Even formal presentations allow for gestures that are purposeful, spontaneous, and natural.

In your presentation to the Maclay faculty, you plan to stand at a podium. But during a staff meeting at the Office of Faculty-Student Mentoring Programs, you would stand closer to your coworkers, and would probably be more animated.

Avoiding Annoying Mannerisms

Be aware of your unique **mannerisms** (recurring or unnatural movements of your voice or body) that can be annoying, such as raising your voice and eyebrows as if you are talking to children; playing with your car keys, a pen, or equipment; or fidgeting, rocking, and pacing. All of these mannerisms can communicate nervousness, as well as detract from your presentation.

> **Tip**
>
> The most common, annoying verbal mannerism is excessive use of "a," "um," "like," and "ya know."

Using Non-Verbal Communication | Reference Window

- Establish eye contact by looking directly at listeners and focusing on a particular person.
- Use your natural speaking voice and a conversational manner. Vary the pitch, rate, and volume of your voice. Breathe deeply.
- Stand tall and keep your hands at your side.
- Use natural gestures.
- Avoid recurring movements that can be annoying and mannerisms, such as rocking and pacing.

After you practice your presentation to the Maclay faculty in front of a friend, she points out that you kept clicking the clip on your pen. You make a note to leave your pen in your backpack during your presentation.

Giving Collaborative or Team Presentations

Collaborative presentations (giving your presentation as part of a group or team) are becoming a common occurrence. Because much of the work in business and industry is collaborative, it's only natural that presentations often are given as a team. The benefits of collaborative presentations include the following:

- Giving more people valuable experience. Collaborative presentations involve more people and give each member of a team experience in communicating ideas.

- Providing more workers with exposure and the rewards of a task accomplished.
- Allowing for a greater range of expertise and ideas.
- Enabling more discussion.
- Presenting greater variety in presentation skills and delivery styles.

A successful collaborative or team presentation depends on your group's ability to plan thoroughly and practice together. The following suggestions are meant to help you have a successful group presentation:

- Plan for the transitions between speakers.
- Observe time constraints.
- Show respect for everyone and for his or her ideas.
- Involve the whole team in your planning.
- Be sensitive to personality and cultural differences.

Figure 2-25 **Team presentation**

Figure 2-26 provides a basic worksheet for practicing and delivering your presentation.

Presentation Delivery worksheet | Figure 2-26

Presentation Delivery Worksheet

What delivery method is the most appropriate for your purpose, audience, and situation?

☐ Written or memorized delivery chronology

☐ Extemporaneous delivery

☐ Impromptu delivery

What questions will your audience probably ask?

What are your audience's needs?

What do you enjoy most in a presentation? How can you implement this in your own presentation?

Team Presentation
Transitions between speakers:
Time allotted for each speaker:

Rehearsal Checkoff

☐ Practiced presentation in front of friends or sample audience.

☐ Asked friends for suggestions and feedback on presentation.

☐ Timed your presentation. Time in minutes:

☐ Practiced with visual aids.

☐ Gave particular attention to introduction, main points, and conclusion.

Evaluation by Your Sample Audience			
Established eye contact with audience	☐ Excellent	☐ Good	☐ Needs improvement
Used natural voice	☐ Excellent	☐ Good	☐ Needs improvement
Used conversational manner	☐ Excellent	☐ Good	☐ Needs improvement
Varied pitch, rate, and volume of voice	☐ Excellent	☐ Good	☐ Needs improvement
Stood up straight	☐ Excellent	☐ Good	☐ Needs improvement
Appeared relaxed	☐ Excellent	☐ Good	☐ Needs improvement
Used proper grammar and pronunciation	☐ Excellent	☐ Good	☐ Needs improvement
Well dressed and groomed	☐ Excellent	☐ Good	☐ Needs improvement
Used natural gestures and movements	☐ Excellent	☐ Good	☐ Needs improvement
Free of annoying mannerisms	☐ Excellent	☐ Good	☐ Needs improvement

Setting Up for Your Presentation

Even the best-planned and practiced presentation can fail if your audience can't see or hear your presentation, or if they're uncomfortable. That's why it's important to include the **setup**, or physical arrangements, for your presentation as a critical element of preparation. Of course, there are some things over which you have no control. If you're giving your presentation as part of a professional conference, you can't control whether the room you're assigned is the right size for your audience. Sometimes (but certainly not always) you can't control what projection systems are available, the thermostat setting in the room, or the quality of the speaker system. But you can control many of the factors that could interfere with or enhance the success of your presentation, if you consider them in advance.

You've probably attended a presentation where the speaker stepped up to the microphone only to find that it wasn't turned on. Or, the speaker turned on the overhead projector to find that the bulb was burned out. Or, the speaker had to wait while the facilities staff adjusted the focus on the slide projector. Much of the embarrassment and lost time can be prevented if the speaker plans ahead and makes sure the equipment works.

Figure 2-27 | **Setting up for the presentation**

Even when the equipment works, it might not work the same as equipment with which you are familiar. One way to prevent this problem is to use your own equipment, or practice in advance with the available equipment. When you must use the available equipment but can't practice with it in advance, you should prepare for the worst and plan ahead.

InSight | **Planning Ahead**

Here are a few suggestions for planning ahead:

- Contact the facilities staff before your presentation to make sure they have the equipment you need. Also make sure the equipment is scheduled for the time and place of your presentation.
- Make sure your equipment is compatible with the facilities at your presentation site. For instance, what version is the software installed on the computer you'll use?
- Take backup supplies of chalk, markers, and extension cords.
- If you plan to use visuals requiring a sophisticated projection system, bring along other visuals, such as overhead transparencies or handouts, as a backup in the event that the computer or slide projector fails.
- If possible, arrive early and test the equipment. Allow yourself enough time before your presentation to practice with the equipment and contact technical staff if problems occur.
- Use a Facilities Checklist to help you anticipate and prevent problems.

Not all of the facilities are under your control. In your presentation to the Maclay faculty, you will have access to the facilities staff, but you won't be authorized to change things like temperature settings or the arrangement of chairs. On the other hand, during your staff meetings at the Office of Faculty-Student Mentoring Programs, you can move the chairs away from the table and into a semicircle, and you can adjust the temperature controls to make the room more comfortable.

Using a Facilities Checklist

Using a Facilities Checklist, a list of things to bring or do to set up for your presentation, will help you ensure that your audience is comfortable and your equipment works. Planning ahead will also help you prevent many potential problems. The Facilities Checklist divides the areas you should consider in setting up your presentation into the following categories: room, layout, equipment, presentation materials, supporting services, and skills. See Figure 2-28.

Facilities Checklist | Figure 2-28

Facilities Checklist

Room	
	☐ Is the room the right size?
	☐ Is the lighting adequate?
	☐ Is the ventilation working properly?
	☐ Is the temperature setting comfortable?
	☐ Is the room free of distracting noises?
Layout	☐ Are the chairs arranged how you want them?
	☐ Are the stand, podium, and microphone set up properly?
	☐ Is the lighting set properly for your type of visuals?
Equipment	☐ Is the electricity on?
	☐ Are there needed extension cords?
	☐ Are all the light bulbs functioning?
	☐ Does the overhead projector, slide projector, or computer projector or Internet connection work properly?
	☐ Is the microphone working with its volume properly adjusted?
	☐ Is the microphone adjusted to the right height?
	☐ Are electrical cords arranged so you don't get entangled in them or trip over them?
	☐ For large presentation rooms, are there microphones set up in the audience for questions and comments, and do they all work properly?

Presentation Materials	
	☐ Do you have all your visuals (slides, overheads, electronic presentation, handouts, or demonstration items)?
	☐ Do you have a pointer?
	☐ If you're using a laser pointer, is it working properly?
	☐ Is a tripod available for your poster or notepad?
	☐ Are there thumbtacks, pins, or tape for your poster or signs?
	☐ Are your slides properly loaded into the slide projector carousel or slide tray?
	☐ Do you have a chalkboard, white board, or notepad and chalk or pens?
Supporting Services	☐ Do you have drinking water?
	☐ Does the audience have notepaper and pens?
	☐ Does the entrance to the presentation room give information about the speaker or session being held there?
	☐ Do you know how to handle audiovisual, lighting, or sound problems in the event something goes wrong?
Skills	☐ Do you know how to work the audiovisual equipment?
	☐ Do you know how to adjust the house lights?
	☐ Do you know how to use the mobile microphone?
	☐ Do you know how to adjust the microphone volume?
	☐ Do you know how much room you have on the podium so you don't fall off?
	☐ Do you know how to access the Internet?

In considering the room in which you'll give your presentation, you'll want to check whether the room is properly ventilated, adequately lighted, and free from distracting noises, such as clanking of dishes in the kitchen, hammering and sawing by work crews, or interference from the speakers in adjacent rooms.

In considering the layout of the room, you'll want to make sure the chairs are arranged so that everyone in the audience can see and hear your presentation. You'll also want to make sure the microphone stand provides enough room for your notes, or that the equipment, such as the overhead projector, is close enough that you won't have to walk back and forth to your notes.

In considering the equipment, you'll want to check to make sure all the needed equipment is available and functioning properly. You'll also want to make sure you have adequate space for your equipment and access to electrical outlets. You might want to make arrangements for extra bulbs for the projector or overhead, or bring your own.

In considering the presentation materials, you'll want to make sure that you have chalk or markers for the chalkboard and white board, an easel to support your visuals, or thumbtacks you can use to mount your visuals on the wall or a poster board. You'll also want to make sure you have a glass of water in case your throat gets dry.

As you go through the Facilities Checklist, you find that everything you need is available for your presentation to the faculty at Maclay University. You feel confident knowing that you have done everything possible on your part to prepare for your presentation. When the presentation time comes, you deliver your message with a natural, clear voice, and keep eye contact with your audience. Your audience responds favorably to your presentation, asks meaningful questions for which you are prepared, and compliments you on a job well done. Your presentation is a success in every way.

Evaluating Your Performance

You should have been evaluating your presentation all along and you may have even asked friends or colleagues to give you feedback as you practiced your presentation. So it would be easy to be satisfied with your performance and not stop to think about it afterwards. But, an important step in any presentation (and the step that is most often left out) is to review your performance after it is over to determine how you can improve your next presentation.

Figure 2-29	Evaluating your performance

You might want to ask a member of your audience to evaluate your presentation (either during the presentation or after it) using the Presentation Evaluation sheet given in Figure 2-30. Having written feedback or a numerical score for each aspect of your presentation can be especially helpful in highlighting where you have room for improvement. Or you might want to reflect upon your presentation using the same evaluation criteria. In any case, evaluating your performance and setting goals for improvement ensures that your next presentation will be even better than your first one.

Evaluation of Oral Presentation

Content (10 points)

Topic was relevant and focused	5	4	3	2	1
Information was credible and reliable	5	4	3	2	1

Organization (20 points)

Main points were identified and supported	5	4	3	2	1
Overviews were helpful	5	4	3	2	1
Introduction was interesting	5	4	3	2	1
Conclusion was concise	5	4	3	2	1

Delivery (20 points)

Visuals increased understanding of topic	5	4	3	2	1
Speaker established eye contact	5	4	3	2	1
Speaker used natural voice and movements	5	4	3	2	1
Speaker used proper grammar and pronunciation	5	4	3	2	1

Total (50 points)

Strengths of the Presentation:

Suggestions:

Session 2.2 Quick Check | Review

1. List and define three common presentation delivery methods.
2. Which delivery method(s) are appropriate if you must speak under a strict time limit and want to use specific wording in your presentation?
3. Which delivery method(s) are appropriate if you're asked to speak on the spur of the moment?
4. Which delivery method(s) are appropriate if you want audience participation?
5. True or False: You should avoid questions from the audience because it shows that your audience didn't pay attention to your presentation.
6. List the most important way to overcome nervousness about giving a presentation.
7. Define non-verbal communication and give one example.
8. Give an example of a filler word you should avoid in your presentation.

Review | Tutorial Summary

In this tutorial, you learned the benefits of using visuals in your presentation and how to select the most appropriate visual for your purpose. You learned the strengths and weaknesses of visuals such as tables, graphs, charts, and illustrations and how to select the most appropriate visuals for your presentation. You learned how to create and present effective visuals. You also learned how to choose an appropriate delivery method for giving your presentation, how to prepare for questions from the audience, and how to overcome nervousness. You learned ways to practice your presentation and improve your delivery, including using proper grammar, pronunciation, and non-verbal communication. You learned how to give a collaborative or team presentation. Finally, you learned how to set up for your presentation and to use a facilities checklist.

Key Terms

bar graph	flowchart	nonverbal communication
chart	graph	organizational chart
clip art	illustration	photograph
collaborative presentation	impromptu presentation	pie chart
column graph	line drawing	setup
delivery method	line graph	storyboard
diagram	mannerism	table
extemporaneous	map	visual
presentation	memorized presentation	written presentation

Practice		Review Assignments

Using the skills you leaned in this tutorial, you'll help a new student employee to prepare and give three presentations.

Juan Lopez de Arroyo is a new student employee with the Office of Faculty-Student Mentoring Programs. You've been asked to help him prepare and give three presentations about mentoring.

The first presentation will be a 20-minute presentation to staff of the Faculty Center (approximately 5 people). Your purpose in this presentation is to inform the Faculty Center about the goals and purposes of the Office of Faculty-Student Mentoring Programs. The presentation will take place in a small conference room in the Maclay Student Center in Tallahassee, Florida, which is fully equipped with the latest technology.

The second presentation will be a 10-minute presentation to directors of the Office of Faculty-Student Mentoring Programs. The purpose of the presentation is to suggest additional mentoring programs that could be funded from a $40,000 donation given to the university by an anonymous donor. The presentation will take place in the 100-year-old Board of Directors board room. It has electricity, but no computer projection equipment.

The third presentation will be a 30-minute presentation to 45 students who will be presenting their mentored research projects at the annual Mentored Research Fair. Your purpose in this presentation is to explain the purpose of the Research Fair and to show students how to display the results of their research in an interesting manner. The presentation will take place in the large banquet hall where the Research Fair will take place.

Complete the following steps (note that your instructor may provide you with files containing the different worksheets you need to complete):

1. Determine the differences and similarities between the three presentations in terms of their purposes. Complete a Purpose and Outcomes Worksheet for each of the three types of presentations.
2. Complete an Audience Analysis Worksheet for each presentation.
3. Determine how the type of information you will present in each presentation will affect the visuals that you would use. Complete a Situation and Media Assessment Worksheet for each presentation.
4. Determine how your purpose and the type of information you will be presenting in each of these presentations will affect the visuals that you use. Complete a Presentation Visuals Worksheet for each presentation, using a numerical table for the first presentation, a graph for the second presentation, and a chart for the third presentation.

5. Explain how your purpose, audience, and situation would affect the delivery method you would use for each presentation. Complete a Presentation Delivery Worksheet for each presentation.
6. Create a storyboard showing an idea and visual for one presentation.
7. List two questions you think the audience might ask for each presentation.
8. Give an example of how your nervousness might vary for the presentations. Explain what you would do to overcome your nervousness.
9. Describe what you would wear for each presentation.
10. Using the Facilities Checklist, determine one aspect you can control and one you can't control for each presentation.

| Apply | **Case Problem 1** |

Apply information you learned in the tutorial to prepare a presentation for a catering company.

Outer Banquets   Outer Banquets is a theme-based banquet facility in the Outer Banks of Cape Hatteras, North Carolina. Outer Banquets takes advantage of the beautiful scenery and recreation facilities of the Outer Banks (including the many lighthouses for which the area is famous) to provide banquets for business groups and families visiting the area. Outer Banquets creates everything from a full-course banquet to a simple picnic. Hannah Stemme, one of the founders of Outer Banquets, asks you to help prepare three presentations.

The first presentation will be a 20-minute presentation to sales personnel (approximately 15 people). Your purpose in this presentation is to inform the sales staff about several new theme meals Outer Banquets can cater so that the sales staff can market Outer Banquets facilities. The presentation will take place at company headquarters in a large conference room. The conference room does not have a computer projection system, but does have a slide projector.

The second presentation will be a 10-minute presentation to approximately 45 potential participants. Your purpose in this presentation is to persuade your audience to consider Outer Banquets' for their corporate retreat, and to contact your sales staff for further details. The presentation will take place at a national retailers' conference in the ballroom of a large hotel. The hotel has a computer projection system, as well as a slide projector.

The third presentation will be a 40-minute presentation to four staff members who'll handle the reservations for Outer Banquets' summer events. Your purpose in this presentation is to demonstrate how to greet, seat, and attend to guests during the meals. The presentation will take place in a small conference room. There is no slide projector or computer projection system in the conference room, but there is a large white board.

Complete the following steps (note that your instructor may provide you with files containing the different worksheets you need to complete):

1. Complete a Purpose and Outcomes Worksheet for each presentation.
2. Explain the differences and similarities between the audiences for the three presentations, including any general demographics that you can determine. Complete an Audience Analysis Worksheet for each presentation.
3. Determine how the settings for these presentations would probably affect your audience's expectations and the appropriate level of formality. Determine appropriate and inappropriate media for each presentation.
4. Complete a Situation and Media Assessment Worksheet for each presentation.
5. Complete a Focus and Organization Worksheet to determine an appropriate organizational pattern for each presentation and organize the text in your presentations accordingly.
6. Explain how your purpose, audience, and setting would affect the visuals you would use. Complete a Presentation Visuals Worksheet for each presentation.
7. Determine what visual you could use to show sales personnel that the number of participants has decreased in the last year. Determine what visual you could use to convince potential participants that they would enjoy attending a banquet at Outer Banks. Determine what visual you could use to show the staff how to seat and greet banquet participants.
8. Create a storyboard showing an idea and visual for one presentation.
9. Using a Presentation Delivery Worksheet, specify which delivery method you would use for each presentation, and list one question you think the audience might ask for each presentation. Also explain how your level of nervousness might differ for each presentation, and what you would do to overcome your nervousness.
10. Using a Facilities Checklist for each presentation, list two setup details you would want to check for each presentation.

Research | Case Problem 2

Use the Internet to collect information for a presentation about small business startups.

LinzBizWhiz Maya Lin established LinzBizWhiz to help people start up small businesses. Obtain information for your presentation by going to the library and resources on small businesses at the U.S. Small Business Administration (SBA) site at *www.sba.gov* or other business sites. You're asked to create three presentations.

The purpose of the first presentation is to inform your listeners of the successful economic environment for small businesses. Your presentation will be given to 50 attendees at an entrepreneurial conference held in a large conference room in a local hotel. There is no computer projection system or slide projector available at the hotel, but your company has an overhead projector you could take to the conference.

The purpose of the second presentation is to persuade your audience of the need for local small business owners to become familiar with and abide by federal laws and regulations regarding small businesses. Your audience consists of five business owners attending a training session held at the LinzBizWhiz offices. There is a slide projector, computer projection system, and blackboard.

The third presentation, demonstrating how to write a business plan, is geared for student entrepreneurs. Your audience consists of 30 students who would like to begin their own businesses. You should base your media selection upon the facilities at your school and classroom.

Complete the following steps (note that your instructor may provide you with files containing the different worksheets you need to complete):

1. Complete a Purpose and Outcomes Worksheet for each presentation.
2. Determine the differences and similarities between the above three groups in terms of their age, education level, and familiarity with the subject. Complete an Audience Analysis Worksheet for each presentation.
3. Determine how the settings for these presentations would affect your audience's expectations, and the appropriate level of formality. Complete a Situation and Media Assessment Worksheet for each presentation.
4. Determine appropriate and inappropriate media for each presentation.
5. Complete a Focus and Organizational Worksheet to determine an appropriate organizational pattern, and organize the text in your presentation accordingly.
6. Determine how your purpose, audience, and setting for each presentation would affect the visuals you use. Complete a Presentation Visuals Worksheet for each presentation, giving an example of an appropriate visual for each presentation.
7. Create a storyboard showing an idea and visual for one presentation.

8. Using a Presentation Delivery Worksheet, identify which delivery method you would use for each presentation. List two questions you think the audience might ask for each presentation. Explain how your level of nervousness might differ for each presentation, and what you would do to overcome your nervousness.

9. Complete a Facilities Checklist for each presentation, determining two things you should check for each presentation.

| Apply | **Case Problem 3** |

Apply information you learned in the tutorial to prepare a presentation about healthy food.

Greens and Grains   Greens and Grains health food store in Lexington, Kentucky, sells natural and organic foods to shoppers who seek quality products without any hydrogenated oils, artificial colors, flavors, or preservatives. The store also offers a gourmet deli, as well as a full-service bakery. Jordon Haydel, owner of Greens and Grains, has asked you to give some presentations for him.

The purpose of the first presentation is to inform approximately 15 interested shoppers at the local Greens and Grains store about additions to the bakery, bulk foods, deli, and holistic health foods sections of the store. Your 20-minute presentation will be given in the store's small theatre, which has a white board and a computer projection system.

The purpose of the second presentation is to discuss the benefits of using soy in cooking. The presentation will be given to approximately 60 high school home economics teachers attending a national teaching convention being held in Lexington. Your 30-minute presentation will be given in a hotel conference room that has an overhead projector and a slide projector.

The purpose of the third presentation is to inform five purchasing agents about products that customers at Greens and Grains have requested. Your 10-minute presentation will be held in a small conference room that has an overhead projector and a white board.

Complete the following steps (note that your instructor may provide you with files containing the different worksheets you need to complete):

1. Complete a Purpose and Outcomes Worksheet for each presentation.

2. Determine the differences and similarities between the above three groups in terms of their age, educational level, and familiarity with the subject. Complete an Audience Analysis Worksheet for each presentation.

3. Determine how the settings for these presentations would affect your audience's expectations, and the appropriate level of formality. Complete a Situation and Media Assessment Worksheet for each presentation.

4. Determine appropriate and inappropriate media for each presentation.

5. Complete a Focus and Organization Worksheet to determine an appropriate organizational pattern, and organize the text in your presentation accordingly.

6. Explain how your purpose, audience, and setting for each presentation would affect the visuals you would use. Complete a Presentation Visuals Worksheet for each presentation.

7. Create a storyboard showing an idea and a visual for one presentation.

8. Using a Presentation Delivery Worksheet, specify which delivery method you would use for each presentation. List one question you think the audience might ask for each presentation. Explain how your level of nervousness might differ for each presentation, and what you would do to overcome your nervousness.

9. Complete a Facilities Checklist for each presentation, determining which items on the checklist would apply to each presentation.

Research | **Case Problem 4**

Use the Internet to collect information for a presentation about satellite radio stations.

Satellite Radio Stations   Satellite radio is becoming increasingly popular because it allows listeners to have access to their favorite music, sports programs, and talk shows from anywhere in the country and at any time. Working with one or two other members of your class, create a five- to seven-minute presentation on satellite radio stations for your classmates. You could get ideas for your presentation by going to various sites on the Internet. To begin looking for information, start at a search engine Web page such as *www.google.com* or *www.yahoo.com* and search on the words "satellite radio" and "satellite radio stations."

Complete the following steps (note that your instructor may provide you with files containing the different worksheets you need to complete):

1. Decide what type of presentation you'll give.

2. Complete a Purpose and Outcomes Worksheet for your presentation.

3. Define your audience according to its general demographic features of age, gender, educational level, and familiarity with your topic. Complete an Audience Analysis Worksheet for your presentation.

4. Assess the situation for your presentation by describing the setting and size of your audience. Complete a Situation and Media Assessment Worksheet.

5. Select appropriate media for your presentation and explain why they are appropriate.

6. Complete a Focus and Organization Worksheet, and organize the text in your presentation accordingly.

7. Determine two ways you could focus your presentation and limit the scope of your topic.

8. Determine a method for gaining your audience's attention, and write an introduction using that method.

9. Create an advance organizer or overview for your presentation.

10. Identify at least two sources for information on your topic and consult those sources. Include at least one information source from the Internet.

11. Select an appropriate organizational pattern for your presentation.

12. Identify four transitional phrases that you'll use in your presentation.

13. Write a summary for your presentation recapping the key ideas.

14. Complete a Presentation Visuals Worksheet.

15. Create an appropriate visual for your presentation.

16. Using the Presentation Delivery Worksheet, decide on an appropriate presentation style. Write a list of questions you think your classmates will ask.

17. Practice your presentation in front of another group in your class, and ask your classmates to complete the evaluation section of the Presentation Delivery Worksheet.

18. Complete a Facilities Checklist for your presentation.

19. Set up your classroom and give your presentation to your classmates.

Session 2.1

1. a. organize information in horizontal rows and vertical columns
   b. show the relationship of two variables along a horizontal and a vertical axis
   c. show the relationship of variables without using a coordinate system
   d. show relationships that aren't numerical

2. a. table (strengths): effective for making facts and details accessible, organizing data by categories, summarizing results and recommendations, and comparing sets of data; (weaknesses): not effective for showing change across time, trends, procedures, or spatial relationships
   b. graph (strengths): effective for comparing one quantity to another, showing changes over time, and indicating patterns or trends; (weaknesses): not effective for showing organizational hierarchy, procedures or work flow, parts and wholes, or spatial relationships
   c. chart (strengths): effective for comparing parts to the whole, explaining organizations, and showing chronology, procedures, and work flow; (weaknesses): not effective for showing changes over time or percentages
   d. illustration (strengths): effective for showing how things appear, the assembly and relationship of parts and processes to each other, and spatial relationships; (weaknesses): not effective for summarizing data, providing chronology, or showing processes

3. a., b., and c.

4. d.

5. c.

6. b.

7. b., c., and d.

8. a technique from movie industry showing dialogue and accompanying camera shots and special effects; list idea you're discussing on left side of sheet and the accompanying visual on the right side of the sheet

Session 2.2

1. written or memorized presentation—write out presentation and read it word for word or memorize it; extemporaneous presentation—speak from a few notes or outline; impromptu presentation—speak without notes or outline, or off-the-cuff

2. written or memorized presentation

3. impromptu presentation

4. extemporaneous presentation, impromptu presentation

5. False; questions probably mean your audience listened and was interested in what you had to say.

6. planning, preparation, and practice

7. conveying a message without talking; appearance, posture, body movement, gestures, and mannerisms

8. "uh," "um," "you know," "er," "a," "like"

Ending Data Files

There are no ending Data Files needed for this tutorial.

Reality Check

Most college students have to take a first-year writing class, an advanced writing class, or both. Typically a college writing class is designed to help you improve your ability to understand and interpret college-level readings, explain your own ideas in relation to the readings, and focus those ideas into a source-based, thesis-driven essay or research paper. Many times you must present a summary of your work as an oral presentation to a small group of your classmates or to your entire writing class. To create a classroom presentation, do the following:

1. Select a topic or use ideas from a paper you've written for a presentation to your writing class. Complete a Purpose and Outcomes Worksheet for your presentation.
2. Determine where your presentation will be given and what media will be available.
3. Complete a Situation and Media Assessment Worksheet for your presentation.
4. Determine how to focus your topic for this particular audience. Complete a Focus and Organization Worksheet.
5. Determine an appropriate organizational pattern for your presentation.
6. Determine a method for gaining your audience's attention, and write an introduction using that method.
7. Create an advance organizer or overview for your presentation.
8. Identify at least two sources for information on your topic and consult those sources. Include at least one information source from the Internet.
9. Identify four transitional phrases to use in your presentation.
10. Write a summary for your presentation recapping the key ideas.
11. Complete a Presentation Visuals Worksheet.
12. Create an appropriate visual for your presentation.
13. Using the Presentation Delivery Worksheet, decide on an appropriate presentation style. Write a list of questions, you think your classmates will ask.
14. Practice your presentation in front of another group in your class, and ask your classmates to complete the evaluation section of the Presentation Delivery Worksheet.
15. Complete a Facilities Checklist for your presentation.
16. Set up your classroom and give your presentation to your class or at some other venue, as the opportunity presents itself.

Objectives

- Develop file management strategies
- Explore files and folders
- Create, name, copy, move, and delete folders
- Name, copy, move, and delete files
- Work with compressed files

Managing Your Files

Creating and Working with Files and Folders in Windows Vista

Case | Distance Learning Company

The Distance Learning Company specializes in distance-learning courses for people who want to participate in college-level classes to work toward a degree or for personal enrichment. Distance learning is formalized education that typically takes place using a computer and the Internet, replacing normal classroom interaction with modern communications technology. The company's goal is to help students gain new skills and stay competitive in the job market. The head of the Customer Service Department, Shannon Connell, interacts with the Distance Learning Company's clients on the phone and from her computer. Shannon, like all other employees, is required to learn the basics of managing files on her computer.

In this tutorial, you'll work with Shannon to devise a strategy for managing files. You'll learn how Windows Vista organizes files and folders, and you'll examine Windows Vista file management tools. You'll create folders and organize files within them. You'll also explore options for working with compressed files.

Starting Data Files

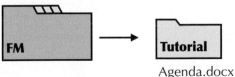

FM →

Tutorial
Agenda.docx
Holiday.bmp
Members.htm
New Logo.bmp
Proposal.docx
Resume.docx
Stationery.bmp
Vinca.jpg

Review
Billing.xlsx
Car Plan.xlsx
Commissions.xlsx
Contracts.xlsx
Customers.xlsx
Loan.docx
Photos.pptx
Speech.wav
Water lilies.jpg

Case1
Inv Feb.xlsx
Inv Jan.xlsx
Inv March.xlsx
Painting-Agenda.docx
Painting-Eval.docx
Painting-Manual.docx
Paris.jpg
Still Life.jpg

Organizing Files and Folders

Knowing how to save, locate, and organize computer files makes you more productive when you are working with a computer. A **file**, often referred to as a **document**, is a collection of data that has a name and is stored on a computer. After you create a file, you can open it, edit its contents, print it, and save it again—usually using the same program you used to create it. You organize files by storing them in **folders**, which are containers for your files. You need to organize files so that you can find them easily and work efficiently.

A file cabinet is a common metaphor for computer file organization. A computer is like a file cabinet that has two or more drawers—each drawer is a storage device, or **disk**. Each disk contains folders that hold documents, or files. To make it easy to retrieve files, you arrange them logically into folders. For example, one folder might contain financial data, another might contain your creative work, and another could contain information you're collecting for an upcoming vacation.

A computer can store folders and files on different types of disks, ranging from removable media—such as **USB drives** (also called USB flash drives), **compact discs (CDs)**, and **digital video discs (DVDs)**—to **hard disks**, or fixed disks, which are permanently stored on a computer. Hard disks are the most popular type of computer storage because they can contain many gigabytes of data and are economical.

To have your computer access a removable disk, you must insert the disk into a **drive**, which is a computer device that can retrieve and sometimes record data on a disk. See Figure 1. A hard disk is already contained in a drive, so you don't need to insert it each time you use the computer.

Figure 1 ▶ **Comparing drives and disks**

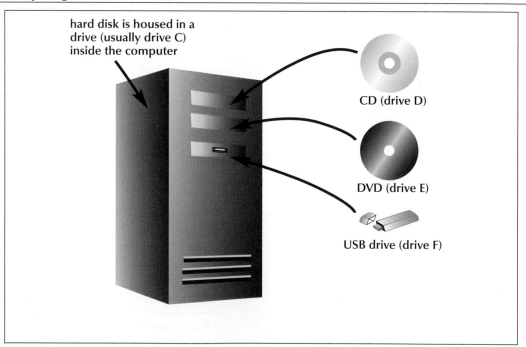

hard disk is housed in a drive (usually drive C) inside the computer

CD (drive D)

DVD (drive E)

USB drive (drive F)

A computer distinguishes one drive from another by assigning each a drive letter. The hard disk is usually assigned to drive C. The remaining drives can have any other letters, but are usually assigned in the order that the drives were installed on the computer—so your USB drive might be drive D or drive F. Most contemporary computers have ports for more than one USB drive.

Understanding the Need for Organizing Files and Folders

Windows Vista stores thousands of files in many folders on the hard disk of your computer. These are system files that Windows Vista needs to display the desktop, use drives, and perform other operating system tasks. To ensure system stability and find files quickly, Windows Vista organizes the folders and files in a hierarchy, or **file system**. At the top of the hierarchy, Windows Vista stores folders and important files that it needs when you turn on the computer. This location is called the **root directory**, and is usually drive C (the hard disk). The term "root" refers to another popular metaphor for visualizing a file system—an upside-down tree, which reflects the file hierarchy that Windows Vista uses. In Figure 2, the tree trunk corresponds to the root directory, the branches to the folders, and the leaves to the files.

Windows file hierarchy | **Figure 2**

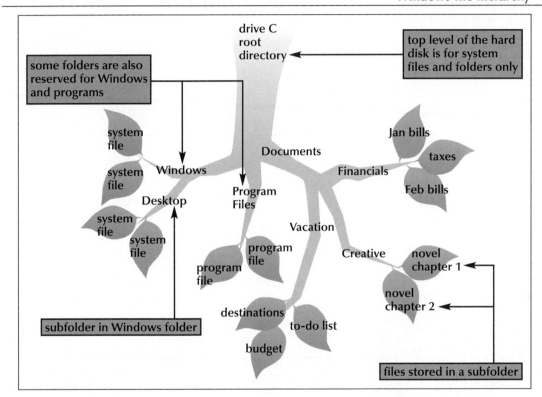

Note that some folders contain other folders. An effectively organized computer contains a few folders in the root directory, and those folders contain other folders, also called **subfolders**.

The root directory, or top level, of the hard disk is for system files and folders only—you should not store your own work here because it could interfere with Windows or a program. (If you are working in a computer lab, you might not be allowed to access the root directory.)

Do not delete or move any files or folders from the root directory of the hard disk—doing so could mean that you cannot run or start the computer. In fact, you should not reorganize or change any folder that contains installed software because Windows Vista expects to find the files for specific programs within certain folders. If you reorganize or change these folders, Windows Vista cannot locate and start the programs stored in that folder. Likewise, you should not make changes to the folder that contains the Windows Vista operating system (usually named Windows or Winnt).

Because the top level of the hard disk is off-limits for your files—the ones that you create, open, and save on the hard disk—you must store your files in subfolders. If you are working on your own computer, you should store your files within the Documents folder. If you are working in a computer lab, you will probably use a different location that your instructor specifies. If you simply store all your files in one folder, however, you will soon have trouble finding the files you want. Instead, you should create folders within a main folder to separate files in a way that makes sense for you.

Likewise, if you store most of your files on removable media, such as USB drives, you need to organize those files into folders and subfolders. Before you start creating folders, whether on a hard disk or removable disk, you should plan the organization you will use.

Developing Strategies for Organizing Files and Folders

The type of disk you use to store files determines how you organize those files. Figure 3 shows how you could organize your files on a hard disk if you were taking a full semester of distance-learning classes. To duplicate this organization, you would open the main folder for your documents, create four folders—one each for the Basic Accounting, Computer Concepts, Management Skills II, and Professional Writing courses—and then store the writing assignments you complete in the Professional Writing folder.

| Figure 3 | Organizing folders and files on a hard disk |

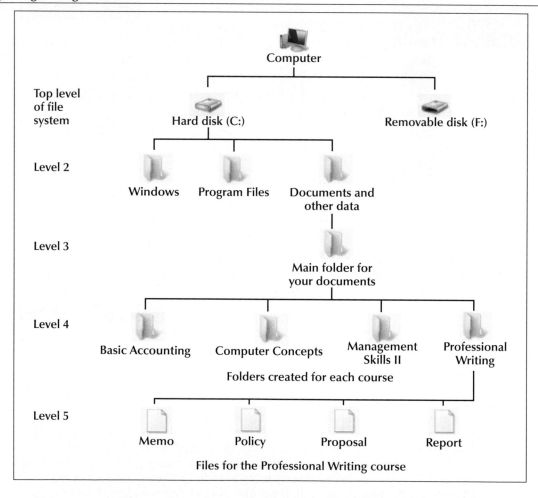

If you store your files on removable media, such as a USB drive or rewritable CD, you can use a simpler organization because you do not have to account for system files. In general, the larger the medium, the more levels of folders you should use because large media can store more files, and, therefore, need better organization. For example, you could organize your files on a 128-MB USB drive. In the top level of the USB drive, you could create folders for each general category of documents you store—one each for Courses, Creative, Finan-cials, and Vacation. The Courses folder could then include one folder for each course, and each of those folders could contain the appropriate files.

If you work on two computers, such as one computer at an office or school and another computer at home, you can duplicate the folders you use on both computers to simplify transferring files from one computer to another. For example, if you have four folders in your Documents folder on your work computer, you would create these same four folders on your removable media as well as in the Documents folder of your home computer. If you change a file on the hard disk of your home computer, you can copy the most recent version of the file to the corresponding folder on your removable media so that it is available when you are at work. You also then have a **backup**, or duplicate copy, of important files that you need.

Planning Your Organization

Now that you've explored the basics of organizing files on a computer, you can plan the organization of your files for this book by writing in your answers to the following questions:

1. How do you obtain the files for this book (on a USB drive from your instructor, for example)?_____
_____

2. On what drive do you store your files for this book (drive A, C, D, for example)?
_____

3. Do you use a particular folder on this drive? If so, which folder do you use?_____
_____

4. Is this folder contained within another folder? If so, what is the name of that main folder?_____

5. On what type of disk or drive do you save your files for this book (hard disk, USB drive, CD, or network drive, for example)?_____

If you cannot answer any of these questions, ask your instructor for help.

Exploring Files and Folders

Windows Vista provides two tools for exploring the files and folders on your computer—Windows Explorer and the Computer window. Both display the contents of your computer, using icons to represent drives, folders, and files. However, by default, each presents a slightly different view of your computer. **Windows Explorer** shows the files, folders, and drives on your computer, making it easy to navigate, or move from one location to another within the file hierarchy. The **Computer** window shows the drives on your computer and makes it easy to perform system tasks, such as viewing system information. Most of the time, you use one of these tools to open a **folder window** that displays the files and subfolders in a folder.

The Windows Explorer and Computer windows are divided into two sections, called **panes**. The left pane is the **Navigation pane**. It contains a **Favorite Links list**, which can provide quick access to the folders you use often, and a **Folders list**, which shows the hierarchy of the folders and other locations on your computer. The right pane lists the contents of these folders and other locations. If you select a folder in the left pane, for example, the files stored in that folder appear in the right pane.

Tip

The term "folder window" refers to any window that displays the contents of a folder, including the Computer, Windows Explorer, and Recycle Bin windows. In all of these windows, you can use the same techniques to display folders and their contents, navigate your computer, and work with files.

If the Folders list showed all the folders on your computer at once, it could be a very long list. Instead, you open drives and folders only when you want to see what they contain. If a folder contains subfolders, an expand icon ▷ appears to the left of the folder icon. (The same is true for drives.) To view the folders contained in an object, you click the expand icon. A collapse icon ◢ then appears next to the folder icon; click the collapse icon to hide the folder's subfolders. To view the files contained in a folder, you click the folder icon, and the files appear in the right pane. See Figure 4.

Figure 4   **Viewing folder contents in Windows Explorer**

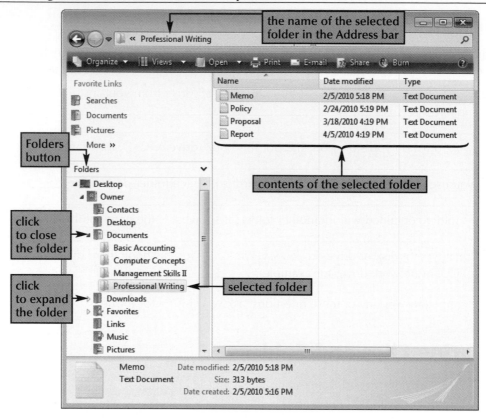

Tip

To display or hide the Folders list in a folder window, click the Folders button in the Navigation pane.

Using the Folders list helps you navigate your computer and orients you to your current location. As you move, copy, delete, and perform other tasks with the files in the right pane of a folder window, you can refer to the Folders list to see how your changes affect the overall organization.

Both Windows Explorer and the Computer window let you view, organize, and access the drives, folders, and files on your computer. In addition to using the Folders list, you can navigate your computer in other ways:

• **Opening drives and folders in the right pane**: To view the contents of a drive or folder, double-click the drive or folder icon in the right pane of a folder window.
• **Using the Address bar**: Use the Address bar to navigate to a different folder. The Address bar displays your current folder as a series of locations separated by arrows. Click a folder name or an arrow button to navigate to a different location.

- **Clicking the Back, Forward, and Recent Pages buttons**: Use the Back, Forward, and Recent Pages buttons to navigate to other folders you have already opened. After you change folders, use the Back button to return to the original folder or click the Recent Pages button to navigate to a location you've visited recently.
- **Using the Search box**: To find a file or folder stored in the current folder or its subfolders, type a word or phrase in the Search box. The search begins as soon as you start typing. Windows finds files based on text in the filename, text within the file, and other characteristics of the file, such as tags (descriptive words or phrases you add to your files) or the author.

These navigation controls are available in Windows Explorer, Computer, and other folder windows, including many dialog boxes. In fact, all of these folder windows share common tools. By default, when you first open Computer, it shows all the drives available on your computer, whereas Windows Explorer shows the folders on your computer. However, by changing a single setting, you can make the two windows interchangeable. If you open the Folders list in Computer, you have the same setup as Windows Explorer. Likewise, if you close the Folders list in the Windows Explorer window, you have the same setup as in the Computer window.

Shannon prefers to use Windows Explorer to manage her files. You'll use Windows Explorer to manage files in the rest of this tutorial.

Using Windows Explorer

Windows Vista also provides a folder for your documents—your **personal folder**, which is designed to store the files and folders you work with regularly and is labeled with the name you use to log on to Windows Vista, such as Shannon. On your own computer, this is where you can keep your data files—the memos, videos, graphics, music, and other files that you create, edit, and manipulate in a program. Windows Vista provides a few built-in folders in your personal folder, including Music (for songs and other music files), Pictures (for photos and other image files), and Documents (for text, spreadsheets, presentations, and other files you create). If you are working in a computer lab, you might not have a personal folder or be able to access the Documents folder, or you might have a personal folder or be able to store files there only temporarily because that folder is emptied every night. Instead, you might permanently store your Data Files on removable media or in a different folder on your computer or network.

When you start Windows Explorer from the All Programs menu, it opens to the Documents folder by default. If you cannot access the Documents folder, the screens you see as you perform the following steps will differ. However, you can still perform the steps accurately.

To examine the organization of your computer using Windows Explorer:

▶ 1. Click the **Start** button 🌐 on the taskbar, click **All Programs**, click **Accessories**, and then click **Windows Explorer**. The Windows Explorer window opens.

▶ 2. Scroll the Folders list, point to the **Folders list**, and then click the **expand** icon ▷ next to the Computer icon. The drives and other useful locations on your computer appear under the Computer icon, as shown in Figure 5. The contents of your computer will differ.

Figure 5 ▶ **Viewing the contents of your computer**

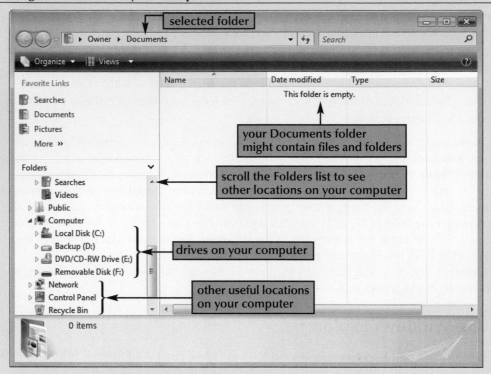

▶ **3.** Click the **expand** icon ▷ next to the Local Disk (C:) icon. The contents of your hard disk appear under the Local Disk (C:) icon.

Trouble? If you do not have permission to access drive C, skip Step 3 and read but do not perform the remaining steps.

Documents is still the selected folder. To view the contents of an object in the right pane, you can click the object's icon in the Folders list.

▶ **4.** If necessary, scroll up the list, and then click the **Public** folder in the Folders list. Its contents appear in the right pane. Public is a built-in Windows Vista folder that contains folders any user can access on this computer.

Navigating to Your Data Files

The **file path** is a notation that indicates a file's location on your computer. The file path leads you through the Windows file system to your file. For example, the Holiday file is stored in the Tutorial subfolder of the FM folder. If you are working on a USB drive, for example, the path to this file might be as follows:

F:\FM\Tutorial\Holiday.bmp

This path has four parts, and each part is separated by a backslash (\ ):

- **F**: The drive name; for example, drive F might be the name for the USB drive. If this file were stored on the hard disk, the drive name would be C.
- **FM**: The top-level folder on drive F.
- **Tutorial**: A subfolder in the FM folder.
- **Holiday.bmp**: The full filename with the file extension.

If someone tells you to find the file F:\FM\Tutorial\Holiday.bmp, you know you must navigate to your USB drive, open the FM folder, and then open the Tutorial folder to find the Holiday file. By default, the Address bar includes arrow buttons instead of back-slashes when displaying a path. To navigate to a different folder in the FM folder, for example, you can click the arrow button to right of FM in the Address bar, and then click the folder name.

You can use Windows Explorer to navigate to the Data Files you need for the rest of this tutorial. Refer to the information you provided in the "Planning Your Organization" section and note the drive on your system that contains your Data Files. In the following steps, this is drive F, a USB drive. If necessary, substitute the appropriate drive on your system when you perform the steps.

To navigate to your Data Files:

▶ **1.** Make sure your computer can access your Data Files for this tutorial. For example, if you are using a USB drive, insert the drive into the USB port.

Trouble? If you don't have the Data Files, you need to get them before you can proceed. Your instructor will either give you the Data Files or ask you to obtain them from a specified location (such as a network drive). In either case, be sure that you make a backup copy of your Data Files before you start using them, so that the original files will be available on your copied disk in case you need to start over because of an error or problem. If you have any questions about the Data Files, see your instructor or technical support person for assistance.

▶ **2.** In the Windows Explorer window, click the **expand** icon ▷ next to the drive containing your Data Files, such as Removable Disk (F:). A list of the folders on that drive appears.

▶ **3.** If the list of folders does not include the FM folder, continue clicking the **expand** icon ▷ to navigate to the folder that contains the FM folder.

▶ **4.** Click the **expand** icon ▷ next to the FM folder, and then click the **FM** folder. Its contents appear in the Folders list and in the right pane of the Windows Explorer window. The FM folder contains the Case1, Review, and Tutorial folders, as shown in Figure 6. The other folders on your system might vary.

Figure 6   Navigating to the FM folder

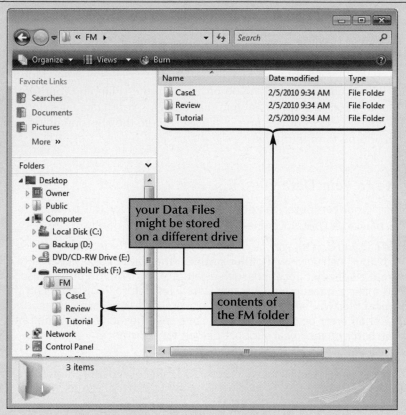

> **5.** In the left pane, click the **Tutorial** folder. The files it contains appear in the right pane. You want to view them as a list.

> **6.** Click the **Views button arrow** on the toolbar, and then click **List**. The files appear in List view in the Windows Explorer window. See Figure 7.

Figure 7   Files in the Tutorial folder in List view

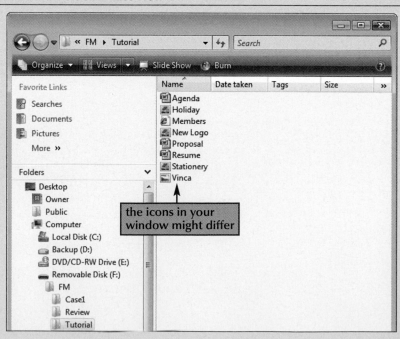

The file icons in your window depend on the programs installed on your computer, so they might be different from the ones shown in Figure 7.

Working with Folders and Files

After you devise a plan for storing your files, you are ready to get organized by creating folders that will hold your files. For this tutorial, you create folders in the Tutorial folder. When you are working on your own computer, you usually create folders within the Documents folder in your personal folder.

Examine the files shown in Figure 7 again and determine which files seem to belong together. Holiday, New Logo, and Vinca are all graphics files containing pictures or photos. The Resume and Stationery files were created for a summer job hunt. The other files were created for a neighborhood association to update a playground.

One way to organize these files is to create three folders—one for graphics, one for the job hunt files, and another for the playground files. When you create a folder, you give it a name, preferably one that describes its contents. A folder name can have up to 255 characters, except / \ : * ? " < > or |. Considering these conventions, you could create three folders as follows:

- **Graphics folder**: Holiday, New Logo, and Vinca files
- **Job Hunt folder**: Resume and Stationery files
- **Playground folder**: Agenda, Proposal, and Members files

Guidelines for Creating Folders | InSight

- **Keep folder names short and familiar**: Long filenames can be cut off in a folder window, so use names that are short but clear. Choose names that will be meaningful later, such as project names or course numbers.
- **Develop standards for naming folders**: Use a consistent naming scheme that is clear to you, such as one that uses a project name as the name of the main folder, and includes step numbers in each subfolder name, such as 01Plan, 02Approvals, 03Prelim, and so on.
- **Create subfolders to organize files**: If a file listing in a folder window is so long that you must scroll the window, consider organizing those files into subfolders.

Creating Folders

You've already seen folder icons in the windows you've examined. Now, you'll create folders in the Tutorial folder using the Windows Explorer toolbar.

Creating a Folder | Reference Window

- In the left pane, click the drive or folder where you want to create a folder.
- Click the Organize button on the toolbar, and then click New Folder (*or* right-click a blank area in the folder window, point to New, and then click Folder).
- Type a name for the folder, and then press the Enter key.

Next you will create three folders in your Tutorial folder. The Windows Explorer window should show the contents of the Tutorial folder in List view.

To create folders in a folder window:

▶ **1.** Click the **Organize** button on the toolbar, and then click **New Folder**. A folder icon with the label "New Folder" appears in the right pane. See Figure 8.

Figure 8 | Creating a folder in the Tutorial folder

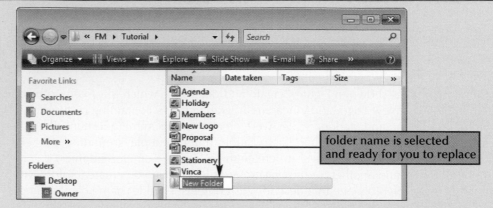

Trouble? If the "New Folder" name is not selected, right-click the new folder, click Rename, and then continue with Step 2.

Windows Vista uses "New Folder" as a placeholder, and selects the text so that you can replace it with the name you want.

▶ **2.** Type **Graphics** as the folder name, and then press the **Enter** key. The new folder is named "Graphics" and is the selected item in the right pane.

You are ready to create a second folder. This time, you'll use a shortcut menu to create a folder.

▶ **3.** Right-click a blank area near the Graphics folder, point to **New** on the shortcut menu, and then click **Folder**. A folder icon with the label "New Folder" appears in the right pane with the "New Folder" text selected.

▶ **4.** Type **Job Hunt** as the name of the new folder, and then press the **Enter** key.

▶ **5.** Using the toolbar or the shortcut menu, create a folder named **Playground**. The Tutorial folder contains three new subfolders.

Moving and Copying Files and Folders

If you want to place a file into a folder from another location, you can either move the file or copy it. **Moving** a file removes it from its current location and places it in a new location you specify. **Copying** places the file in both locations. Windows Vista provides several techniques for moving and copying files. The same principles apply to folders—you can move and copy folders using a variety of methods.

Reference Window | **Moving a File or Folder**

- Right-click and drag the file or folder you want to move to the destination folder.
- Click Move Here on the shortcut menu.

or

- Right-click the file or folder you want to move, and then click Cut on the shortcut menu.
- Navigate to and right-click the destination folder, and then click Paste on the shortcut menu.

Next, you'll move the Agenda, Proposal, and Members files to the Playground folder.

To move a file using the right mouse button:

1. Point to the **Agenda** file in the right pane, and then press and hold the *right* mouse button.

2. With the right mouse button still pressed down, drag the **Agenda** file to the **Playground** folder. When a "Move to Playground" ScreenTip appears, release the button. A shortcut menu opens.

3. With the left mouse button, click **Move Here** on the shortcut menu. The Agenda file is removed from the main Tutorial folder and stored in the Playground subfolder.

   Trouble? If you release the mouse button before dragging the Agenda file to the Playground folder, the shortcut menu opens, letting you move the file to a different folder. Press the Esc key to close the shortcut menu without moving the file, and then repeat Steps 1 through 3.

4. In the right pane, double-click the **Playground** folder. The Agenda file is in the Playground folder.

5. In the left pane, click the **Tutorial** folder to see its contents. The Tutorial folder no longer contains the Agenda file.

The advantage of moving a file or folder by dragging with the right mouse button is that you can efficiently complete your work with one action. However, this technique requires polished mouse skills so that you can drag the file comfortably. Another way to move files and folders is to use the **Clipboard**, a temporary storage area for files and information that you have copied or moved from one place and plan to use somewhere else. You can select a file and use the Cut or Copy commands to temporarily store the file on the Clipboard, and then use the Paste command to insert the file elsewhere. Although using the Clipboard takes more steps, some users find it easier than dragging with the right mouse button.

You'll move the Resume file to the Job Hunt folder next.

To move files using the Clipboard:

1. Right-click the **Resume** file, and then click **Cut** on the shortcut menu. Although the file icon is still displayed in the folder window, Windows Vista removes the Resume file from the Tutorial folder and stores it on the Clipboard.

2. In the Folders list, right-click the **Job Hunt** folder, and then click **Paste** on the shortcut menu. Windows Vista pastes the Resume file from the Clipboard to the Job Hunt folder. The Resume file icon no longer appears in the folder window.

3. In the Folders list, click the **Job Hunt** folder to view its contents in the right pane. The Job Hunt folder now contains the Resume file.

   You'll move the Stationery file from the Tutorial folder to the Job Hunt folder.

4. Click the **Back** button ⬅ on the Address bar to return to the Tutorial folder, right-click the **Stationery** file in the folder window, and then click **Cut** on the shortcut menu.

5. Right-click the **Job Hunt** folder, and then click **Paste** on the shortcut menu.

▶ **6.** Click the **Back** button ⬅ on the Address bar to return to view the contents of the Job Hunt folder. It now contains the Resume and Stationery files. See Figure 9.

Figure 9 **Moving files**

▶ **7.** Click the **Forward** button ➡ to return to the Tutorial folder.

You can also copy a file using the same techniques as when you move a file—by dragging with the right mouse button or by using the Clipboard. You can copy more than one file at the same time by selecting all the files you want to copy, and then clicking them as a group. To select files that are listed together in a window, click the first file in the list, hold down the Shift key, click the last file in the list, and then release the Shift key. To select files that are not listed together, click one file, hold down the Ctrl key, click the other files, and then release the Ctrl key.

Reference Window | **Copying a File or Folder**

- Right-click and drag the file or folder you want to copy to the destination folder.
- Click Copy Here on the shortcut menu.

or

- Right-click the file or folder you want to copy, and then click Copy on the shortcut menu.
- Navigate to the destination folder.
- Right-click a blank area of the destination folder window, and then click Paste on the shortcut menu.

You'll copy the three graphics files from the Tutorial folder to the Graphics folder now.

To copy files using the shortcut menu:

▶ **1.** In the Tutorial window, click the **Holiday** file.

▶ **2.** Hold down the **Ctrl** key, click the **New Logo** file, click the **Vinca** file, and then release the **Ctrl** key. Three files are selected in the Tutorial window.

▶ **3.** Right-click a selected file, and then click **Copy** on the shortcut menu.

▶ **4.** In the right pane, double-click the **Graphics** folder to open it.

▶ **5.** Right-click a blank area in the right pane, and then click **Paste** on the shortcut menu. Windows Vista copies the three files to the Graphics folder.

▶ **6.** Switch to List view, if necessary.

Now that you are familiar with two ways to copy files, you can use the technique you prefer to copy the Proposal and Members files to the Playground folder.

To copy the two files:

▶ **1.** In the Graphics folder window, click the **Back** button ⬅ on the toolbar to return to the Tutorial folder.

▶ **2.** Use any technique you've learned to copy the **Proposal** and **Members** files from the Tutorial folder to the Playground folder.

You can move and copy folders in the same way that you move and copy files. When you do, you move or copy all the files contained in the folder.

Naming and Renaming Files

As you work with files, pay attention to **filenames**—they provide important information about the file, including its contents and purpose. A filename such as Car Sales.docx has three parts:

- **Main part of the filename**: The name you provide when you create a file, and the name you associate with a file
- **Dot**: The period (.) that separates the main part of the filename from the file extension
- **File extension**: Usually three or four characters that follow the dot in the filename

The main part of a filename can have up to 260 characters—this gives you plenty of room to name your file accurately enough so that you'll know the contents of the file just by looking at the filename. You can use spaces and certain punctuation symbols in your filenames. Like folder names, however, filenames cannot contain the symbols \ / ? : * " < > | because these characters have special meaning in Windows Vista.

A filename might display an **extension**—three or more characters following a dot—that identifies the file's type and indicates the program in which the file was created. For example, in the filename Car Sales.docx, the extension "docx" identifies the file as one created by Microsoft Office Word 2007, a word-processing program. You might also have a file called Car Sales.xlsx—the "xlsx" extension identifies the file as one created in Microsoft Office Excel 2007, a spreadsheet program. Though the main parts of these filenames are identical, their extensions distinguish them as different files. You usually do not need to add extensions to your filenames because the program that you use to create the file adds the file extension automatically. Also, although Windows Vista keeps track of extensions, not all computers are set to display them.

Be sure to give your files and folders meaningful names that help you remember their purpose and contents. You can easily rename a file or folder by using the Rename command on the file's shortcut menu.

Guidelines for Naming Files | InSight

The following are a few suggestions for naming your files:

- **Use common names**: Avoid cryptic names that might make sense now, but could cause confusion later, such as nonstandard abbreviations or imprecise names like Stuff08.
- **Don't change the file extension**: When renaming a file, don't change the file extension. If you do, Windows might not be able to find a program that can open it.
- **Find a comfortable balance between too short and too long**: Use filenames that are long enough to be meaningful, but short enough to read easily on the screen.

Next, you'll rename the Agenda file to give it a more descriptive name.

To rename the Agenda file:

▶ **1.** In the Tutorial folder window, double-click the **Playground** folder to open it.

▶ **2.** Right-click the **Agenda** file, and then click **Rename** on the shortcut menu. The file-name is highlighted and a box appears around it.

▶ **3.** Type **Meeting Agenda**, and then press the **Enter** key. The file now appears with the new name.

Trouble? If you make a mistake while typing and you haven't pressed the Enter key yet, press the Backspace key until you delete the mistake, and then complete Step 3. If you've already pressed the Enter key, repeat Steps 1 through 3 to rename the file again.

Trouble? If your computer is set to display file extensions, a message might appear asking if you are sure you want to change the file extension. Click the No button, right-click the Agenda file, click Rename on the shortcut menu, type "Meeting Agenda.docx", and then press the Enter key.

All the files in the Tutorial folder are now stored in appropriate subfolders. You can streamline the organization of the Tutorial folder by deleting the files you no longer need.

Deleting Files and Folders

Tip

To retrieve a deleted file from the hard disk, double-click the Recycle Bin, right-click the file you want to retrieve, and then click Restore.

You should periodically delete files and folders you no longer need so that your main folders and disks don't get cluttered. In the Computer window or Windows Explorer, you delete a file or folder by deleting its icon. Be careful when you delete a folder, because you also delete all the files it contains. When you delete a file from a hard disk, Windows Vista removes the filename from the folder, but stores the file contents in the Recycle Bin. The **Recycle Bin** is an area on your hard disk that holds deleted files until you remove them permanently; an icon on the desktop allows you easy access to the Recycle Bin. If you change your mind and want to retrieve a file deleted from your hard disk, you can use the Recycle Bin to recover it or return it to its original location. However, after you empty the Recycle Bin, you can no longer recover the files that were in it.

When you delete a file from removable media, it does not go into the Recycle Bin. Instead, it is deleted as soon as its icon disappears—and you cannot recover it.

Shannon reminds you that because you copied the Holiday, New Logo, Proposal, Members, and Vinca files to the Graphics and Playground folders, you can safely delete the original files in the Tutorial folder. As with moving, copying, and renaming files and folders, you can delete a file or folder in many ways, including using a shortcut menu.

To delete files in the Tutorial folder:

▶ **1.** Use any technique you've learned to navigate to and open the **Tutorial** folder.

▶ **2.** Click **Holiday** (the first file in the file list), hold down the **Shift** key, click **Vinca** (the last file in the file list), and then release the **Shift** key. All the files in the Tutorial folder are now selected. None of the subfolders should be selected.

▶ **3.** Right-click the selected files, and then click **Delete** on the shortcut menu. Windows Vista asks if you're sure you want to delete these files.

▶ **4.** Click the **Yes** button.

So far, you've moved, copied, renamed, and deleted files, but you haven't viewed any of their contents. To view file contents, you can preview or open the file. When you double-click a file in a folder window, Windows Vista starts the appropriate program and opens the file. To preview the file contents, you can select the file in a folder window, and then open the Preview pane by clicking the Organize button, pointing to Layout, and then clicking Preview Pane.

Working with Compressed Files

If you transfer files from one location to another, such as from your hard disk to a removable disk or vice versa, or from one computer to another via e-mail, you can store the files in a **compressed (zipped) folder** so that they take up less disk space. You can then transfer the files more quickly. When you create a compressed folder, Windows Vista displays a zipper on the folder icon.

You compress a folder so that the files it contains use less space on the disk. Compare two folders—a folder named Pictures that contains about 8.6 MB of files and a compressed folder containing the same files, but requiring only 6.5 MB of disk space. In this case, the compressed files use about 25 percent less disk space than the uncompressed files.

You can create a compressed folder using the Compressed (zipped) Folder command on the New submenu of the shortcut menu in a folder window. Then, you can compress files or other folders by dragging them into the compressed folder. You can open files directly from a compressed folder, although you cannot modify the file. To edit and save a compressed file, you must extract it first. When you **extract** a file, you create an uncompressed copy of the file and folder in a folder you specify. The original file remains in the compressed folder.

If a different compression program has been installed on your computer, such as WinZip or PKZIP, the Compressed (zipped) Folder command might not appear on the New submenu. Instead, it might be replaced by the name of your compression program. In this case, refer to your compression program's Help system for instructions on working with compressed files.

Shannon suggests you compress the files and folders in the Tutorial folder so that you can more quickly transfer them to another location.

To compress the folders and files in the Tutorial folder:

▶ **1.** If necessary, navigate to the Tutorial folder.

▶ **2.** Right-click a blank area of the right pane, point to **New** on the shortcut menu, and then click **Compressed (zipped) Folder**. A new compressed folder with a zipper icon appears in the Tutorial window. See Figure 10. Your window might appear in a different view.

Creating a compressed folder ◀ Figure 10

Trouble? If the Compressed (zipped) Folder command does not appear on the New submenu, a different compression program is probably installed on your computer. Click a blank area of the Tutorial window to close the shortcut menu, and then read but do not perform the remaining steps.

▶ **3.** Type **Final Files**, and then press the **Enter** key. Windows Vista names the compressed folder in the Tutorial folder.

▶ **4.** Click the **Graphics** folder, hold down the **Shift** key, click the **Playground** folder in the right pane, and then release the **Shift** key. Three folders are selected in the Tutorial window.

▶ **5.** Drag the three folders to the **Final Files** compressed folder. Windows Vista copies the files to the folder, compressing them to save space.

You open a compressed folder by double-clicking it. You can then move and copy files and folders in a compressed folder, although you cannot rename them. When you extract files, Windows Vista uncompresses and copies them to a location that you specify, preserving the files in their folders as appropriate.

To extract the compressed files:

▶ **1.** Right-click the **Final Files** compressed folder, and then click **Extract All** on the shortcut menu. The Extract Compressed (Zipped) Folders dialog box opens.

▶ **2.** Press the **End** key to deselect the path in the text box, press the **Backspace** key as many times as necessary to delete "Final Files," and then type **Extracted**. The final three parts of the path in the text box should be "\FM\Tutorial\Extracted." See Figure 11.

Figure 11 | **Extracting compressed files**

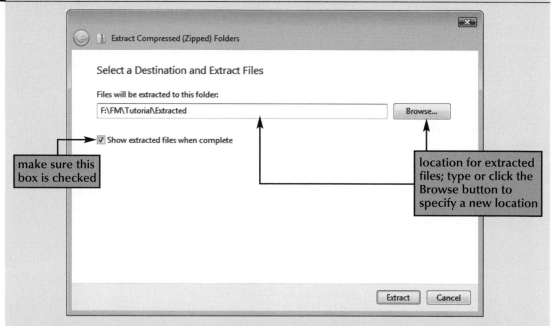

▶ **3.** Make sure the **Show extracted files when complete** check box is checked, and then click the **Extract** button. The Extracted folder opens, showing the Graphics, Job Hunt, and Playground folders.

▶ **4.** Open each folder to make sure it contains the files you worked with in this tutorial.

▶ **5.** Close all open windows.

Quick Check | Review

1. What do you call a named collection of data stored on a disk?
2. Name two types of removable media for storing files.
3. The letter C is typically used for the _____ drive of a computer.
4. What are the two tools that Windows Vista provides for exploring the files and folders on your computer?
5. What is the notation you can use to indicate a file's location on your computer?
6. True or False: The advantage of moving a file or folder by dragging with the right mouse button is that you can efficiently complete your work with one action.
7. What part of a filename indicates the file type and program that created it?
8. Is a file deleted from a compressed folder when you extract it?

Tutorial Summary | Review

In this tutorial, you examined Windows Vista file organization, noting that you need to organize files and folders to work efficiently. You learned about typical file management strategies, including how to organize files and folders by creating folders, moving and copying files, and renaming and deleting files. You also learned how to copy files to a compressed (zipped) folder, and then extract files from a compressed folder.

Key Terms

backup	extract	move
Clipboard	Favorite Links list	Navigation pane
compact disc (CD)	file	pane
compressed (zipped) folder	file path	personal folder
Computer	file system	Recycle Bin
copy	filename	root directory
disk	folder	subfolder
document	folder window	USB drive
drive	Folders list	Windows Explorer
extension	hard disk	

Practice	**Review Assignments**

Practice the skills you learned in the tutorial.

Data Files needed for the Review Assignments: Billing.xlsx, Car Plan.xlsx, Commissions.xlsx, Contracts.xlsx, Customers.xlsx, Loan.docx, Photos.pptx, Speech.wav, Water lilies.jpg

Complete the following steps, recording your answers to any questions:

1. Use the Computer window or Windows Explorer as necessary to record the following information:
   - Where are you supposed to store the files you use in the Review Assignments for this tutorial?
   - Describe the method you will use to navigate to the location where you save your files for this book.
   - Do you need to follow any special guidelines or conventions when naming the files you save for this book? For example, should all the filenames start with your course number or tutorial number? If so, describe the conventions.
   - When you are instructed to open a file for this book, what location are you supposed to use?
   - Describe the method you will use to navigate to this location.
2. Use the Computer window or Windows Explorer to navigate to and open the FM\Review folder provided with your Data Files.
3. Examine the nine files in the Review folder included with your Data Files, and then answer the following questions:
   - How will you organize these files?
   - What folders will you create?
   - Which files will you store in these folders?
   - Will you use any built-in Windows folders? If so, which ones? For which files?
4. In the Review folder, create three folders: Business, Finances, and Project.
5. Move the **Billing**, **Commissions**, **Contracts**, and **Customers** files from the Review folder to the Business folder.
6. Move the **Car Plan** and **Loan** files to the Finances folder.
7. Copy the remaining files to the Project folder.
8. Delete the files in the Review folder (do *not* delete any folders).
9. Rename the **Speech** file in the Project folder to **Ask Not**.
10. Create a compressed (zipped) folder in the Review folder named **Final Review** that contains all the files and folders in the Review folder.
11. Extract the contents of the Final Review files folder to a new folder named **Extracted**. (*Hint:* The file path will end with "\FM\Review\Extracted.")
12. Locate all copies of the **Loan** file in the subfolders of the Review folder. In which locations did you find this file?
13. Close all open windows.
14. Submit the results of the preceding steps to your instructor, either in printed or electronic form, as requested.

Apply		Case Problem 1

Use the skills you learned in the tutorial to manage files and folders for an arts organization.

Data Files needed for this Case Problem: Inv Feb.xlsx, Inv Jan.xlsx, Inv March.xlsx, Painting–Agenda.docx, Painting–Eval.docx, Painting–Manual.docx, Paris.jpg, Still Life.jpg

Jefferson Street Fine Arts Center   Rae Wysnewski owns the Jefferson Street Fine Arts Center (JSFAC) in Pittsburgh, and offers classes and gallery, studio, and practice space for aspiring and fledgling artists, musicians, and dancers. Rae opened JSFAC two years ago, and this year the center has a record enrollment in its classes. She hires you to teach a painting class and to show her how to manage her files on her new Windows Vista computer. Complete the following steps:

1. In the FM\Case1 folder in your Data Files, create two folders: Invoices and Painting Class.
2. Move the **Inv Jan**, **Inv Feb**, and **Inv March** files from the Case1 folder to the Invoices folder.
3. Rename the three files in the Invoices folder to remove "Inv" from each name.
4. Move the three text documents from the Case1 folder to the Painting Class folder. Rename the three documents, using shorter but still descriptive names.
5. Copy the remaining files to the Painting Class folder.
6. Switch to Details view, if necessary, and then answer the following questions:
   a. What is the largest file in the Painting Class folder?
   b. How many files in the Painting Class folder are JPEG images?
7. Delete the **Paris** and **Still Life** files from the Case1 folder.
8. Open the Recycle Bin folder by double-clicking the Recycle Bin icon on the desktop. Do the Paris and Still Life files appear in the Recycle Bin folder? Explain why or why not. Close the Recycle Bin window.
9. Copy the Painting Class folder to the Case1 folder. The duplicate folder appears as "Painting Class – Copy." Rename the Painting Class – Copy folder as **Graphics**.
10. Delete the text files from the Graphics folder.
11. Delete the **Paris** and **Still Life** files from the Painting Class folder.
12. Close all open windows, and then submit the results of the preceding steps to your instructor, either in printed or electronic form, as requested.

Challenge		Case Problem 2

Extend what you've learned to discover other methods of managing files for a social service organization.

There are no Data Files needed for this Case Problem.

First Call Outreach   Victor Crillo is the director of a social service organization named First Call Outreach in Toledo, Ohio. Its mission is to connect people who need help from local and state agencies to the appropriate service. Victor has a dedicated staff, but they are all relatively new to Windows Vista. In particular, they have trouble finding files that they have saved on their hard disks. He asks you to demonstrate how to find files in Windows Vista. Complete the following:

⊕ EXPLORE

1. Windows Vista Help and Support includes topics that explain how to search for files on a disk without looking through all the folders. Click the Start button, click Help and Support, and then use one of the following methods to locate topics on searching for files.
   • In the Windows Help and Support window, click the Windows Basics icon. Click the Working with files and folders link. In the "In this article" list, clicking Finding your files.

- In the Windows Help and Support window, click the Table of Contents icon. (If necessary, click the Home icon first, and then click the Table of Contents icon.) the Files and folders link, and then click Working with files and folders. In the "In this article" list, click Finding your files.
- In the Search Help box, type **searching for files**, and then press the Enter key. Click the Find a file or folder link. In the article, click the Show all link.

 EXPLORE

2. Read the topic and click any See also or For more information links in the topic, if necessary, to provide the following information:
   a. Where is the Search box located?
   b. Do you need to type the entire filename to find the file?
   c. Name three file characteristics you can use as search options.

EXPLORE

3. Use the Windows Vista Help and Support window to locate topics related to managing files and folders. Write out two procedures for working with files and folders that were not covered in the tutorial.

4. Submit the results of the preceding steps to your instructor, either in printed or electronic form, as requested.

Assess | SAM Assessment and Training

SAM

If you have a SAM user profile, you may have access to hands-on instruction, practice, and assessment of the skills covered in this tutorial. Log in to your SAM account (**http://sam2007.course.com**) to launch any assigned training activities or exams that relate to the skills covered in this tutorial.

Review | Quick Check Answers

1. file
2. USB drives, CDs, and DVDs
3. hard disk
4. Windows Explorer and the Computer window
5. file path
6. True
7. extension
8. No

Ending Data Files

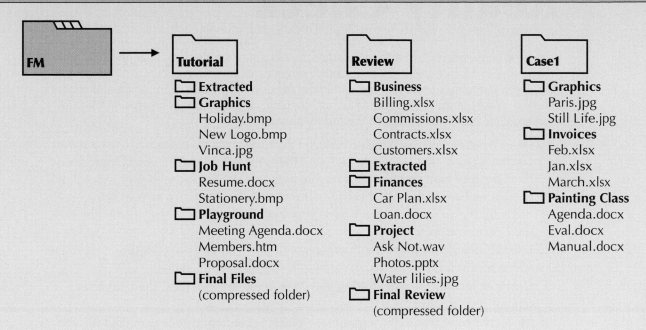

FM →

Tutorial
- **Extracted**
- **Graphics**
  - Holiday.bmp
  - New Logo.bmp
  - Vinca.jpg
- **Job Hunt**
  - Resume.docx
  - Stationery.bmp
- **Playground**
  - Meeting Agenda.docx
  - Members.htm
  - Proposal.docx
- **Final Files**
  - (compressed folder)

Review
- **Business**
  - Billing.xlsx
  - Commissions.xlsx
  - Contracts.xlsx
  - Customers.xlsx
- **Extracted**
- **Finances**
  - Car Plan.xlsx
  - Loan.docx
- **Project**
  - Ask Not.wav
  - Photos.pptx
  - Water lilies.jpg
- **Final Review**
  - (compressed folder)

Case1
- **Graphics**
  - Paris.jpg
  - Still Life.jpg
- **Invoices**
  - Feb.xlsx
  - Jan.xlsx
  - March.xlsx
- **Painting Class**
  - Agenda.docx
  - Eval.docx
  - Manual.docx

Reality Check

Now that you have reviewed the fundamentals of managing files, organize the files and folders you use for course work or for other projects on your own computer. Be sure to follow the guidelines presented in this tutorial for developing an organization strategy, creating folders, naming files, and moving, copying, deleting, and compressing files. To manage your own files, complete the following tasks:

1. Use a program such as Word or Notepad to create a plan for organizing your files. List the types of files you work with, and then determine whether you want to store them on your hard disk or on removable media. Then sketch the folders and subfolders you will use to manage these files. If you choose a hard disk as your storage medium, make sure you plan to store your work files and folders in a subfolder of the Documents folder.

2. Use Windows Explorer or the Computer window to navigate to your files. Determine which tool you prefer for managing files, if you have a preference.

3. Create or rename the main folders you want to use for your files. Then create or rename the subfolders you will use.

4. Move and copy files to the appropriate folders according to your plan, and rename and delete files as necessary.

5. Create a backup copy of your work files by creating a compressed file and then copying the compressed file to a removable disk, such as a USB flash drive.

6. Submit your finished plan to your instructor, either in printed or electronic form, as requested.

Objectives

- Explore the programs that comprise Microsoft Office
- Start programs and switch between them
- Explore common window elements
- Minimize, maximize, and restore windows
- Use the Ribbon, tabs, and buttons
- Use the contextual tabs, Mini toolbar, and shortcut menus
- Save, close, and open a file
- Use the Help system
- Print a file
- Exit programs

Getting Started with Microsoft Office 2007

Preparing a Meeting Agenda

Case | Recycled Palette

Recycled Palette, a company in Oregon founded by Ean Nogella in 2006, sells 100 percent recycled latex paint to both individuals and businesses in the area. The high-quality recycled paint is filtered to industry standards and tested for performance and environmental safety. The paint is available in both 1 gallon cans and 5 gallon pails, and comes in colors ranging from white to shades of brown, blue, green, and red. The demand for affordable recycled paint has been growing each year. Ean and all his employees use Microsoft Office 2007, which provides everyone in the company with the power and flexibility to store a variety of information, create consistent files, and share data. In this tutorial, you'll review how the company's employees use Microsoft Office 2007.

Starting Data Files

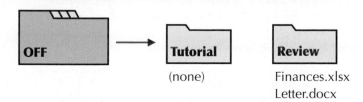

OFF → Tutorial (none)

Review
Finances.xlsx
Letter.docx

Exploring Microsoft Office 2007

Microsoft Office 2007, or **Office**, is a collection of Microsoft programs. Office is available in many suites, each of which contains a different combination of these programs. For example, the Professional suite includes Word, Excel, PowerPoint, Access, Outlook, and Publisher. Other suites are available and can include more or fewer programs (for additional information about the available suites, go to the Microsoft Web site). Each Office program contains valuable tools to help you accomplish many tasks, such as composing reports, analyzing data, preparing presentations, compiling information, sending e-mail, and planning schedules.

Microsoft Office Word 2007, or **Word**, is a computer program you use to enter, edit, and format text. The files you create in Word are called **documents**, although many people use the term *document* to refer to any file created on a computer. Word, often called a word processing program, offers many special features that help you compose and update all types of documents, ranging from letters and newsletters to reports, brochures, faxes, and even books—all in attractive and readable formats. You can also use Word to create, insert, and position figures, tables, and other graphics to enhance the look of your documents. For example, the Recycled Palette employees create business letters using Word.

Microsoft Office Excel 2007, or **Excel**, is a computer program you use to enter, calculate, analyze, and present numerical data. You can do some of this in Word with tables, but Excel provides many more tools for recording and formatting numbers as well as performing calculations. The graphics capabilities in Excel also enable you to display data visually. You might, for example, generate a pie chart or a bar chart to help people quickly see the significance of and the connections between information. The files you create in Excel are called **workbooks** (commonly referred to as spreadsheets), and Excel is often called a spreadsheet program. The Recycled Palette accounting department uses a line chart in an Excel workbook to visually track the company's financial performance.

Microsoft Office Access 2007, or **Access**, is a computer program used to enter, maintain, and retrieve related information (or data) in a format known as a database. The files you create in Access are called **databases**, and Access is often referred to as a database or relational database program. With Access, you can create forms to make data entry easier, and you can create professional reports to improve the readability of your data. The Recycled Palette operations department tracks the company's inventory in a table in an Access database.

Microsoft Office PowerPoint 2007, or **PowerPoint**, is a computer program you use to create a collection of slides that can contain text, charts, pictures, sound, movies, multimedia, and so on. The files you create in PowerPoint are called **presentations**, and PowerPoint is often called a presentation graphics program. You can show these presentations on your computer monitor, project them onto a screen as a slide show, print them, share them over the Internet, or display them on the World Wide Web. You can also use PowerPoint to generate presentation-related documents such as audience handouts, outlines, and speakers' notes. The Recycled Palette marketing department has created an effective slide presentation with PowerPoint to promote its paints to a wider audience.

Microsoft Office Outlook 2007, or **Outlook**, is a computer program you use to send, receive, and organize e-mail; plan your schedule; arrange meetings; organize contacts; create a to-do list; and jot down notes. You can also use Outlook to print schedules, task lists, phone directories, and other documents. Outlook is often referred to as an information management program. The Recycled Palette staff use Outlook to send and receive e-mail, plan their schedules, and create to-do lists.

Although each Office program individually is a strong tool, their potential is even greater when used together.

Integrating Office Programs

One of the main advantages of Office is **integration**, the ability to share information between programs. Integration ensures consistency and accuracy, and it saves time because you don't have to reenter the same information in several Office programs. The staff at Recycled Palette uses the integration features of Office daily, including the following examples:

- The accounting department created an Excel bar chart on the previous two years' fourth-quarter results, which they inserted into the quarterly financial report created in Word. They included a hyperlink in the Word report that employees can click to open the Excel workbook and view the original data.
- The operations department included an Excel pie chart of sales percentages by paint colors on a PowerPoint slide, which is part of a presentation to stockholders.
- The marketing department produced a mailing to promote its recycled paints to local contractors and designers by combining a form letter created in Word with an Access database that stores the names and addresses of these potential customers.
- A sales representative wrote a letter in Word about an upcoming promotion for new customers and merged the letter with an Outlook contact list containing the names and addresses of prospective customers.

These are just a few examples of how you can take information from one Office program and integrate it with another.

Starting Office Programs

You can start any Office program by clicking the Start button on the Windows taskbar, and then selecting the program you want from the All Programs menu. As soon as the program starts, you can immediately begin to create new files or work with existing ones. If an Office program appears in the most frequently used programs list on the left side of the Start menu, you can click the program name to start the program.

Starting Office Programs | Reference Window

- Click the Start button on the taskbar.
- Click All Programs.
- Click Microsoft Office.
- Click the name of the program you want to start.

or

- Click the name of the program you want to start in the most frequently used programs list on the left side of the Start menu.

You'll start Excel using the Start button.

To start Excel and open a new, blank workbook:

▶ 1. Make sure your computer is on and the Windows desktop appears on your screen.

Trouble? If your screen varies slightly from those shown in the figures, your computer might be set up differently. The figures in this book were created while running Windows Vista with the Aero feature turned off, but how your screen looks depends on the version of Windows you are using, the background settings, and so forth.

Windows XP Tip

The Start button is the green button with the word "start" on it, located at the bottom left of the taskbar.

▶ **2.** Click the **Start** button ⊕ on the taskbar, and then click **All Programs** to display the All Programs menu.

▶ **3.** Click **Microsoft Office** on the All Programs list, and then point to **Microsoft Office Excel 2007**. Depending on how your computer is set up, your desktop and menu might contain different icons and commands.

Trouble? If you don't see Microsoft Office on the All Programs list, click Microsoft Office Excel 2007 on the All Programs list. If you still don't see Microsoft Office Excel 2007, ask your instructor or technical support person for help.

▶ **4.** Click **Microsoft Office Excel 2007**. Excel starts, and a new, blank workbook opens. See Figure 1.

Figure 1 New, blank Excel workbook

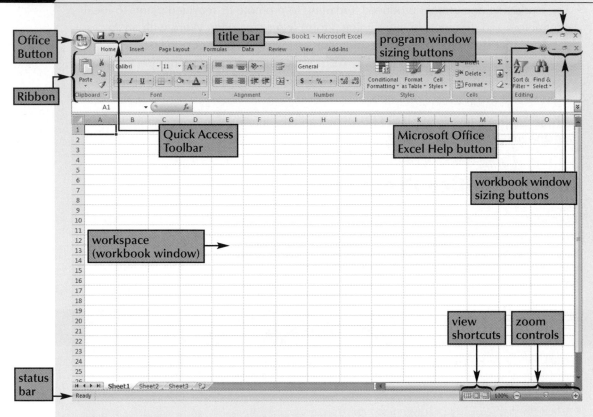

Trouble? If the Excel window doesn't fill your entire screen, the window is not maximized, or expanded to its full size. You'll maximize the window shortly.

You can have more than one Office program open at once. You'll use this same method to start Word and open a new, blank document.

To start Word and open a new, blank document:

▶ **1.** Click the **Start** button ⊕ on the taskbar, click **All Programs** to display the All Programs list, and then click **Microsoft Office**.

Trouble? If you don't see Microsoft Office on the All Programs list, click Microsoft Office Word 2007 on the All Programs list. If you still don't see Microsoft Office Word 2007, ask your instructor or technical support person for help.

▶ **2.** Click **Microsoft Office Word 2007**. Word starts, and a new, blank document opens. See Figure 2.

New, blank document in Word ◄ **Figure 2**

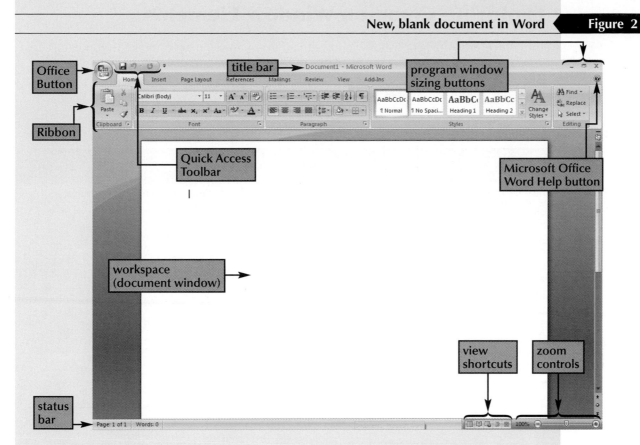

Trouble? If the Word window doesn't fill your entire screen, the window is not maximized. You'll maximize the window shortly.

Switching Between Open Programs and Files

Two programs are running at the same time—Excel and Word. The taskbar contains buttons for both programs. When you have two or more programs running or two files within the same program open, you can use the taskbar buttons to switch from one program or file to another. The button for the active program or file is darker. The employees at Recycled Palette often work in several programs at once.

To switch between Word and Excel files:

▶ 1. Click the **Microsoft Excel – Book1** button on the taskbar. The active program switches from Word to Excel. See Figure 3.

Excel and Word programs opened simultaneously ◄ **Figure 3**

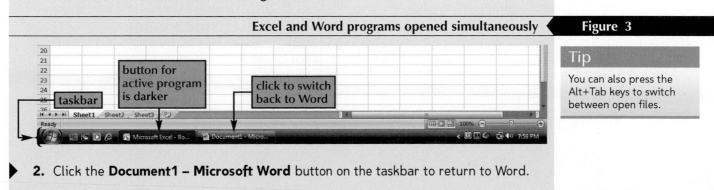

Tip

You can also press the Alt+Tab keys to switch between open files.

▶ 2. Click the **Document1 – Microsoft Word** button on the taskbar to return to Word.

Exploring Common Window Elements

The Office programs consist of windows that have many similar features. As you can see in Figures 1 and 2, many of the elements in both the Excel program window and the Word program window are the same. In fact, all the Office programs have these same elements. Figure 4 describes some of the most common window elements.

Figure 4   **Common window elements**

Element	Description
Office Button	Provides access to document-level features and program settings
Quick Access Toolbar	Provides one-click access to commonly used commands, such as Save, Undo, and Repeat
Title bar	Contains the name of the open file, the program name, and the sizing buttons
Sizing buttons	Resize and close the program window or the workspace
Ribbon	Provides access to the main set of commands organized by task into tabs and groups
Microsoft Office Help button	Opens the Help window for that program
Workspace	Displays the file you are working on (Word document, Excel workbook, Access database, or PowerPoint slide)
Status bar	Provides information about the program, open file, or current task as well as the view shortcuts and zoom controls
View shortcuts	Change how a file is displayed in the workspace
Zoom controls	Magnify or shrink the content displayed in the workspace

Because these elements are the same in each program, after you've learned one program, it's easy to learn the others. The next sections explore these common features.

Resizing the Program Window and Workspace

There are three different sizing buttons. The Minimize button ▬ , which is the left button, hides a window so that only its program button is visible on the taskbar. The middle button changes name and function depending on the status of the window—the Maximize button ▢ expands the window to the full screen size or to the program window size, and the Restore Down button ▭ returns the window to a predefined size. The Close button ✕ , on the right, exits the program or closes the file. Excel has two sets of sizing buttons. The top set controls the program window and the lower set controls the workspace. The workspace sizing buttons look and function in exactly the same way as the program window sizing buttons, except the button names change to Minimize Window and Restore Window when the workspace is maximized.

Most often, you'll want to maximize the program window and workspace to take advantage of the full screen size you have available. If you have several files open, you might want to restore down their windows so that you can see more than one window at a time, or you might want to minimize programs or files you are not working on at the moment. You'll try minimizing, maximizing, and restoring down windows and workspaces now.

To resize windows and workspaces:

1. Click the **Minimize** button [—] on the Word title bar. The Word program window reduces to a taskbar button. The Excel program window is visible again.

2. If necessary, click the **Maximize** button [□] on the Excel title bar. The Excel program window expands to fill the screen.

3. Click the **Restore Window** button [❐] in the lower set of Excel sizing buttons. The workspace is resized and is now smaller than the full program window. See Figure 5.

Resized Excel window and workspace ◄ **Figure 5**

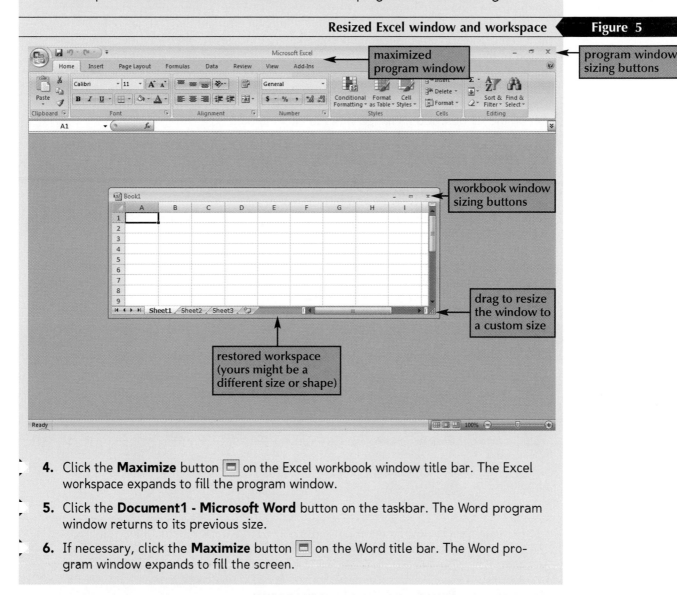

4. Click the **Maximize** button [□] on the Excel workbook window title bar. The Excel workspace expands to fill the program window.

5. Click the **Document1 - Microsoft Word** button on the taskbar. The Word program window returns to its previous size.

6. If necessary, click the **Maximize** button [□] on the Word title bar. The Word program window expands to fill the screen.

The sizing buttons give you the flexibility to arrange the program and file windows on your screen to best fit your needs.

Getting Information from the Status Bar

The **status bar** at the bottom of the program window provides information about the open file and current task or selection. It also has buttons and other controls for working with the file and its content. The status bar buttons and information displays are specific to the individual programs. For example, the Excel status bar displays summary information about a selected range of numbers (such as their sum or average), whereas the Word status bar shows the current page number and total number of words in a document. The right side of the status bar includes buttons that enable you to switch the workspace view in Word, Excel, PowerPoint, and Access as well as zoom the workspace in Word, Excel, and PowerPoint. You can customize the status bar to display other information or hide the **default** (original or preset) information.

Switching Views

Each program has a variety of views, or ways to display the file in the workspace. For example, Word has five views: Print Layout, Full Screen Reading, Web Layout, Outline, and Draft. The content of the file doesn't change from view to view, although the presentation of the content will. In Word, for example, Page Layout view shows how a document would appear as the printed page, whereas Web Layout view shows how the document would appear as a Web page. You can quickly switch between views using the shortcuts at the right side of the status bar. You can also change the view from the View tab on the Ribbon. You'll change views in later tutorials.

Zooming the Workspace

Zooming is a way to magnify or shrink the file content displayed in the workspace. You can zoom in to get a closer look at the content of an open document, worksheet, or slide, or you can zoom out to see more of the content at a smaller size. There are several ways to change the zoom percentage. You can use the Zoom slider at the right of the status bar to quickly change the zoom percentage. You can click the Zoom level button to the left of the Zoom slider in the status bar to open the Zoom dialog box and select a specific zoom percentage or size based on your file. You can also change the zoom settings using the Zoom group in the View tab on the Ribbon.

Reference Window	**Zooming the Workspace**

- Click the Zoom Out or Zoom In button on the status bar (or drag the Zoom slider button left or right) to the desired zoom percentage.

or

- Click the Zoom level button on the status bar.
- Select the appropriate zoom setting, and then click the OK button.

or

- Click the View tab on the Ribbon, and then in the Zoom group, click the zoom setting you want.

The figures shown in these tutorials are zoomed to enhance readability. You'll zoom the Word and Excel workspaces.

To zoom the Word and Excel workspaces:

▶ 1. On the Zoom slider on the Word status bar, drag the **slider button** to the left until the Zoom percentage is **10%**. The document reduces to its smallest size, which makes the entire page visible but unreadable. See Figure 6.

Word document zoomed to 10% | Figure 6

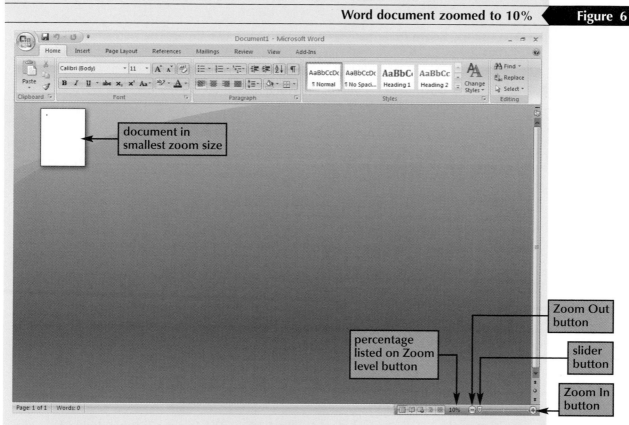

You'll zoom the document so its page width fills the workspace.

▶ **2.** Click the **Zoom level** button `10%` on the Word status bar. The Zoom dialog box opens. See Figure 7.

Zoom dialog box | Figure 7

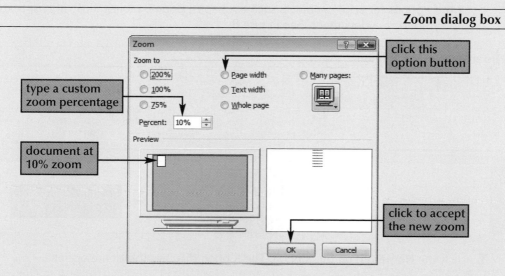

▶ **3.** Click the **Page width** option button, and then click the **OK** button. The Word document magnifies to its page width to match the rest of the Word figures shown in these tutorials.

Now, you'll zoom the workbook to 120%.

▶ **4.** Click the **Microsoft Excel – Book1** button on the taskbar. The Excel program window is displayed.

▶ **5.** Click the **Zoom In** button ⊕ on the status bar two times. The workspace magnifies to 120%. This is the zoom percentage that matches the rest of the Excel figures shown in these tutorials.

▶ **6.** Click the **Document1 – Microsoft Word** button on the taskbar. The Word program window is displayed.

Using the Ribbon

The **Ribbon** at the top of the program window just below the title bar is the main set of commands that you click to execute tasks. The Ribbon is organized into tabs. Each **tab** has commands related to particular activities. For example, in Word, the Insert tab on the Ribbon provides access to all the commands for adding objects such as shapes, pages, tables, illustrations, text, and symbols to a document. Although the tabs differ from program to program, the first tab in each program, called the Home tab, contains the commands for the most frequently performed activities, including cutting and pasting, changing fonts, and using editing tools. In addition, the Insert, Review, View, and Add-Ins tabs appear on the Ribbon in all the Office programs except Access, although the commands they include might differ from program to program. Other tabs are program specific, such as the Design tab in PowerPoint and the Datasheet tab in Access.

To use the Ribbon tabs:

▶ **1.** In Word, point to the **Insert** tab on the Ribbon. The Insert tab is highlighted, though the Home tab with the options for using the Clipboard and formatting text remains visible.

▶ **2.** Click the **Insert** tab. The Ribbon displays the Insert tab, which provides access to all the options for adding objects such as shapes, pages, tables, illustrations, text, and symbols to a document. See Figure 8.

| Figure 8 | Insert tab on the Ribbon |

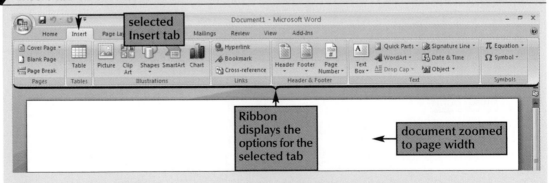

▶ **3.** Click the **Home** tab on the Ribbon. The Ribbon displays the Home options.

Clicking Button Icons

Each **button**, or icon, on the tabs provides one-click access to a command. Most buttons are labeled so that you can easily find the command you need. For the most part, when you click a button, something happens in your file. If you want to repeat that action, you click the button again. Buttons for related commands are organized on a tab in **groups**. For example, the Clipboard group on the Home tab includes the Cut, Copy, Paste, and Format Painter buttons—the commands for moving or copying text, objects, and formatting.

Buttons can be toggle switches: one click turns on the feature and the next click turns off the feature. While the feature is on, the button remains colored or highlighted to remind you that it is active. For example, in Word, the Show/Hide button on the Home tab in the Paragraph group displays the nonprinting screen characters when toggled on and hides them when toggled off.

Some buttons have two parts: a button that accesses a command and an arrow that opens a menu of all the commands available for that task. For example, the Paste button on the Home tab includes the default Paste command and an arrow that opens the menu of all the Paste commands—Paste, Paste Special, and Paste as Hyperlink. To select a command on the menu, you click the button arrow and then click the command on the menu.

The buttons and groups change based on your monitor size, your screen resolution, and the size of the program window. With smaller monitors, lower screen resolutions, and reduced program windows, buttons can appear as icons without labels and a group can be condensed into a button that you click to display the group options. The figures in these tutorials were created using a screen resolution of 1024 × 768 and, unless otherwise specified, the program and workspace windows are maximized. If you are using a different screen resolution or window size, the button icons on the Ribbon might show more or fewer button names, and some groups might be condensed into buttons.

You'll type text in the Word document, and then use the buttons on the Ribbon.

To use buttons on the Ribbon:

▶ **1.** Type **Recycled Palette**, and then press the **Enter** key. The text appears in the first line of the document and the insertion point moves to the second line.

   Trouble? If you make a typing error, press the Backspace key to delete the incorrect letters, and then retype the text.

▶ **2.** In the Paragraph group on the Home tab, click the **Show/Hide** button ¶. The nonprinting screen characters appear in the document, and the Show/Hide button remains toggled on. See Figure 9.

   Trouble? If the nonprinting characters are removed from your screen, the Show/Hide button ¶ was already selected. Repeat Step 2 to show the nonprinting screen characters.

Button toggled on ◀ **Figure 9**

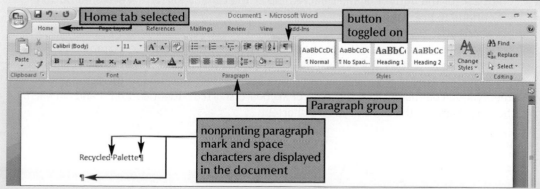

3. Drag to select all the text in the first line of the document (but not the paragraph mark).

4. In the Clipboard group on the Home tab, click the **Copy** button. The selected text is copied to the Clipboard.

▶ 5. Press the ↓ key. The text is deselected and the insertion point moves to the second line in the document.

▶ 6. In the Clipboard group on the Home tab, point to the top part of the **Paste** button. Both parts of the Paste button are highlighted, but the icon at top is darker to indicate it will be clicked if you press the mouse button.

▶ 7. Point to the **Paste button arrow**. The button arrow is now darker.

▶ 8. Click the **Paste button arrow**. A menu of paste commands opens. See Figure 10. To select one of the commands on the list, you click it.

Figure 10	Two-part Paste button

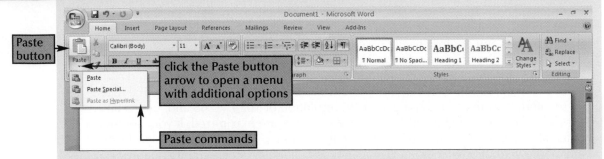

▶ 9. Click **Paste**. The menu closes, and the text is duplicated in the second line of the document.

As you can see, you can quickly access commands and turn features on and off with the buttons on the Ribbon.

Keyboard shortcuts can help you work faster and more efficiently. A **keyboard shortcut** is a key or combination of keys you press to access a tool or perform a command. To quickly access options on the Ribbon, the Quick Access Toolbar, and the Office Button without removing your hands from the keyboard:

1. Press the Alt key. Key Tips appear that list the keyboard shortcut for each Ribbon tab, each Quick Access Toolbar button, and the Office Button.
2. Press the key for the tab or button you want to use. An action is performed or Key Tips appear for the buttons on the selected tab or the commands for the selected button.
3. Continue to press the appropriate key listed in the Key Tip until the action you want is performed.

You can also use keyboard shortcuts to perform specific commands. For example, Ctrl+S is the keyboard shortcut for the Save command (you hold down the Ctrl key while you press the S key). This type of keyboard shortcut appears in ScreenTips next to the command's name. Not all commands have this type of keyboard shortcut. Identical commands in each Office program use the same keyboard shortcut.

Using Galleries and Live Preview

A button can also open a **gallery**, which is a grid or menu that shows a visual representation of the options available for that command. For example, the Bullet Library gallery in Word shows an icon of each bullet style you can select. Some galleries include a More button that you click to expand the gallery to see all the options in it. When you hover the pointer over an option in a gallery, **Live Preview** shows the results you would achieve in your file if you clicked that option. To continue the bullets example, when you hover over a bullet style in the Bullet Library gallery, the current paragraph or selected text previews that bullet style. By moving the pointer from option to option, you can quickly see the text set with different bullet styles; you can then select the style that works best for your needs.

To use a gallery and Live Preview:

▶ **1.** In the Paragraph group on the Home tab, click the **Bullets button arrow** ☷▾. The Bullet Library gallery opens.

▶ **2.** Point to the **check mark bullet** style. Live Preview shows the selected bullet style in your document, so you can determine if you like that bullet style. See Figure 11.

Live Preview of bullet style ◀ **Figure 11**

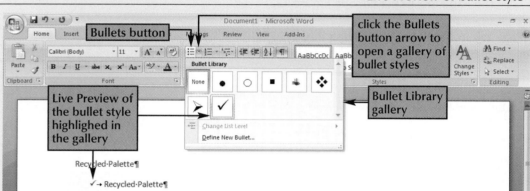

▶ **3.** Place the pointer over each of the remaining bullet styles and preview them in your document.

You don't want to add bullets to your document right now, so you'll close the Bullet Library gallery and deselect the Bullets button.

▶ **4.** Press the **Esc** key on the keyboard. The Bullet Library gallery closes and the Bullets button is deselected.

▶ **5.** Press the **Backspace** key on the keyboard to delete the text "Recycled Palette" on the second line.

Galleries and Live Preview let you quickly see how your file will be affected by a selection.

Opening Dialog Boxes and Task Panes

The button to the right of the group names is the **Dialog Box Launcher**, which you click to open a task pane or dialog box that provides more advanced functionality for that group of tasks. A **task pane** is a window that helps you navigate through a complex task or feature. For example, the Clipboard task pane allows you to paste some or all of the items that have been cut or copied from any Office program during the current work session and the Research task pane allows you to search a variety of reference resources from within a file. A **dialog box** is a window from which you enter or choose settings for how you want to perform a task. For example, the Page Setup dialog box in Word contains options for how you want a document to look. Some dialog boxes organize related information into tabs, and related options and settings are organized into groups, just as they are on the Ribbon. You select settings in a dialog box using option buttons, check boxes, text boxes, lists, and other controls to collect information about how you want to perform a task.

In Excel, you'll use the Dialog Box Launcher for the Page Setup group to open the Page Setup dialog box.

To open the Page Setup dialog box using the Dialog Box Launcher:

▶ **1.** Click the **Microsoft Excel – Book1** button on the taskbar to switch from Word to Excel.

▶ **2.** Click the **Page Layout** tab on the Ribbon.

▶ **3.** In the Page Setup group, click the **Dialog Box Launcher**, which is the small button to the right of the Page Setup group name. The Page Setup dialog box opens with the Page tab displayed. See Figure 12.

| Figure 12 | Page tab in the Page Setup dialog box |

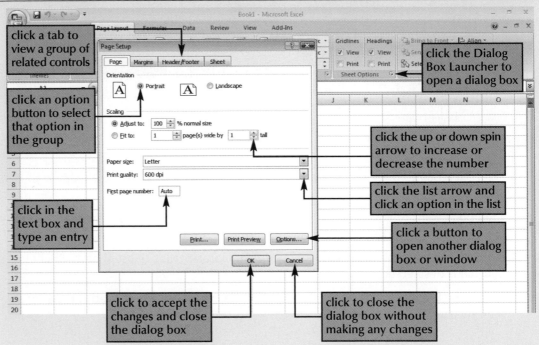

▶ **4.** Click the **Landscape** option button. The workbook's page orientation changes to a page wider than it is long.

▶ **5.** Click the **Sheet** tab. The dialog box displays options related to the worksheet. You can click a check box to turn an option on (checked) or off (unchecked). You can check more than one check box in a group, whereas you can select only one option button in a group.

▶ **6.** In the Print group, click the **Gridlines** check box and the **Row and column headings** check box. Check marks appear in both check boxes, indicating that these options are selected.

You don't want to change the page setup right now, so you'll close the dialog box.

▶ **7.** Click the **Cancel** button. The dialog box closes without making any changes to the page setup.

Using Contextual Tools

Some tabs, toolbars, and menus come into view as you work. Because these tools become available only as you might need them, the workspace on your screen remains more open and less cluttered. However, tools that appear and disappear as you work can be distracting and take some getting used to.

Displaying Contextual Tabs

Any object that you can select in a file has a related contextual tab. An **object** is anything that appears on your screen that can be selected and manipulated as a whole, such as a table, a picture, a text box, a shape, a chart, WordArt, an equation, a diagram, a header, or a footer. A **contextual tab** is a Ribbon tab that contains commands related to the selected object so you can manipulate, edit, and format that object. Contextual tabs appear to the right of the standard Ribbon tabs just below a title label. For example, Figure 13 shows the Table Tools contextual tabs that appear when you select a table in a Word document. Although the contextual tabs appear only when you select an object, they function in the same way as standard tabs on the Ribbon. Contextual tabs disappear when you click elsewhere on the screen and deselect the object. Contextual tabs can also appear as you switch views. You'll use contextual tabs in later tutorials.

Table Tools contextual tabs ◄ Figure 13

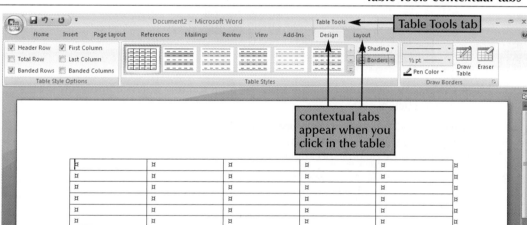

Accessing the Mini Toolbar

The **Mini toolbar** is a toolbar that appears next to the pointer whenever you select text, and it contains buttons for the most commonly used formatting commands, such as font, font size, styles, color, alignment, and indents that may appear in different groups or tabs on the Ribbon. The Mini toolbar buttons differ in each program. A transparent version of the Mini toolbar appears immediately after you select text. When you move the pointer over the Mini toolbar, it comes into full view so you can click the appropriate formatting button or buttons. The Mini toolbar disappears if you move the pointer away from the toolbar, press a key, or press a mouse button. The Mini toolbar can help you format your text faster, but initially you might find that the toolbar disappears unexpectedly. All the commands on the Mini toolbar are also available on the Ribbon. Be aware that Live Preview of selected styles does not work in the Mini toolbar.

You'll use the Mini toolbar to format text you enter in the workbook.

Tip

You can turn off the Mini toolbar and Live Preview in Word, Excel, and PowerPoint. Click the Office Button, click the Options button at the bottom of the Office menu, uncheck the first two check boxes in the Popular category, and then click the OK button.

To use the Mini toolbar to format text:

▶ 1. If necessary, click cell **A1** (the rectangle in the upper-left corner of the worksheet).

▶ 2. Type **Budget**. The text appears in the cell.

▶ 3. Press the **Enter** key. The text is entered in cell A1 and cell A2 is selected.

▶ 4. Type **2008**, and then press the **Enter** key. The year is entered in cell A2 and cell A3 is selected.

You'll use the Mini toolbar to make the word in cell A1 boldface.

▶ 5. Double-click cell **A1** to place the insertion point in the cell. Now you can select the text you typed.

▶ 6. Double-click **Budget** in cell A1. The selected text appears white in a black background, and the transparent Mini toolbar appears directly above the selected text. See Figure 14.

Figure 14	Transparent Mini toolbar

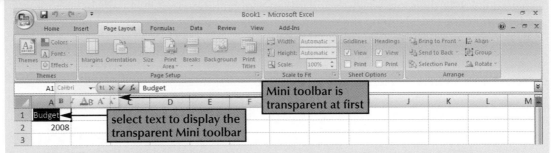

▶ 7. Move the pointer over the Mini toolbar. The Mini toolbar is now completely visible, and you can click buttons.

Trouble? If the Mini toolbar disappears, you probably moved the pointer to another area of the worksheet. To redisplay the Mini toolbar, repeat Steps 5 through 7, being careful to move the pointer directly over the Mini toolbar in Step 7.

▶ 8. Click the **Bold** button **B** on the Mini toolbar. The text in cell A1 is bold and the Mini toolbar remains visible so you can continue formatting the selected text. See Figure 15.

Tip

You can redisplay the Mini toolbar if it disappears by right-clicking the selected text.

Figure 15	Mini toolbar with the Bold button selected

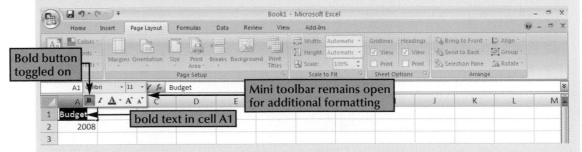

You don't want to make any other changes, so you'll close the Mini toolbar.

▶ 9. Press the **Enter** key. The Mini toolbar disappears and cell A2 is selected.

Opening Shortcut Menus

A **shortcut menu** is a list of commands related to a selection that opens when you click the right mouse button. Each shortcut menu provides access to the commands you'll most likely want to use with the object or selection you right-click. The shortcut menu includes commands that perform actions, commands that open dialog boxes, and galleries of options that provide Live Preview. The Mini toolbar also opens when you right-click. If you click a button on the Mini toolbar, the rest of the shortcut menu closes while the Mini toolbar remains open so you can continue formatting the selection. Using a shortcut menu provides quick access to the commands you need without having to access the tabs on the Ribbon. For example, you can right-click selected text to open a shortcut menu with a Mini toolbar, text-related commands, such as Cut, Copy, and Paste, as well as other program-specific commands.

You'll use a shortcut menu in Excel to delete the content you entered in cell A1.

To use a shortcut menu to delete content:

▶ 1. Right-click cell **A1**. A shortcut menu opens, listing commands related to common tasks you'd perform in a cell, along with a Mini toolbar. See Figure 16.

Shortcut menu with Mini toolbar ◀ **Figure 16**

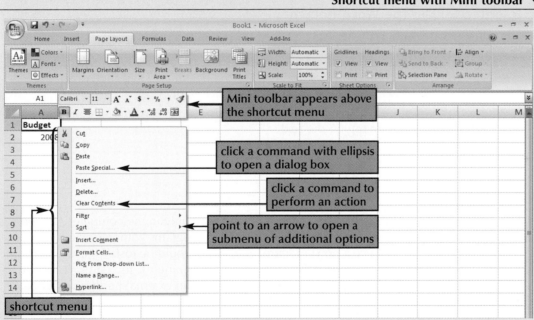

You'll use the Clear Contents command to delete the bold text from cell A1.

▶ 2. Click **Clear Contents** on the shortcut menu. The shortcut menu closes, the Mini toolbar disappears, and the formatted text is removed from cell A1.

You'll use the Clear Contents command again to delete the year from cell A2.

▶ 3. Right-click cell **A2**, and then click **Clear Contents** on the shortcut menu. The year is removed from cell A2.

Shortcut menus enable you to quickly access commands that you're most likely to need in the context of the task you're performing.

Tip

Press the Esc key to close an open menu, shortcut menu, list, gallery, and so forth without selecting an option.

Working with Files

The most common tasks you perform in any Office program are to create, open, save, and close files. The processes for these tasks are basically the same in all the Office programs. In addition, there are several methods for performing most tasks in Office. This flexibility enables you to use Office in a way that best fits how you like to work.

The **Office Button** provides access to document-level features, such as creating new files, opening existing files, saving files, printing files, and closing files, as well as the most common program options, called **application settings**. The **Quick Access Toolbar** is a collection of buttons that provide one-click access to commonly used commands, such as Save, Undo, and Repeat.

To begin working in a program, you need to create a new file or open an existing file. When you start Word, Excel, or PowerPoint, the program opens along with a blank file—ready for you to begin working on a new document, workbook, or presentation. When you start Access, the Getting Started with Microsoft Access window opens, displaying options for creating a new database or opening an existing one.

Ean has asked you to continue working on the agenda for the stockholder meeting. You already started typing in the document that opened when you started Word. Next, you will enter more text in the Word document.

To enter text in the Word document:

▶ 1. Click the **Document1 – Microsoft Word** button on the taskbar to activate the Word program window.

▶ 2. Type **Meeting Agenda** on the second line of the document, and then press the **Enter** key. The text you typed appears in the document.

   Trouble? If you make a typing error, press the Backspace key to delete the incorrect letters, and then retype the text.

Saving a File

As you create and modify Office files, your work is stored only in the computer's temporary memory, not on a hard disk. If you were to exit the programs without saving, turn off your computer, or experience a power failure, your work would be lost. To prevent losing work, save your file to a disk frequently—at least every 10 minutes. You can save files to the hard disk located inside your computer, a floppy disk, an external hard drive, a network storage drive, or a portable storage disk, such as a USB flash drive.

Reference Window | Saving a File

To save a file the first time or with a new name or location:
- Click the Office Button, and then click Save As (or for an unnamed file, click the Save button on the Quick Access Toolbar or click the Office Button, and then click Save).
- In the Save As dialog box, navigate to the location where you want to save the file.
- Type a descriptive title in the File name box, and then click the Save button.

To resave a named file to the same location:
- Click the Save button on the Quick Access Toolbar (or click the Office Button, and then click Save).

The first time you save a file, you need to name it. This **filename** includes a descriptive title you select and a file extension assigned by Office. You should choose a descriptive title that accurately reflects the content of the document, workbook, presentation, or database, such as "Shipping Options Letter" or "Fourth Quarter Financial Analysis." Your descriptive title can include uppercase and lowercase letters, numbers, hyphens, and spaces in any combination, but not the following special characters: ? " / \ < > * | and :. Each filename ends with a **file extension**, a period followed by several characters that Office adds to your descriptive title to identify the program in which that file was created. The default file extensions for Office 2007 are .docx for Word, .xlsx for Excel, .pptx for PowerPoint, and .accdb for Access. Filenames (the descriptive title and the file extension) can include a maximum of 255 characters. You might see file extensions depending on how Windows is set up on your computer. The figures in these tutorials do not show file extensions.

You also need to decide where to save the file—on which disk and in what folder. A **folder** is a container for your files. Just as you organize paper documents within folders stored in a filing cabinet, you can organize your files within folders stored on your computer's hard disk or a removable disk, such as a USB flash drive. Store each file in a logical location that you will remember whenever you want to use the file again. The default storage location for Office files is the Documents folder; you can create additional storage folders within that folder or navigate to a new storage location.

You can navigate the Save As dialog box by clicking a folder or location on your computer in the Navigation pane along the left side of the dialog box, and then double-clicking folders in the file list until you display the storage location you want. You can also navigate to a storage location with the Address bar, which displays the current file path. Each location in the file path has a corresponding arrow that you can click to quickly select a folder within that location. For example, you can click the Documents arrow in the Address bar to open a list of all the folders in the Documents folder, and then click the folder you want to open. If you want to return to a specific spot in the file hierarchy, you click that folder name in the Address bar. The Back and Forward buttons let you quickly move between folders.

Tip

Office adds the correct file extension when you save a file. Do not type one in the descriptive title, or you will create a duplicate (such as Meeting Agenda. docx.docx).

Windows XP Tip

The default storage location for Office files is the My Documents folder.

Saving and Using Files with Earlier Versions of Office | InSight

The default file types in Office 2007 are different from those used in earlier versions. This means that someone using Office 2003 or earlier cannot open files created in Office 2007. Files you want to share with earlier Office users must be saved in the earlier formats, which use the following extensions: .doc for Word, .xls for Excel, .mdb for Access, and .ppt for PowerPoint. To save a file in an earlier format, open the Save As dialog box, click the Save as type list arrow, and then click the appropriate 97-2003 format. A compatibility checker reports which Office 2007 features or elements are not supported by the earlier version of Office, and you can choose to remove them before saving. You can use Office 2007 to open and work with files created in earlier versions of Office. You can then save the file in its current format or update it to the Office 2007 format.

The lines of text you typed are not yet saved on disk. You'll do that now.

To save a file for the first time:

▶ **1.** Click the **Save** button 🔲 on the Quick Access Toolbar. The Save As dialog box opens because you have not yet saved the file and need to specify a storage location and filename. The default location is set to the Documents folder, and the first few words of the first line appear in the File name box as a suggested title.

▶ **2.** In the Navigation pane, click the link for the location that contains your Data Files, if necessary.

Trouble? If you don't have the starting Data Files, you need to get them before you can proceed. Your instructor will either give you the Data Files or ask you to obtain them from a specified location (such as a network drive). In either case, make a backup copy of the Data Files before you start so that you will have the original files available in case you need to start over. If you have any questions about the Data Files, see your instructor or technical support person for assistance.

▶ **3.** Double-click the **OFF** folder in the file list, and then double-click the **Tutorial** folder. This is the location where you want to save the document.

Next, you'll enter a more descriptive title for the filename.

▶ **4.** Type **Meeting Agenda** in the File name box. See Figure 17.

Figure 17 ▶ Completed Save As dialog box

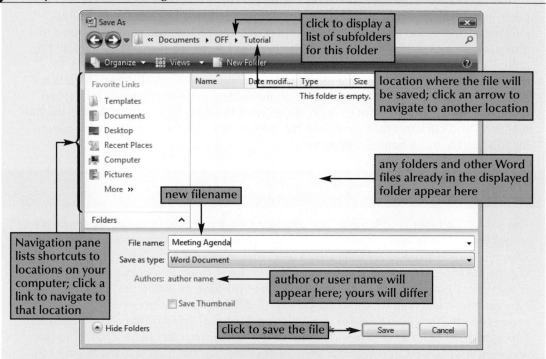

Trouble? If the .docx file extension appears after the filename, your computer is configured to show file extensions. Continue with Step 5.

▶ **5.** Click the **Save** button. The Save As dialog box closes, and the name of your file appears in the title bar.

The saved file includes everything in the document at the time you last saved it. Any new edits or additions you make to the document exist only in the computer's memory and are not saved in the file on the disk. As you work, remember to save frequently so that the file is updated to reflect the latest content of the document.

Because you already named the document and selected a storage location, the Save As dialog box doesn't open whenever you save the document again. If you want to save a copy of the file with a different filename or to a different location, you reopen the Save As dialog box by clicking the Office Button, and then clicking Save As. The previous version of the file remains on your disk as well.

You need to add your name to the agenda. Then, you'll save your changes.

To modify and save the Word document:

▶ 1. Type your name, and then press the **Enter** key. The text you typed appears on the next line.

▶ 2. Click the **Save** button 🔲 on the Quick Access Toolbar to save your changes.

Closing a File

Although you can keep multiple files open at one time, you should close any file you are no longer working on to conserve system resources as well as to ensure that you don't inadvertently make changes to the file. You can close a file by clicking the Office Button and then clicking the Close command. If that's the only file open for the program, the program window remains open and no file appears in the window. You can also close a file by clicking the Close button in the upper-right corner of the title bar or double-clicking the Office Button. If that's the only file open for the program, the program also closes.

As a standard practice, you should save your file before closing it. However, Office has an added safeguard: If you attempt to close a file without saving your changes, a dialog box opens, asking whether you want to save the file. Click the Yes button to save the changes to the file before closing the file and program. Click the No button to close the file and program without saving changes. Click the Cancel button to return to the program window without saving changes or closing the file and program. This feature helps to ensure that you always save the most current version of any file.

You'll add the date to the agenda. Then, you'll attempt to close it without saving.

To modify and close the Word document:

▶ 1. Type today's date, and then press the **Enter** key. The text you typed appears below your name in the document.

▶ 2. In the upper-left corner of the program window, click the **Office Button** . A menu opens with commands for creating new files, opening existing files, saving files, printing files, and closing files.

▶ 3. Click **Close**. A dialog box opens, asking whether you want to save the changes you made to the document.

▶ 4. Click the **Yes** button. The current version of the document is saved to the file, and then the document closes. Word is still running.

After you have a program open, you can create additional new files for the open program or you can open previously created and saved files.

Opening a File

When you want to open a blank document, workbook, presentation, or database, you create a new file. When you want to work on a previously created file, you must first open it. Opening a file transfers a copy of the file from the storage disk (either a hard disk or a portable disk) to the computer's memory and displays it on your screen. The file is then in your computer's memory and on the disk.

Reference Window | **Opening an Existing File or Creating a New File**

- Click the Office Button, and then click Open.
- In the Open dialog box, navigate to the storage location of the file you want to open.
- Click the filename of the file you want to open.
- Click the Open button.

or

- Click the Office Button, and then click a filename in the Recent Documents list.

or

- Click the Office Button, and then click New.
- In the New dialog box, click Blank Document, Blank Workbook, Blank Presentation, or Blank Database (depending on the program).
- Click the Create button.

Ean asks you to print the agenda. To do that, you'll reopen the file.

To open the existing Word document:

1. Click the **Office Button** , and then click **Open**. The Open dialog box, which works similarly to the Save As dialog box, opens.

Windows XP Tip

To navigate to a location in the Open dialog box, you use the Look in arrow.

2. Use the Navigation pane or the Address bar to navigate to the **OFF\Tutorial** folder included with your Data Files. This is the location where you saved the agenda document.

3. Click **Meeting Agenda** in the file list. See Figure 18.

Figure 18 Open dialog box

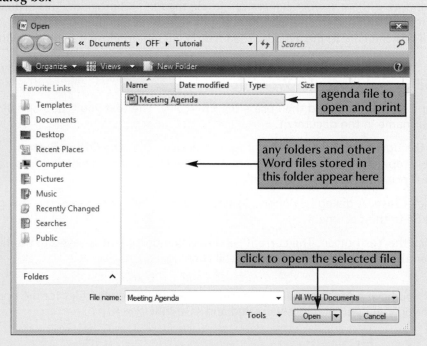

4. Click the **Open** button. The agenda file opens in the Word program window.

Next, you'll use Help to get information about printing files in Word.

Getting Help

If you don't know how to perform a task or want more information about a feature, you can turn to Office itself for information on how to use it. This information, referred to simply as **Help**, is like a huge encyclopedia available from your desktop. You can get Help in ScreenTips, from the Help window, and in Microsoft Office Online.

Viewing ScreenTips

ScreenTips are a fast and simple method you can use to get help about objects you see on the screen. A **ScreenTip** is a box with the button's name, its keyboard shortcut if it has one, a description of the command's function, and, in some cases, a link to more information. Just position the mouse pointer over a button or object to view its ScreenTip. If a link to more information appears in the ScreenTip, press the F1 key while the Screen-Tip is displayed to open the Help window with the appropriate topic displayed.

To view ScreenTips:

▶ **1.** Point to the **Microsoft Office Word Help** button ⊚. The ScreenTip shows the button's name, its keyboard shortcut, and a brief explanation of the button. See Figure 19.

ScreenTip for the Help button ◀ **Figure 19**

▶ **2.** Point to other buttons on the Ribbon to display their ScreenTips.

Using the Help Window

For more detailed information, you can use the **Help window** to access all the Help topics, templates, and training installed on your computer with Office and available on Microsoft Office Online. **Microsoft Office Online** is a Web site maintained by Microsoft that provides access to the latest information and additional Help resources. For example, you can access current Help topics, templates of predesigned files, and training for Office. To connect to Microsoft Office Online, you need Internet access on your computer. Otherwise, you see only those topics stored locally.

Reference Window | Getting Help

- Click the Microsoft Office Help button (the button name depends on the Office program).
- Type a keyword or phrase in the "Type words to search for" box, and then click the Search button.
- Click a Help topic in the search results list.
- Read the information in the Help window. For more information, click other topics or links.
- Click the Close button on the Help window title bar.

You open the Help window by clicking the Microsoft Office Help button located below the sizing buttons in every Office program. Each program has its own Help window from which you can find information about all the Office commands and features as well as step-by-step instructions for using them. You can search for information in the Help window using the "Type words to search for" box and the Table of Contents pane.

The "Type words to search for" box enables you to search the Help system using keywords or phrases. You type a specific word or phrase about a task you want to perform or a topic you need help with, and then click the Search button to search the Help system. A list of Help topics related to the keyword or phrase you entered appears in the Help window. If your computer is connected to the Internet, your search results come from Microsoft Office Online rather than only the Help topics stored locally on your computer. You can click a link to open a Help topic with step-by-step instructions that will guide you through a specific procedure and/or provide explanations of difficult concepts in clear, easy-to-understand language. For example, if you type "format cell" in the Excel Help window, a list of Help topics related to the words you typed appears in the Help window. You can navigate through the topics you've viewed using the buttons on the Help window toolbar. These buttons—including Back, Forward, Stop, Refresh, Home, and Print—are the same as those in the Microsoft Internet Explorer Web browser.

You'll use the "Type words to search for" box in the Help window to obtain more information about printing a document in Word.

To use the "Type words to search for" box:

► 1. Click the **Microsoft Office Word Help** button . The Word Help window opens.

► 2. Click the **Type words to search for** box, if necessary, and then type **print document**. You can set where you want to search.

► 3. Click the **Search button arrow**. The Search menu shows the online and local content available.

4. If your computer is connected to the Internet, click **All Word** in the Content from Office Online list. If your computer is not connected to the Internet, click **Word Help** in the Content from this computer list.

5. Click the **Search** button. The Help window displays a list of topics related to your keywords. See Figure 20.

Search results displaying Help topics **Figure 20**

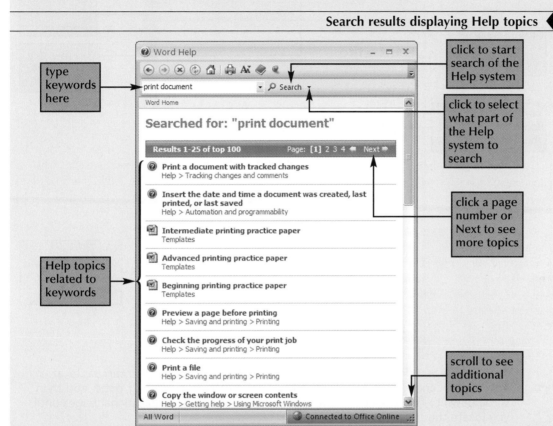

Trouble? If your search results list differs from the one shown in Figure 20, your computer is not connected to the Internet or Microsoft has updated the list of available Help topics since this book was published. Continue with Step 6.

6. Scroll through the list to review the Help topics.

7. Click **Print a file**. The Help topic is displayed in the Help window so you can learn more about how to print a document. See Figure 21.

Figure 21 > Print a file Help topic

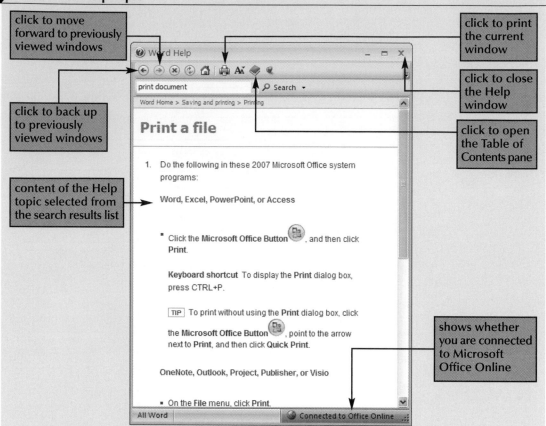

click to move forward to previously viewed windows

click to print the current window

click to close the Help window

click to back up to previously viewed windows

click to open the Table of Contents pane

content of the Help topic selected from the search results list

shows whether you are connected to Microsoft Office Online

Trouble? If you don't see the Print a file Help topic on page 1, its current location might be on another page. Click the Next link to move to the next page, and then scroll down to find the Print a file topic, repeating to search additional pages until you locate the topic.

▶ **8.** Read the information.

Another way to find information in the Help system is to use the Table of Contents pane. The Show Table of Contents button on the Help window toolbar opens a pane that displays a list of the Help system content organized by subjects and topics, similar to a book's table of contents. You click main subject links to display related topic links. You click a topic link to display that Help topic in the Help window. You'll use the Table of Contents to find information about getting help in Office.

To use the Help window table of contents:

▶ **1.** Click the **Show Table of Contents** button on the Help window toolbar. The Table of Contents pane opens on the left side of the Help window.

▶ **2.** Click **Getting help** in the Table of Contents pane, scrolling up if necessary. The Getting help "book" opens, listing the topics related to that subject.

▶ **3.** Click the **Work with the Help window** topic, and then click the **Maximize** button ☐ on the title bar. The Help topic is displayed in the maximized Help window, and you can read the text to learn more about the various ways to obtain help in Word. See Figure 22.

Table of Contents pane in the Help window ◀ **Figure 22**

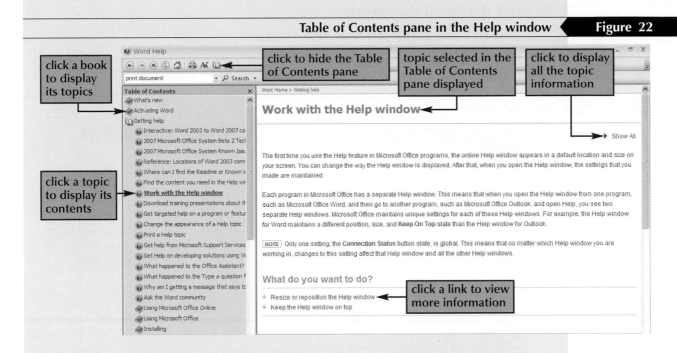

Trouble? If your search results list differs from the one shown in Figure 22, your computer is not connected to the Internet or Microsoft has updated the list of available Help topics since this book was published. Continue with Step 4.

▶ **4.** Click **Using Microsoft Office Online** in the Table of Contents pane, click the **Get online Help, templates, training, and additional content** topic to display information about that topic, and then read the information.

▶ **5.** Click the links within this topic and read the information.

▶ **6.** Click the **Close** button ☒ on the Help window title bar to close the window.

Printing a File

At times, you'll want a paper copy of your Office file. The first time you print during each session at the computer, you should use the Print command to open the Print dialog box so you can verify or adjust the printing settings. You can select a printer, the number of copies to print, the portion of the file to print, and so forth; the printing settings vary slightly from program to program. If you want to use the same default settings for subsequent print jobs, you can use the Quick Print button to print without opening the dialog box.

Printing a File | Reference Window

- Click the Office Button, and then click Print.
- Verify the print settings in the Print dialog box.
- Click the OK button.

or

- Click the Office Button, point to Print, and then click Quick Print.

Now that you know how to print, you'll print the agenda for Ean.

To print the Word document:

▶ **1.** Make sure your printer is turned on and contains paper.

▶ **2.** Click the **Office Button** (), and then click **Print**. The Print dialog box opens. See Figure 23.

Figure 23 ▶ **Print dialog box**

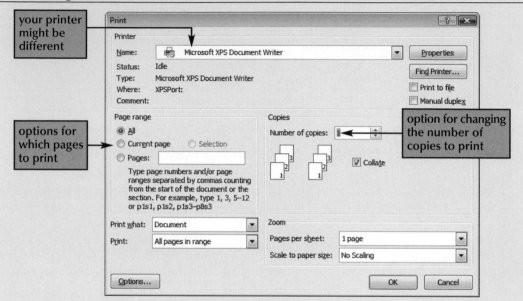

your printer might be different

options for which pages to print

option for changing the number of copies to print

> **Trouble?** If a menu of Print commands opens, you clicked the Print button arrow on the two-part Print button. Click Print on the menu to open the Print dialog box.

▶ **3.** Verify that the correct printer appears in the Name box in the Printer group. If necessary, click the **Name** arrow, and then click the correct printer from the list of available printers.

▶ **4.** Verify that **1** appears in the Number of copies box.

▶ **5.** Click the **OK** button to print the document.

> **Trouble?** If the document does not print, see your instructor or technical support person for help.

Exiting Programs

When you finish working with a program, you should exit it. As with many other aspects of Office, you can exit programs with a button or a command. You'll use both methods to exit Word and Excel. You can use the Exit command to exit a program and close an open file in one step. If you haven't saved the final version of the open file, a dialog box opens, asking whether you want to save your changes. Clicking the Yes button saves the open file, closes the file, and then exits the program.

To exit the Word and Excel programs:

▶ **1.** Click the **Close** button on the Word title bar to exit Word. The Word document closes and the Word program exits. The Excel window is visible again.

Trouble? If a dialog box opens, asking if you want to save the document, you might have inadvertently made a change to the document. Click the No button.

▶ **2.** Click the **Office Button** 🔘, and then click **Exit Excel**. A dialog box opens, asking whether you want to save the changes you made to the workbook. If you click the Yes button, the Save As dialog box opens and Excel exits after you finish saving the workbook. This time, you don't want to save the workbook.

▶ **3.** Click the **No** button. The workbook closes without saving a copy, and the Excel program exits.

Exiting programs after you are done using them keeps your Windows desktop uncluttered for the next person using the computer, frees up your system's resources, and prevents data from being lost accidentally.

Quick Check | Review

1. What Office program would be best to use to create a budget?
2. How do you start an Office program?
3. Explain the difference between Save and Save As.
4. How do you open an existing Office file?
5. What happens if you open a file, make edits, and then attempt to close the file or exit the program without saving the current version of the file?
6. What are two ways to get Help in Office?

Tutorial Summary | Review

You have learned how to use features common to all the programs included in Microsoft Office 2007, including starting and exiting programs; resizing windows; using the Ribbon, dialog boxes, shortcut menus, and the Mini toolbar; opening, closing, and printing files; and getting Help.

Key Terms

Access	Help window	Office Button
application settings	integration	Outlook
button	keyboard shortcut	PowerPoint
contextual tab	Live Preview	presentation
database	Microsoft Office 2007	Quick Access Toolbar
default	Microsoft Office Access 2007	Ribbon
dialog box	Microsoft Office Excel 2007	ScreenTip
Dialog Box Launcher	Microsoft Office Online	shortcut menu
document	Microsoft Office	status bar
Excel	Outlook 2007	tab
file extension	Microsoft Office	task pane
filename	PowerPoint 2007	Word
folder	Microsoft Office Word 2007	workbook
gallery	Mini toolbar	zoom
group	object	
Help	Office	

Practice	**Review Assignments**

Practice the skills you learned in the tutorial.

Data Files needed for the Review Assignments: Finances.xlsx, Letter.docx

You need to prepare for an upcoming meeting at Recycled Palette. You'll open and print documents for the presentation. Complete the following:

1. Start PowerPoint.
2. Use the Help window to search Office Online for the PowerPoint demo "Demo: Up to Speed with PowerPoint 2007." (*Hint*: Use "demo" as the keyword to search for, and make sure you search All PowerPoint in the Content from Office Online list. If you are not connected to the Internet, continue with Step 3.) Open the Demo topic, and then click the Play Demo link to view it. Close Internet Explorer and the Help window when you're done.
3. Start Excel.
4. Switch to the PowerPoint window using the taskbar, and then close the presentation but leave open the PowerPoint program. (*Hint:* Click the Office Button and then click Close.)
5. Open a new, blank PowerPoint presentation from the New Presentation dialog box.
6. Close the PowerPoint presentation and program using the Close button on the PowerPoint title bar; do not save changes if asked.
7. Open the **Finances** workbook located in the OFF\Review folder included with your Data Files.
8. Use the Save As command to save the workbook as **Recycled Palette Finances** in the OFF\Review folder.
9. Type your name, press the Enter key to insert your name at the top of the worksheet, and then save the workbook.
10. Print one copy of the worksheet using the Print button on the Office Button menu.
11. Exit Excel using the Office Button.
12. Start Word, and then open the **Letter** document located in the OFF\Review folder included with your Data Files.
13. Use the Save As command to save the document with the filename **Recycled Palette Letter** in the OFF\Review folder.
14. Press and hold the Ctrl key, press the End key, and then release both keys to move the insertion point to the end of the letter, and then type your name.
15. Use the Save button on the Quick Access Toolbar to save the change to the Recycled Palette Letter document.
16. Print one copy of the document, and then close the document.
17. Exit the Word program using the Close button on the title bar.

Review | **Quick Check Answers**

1. Excel
2. Click the Start button on the taskbar, click All Programs, click Microsoft Office, and then click the name of the program you want to open.
3. Save updates a file to reflect its latest contents using its current filename and location. Save As enables you to change the filename and storage location of a file.
4. Click the Office Button, and then click Open.
5. A dialog box opens asking whether you want to save the changes to the file.
6. Two of the following: ScreenTips, Help window, Microsoft Office Online

Ending Data Files

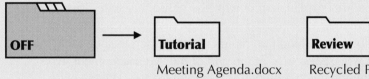

Meeting Agenda.docx

Recycled Palette Finances.xlsx
Recycled Palette Letter.docx

Reality Check

At home, school, or work, you probably complete many types of tasks, such as writing letters and balancing a checkbook, on a regular basis. You can use Microsoft Office to streamline many of these tasks.

Note: Please be sure *not* to include any personal information of a sensitive nature in the documents you create to be submitted to your instructor for this exercise. Later on, you can update the documents with such information for your own personal use.

1. Start Word, and open a new document, if necessary.
2. In the document, type a list of all the personal, work, and/or school tasks you do on a regular basis.
3. For each task, identify the type of Office file (document, workbook, presentation, or database) you would create to complete that task. For example, you would create a Word document to write a letter.
4. For each file, identify the Office program you would use to create that file, and explain why you would use that program. For example, Word is the best program to use to create a document for a letter.
5. Save the document with an appropriate filename in an appropriate folder location.
6. Use a Web browser to visit the Microsoft Web site at *www.microsoft.com* and research the different Office 2007 suites available. Determine which suite includes all the programs you need to complete the tasks on your list.
7. At the end of the task list you created in your Word document, type which Office suite you decided on and a brief explanation of why you chose that suite. Then save the document.
8. Double-click the Home tab on the Ribbon to minimize the Ribbon to show only the tab names and extend the workspace area. At the end of the Word document, type your opinion of whether minimizing the Ribbon is a helpful feature. When you're done, double-click the Home tab to display the full Ribbon.
9. Print the finished document, and then submit it to your instructor.

Creating a Presentation

Presenting Information About a Recreational Timeshare Company

Case | Share-My-Toys, Inc.

After Sandra Corwin graduated from Idaho State University with a degree in business administration, she worked for a large company, Anaconda Kayaks and Canoes, in Redding, California. After several years, she decided to return to her home town of Montpelier, Idaho, and start her own business. Montpelier is located near Bear Lake and other recreational areas in southeastern Idaho and western Wyoming, and Sandra grew up participating in camping, hiking, snowmobiling, boating, and other water sports. During that time, she noticed that her family often borrowed outdoor recreational equipment from family and friends, but now, because of the population increase in the area and the rise in equipment costs, many people don't have access to the equipment to do the activities that she enjoyed as a youth.

With these ideas in mind and her experience in the outdoor equipment industry, Sandra started the company Share-My-Toys, Inc., which specializes in selling timeshares for recreational equipment, including ski boats, wave runners, snowmobiles, recreational vehicles (RVs), and all-terrain vehicles (ATVs). The company would allow everyone, even those of modest means or few family members in the area, to have access to a wide range of outdoor activities.

In this tutorial, you'll first examine a presentation that Sandra created for potential members. Viewing this file will help you to become familiar with **Microsoft Office PowerPoint 2007** (or simply **PowerPoint**). You'll then create a presentation for Sandra that describes her business plan for Share-My-Toys to banks and potential investors. The presentation you create will be based on content that PowerPoint suggests by using a template. You'll modify the text in the presentation, and you'll add and delete slides. You'll check the spelling of the presentation, and then you'll view the completed slide show. Finally, you'll save the slide show and print handouts.

Starting Data Files

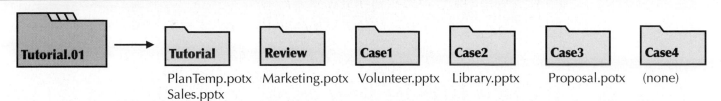

Tutorial.01 → Tutorial · Review · Case1 · Case2 · Case3 · Case4

PlanTemp.potx   Marketing.potx   Volunteer.pptx   Library.pptx   Proposal.potx   (none)
Sales.pptx

Session 1.1

What Is PowerPoint?

PowerPoint is a powerful presentation graphics program that provides everything you need to produce an effective presentation in the form of on-screen slides, a slide presentation on a Web site, or black-and-white or color overheads. You might have already seen your instructors use PowerPoint presentations to enhance their classroom lectures.

Using PowerPoint, you can prepare each component of a presentation: individual slides, speaker notes, an outline, and audience handouts. The presentation you'll create for Sandra will include slides, notes, and handouts.

To start PowerPoint:

1. Click the **Start** button 🌀 on the taskbar, click **All Programs**, click **Microsoft Office**, and then click **Microsoft Office PowerPoint 2007**. PowerPoint starts and the PowerPoint window opens. See Figure 1-1.

   Trouble? If you don't see Microsoft Office PowerPoint 2007 on the Microsoft Office submenu, look for it on a different submenu or on the All Programs menu. If you still cannot find it, ask your instructor or technical support person for help.

Figure 1-1 | **Blank PowerPoint window**

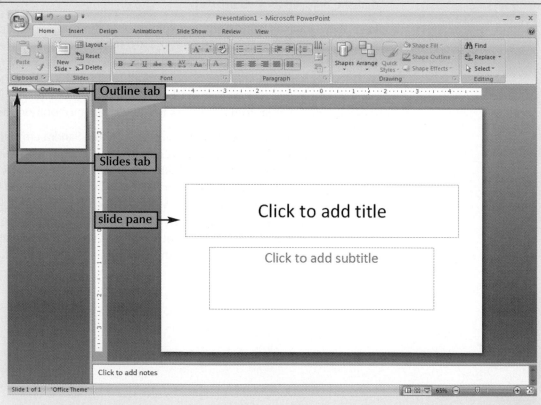

Opening an Existing PowerPoint Presentation

Before you prepare the presentation on Share-My-Toys, Sandra suggests that you view an existing presentation that she recently prepared so that you can see examples of PowerPoint features. When you examine the presentation, you'll learn about some PowerPoint capabilities that can help make your presentations more interesting and effective. You'll open the presentation now.

To open the existing presentation:

▶ **1.** Make sure you have access to the Data Files in the Tutorial.01 folder.

Trouble? If you don't have the starting Data Files, you need to get them before you can proceed. Your instructor will either give you the Data Files or ask you to obtain them from a specified location (such as a network drive). In either case, make a backup copy of your Data Files before you start so that you will have the original files available in case you need to start over. If you have any questions about the Data Files, see your instructor or technical support person for assistance.

▶ **2.** In the upper-left corner of the PowerPoint window, click the **Office Button** . A menu of commands appears.

▶ **3.** Click **Open** to display the Open dialog box.

▶ **4.** Expand the Folders list, if necessary, and then navigate to the **Tutorial.01\Tutorial** folder included with your Data Files.

▶ **5.** Click **Sales**, and then click the **Open** button to display Sandra's presentation. The presentation opens in Normal view. See Figure 1-2. Notice, on the left side of the status bar, that you are on the first slide of a presentation that contains nine slides.

PowerPoint window with presentation ◀ Figure 1-2

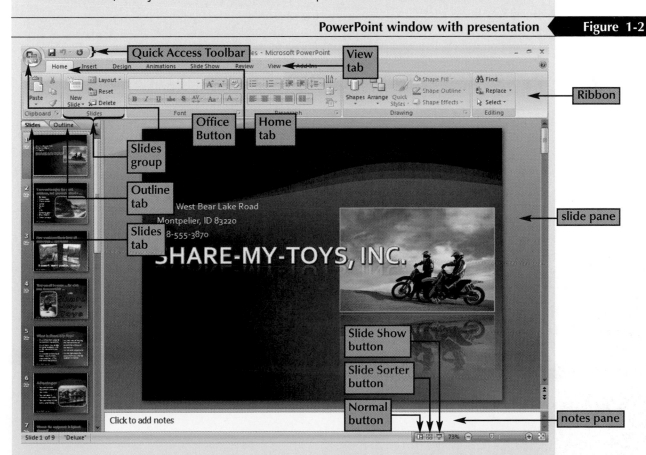

Trouble? If you see filename extensions on your screen (such as ".pptx" appended to "Sales" in the filename), don't be concerned; they won't affect your work.

Switching Views and Navigating a Presentation

The PowerPoint window contains features common to all Windows programs, as well as features specific to PowerPoint. One obvious difference between the PowerPoint window and other Office programs is that the PowerPoint window is divided into sections. The large section in the center of the screen is the slide pane. The **slide pane** shows the current slide as it will look during your slide show. When you type text or insert graphics on your slide, you'll mainly use the slide pane. Just below the slide pane is the notes pane. The **notes pane** contains notes (also called speaker notes) for the presenter; for example, the notes pane might contain specific points to cover or phrases to say during the presentation. During a slide show, the audience does not see the contents of the notes pane.

To the left of the slide pane, you can see another pane that contains two tabs, the Slides tab and the Outline tab. The **Slides tab** is on top when you first start PowerPoint. It shows a column of numbered slide **thumbnails** (miniature images) so you can see a visual representation of several slides at once. You can use the Slides tab to jump quickly to another slide in the slide pane by clicking the desired slide. The **Outline tab** shows an outline of the titles and text of each slide of your presentation.

At the lower right of the PowerPoint window, on the status bar to the left of the Zoom slider, are three buttons you can use to switch views: the Normal button [⊞] , the Slide Sorter button [⊞] , and the Slide Show button [⬚] . These three buttons allow you to change the way you view a presentation. PowerPoint is currently in Normal view. **Normal view** is best for working with the content of the slides. You can see how the text and graphics look on each individual slide, and you can examine the outline of the entire presentation. When you switch to **Slide Sorter view**, the pane that contains the Slides and Outline tabs disappears from view and all the slides appear as thumbnails. Slide Sorter view is an easy way to reorder the slides or set special features for your slide show. **Slide Show view** is the view in which you run the slide show presentation and the slide fills the entire screen. The View tab on the Ribbon also contains buttons for Normal, Slide Sorter, and Slide Show views, as well as for other views of the PowerPoint presentation, including Notes Page view.

Next, you'll examine Normal and Slide Sorter views. PowerPoint is currently in Normal view with Slide 1 in the slide pane.

To examine the presentation in Normal and Slide Sorter views:

▶ **1.** In the pane that contains the Slides tab, click the **Slide 2** thumbnail. Slide 2 appears in the slide pane.

▶ **2.** Click the **Next Slide** button [⬚] at the bottom of the vertical scroll bar on the right side of the slide pane. Slide 3 appears in the slide pane.

▶ **3.** Drag the scroll box in the slide pane vertical scroll bar down to the bottom of the scroll bar. Notice the ScreenTip that appears as you drag. It identifies the slide number and the title of the slide at the current position.

▶ **4.** In the pane that contains the Slides and Outline tabs, click the **Outline** tab. The text outline of the slides appears in the Outline tab.

▶ **5.** Drag the scroll box in the vertical scroll bar of the Outline tab up to the top of the scroll bar, and then, in the Outline tab, click the **slide icon** [▬] next to Slide 3. Slide 3 again appears in the slide pane.

▶ **6.** In the pane that contains the Slides and Outline tabs, click the **Slides** tab. The Outline tab disappears behind the Slides tab.

▶ **7.** On the status bar, to the left of the Zoom slider, click the **Slide Sorter** button 🔠 . Slide Sorter view appears, and Slide 3 has a colored frame around it to indicate that it is the current slide.

▶ **8.** Position the pointer over the **Slide 2** thumbnail. A colored frame appears around Slide 2.

▶ **9.** Click the **Slide 2** thumbnail to make it the current slide. The colored frame disappears from Slide 3 and stays around Slide 2.

▶ **10.** Double-click the **Slide 1** thumbnail. The view switches back to Normal view and Slide 1 appears in the slide pane. You could also have clicked the Normal button on the status bar to switch back to Normal view.

Now that you're familiar with the PowerPoint window, you're ready to view Sandra's presentation. You'll do this in Slide Show view.

Viewing a Presentation in Slide Show View

Slide Show view is the view you use when you present an on-screen presentation to an audience. When you click the Slide Show button on the status bar, the slide show starts beginning with the current slide (the slide currently in the slide pane in Normal view or the selected slide in Slide Sorter view). When you click the Slide Show button on the View tab on the Ribbon or press the F5 key, the slide show starts at the beginning of the presentation—at Slide 1—even if Slide 1 is not the current slide. In a slide show, the slides fill the screen; no toolbars or other Windows elements are visible on the screen.

In Slide Show view, you move from one slide to the next by pressing the Spacebar, clicking the left mouse button, or pressing the → key. In addition, PowerPoint provides a method for jumping from one slide to any other slide in the presentation during the slide show: You can right-click anywhere on the screen, point to Go to Slide on the shortcut menu, and then, in the list that appears, click one of the slide titles to jump to that slide.

When you prepare a slide show, you can add special effects to the show. For example, you can add **slide transitions**, the manner in which a new slide appears on the screen during a slide show. You can also add **animations** to the elements on the slide; that is, a text or graphic object on the slide can appear on the slide in a special way or have a sound effect associated with it. A special type of animation is **progressive disclosure**, a technique in which each element on a slide appears one at a time after the slide background appears. Animations draw the audience's attention to the particular item on the screen.

You can also add a footer on the slides. A **footer** is a word or phrase that appears at the bottom of each slide in the presentation.

You want to see how Sandra's presentation will appear when she shows it in Slide Show view to a potential Share-My-Toys member. You'll then have a better understanding of how Sandra used PowerPoint features to make her presentation informative and interesting.

To view the presentation in Slide Show view:

▶ **1.** On the status bar, to the left of the Zoom slider, click the **Slide Show** button 🖵 . The slide show begins by filling the entire viewing area of the screen with Slide 1 of Sandra's presentation. When you click the Slide Show button on the status bar, the slide show starts from the current slide. Watch as the slide title moves across the screen from left to right and right to left, the address block moves down the screen, and the picture of dirt bikers moves up the screen.

Tip

To start the slide show from the first slide no matter what the current slide is, click the View tab on the Ribbon, and then, in the Presentation Views group, click the Slide Show button, or press the F5 key.

As you view this first slide, you can already see some of the types of elements that PowerPoint allows you to place on a slide: text in different styles, sizes, and colors; graphics; and a background design. You also saw an example of an animation when you watched the slide title scroll across the screen and other elements move onto the screen. You can also see other special effects: text shadows, text reflection, and photo reflection.

2. Press the **Spacebar**. The slide show goes from Slide 1 to Slide 2. See Figure 1-3. Notice that during the transition from Slide 1 to Slide 2, Slide 2 appeared as if it were a wheel with four spokes spinning onto the screen.

| Figure 1-3 | Slide 2 in Slide Show view |

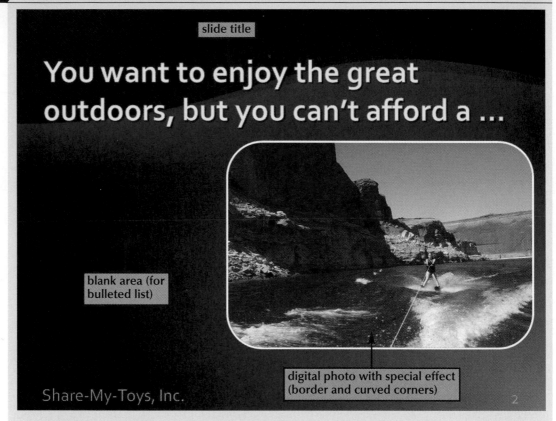

Trouble? If you missed the transition from Slide 1 to Slide 2, or if you want to see it again, press the ← key twice to redisplay Slide 1, and then press the Spacebar to go to Slide 2 again.

Notice in Figure 1-3 that Slide 2 displays (1) a colored background that varies in color across various sections of the slide, (2) a title in large, pale yellow text with a black **drop shadow** (a thin shadow on one side of the characters), (3) a photograph with a white border and curved corners of a woman on water skis, and (4) a blank area to the left of the photo. A bulleted list will appear in the blank area after you press the Spacebar. Also note that the slide number appears in the lower-right corner of the slide.

3. Press the **Spacebar**. The bulleted list moves onto the slide. Now you can see 10 items—the list of recreational equipment available through Share-My-Toys, Inc. They "flew" onto the screen in progressive disclosure—one item at a time—without your having to press the Spacebar to reveal each item.

4. Click the left mouse button. Slide 3 appears on screen. During the transition from Slide 2 to Slide 3, you again see a spinning wheel with four spokes that covers up one slide and reveals the next slide. After the slide appears on the screen, you see two photographs slowly move onto the slide, a houseboat from the left and a kayak from the right. These photos each have three PowerPoint special effects applied to them: They are positioned at an angle, have beveled edges, and show reflections below them. PowerPoint supports many special effects for pictures that you insert into a presentation.

5. Press the **Spacebar** to go to Slide 4. A picture of a woman in a boat and the slide title appear on screen, followed by the twirling text "Share-My-Toys." This is an example of custom animation.

6. Proceed to the next slide by clicking the left mouse button or pressing the **Spacebar**. The title of Slide 5 appears on the screen, with a large blank area below the title. You can't see any of the items of the bulleted list yet, but through progressive disclosure, you'll display the bulleted items one at a time.

7. Press the **Spacebar**. A bulleted item flies onto the slide from the bottom of the screen. Notice that the bullet itself is a red diamond and the text is white.

8. Press the **Spacebar** again. The next bulleted item appears on the slide. As this item appears, the previous item dims. Dimming the previous bulleted items helps focus the audience's attention on the current bulleted item.

9. Press the **Spacebar** four more times, reading the bulleted text as it appears on the screen, and a fifth time to dim the final bulleted item. Notice that this bulleted list is a two-column list.

> **Tip**
>
> To end a slide show before you reach the last slide, press the Esc key

---

Using Conservative Animations in Formal Presentations | InSight

Flashy or flamboyant animations are acceptable for informal, fun-oriented presentations but would not be appropriate in a formal business, technical, or educational presentation. These types of presentations should be more conservative. When you are creating a formal presentation, it's best not to include superfluous animations that might detract from your message.

So far, you've seen several important PowerPoint features: slide transitions, progressive disclosure, animations, and special photographic effects. Now you'll finish the presentation and see more special effects, including custom animations, simple drawings, and a chart.

To continue viewing the slide show:

1. Press the **Spacebar** to go to Slide 6, and then press the **Spacebar** three more times to reveal the three bulleted list items in progressive disclosure. This time, the items are not dimmed as others appear on the slide.

2. Advance to Slide 7, where you see first the slide title and then a chart appear on the slide. PowerPoint has powerful features that allow you to add a wide variety of different types of charts and apply special effects to them.

3. Press the **Spacebar** to go to Slide 8. Here, you see the title and a simple drawing of a face in the middle of the slide. PowerPoint drawing tools let you draw simple pictures and diagrams for your presentations. This slide also demonstrates other drawing objects and animations. After you press the Spacebar in the next step to reveal the rest of the objects on this slide, watch the eyes of the face as you read the items in the flow diagram.

▶ **4.** Press the **Spacebar** to initiate the animation of the flow diagram.

   Trouble? If you want to watch the animations again, press the ← key, and then press the Spacebar to animate the diagram.

▶ **5.** Press the **Spacebar** to move to Slide 9, the final slide, and then press the **Spacebar** again. A black, nearly blank slide appears with small text at the top identifying the end of the presentation.

▶ **6.** Press the **Spacebar** one more time to exit Slide Show view and return to the view from which you started the slide show, in this case, Normal view.

▶ **7.** In the upper-left corner of the window, click the **Office Button** (⊞), and then click **Close**.

As you can see from this slide show, PowerPoint has many powerful features. You'll learn how to use many of these features in your own presentations as you work through these tutorials.

You're now ready to create a presentation for Sandra, which she plans to give to bankers and potential investors. The presentation will include the business plan for Share-My-Toys. Before you begin, however, you need to plan the presentation.

Planning a Presentation

Planning a presentation before you create it improves the quality of your presentation, makes your presentation more effective and enjoyable, and, in the long run, saves you time and effort. As you plan your presentation, you should answer several questions: What is my purpose or objective for this presentation? What type of presentation is needed? Who is the audience? What information does that audience need? What is the physical location of my presentation? What is the best format for presenting the information contained in this presentation, given its location?

In planning your presentation, you should determine the following aspects:

• **Purpose of the presentation**: To acquire loans and investment funds for Share-My-Toys
• **Type of presentation**: Business plan (a summary of the operational and financial objectives of a business, including detailed plans and budgets showing how the objectives will be realized)
• **Audience for the presentation**: Local banks and potential investors
• **Audience needs**: To understand the mission, objectives, budgets, marketing, resources, and so forth, for Share-My-Toys
• **Location of the presentation**: Small conference room
• **Format**: Oral presentation accompanied by an electronic slide show of 6 to 8 slides

You have carefully planned your presentation. Now you'll use a PowerPoint template to create it.

Using Templates

PowerPoint helps you quickly create effective presentations by using a **template**, a PowerPoint file that contains the colors, background format, font styles, and accent colors for a presentation. Templates can also contain sample text. After you start creating a presentation with a given template, you can make changes to the design features and the text of the template. As you will see, each slide in a template has a predetermined way of organizing the objects on a slide.

When you create a presentation from a template, you can use a template that you or someone else designed, or you can use a template that you download from Microsoft Office Online. In this tutorial, you'll use a template that Sandra created while she worked for Anaconda Kayaks and Canoes in California. The slides in templates usually have existing text. The purpose of this text is to guide you in selecting and inserting the proper text content into your presentation. You'll now open the template.

Selecting a Template from Microsoft Office Online | InSight

To find many more templates, it's a good idea to look on Microsoft Office Online, which provides a variety of template categories to help you select the correct template for your presentation needs, including agendas, award certificates, calendars, design, reports, resumés, schedules, and so forth. After you select a category, you can examine and download different templates to see which you like the most. You can also view user ratings of the various templates, based on the feedback from hundreds, and, in some cases, even thousands, of users.

To use a template in starting a presentation:

▶ **1.** Click the **Office Button** 🏢, and then click **New**. The New Presentation dialog box opens. See Figure 1-4. You'll now select the template that Sandra created.

New Presentation dialog box | **Figure 1-4**

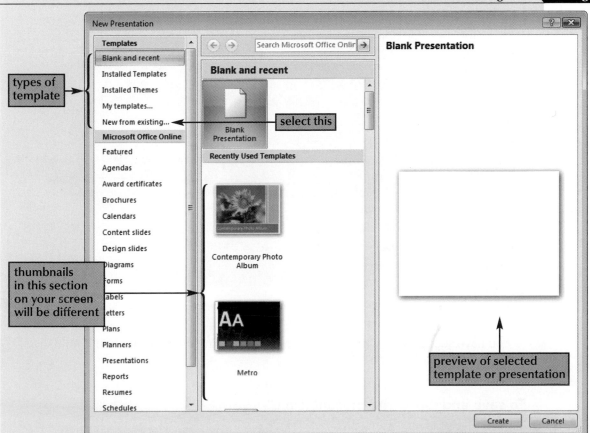

▶ **2.** In the pane on the left side of the New Presentation dialog box, click **New from existing** in the list under Templates. The New from Existing Presentation dialog box opens.

▶ **3.** Navigate to the **Tutorial.01\Tutorial** folder included with your Data Files.

▶ **4.** Double-click **PlanTemp**.

The Business plan presentation template contains text on the slides to help you insert your business plan information. See Figure 1-5. PlanTemp is a PowerPoint template file, not a presentation file, but when you click New from existing in the New Presentation dialog box, you are allowed to choose from all PowerPoint files in the current folder. Notice that the filename in the title bar is "Presentation2" instead of the name of the file you opened "PlanTemp." This indicates that this is the second presentation of your current session, but that you opened a template or another presentation as a template.

Trouble? If the number in the filename on the title bar is a number other than 2 (such as "Presentation3"), don't worry about it. It just means that you have opened or created more than two presentations during this session.

Figure 1-5 ▶ **PowerPoint window with business plan presentation**

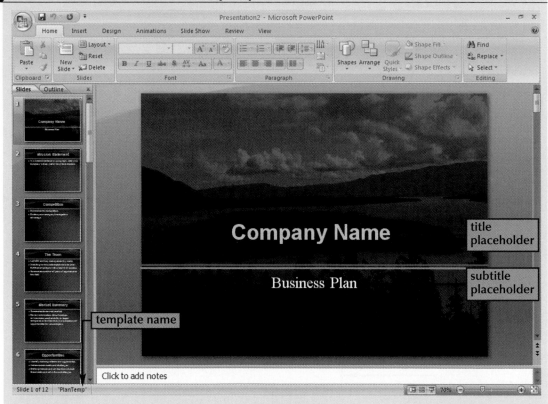

You have successfully started a new presentation using the template. You'll now save the presentation to your disk.

To save and name the presentation:

▶ **1.** On the Quick Access Toolbar, click the **Save** button 🖫 . The Save As dialog box opens.

▶ **2.** Expand the Folders list, if necessary, and then navigate to the **Tutorial.01\Tutorial** folder included with your Data Files, if necessary.

▶ **3.** In the File name text box, click immediately after Company Name, the default file-name, press the **Backspace** key enough times to delete the default filename, and then type **Business Plan**.

▶ **4.** At the bottom of the dialog box, click the **Save** button. PowerPoint saves the presentation as Business Plan and displays that name in the title bar of the PowerPoint window.

In the next session, you'll edit the text of Sandra's template, as well as create notes.

Session 1.1 Quick Check | Review

1. Describe the components of a PowerPoint presentation.
2. Name and describe the three panes in the PowerPoint window in Normal view.
3. Define or describe the following:
   a. slide pane
   b. progressive disclosure
   c. slide transition
   d. template
   e. layout
4. What are some of the questions that you should answer when planning a presentation?
5. Describe the purpose of the existing text in a template.
6. Describe Slide Show view.

Session 1.2

Modifying a Presentation

Now that you've started a presentation using a template with existing text, you're ready to edit the words in the presentation to fit Sandra's specific needs. You'll keep the presentation design, which includes the dark blue background and the size and color of the text.

The template includes the title slide, as well as other slides, with suggested text located in placeholders. A **placeholder** is a region of a slide, or a location in an outline, reserved for inserting text or graphics. To edit the template outline to fit Sandra's needs, you must insert text or objects into the placeholders one at a time. Text placeholders are a special kind of **text box**, which is an object that contains text. You can edit and format text in a text box or you can manipulate the text box as a whole. When you manipulate the text box as a whole, the text box is treated as an object, something that can be manipulated or resized as a unit.

When the text box is **active**, you can add or revise the text in it and the box appears with dashed lines and sizing handles around the text. **Sizing handles** are small circles and squares that appear at each corner and on each side of the active box that you can drag to make a text box or other object larger or smaller on the slide. When the entire text box is selected as a single object, you can apply effects to all of the text inside it and the text box appears as a solid line with sizing handles.

Many of the slides in your presentation for Share-My-Toys contain bulleted lists. A **bulleted list** is a list of "paragraphs" (words, phrases, sentences, or paragraphs) with a special character (dot, dash, circle, box, star, or other character) to the left of each paragraph. A **bulleted item** is one paragraph in a bulleted list. Bullets can appear at different outline levels. A **first-level bullet** is a main paragraph in a bulleted list; a **second-level bullet**—sometimes called a **subbullet**—is a bullet beneath (and indented from) a first-level bullet. Using bulleted lists reminds both the speaker and the audience of the main points of the presentation. In addition to bulleted lists, PowerPoint also supports numbered lists. A **numbered list** is a list of paragraphs that are numbered consecutively on the slide.

When you edit the text on the slides, keep in mind that the bulleted lists aren't meant to be the complete presentation; instead, they should emphasize the key points to the audience and remind the speaker of the points to emphasize. In all your presentations, you should follow the **6 x 6 rule** as much as possible: Keep each bulleted item to no more than six words, and don't include more than six bulleted items on a slide. This is, however, just a general guideline. You'll sometimes have slides with seven or eight bulleted items, and sometimes have items with more than six words. Never sacrifice clarity and purpose for brevity.

InSight | Creating Effective Text Presentations

- Think of your text presentation as a visual map of your oral presentation. Show your organization by using overviews, making headings larger than subheadings, and including bulleted lists to highlight key points and numbered steps to show sequences.
- Follow the 6 × 6 rule: Use six or fewer items per screen, and use phrases of six or fewer words. Omit unnecessary articles, pronouns, and adjectives.
- Keep phrases parallel. For example, if one bulleted item starts with a verb (such as "Summarize"), all the other bulleted items should start with a verb (such as "Include," "List," or "Review"). Or, if one bulleted list is a complete sentence, all the items should be complete sentences.
- Make sure your text is appropriate for your purpose and audience.

Sandra reviewed the presentation template with its existing text, and she has several suggestions to customize it for the presentation she wants you to create. First, she wants you to replace the placeholder text with information about Share-My-Toys. She also wants you to delete unnecessary slides and change the order of the slides in the presentation. You'll start by editing the text on the slides.

Editing Slides

Most of the slides in the presentation contain two placeholder text boxes. The slide **title text** is a text box at the top of the slide that gives the title of the information on that slide; the slide **content** is a large box in which you type a bulleted or numbered list or insert some other kind of object. In this presentation, you'll modify or create title text in some of the slides and modify the content text in all the slides that you keep in the presentation.

To edit the template text to fit Sandra's needs, you must select text in each of the placeholders, and then replace that text with other text. You'll now begin to edit and replace the text to fit Sandra's presentation. The first text you'll change is the title placeholder on the first (title) slide.

To edit and replace text in the first slide:

▶ **1.** If you took a break after the previous session, make sure PowerPoint is running, and then open the presentation **Business Plan** located in the Tutorial.01\Tutorial folder included with your Data Files. Slide 1 appears in the slide pane and the Slides tab is on top in the pane on the left.

> **Trouble?** If the Slides tab isn't on top in the pane on the left, click it to make the entire tab appear.

▶ **2.** Position the pointer over the title text (currently "Company Name") in the slide pane so that the pointer changes to Ⅰ, and then drag it across the text to select it. See Figure 1-6. The text box becomes active, as indicated by the dashed lines around the box and the sizing handles at each corner and on each side of the text box, and the text becomes highlighted, as indicated by the gray box around it. The Mini toolbar appears because you used the mouse to select the text.

Selecting placeholder text **Figure 1-6**

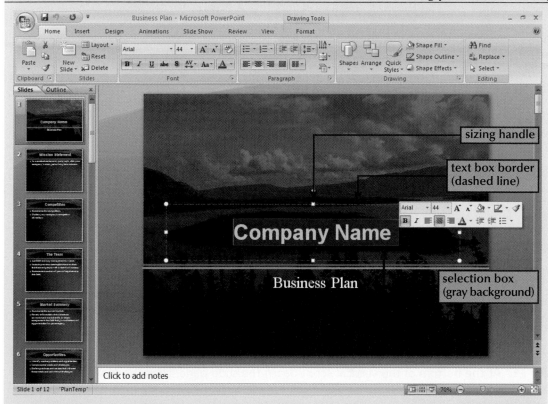

▶ **3.** Type **Share-My-Toys**. As soon as you start to type, the selected text disappears, and the typed text appears in its place. Now the title slide has the title Sandra wants for your presentation.

▶ **4.** Select the subtitle text ("Business Plan"), and then type your first and last name (so your instructor can identify you as the author of this presentation), and then click anywhere else on the slide to make the text box inactive. The dashed lines and sizing handles around the text box disappear. See Figure 1-7. (The figures in this book will show the name Sandra Corwin.)

Figure 1-7   Slide 1 after replacing placeholders with user text

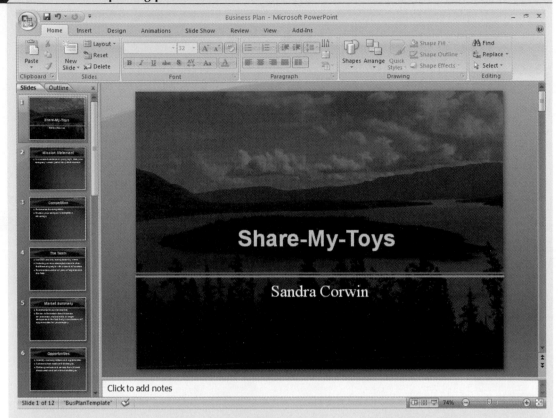

Trouble? If PowerPoint marks your name with a red wavy underline, this indicates that the word is not found in the PowerPoint dictionary. Ignore the wavy line for now; you'll learn how to deal with this later in this tutorial.

You'll now edit Slides 2 through 12 by replacing the placeholder text and adding new text, and by deleting slides that don't apply to your presentation. You'll edit text not only in the slide pane but also in the Outline tab.

To edit the text in the slides:

▶ **1.** At the bottom of the vertical scroll bar in the slide pane, click the **Next Slide** button ⬇. Slide 2 appears in the slide pane.

▶ **2.** Drag across the text in the bulleted item to select all the text in that item.

Now you're ready to type the Share-My-Toys mission statement.

▶ **3.** Type **Share-My-Toys is a start-up company that sells timeshares of recreational equipment for outdoor activities in southeastern Idaho and western Wyoming**. (including the period).

▶ **4.** Click in a blank space in the slide pane, just outside the edge of the slide, to make the text box inactive.

Trouble? If you clicked somewhere on the slide and selected another object (the other text box), click another place on the slide, preferably just outside the edge of the text box, to deselect all items.

Now you're going to edit the text in the Outline tab.

To edit the text using the Outline tab:

1. Click the **Next Slide** button ⊻ to go to Slide 3.

2. In the pane that contains the Slides and Outline tabs, click the **Outline** tab. In the Outline tab, you can see the text on each of the slides, but not the slide design. The Slide 3 slide icon is highlighted because Slide 3 is the current slide.

3. In the Outline tab, drag to select the text **Summarize the competition.**, located just below the title of Slide 3. The text is highlighted with a light-blue background.

4. Type **Southeastern Idaho has several recreational equipment rental companies but no timeshare companies.** (including the period). Notice that as you type, the text changes on the slide in the slide pane as well as in the Outline tab where you are typing.

5. In the Outline tab, select the text of the second bulleted paragraph ("Outline your company's competitive advantage.").

6. Type **SMT has a wider range and greater inventory of equipment.** (including the period).

With the insertion point at the end of the second bulleted item, you're ready to create additional bulleted items.

To create additional bulleted items:

1. With the insertion point blinking at the end of the last bulleted item (after the period) in the Outline tab, press the **Enter** key. PowerPoint creates a new bullet and leaves the insertion point to the right of the bullet, waiting for you to type the text.

2. Type **Timeshare gives members ownership.** (including the period), and then press the **Enter** key.

3. To the right of the new bullet, type **Membership fees provide needed business capital.** (including the period), and press the **Enter** key.

   Now you'll switch back to typing in the slide pane.

4. In the slide pane, click just below the last bulleted item. The new bullet you inserted in the Outline tab comes into view, and the insertion point is blinking to the right of it.

5. Type **Members get more use of equipment for less money.** (including the period). Notice that as you typed, PowerPoint automatically adjusts the size of the text in the slide pane so that the bulleted text fits within the text box on the slide.

6. Click a blank area of the slide to deselect the bulleted list text box. The completed Slide 3 should look like Figure 1-8.

Figure 1-8 Completed Slide 3

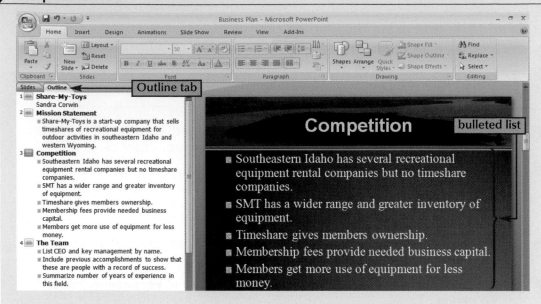

You're now ready to edit the text on another slide and create subbullets.

To create subbullets:

1. Click the **Next Slide** button to move to Slide 4.

2. Select all the text (all three bulleted items) in the slide pane, and then type **Sandra Corwin, CEO** (with no period). Now you want to add subbullets to provide information about Sandra, in addition to the fact that she is the company CEO (chief executive officer).

3. Press the **Enter** key to insert a new bullet, and then press the **Tab** key. The new bullet changes to a subbullet. In the design used in this presentation, subbullets are a gold-colored filled circle.

> **Tip**
>
> To move a bullet down a level, you can also click the Increase List Level button in the Paragraph group on the Home tab.

4. Type **B.S., Business Administration, Idaho State University**, and then press the **Enter** key. As you can see, PowerPoint automatically creates a new bullet at the same level as the previous bullet (in this case, the second-level), not a first-level bullet. You're now ready to type the next item to describe Sandra's qualifications.

5. Type **Product Manager, Anaconda Kayaks and Canoes, Redding, CA, 6 years**, and then press the **Enter** key to display another subbullet.

   Next you want to input information about Ernesto Candelaria, the chief financial officer (CFO) for Share-My-Toys. Because this information is not related to the previous first-level bullet, it should not be listed as a subbullet under that first-level bullet.

> **Tip**
>
> To move a bullet up a level, you can also press the Shift+Tab keys.

6. In the Paragraph group on the Home tab, click the **Decrease List Level** button. The bullet is converted from a second-level to a first-level bullet.

7. Type **Ernesto Candelaria, CFO**, and then press the **Enter** key. Now you want to provide information about Ernesto, so you will convert this first-level bullet to a second-level bullet.

8. In the Paragraph group on the Home tab, click the **Increase List Level** button.

> **9.** Type **M.S., Accountancy, University of Montana**, and then press the **Enter** key.

> **10.** Type **CPA for KPMG Accounting Firm, 12 years**, and then press the **Enter** key.

> **11.** Type **Private CPA, Montpelier, ID, 7 years**, then click a blank area of the slide. You have completed editing Slide 4. See Figure 1-9.

Completed Slide 4 | **Figure 1-9**

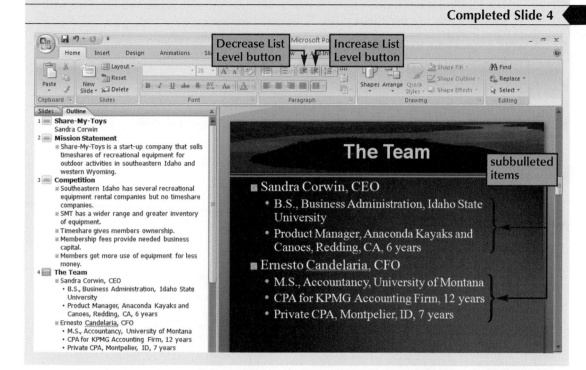

Sandra suggests that you delete Slides 5 ("Market Summary"), 6 ("Opportunities"), and 7 ("Business Concept") because she is trying to keep the presentation short and because the Market Summary slide implies the desired business opportunities and gives the basic business concept. Besides, she plans to have a handout for her audience with a market summary and other business ideas.

Deleting Slides

When creating a presentation, you'll often delete slides. A template might provide slides that you don't think are necessary, or you might create slides that you no longer want. Keep in mind that after you delete a slide, you can recover it by immediately clicking the Undo button on the Quick Access Toolbar.

Deleting Slides | Reference Window

- In Normal view, go to the slide you want to delete so it appears in the slide pane, and then click the Delete button in the Slides group on the Home tab.

or

- Click the desired slide thumbnail in the Slides tab, click the slide icon in the Outline tab, or in Slide Sorter view, select the slides you want to delete, and then press the Delete key.

To delete slides 5 through 7:

▶ 1. Go to Slide 5, and then, in the Slides group on the Home tab, click the **Delete** button. Slide 5 disappears and what was Slide 6 becomes Slide 5 and appears in the slide pane. You'll delete this Slide 5 using a different method.

▶ 2. In the pane that contains the Slides and Outline tab, click the **Slides** tab to display it. The Outline tab is hidden behind the Slides tab, and the Slides tab appears with thumbnails of all of the slides. Slide 5 ("Opportunities") is selected.

▶ 3. With Slide 5 selected in the Slides tab, press the **Delete** key. The "Opportunities" slide is deleted and the new Slide 5 ("Business Concept") appears in the slide pane.

▶ 4. Delete Slide 5 ("Business Concept"). The new Slide 5 becomes the "Goals and Objectives" slide.

▶ 5. Select all the bulleted text in the new Slide 5 and replace it with the text shown in Figure 1-10.

Figure 1-10	Completed new Slide 5

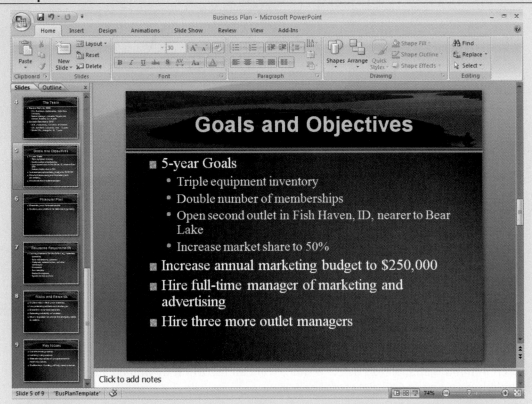

Now Sandra wants you to delete Slides 6 ("Financial Plan") and 7 ("Resource Requirements").

▶ 6. In the Slides tab, click **Slide 6** to select it, press and hold the **Shift** key, click **Slide 7** in the Slides tab, and then release the **Shift** key. Slides 6 and 7 are both selected in the Slides tab.

▶ 7. In the Slides group on the Home tab, click the **Delete** button. The two slides disappear, leaving a total of seven slides in the presentation.

Now you'll finish editing the presentation and save your work.

▶ **8.** Replace the text on Slide 6 ("Risks and Rewards") with the text shown in Figure 1-11.

Completed Slide 6 ◀ **Figure 1-11**

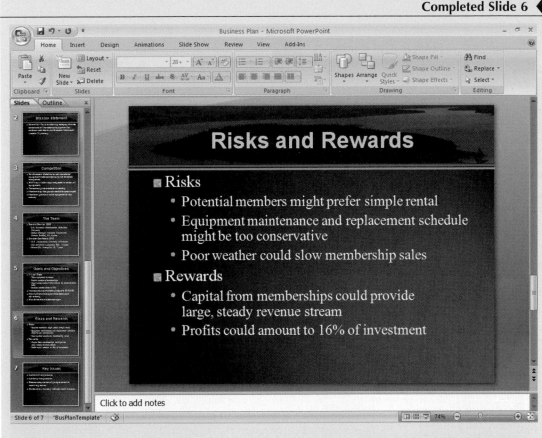

▶ **9.** Delete Slide 7 ("Key Issues").

▶ **10.** On the Quick Access Toolbar, click the **Save** button 🖫 to save the presentation.

Sandra reviews your presentation and wants you to add a slide at the end of the presentation stating what action she wants the audience to take as a result of your presentation.

Adding a New Slide and Choosing a Layout

Sandra suggests that you add a new slide at the end of the presentation with contact information for Share-My-Toys. When you add a new slide, PowerPoint formats the slide using a **layout**, which is a predetermined way of organizing the objects on a slide including placeholders for title text and other objects (bulleted lists, photographs, clip art, charts, and so forth). PowerPoint supports nine built-in layouts, including Title Slide (placeholders for a title and a subtitle, usually used as the first slide in a presentation); Title and Content (the default slide layout, with a title and a bulleted list or other object placeholder); Two Content (same as Title and Text, but with two side-by-side columns for text or other objects); and Title Only (includes only one placeholder, for the slide title). A content placeholder can contain not only a bulleted list, but can also contain a table, graph, chart, clip-art picture, photograph, or some other graphic object.

When you insert a new slide, it appears after the current slide, with the default layout, Title and Content. To use a different layout, you click the Layout button in the Slides group on the Home tab. You'll now insert a new slide at the end of your presentation with the contact information.

To insert the new slide at the end of the presentation:

▶ 1. Because you want to add a slide after Slide 6, make sure Slide 6 is still in the slide pane.

▶ 2. In the Slides group on the Home tab, click the **New Slide** button. A new Slide 7 appears in the slide pane with the default layout (Title and Content) applied. See Figure 1-12.

Figure 1-12 | A new slide with the Title and Content placeholders

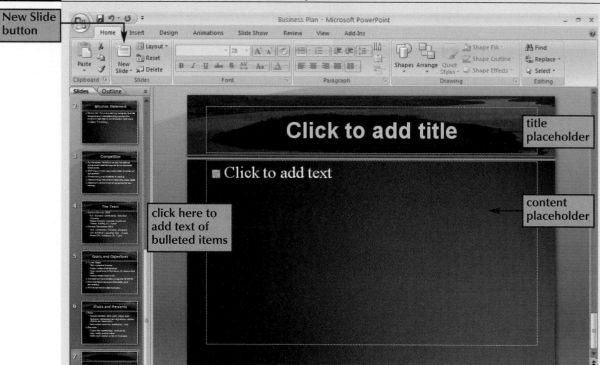

Trouble? If a gallery of choices appeared when you clicked the New Slide button, you clicked the arrow under the button instead of clicking the button itself. Click anywhere in the slide pane to close the menu, and then repeat Step 2, this time being careful to click the icon on the button, above the words "New Slide."

The Title and Text layout was applied to the new slide because the previous slides contain only bulleted lists. You'll accept the default layout for this slide. The new slide contains a blank title text placeholder, which means that you don't need to select the text on the slide to replace it with your text. After you enter your text, the dotted line outlining the edge of the text box will disappear.

▶ 3. Click anywhere in the title text placeholder in the slide pane, where it says "Click to add title." The title placeholder instructions ("Click to add title") disappear and the insertion point blinks at the left of the title text box.

▶ 4. Type **How to Conntact Share-My-Toys** (with no period). Make sure you type "Conntact" with two *n*s in the middle. You'll correct this misspelling later.

5. Click to the right of the bullet in the content placeholder. The placeholder text ("Click to add text") disappears, and the insertion point appears just to the right of the bullet.

6. Type **There are three ways too contact us.** (including the period). Make sure you type the incorrect word "too" instead of the correct word "to." You'll correct this problem later.

7. Press the **Enter** key, type **Call Sandra Corwin, CEO, at 208-555-3870, ext. 110**, and then press the **Enter** key.

8. Type **Or call Ernesto Candelaria, CFO, at ext. 210**, and then press the **Enter** key.

9. Type **Or visit our Web site at www.share-my-toys.com**, and then press the **Spacebar**.

   When you press the Spacebar after typing the Web site address, PowerPoint automatically changes the Web site address (the URL) to a link. It formats the link by changing its color and underlining it. When you run the slide show, you can click this link to jump to that Web site if you are connected to the Internet. The URL is split between two lines. You can force it to start on a new line without inserting a new bullet by pressing the Shift and Enter keys at the same time.

10. Click immediately before the "www", press and hold the Shift key, and then press the Enter key. The line is broken in front of the URL and the entire URL appears on its own line.

11. On the Quick Access Toolbar, click the **Save** button 🔲 to save the changes to your presentation.

Contact Information in a Printed Presentation | InSight

In a business presentation, the printed presentation should always include contact information so that audience members know how to contact the presenter. The information should include all the ways that someone might want to contact the presenter: the presenter's name, office phone number, cell phone number, e-mail addresses, mailing address, and company Web site. If the presenter is not the only contact person at the company, or not the best contact person, include information about other people—sales representatives, marketing personnel, accountants, or other employees.

You have inserted a new slide at the end of the presentation and added text to the slide. Next you'll create a new slide by promoting text from an existing slide in the Outline tab.

Promoting, Demoting, and Moving Outline Text

You can modify the text of a slide in the Outline tab as well as in the slide pane. Working in the Outline tab gives you more flexibility because you can see the outline of the entire presentation, not only the single slide currently in the slide pane. Working in the Outline tab also allows you to easily move text from one slide to another or to create a new slide by promoting bulleted items from a slide so that they become the title and content on a new slide.

To **promote** an item means to raise the outline level of that item, for example, to change a bulleted item into a slide title or to change a second-level bullet into a first-level bullet. When you promote an item, you are changing the outline level from a higher number to a lower number. A slide title is at the first outline level, a bulleted item is at the second outline level, and a subbullet is at the third outline level. To **demote** an item means to decrease the outline level (but to increase the level number)—for example, to change a slide title into a bulleted item on the previous slide or to change a first-level bullet into a second-level bullet. You'll begin by promoting a bulleted item to a slide title, thus creating a new slide.

To create a new slide by promoting outline text:

▶ **1.** In the pane that contains the Slides and Outline tab, click the **Outline** tab. The outline of the presentation appears.

Now you're ready to promote outline text. Sandra wants you to divide Slide 5 ("Goals and Objectives") into two slides, one for "Goals" and the other for "Objectives."

▶ **2.** In the Outline tab, move the pointer over the bullet to the left of the "5-year Goals" bullet in Slide 5 so that the pointer becomes ⊕, and then click the bullet. The text for that bullet and all its subbullets is selected.

Trouble? If you can't see Slide 5 in the Outline tab, drag the scroll box in the Outline tab up until you can see Slide 5.

Now you'll promote the selected text so that it becomes the title text and first-level bullets on a new slide.

▶ **3.** Click the **Decrease List Level** button 🔄 in the Paragraph group. PowerPoint promotes the selected text one level. Because the bullet you selected was a first-level bullet, the first-level bullet is promoted to a slide title on a new Slide 6, and the second-level bullets become first-level bullets on the new slide. See Figure 1-13. Remember, when you promote text, the outline list level number *decreases*—in this case, from 2 to 1—so you click the Decrease List Level button to decrease the level number.

Figure 1-13	New Slide 6 after promoting text

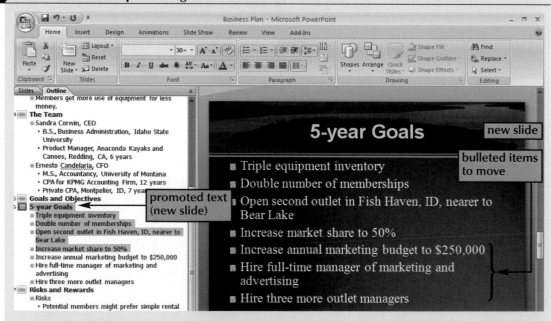

Now you'll edit text and move a bulleted item from Slide 6 to Slide 5.

▶ **4.** In the Outline tab, click to the left of "Objectives" in the slide title of Slide 5, and then press the **Backspace** key as many times as necessary to delete "Goals and."

▶ **5.** In the Outline tab in the title of Slide 6, change "year" to "Year".

▶ **6.** In the Outline tab, point to the bullet icon to the left of "Increase market share to 50%" in Slide 6, press and hold down the left mouse button, and then drag the bullet and its text up until the horizontal line is below the slide title "Objectives," as shown in Figure 1-14.

Tip

To select bulleted items or objects that are not adjacent to one another, press and hold the Ctrl key instead of the Shift key while clicking.

Moving a slide in Slide Sorter view ◀ **Figure 1-14**

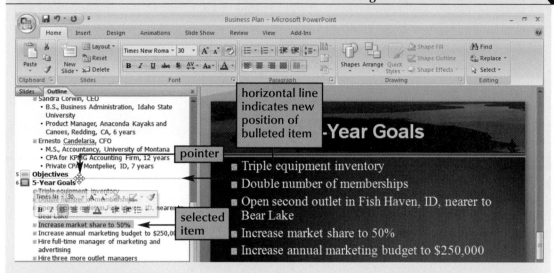

▶ **7.** Using the same procedure as in Step 6, drag the last three bulleted items in Slide 6 onto slide 5.

Sandra looks at your presentation. It meets Sandra's goal for a short presentation of seven to eight slides, but she suggests that you move the current Slide 5 ("Objectives") after Slide 6 ("5-Year Goals"). You could make this change in the Outline tab by dragging the slide icon for Slide 5 above the slide icon for Slide 7. Instead, you'll move the slide in Slide Sorter view.

Moving Slides in Slide Sorter View

In Slide Sorter view, PowerPoint displays all the slides as thumbnails, so that several slides can appear on the screen at once. This view not only provides you with a good overview of your presentation, but also allows you to easily change the order of the slides and modify the slides in other ways.

To move Slide 5:

▶ **1.** On the status bar, click the **Slide Sorter** button ⬛. You now see your presentation in Slide Sorter view. A thick colored frame appears around Slide 5, indicating that the slide is selected.

▶ **2.** Point to **Slide 5**, and then drag Slide 5 so that the vertical line position marker appears on the left side of Slide 7, as shown in Figure 1-15.

Figure 1-15 ▶ **Moving a slide in Slide Sorter view**

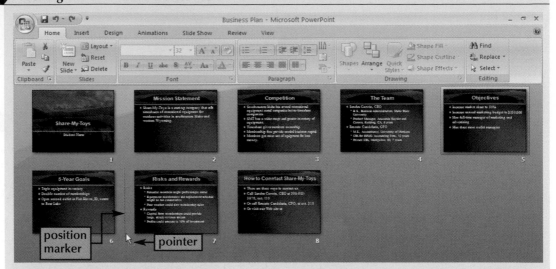

▶ **3.** Release the mouse button. The old Slide 5 is now Slide 6.

▶ **4.** On the status bar, click the **Normal** button 🖽 to return to Normal view, and then in the pane that contains the Outline and Slides tab, click the Slides tab.

Your next task is to check the spelling of the text in your presentation.

Checking the Spelling in a Presentation

Before you print or present a slide show, you should always perform a final check of the spelling of all the slides in your presentation. This helps to ensure that your presentation is accurate and professional looking.

PowerPoint performs two types of spell check. The standard type is when PowerPoint finds a word that's not in its dictionary. The word is then underlined with a red wavy line in the slide pane. The other type is called **contextual spelling**, which checks the context in which a word is used, and marks it with a red wavy line even though the word is in the dictionary. For example, if you type "their" when you mean "there" (or vice versa), or type "too" when you mean "to" (or vice versa), PowerPoint might flag the error. Of course, a computer program can't be 100 percent correct in determining the correct context, especially in bulleted items that are incomplete sentences, so you still have to carefully proofread your presentation.

When you right-click a word marked with the red wavy line, PowerPoint displays suggestions for alternate spellings as well as commands for ignoring the misspelled word or opening the Spelling dialog box. You can also click the Spelling button in the Proofing group on the Review tab on the Ribbon to check the spelling in the entire presentation. You'll now check the spelling in the Share-My-Toys presentation.

To check the spelling in the presentation:

▶ **1.** Click the **Office Button** 🔘, click the **PowerPoint Options** button, click **Proofing** in the left pane, make sure the **Use contextual spelling** check box is selected, and then click the **OK** button.

▶ **2.** Go to **Slide 8**. The spelling check always starts from the current slide.

▶ **3.** Click the **Review** tab on the Ribbon. The Ribbon changes to display the commands available for reviewing and correcting your presentation.

▶ **4.** In the Proofing group on the Review tab, click the **Spelling** button. The Spelling dialog box opens. The word you purposely mistyped earlier, "Conntact," is highlighted in the slide pane and listed in the Spelling dialog box in the Not in Dictionary text box. Two suggested spellings appear in the Suggestions list box, and the selected word in the Suggestions list box appears in the Change to text box. See Figure 1-16.

Checking the spelling in the presentation ◀ **Figure 1-16**

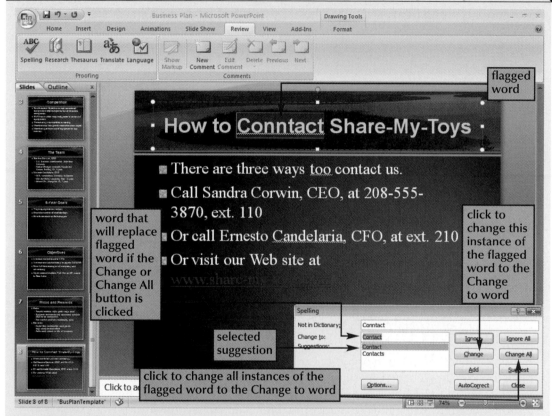

▶ **5.** With "Contact" selected in the Suggestions list box and listed in the Change to text box, click the **Change** button in the Spelling dialog box. If you knew that you misspelled that word throughout your presentation, you could click the Change All button to change all of the instances of the misspelling in the presentation to the corrected spelling.

The word is corrected, and the next word in the presentation that PowerPoint flags is "too" in the first bulleted item. This word is in PowerPoint's dictionary, but it is contextually misspelled.

▶ **6.** With "to" selected in the Suggestions list box and in the Change to text box, click the **Change** button. The correct word appears on the slide.

Next, PowerPoint stops at the word "Candelaria." This word, however, is not misspelled; it is a surname.

Trouble? If PowerPoint doesn't flag "Candelaria," someone might have added it to the PowerPoint dictionary. Read Step 7 but don't do anything, and then continue with Step 8.

▶ **7.** Click the **Ignore All** button. The word is not changed on the slide. If you wanted to ignore only this instance of that word in the presentation, you could click the Ignore button instead of the Ignore All button.

PowerPoint continues checking the presentation for misspelled words. When it reaches the final slide, it cycles back to the first slide and continues searching until it reaches the slide prior to the one you started checking. When it doesn't find any other words that aren't in the PowerPoint dictionary, a dialog box opens telling you that the spelling check is complete.

Trouble? If another word in the presentation is flagged as misspelled, select the correct spelling in the Suggestions list, and then click the Change button. If your name on Slide 1 is flagged, click the Ignore button.

▶ **8.** In the dialog box, click the **OK** button. The dialog box closes.

▶ **9.** On the Quick Access Toolbar, click the **Save** button 🔲 to save the changes to your presentation.

After you check the spelling, you should always reread your presentation; the spell checker, even with the contextual spelling feature, doesn't catch every instance of a misused word.

Sandra is pleased with how you have edited your presentation slides, but she thinks the word "large" in Slide 7 might not be precise enough. She asks you to find an appropriate replacement word.

Using the Research Task Pane

PowerPoint enables you to search online services or Internet sites for additional help in creating a presentation. Using these resources helps you make your presentations more professional. For example, you could look up specific words in a thesaurus. A **thesaurus** contains a list of words and their synonyms, antonyms, and other related words. Using a thesaurus is a good way to add variety to the words you use or to choose more precise words. You could also look up information in online dictionaries, encyclopedias, news services, libraries, and business sites.

You access the Research task pane by clicking the Review tab on the Ribbon, and then clicking either the Research or the Thesaurus button in the Proofing group. When you click the Research button, the search is executed in all available sources. When you click the Thesaurus button, the search is automatically restricted to just the thesaurus.

You'll begin by using the thesaurus. You'll now look for synonyms for "large."

To do research using the thesaurus:

▶ **1.** Go to **Slide 7**, and then, in the slide pane, in the first subbullet under "Rewards," click anywhere in the word "large." The thesaurus lets you completely select the word or simply position the insertion point anywhere within the word.

▶ **2.** In the Proofing group on the Review tab, click the **Thesaurus** button. PowerPoint selects the word "large," and the Research task pane opens with the word "large" in the Search for text box and Thesaurus: English (U.S.) listed in the box under the Search for text box. Below that, the task pane displays synonyms for "large" found in the built-in thesaurus.

▶ **3.** In the list of synonyms, below the bold entry "sizeable (adj.)," position the pointer over the word **significant**. A box appears around the term, and an arrow appears at the right end of the box.

▶ **4.** Click the arrow in the box. A menu opens, as shown in Figure 1-17.

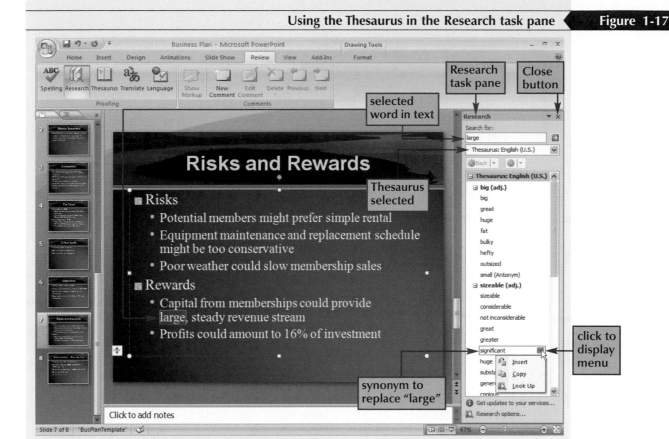

Using the Thesaurus in the Research task pane | Figure 1-17

▶ **5.** Click **Insert**. The word "significant" replaces "large" on the slide.

▶ **6.** In the task pane title bar, click the **Close** button ⊠. The Research task pane closes.

When you show the presentation to Sandra, she is satisfied. Now you're ready to create notes for Sandra's presentation to help her remember important points during the slide show.

Creating Speaker Notes

Notes (also called **speaker notes**) help the speaker remember what to say when a particular slide appears during the presentation. They appear in the notes pane below the slide pane in Normal view; they do not appear during the slide show. You can also print notes pages with a picture of and notes about each slide.

You'll create notes for only a few of the slides in the presentation. For example, Sandra wants to remember the names of the Share-My-Toys' competitors when she displays Slide 3. You'll create a note reminding her to mention the names of the competitors.

To create notes:

▶ **1.** Go to **Slide 3**. The notes pane currently contains placeholder text.

▶ **2.** Click in the notes pane, and then type **Rental companies include A-1 Recreation Rentals, Boats4Rent, and Camping Gear To Go**. See Figure 1-18.

Figure 1-18 ▸ Notes on Slide 3

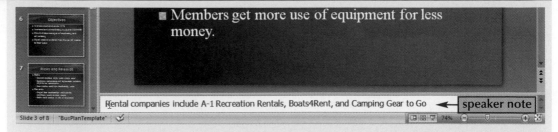

Now Sandra wants you to add a note on Slide 6 to remind her to give the audience a handout on marketing plans.

▸ 3. Go to **Slide 6**, click in the notes pane, and then type **Pass out marketing plan handouts**.

▸ 4. Save the changes to the presentation.

Before Sandra gives her presentation, she'll print the notes of the presentation so she'll have them available during her presentations. You can now view the completed presentation to make sure that it is accurate, informative, and visually pleasing.

To view the slide show:

▸ 1. Click the **View** tab on the Ribbon, and then, in the Presentation Views group, click the **Slide Show** button. The slide show starts from Slide 1.

▸ 2. Proceed through the slide show as you did earlier, clicking the left mouse button or pressing the Spacebar or the right arrow key to advance from one slide to the next.

▸ 3. If you see a problem on one of your slides, press the **Esc** key to leave the slide show and display the current slide on the screen in Normal view, fix the problem on the slide, save your changes, and then click the **Slide Show** button 🖵 on the status bar to resume the slide show from the current slide.

▸ 4. When you reach the end of your slide show, press the **Spacebar** to move to the blank screen, and then press the **Spacebar** again to return to Normal view.

You're now ready to preview and print your presentation.

Previewing and Printing a Presentation

Before you give your presentation, you might want to print it. PowerPoint provides several printing options. For example, you can print the slides in color using a color printer; print in grayscale or pure black and white using a black-and-white printer; or print the notes pages (the speaker notes printed below a picture of the corresponding slide). You can also print handouts with 2, 3, 4, 6, or 9 slides per page. **Handouts** are printouts of the slides themselves; these can be arranged with several slides printed on a page. Some presenters like to give the audience handouts so that they can more easily take notes during the presentation. Finally, you can also format and then print the presentation onto overhead transparency film (available in most office supply stores).

If you're going to print your presentation on a black-and-white printer, you should first preview the presentation to make sure the text will be legible. You also need to make sure that any graphics on the background do not make it difficult to read the text on the slides. You'll use Print Preview to see the slides as they will appear when they are printed.

To preview the presentation and hide background graphics:

▶ **1.** Click the **Office Button** 🔘, and then point to the **Print** button. The pane on the right side of the menu changes to include print options.

▶ **2.** In the pane on the right of the menu, click **Print Preview**. The Preview window appears, displaying Slide 1. Notice that the only tab on the Ribbon is the Print Preview tab.

▶ **3.** In the Print group on the Print Preview tab, click the **Options** button, point to **Color/Grayscale**, and then click **Grayscale**. The current slide is displayed in grayscale. See Figure 1-19. As you can see, the text is illegible in grayscale. You'll now fix that problem in preparation to print your presentation in black and white.

Print Preview window showing Slide 1 in grayscale ◀ **Figure 1-19**

▶ **4.** In the Preview group on the Print Preview tab, click the **Close Print Preview** button to return to Normal view.

▶ **5.** On the status bar, click the **Slide Sorter** button 🔠, click **Slide 1**, if necessary, press and hold the **Shift** key, and then click **Slide 8**. All the slides are selected.

▶ **6.** Click the **Design** tab on the Ribbon, and then, in the Background group, click the **Hide Background Graphics** check box. The background images and lines on the slides disappear.

Now you're ready to return to Print Preview and continue to view how your presentation will look when you print it.

To preview and print your presentation:

▶ **1.** Return to Print Preview and set the Options to Grayscale as you did previously. Now you can read the text of your presentation.

▶ **2.** In the Preview group on the Print Preview tab, click the **Next Page** button. Slide 2 appears in the Print Preview window.

Next you will change the option to print handouts.

▶ **3.** In the Page Setup group on the Print Preview tab, click the **Print What** arrow, and then click **Handouts (4 Slides Per Page)**. The preview changes to display four slides on a page.

▶ **4.** In the Print group on the Print Preview tab, click the **Print** button. The Print dialog box opens. See Figure 1-20.

Figure 1-20 ▶ **Print dialog box**

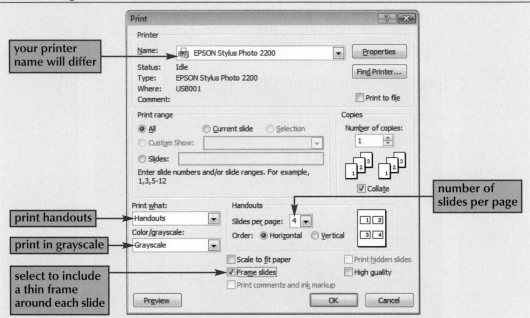

your printer name will differ

print handouts

print in grayscale

select to include a thin frame around each slide

number of slides per page

▶ **5.** Compare your dialog box to the one shown in Figure 1-20, make any necessary changes, and then click the **OK** button to print the handouts on two pages. The Print dialog box closes, and the slides print as handouts, four slides per page.

Now you're ready to print the notes.

▶ **6.** In the Page Setup group on the Print Preview tab, click the **Print What** arrow, and then click **Notes Pages**. The current slide is displayed as a notes page, with the slide on the top and space for notes on the bottom.

▶ **7.** Drag the scroll box on the vertical scroll bar down until the ScreenTip identifies the current slide as Page 3 of 8. This is one of the slides to which you added notes.

▶ **8.** In the Print group, click the **Print** button to open the Print dialog box again.

▶ **9.** In the Print range section of the Print dialog box, click the **Slides** option button, click in the text box to the right of the Slides option button, and then type **3,6** (with no space before or after the comma). These are the only slides with notes on them, so you do not need to print all eight slides as notes pages.

▶ **10.** Click the **OK** button to print the notes. Slides 3 and 6 print on two pieces of paper as notes pages.

11. In the Preview group, click the **Close Print Preview** button. The view returns to Slide Sorter view. In Slide Sorter view, the slides appear on the screen in several rows, depending on the current zoom percentage shown next to the Zoom slider (located in the lower-right corner of the PowerPoint window) and on the resolution and size of your monitor.

12. On the Zoom slider, drag the slider tab to the right, until the zoom is about 90%. See Figure 1-21.

Completed presentation in Slide Sorter view | Figure 1-21

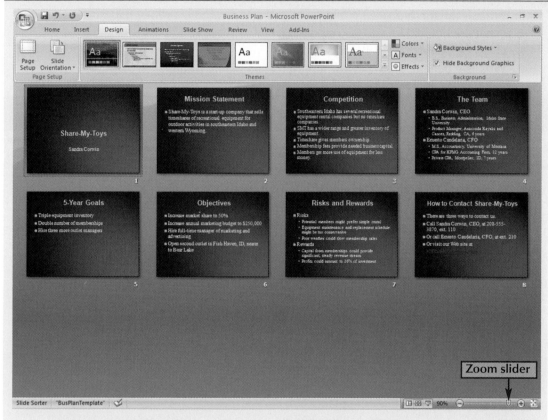

Trouble? If all the slides are not visible on your monitor after setting the Zoom to 90%, drag the Zoom slider to the left until you can see all of the slides.

13. Compare your printed handouts (with their four slides per page) with the slides shown in Slide Sorter view.

14. Save the presentation in Slide Sorter view. When Sandra opens the presentation, it will appear in Slide Sorter view.

15. In the upper-right corner of the PowerPoint window, click the **Close** button ☒ on the title bar.

You have created a presentation using a template, edited it according to Sandra's wishes, and created and printed notes and handouts. Sandra thanks you for your help; she believes that your work will enable her to make an effective presentation to banks and potential investors.

Review | **Session 1.2 Quick Check**

1. Explain how to do the following in the Outline tab:
   a. move text up
   b. delete a slide
   c. change a first-level bullet to a second-level bullet
2. What does it mean to promote a bulleted item in the Outline tab? To demote a bulleted item?
3. Explain a benefit of using the Outline tab rather than the slide pane.
4. What is the thesaurus?
5. What are notes? How do you create them?
6. Describe contextual spell checking.
7. Why is it beneficial to preview a presentation before printing it?

Review | **Tutorial Summary**

In this tutorial, you learned how to plan and create a PowerPoint presentation by modifying template slides. You learned how to edit the text in both the Outline tab and the slide pane; add a new slide and choose a slide layout; delete slides; and promote, demote, and move text in your outline. You also learned how to check the spelling in your presentation, create speaker notes, and preview and print your presentation.

Key Terms

6 × 6 rule	layout	slide pane
active	Normal view	Slide Show view
animation	note (speaker note)	Slide Sorter view
bulleted item	notes pane	slide transitions
bulleted list	numbered list	Slides tab
content	Outline tab	subbullet
contextual spelling	placeholder	template
demote	PowerPoint	text box
drop shadow	progressive disclosure	thesaurus
first-level bullet	promote	thumbnail
footer	second-level bullet	title text
handout	sizing handle	

| Practice | **Review Assignments** |

Practice the skills you learned in the tutorial using the same case scenario.

Data File needed for the Review Assignments: Marketing.potx

Calista Dymock, the new director of marketing at Share-My-Toys, asks you to prepare a PowerPoint presentation explaining the new marketing strategy. She recommends that you start with an existing template prepared by Sandra Corwin in her previous job. Your job is to edit the presentation according to Calista's instructions. Complete the following steps:

1. Start a new PowerPoint presentation using the existing template **Marketing** located in the Tutorial.01\Review folder where your Data Files are located, and then save the presentation as **Marketing Plan** in the Tutorial.01\Review folder.

2. In Slide 1, replace the text "[Product or Service Name]" with **Share-My-Toys Membership**, and then change the "[Your Name]" subtitle to your name.

3. Go to Slide 2, and then replace all the content text with the following first-level bulleted items: **Current memberships: 218**, **Maximum memberships: 800**, and **Current members live in:**.

4. Below "Current members live in," add the following second-level bulleted items: **Montpelier, ID**, **Soda Springs, ID**, and **Fish Haven, ID**.

5. Below the three second-level bullets, add the following first-level bulleted item: **Additional target locations**, and below that, the following second-level bulleted items: **Preston, ID**, **Logan, UT**, and **Afton, WY**.

6. Go to Slide 3 ("Product Definition"), replace the bulleted item with **Membership in Share-My-Toys provides the following services:**, and then below that, insert the subbullets **Unlimited use of equipment** and **Free service, maintenance, and replacement of equipment**.

7. Below the subbullets, add the first-level item **Membership lasts for three years**.

8. Go to Slide 4 ("Competition"), and then replace the bulleted text with the following first-level bulleted items: **Retail recreational equipment stores** and **Recreational equipment rental companies**.

9. Delete Slide 5 ("Positioning"), and then on the new Slide 5, change the title "Communication Strategies" to **Overcoming Disadvantages**, and replace the first-level bulleted items with **Institute low-interest monthly payment program**, and **Open distribution centers in more cities**.

10. Go to Slide 6 ("Public Relations"), and then replace the content text with the first-level bulleted items **Hold public ATV and dirt-bike safety courses** and **Participate in local outdoorsman radio talk shows**.

11. Go to Slide 7 ("Advertising"), and then replace the bulleted items with the first-level bulleted items: **Local radio**, **Local TV**, **Local newspapers**, and **Advertisement mailers**.

12. Go to Slide 8 ("Success Metrics"), and then replace the bulleted items with the first-level bulleted items **Sell 200 memberships per year**, **Maintain high customer satisfaction**, **Develop indirect earnings**, **Interest on membership monthly payment program**, **Sales of used, out-of-date equipment**.

13. Go to Slide 2 and add **Explain how often equipment will need to be replaced.** as a note, and then go to Slide 3 and add **Explain that we must set a maximum number of memberships to ensure that members get the equipment they want.** as a note.

14. Delete Slide 9, leaving eight slides in the presentation.

15. Switch to Slide Sorter view, move Slide 7 ("Advertising") before Slide 6 ("Public Relations"), and then move Slide 8 ("Success Metrics") to become the new Slide 2.

16. Double-click Slide 3 ("Market Summary") to switch to Normal view, and then click the Outline tab in the pane on the left.

17. In the Outline tab, click the bullet icon next to "Additional target locations," and then, in the Paragraph group on the Home tab, click the Decrease List Level button so that it becomes a new slide. In the new slide title, change the "t" in "target" and the "l" in "locations" to uppercase so that the title words are capitalized.

18. In the Outline tab, in Slide 3, drag the "Maximum Members: 800" bullet up so it becomes the first bulleted item.

19. In the Outline tab, in Slide 2 ("Success Metrics"), select the final two bulleted items, and then demote them so they become subbullets under "Develop indirect earnings."

20. Use the spelling checker, along with your own proofreading to check spelling in the presentation. Change misspelled words and ignore flagged words that are spelled correctly.

21. Go to Slide 9 and then use the thesaurus to replace the word "hold" with an appropriate synonym.

22. View the presentation in Slide Show view. Look carefully at each slide and check the content. If you see any errors of formatting problems, press the Esc key to end the slide show, fix the error, and then start the slide show again.

23. Switch to Slide Sorter view, adjust the zoom so that the thumbnails are maximum size yet still all visible at once on the screen, and then save the presentation using the default filename.

24. Preview the presentation in grayscale, and then print the presentation in grayscale as handouts, four slides per page.

25. Print Slides 2 and 3 as notes pages in grayscale, and then close the file.

Apply	**Case Problem 1**

Apply the skills you learned in this tutorial to modify a presentation for a pharmaceutical research lab.

Data File needed for this Case Problem: Volunteer.pptx

Department of Social Services, Yosemite Regional Hospital Mercedes Cirillo is head of Volunteer Services at Yosemite Regional Hospital in Wawona, CA. One of her jobs is to recruit and train hospital volunteers. Volunteer positions include Family Surgical Liaison, Family Waiting Area Liaison, Hospitality and Escort Volunteer, Volunteer Information Ambassador, Book Cart and Special Requests Volunteer, Flower Shop Assistant, and Pastoral Care Volunteer. Mercedes wants to give a PowerPoint presentation to individuals, couples, church groups, and service organizations on opportunities and requirements for volunteer service at the hospital. She has a rough draft of a presentation and asks you to help her revise the presentation. Complete the following steps:

1. Start PowerPoint and open the file **Volunteer** located in the Tutorial.01\Case1 folder with your Data Files.

2. Click the Office Button, click Save As, and then save the presentation using the filename **Hospital Volunteers** in the Tutorial.01\Case1 folder.

3. In Slide 1, change the name "Mercedes Cirillo" to your name.

4. Delete Slide 3.

5. In Slide Sorter view, move Slide 5 so it becomes Slide 3.

6. In Normal view, in Slide 2, add a new bulleted item to the end of the bulleted list, with the text **Volunteers work in almost all departments within the hospital.**

7. In the notes pane of Slide 2, add the speaker note, **Departments that don't have volunteers include Food Services, Medical Research, Security, Custodial Services, and others.**

8. In Slide 3, after the second bulleted item ("Select a desired volunteer position"), insert the bulleted item **Pick up application form from Volunteer Services office.**

⊕ EXPLORE

9. In Slide 3, AutoFit the text to the placeholder so that the last bulleted item isn't too close to the bottom of the slide. To do this, make sure the insertion point is in the main text box (the bulleted list), click the AutoFit Options button that appears to the left of the new bulleted item, and then, on the menu that opens, click the AutoFit Text to Placeholder option button.

10. In the notes pane of Slide 3, add the speaker note, **Announce that I have application forms with me.**

11. In Slide 4, use the Outline tab to move the bulleted items "Book Cart Volunteer" and "Special Requests Volunteer" down below "Gift Shop Assistant" (but above "Pastoral Care Volunteer").

12. In Slide 5, click the insertion point in the Outline tab just before the phrase "4 hours per week," and press the Enter key to make that phrase a new bullet.

13. Demote the phrases "4 hours per week" and "3-month commitment" to second-level bullets under "Minimum volunteer time."

14. After Slide 5, insert a new Slide 6.

15. In Slide 6, insert the title text **Before You Decide to Volunteer**, and then insert the following first-level bulleted items: **Understand the time commitment to do a particular job.**; **Base your decision on your interests, skills, and schedule.**; **Know HIPA laws regarding confidentiality.**; and **Be willing to learn and to give and receive feedback.**

16. Check the spelling throughout the presentation, including contextual spelling. Change misspelled words to the correct spelling, and ignore any words (such as proper names) that are spelled correctly but are not in the built-in dictionary.

17. Read each slide, proofreading for spelling errors that the spelling checker didn't detect. Notice that, on Slide 2, the word "weak" should be "week." Contextual spelling failed to detect this error, probably because the bulleted items are not complete sentences. Make that change and correct any other spelling errors you find.

18. View the presentation in Slide Show view.

19. Preview the presentation in grayscale. Remove the background graphics if necessary. Save your changes.

20. Print the presentation in grayscale as handouts with four slides per page.

21. Print notes pages for Slides 2 and 3 (the only ones that have speaker notes).

22. Close the file.

| Apply | **Case Problem 2** |

Apply the skills you learned to modify an existing presentation.

Data File needed for this Case Problem: Library.pptx

Carriage Path Public Library   Davion McGechie is head of the Office of Community Outreach Services for the Carriage Path Public Library in Milford, Connecticut. Davion and his staff coordinate outreach services and develop programs in communities throughout the Long Island Sound. These services and programs depend on a large volunteer staff. Davion wants you to help him create a PowerPoint presentation to train his staff. Complete the following steps:

1. Open the file **Library** in the Case2 folder in the Tutorial.01 folder of your Data Files, and then save it back to the same folder using the filename **Library Outreach**.

2. In Slide 1, replace the subtitle placeholder ("Davion McGechie, Director") with your name.

3. In Slide 2, add the speaker's note **Mention that community groups include ethnic neighborhood councils, religious organizations, and civic groups.**

4. Add a fourth bulleted item to Slide 2: **To implement outreach programs in the surrounding communities**.

5. Move the second bulleted item in Slide 2 ("To provide staff training") so that it becomes the last bulleted item.

6. In Slide 3, make "Four central libraries with in-depth collections" and "Six neighborhood branch libraries" second-level bulleted items below the first bullet.

7. Promote the bulleted item "Special Events & Programs" and its subbullets so that they become a new slide.

⊕ **EXPLORE**　　8. In the Slides tab, drag Slide 6 ("Branch Libraries") above Slide 5.

9. Add a new slide at the end (Slide 8) with the title **Volunteer Opportunities**.

10. On Slide 8, create three bulleted items with the first line **Literacy Instructors**, the second line **Computer Instructors**, and the third line **Children's Hour Story Tellers**.

11. Under the third bullet, add the subbullets **After-school story hour** and **Bookmobile story hour**.

⊕ **EXPLORE**　　12. Click the word "Instructors" in the first bulleted item, and then use the thesaurus to select a synonym. (*Hint*: The thesaurus can't find a synonym for a plural word, so click the Related Word "instructor" in the Research task pane to look up a synonym for the singular form of the word.) Make sure you pluralize the replacement word, if necessary.

13. Check the spelling in the presentation. Correct any spelling errors and ignore any words that are spelled correctly.

14. View the presentation in Slide Show view.

15. Save the presentation using its default filename.

16. Preview the presentation in grayscale, and then print the presentation in grayscale as handouts with four slides per page.

17. Print Slide 2 as a notes page.

18. Close the file.

| Create | **Case Problem 3** |

Create a new presentation about a marketing company by using and expanding on the skills you learned in this tutorial.

Data File needed for this Case Problem: Proposal.potx

AfterShow, Inc.　Karla Brown is president of AfterShow, Inc., a company that markets specialized merchandise to attendees at trade shows, training seminars, and other large business events. For example, after a recent trade show of the American Automobile Manufacturers, AfterShow mailed advertisement flyers and made phone calls to the trade show participants to sell them art pieces (mostly bronze sculptures) depicting antique automobiles. In another case, after a large business seminar in which the keynote speakers were famous business leaders and athletes, AfterShow contacted participants in an effort to sell them autographed books written by the speakers. Karla asked you to create a presentation to be given to event organizers in an effort to work with those organizers in developing an after-show market and profit-sharing program. The slides in your complete presentation should look like the slides in Figure 1-22. The following instructions will help you in creating the slide show. Read all the steps before you start creating your presentation.

Figure 1-22

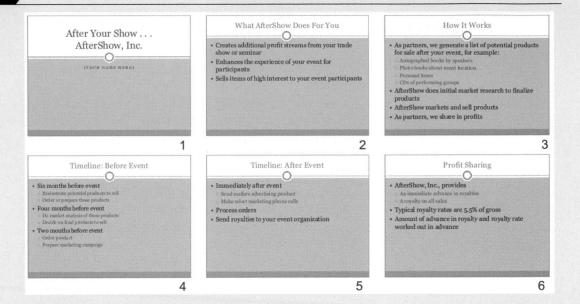

Complete the following steps:

1. Create a new presentation based on the template **Proposal** located in the Tutorial.01\Case3 folder included with your Data Files.
2. Save the file as **AfterShow** to the same folder.
3. After starting the presentation with the "Proposal" template, add slides, titles, and bulleted text as you learned in this tutorial.
4. In Slide 1, replace the placeholder "[Your name here]" with your name.
5. Promote and demote text as needed to produce the bulleted lists.
6. Delete any unnecessary slides.
7. Read through your presentation and make sure your ideas are presented clearly. Consider using the thesaurus to find words to enliven your presentation.
8. Check the spelling, including contextual spelling, in the final presentation, and examine the slides in Slide Show view.
9. Save the completed presentation using the default name and location.
10. Preview the presentation in grayscale, and delete the background objects, if necessary, to make the text legible.
11. Print the final presentation in grayscale as handouts with six slides per page.

| Research | **Case Problem 4** |

Use the Internet to research MP3 players and use PowerPoint's Help system to find out how to format text.

There are no Data Files needed for this Case Problem.

Review of a Portable Digital Audio Player   Your assignment is to prepare a review of a portable digital audio player (for example, an MP3 player) for presentation to the class. If you are not familiar with what portable digital audio players are, you might want to search the Internet or talk to other students for an explanation of what they are, how they work, and why so many people like them. You should then search the Internet for information or reviews about various brands and models of digital audio players. Alternatively, if you own a portable digital audio player, you could search the Internet for information about your player. You should organize your information into a PowerPoint presentation, with at least six slides. (Your instructor might also assign you to give an oral presentation based on your PowerPoint file.) Complete the following steps:

1. Go to Google.com, Yahoo.com, or some other Web site that allows you to search the Web, and search using such terms as **digital audio player review** or **MP3 player review**. You should read about various brands of players to get an idea of the most popular sellers.

2. Select one brand and model of digital audio player; search the Internet for more information and reviews about that player.

⊕ EXPLORE

3. Create a new presentation based on a template you can download from Microsoft Office Online. To do this, make sure you are connected to the Internet, open the New Presentation dialog box, on the left, under Microsoft Office Online, click Presentations, and then in the pane in the middle of the dialog box, click the Business link. Scroll down the list in the pane in the middle of the dialog box until you find the template titled "Product overview presentation" with an orange background and a wide pale blue stripe on the left, click it, and then click the Download button. In the dialog box that opens asking you to validate your copy of Microsoft Office, click the Continue button. After the template downloads and opens, the PowerPoint Help window opens with information about the template. Read this, and then click the Close button in the Help window title bar.

4. Save the presentation in the Tutorial.01\Case4 folder included with your Data Files, using the filename **Review**.

5. Replace the title placeholder text "Product Name" with the brand and model of your selected digital audio player. For example, the title might be something like "Apple iPod" or "Creative Zen Micro Photo 4GB MP3 Player."

6. Replace the subtitle text "Insert Product Photograph Here" with your full name. You won't include a photograph of your selected digital audio player. You can also ignore the little box labeled "Your Logo Here."

7. In Slide 2 ("Overview"), include basic information about the digital audio players in the bulleted list. The information might include brand name, model name or number, capacity (for example, 128 MB or 256 MB), retail price, and street price.

8. In Slide 3 ("Features & Benefits"), delete part of the title so it just says "Features." Replace the bulleted list placeholder text with specific features such as number of tunes the player holds, total playing time, expansion slots, battery life, auxiliary features (for example, pictures, calendar, videos), and so forth.

9. Delete Slide 4 ("Applications").

10. In what is now Slide 4 ("Specifications"), list technical specifications (for example, size, weight, interface).

11. In Slide 5 ("Pricing"), give the manufacturer's suggested retail price (MSRP) and examples of online or in-store prices (for example, from Buy.com, Amazon.com, and Circuit City).

12. Delete Slide 6.

13. Create at least three new slides, using the topics **Ease of Use**, **Desktop Computer Software**, and **Reviewers' Comments**. (Feel free to change the wording of these titles.)

⊕ EXPLORE

14. Use the Research task pane (click the Review tab and then, in the Proofing group, click the Research button) to find additional information about the topic of the digital audio player you've chosen. (*Hint*: In the Research task pane, type the phrase **digital audio player** into the Search for text box, make sure your computer is connected to the Internet, and then select All Research Sites in the box below the Search for text box.) You might or might not find anything useful about digital audio players.

15. Create a slide titled **Summary and Recommendations** as the final slide in your presentation, giving your overall impression of the player and your recommendation for whether the player is worth buying.

16. View the presentation on the Outline tab. If necessary, change the order of the bulleted items on the slides, or change the order of the slides.

 EXPLORE

17. If there are any slides with more than about six or seven bulleted items, split the slide in two. If there are any slides in which the text extends below the bulleted list text box, fix the problem. (*Hint*: In either case, click to place the insertion point in the body text box, click the AutoFit Options that appears near the lower-left corner of the text box, and then click the appropriate command on the menu.)

18. Go through all the slides, correcting problems of case (capitalization), punctuation, number of bulleted items per slide, and number of lines per bulleted item.

19. Check the spelling of your presentation.

20. View the presentation in Slide Show view. If you see any typographical errors or other problems, stop the slide show, correct the problems, and then continue the slide show. If you find slides that aren't necessary, delete them.

21. Preview the presentation in grayscale, and then print the presentation in grayscale as handouts with four slides per page. Print speaker notes if you created any, and then close the file.

Research | Internet Assignments

Go to the Web to find information you can use to create presentations.

The purpose of the Internet Assignments is to challenge you to find information on the Internet that you can use to work effectively with this software. The actual assignments are updated and maintained on the Course Technology Web site. Log on to the Internet and use your Web browser to go to the Student Online Companion for New Perspectives Office 2007 at **www.course.com/np/office2007**. Then navigate to the Internet Assignments for this tutorial.

Assess | SAM Assessment and Training

SAM

If you have a SAM user profile, you may have access to hands-on instruction, practice, and assessment of the skills covered in this tutorial. Log in to your SAM account (**http://sam2007.course.com**) to launch any assigned training activities or exams that relate to the skills covered in this tutorial.

Review | Quick Check Answers

Session 1.1

1. A presentation's components can consist of individual slides, speaker notes, an outline, and audience handouts.

2. The slide pane shows the slide as it will look during your slide show. The notes pane contains speaker notes. The third pane, to the left of the slide pane, contains two tabs: The Outline tab shows an outline of your presentation; the Slides tab displays thumbnails of each slide.

3. (a) shows the current slide as it will look during your slide show; (b) a feature that causes each element on a slide to appear one at a time; (c) the manner in which a new slide appears on the screen during a slide show; (d) a file that contains the colors and format of the background and the font style of the titles, accents, and sample text; (e) a predetermined way of organizing the objects on a slide

4. What is my purpose or objective? What type of presentation is needed? Who is my audience? What is the physical location of my presentation? What is the best format for my presentation?

5. The existing text provides a guide in selecting and inserting the proper text content into your presentation.

6. The view you use to present an on-screen presentation to an audience.

Session 1.2

1. (a) Click a slide or bullet icon, and then drag the selected item up. (b) Right-click the slide icon of the slide to be deleted, and then click Delete Slide on the shortcut menu. (c) In the Outline tab, click the slide or bullet icon, and then click the Decrease List Level button.

2. Promote means to decrease the level (for example, from level two to level one) of an outline item; demote means to increase the level of an outline item.

3. In the Outline tab, you can see the text of several slides at once, which makes it easier to work with text. In the slide pane, you can see the design and layout of the slide.

4. The thesaurus is a list of words and their synonyms, antonyms, and other related words.

5. Notes are notes for the presenter. They appear in the notes pane in Normal view or you can print notes pages, which contain a picture of and notes about each slide.

6. A feature in which spelling is checked in the context of how the words are used.

7. By previewing your presentation, you make sure that the slides are satisfactory, and that the presentation is legible in grayscale if you use a monochrome printer.

Ending Data Files

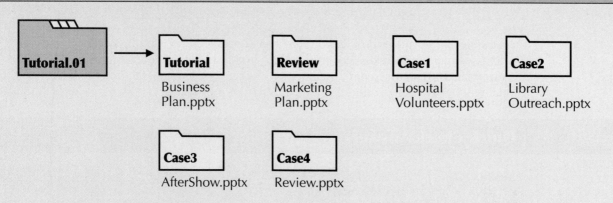

Tutorial.01 → Tutorial
Business Plan.pptx

Review
Marketing Plan.pptx

Case1
Hospital Volunteers.pptx

Case2
Library Outreach.pptx

Case3
AfterShow.pptx

Case4
Review.pptx

Applying and Modifying Text and Graphic Objects

Preparing a Presentation About a Travel Company

Case | Alaskan Cruises and Land Tours

Chad Morley visited Alaska for the first time in 1978, fell in love with it, and stayed to live in Anchorage. He later graduated from the University of Alaska with a degree in travel and tourism, worked as a travel agent for several years, and now works for Alaskan Cruises and Land Tours (ACLT), a company based in Fairbanks and with offices in Anchorage and Juneau. ACLT is not a travel agency but is a travel operator or wholesaler; the company arranges travel packages for travel agencies to sell to their customers. Chad's job entails educating travel agents throughout the United States and Canada about ACLT.

In this tutorial, you'll create a presentation based on a design theme, apply a design theme to an existing presentation, and then enhance the presentation by adding graphics to the slides.

Starting Data Files

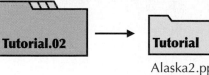

Tutorial.02 →	Tutorial	Review	Case1	Case2	Case3	Case4
	Alaska2.pptx	AKRibbon.jpg	Balmoral.jpg	Campsite.jpg	BodieLH.jpg	Camera01.jpg
	AKPanel.jpg	LandTour.pptx	Castles.pptx	Meadow.jpg	LHBase.jpg	Camera02.jpg
	Ship.jpg	Naturalist.jpg	Edinburgh.jpg	Men.jpg	LHPanel.jpg	Camera03.jpg
	Glacier.jpg			Outfitter.pptx	LHStairs.jpg	ManCam.jpg
				Panel.jpg	LHTop.jpg	
				River.jpg	Ocracoke.jpg	
					Sizemore.jpg	

Session 2.1

Planning a Presentation

Before creating his text presentation, Chad and his staff planned the presentation as follows:

- **Purpose of the presentation**: To encourage travel agents to sell travel packages from Alaska Cruises and Land Tours
- **Type of presentation**: An on-screen (electronic) information presentation
- **Audience**: Travel agents
- **Location of presentation**: Offices and conference rooms
- **Audience needs**: To understand the general features and services of ACLT
- **Format**: One speaker presenting an on-screen slide show consisting of about 12 slides

After planning the presentation, Chad and his staff discuss how they want the slides to look.

Creating a New Presentation from a Theme

Plain white slides with normal text (such as black Times New Roman or Calibri) often fail to hold an audience's attention. In today's information age, audiences expect more interesting color schemes, fonts, graphics, and other effects.

To make it easy to add color and style to your presentations, PowerPoint supports themes. A **theme** is the overall design of a presentation. It includes preset colors, fonts, and other design elements. The **theme colors** are the colors used for background, title text, body text, accents, and other elements of a slide, including text formats, background colors and objects, and graphics in the presentation. The **theme fonts** are two fonts or font styles, one for the titles (or headings) and one for the main body text. In some themes, the title and body fonts are the same, just different sizes and possibly different colors; in others, the two fonts and font styles are different, as well as the sizes and colors. Some themes include graphics as part of the slide background. A **graphic** is a picture, clip art, photograph, shape, design, graph, chart, or diagram. A graphic, like a text box, is an object. Chad asks you to create a new presentation with a design from an installed theme, so that he can see what it looks like.

InSight	Creating a "Blank" Presentation

In PowerPoint, you can create a blank presentation. To do this, you click Blank Presentation in the New Presentation dialog box, and then click Create. It is not exactly accurate, however, to call it a blank presentation. Even though it is called a "blank" presentation, the presentation that is created actually has the Office theme applied. The Office theme has theme colors, fonts, and font styles, just like any other theme.

Creating a New Presentation | Reference Window

Creating a New Presentation | Reference Window

- Click the Office Button, and then click New.
- In the Templates list on the left of the New Presentation dialog box, click Blank and recent, and then, in the Blank and recent pane in the middle of the dialog box, click the Blank Presentation icon to create a new presentation with the Office theme *or* in the Templates list on the left of the New Presentation dialog box, click Installed Themes, and then, in the Installed Themes pane in the middle of the dialog box, click one of the themes.
- Click the Create button.

You'll begin enhancing Chad's presentation by using an installed theme.

To create a new presentation with an installed theme:

▶ **1.** Start PowerPoint, click the **Office Button** 🔘, and then click **New**. The New Presentation dialog box opens.

▶ **2.** Click **Installed Themes** in the Templates pane of the dialog box. PowerPoint lists the installed themes in the middle pane in the dialog box. See Figure 2-1.

Gallery of installed themes ◀ Figure 2-1

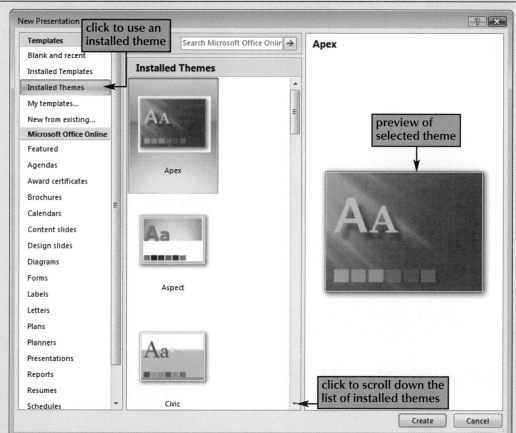

Tip

To create a presentation based on the Office theme, click Blank and recent in the Templates list on the left of the dialog box, and then click the Blank Presentation icon.

▶ **3.** Scroll down the list in the Installed Themes pane until you see Metro, and then click the **Metro** icon.

▶ **4.** Click the **Create** button in the lower-right corner of the dialog box. A new presentation is created with the Metro theme applied. Slide 1 appears in the slide pane with the Title Slide layout applied. See Figure 2-2.

Figure 2-2   Slide 1 with Metro theme

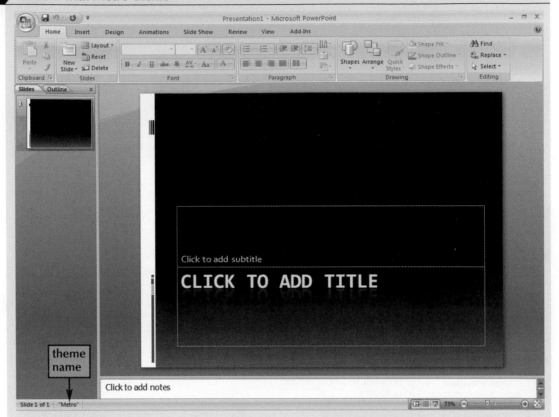

5. In the slide pane, click in the **title** placeholder, and then type **Alaskan Cruises and Land Tours**.

6. Click in the **subtitle** placeholder, and then type your own name. (The figures in this tutorial will show the name Chad Morley.)

7. Save the presentation as **Alaska** in the Tutorial.02\Tutorial folder included with your Data Files.

8. In the upper-left corner of the window, click the **Office Button** 🔘, and then click **Close** to close the presentation but leave PowerPoint running.

Chad takes the new presentation you created, adds more slides to the presentation, and saves the file as Alaska2. After looking at the Metro theme, he decides he would like to use a different theme. You'll change the theme now.

Applying a New Theme

The theme you choose for your presentation should reflect the content and the intended audience. For example, if you are presenting a new curriculum to a group of elementary school teachers, you might choose a theme that uses bright, primary colors. On the other hand, if you are presenting a new marketing plan to a mutual fund company, you might choose a plain-looking theme that uses dark colors formatted in a way that appears sophisticated. To help you decide, you can see how your presentation will look with a new theme by using Live Preview in the themes gallery.

Although Chad's presentation is serious, he wants to make the cruises and tours seem attractive to travel agents. He decides that he wants to use a design theme more representative of an Alaskan cruise and add some graphics representing Alaska.

Applying a Different Theme | Reference Window

- Click the Design tab.
- In the Themes group, click the scroll arrows to scroll through the themes or click the More button to display all of the themes in the gallery.
- Click one of the themes in the gallery.

To change the design theme:

1. Open the presentation file **Alaska2** from the Tutorial.02\Tutorial folder included with your Data Files.

2. Save the file in the same folder using the filename **Alaskan Tours**. The presentation title slide appears in the slide pane.

3. Click the **Design** tab on the Ribbon. The Ribbon changes to display options for setting or modifying the presentation design.

4. In the Themes group, click the **More** button to display the entire gallery of available design themes. The Office theme is listed first, and then the rest of the themes are in alphabetical order.

5. Point to the **Apex** theme (the second theme in the first row in the gallery), but do not click the mouse button. The Live Preview feature changes the design and colors on the slide in the slide pane to the Apex theme colors.

6. Point to the **Flow** theme, as shown in Figure 2-3.

Live Preview of the Flow theme in the Themes gallery | Figure 2-3

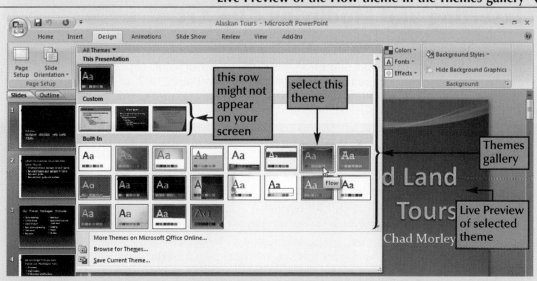

7. Click the **Flow** theme. All of the slides in the presentation are changed to the design and colors of the Flow theme.

As you can see, the title slide has a dusky blue background with varying color, and a background graphic of some waves across the top of the slide, and Slides 2 through 12 have a white background with the same graphic across the top. Next, you'll add graphics to some of the slides.

Understanding Graphics

Graphics add information, clarification, emphasis, variety, and even pizzazz to a Power-Point presentation. PowerPoint enables you to include many types of graphics in your presentation: graphics created using another Windows program; scanned photographs, drawings, and cartoons; and other picture files or clip art located on a CD or other disk. You can also create graphics using the Drawing tools in PowerPoint. In addition, you can add graphical bullets to a bulleted list.

InSight	**Using Graphics Effectively**

You should remember the following points when using graphics:
- Use graphics to present information that words can't communicate effectively, to pique interest and motivate the reader, and to increase understanding and retention of information.
- Consider your audience (their jobs, experiences, education, and culture) in selecting appropriate graphics.
- Consider your purpose and the type of information you'll be presenting in choosing the type of graphic you'll use.
- Consider file size when choosing graphics. Some clip-art images are significantly larger than others and use more disk space.

You will begin by adding clip art to your presentation, and then you'll add a digital photograph.

Inserting and Modifying Clip Art

Slide 2, "What is Alaskan Cruises and Land Tours?", has four bulleted items of text. Chad wants to insert clip art to add interest to this slide. In PowerPoint, **clip art** refers specifically to images in the gallery that is installed with PowerPoint 2007, or images that are available from Microsoft Office Online. You'll search for clip art that illustrates travel.

Reference Window	**Inserting Clip Art on a Slide**

- Switch to a layout that includes a content placeholder, and then, in the content place-holder, click the Clip Art button; *or*, click the Insert tab on the Ribbon, and then, in the Illustrations group, click the Clip Art button.
- In the Clip Art task pane, type a search term in the Search for text box, and then click the Go button.
- In the task pane, click the clip art that you want to insert into the slide.

Inserting Clip Art

The best way to add clip art to a slide is to use a slide layout that has a placeholder for clip art. You'll now change the existing slide layout and then add clip art.

To change the layout of a slide and add clip art:

▶ 1. Go to **Slide 2** ("What is Alaskan Cruises and Land Tours?"), and then click the **Home** tab on the Ribbon.

▶ 2. In the Slides group, click the **Layout** button, and then click the **Two Content** layout. The bulleted list moves to the left side of the slide in the slide pane, and a second content placeholder appears in the center of the slide.

▶ 3. In the content placeholder, click the **Clip Art** button 🔲. The Clip Art task pane appears on the right side of the PowerPoint window. See Figure 2-4.

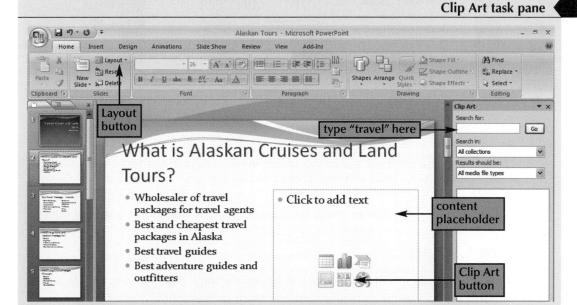

Now you'll search for an appropriate clip-art image.

▶ 4. At the top of the Clip Art task pane, click in the Search for text box, type **travel**, click the **Results should be** list arrow, make sure the **Clip Art** check box is selected, and then click the **Go** button to the right of the Search for text box. PowerPoint displays at least three clip-art images that are associated with the word "travel." (Depending on how Office was installed on your computer or if you are connected to the Internet, you might see many more clip-art images.)

▶ 5. In the Clip Art task pane, click the clip art of a globe and a suitcase. The content placeholder disappears from the slide, and the clip art you selected appears in its place. Note that it is selected, as indicated by the selection handles in the corners and on the sides. See Figure 2-5.

Trouble? If the clip-art image is inserted into the slide without replacing the placeholder, delete the clip-art image, select the content placeholder again, and then click the thumbnail in the Clip Art task pane.

Figure 2-5 **Clip art inserted on the slide**

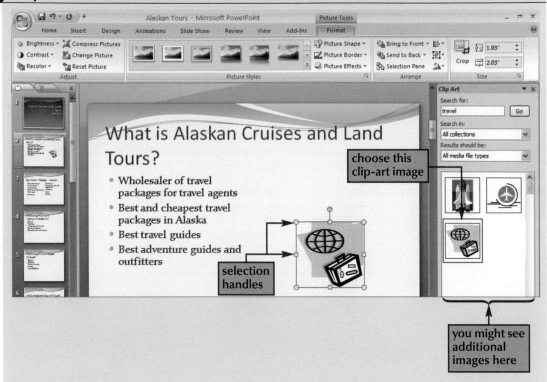

Trouble? If you don't see the image shown in Figure 2-5 in the task pane, scroll down the list. If you still can't find it, use another clip-art image.

Now, you'll modify this clip-art image by changing its size and adding a special effect.

Resizing Clip Art

Chad feels that the clip-art image in Slide 2 is too small. You'll now increase the size of the clip art.

To resize the clip art:

Tip

When you resize a picture, you'll usually want to drag a corner resize handle to maintain the ratio of the width to the height.

1. Position the pointer over the upper-right corner sizing handle of the clip art so that the pointer changes to ↗, and then drag the handle up and to the right until the image is about twice its original size. Don't worry about getting the exact size.

2. Position the pointer anywhere on top of the selected clip art except on top of a sizing handle so that the pointer changes to ↖, and then drag the entire clip-art image on the slide to position it so that its upper edge is level with the first bulleted item and its right edge is about one inch from the right edge of the slide.

3. Click a blank area of the slide to deselect the image. See Figure 2-6.

Slide 2 with resized and repositioned clip art ◀ Figure 2-6

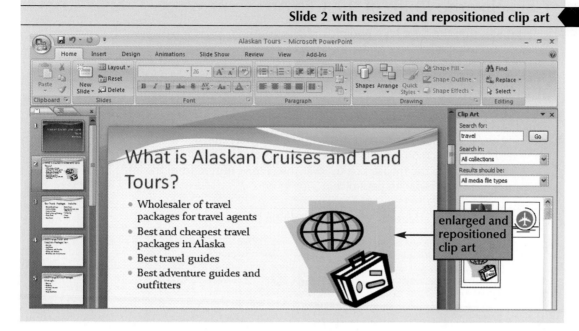

With the clip-art image inserted and resized, you're ready to add special effects.

Modifying the Picture Style of an Image

Chad thinks that, to add interest, you should modify the clip art so that it looks like it is reflecting into a mirror.

To modify the picture style:

▶ 1. Click the **clip art** to select it. The sizing handles and selection line appear around the image. Notice that PowerPoint adds a Picture Tools contextual tab to the Ribbon—the Format tab—indicating that, when you click the tab, you'll see picture tools on the Ribbon.

▶ 2. Click the **Format** tab (below "Picture Tools" on the Ribbon), if necessary, to display commands for formatting pictures.

▶ 3. In the Picture Styles group, click the **Reflected Rounded Rectangle** (the fifth thumbnail from the left). You will see the name of the picture style in a ScreenTip when you rest the mouse pointer over the thumbnail. A reflection of the image appears below the clip art. Chad now wants you to add a border that is included with the Reflected Rounded Rectangle style.

▶ 4. In the Picture Styles group, click the **Picture Border** button. A palette of color tiles and a menu for picture borders appears. You'll use this palette to select the color of the border; you could also use the menu to make the border line thicker (increase its weight), or change it from a solid line to a dashed style.

▶ 5. On the Picture Border palette, point to **Dark Teal, Text 2** (the fourth tile from the left under Theme Colors).

▶ 6. Click the **Dark Teal, Text 2** tile, and then click a blank area of the slide to deselect the clip-art image. The clip art now has a thin, dark teal border around the image.

Now you're ready to change some of the colors in the clip art.

Changing the Color of the Clip Art

Chad thinks that the light blue and green colors of the clip art look too washed out, so he asks you to change them to darker colors.

To change the color of clip art:

▶ 1. Click the **clip art** to select it.

▶ 2. In the Adjust group on the Format tab, click the **Recolor** button, and then, in the Dark Variations section of the gallery, click **Accent color 1 Dark** (as shown in the ScreenTip when you move the mouse pointer over the second button from the left). The clip-art image is recolored with dark blues. See Figure 2-7.

Figure 2-7 ▶ **Slide 2 after adding effects and recoloring clip art**

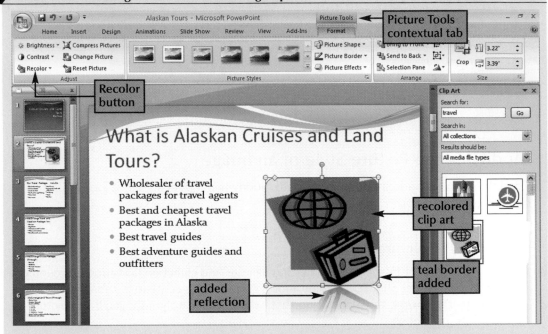

▶ 3. In the Clip Art task pane title bar, click the **Close** button ✖. The task pane closes and the size of the slide in the slide pane increases.

▶ 4. On the Quick Access Toolbar, click the **Save** button 🖫 to save your changes.

You'll continue modifying the presentation by adding pictures to some of the slides.

Inserting Bitmapped Images

To add a picture to a slide, the picture must be a computer file located on an electronic medium, such as a memory card, CD, or hard disk. Picture files are generated by taking photographs with a digital camera, scanning photographs taken with conventional cameras, or pictures drawn using graphics software (such as Microsoft Paint). These types of picture files are bitmapped images. A **bitmapped image** is a grid (or "map") of colored dots that form a picture. The colored dots are called **pixels**, which stands for picture elements. Bitmapped images occur in different formats, the most popular of which have the filename extensions **.bmp** (which are uncompressed bitmapped images), **.tif** (which are tagged uncompressed bitmapped images), **.gif** (which are compressed bitmapped images), or **.jpg** (which are another type of compressed bitmap image).

In addition to using the current background graphic of the Flow design theme, Chad wants you to use a photograph, in the form of a bitmapped image, which shows scenes of Alaska. To get the bitmapped file of the scenes of Alaska, the company graphics artist took pictures with a digital camera and then used image-editing software to combine several pictures into one.

Inserting a Bitmapped Image on a Slide | Reference Window

- Switch to a layout that includes a content placeholder, and then, in the content placeholder, click the Insert Picture from File button; or, click the Insert tab on the Ribbon, and then, in the Illustrations group, click the Picture button.
- Navigate to the folder containing the desired picture file.
- Double-click the picture file that you want to insert on the slide.

Inserting digital photographs (from now on simply called "pictures") on your slides is similar to inserting clip art. Chad wants you to add digital photographs to some of the slides.

To insert a picture on a slide:

▶ **1.** Go to **Slide 4** so that it appears in the slide pane. The Home tab becomes the active tab on the Ribbon.

▶ **2.** In the Slides group, click the **Layout** button, and then click the **Two Content** layout.

▶ **3.** In the content placeholder on the right side of the slide, click the **Insert Picture from File** button 🖻 . The Insert Picture dialog box opens.

▶ **4.** Navigate to the **Tutorial.02\Tutorial** folder included with your Data Files, click the picture file **Glacier**, and then click the **Insert** button. The picture appears in the slide pane in place of the content placeholder. See Figure 2-8.

Slide 4 after inserting picture | **Figure 2-8**

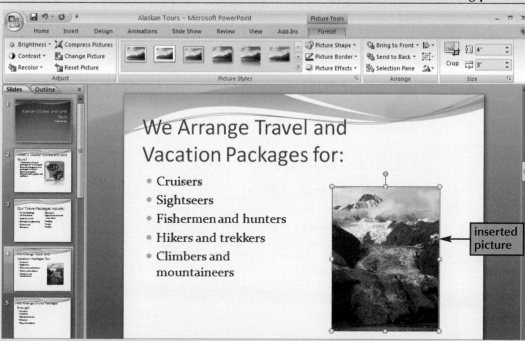

▶ **5.** Go to **Slide 5**, change the slide layout to the **Two Content** layout, and then insert the picture file **Ship**, stored in the Tutorial.02\Tutorial folder.

6. Drag the image of the cruise ship up until its top edge is aligned with the top edge of the first bulleted item, and then save your changes to the presentation.

Modifying the Slide Master

A **master** is a slide that contains the elements and styles of the design theme, including the text and other objects that appear on all the slides of the same type. Masters never appear when you show or print a presentation. PowerPoint presentations have three major types of masters: the **Slide Master**, which includes the various layouts and designs on the presentation slides; the **Handouts Master**, which contains the objects that appear on all the printed handouts; and the **Notes Master**, which contains the objects that appear on the notes pages.

The Slide Master includes masters for the different layouts available in the presentation, including the Title Slide Layout master (usually used by Slide 1, the title slide), the Title and Content Layout master (used by slides with a bulleted list, clip art, or another kind of graphic), and the Two Content Layout master (used by slides with two bulleted lists, one bulleted list and one graphic, or two graphics). If you modify the Slide Master, the changes usually affect all of the slides in the presentation. If you modify an individual layout master, the changes affect only slides that have that layout applied.

You use the slide masters so that all the slides in the presentation have a similar design and appearance. This ensures that your presentation is consistent. To make changes to the masters, you need to switch to Slide Master view. You'll do this now.

To switch to Slide Master view:

1. Click the **View** tab, and then in the Presentation Views group, click the **Slide Master** button. The view changes to Slide Master view and a new tab, the Slide Master tab, appears on the Ribbon to the left of the Home tab. See Figure 2-9.

| Figure 2-9 | Two Content Layout master selected in Slide Master view |

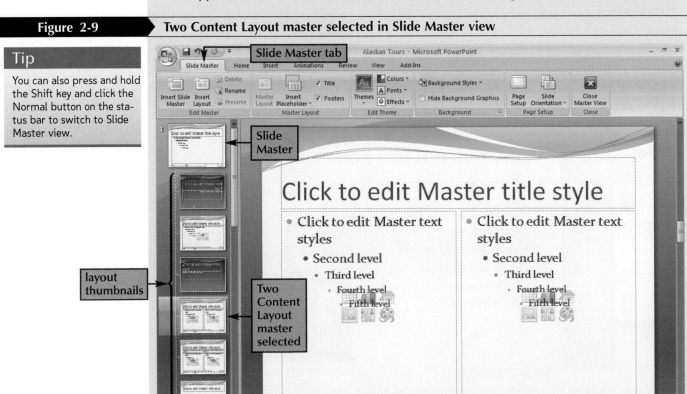

As you can see from the thumbnail slides in the pane on the left side of the window, Slide Master view includes the Slide Master thumbnail at the top and several layouts below it. The Two Content Layout thumbnail is currently selected because you switched to Slide Master view from Slide 5, which has the Two Content layout applied.

2. In the pane at the left of the window, click the **Title and Content Layout** thumbnail, the third thumbnail from the top (the second layout thumbnail). The slide pane now displays the master for the Title and Content layout.

You can modify master slides by changing the size and design of the title and body text, adding or deleting graphics, changing the background, and making other modifications.

Modifying Slide Masters | Reference Window

- Click the View tab on the Ribbon, and then, in the Presentation Views group, click the Slide Master button, *or* press and hold the Shift key, and then, on the status bar, click the Normal button.
- Click the Slide Master or the layout master thumbnail that you want to modify.
- Make changes to the master, such as changing the background color; modifying the text size, color, font, or alignment; inserting clip art, bitmapped images, or other graphics; changing the size or location of text placeholders; and so forth.
- In the Close group, click the Close Master View button *or*, on the status bar, click the Normal button.

You'll now insert the image of Alaska into a master slide. To add the new bitmapped image to all the slides in the presentation that have the Title and Content layout applied, you'll insert it on the Slide Master in Slide Master view. To insert a bitmapped image on just one slide, you use the same procedure in Normal view.

To insert a graphic on a Slide Master:

1. Click the **Insert** tab on the Ribbon, and then, in the Illustrations group, click the **Picture** button. The Insert Picture dialog box opens to the Tutorial.02\Tutorial folder.

2. Click the picture file **AKPanel**, and then click the **Insert** button. The image is inserted on your Slide Master in the middle of the slide.

3. Position the pointer over the bitmapped image so that it changes to 🕂, and then drag the image to the left edge of the slide. See Figure 2-10.

Figure 2-10 **Title and Content Layout master with bitmapped image**

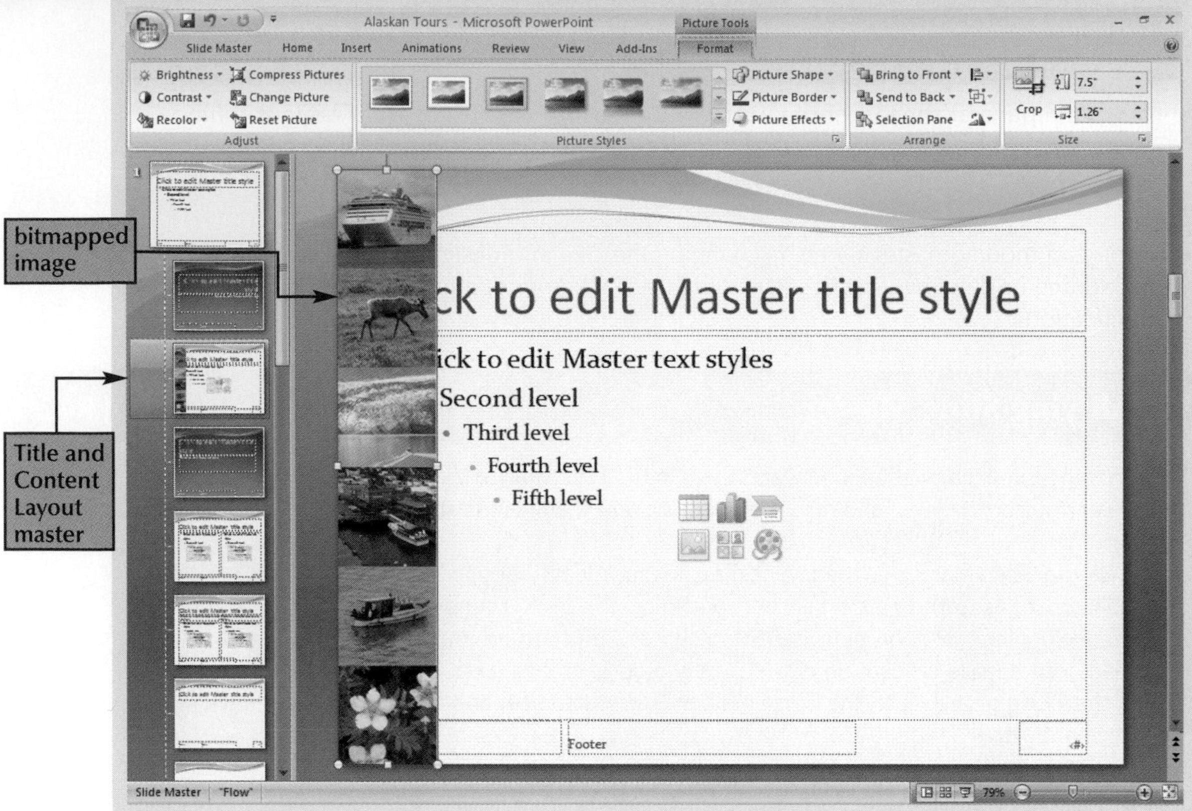

Modifying Text Placeholders

The picture that you just inserted overlaps the text boxes that hold the slide title and bul-leted list. You'll want to resize the text box so its left edge is to the right of the picture. To resize a text box, you need to select it, and then you drag a sizing handle. You'll resize the placeholder text boxes on the Slide Master by dragging a sizing handle.

To change the title and text placeholders on the Slide Master:

▶ 1. In the slide pane, click the edge of the title placeholder, which currently contains the text "Click to edit Master title style" partially obscured by the bitmapped image. Siz-ing handles appear around the placeholder text box and the border around the text box changes from a dashed line to a solid line to indicate that the entire object is selected. You can see the left edge of the selection box even though the left edge of the title placeholder is obscured by the picture you inserted.

Trouble? If the box surrounding the placeholder is composed of lines with dots and dashes, the text box is active, not selected. Click the edge of the text box to change it to a solid line.

▶ 2. Drag the left-middle sizing handle to the right until the left edge of the place-holder is just to the right of the bitmapped image.

▶ 3. Click the edge of the content placeholder (located just below the title placeholder), and then drag its left-middle sizing handle to the right, so that its left edge aligns the with left edge of the title placeholder. See Figure 2-11.

Title and Content Layout master with resized placeholders ◀ Figure 2-11

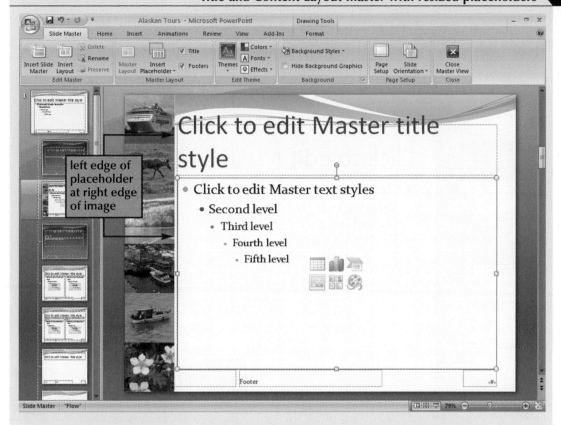

Three text placeholders are at the bottom of the Slide Master. These make up the **footer**—text that appears at the bottom of each slide. The placeholder on the left is for the date, the placeholder in the middle is for custom text that you insert, and the placeholder on the right displays the current slide number. Chad doesn't want the date to be displayed in this presentation, so you'll delete the date placeholder. This will give you room to reposition the other two footer placeholders more attractively. You want this change to affect all the slides in the presentation, so you first need to switch to the Slide Master.

To delete and reposition text placeholders:

▶ 1. At the top of the pane at the left of the window, click the Slide Master (the top thumbnail). When you point to it, you see that its ScreenTip contains the name of the current theme, in this case, it is the Flow Slide Master.

▶ 2. In the slide pane, click the edge of the leftmost footer placeholder (the one with the word "Date" in it). The border changes to a solid line. If you left this placeholder here and selected the option to show this box on slides in the presentation, it would display the current date on each slide.

▶ 3. Press the **Delete** key to delete the Date placeholder.

   Trouble? If nothing happened when you pressed the Delete key, you didn't select the entire object. Click the edge of the placeholder so that the border changes to a solid line, and then repeat Step 3.

▶ 4. Select the center footer placeholder (it contains the word "Footer").

▶ 5. Press the ← key as many times as necessary to move the footer placeholder so its left edge is aligned with the left edge of the text placeholder above it. See Figure 2-12.

Figure 2-12 | Slide Master with modified footer placeholder

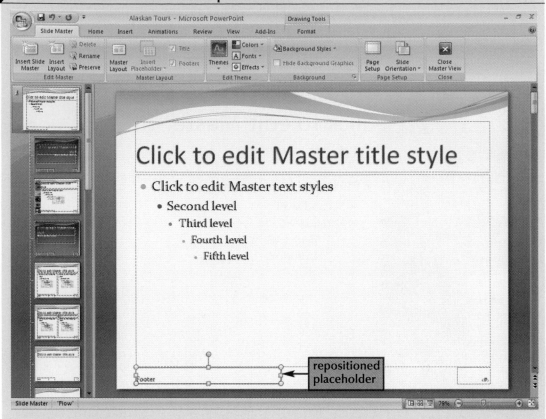

Now you need to fix the alignment of the Footer placeholder on the Title and Content Layout master.

▶ **6.** In the pane at the left of the window, click the **Title and Content Layout** thumbnail, in the slide pane, select the Footer placeholder, and then press the → key as many times as necessary to move the footer placeholder so its left edge is aligned with the left edge of the text placeholder above it.

▶ **7.** Save your changes.

Be aware that, even though you have modified the footer placeholders, you haven't yet added the text of the footers nor have you told PowerPoint to display the slide numbers. You'll do that later.

After you insert the graphic into the master slides, Chad decides that you should change the font color of the title text to yellow.

Modifying Text on a Slide

In PowerPoint, text is described in terms of the font, font size, and font style. A **font** is the design of a set of characters. Some names of fonts include Arial, Times New Roman, Verdana, and Cambria. Font size is measured in **points**. Text in a book is typically printed in 10- or 12-point type. **Font style** refers to special attributes applied to the characters; for example, bold and italic are font styles.

Chad wants you to change the font style of the title text in most of the layouts from normal to bold, and the color of the title text in the Title Slide layout from light blue to yellow. To change the format of all the text in a text box, you first need to select the text box. As you learned in Tutorial 1, to do this, you click the edge of it to change the text box border from a dashed line to a solid line. This is different than clicking inside a text box, which makes the box active—that is, ready to accept text that you type or paste. Remember that making a text box active is not the same as selecting the text box. When you select a text box (and the border changes to a solid line), any formatting changes you make are global formatting changes and are applied to all of the text in the text box. When you select specific text within the active text box and make formatting changes, the changes are local formatting changes applied only to the selected text in the text box.

You'll now select text boxes in the masters to change the font on all the slides.

To modify the font color in text boxes on a slide:

1. In the pane at the left of the window, click the **Flow Slide Master** thumbnail at the top of the list, and then, in the slide pane, select the **title text placeholder**.

2. Click the **Home** tab on the Ribbon, and then, in the Font group, click the **Bold** button ⬚B⬚ . The text in the title text placeholder on the Slide Master becomes bold.

3. In the pane on the left of the window, click the **Title Slide Layout** thumbnail (the second one in the list).

4. Position the pointer directly on top of the border of the title text placeholder, and then right-click. The border line becomes solid, indicating that the entire object is selected, and a shortcut menu and the Mini toolbar appear.

   Trouble? If the border line is still dotted and the Mini toolbar did not appear, you did not right-click directly on top of the border line. Click a blank area of the slide to close the shortcut menu, and then repeat Step 4.

5. On the Mini toolbar, click the **Font Color button arrow** ⬚A ▾⬚ , and then, in the Standard Colors section at the bottom of the palette of colors that opens, click the **Yellow** tile. The text in the placeholder becomes yellow to match the color of the flowers in the pictures on the Title and Content layout master.

6. Click the **Slide Master** tab on the Ribbon, and then, in the Close group, click the **Close Master View** button. Slide 1 appears in the slide pane in Normal view. You can see the result of one of the changes you made in Slide Master view; the title text on the title slide is yellow. You can't see the changes to the footer because you need to explicitly display the contents of the footer placeholders. You'll do that later in this tutorial.

7. Save your changes to the presentation.

Selecting Appropriate Font Colors | InSight

Be careful as you select font colors to make sure your text is easy to read when your presentation is projected onto a screen. Font colors that work well are dark colors on a light background, or light colors on a dark background. Avoid red text on a blue background (and vice versa), or blue text on a green background (and vice versa), unless the shades of those colors are in strong contrast. For example, red on blue often looks good up close on your computer monitor, but it is almost totally illegible to an audience watching your presentation on a screen in a darkened room. You should also avoid using red/green combinations, which color-blind people find illegible.

Applying a Second Theme

Normally, all your slides in one presentation will have the same theme. On occasion, however, you might want to apply a second theme to only one, or a few, of the slides in your presentation. Chad wants you to change the theme for Slide 12, "Contact Us" from the modified Flow design theme to the Technic theme. He wants this slide to stand out from the others because it lists the contact information.

To apply a second theme to a presentation:

▶ 1. Go to **Slide 12** ("Contact Us"), and then click the **Design** tab on the Ribbon to display options for modifying the presentation design.

▶ 2. In the Themes group, click the **More** button to display the Themes gallery. You can choose one of the themes that comes with PowerPoint, or, if you have created and saved your own theme, you can click Browse for Themes at the bottom of the menu to open a dialog box similar to the Open dialog box and choose a theme saved on your computer. You can also search for themes on Microsoft Office Online.

▶ 3. Right-click the **Technic** theme (the first theme in the third row), and then click **Apply to Selected Slides**. Because Slide 12 is the only selected slide, the Technic design theme is applied only to that slide. See Figure 2-13.

| Figure 2-13 | Slide 12 with Technic design theme applied |

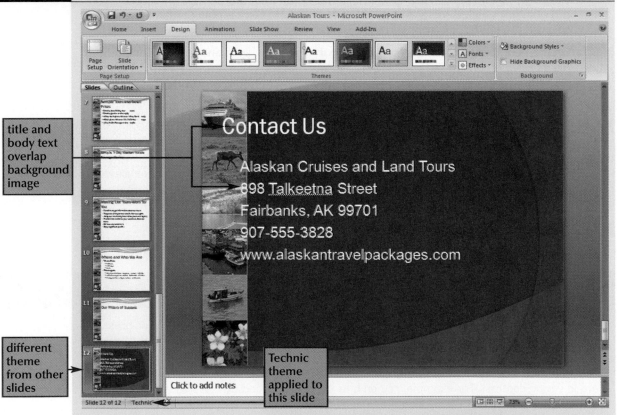

title and body text overlap background image

different theme from other slides

Technic theme applied to this slide

Trouble? If your screen resolution is different from the resolution used in this book, the Technic theme might be in a different position.

You applied the Technic design theme to only one slide in the presentation. The modified Flow design remains on the other slides.

The title and bulleted text again overlap the bitmapped image. In this case, however, you will change the placeholder on this slide rather than on the Slide Master because this is the only slide using the Technic theme.

To resize the placeholder:

▶ **1.** Click anywhere on the title text, press and hold the **Shift** key, and then click the bulleted list text box. Both text boxes are selected.

▶ **2.** Drag the left-middle sizing handle of either of the text boxes to the right until their left edges are just to the right of the bitmapped image.

▶ **3.** Click a blank area of the slide to deselect the text boxes. See Figure 2-14.

Slide 12 after moving text boxes ◄ **Figure 2-14**

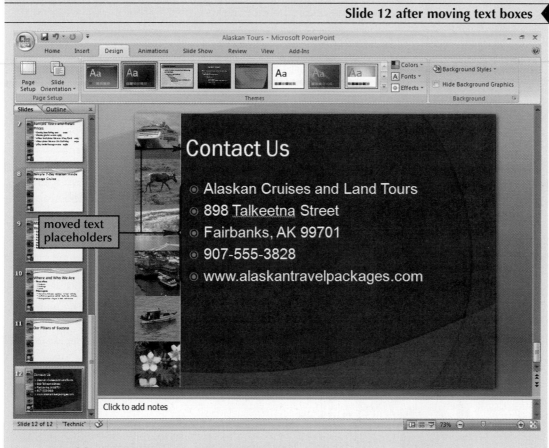

Trouble? If your slide doesn't look like Figure 2-14, make adjustments now.

Now, Chad instructs you to modify the slide with prices of some of the major tours that Alaskan Cruises and Land Tours sells to travel agencies. He wants you to align the dollar amounts on the slide.

Adding and Modifying Tab Stops

A **tab** adds space between the left margin and the beginning of the text on a particular line, or between the text in one column and the text in another column. (When you create several long columns of data, however, you probably want to use a table instead of tabs.) For example, when Chad typed the text in Slide 7, he typed the tour description and a colon, pressed the Tab key to add space, and then typed the dollar amounts. A **tab stop** is the location where the insertion point moves to (including any text to the right of it) when you press the Tab key. The default tab stops on a slide are set at one-inch intervals. You can add your own tab stops to override the default tab stops to align text on a slide. You can set tab stops so that the text left-aligns, right-aligns, center-aligns, or aligns on a decimal point.

The default tab stops on the ruler are left tabs, which position the left edge of text at the tab stop and extend the text to the right. However, you want to align the right sides of the dollar amounts in a new Slide 7, so you want to use a right tab stop, which positions the right edge of text at the tab stop and extends the text to the left. You'll change the tab stops on Slide 7 now.

To change the tab stops:

▶ 1. Go to **Slide 7**, click the **View** tab on the Ribbon, and then, in the Show/Hide group, click the **Ruler** check box to insert a check mark. Horizontal and vertical rulers appear along the top and left edges of the slide pane.

   Trouble? If a check mark already appears in the Ruler check box, the rulers were already visible on your screen. If you clicked the Ruler check box to remove the check mark, you hid the rulers; in this case, click it again to insert a check mark.

▶ 2. Click anywhere in the bulleted list text box. The default tab stops for the body text are set every inch and appear as light gray rectangles, or hash marks, under the ruler. (The hash marks are very light.) The Left Tab button [L] appears in the upper-left corner of the slide pane, to the left of the horizontal ruler. When Chad typed the text on this slide, he pressed the Tab key after typing the colon in each line, so the dollar amounts on each line are aligned at the next available tab stop. See Figure 2-15.

Figure 2-15 ▶ **Slide 7 with ruler and tab stops**

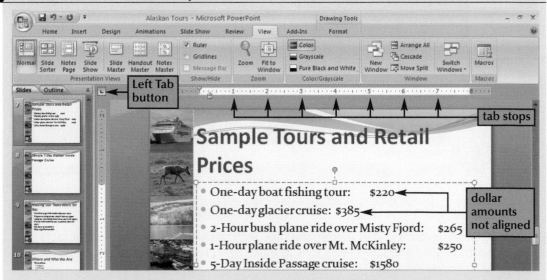

Trouble? If a button other than the Left Tab button [L] appears to the left of the horizontal ruler, click that button as many times as necessary until the Left Tab button [L] appears.

3. Click the **Left Tab** button so that the button changes to the Center Tab button, click the **Center Tab** button to change it to the Right Tab button. Clicking the Tab button cycles through the various tabs; if you clicked the Tab button again, the Decimal Tab button would appear, and if you clicked once more, the Left Tab button would appear again.

4. Position the pointer immediately before the word "One-day" in the first bulleted item, and then drag to the bottom of the body text to select all of the bulleted items. The selected text is highlighted.

5. Click just to the left of the 8-inch mark in the white area of the horizontal ruler. A new, right tab stop appears at the location you clicked; the default tab stops to the left of the new tab stop are removed; and the dollar amounts in the body text box become right-aligned at the new tab stop. See Figure 2-16.

Aligned text after inserting a right tab stop ◄ Figure 2-16

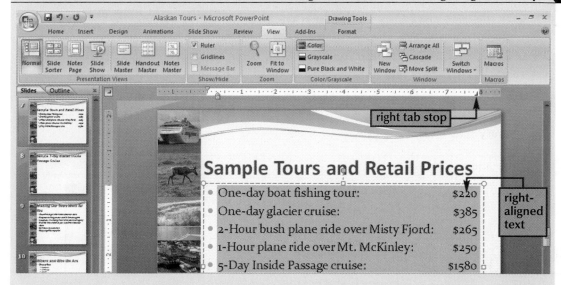

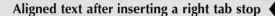

Trouble? If you used the wrong type of tab, drag the new tab stop off the ruler to delete it, click the Tab button as many times as necessary to display the Right Tab button, and then repeat Steps 4 and 5. If you clicked in the wrong place on the ruler, drag the tab stop character to the right or left until it's positioned where you want it.

6. In the Show/Hide group on the View tab, click the **Ruler** check box to remove the check mark. The rulers are removed from the slide pane.

7. Click a blank area of the slide pane to deselect the text box, and then save your changes.

Next, you'll insert footers and display the slide numbers.

Inserting Footers and Slide Numbers

A **header** is text that appears at the top of each slide and, as you might recall, a footer is text that appears at the bottom of each slide. PowerPoint provides a footer placeholder on the Slide Master, and both header and footer placeholders on the Notes and Handout Masters.

As part of the overall slide design, Chad wants you to include footers and the current slide number on each slide, except the title slide. You already deleted the Date footer placeholder in the Slide Master.

To insert a footer into your presentation:

▶ **1.** Click the **Insert** tab, and then, in the Text group, click the **Header & Footer** button. The Header and Footer dialog box opens with the Slide tab on top. In the Preview box in the lower-right corner of the dialog box, you can see rectangles at the bottom of the preview slide. These rectangles correspond to footer and slide number placeholders.

▶ **2.** In the dialog box, click the **Slide number** check box to select it. The right rectangle in the Preview box turns black to indicate that the contents of this placeholder—in this case, the slide number—will appear on each slide.

▶ **3.** In the dialog box, click the **Footer** check box. In the Preview box, the rectangle on the left turns black. The insertion point is blinking in the Footer text box.

▶ **4.** In the Footer text box, type **Alaskan Tours 2010**. This text will appear on all of the slides. Often, the title slide looks better without footers.

▶ **5.** Click the **Don't show on title slide** check box to select it. See Figure 2-17. Now, the slide number and the text you typed in the Footer text box will appear on every slide except the title slide.

| Figure 2-17 | Header and Footer dialog box |

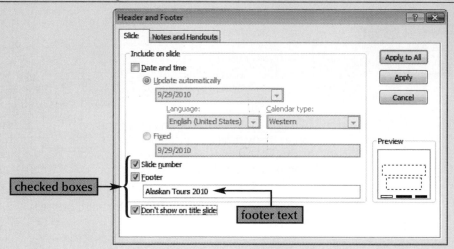

▶ **6.** Click the **Apply to All** button. The dialog box closes and all the slides (except the title slide, Slide 1) now contain the footer you typed and the slide number.

▶ **7.** Go to Slide 1 to see that the footer does not appear on the slide, and then save your changes.

The text of the footer is too small for an audience to read, but not too small for the presenter. If you wanted the audience to be able to read this text, you would modify the font size of the placeholders on the Slide Master.

You completed most of Chad's presentation. In Session 2.2, you'll finalize the slides by creating a table, diagram, and simple drawing.

1. List three situations in which you can use graphics effectively.
2. What is the name of the PowerPoint feature that gives your presentation an overall design, including colors, fonts, and other design elements?
3. How would you change the size of a clip art, picture, or text box?
4. What are tabs? What are tab stops? Describe how to insert a right tab stop on the ruler.
5. List four criteria for selecting an appropriate type of graphic.
6. What is a picture style in PowerPoint? How do you modify the picture style of an inserted picture?

Session 2.2

Creating a Table in a Slide

Chad wants you to insert a new slide with a table listing a typical cruise itinerary. A **table** is information arranged in horizontal rows and vertical columns. The area where a row and column intersect is called a **cell**. Each cell contains one piece of information and is identified by a column and row label; for example, the cell in the upper-left corner of a table is cell A1 (column A, row 1), the cell to the right of that is B1, the cell below A1 is A2, and so forth. A table's structure is indicated by borders, which are lines that outline the rows and columns.

Inserting a Table | Reference Window

- Switch to a layout that includes a content placeholder, and then, in the content placeholder, click the Insert Table button, *or* click the Insert tab on the Ribbon, in the Tables group, click the Table button, and then click a box in the grid that opens to create a table or click Insert Table on the menu.
- If the Insert Table dialog box is open, specify the desired table size—the numbers of columns and rows—and then click the OK button.
- Add information to the cells. Use the Tab key to move from one cell to the next, and the Shift+Tab keys to move to previous cells.
- Use the Table Styles Gallery to select a table style.

The itinerary table you'll create needs to have four columns: one for the day of the cruise (you'll show a seven-day cruise), one for the departure or arrival port of call, one for the time of arrival, and one for the time of departure. The table needs to have eight rows: one row for column labels, and seven rows for the data

To create a table:

1. If you took a break after the previous session, make sure PowerPoint is running, and then open the presentation you created in Session 2.1, **Alaskan Tours** located in the Tutorial.02\Tutorial folder included with your Data Files or in a location specified by your instructor.

2. Go to **Slide 8** ("Sample 7-Day Alaskan Inside Passage Cruise").

3. In the slide pane in the content placeholder, click the **Insert Table** button 🏢. The Insert Table dialog box opens.

4. In the Number of columns text box, type **4**, press the **Tab** key to move the insertion point to the Number of rows text box, type **8**, and then click the **OK** button. A table made up of four columns and eight rows is inserted in the slide with the insertion point blinking in the first cell (cell A1), and the Table Tools contextual tabs appear on the Ribbon. See Figure 2-18.

Figure 2-18 ▶ **Slide 8 with empty table**

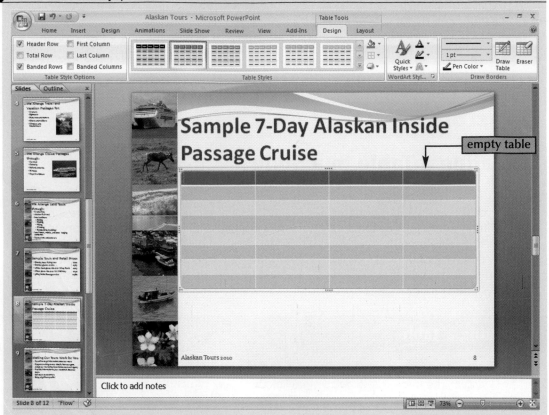

Trouble? If the table doesn't have four columns and eight rows, click the Undo button 🔄 on the Quick Access Toolbar to undo your creation of the table, and then repeat Steps 3 and 4.

Now you're ready to fill the blank cells with information. To enter data in a table, you click in the cell in which you want to enter data. Use the Tab and arrow keys to move from one cell to another. To add a new row at the bottom of the table, move the insertion point to the last cell in the table, and then press the Tab key. A new row is inserted automatically.

To add information to the table:

1. With the insertion point blinking in the upper-left cell, type **Day**, press the **Tab** key to move to cell B1, type **Port**, press the **Tab** key to move to cell C1, type **Arrival**, press the **Tab** key to move to cell D1 (the last cell in the first row), and then type **Departure**. This completes the column labels.

2. Press the **Tab** key. The insertion point moves to cell A2.

3. Type **1** (the number one), and then press the **Tab** key to move to cell B2.

4. Type **Vancouver, BC** in cell B2, press the **Tab** key twice, leaving cell C2 blank and placing the insertion point in cell D2.

5. Type **4:00 pm** in cell D2. This completes the first row of data.

6. Press the **Tab** key to move to cell A3, complete the information in the rest of the cells, as shown in Figure 2-19, and then click a blank area of the slide to deselect the table.

Slide 8 with table of information | Figure 2-19

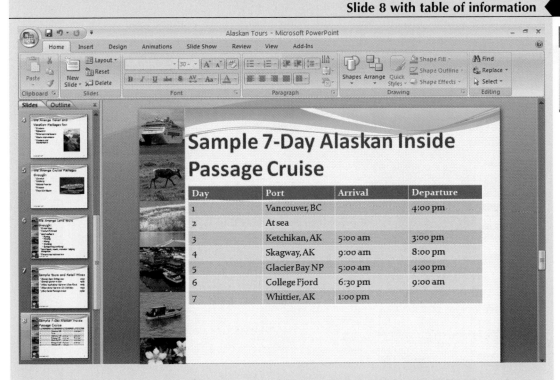

Tip

For readability, a table on a slide should rarely have more than five columns or eight rows of data.

Trouble? If you have a blank row at the bottom of your table, you probably pressed the Tab key after entering the data in the last cell, which inserted a new, blank row at the bottom of the table. On the Quick Access Toolbar, click the Undo button to undo the creation of the extra row.

Chad now wants you to change the table style to better match the presentation theme.

Changing the Table Style

PowerPoint comes with built-in table styles for each theme. Table styles include the borders around the table and cells and color schemes. You can use Live Preview to see how your table will look with different table styles. You want to apply a style with banded rows, horizontal and vertical borders, and blue-green colors to match the colors and style of the presentation and to add visual interest.

To change the table style:

1. Click anywhere in the table to select it. The two Table Tools contextual tabs appear again on the Ribbon.

2. Under the Table Tools label on the Ribbon, click the **Design** tab, if necessary. Design tools for working with tables appear.

Trouble? If you accidentally clicked the Design tab next to the Insert tab, you will not see the table styles. Click the Design tab farther to the right; it has the Table Tools label above it.

▶ **3.** In the Table Style Options group, make sure the **Header Row** and the **Banded Rows** check boxes are selected, and the other check boxes are deselected.

▶ **4.** In the Table Styles group, click the **More** button, point to several of the table styles and watch the table on the slide change to reflect the style you are pointing to, and then click the **Themed Style 1 - Accent 4** style, which is the fifth thumbnail from the left in the first row, under Best Match for Document. See Figure 2-20.

Figure 2-20 Table after applying a table style

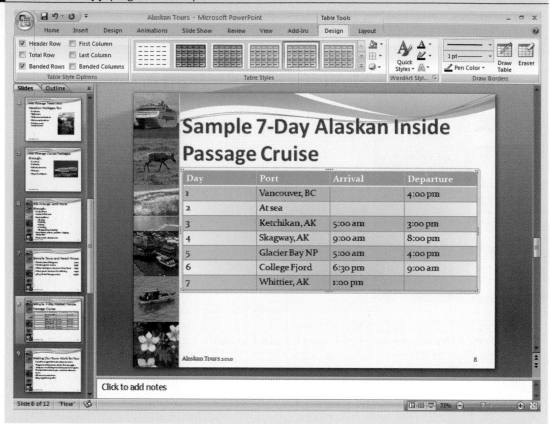

Applying Table Effects

You can add more visual interest to your table by applying one or more special effects. For example, Chad thinks the table would look more professional if the cells were beveled. A **cell bevel** is a three-dimensional effect on the edges of the cells.

To apply a cell bevel to the table:

▶ **1.** Drag the pointer from cell A1 (upper left) to cell D8 (lower right) to select all the cells.

▶ **2.** In the Table Styles group, click the **Effects** button ⬜▾, point to **Cell Bevel**, and then click the **Circle** button, which is the first button in the first row under Bevel in the gallery. The darker-green cells in the table have a beveled effect. PowerPoint automatically bevels only every other row with this table style.

▶ **3.** Click a blank area of the slide pane to deselect the table.

Using other options in the Table Styles group, you could change the shading with selected cells or change the border style around selected cells.

Changing the Table Layout

After you insert data into a table, you usually need to adjust the layout so it fits nicely on the slide and is readable. Commands on the Table Tools Layout tab on the Ribbon let you remove rows, add and remove columns, combine cells, split cells, position text in cells, and perform other modifications to the table. As you can see, all four columns of the table are of equal width, but the width of the data in column A is less than in the other columns. Furthermore, column A might be more readable if the numbers were centered in the cells.

To change the table layout:

1. Position the pointer on the divider between the first two columns (columns A and B) so that the pointer changes to ←‖→.

2. Drag the border between columns A and B to the left until column A is about one-third the size of the rest of the columns.

3. Position the pointer just above the top of column A so that the pointer changes to ↓, and then click to select the entire column.

4. Click the **Layout** tab on the Ribbon. The Ribbon displays options that allow you to change the layout of the rows and columns of the table.

5. In the Alignment group, click the **Center** button ≣. The contents of the cells in the first column are center-aligned in the cells.

6. Deselect the table. See Figure 2-21.

Table after changing the layout of column A ◄ Figure 2-21

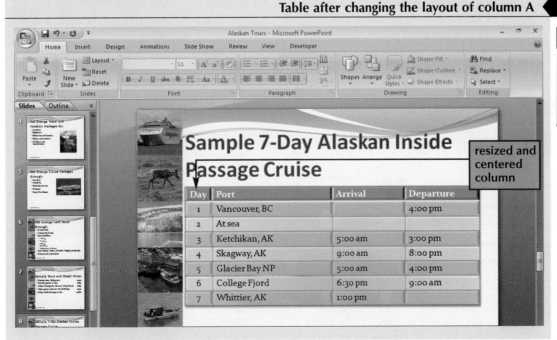

Tip

Right-click anywhere on the table to see a shortcut menu containing commands specific to working with tables.

You have completed the table that shows a sample cruise itinerary for the Alaskan Inside Passage. Your next task is to create a diagram on Slide 9 to show the process by which travel agents sell Alaskan Cruises and Land Tours products.

Creating a Diagram on a Slide

PowerPoint allows you to create the following types of diagrams on slides:

- **List diagram**: Shows a list of items in a graphical representation
- **Process diagram**: Shows a sequence of steps in a process
- **Cycle diagram**: Shows a process that has a continuous cycle
- **Hierarchy diagram** (including **organization charts**): Shows the relationship between individuals or units within an organization
- **Relationship diagrams** (including **Venn diagrams**, **radial diagrams**, and **target diagrams**): Show the relationship between two or more elements
- **Matrix diagram**: Shows information in a matrix or grid
- **Pyramid diagram**: Shows foundation-based relationships

To create diagrams, you use SmartArt, a feature that allows you to create diagrams easily and quickly. In the Alaskan Cruises and Land Tours presentation, Chad wants you to convert the bulleted items in Slide 9 ("Making Our Tours Work for You") into a process to show the steps in using ACLT services. This graphic will be a strong visual reminder to travel agents of the benefits of using ACLT tours.

To create a process diagram using SmartArt:

▶ 1. Go to **Slide 9**, and then, in the slide pane, click anywhere in the bulleted list.

▶ 2. If necessary, click the **Home** tab, and then, in the Paragraph group, click the **Convert to SmartArt Graphic** button 🔽. A gallery opens displaying various SmartArt graphic styles.

▶ 3. Click **More SmartArt Graphics**. The Choose a SmartArt Graphic dialog box opens.

▶ 4. In the list of diagram types on the left of the dialog box, click **Process**. The gallery in the middle of the dialog box changes to display various types of process diagrams. See Figure 2-22.

Figure 2-22 ▶ **Choose a SmartArt Graphic dialog box**

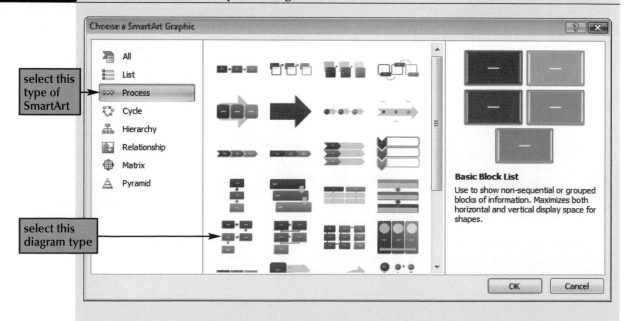

5. Click the **Basic Bending Process** icon, and then click the **OK** button to add the selected SmartArt to Slide 9. See Figure 2-23.

Trouble? If you don't see the panel to the left of the diagram, click the left arrowhead located on a small tab on the left edge of the diagram placeholder.

Slide 9 with process diagram — Figure 2-23

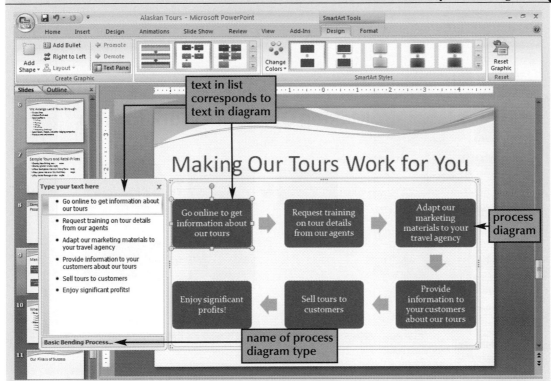

The process diagram appears on the slide, and the text of the original bulleted list appears in the boxes in the graphic. The text in each box also appears in a bulleted list to the left of the slide. The label at the bottom of this list identifies the graphic as the Basic Bending Process graphic. You can edit the text in the boxes, or you can edit the bulleted list on the left just as you would edit any list. Chad decides he doesn't need the last box in the diagram.

6. In the list on the left of the graphic, select all the text of the last bullet, and then press the **Delete** key. The bullet is removed from the list, and the corresponding box is removed from the slide.

7. In the upper-right corner of the bulleted list box, click the **Close** button ☒ . The bulleted list closes and you see a small tab on the left edge of the SmartArt selection box. You can click this tab to display the bulleted list again. You can also use options on the SmartArt Tools contextual Design tab to apply special effects to the diagram.

8. Click the **Design** tab, if necessary, under SmartArt Tools on the Ribbon, and then, in the SmartArt Styles group, click the **More** button to open the gallery of styles available for the graphic.

Trouble? If you don't see the SmartArt Styles group, you probably clicked the Design tab next to the Insert tab. Make sure the SmartArt in the slide pane is selected, and then click the Design tab on the right of the Ribbon, under SmartArt Tools.

9. In the gallery, click the **Metallic Scene** icon (the second icon in the last row under 3-D). The style of the graphic changes to the one you chose.

> **10.** Click anywhere outside the process diagram to deselect it, and then save your changes to the presentation. See Figure 2-24.

Figure 2-24 | **Slide 9 with completed process diagram**

As with any text, you can change the font attributes of the text in the boxes in the diagram; for example, you can make the text bold or change the font.

This completes the process diagram on Slide 9. When Chad uses this slide show to give a presentation, he'll discuss each of these steps and show his potential clients how to do each step. Chad now asks you to create a simple drawing on Slide 11.

Creating and Manipulating a Shape

For the last graphic to be included in his presentation, Chad asks you to add an inverted triangle with text to a new Slide 11. The labels on each side of the triangle list the three features of Chad's company that he wants to emphasize—superior tours, excellent guides, and reasonable prices. The triangle shows that each of these three is equally important in the success achieved by travel agents as they use ACLT products.

To create the triangle, you'll use a tool in the Shapes group on the Insert tab. When you click the Insert button, you are presented with a gallery of ready-made (built-in) shapes.

To insert a ready-made shape on a slide:

> **1.** Go to **Slide 11**, click the **Home** tab on the Ribbon if necessary, and then change the layout to **Title Only**, so that the slide has no content placeholder below the title. You want to draw the triangle in a blank area of the slide.

▶ **2.** Click the **Insert** tab on the Ribbon, and then, in the Illustrations group, click the **Shapes** button.

▶ **3.** Under Basic Shapes in the menu, click the **Isosceles Triangle** button △ (the third button in the first row under Basic Shapes), and then position the pointer over the slide in the slide pane. The pointer changes to ╋.

▶ **4.** Position ╋ approximately one inch below the "s" in "Pillars" (in the title of the slide), press and hold down the **Shift** key, and then click and hold the mouse button and drag the pointer down and to the right. The outline of a triangle appears as you drag. Pressing the Shift key while you drag makes the triangle equilateral—the three sides are of equal length.

▶ **5.** Release the mouse button and the Shift key when your triangle is approximately the same size and shape as the one shown in Figure 2-25.

Tip

To draw an equilateral triangle, circle, or square, hold down the Shift key while you drag the pointer after selecting the triangle, oval, or rectangle shape, respectively.

Slide 11 with an equilateral triangle ◀ **Figure 2-25**

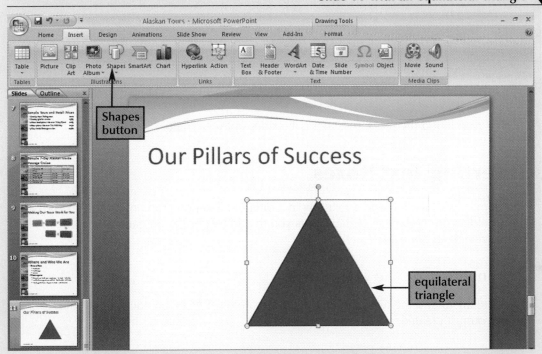

Trouble? If your triangle doesn't look like the one in Figure 2-25, you can move it by dragging it to a new location, resize or change its shape by dragging one or more of the sizing handles, or you can press the Delete key to delete your triangle, and then repeat Steps 2 through 5 to redraw it.

In addition to the sizing handles, the selected triangle has a yellow diamond and a green circle at its top. The yellow diamond is an **adjustment handle**; if you drag it, the shape of the tip of the triangle changes without changing the overall size of the object. The green circle is the **rotate handle**, which you can drag to rotate the shape.

The default color of the drawn object is the blue color from the set of theme colors, but Chad prefers a different color and style. Notice that the Drawing Tools contextual tab, Format, appears on the Ribbon when the shape you drew is selected.

To change the shape style:

▶ **1.** With the triangle still selected, click the **Format** tab on the Ribbon, and then, in the Shape Styles group, click the **More** button to display a gallery of shape styles.

▶ **2.** Click the **Intense Effect – Accent 6** style (the last column in the last row). The shape now has a shaded greenish color with a small shadow on the bottom and right side.

The triangle is the desired size and color, but Chad wants you to flip (invert) the triangle so that it points down instead of up. You can use commands in the Arrange group on the Ribbon to rotate and flip objects.

To flip an object:

▶ **1.** With the triangle still selected, in the Arrange group on the Ribbon, click the **Rotate** button.

▶ **2.** Click **Flip Vertical**.

▶ **3.** Click a blank region in the slide pane to deselect the triangle.

▶ **4.** Save your changes to the presentation.

Now you'll add the text labels along the sides of the triangle.

Inserting Text Boxes

Sometimes, you need to add a text box in a different location than any of the text box placeholders on the layouts. Chad wants you to add text boxes on each of the three sides of the triangle in Slide 11.

Adding Text to the Diagram

You're ready to add the text naming the three features of ACLT on each side of the triangle you just created.

To add a text box to the slide:

▶ **1.** Click the **Insert** tab on the Ribbon, in the Text group click the **Text Box** button, and then position the pointer over the slide. The pointer changes to ↓ .

▶ **2.** Position ↓ so it is just above and centered on the top side of the triangle, and then click. The position doesn't have to be exact. A small text box appears above the triangle with the insertion point blinking in it, and the Home tab becomes active on the Ribbon.

Trouble? If the insertion point is blinking in the middle of the triangle instead of in a new text box above the triangle, you clicked the edge of the triangle. On the Quick Access Toolbar, click the Undo button 🔄 , and then repeat Steps 1 and 2.

▶ **3.** Type **Superior Tours**.

▶ **4.** Insert another text box to the right of the triangle, and then type **Excellent Guides**.

▶ **5.** Insert a third text box to the left of the triangle, in the Paragraph group on the Home tab click the **Align Right** button 📰 , and then type **Reasonable Prices**.

▸ **6.** Use the Shift key to select the three text boxes that you created, and then change the font size to **24** points.

▸ **7.** Click a blank area of the slide to deselect the text boxes. Your slide should now look similar to the slide in Figure 2-26.

Text boxes added around the triangle ◂ **Figure 2-26**

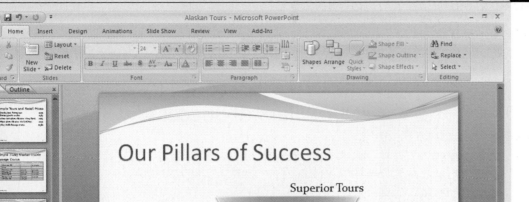

Trouble? If your text boxes are not positioned exactly as shown in Figure 2-26, don't worry. You'll reposition them in the next set of steps.

Next, you'll rotate the text boxes to make them parallel to the sides of the triangle.

Rotating and Moving Objects

The method for rotating text is similar to the one for rotating graphics (or rotating any other object). You use the Rotate or Flip commands on the Drawing Tools contextual Format tab on the Ribbon, or you drag the rotate handle on the object. You will rotate the text boxes on the left and right sides of the triangle.

To rotate and move the text boxes:

▸ **1.** Click anywhere within the "Excellent Guides" text box. The sizing handles and the green rotate handle appear around the text box.

▸ **2.** Position the pointer over the rotate handle. The pointer becomes ↻.

▸ **3.** Press and hold the **Shift** key, and then drag the rotate handle counterclockwise until the top edge of the box is parallel to the right edge of the triangle. Holding down the Shift key makes the rotation occur in 15-degree increments.

4. Drag the "Excellent Guides" text box to position it against and centered on the right edge of the triangle. See Figure 2-27.

Figure 2-27 | **Slide 11 with rotated and repositioned text box**

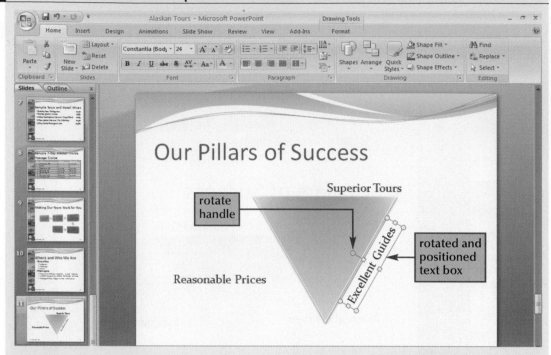

Trouble? If the edge of the text box isn't parallel to the edge of the triangle, you can repeat Steps 2 and 3 to fix the rotation. If necessary, try it without pressing the Shift key.

Trouble? If the text box jumps from one location to another as you drag it, and you can't position it exactly where you want it, hold down the Alt key as you drag the box. (The Alt key temporarily disables a feature that forces objects to snap to invisible gridlines on the slide.)

5. Rotate the "Reasonable Prices" text box clockwise so that the top edge of the text is parallel to the left edge of the triangle, and then position the text box so it's against and centered on the left edge of the triangle.

6. Adjust the position of (but don't rotate) the "Superior Tours" text box so it's centered over the triangle.

7. Click a blank area of the slide pane to deselect the text box. Your slide should look like the slide in Figure 2-28.

Slide 11 with completed diagram | Figure 2-28

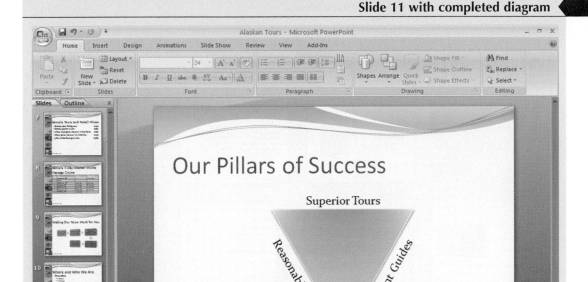

8. Save your changes to the presentation.

You have completed Chad's presentation. As usual, you should finalize your presentation by checking the spelling, viewing it in Slide Show view, and saving the presentation so you can submit it to your instructor, either in printed or electronic form, as requested.

To check and view the presentation:

1. Click the **Review** tab on the Ribbon, and then, in the Proofing group, click the **Spelling** button to start checking the spelling of your presentation. Decide how to handle each word that is flagged because it was not found in the PowerPoint dictionary. (In most cases, you should click the **Ignore All** button because the words are proper nouns, such as "Talkeetna.")

2. Go to Slide 1, and then in the status bar, click the **Slide Show** button 🖵. The slide show starts.

3. Press the **spacebar** or click the mouse button to advance through the slide show.

4. If you see any problems while you are watching the slide show, press the **Esc** key to exit the slide show and return to Normal view, make the necessary corrections, and then return to Slide Show view.

5. Switch to Slide Sorter view, increase the zoom so that the slide thumbnails are as large as possible but still all appear within the Slide Sorter window (about 90% zoom), and then save your changes to the presentation. Compare your presentation to Figure 2-29.

Figure 2-29 **Completed presentation in Slide Sorter view**

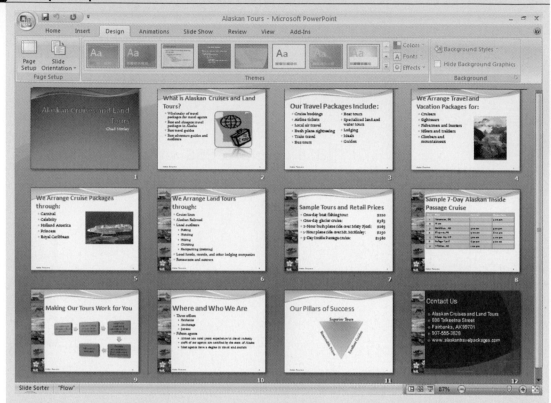

6. Submit the finished presentation to your instructor, either in printed or electronic form, as requested, and then close the presentation.

Chad is pleased with the additions and modifications you made to the presentation. He is eager to give the presentation to travel agents.

Review | **Session 2.2 Quick Check**

1. How do you add a table to a slide?
2. Where is cell A1 in a table?
3. Describe SmartArt.
4. What is a process diagram?
5. How do you add a text box to a slide?
6. How do you draw a shape, such as a rectangle or a circle, on a slide?
7. How do you rotate or flip an object?

Tutorial Summary | Review

In this tutorial, you learned how to create a new presentation using a design theme and how to apply a new design theme to selected slides or to all the slides in the presentation. You learned how to insert, format, and resize graphics, including clip art and pictures. You also learned how to modify the design theme in the Slide and Title Masters. You learned how to add tab stops to align text on a slide. You learned how to insert footer information on slides. Finally, you also learned how to insert a table, a diagram, a shape, and a text box on slides.

Key Terms

adjustment handle	graphic	Slide Master
bitmapped image	Handouts Master	tab
cell	header	tab stop
cell bevel	master	table
clip art	Notes Master	theme
font	pixels	theme colors
font style	points	theme fonts
footer	rotate handle	

| Practice | **Review Assignments** |

Get hands-on practice of the skills you learned in the tutorial using the same case scenario.

Data Files needed for the Review Assignments: AKRibbon.jpg, LandTour.pptx, Naturalist.jpg

In addition to the presentation on general information about Alaskan Cruises and Land Tours, Chad wants presentations on information about the specific cruises and land tours that his company operates. He asks you to create a PowerPoint presentation on one of the Alaskan land tours. Do the following:

1. Open the file **LandTour**, located in the Tutorial.02\Review folder included with your Data Files, and then save the file as **Denali Tours** in the same folder.
2. Apply the Module theme.
3. Replace "Chad Morley" in the subtitle in Slide 1 with your name.
4. Add the footer "Denali Land Tours" and slide numbering to all the slides except Slide 1.
5. Switch to Slide Master view, and then, in the Title Slide Layout, insert the picture file **AKRibbon**, located in the Tutorial.02\Review folder. Position the graphic along the bottom of the slide. It will cover up the footer and page number placeholders, which is no problem because those items don't appear on the title slide. Close Slide Master view when you are finished.
6. In Slide 2, change the layout so you can place clip art to the right of the bulleted list, and then insert a clip-art image of a yellow bus (by searching for **bus** in the Clip Art task pane). Close the Clip Art task pane.
7. Increase the size of the clip art so it's approximately double its original width, and then move the clip art so its top is aligned with the top of the first bulleted item.
8. Recolor the clip art to Accent color 2 Dark (in the Dark Variations section of the Recolor menu).
9. In Slide 3, change the layout so you can place a picture on the right, insert the picture file **Naturalist** located in the Tutorial.02\Review folder, and then apply the picture style Reflected Rounded Rectangle.
10. Increase the size of the Naturalist picture until the picture height is about the same height as the entire bulleted list.
11. In Slide 4, convert the bulleted list to the Continuous Block Process SmartArt graphic.
12. In Slide 5, insert a table of the appropriate size and add the text as follows:

Days in Denali	Without Flight Over McKinley	With Flight Over McKinley
1	$125	N/A
2	$200	$425
3	$280	$490

13. Center-align the text and numbers in column 1, and then right-align the text and numbers in columns 2 and 3.
14. Reduce the width of column A until it is so narrow that "Days in" is on one line and "Denali" is on a second line in cell A1.
15. Reduce the column widths of columns B and C until "Over McKinley" in each of the cells B1 and C1 is on a second line of text. (*Hint*: You might have to make several adjustments to the border lines to get the column widths as you want them.)
16. Position the (now much smaller) table in the center of the white background on the slide. You don't need to center it exactly.
17. Make sure Header Row and Banded Rows are checked in the Table Style Options group of the Design tab, and then change the table style to Dark Style 1 – Accent 1.

18. In Slide 6, use a right tab stop to align the dollar amounts along the right edge of the slide.

19. Change the layout of Slide 7 to Title Only, draw a Regular Pentagon (hold down the Shift key while drawing so that all five corners stay the same angle), and then position the pentagon in the middle of the white area of the slide.

20. Flip the pentagon so a flat edge is on top and a corner is pointing down.

21. Insert a text box on each side of the pentagon, starting with the top of the pentagon and going clockwise around it, with the phrases "Exciting tours," "Low prices," "Expert guides," "Full amenities," and "Flexible schedules."

22. Rotate and reposition these text boxes so they are flush with their respective sides of the pentagon. Press the Alt key if you need to override the snap-to-grid feature.

23. To Slide 8 only, apply the design theme titled "Trek."

24. Check the spelling in the presentation, view the slide show, fix any problems you see, and then save your changes.

25. Submit the complete presentation to your instructor, either in printed or electronic form, as requested, and then close the file.

| Apply | | **Case Problem 1** |

Apply information you used in this tutorial to create a presentation on castles of Scotland.

Data Files needed for this Case Problem: Balmoral.jpg, Castles.pptx, Edinburgh.jpg

Castles of Scotland   Moyra Torphins is a sales representative for Johnson Hodges Incorporated (JHI), a sales promotions company in Scarsdale, New York. JHI provides incentives packages and giveaways for large companies that hold internal sales competitions. Moyra, originally from Scotland, has been assigned to do research on castles in Scotland and to present her research to the other sales representatives. You will help her prepare a PowerPoint presentation on castles of Scotland. Do the following:

1. Open the file **Castles**, located in the Tutorial.02\Case1 folder included with your Data Files, and then save the file to the same folder using the filename **Scottish Castles**.

2. Apply the design theme titled "Foundry," and then replace the subtitle in Slide 1 with your name.

3. In the Foundry Slide Master, change the title text so it's the light-blue theme (Sky Blue, Accent 3) color.

4. Add the footer "Scottish Castles" and slide numbering to all the slides, even the first one.

5. In Slide 2, use SmartArt to convert the bulleted list to a Venn diagram. Select Basic Venn in the SmartArt gallery.

6. Change the font size of the Venn diagram text boxes to 24 points. If necessary, insert a hyphen between the two *m*s in "Accommodations," so that PowerPoint will split the word at the desired location.

7. Near the upper-left side of the Venn diagram, insert a text box with the phrase "The Intersection of Success." Change the text to 20-point, light-green (Light Green, Accent 2) text.

8. Decrease the width and increase the height of the text box so that "The Intersection" is on one line and "of Success" is on another line.

9. Draw a 3-point black arrow from the text box to the center of the Venn diagram where the three circles overlap. (*Hint*: Choose an arrow in the Lines section of the Shapes gallery on the Home or Insert tab. After drawing it, click the Format tab, then click Shape Outline to change the color and weight.)

EXPLORE

10. In Slide 3, change the layout to Two Content, and then insert a clip-art image that deals with travel (for example, a picture of luggage or an airplane). If necessary, recolor the image to match the slide color scheme. If necessary, use the AutoFit option to fit the text in the placeholder. Resize the clip art to fit nicely on the right of the slide.

11. In Slide 4, insert the following table:

Castle	Nearest Major City	Approx. Year(s) of Construction	Open to Public
Balmoral	Aberdeen	1854	Mar to Aug 1
Craigievar	Aberdeen	1626	All year
Edinburgh	Edinburgh	1058-1093	All year
Fraser	Aberdeen	1575-1636	All year
Urquhart	Inverness	1230	All year

12. Center the text within the cells of the table.

13. Change the table design to Dark Style 1 – Accent 2.

14. Apply the Soft Round cell bevel effect to the table.

15. In Slides 5 and 6, change the layouts as needed, and insert the appropriate picture of the castle from the pictures in the Tutorial.02\Case1 folder. If the text doesn't fit well to the left of the picture, click the AutoFit Options button (located in the lower-left corner of the active text box), and select AutoFit Text to Placeholder, and then, if you desire, change the size of the textbox.

16. To each of the pictures, apply the picture style Simple Frame, White.

17. In Slide 7, insert a right tab stop on the ruler to align the mile amounts along the right edge of the slide.

18. Check the spelling, view the slide show, fix any problems you see, and then save the presentation using the default filename.

19. Submit the complete presentation to your instructor, either in printed or electronic form, as requested, and then close the file.

Challenge | Case Problem 2

Learn new PowerPoint skills as you modify a presentation for a backpacking outfitter company.

Data Files needed for this Case Problem: Campsite.jpg, Meadow.jpg, Men.jpg, Outfitter.pptx, Panel.jpg, River.jpg

The Backpacker's Outfitter Several years ago, Blake Stott received an M.S. degree in recreation management and started a new company, The Backpacker's Outfitter, which provides products and services for hiking, mountain climbing, rock climbing, and camping. The services include guided backpacking and climbing expeditions and courses on climbing and backpacking. The products include backpacking and climbing equipment and supplies. Blake uses PowerPoint to give presentations to businesses, youth groups (including Girl Scouts and Boy Scouts), clubs, and other organizations. He asks you to help him prepare a PowerPoint presentation explaining his products and services. Do the following:

1. Open the presentation **Outfitter**, located in the Tutorial.02\Case2 folder included with your Data Files, and then save the file to the same folder using the filename **Backpacker's Outfitter**.

2. On Slide 1, change the subtitle from "Blake Stott" to your name.

3. Apply the built-in design theme titled "Solstice."

EXPLORE　　4. In the Solstice Slide Master, select and delete the three circular objects located in the upper-left corner. Keep the tan textured rectangle on the left.

5. In the same Slide Master, insert the picture file **Panel**, and then position it over the left tan panel, so that it's centered between the left and right edges of the tan rectangle and so that the picture's top is at the same height as the top of the title text placeholder. (*Hint*: If you have difficulty positioning the picture exactly where you want it—the picture might "snap" to the edge of the screen or "snap" to the edge of the tan panel as you try to move it—hold down the Alt key as you move the picture with the mouse. The Alt key overrides the "snap" feature.)

6. Still in the Slide Master, delete the Date placeholder (located at the bottom of the slide), and then move the footer placeholder so its left edge is aligned with the left edge of the bulleted list placeholder.

7. Change the font size of the footer and slide number text boxes to 20 points. Increase the width of the slide number text box so that the symbol "<#>" fits on one line.

EXPLORE　　8. In the layout masters Title Slide Layout, Title and Content Layout, and Two Content Layout, delete the Date placeholder. Delete the little circle objects from the Title Slide layout.

EXPLORE　　9. In the Two Content Layout master, change the paragraph spacing and the space before and after each line of text. Select both bulleted list text box placeholders, click the Home tab if necessary, in the Paragraph group, click the Line Spacing button, and then click Line Spacing Options. In the Paragraph dialog box, in the Spacing section, set the value in the Before text box to 0, and then set the value in the Line Spacing text box to Single, if necessary.

10. Close Master view, and then insert the footer "Backpacker's Outfitter" and turn on slide numbering for all the slides except the first one.

11. In Slide 2, change the slide layout to Two Content, and then add the bitmapped image **River** to the content placeholder.

12. Change the image to the picture style called Rotated, White. Adjust the location of the picture so it's centered between the left edge of the bulleted list text box and the right edge of the slide.

13. Repeat Steps 11 and 12 for Slide 5, except insert the image **Men**. Move the picture so it and its frame and shadow appear within the boundaries of the slide, and then decrease the width of the bulleted list text box so the picture doesn't overlap the text.

14. In Slide 4, change the layout to Two Content, and then modify the size and shape of the content placeholders so that they are horizontal rectangles, and so that the one currently on the left is positioned above the one currently on the right.

EXPLORE　　15. Add the bitmapped image **Campsite** to the lower content placeholder. Adjust the width of the image to five inches, keeping the ratio of the width to the height fixed. (*Hint*: With the picture selected, click the Format tab, if necessary, and then in the Size group, change the width to five inches. The height will automatically change to maintain the ratio of width to height.)

16. Position the picture so it's centered between the left and right edges of the white background of the slide and between the bottom of the bulleted list and the footer.

17. In Slide 8, change the layout to Two Content, and then repeat Steps 15 and 16 for Slide 8, except insert the image **Meadow** and increase its size to five and a half inches. Make sure the picture and text don't overlap.

EXPLORE　　18. In Slide 6, reapply the Two Content layout so that the left bulleted list doesn't overlap the graphic on the left. (*Hint*: To reapply the layout, you do the same steps as you did to apply the Two Content layout.)

19. Insert a new Slide 7 with the Title Only layout. Type **Phases of a Successful Backpacking Trip** as the title. Draw a large, equilateral, Regular Pentagon in the middle of the blank area of the slide below the title, and then invert the pentagon so it's pointed down and change its fill color to orange (labeled Gold, Accent 2 in the ScreenTip), if necessary.

20. Add 18-point Verdana (or Arial if your computer doesn't have Verdana) text just outside the pentagon on each of its five sides, using the phrases (starting at the top of the pentagon and going clockwise): "Planning," "Conditioning," "Training," "Equipment," and "Trip Site."

21. Rotate the text boxes so they are parallel to their respective sides of the pentagon. Adjust the size of the pentagon and the position of the text so that each phrase is centered along an edge, and almost resting on the shape.

22. Insert a new Slide 8 with the Title and Content layout, type the title **Prices of Major Items**, insert a table with two columns and five rows, and then add the text as follows:

Item	Typical Price
Backpack	$180
Tent	$150
Sleeping bag	$100
Boots	$160

✦ EXPLORE   23. Add a new row with **Total** in the left column and $590 in the right column. (*Hint*: To add a row to an existing table, click in the last cell, in this case cell B5, and then press the Tab key.)

24. Right-align the text and numbers in column 2.

✦ EXPLORE   25. Adjust the widths of both columns at once so the text just fits without wrapping, and then center the table in the white area of the slide. (*Hint*: To reduce the width of both columns at once, drag the right edge of the table at the location where you see a vertical row of three dots.)

26. Change the table style to Dark Style 1 – Accent 1.

27. Check the spelling, view the slide show, fix any problems you see, and then save your changes.

28. Submit the completed presentation in printed or electronic form, as requested by your instructor, and then close the file.

| Create | **Case Problem 3** |

Create a new presentation about lighthouses by using and expanding on the skills you learned in this tutorial.

Data Files needed for this Case Problem: BodieLH.jpg, LHBase.jpg, LHPanel.jpg, LHStairs.jpg, LHTop.jpg, Ocracoke.jpg, Sizemore.jpg

Historic Preservation of Lighthouses   Ardith Sizemore is a field representative for the Division of Historic Preservation for the Massachusetts State Historical Society. She travels throughout the eastern seaboard to visit lighthouses of historical significance. She gathers information about the lighthouses from local libraries and other resources, helps direct the creation of the museum-type displays at the lighthouses, and preserves historical documents about the lighthouses. One of her goals is to have lighthouses placed on the National Registry of Historical Places by the United States Department of the Interior. Often, she presents information about lighthouses in a certain area. She has asked you to prepare a PowerPoint presentation on lighthouses of the Outer Banks of North Carolina. The nine slides in your completed presentation should look like the slides shown in Figure 2-30.

Figure 2-30

The following information will help you in creating the slide show. Read all the steps before you start creating your presentation. Start by creating a new presentation.

⊕ EXPLORE

1. Use the Deluxe theme. If this theme is not available in the Themes gallery on your computer, it is available from Microsoft Office Online. After you create a blank presentation, open the Themes gallery, make sure you are connected to the Internet, and then click More Themes on Microsoft Office Online. In the browser window that opens, click in the Search Templates text box, type Deluxe, and then press the Enter key. In the list of results, click the Deluxe theme, and then follow the on-screen instructions for downloading the theme. If a Microsoft Office Word window opens, close it and then close your browser window. Open the Themes gallery again and apply the Deluxe theme.

2. The picture LHPanel is inserted into the Deluxe Slide Master (and the other Slide Master, as needed) so that the picture appears on the left edge of every slide.

3. The LHPanel picture is recolored with the Dark Variation called Accent color 6 Dark and resized as tall as the slide.

⊕ EXPLORE

4. The LHPanel picture is modified so that it has a 25-point "soft edge," which means that a 25-point region around the edges becomes partially or totally transparent to blend in with the background. (*Hint*: Use the Soft Edges effect in the Picture Effects menu of the Picture Styles group on the Picture Tools Format tab.)

5. The slide masters are modified so that:
   a. the placeholders don't overlap the LHPanel picture.
   b. the font size of the footer and slide number are 24 points.

    c.   the placeholder for the date is removed from all the pertinent layout slide masters.

    d.   the placeholder for the footer is positioned as shown in the figure.

    e.   the title placeholder is positioned up higher on the slide, and the size of the content placeholder(s) is expanded to give it more area on the slides.

    f.   the title and content placeholders are aligned with the slide-number text box below them.

6. Most slides contain a picture (in addition to the LHPanel picture on the slide masters). You'll find all these images in the Tutorial.02\Case3 folder. You should use each image once.

7. The picture style used is Drop Shadow Rectangle.

8. Some of the pictures include a caption, which you can insert using a text box.

9. The text at the bottom of the slides is a footer and an automatic slide number.

10. The table style is modified to Themed Style 1- Accent 5.

⊕ **EXPLORE**　11. The header (top) row of the table is modified is center-aligned and bottom-aligned. (*Hint*: Use the buttons in the Alignment group on the Layout tab (located below Table Tools when the table is selected).)

12. Remember to check the spelling in the final presentation, and then view the slide show.

13. Submit the completed presentation in printed or electronic form, as requested by your instructor, and then close the file.

14. Save the file as **Lighthouses** to the Tutorial.02\Case3 folder.

| Research | **Case Problem 4** |

Use the Internet to collect information about a digital camera and create a new presentation based on this information.

Data Files needed for this Case Problem: Camera01.jpg, Camera02.jpg, Camera03.jpg, ManCam.jpg

Digital Cameras　Your assignment is to prepare a description of a digital camera for a presentation to the class. If you're not familiar with digital cameras, you might want to search the Internet to learn more about them and to find out why they have become so popular. You should then search the Internet for information or reviews about a particular brand and model of digital camera. Alternatively, if you own a digital camera, you could search the Internet for information about your camera. You should organize your information into a PowerPoint presentation, with at least eight slides. Use the photos supplied in the Tutorial.02\Case4 folder included with your Data Files as needed to add interest to your presentation. (Your instructor might also assign you to give an oral presentation based on your PowerPoint file.) Do the following:

1. Gather information on a particular digital camera of your own choice. A suggested Web site is www.dpreview.com, but you will probably want to find others that describe and review digital cameras.

2. Create a new PowerPoint presentation based on an appropriate design theme. Type the brand and model of the camera on the title slide, and then type your name as the subtitle.

3. Create one or two slides with general information about digital cameras or digital photography.

4. Create at least three slides with information about the camera you have chosen. Your slides might include information about the body and design, lens, operation, picture resolution options, picture format options, storage card, battery, viewfinder, LCD (liquid crystal display), boot-up time, retake time, automatic and manual features, upload method, or software. The information might also include lists of advantages and disadvantages. Before starting to create the slides, consider your audience and audience needs: How much technical information do they want? What kinds of information do they need if they might consider buying the camera?

5. Modify the Slide Master by adding a text box or graphics object, changing the font attributes, or making some other desired change that will appear on all the slides.

6. Include the slide number and an appropriate footer on each slide, except the first title slide. In the Slide Master, change the font style, size, color, or position of the footer and slide number text.

7. If your presentation is about your own camera, include sample photographs that you've taken with the camera.

8. If possible, include a photo of the camera itself.

9. Include in your presentation at least one clip-art image.

10. Recolor the clip-art image with a different shade.

11. Include a table in your presentation. You might include a table of features, with the feature name (Price, Body material, Sensor, Image Sizes, File Format, Lens, and so forth) in the left column, and the corresponding feature data in the right column.

12. Include at least one drawing or graphic. For example, you might create a process diagram for the process of setting up the camera, or you might create a Venn diagram showing how the elements of taking a good photograph come together.

13. Apply a second design theme to one of the slides.

14. Check the spelling in your presentation, view the slide show, and then save the presentation to the Tutorial.02\Case4 folder using the filename **Digital Camera**.

15. Submit the completed presentation in printed or electronic form, as requested by your instructor, and then close the file.

Research | **Internet Assignments**

Go to the Web to find information you can use to create presentations.

The purpose of the Internet Assignments is to challenge you to find information on the Internet that you can use to work effectively with this software. The actual assignments are updated and maintained on the Course Technology Web site. Log on to the Internet and use your Web browser to go to the Student Online Companion for New Perspectives Office 2007 at **www.course.com/np/office2007**. Then navigate to the Internet Assignments for this tutorial.

Assess | **SAM Assessment and Training**

If you have a SAM user profile, you may have access to hands-on instruction, practice, and assessment of the skills covered in this tutorial. Log in to your SAM account (**http://sam2007.course.com**) to launch any assigned training activities or exams that relate to the skills covered in this tutorial.

Review | **Quick Check Answers**

Session 2.1

1. (a) to present information that words can't communicate effectively; (b) to interest and motivate the reader; and (c) to increase understanding and retention
2. design theme
3. drag a sizing handle
4. Tabs add space between the left margin and the beginning of the text on a particular line, or between the text in one column and the text in another column. Tab stops are the locations where text moves when you press the Tab key. Click the Tab button until the Right Tab button appears, and then click the desired location on the ruler.
5. Consider (a) your audience (jobs, experiences, education, culture); (b) your purpose (to inform, instruct, identify, motivate); (c) the type of information on the slide (numerical values, logical relationships, procedures and processes, and visual and spatial characteristics); and (d) the file size of the graphic.
6. A special effect (such as border or reflection) applied to a picture on a slide. Select the picture, and then in the Picture Styles group of the Format tab, click the desired style.

Session 2.2

1. Click the Insert Table button in the Content placeholder of a slide, set the desired number of columns and rows, insert information into the cells, and modify the table format as desired.
2. upper-left corner
3. a command that automatically converts a bulleted list to a diagram
4. a diagram that shows a step-by-step procedure
5. Click the Text Box button in the Text group on the Insert tab, and click or drag at the desired location in the slide.
6. Click the button for the desired shape in the Shapes group of the Insert tab, move the pointer into the slide pane, and then drag the pointer to draw the figure.
7. Select the shape, click the Format tab (if necessary), click the Rotate button arrow, and then click the appropriate command, or drag the rotate handle of the object in the slide pane.

Ending Data Files

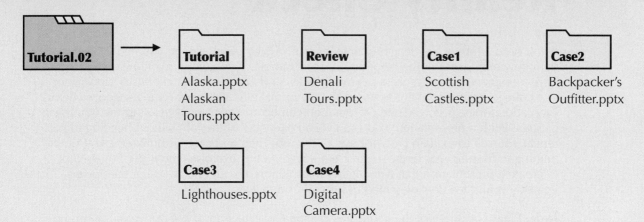

Tutorial.02

Tutorial
Alaska.pptx
Alaskan
Tours.pptx

Review
Denali
Tours.pptx

Case1
Scottish
Castles.pptx

Case2
Backpacker's
Outfitter.pptx

Case3
Lighthouses.pptx

Case4
Digital
Camera.pptx

Reality Check

If you hold a job for any length of time, as part of your employment, you might have to train new employees in their work tasks. For example, if you work in a library, you might have to explain how to process returned books, or if you work in a chemistry stockroom at a college, you might have to describe how to make up solutions for the school's chemistry laboratories. A PowerPoint presentation can be an effective way to start the training process. With a presentation, you can give an overview of the job without needing to repeat yourself to explain basic aspects of the job. Then you can customize the rest of the training to fit the needs of the specific employee. In this exercise, you'll use PowerPoint to create a presentation that will contain information of your choice, using the PowerPoint skills and features presented in Tutorials 1 and 2.

Note: Please be sure *not* to include any personal information of a sensitive nature in the documents you create to be submitted to your instructor for this exercise. Later on, you can update the documents with such information for your own personal use.

1. Create a new PowerPoint presentation based on a theme of your choice. Choose a theme that is relevant to the job you are describing and to your audience.
2. On Slide 1, make the presentation title the same as the title of your job or the job for which you are giving the training. Add your name as a subtitle.
3. On the Slide Master, add the logo of the business for which you are creating your presentation. You can usually get a digital image of the logo from the business's Web site.
4. Look at each of the layout masters. Is the logo appropriately placed on each one? If not, move it.
5. Create a new slide for each major category of tasks. For example, task categories for a library job might be "Punching In", "Checking in with Your Supervisor", "Gathering Books from Drop-Off Stations", "Scanning Returned Books into the Computer", "Checking Books for Damage or Marks", "Processing Abused Books," "Processing Late Books", "Sorting Books", "Shelving Books," and "Punching Out."
6. On each slide, create a bulleted list to explain the particular task category or to provide the steps required to perform the task.
7. Where applicable, include clip art or a photograph. For example, you might include a photograph of the punch clock (time clock) used by hourly workers in the library, or a photograph of a book with serious damage relative to one with normal wear.
8. If certain jobs require a set process, convert a bulleted list into a process diagram using SmartArt graphics.
9. On at least one of the slides, create a table. The table might contain, for example, the headings "Task" (name of the task), "Time Allotted" (time allotted each day or week to perform that task), "Tools" (the supplies, software, or other tools needed to complete the task), or other headings.
10. On one or more slides, insert a shape, such as a rectangle, triangle, circle, arrow or star. For example, you might want to place a small colored star next to a particularly important step in carrying out a task.
11. Re-evaluate the theme you chose. Do you think it is still appropriate? Does it fit the content of your presentation? If not, apply a different theme.
12. Check the spelling, including contextual spelling, of your presentation. Proofread your presentation. Use the thesaurus if you think you could find a better word to substitute for any of your original words.
13. Save the presentation, and submit the completed presentation to your instructor in printed or electronic form, as requested.

Objectives

Session 3.1
- Insert slides from another presentation
- Create and apply a custom theme
- Add a background picture
- Customize bullets
- Add a textured background

Session 3.2
- Apply sound clips and a movie
- Create and format a chart (graph)
- Create, modify, and format an organization chart
- Apply slide transitions and animations
- Use the pointer pen during a slide show
- Hide slides in a presentation
- Prepare a presentation to run on another computer
- Give a presentation in podium mode

Adding Special Effects to a Presentation

Preparing and Customizing a Sales Presentation

Case | Classic Flowers, Inc.

Sophie De Graff is a horticulturalist who works as the sales manager at Classic Flowers, Inc., in Bainbridge, Georgia. Classic Flowers grows and distributes flowers to retail stores throughout Georgia. One of Sophie's responsibilities is to obtain and manage new accounts. This involves giving sales presentations to large retail stores (Sam's Club, Costco, Wal-Mart, Piggly Wiggly, Kroger, and so forth) that have floral departments. Sophie wants you to help her prepare the Microsoft PowerPoint presentation. She emphasizes the importance of preparing a high-quality presentation that includes a custom theme, graphics, sound effects, animations, charts, graphs, and other elements to maximize the visual effects of the presentation.

In this tutorial, you'll insert slides from one presentation into another presentation; create a custom theme; add a digital image, movie, and sound clip to slides; create a graph and organization chart; apply special visual effects to the slides; learn how to give the slides show in podium mode; and save the presentation to a CD so it can be run on another computer.

Starting Data Files

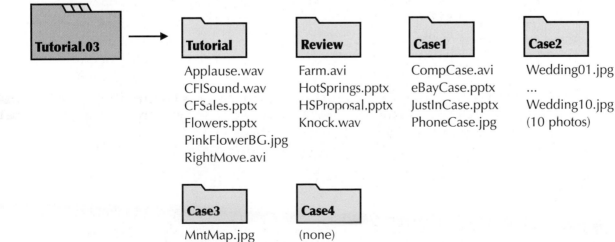

Tutorial.03 → **Tutorial**
Applause.wav
CFISound.wav
CFSales.pptx
Flowers.pptx
PinkFlowerBG.jpg
RightMove.avi

Review
Farm.avi
HotSprings.pptx
HSProposal.pptx
Knock.wav

Case1
CompCase.avi
eBayCase.pptx
JustInCase.pptx
PhoneCase.jpg

Case2
Wedding01.jpg
...
Wedding10.jpg
(10 photos)

Case3
MntMap.jpg
MntPlateau1.jpg
MntPlateau2.jpg

Case4
(none)

Planning the Presentation

Before you begin to create Sophie's slide show, she discusses with you the purpose of, and the audience for, her presentation:

- **Purpose of the presentation**: To present information about products and services of Classic Flowers
- **Type of presentation**: Persuasive (sales)
- **Audience**: Floral department managers and store managers
- **Audience needs**: Details of products and services and information on potential profits
- **Location of the presentation**: Small meeting rooms
- **Format**: On-screen slide show

With this general plan for the presentation, Sophie prepares the text and some of the pictures for the sales presentation.

Inserting Slides from Another Presentation

After Sophie discusses her presentation planning with you, she gives you two presentation files: Flowers, which contains the text and some pictures to include with her sales presentation, and CFSales, a presentation that includes additional information about Classic Flowers's sales. First, you'll open the Flowers presentation and look through it to see what information Sophie has already included. Then, you'll add slides to it from the CFSales presentation.

To insert slides from another presentation, you first need to open the presentation to which you want to add the slides. Then, you use the Reuse Slides command on the New Slide menu to insert specific slides from any other presentation. If the inserted slides have a different design than the current presentation, the design of the current presentation will override the design of the inserted slides.

Inserting Slides from Another Presentation | Reference Window

- Go to the slide in your current presentation after which you want to insert the slides from another presentation.
- In the Slides group on the Home tab, click the New Slide button arrow.
- Click Reuse Slides to display the Reuse Slides task pane.
- In the task pane, click the Browse button, and then click Browse File to open the Browse dialog box.
- Navigate to the location of the presentation that contains the slides you want to insert into the presentation in the PowerPoint window, click the file, and then click the OK button.
- In the task pane, select or deselect the Keep source formatting check box to retain or not retain the formatting of the slides you want to import.
- Click each slide that you want inserted into your presentation.

To open the Flowers presentation and save it with a new name:

▶ **1.** Start PowerPoint, and then open the file **Flowers** located in the **Tutorial.03\Tutorial** folder included with your Data Files.

▶ **2.** Change the subtitle ("Sophie De Graff") to your name.

▶ **3.** Save the presentation file as **Flower Sales** in the Tutorial.03\Tutorial folder. See Figure 3-1.

Slide 1 of Flower Sales ◀ **Figure 3-1**

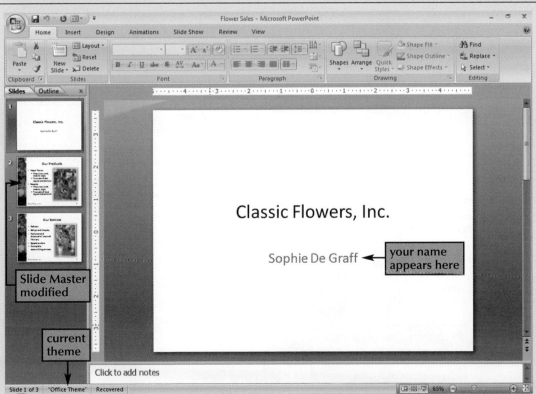

> 4. Look through the three slides of the presentation so you have an idea of its current content. Notice that the presentation has a modified blank Office theme (black text on white background), with the Calibri font for the slide titles and body text. The modifications to the Office theme include the long, slender photograph ("panel") of pink flowers on the slides with bulleted lists, resized placeholders for the body text, and inserted and modified footer and slide number.

Your first task is to insert slides from the presentation file CFSales. Sophie tells you that she wants you to insert all five slides from CFSales.

To insert slides from one presentation into another:

1. Go to **Slide 3** of Flower Sales. When you insert slides from another presentation, they are inserted after the current slide.

2. In the Slides group on the Home tab, click the **New Slide button arrow**. A menu appears with slide layouts for the Office theme and other items.

3. Click **Reuse Slides**. The Reuse Slides task pane opens on the right side of the window.

4. In the task pane, click the **Browse** button, and then click **Browse File**. The Browse dialog box opens.

5. Navigate to the **Tutorial.03\Tutorial** folder, and then double-click **CFSales**. The five slides from the CFSales presentation appear in the Reuse Slides task pane. See Figure 3-2.

Figure 3-2 ▶ **Slide 3 and the Reuse Slides task pane**

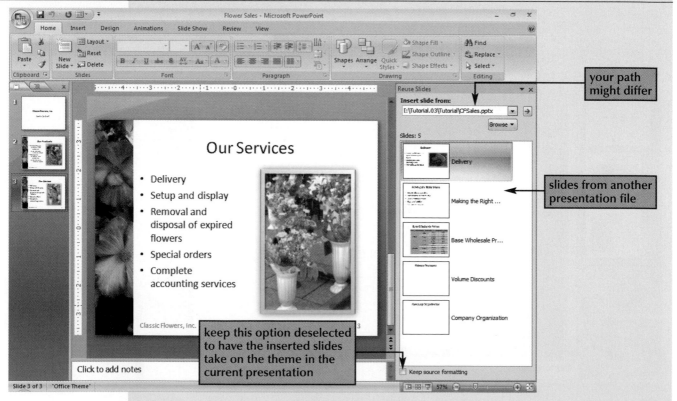

▶ **6.** At the bottom of the task pane, make sure the **Keep source formatting** check box is unchecked. You don't want to keep the formatting of the inserted slides, but rather you want the new slides to take on the formatting (the theme) of the current Flower Sales presentation.

▶ **7.** Point to the first slide, "Delivery," in the task pane. The slide increases in size so that you can read its content.

▶ **8.** Click the **Delivery** slide. It is inserted into the Flower Sales presentation after the current slide (Slide 3).

▶ **9.** Insert the other four slides, one at a time. See Figure 3-3.

Slide 8 after inserting five slides from another presentation ◀ **Figure 3-3**

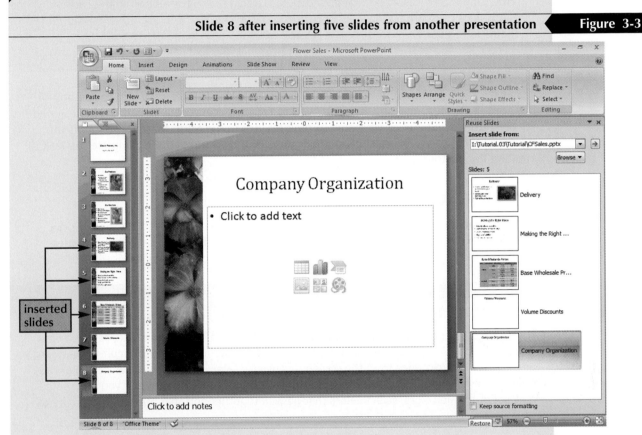

▶ **10.** In the task pane title bar, click the **Close** button ☒.

The five slides from CFSales are now Slides 4 through 8 of Flower Sales. Some of the new slides contain bulleted lists or a table of sales information; others contain only a title. Notice that the newly inserted slides take on the modified Office theme of the current presentation.

With most of the slides now created for the presentation, you're ready to create a custom theme.

Creating a Custom Theme

As you recall, a theme is a presentation design that contains the color, attributes, and format for the titles, bulleted lists, other text, and background for the presentation. You have already used several themes that come with PowerPoint. Sometimes, however, you'll want to design your own, custom theme. After you create a custom theme, you can save the presentation as a normal PowerPoint presentation file and then create a new presentation based on the customized presentation, or you can save a presentation as an Office theme, which you can easily apply to other presentations.

Reference Window | **Creating and Saving a Custom Theme**

- Using an existing or new presentation, create the desired theme colors, bullets, fonts, background color, and background graphics.
- Click the Office Button, click Save As to open the Save As dialog box, click the Save as type arrow, and then click Office Theme; *or* click the Design tab on the Ribbon, in the Themes group, click the More button, and then click Save Current Theme to open the Save Current Theme dialog box with Office Theme already selected in the Save as type box.
- Navigate to the desired location, type a filename, and then click the Save button.

Tip

You can press the F12 key to open the Save As dialog box.

For the sales presentation for Classic Flowers, Sophie doesn't want you to use any of the built-in themes; instead, she wants you to create a completely original one designed for her business. She likes the panel of pink flowers in the Slide Master and wants the new theme to match the subject and the colors of the picture. You'll complete the task of creating the custom theme.

Creating Custom Theme Colors

Theme colors are coordinating colors that make up the background, title fonts, body fonts, and other elements of the presentation. Each of the built-in PowerPoint themes, including the default Office theme, has a set of colors associated with it.

InSight | Selecting Theme Colors

It's easy to select colors that don't match or make text illegible; for example, red text on a blue background might seem like a good combination, but it's actually difficult to read for an audience at a distance from the screen. It's usually safer, therefore, to select one of the built-in theme colors and stick with it, or make only minor modifications. If you do create a new set of theme colors, select colors that go well together and that maximize legibility of your slides.

The PowerPoint theme colors are a set of 12 colors that have general purposes. These are the 12 colors:

- **Text/Background – Dark 1**, **Text/Background – Light 1**, **Text/Background – Dark 2**, and **Text/Background – Light 2**: These four colors provide you with two possible schemes for light text on a dark background and two possible schemes for dark text on a light background. In practice, you would never select dark text on dark background or light text on light background.
- **Accent 1** through **Accent 6**: These six colors provide colors for lines, shapes, charts, tables, shadows, picture borders, and other objects that might appear on your presentation slides.
- **Hyperlink**: This is the default color for hyperlinked text.
- **Followed hyperlink**: This is the default color for hyperlinks that have been followed. In other words, if you click on a hyperlink and thereby jump to another location, when you return to the original slide, the color of the hyperlink text will be changed to indicate that you have followed that hyperlink.

After you have specified a coordinated set of theme colors, they will appear by default in text and objects, but you can use any of the 12 colors to change the default color of text, fills, shadows, and so forth.

The current presentation uses the color theme called "Office," which is the default set of colors used when the Office theme is applied. The default background color is white and the default text color is black (except for the gray subtitle on the title slide). Sophie feels that this simple theme doesn't fit well with the sales presentation on potted flowers and bouquets. In fact, as you look at the pictures of the flowers in Sophie's presentations, you see mostly warm colors—pinks, reds, violets, oranges, and yellows—so you'll create a set of theme colors using those colors, as well as some greens to match leaf colors and to offer contrast.

You can create the theme colors with any slide in the slide pane, but here you'll want to move to Slide 2 so you can see how the color changes appear on a slide that contains bulleted text and a photograph. You'll create the theme colors now.

To create custom theme colors:

▶ **1.** Go to **Slide 2**, so that a bulleted-list slide appears in the slide pane.

▶ **2.** Click the **Design** tab on the Ribbon. The Ribbon changes to display the available themes, the Colors button, the Fonts button, and others.

▶ **3.** In the Themes group, click the **Colors** button to display the Colors menu. See Figure 3-4. PowerPoint displays the built-in color sets, a set of eight color tiles, for each of the built-in themes. The eight tiles correspond to the second two Text/Background colors and the six accent colors.

Viewing the Colors menu ◁ **Figure 3-4**

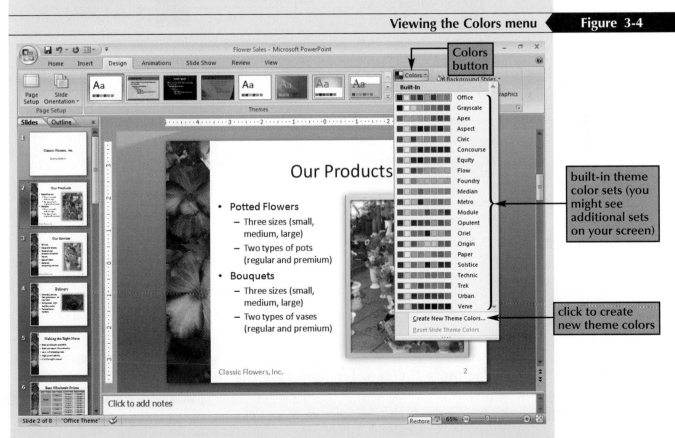

▶ 4. Click **Create New Theme Colors** at the bottom of the Colors menu. The Create New Theme Colors dialog box opens. Here, you can see color tiles representing each of the 12 theme colors of the Office theme. The Sample section of the dialog box shows sample slides with dark and light backgrounds. You'll change most of these colors, beginning with the Text/Background – Dark 1 color, which you'll change to dark green.

▶ 5. Click the **Text/Background – Dark 1** button to display the Theme Colors palette. Because no dark-green tile appears in the palette, you'll look at more colors.

▶ 6. At the bottom of the palette, click **More Colors** to display the Colors dialog box, and then, if necessary, click the **Standard** tab. See Figure 3-5.

Figure 3-5 **Colors dialog box with theme colors**

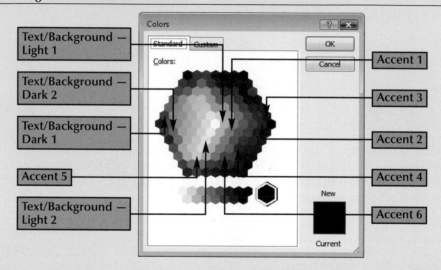

▶ 7. Click the dark-green tile for Text/Background – Dark 1 as indicated in Figure 3-5, and then click the **OK** button. The Colors dialog box closes. The Text/Background – Dark 1 color changes from black to dark green, and the title text in the right panel in the Sample area of the Create New Theme Colors dialog box changes to dark green also.

You'll now change the color of the light text on the dark background from white to light pink.

▶ 8. Click the **Text/Background – Light 1** button to display the Theme Colors gallery again. The lightest pink tile in the gallery is not light enough.

▶ 9. Click **More Colors**, click the light-pink tile shown in Figure 3-5, and then click the **OK** button. The title text on the dark background in the panel on the left in the Sample area changes to light pink.

So far, you have changed the first two theme colors. You'll now change several of the others.

To change more theme colors and save the custom colors:

▶ 1. With the Create New Theme Colors dialog box still open, click the **Text/Background – Dark 2** button, click **More Colors**, click the **Standard** tab, click the green tile as indicated in Figure 3-5, and then click the **OK** button.

2. Change each of the next seven theme colors to the color indicated in Figure 3-5. (Do not change the Hyperlink or Followed Hyperlink colors.)

3. In the Create New Theme Colors dialog box, select all of the text in the **Name** text box, and then type **Flower**. See Figure 3-6.

Create New Theme Colors dialog box with new colors | **Figure 3-6**

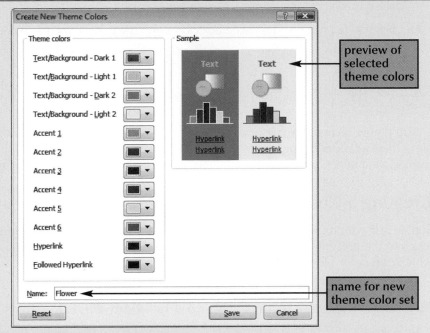

Trouble? If you clicked the Save button before you changed the name, you can edit it. On the Design tab, in the Themes group, click the Colors button, and then locate the custom theme you created. It will appear at the top of the menu and will be named "Custom" followed by a number. Right-click the custom theme, and then, on the shortcut menu, click Edit. Continue with Step 4.

4. Click the **Save** button in the Create New Theme Colors dialog box. The dialog box closes and the theme is applied.

5. In the Themes group, click the **Colors** button. The Flower custom color theme you created appears at the top of the list under "Custom."

6. Press the **Esc** key to close the menu.

7. Save the presentation using the default name.

As you can see in Slide 2, the title and body text are now dark green and the background is light pink. If you look at the slide thumbnails in the pane on the left, you see that those slides also have dark-green text with light-pink background.

Deleting Custom Theme Colors

You can delete a custom theme or theme colors. If you've applied the theme or the theme colors to a presentation, and then saved that presentation, the theme and colors will still be applied to that presentation even if you delete the theme or theme colors from the hard drive. You'll delete the custom theme colors you created. To access the Colors menu, a presentation must be open.

To delete custom theme colors:

▶ **1.** Click the **Design** tab on the Ribbon, and then, in the Themes group, click the **Colors** button. The Colors menu opens.

▶ **2.** Right-click the **Flower** theme color set at the top of the list under Custom.

▶ **3.** On the shortcut menu, click **Delete**. A dialog box opens asking if you want to delete these theme colors.

▶ **4.** Click the **Yes** button. The dialog box closes and the custom theme colors are deleted.

▶ **5.** In the Themes group, click the **Colors** button. Note that the Flower theme colors are deleted.

▶ **6.** Click a blank area of the window to close the menu.

You'll now change the background style of the slides. You've already used the Create New Theme Colors dialog box to change the background to a solid light pink, but if you want special effects, such as shading, you must use the Background Styles gallery.

Creating a Custom Background

Sophie asks you to add shading to the background to add interest and a professional touch to the presentation. You decide to use a **gradient fill**, which is a type of shading in which one color blends into another or varies from one shade to another.

To change the background style to a gradient fill:

▶ **1.** Make sure **Slide 2** appears in the slide pane and the **Design** tab is the active tab on the Ribbon.

▶ **2.** In the Background group, click the **Background Styles** button. The Background Styles gallery appears. See Figure 3-7.

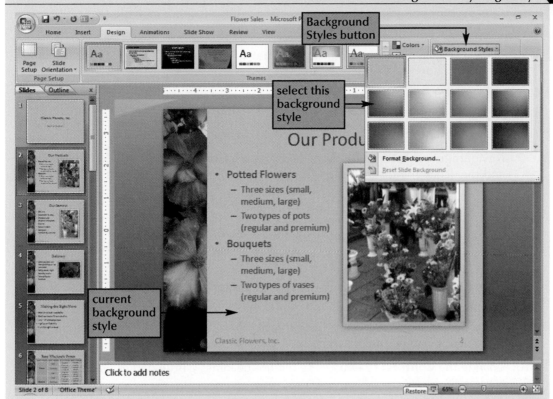

Figure 3-7   Background Styles gallery

The Background Styles gallery includes 12 styles—four solid colors along the top row corresponding to the four Text/Background theme colors and two gradient styles for each of those colors.

▶ **3.** Click **Style 5**, which is the second background style from the top in the first column. The backgrounds of the slides now vary from dark pink (or violet) in the lower-left corner to light pink in the upper-right corner.

▶ **4.** Save the presentation using the default filename.

As you can see from the slide pane and the slide thumbnails in the pane on the left, all of the slides now have a background with a gradient fill. You'll now add a picture to the background of Slide 1.

Adding a Background Picture

Sophie now wants you to add a photo of a bed of flowers to the background of Slide 1. You'll add it to the Title Slide layout in the Slide Master so it becomes part of the design theme. As you might recall, the Slide Master contains the objects that appear on the slide layouts, and the Title Slide layout contains the objects that appear only on the title slide.

To apply a background picture to a slide:

▶ **1.** Click the **View** tab on the Ribbon, and then, in the Presentation Views group, click the **Slide Master** button. Slide Master view opens and the Ribbon changes to display the Slide Master tab.

▶ **2.** Click the **Title Slide Layout** thumbnail, the second thumbnail from the top in the pane on the left.

▶ **3.** In the Background group on the Slide Master tab, click the **Background Styles** button. The Background Styles gallery again appears on the screen.

▶ **4.** Below the gallery in the menu, click **Format Background**. The Format Background dialog box opens with Fill selected in the list on the left.

▶ **5.** Click the **Picture or texture fill** option button. The dialog box changes to display commands for customizing a background with a texture or a picture.

▶ **6.** Click the **File** button. The Insert Picture dialog box opens.

▶ **7.** Navigate to the **Tutorial.03\Tutorial** folder, click the picture file **PinkFlowerBG**, and then click the **Insert** button. The Insert Picture dialog box closes and the picture is inserted into the background of Slide 1 behind the Format Background dialog box.

Sophie likes the background picture, but is concerned that it is too bright and has too much contrast, making it hard for the audience to read the text on the slide. You'll adjust the brightness and contrast.

▶ **8.** Click **Picture** in the left pane of the Format Background dialog box. The dialog box changes to include commands for modifying the picture on the background.

▶ **9.** Drag the **Brightness** slider to the left until the box indicates **–30%**. Watch the picture change behind the dialog box.

▶ **10.** Change the **Contrast** to **–40%**. The picture becomes a little darker but with less contrast.

▶ **11.** Click the **Close** button in the dialog box. See Figure 3-8.

Figure 3-8 | **Picture background in the Title Slide Layout master**

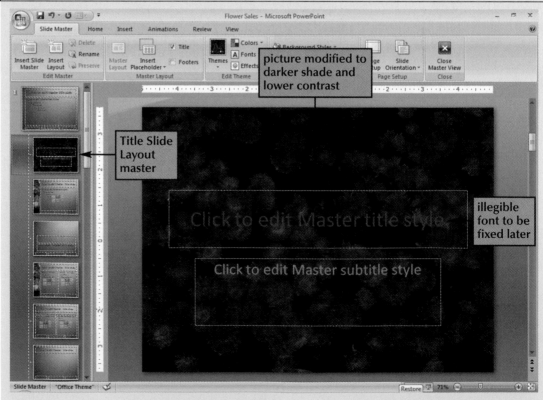

The backgrounds appear as Sophie wants them, but she now wants you to make the title text on the slides stand out more. You'll change the title text font, and then modify its size, style, and color.

Modifying Fonts and Bullets

The font used for all of the text in the presentation is Calibri. This is a good, general-purpose font, but Sophie feels that it doesn't stand out enough as a title font. You'll change the title font, increase its size, and format it as bold. By making the changes in Slide Master view, you'll change the fonts on all the slides in the presentation.

To modify the fonts in Slide Master view:

1. Click the **Office Theme Slide Master**, the large thumbnail at the top of the left pane.

2. Click the edge of the title placeholder, which contains the phrase "Click to edit Master title style." Make sure the title box has a solid line around it, not just a dashed line, so the entire text box is selected.

3. Click the **Home** tab, and then, in the Font group, click the **Font button arrow** to display a menu of fonts.

4. Click **Arial Rounded MT Bold**.

   Trouble? If Arial Rounded MT Bold doesn't appear in your list of fonts, select Arial Black, AvantGarde Md BT, or some other font that stands out.

5. In the Font group, click the **Font Size button arrow**, and then click **48** to increase the font size to 48 points.

   The title fonts on all the slides stand out more now, except on the Title Slide Master, where the dark background with dark text makes the text illegible. You'll fix that problem now.

6. Click the **Title Slide Layout** thumbnail, and then select the title text placeholder, which currently contains dark-green text.

7. Click the **Font Color button arrow** ![A] to display the theme colors palette.

8. Click the **Light Yellow, Background 2** tile, located third from the left in the top row in the palette under Theme Colors.

9. Using the same method, change the subtitle to **Yellow, Accent 5** (located second from the right in the top row of tiles).

10. Deselect the text box. See Figure 3-9.

Figure 3-9 Title Slide Layout master with modified title text

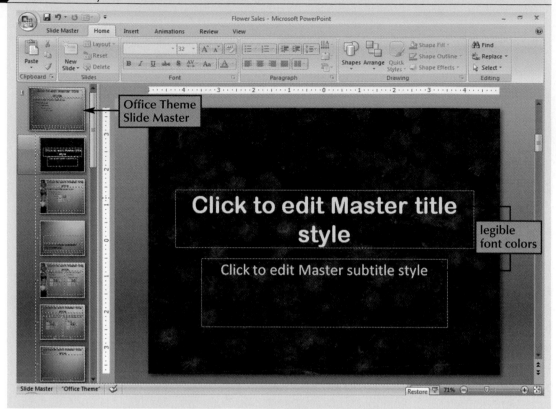

You have changed the font attributes so the title text stands out more. Now you'll change the bullets.

To change the bullets style in Slide Master view:

▶ 1. Click the **Office Theme Slide Master** thumbnail to display the Slide Master in the slide pane.

▶ 2. Click anywhere in the first bulleted item, which says "Click to edit Master text styles."

▶ 3. In the Paragraph group on the Home tab, click the **Bullets button arrow** [icon] to display the Bullets gallery. You could select one of the standard bullets shown here in the gallery, but instead, Sophie wants you to select a picture bullet.

▶ 4. Click **Bullets and Numbering** at the bottom of the Bullets gallery to display the Bullets and Numbering dialog box with the Bulleted tab on top.

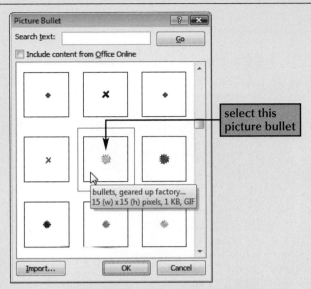

7. Click the bullet indicated in Figure 3-10, and then click the **OK** button. Both dialog boxes close, and the picture bullet you selected becomes the first-level bullet in the body text. Now you'll change the second-level bullet.

8. Click anywhere in the "Second level" line, and then open the Bullets and Numbering dialog box with the Bulleted tab on top.

9. Click the **Filled Square Bullets** style in the top row. Sophie wants you to change the color to the Accent 5 theme color (yellow).

10. Click the **Color** button in the lower-left corner of the dialog box, and then click the **Yellow, Accent 5** tile, the same color you selected for the subtitle text on the Title Master.

11. Click the **OK** button in the Bullets and Numbering dialog box.

12. Select the footer and slide number placeholders at the bottom of the slide, and then change the color of the text to **Yellow, Accent 5**. Deselect the placeholders. See Figure 3-11.

Figure 3-11 **Slide Master with modified bullets**

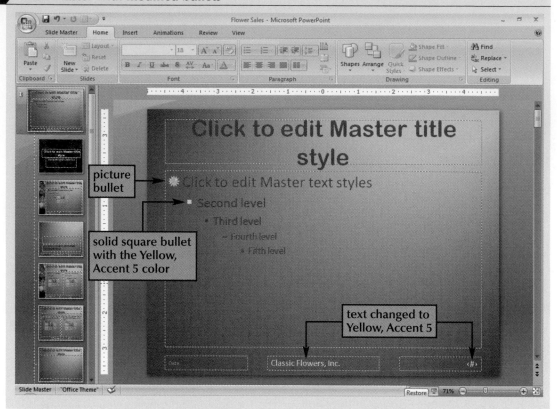

You'll now return to Normal view, see how the slides look, and then save the presentation.

To view the presentation and save it:

▶ **1.** On the status bar, click the **Normal** button ⊞ . Slide Master view closes and the Slide Master tab disappears from the Ribbon. You see the changes you made in Slide 2.

▶ **2.** Go to **Slide 4**. As you can see, the new font didn't automatically change to match the Slide Masters on the slides that you inserted from the other presentation file, and the footer and slide number don't appear on the slide. You'll fix these problems now.

▶ **3.** Click the **Insert** tab on the Ribbon, and then, in the Text group click the **Header & Footer** button. The Header and Footer dialog box opens with the Slide tab on top.

▶ **4.** Click the **Slide number** and **Footer** check boxes to select them, and then click the **Apply to All** button. The dialog box closes and the slide number and footer appear on all the slides.

▶ **5.** Click the **Home** tab, and then, in the Slides group, click the **Reset** button. The Reset button resets the position, size, and formatting of the slide placeholders in the current slide to the default settings, meaning to the settings found in the Slide Masters. Notice that the border on the picture of the rose disappeared because this setting is not part of the Slide Masters. You'll restore the border now.

▶ **6.** Click the picture to select it, and then click the Picture Tools **Format** contextual tab.

7. In the Picture Styles group, click the **Metal Frame** style.

8. Drag the picture up so that its top is aligned with the first bullet in the bulleted list.

9. Proceed through all the slides, and on each slide, as necessary, reset the title font to the Slide Master font and reposition the table in Slide 6.

10. Save the presentation using the default filename.

Your custom theme is now complete, with its customized theme colors, gradient background, new fonts, and pictures of flowers in the background of all the slides. Sophie asks you to save the custom theme so she can apply it to other presentations.

Saving a Custom Theme

In earlier tutorials, you applied built-in themes by clicking the Design tab on the Ribbon to display the Themes group, and then selecting the desired theme. What if you wanted to apply the flower theme in a similar way? That's exactly what Sophie wants to do. To make that possible, she wants you to save the presentation as an Office theme. An **Office theme** is the file type that serves as a design theme. It has the filename extension ".thmx". You can use an Office theme file to apply a custom theme to an existing PowerPoint presentation or you can create a new presentation based on the custom theme.

The default location for saving a PowerPoint presentation as a theme is the Document Themes folder located in the Templates folder, but you can save a theme in any folder. No matter where you save your theme, you can create a new presentation based on that theme by clicking Browse for Themes at the bottom of the Themes gallery.

Understanding the Difference Between a Theme and a Template	InSight

When you save a PowerPoint presentation as a theme, only the design elements (including background graphics) are saved, not the content, that is, not the text or objects applied to the slides. If you want to save a theme with the contents for use in other presentations, you would instead save the presentation as a PowerPoint template.

You've saved your work as a normal PowerPoint presentation. Now you'll save it as a theme, and then test it by creating a new presentation based on this theme.

To save a presentation as a theme:

1. Click the **Office Button** (🔘), and then click **Save As**. The Save As dialog box opens.

2. Click the **Save as type arrow** near the bottom of the dialog box.

3. Click **Office Theme** in the list. The current folder changes to Document Themes, but you want to save your theme file in the same location where you saved Flower Sales (in the Tutorial.03\Tutorial folder included with your Data Files).

4. Change the current folder to the **Tutorial.03\Tutorial** folder included with your Data Files (or to the location where you saved Flower Sales).

> **5.** Edit the text in the File name text box to **Flower**, and then click the **Save** button. PowerPoint saves the file as a theme.

If you had saved the theme to the default Themes folder, it would have appeared as a custom theme in the Themes gallery when you clicked the More button. To delete a custom theme, you right-click it, and then click Delete on the shortcut menu.

You have now created a custom theme that Sophie and others can use with any new presentation.

Using a Custom Theme

You decide to test your new custom theme on a new presentation.

To start a new presentation using a custom theme:

> **1.** Click the **Office Button** 🔘, click **New**, and then with the Blank Presentation selected in the Blank and recent section of the New Presentation dialog box, click the **Create** button. PowerPoint creates a new presentation.

> **2.** Click the **Design** tab on the Ribbon, and then, in the Themes group, click the **More** button.

> **3.** Below the Themes gallery click **Browse for Themes**. The Choose Theme or Themed Document dialog box opens.

> **4.** Navigate to the **Tutorial.03\Tutorial** folder included with your Data Files, and then double-click the Office theme file **Flower**. This is the theme you created and saved. The new presentation now has the Flower theme applied. It has only one slide, the title slide, and it has no text.

> **5.** Close the presentation without saving it. Keep Flower Sales open in PowerPoint.

You can now report to Sophie that your custom theme works as planned. You can still make changes to customize the background of a slide after a theme is applied. You'll make a change to the background of one of the slides now.

Adding a Textured Background

Sophie wants to highlight Slide 6, which contains a table of the base wholesale prices of Classic Flowers's products. She decides that she wants you to add a textured background to the slide. You'll do that now.

Applying a Textured Background | Reference Window

- Go to the slide to which you want to apply the textured background.
- Click the Design tab on the Ribbon.
- In the Background group, click the Background Styles button, and then click Format Background at the bottom of the backgrounds gallery to open the Format Background dialog box.
- Click the Picture or texture file option button.
- Click the Texture button to display a gallery of textured backgrounds.
- Click the desired texture and then click the Close button if you want to apply the textured background just to the current slide, or click the Apply to All button if you want to apply the textured background to all the slides in the presentation.

You'll now apply a "pink tissue paper" texture to the background of Slide 6.

To add a textured background:

▶ 1. Go to **Slide 6**, and then, if necessary, click the **Design** tab on the Ribbon.

▶ 2. In the Background group, click the **Background Styles** button, and then click **Format Background**. The Format Background dialog box opens with Fill selected on the left.

▶ 3. Click the **Picture or texture fill** option button. The dialog box changes to include commands for inserting a picture or a fill.

▶ 4. Click the **Texture button** ▦ ▾ . **A gallery of textured backgrounds appears. As you can see, PowerPoint has 25 built-in textures to choose from.**

▶ 5. Click the **Pink tissue paper** texture, located in row 4, column 3. The background of the slide changes to pink tissue paper behind the dialog box.

▶ 6. Click the **Close** button. See Figure 3-12.

Figure 3-12 **Slide 6 with textured background**

7. Save the presentation using the default filename.

Sophie is pleased with how Slide 6 stands out from the others, and is happy with the progress you're making on the presentation.

Review | **Session 3.1 Quick Check**

1. Describe how you insert slides from one presentation into another.
2. What are theme colors?
3. In creating a custom theme, what are four (or more) elements in your presentation that you might want to change?
4. What is a gradient fill, as it pertains to a slide background?
5. Describe how you save a PowerPoint presentation as an Office theme.
6. How do you apply a textured background to a slide?

Session 3.2

Inserting Sounds and Movies into Your Presentation

PowerPoint allows you to add various types of graphics and sounds to your presentation. You're already familiar with adding clip art, drawn images, and digital photos to a slide. In fact, the original Flowers and CFSales presentation files came with images of flowers and bouquets, and you have already inserted the image of a flower bed into the slide background of the title slide. In addition to still photos and other graphics, you can insert sounds and movies into a presentation.

| **Inserting a Sound into a Presentation** | Reference Window |

- Go to the slide in which you want to insert the sound.
- Click the Insert tab on the Ribbon.
- In the Media Clips group, click the Sound button arrow, and then on the menu, click the desired source of the sound file.
- Select the sound file from a specified folder and click the OK button.
- When asked how you want the sound to start in the slide show, click the Automatically or When Clicked button.

Sophie feels that you can improve the Flower Sales presentation by adding sound clips, a video clip, and other special effects. You'll use sound and video files that are included with your Data Files. In other presentations, you might have to acquire the sounds and videos in other ways. For example, you can do the following:

- Record sound files with a microphone attached to your computer and appropriate software.
- Use a digital camera with video capture or use a video camera to take digital videos.
- Create images or movies using graphics software.
- Download images or sound clips from the Internet.
- Insert images or sounds from the Clip Organizer, which might include sound or movie files that you have made and that you have downloaded from Office Online.
- Use built-in PowerPoint sound effects.

Inserting Sound Clips

Sophie wants you to add two sound clips, a recording of "Welcome to Classic Flowers" and a sound clip of applause. Sophie's recordings are in .wav files, which is the most common file format for short sound clips.

You can add a sound clip to a slide in several ways. You can use the Insert Media Clip button in a content layout placeholder, or you can use the Insert tab on the Ribbon. You'll add the sound files now using the Insert tab.

To add sound clips to the presentation:

▶ **1.** If you took a break after Session 1, start PowerPoint and make sure the Flower Sales presentation is open.

▶ **2.** Go to **Slide 1**, and then click the **Insert** tab on the Ribbon.

▶ **3.** In the Media Clips group, click the **Sound** button. The Insert Sound dialog box opens.

▶ **4.** Navigate to the **Tutorial.03\Tutorial** folder included with your Data Files. This folder contains two sound files, Applause and CFISound.

▶ **5.** Click **CFISound**, and then click the **OK** button. A dialog box opens displaying the question "How do you want the sound to start in the slide show?" Sophie wants the sound to start automatically when she displays Slide 1 in Slide Show view.

▶ **6.** Click the **Automatically** button. The dialog box closes and a sound icon 🔊 appears in the middle of the slide to indicate that a sound clip is available on that slide. Notice that a special effects icon appears below the slide in the Slides tab. See Figure 3-13.

Figure 3-13 ▶ **Slide 1 with sound icon**

▶ **7.** Double-click the **sound** icon 🔊 to play the sound clip. In Slide Show view, the sound will automatically play whenever you display Slide 1. You can also click the sound icon during the slide show to make the sound play again.

Now that you know how to insert a sound clip, Sophie wants you to insert another one in Slide 4.

To add another sound clip:

▶ **1.** Go to **Slide 4** ("Delivery"). Sophie wants you to insert the applause sound clip to celebrate the positive features of the Classic Flowers delivery system.

2. Insert the sound clip **Applause**, located in the **Tutorial.03\Tutorial** folder included with your Data Files, into Slide 4, and again select the **Automatically** button in the dialog box asking how you want the sound clip to start.

3. Double-click the **sound** icon 🔊 to test the sound clip. Sophie doesn't want this sound icon to be visible on the screen during the slide show, so you'll hide it behind the flower picture.

4. Drag the **sound** icon 🔊 so it's located anywhere on top of the framed flower picture on the right of the text.

5. With the sound icon still selected, click the **Format** tab below Picture Tools on the Ribbon.

6. In the Arrange group, click the **Send to Back** button. The selected sound icon disappears behind the flower picture. You can still see the sizing handles of the sound icon.

7. Click a blank area of the slide to deselect the sound icon.

8. Save the presentation using the default filename.

Now, when Sophie uses Flower Sales in a sales presentation, the slide show will have sound effects to add interest.

Inserting a Movie

A **video clip**, or **digital movie**, is an animated picture file. PowerPoint supports various file formats, but the most common one for PowerPoint presentations is the Windows video file, which has the extension ".avi".

Sophie wants you to insert a short video of a chess piece being moved as part of Slide 5, "Making the Right Move."

Inserting a Movie into a Presentation | Reference Window

- Go to the slide in which you want to insert the movie.
- Change the layout to include an empty content layout, and then click the Insert Media Clip button in the content layout placeholder to open the Insert Movie dialog box, *or* click the Insert tab on the Ribbon, in the Media Clips group, click the Movie button. The Insert Movie dialog box opens.
- Navigate to the folder containing the movie, click the movie filename from a specified folder, and then click the OK button.
- When asked how you want the movie or sound to start in the slide show, click the Automatically or When Clicked button.

You can insert a video clip in two different ways. You can change the layout to one of the content layouts, click the Insert Media Clip button, and then use the Insert Movie dialog box, or you can use the Movie button in the Media Clips group on the Insert tab. You'll add the movie now using the Insert Media Clip button in a content layout.

To add a movie to a slide:

1. Go to **Slide 5** ("Making the Right Move") and then, if necessary, click the **Home** tab on the Ribbon.

2. In the Slides group, click the **Layout** button, and then click the **Two Content** layout.

▶ 3. Click the **Insert Media Clip** button 🖼 in the content placeholder. The Insert Movie dialog box opens.

▶ 4. Navigate to the **Tutorial.03\Tutorial** folder included with your Data Files, click **RightMove**, and then click the **OK** button. The dialog box asks if you want to play the movie automatically or when you click the icon.

▶ 5. Click the **Automatically** button. The first frame of the movie appears in the right side of the slide. Now you'll change the Picture Style of the movie.

▶ 6. With the movie frame selected, click the **Format** tab below Picture Tools on the Ribbon.

▶ 7. In the Picture Styles group, click the **Metal Frame** style (the third thumbnail from the left). See Figure 3-14. Now the frame around the movie photo matches the frame around the other pictures in the presentation.

Figure 3-14 ▶ **Slide 5 with movie**

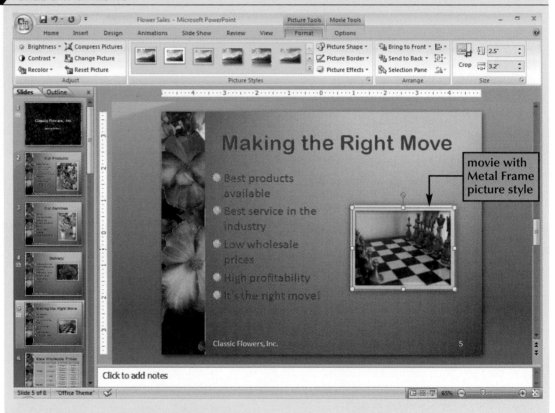

Having inserted the digital movie and changed its picture style, you are now ready to view it.

▶ 8. Double-click the picture of the movie. As you can see, the movie shows a chess player making the first move.

Trouble? If the movie was slow to start, don't worry. On some computers, it might take a moment after you double-click the picture for the movie to begin.

Because you clicked the Automatically button when you inserted the movie, it will play when Slide 5 appears during the slide show.

When you insert a movie, you can choose from a few other options to play the movie. You can play the movie full screen, so that it fills the entire screen. You can also set the movie to Loop Until Stopped, which means the movie will play over and over again until you advance to the next slide in Slide Show view. Finally, you can choose the Rewind the Movie After Playing option, which means that, when it's over, the picture on the slide returns to the first frame of the movie rather than stopping on the last frame. Sophie wants the movie to play full screen.

To set the movie to full-screen viewing:

▶ **1.** Make sure the movie is still selected, and then click the **Options** tab below Movie Tools on the Ribbon, if necessary.

▶ **2.** In the Movie Options group, click the **Play Full Screen** check box. Now you'll see what the movie looks like in Slide Show view.

▶ **3.** On the status bar, click the **Slide Show** button 🖵 to start the slide show from the current slide. Slide 5 appears in Slide Show view and the movie plays once in full screen, ending with the final frame, and the slide appears again on the screen.

▶ **4.** Press the **Esc** key. The slide show terminates and you return to Normal view.

   Trouble? You might need to press the Esc key twice to stop the movie and the slide show.

▶ **5.** Save the presentation using the default filename.

Creating a Chart (Graph)

A **chart**, or **graph**, is a visual depiction of data in a spreadsheet. The **spreadsheet** is a grid of cells in a Microsoft Excel worksheet. **Cells** are the boxes that are organized in rows and columns, in which you can add data and labels. The rows are numbered 1, 2, 3, and so on, and the columns are labeled A, B, C, and so forth. You can use a chart to show an audience data trends and patterns or to visually compare data.

Creating a Chart (Graph) | Reference Window

- Change the slide layout to one of the content layouts, and then click the Insert Chart button in the content placeholder; *or* click the Insert tab, and then, in the Illustrations group, click the Chart button. The Insert Chart dialog box opens.
- Click one of the chart icons in the Insert Chart gallery, and then click the OK button. PowerPoint automatically opens a Microsoft Excel worksheet.
- Edit the information in the worksheet for the data that you want to plot.
- Modify the chart layout, style, format, data, or other features, as desired.
- Click outside the chart area to make the chart inactive.

Sophie now wants you to create a chart in Slide 7. The chart will give the volume discount prices from the base wholesale prices given in Slide 6. You'll create the chart now.

To insert a chart:

▶ **1.** Go to **Slide 7** ("Volume Discounts"), and then click the **Insert Chart** button 📊 in the content placeholder. The Insert Chart dialog box opens, displaying a gallery of charts. See Figure 3-15.

Figure 3-15 Insert Chart dialog box

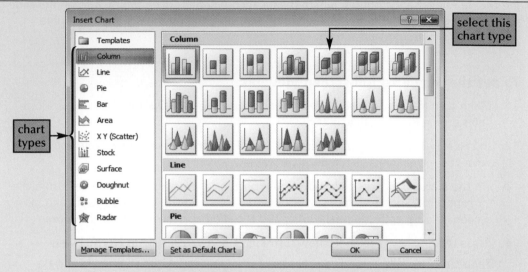

▶ **2.** Click the **Stacked Column in 3D** chart type, which is in the first row, fifth column of the gallery, and then click the **OK** button. PowerPoint inserts a sample chart into Slide 7 and opens a Microsoft Excel worksheet with sample data. See Figure 3-16. You can now use Excel features for inserting and editing data in a worksheet.

Excel spreadsheet with data for chart ◀ Figure 3-16

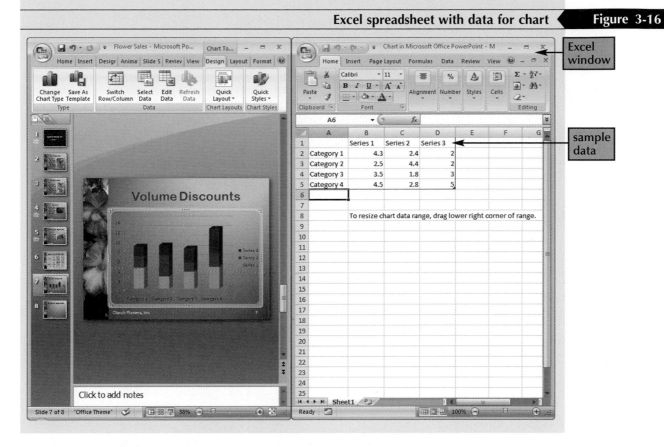

To create the chart for Sophie's presentation, you simply edit the information in the sample spreadsheet on the screen. When you work with a spreadsheet, the cell in which you are entering data is the **active cell**. The active cell has a thick black border around it. In this chart, you want only two columns, one with the number of units ordered (per month) and one with the percent discount. You'll begin by deleting the third and fourth columns of data on the spreadsheet.

To modify the spreadsheet:

▶ **1.** Move the mouse pointer to the top of column C so that the pointer changes to ⬇.

▶ **2.** Click and drag the mouse pointer to select both columns C and D. See Figure 3-17.

Figure 3-17 **Excel spreadsheet with selected columns**

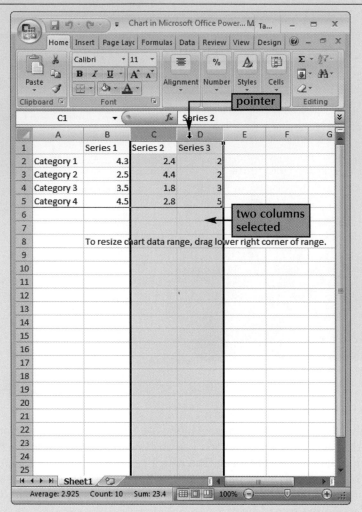

3. Click the **Cells** button on the Home tab in the Excel window, and then click the **Delete** button.

Trouble? If you see the Cells group instead of the Cells button on the Home tab, just click the Delete button located there.

A dialog box opens warning you that a formula in the worksheet contains one or more invalid references.

4. Click the **OK** button. After you finish editing the data, Excel and PowerPoint will fix the problem of invalid references automatically.

5. Click cell **B1**, which currently contains the column label "Series 1."

6. Type **Discount %**, and then press the **Enter** key. Again, you'll get the warning of invalid references, which you will get after each data entry until you finish the chart.

7. Click the **OK** button in the dialog box.

You need to finish modifying the spreadsheet.

To finish modifying the spreadsheet:

1. Click cell **A2** ("Category 1"), type **11-50 Units/Mo**, press the **Enter** key, and then click the **OK** button. The text is entered into cell A2 and cell A3 becomes the active cell. The text in cell A2 is too wide to fit within the cell because the column is too narrow. You'll solve that problem in a moment.

2. Type **51-100 Units/Mo** in cell A3, press the **Enter** key, and then click the **OK** button.

3. Enter **101-300 Units/Mo** in cell A4 and **>300 Units/Mo** in cell A5. Click the **OK** button in the warning dialog box each time it appears.

4. Position the pointer on the divider line between the column A and B headings so that the pointer changes to ↔, and then double-click. The width of column A is automatically resized so that the widest entry in the column fits in its cell.

5. Click the **OK** button in the warning dialog box.

6. Click cell **B2**, type **3**, press the **Enter** key, and then click the **OK** button.

7. Enter **8** in cell B3, **15** in cell B4, and **20** in cell B5, clicking the OK button each time the warning dialog box appears. The new values appear in cells B2 through B5 in Excel and are reflected in the chart in PowerPoint. See Figure 3-18.

Figure 3-18 **Complete Excel spreadsheet with data for chart**

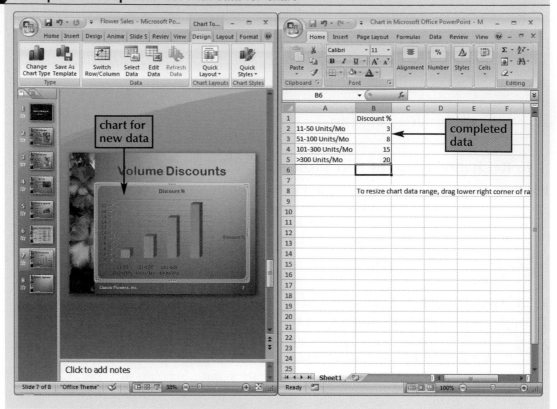

The spreadsheet contains all the necessary data to make the chart. You'll now exit Excel.

To exit Excel and edit the chart:

1. In the title bar in the Excel window, click the **Close** button ⊠. The Excel window closes, the Excel data is saved in the PowerPoint presentation, the PowerPoint window expands to fill the full screen, and the new chart appears in Slide 7. See Figure 3-19.

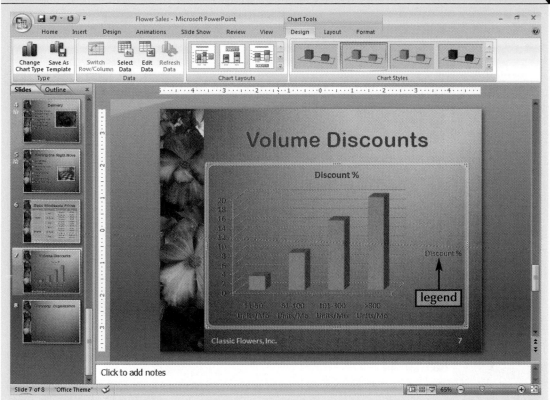

Sophie realizes that the legend on the right side of the chart is unnecessary because all the columns in the chart refer to the discount percentage. You'll now delete the legend.

► **2.** Click the **legend** to the right of the chart columns. The legend is selected.

► **3.** Press the **Delete** key. The legend disappears from the chart, and the graph expands to fill the space that was occupied by the text box you deleted. You'll now change the chart style.

► **4.** If necessary, click the **Design** tab below Chart Tools on the Ribbon.

► **5.** In the Chart Styles group, click **Style 4**, the rightmost style in the Chart Styles gallery. The column colors change from pink to purple.

► **6.** Click outside the chart region to deselect the chart. See Figure 3-20.

Tip

You can also delete the legend using a command on the Ribbon. With the chart selected, click the Layout tab on the Ribbon, in the Labels group click the Legend button, and then click None.

Figure 3-22 **Chart with light-pink background**

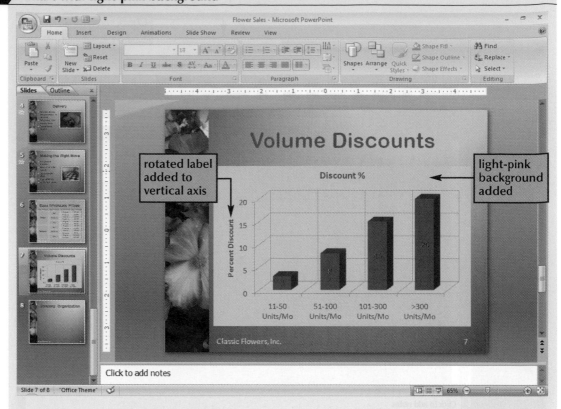

11. Save the presentation.

Sophie is pleased with your chart, which graphically displays the volume discounts offered to customers of Classic Flowers.

Building and Modifying an Organization Chart

Sometimes, potential clients like to know the company organization of Classic Flowers so they know more about the company personnel. Therefore, Sophie wants you to create an organization chart showing key personnel at Classic Flowers. An **organization chart** is a diagram of boxes connected with lines, showing the hierarchy of positions within an organization. Fortunately, PowerPoint provides a feature for easily creating and modifying an organization chart.

| Reference Window

Creating an Organization Chart

- Go to the slide in which you want to insert an organization chart.
- Change the slide layout, if necessary, to one of the content layouts, and then click the Insert SmartArt Graphic button, *or* click the Insert tab, and then, in the Illustrations group, click the SmartArt button. The Choose a SmartArt Graphic dialog box opens.
- Click Hierarchy in the pane on the left side of the dialog box to select the type of SmartArt graphic you want.
- In the SmartArt gallery of hierarchy graphics, click Organization Chart, and then click the OK button.
- In the organization chart boxes, type the personnel names, positions, or other information, as desired.
- Add subordinate and coworker boxes as desired.
- Click anywhere outside the organization chart area.

Now you'll insert an organization chart in Slide 8.

To create an organization chart:

1. Go to **Slide 8** ("Company Organization"), and then click the **Insert SmartArt Graphic** button 📊 in the content placeholder. The Choose a SmartArt Graphic dialog box opens.

2. Click **Hierarchy** in the pane on the left side of the dialog box to display SmartArt only in that category.

3. In the SmartArt gallery of hierarchy graphics, click the **Organization Chart** type (the first chart in the first row), and then click the **OK** button. A sample organization chart, with empty text boxes, appears in the slide.

4. Click in the top (Level 1) box. The placeholder text disappears and the insertion point blinks in the box.

5. Type **Marjory Cordova**, press the **Enter** key, and then type **President and CEO**. The text is difficult to read because it's light pink on darker pink, but you'll fix the problem later.

6. Click the edge of the box just below and to the left of the Level 1 box so that a solid line appears around the box and the entire box is selected. This box represents an assistant to the Level 1, but Sophie doesn't want to show assistants in the organization chart.

7. Press the **Delete** key. The assistant box is deleted from the organization chart.

8. Click in the leftmost subordinate (Level 2) box, type **Darrell McCarty**, press the **Enter** key, and then type **Director of Operations**.

9. Click in the middle Level 2 box, type **Priscilla Rollins**, press the **Enter** key, and then type **Comptroller**.

10. Click the rightmost Level 2 box, type **Sophie De Graff**, press the **Enter** key, and then type **Sales Manager**.

11. Click outside the Level 2 box but inside the organization chart area to deselect the Level 2 box but keep the entire chart selected. See Figure 3-23.

Figure 3-23 | Slide 8 with organization chart

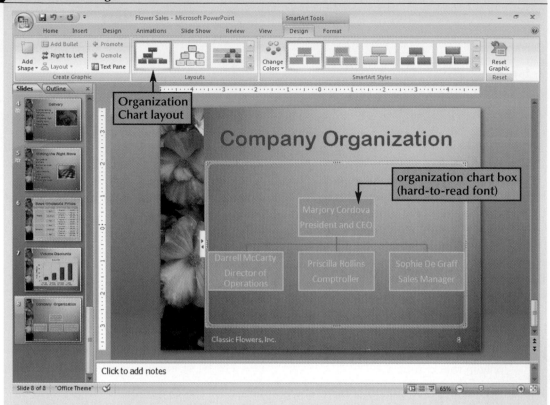

12. Save the presentation.

You have completed part of the organization chart. You'll need to add new boxes, including one more Level 2 box and several subordinate (Level 3) boxes. But first, you'll change the SmartArt style of the organization chart so that the text is more legible.

Changing the Organization Chart Color and Style

To make the text more visible in the organization chart, you could change the text color to, for example, dark green, so it is legible against the pink background, or you could change the background color of the boxes to a darker shade. You'll make the boxes darker.

To change the fill color of the organization chart boxes:

▶ **1.** With the organization chart still selected, click the **Design** tab, if necessary, below SmartArt Tools on the Ribbon.

▶ **2.** In the SmartArt Styles group, click the **Change Colors** button. The Change Colors gallery appears.

▶ **3.** Click the **Dark 2 Fill** icon, the third icon in the first row (under Primary Theme Colors). Now the text is more legible because the boxes have a darker background color. Sophie wants you to add a little interest to the organization chart.

▶ **4.** In the SmartArt Styles group, click the **Intense Effect** style on the far right of the SmartArt Styles gallery. See Figure 3-24.

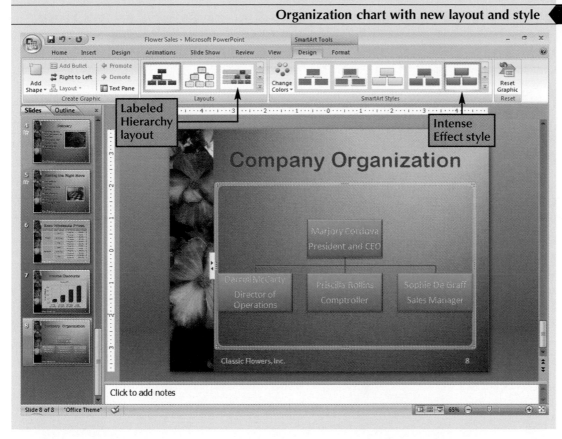

Organization chart with new layout and style ◄ Figure 3-24

Now you're ready to add more organization boxes to your organization chart.

Adding Boxes to an Organization Chart

Sophie now wants you to add a box to the organization chart for Kathleen Bahlmann, the chief horticulturalist for the company. She also reports to Marjory Cordova.

To add boxes to the organization chart:

► **1.** Click the "Priscilla Rollins" box. You'll add a new box to the right of this box.

► **2.** In the Create Graphic group on the Design tab, click the **Add Shape button arrow** to display the Add Shape menu, and then click **Add Shape After**. A new Level 2 box appears between Pricilla Rollins and Sophie De Graff. The new box is selected and ready for you to enter text in it.

► **3.** Type **Kathleen Bahlmann**, press the **Enter** key, and then type **Chief Horticulturalist**. You're now ready to add some Level 3 boxes.

► **4.** With the "Kathleen Bahlmann" box still selected, in the Create Graphic group click the **Add Shape button arrow**, and then click **Add Shape Below**. A box appears below Kathleen Bahlmann.

► **5.** Type **Kyle Wootton**, press the **Enter** key, and then type **Plant Biologist**.

► **6.** Click the "Sophie De Graff" box, and then in the Create Graphic group click the **Add Shape** button. A new box is added below the current box. Clicking the button instead of the arrow below the button inserts the type of box inserted the previous time you clicked the Add Shape button.

▶ **7.** Type **Alberto Pendergrass**, press the **Enter** key, and then type **Sales Rep**.

Sophie doesn't like the way the bent lines look between the Level 2 and Level 3 boxes, so she asks you to modify the style of the chart so that the lines go straight down.

▶ **8.** In the Layouts group, point to each of the three styles in the gallery to see how each one looks.

▶ **9.** Click the **Labeled Hierarchy** button. Now you need to increase the font size within the boxes of the organization chart.

▶ **10.** With the organization chart still selected, click the **Home** tab.

▶ **11.** In the Font group, click the **Font Size button arrow**, click **16**, and then deselect the organization chart. See Figure 3-25.

Figure 3-25	Slide 8 with completed organization chart

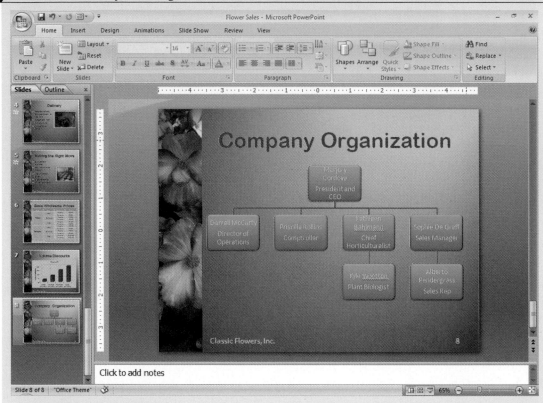

▶ **12.** Save the presentation.

This completes Slide 8 with its organization chart, and completes the text and content of all the slides in the Flower Sales presentation. The only thing left to do is add some special effects and animations.

Applying Special Effects

Special effects—such as fading out of one slide as another appears, animated (moving) text, and sound effects to accompany these actions—can liven up your presentation, help hold your audience's attention, and emphasize key points. On the other hand, special effects can also distract or even annoy your audience. Your goal is to apply special effects conservatively and tastefully so that, rather than making your presentation look gawky and amateurish, they add a professional look and feel to your slide show.

Using Special Effects		InSight

- Don't feel that you must include special effects in your slides. Special effects can distract your audience from the message of the presentation. When in doubt, leave them out.
- If you include transitions, use only one type of transition for all the slides. This will keep your audience from trying to guess what the next transition will be and, instead, will help them stay focused on your message.
- If you include bulleted-list animation, use only one type of animation for all the bulleted lists in the slides. This will keep your presentation consistent and conservative.
- Use sound effects sparingly, just enough to provide emphasis, but not enough to distract the audience from your message.

Sophie wants you to add a few special effects to your presentation. The first special effect that you will add is slide transitions.

Adding Slide Transitions

A slide **transition** is a method of moving one slide off the screen and bringing another slide onto the screen during a slide show. Although applying transitions is usually easier in Slide Sorter view because you can easily select several (or all) slides at once, you can also apply a transition in Normal view.

Adding Slide Transitions		Reference Window

- Switch to Slide Sorter view, and then select the slide(s) to which you want to add a transition.
- Click the Animations tab on the Ribbon.
- In the Transition to This Slide group, click the More button to display the gallery of transition effects.
- Click the desired transition effect in the gallery.
- In the Transition to This Slide group, click the Transition Sound button arrow to insert a sound effect that accompanies each transition.
- In the Transition to This Slide group, click the Transition Speed button arrow to modify the speed of the transition.
- In the Transition to This Slide group, click the Apply To All button to apply the transition to all the slides in the presentation.

You'll add a transition to all the slides in the presentation.

To add a transition effect:

▶ **1.** On the status bar, click the **Slide Sorter** button 🔡 to switch to Slide Sorter view.

▶ **2.** Drag the **Zoom** slider on the status bar to the left to set the zoom to about 95% so you can see all eight slides at once and still have the slides as large as possible.

3. Click the **Animations** tab on the Ribbon. You're going to apply a transition to all the slides in the presentation. You must select at least one slide to make the commands on this tab available.

4. Click **Slide 2**.

5. In the Transition to This Slide group, click the **More** button to display the gallery of slide transitions.

6. Click the **Wipe Right** transition located in the top row, third column under Wipes. PowerPoint previews the transition, and a special effects icon 🌠 appears below the lower-left corner of Slide 2. See Figure 3-26.

Figure 3-26 | **Presentation in Slide Sorter view after applying transition effect**

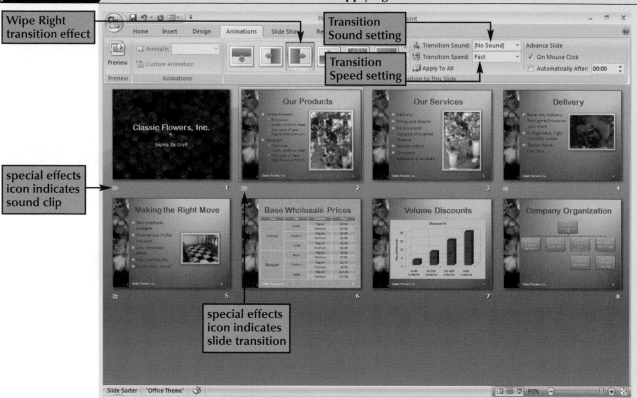

You can change the speed of the transition using the Transition Speed button arrow.

7. In the Transition to This Slide group, click the **Transition Speed button arrow**, and then click **Medium**. This sets the speed at medium, rather than fast or slow. Power-Point previews the transitions so you can see the type of transition and the speed.

8. In the Transition to This Slide group, click the **Transition Sound button arrow**, and then click **Chime**. This causes a chime to be played during the transition while in Slide Show view.

Now that you have set the desired transition, speed, and sound to one slide, you can apply it to all the slides in the presentation.

9. In the Transition to This Slide group, click the **Apply To All** button. As indicated in the ScreenTip for this button, clicking this button applies the transition of the current slide to all the other slides.

10. Click a blank area of the slide sorter pane to deselect the slides. Now you'll test the transition.

▶ **11.** Click the **special effects** icon ⭐ below Slide 2. PowerPoint momentarily displays the Slide 1 image at that location, and then performs the Wipe Right transition to Slide 2.

Now, when Sophie advances from one slide to another during a slide show, each slide will wipe onto the screen as a chime sounds.

Now that you've added transitions to the slides, you're ready to add animation.

Animating Bulleted Lists

A PowerPoint **animation** is a special visual or audio effect applied on a slide to an object, such as a graphic or a bulleted list. For example, you can add an animation to display bulleted items on a slide one item at a time. This process is called **progressive disclosure**. When a slide with a bulleted list has a progressive disclosure animation added, only the slide title appears when you first display the slide in your slide show. Then, when you advance the slide show by clicking the left mouse button (or pressing the spacebar or the → key), the first bulleted item appears. When you advance the slide show again, the second bulleted item appears, and so on. The advantage of this type of animation effect is that you can focus your audience's attention on one item at a time, without the distractions of items that you haven't discussed yet.

Applying an Animation | Reference Window

- In Normal view, select the object to which you want to add an animation effect.
- Click the Animations tab on the Ribbon.
- In the Animations group, click the Animate button arrow to display a menu of animations, and then click the desired animation.

or

- In the Animations group, click the Custom Animation button to open the Custom Animation task pane.
- Click the Add Effect button, point to a style, and then click More Effects to open the Add Entrance Effect dialog box.
- Click the desired effect, and then click the OK button.
- Click the Start arrow to choose when the animation starts.
- Click the Speed arrow to choose the speed of the animation.

Because objects on a slide are animated, not the slide itself, the presentation must be in Normal view and an object must be selected for you to choose an animation.

Applying a Custom Animation to Bulleted Lists

PowerPoint Custom Animation supports four general types of animations: Basic (the simplest and most conservative animations), Subtle (less conservative but unobtrusive), Moderate (moderately simple and moderately conservative animations), and Exciting (more complex and less conservative animations). For academic or business presentations, you should generally stick with Basic or Subtle and sometimes Moderate animations. If you're giving a casual or informal presentation, such as one describing a group game or explaining an exciting travel vacation, you might want to use Exciting animations. For this presentation on flowers, you'll apply a Subtle animation.

Now you'll add an animation effect to the bulleted lists in Sophie's presentation. For some presentations, you might include only one or two animations, but Sophie wants to try various animation effects before she completes her final presentation. Because Sophie wants to add the same animation to all the slides that contain a bulleted list and other content, she'll do it all at once by applying the animation to a master layout.

To add an animation to a Slide Master:

▶ 1. Click the **View** tab on the Ribbon, and then in the Presentation Views group, click the **Slide Master** button.

▶ 2. Click the **Two Content Layout** thumbnail, which is the fifth thumbnail from the top in the pane to the left of the slide pane. The ScreenTip informs you that this layout is used by Slides 2–5.

▶ 3. Click the edge of the left content placeholder of the Slide Master in the slide pane. You have to select the object to which you want to apply an animation.

> **Tip**
>
> You can also click the Custom Animation button in the Animation group to open the Custom Animation task pane.

▶ 4. Click the **Animations** tab on the Ribbon, and then in the Animations group, click the **Animate button arrow**. A menu appears with three general types of animation: Fade, Wipe, and Fly In, and Custom Animation, which you can use to access a wide variety of animation types.

▶ 5. Click **Custom Animation**. PowerPoint displays the Custom Animation task pane on the right side of the PowerPoint window. See Figure 3-27.

Figure 3-27 ▶ Slide Master with Custom Animation task pane

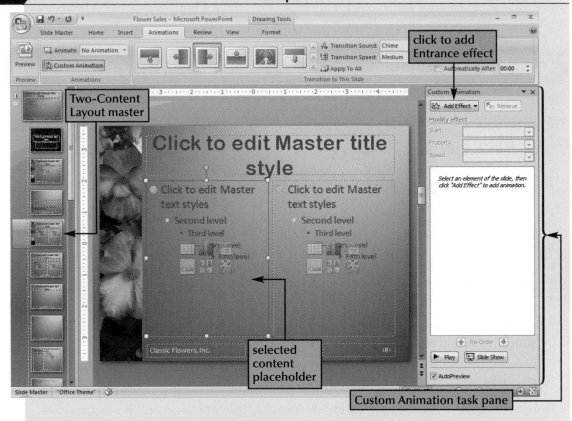

▶ 6. In the Custom Animation task pane, click the **Add Effect** button, point to **Entrance**, and then click **More Effects** at the bottom of the menu. The Add Entrance Effect dialog box opens. This dialog box shows the various built-in animation effects with which an object can enter the slide during a slide show. You'll test an effect now.

▶ 7. Click the **Preview Effect** check box, if necessary, at the bottom of the dialog box so that it's selected. This allows you to click an animation effect in the list and watch the animation in the slide pane.

8. In the Basic section of the dialog box, click **Fly In**. PowerPoint plays the slide transition you applied earlier, including the sound effect, and then animates the text of the bulleted list in the placeholder. As you can see, Fly In causes the text to scroll up into the slide. Feel free to test other animation entrance effects.

   Trouble? If you can't see the list, drag the dialog box out of the way by its title bar.

9. In the Subtle section of the dialog box, click **Expand**. PowerPoint previews the effect for you. You decide to apply this effect to the bulleted lists in the Flower Sales presentation.

10. Click the **OK** button. The object is listed in the task pane. See Figure 3-28. The mouse icon next to the object in the task pane indicates that the animation will occur when you advance the slide show.

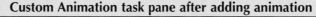

Custom Animation task pane after adding animation | Figure 3-28

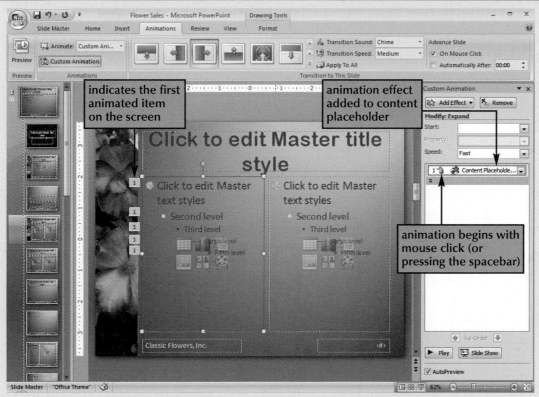

The bulleted items in the left content placeholder are marked with a "1" in little light-blue boxes. This indicates that all five bulleted levels will be animated first among the list of animated objects in this slide. Here, however, you have only one object animated, so you don't see any other numbers besides 1. You'll change that later.

You'll now test the transitions and animation effects you applied to the presentation.

To run a slide show with transitions and animation effects:

1. On the status bar, click the **Slide Show** button to start the slide show. PowerPoint displays Slide 1 with the Wipe Right transition effect, makes the chime sound, and then runs the sound clip "Welcome to Classic Flowers, Inc."

▶ **2.** Press the **spacebar** to go to Slide 2, "Our Products." Notice that the title and picture appear in the slide, but not the bulleted list. It will appear, one item at a time in progressive disclosure, as you press the spacebar or the → key or click the left mouse button.

▶ **3.** Press the **spacebar** to display the first-level bulleted item and the two second-level bulleted items below it. Sophie wants you to set up the animation so that the second-level items also appear one at a time in progressive disclosure. You'll do that by modifying the animation effect.

▶ **4.** Continue pressing the **spacebar** to progress through the slide show, and then return to Slide Master view.

▶ **5.** Save the presentation using the default filename.

Modifying the Bulleted-List Animation

Now you'll change the custom animation so that the second-level bulleted items also appear through progressive disclosure.

To set second-level bulleted items to progressive disclosure:

▶ **1.** In the Custom Animation task pane, click the **Click to expand contents arrow** ⌄ located just below the "Content Placeholder" item listed in the task pane. This expands the list of animation items to show the second- through fifth-level bulleted items.

▶ **2.** In the list of animated items, click **Second level**, and then click the **Start** arrow, near the top of the task pane. A three-item menu appears with *On Click* (meaning that the animation begins when you click the left mouse button or press the Spacebar or the → key), *With Previous* (meaning that the animation occurs with the previous animated item, in this case the first-level bulleted item), and *After Previous* (meaning that the animation occurs after the previous animation).

▶ **3.** Click **On Click**. A mouse icon appears next to the second-level item in the task pane. Now the second- through fifth-level bulleted items will animate as a group, but only after you click the mouse button after the first-level bulleted item has animated onto the screen during a slide show. See Figure 3-29.

Slide Master with second-level animation ◄ Figure 3-29

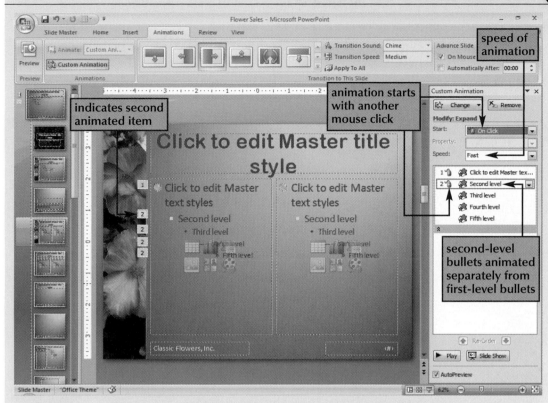

Next, Sophie wants you to add a special feature to the progressive disclosure: dimming after animation. When a bulleted item dims after animation, it changes color, usually to a lighter color, as the next bulleted item animates onto the screen during a slide show.

To set the bulleted items to dim after animation:

▶ **1.** In the Custom Animation task pane, click the **Click to edit Master...** box (the first animated item in the list), and then click the arrow that appears on the right side of that box, which displays a menu of items that allow you to change the animation effect.

▶ **2.** Click **Effect Options** on the menu. The Expand dialog box opens.

▶ **3.** Click the **After animation** arrow, and then click the dark purple color tile, located on the far right in the first row of color tiles.

▶ **4.** Click the **OK** button. PowerPoint plays the animation and demonstrates the dimming after animation.

   Trouble? If you don't see the animation, click the Play button at the bottom of the Custom Animation task pane.

▶ **5.** Repeat this procedure for the second-level bulleted items so that they also dim after animation to the same purple color.

Now you'll view the modified animations.

To view progressive disclosure with dimming after animation:

► **1.** On the status bar, click the **Slide Show** button to start the slide show.

► **2.** Press the **spacebar** to advance to Slide 2, and then press the **spacebar** again to display the first bulleted item. This time, the second-level bulleted items don't automatically appear with the first-level item.

► **3.** Press the **spacebar** again. The first-level bulleted item dims to purple, and the second-level bulleted item appears in the normal color (dark green). See Figure 3-30.

Figure 3-30 ▶ **Slide 2 in Slide Show view**

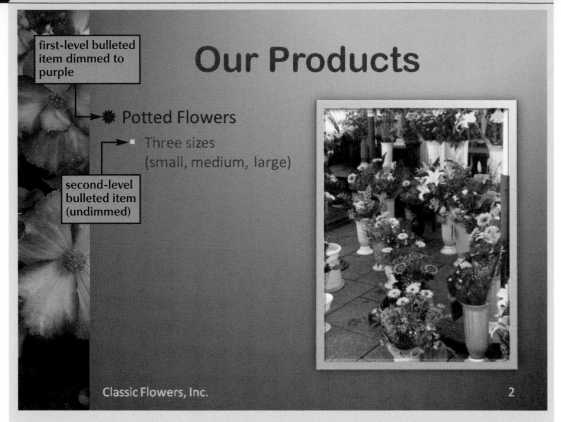

first-level bulleted item dimmed to purple

second-level bulleted item (undimmed)

Our Products

❋ Potted Flowers

▪ Three sizes (small, medium, large)

Classic Flowers, Inc.   2

► **4.** Continue advancing through the slide show for two or three more slides so you can see how the animation works.

► **5.** Press the **Esc** key to terminate the slide show and return to Slide Master view.

► **6.** On the status bar, click the **Normal** button to return to Normal view.

► **7.** Save the presentation.

Applying a Custom Animation to a Chart

Sophie now wants you to apply an animation effect to the chart in Slide 7. You'll use PowerPoint's Custom Animation feature, which works for any type of graphic—chart, graph, pictures, and so forth.

To animate a chart:

1. Go to **Slide 7** ("Volume Discounts"), click anywhere in the chart, and then click the edge of the chart to select the entire object.

2. Make sure the Custom Animation task pane is still open in the PowerPoint window.

3. In the Custom Animation task pane, click the **Add Effect** button. For this animation, rather than selecting a method by which the object enters the screen, you'll select an animation effect that emphasizes an object that already appears on the screen in Slide Show view.

4. Point to **Emphasis**, and then click **More Effects**. The Add Emphasis Effect dialog box opens.

5. In the Moderate section, click **Teeter**. This effect causes the object to teeter back and forth for a second when it appears on the slide.

6. Click the **OK** button.

7. At the top of the task pane, click the **Speed** arrow, and then click **Slow**. The teetering motion will occur slowly.

8. At the top of the task pane, click the **Start** arrow, and then click **With Previous**. The teetering will occur as the slide appears on the screen in Slide Show view, rather than when you click the mouse button after the slide appears.

9. Click the **Play** button at the bottom of the Custom Animation task pane to preview the animations in Slide 7.

10. In the task pane, click the Close button ☒, and then save the presentation.

This completes the presentation. You could edit each slide, one at a time, with custom animations to focus on key information or to add interest and excitement to the slide. But Sophie feels that the presentation has enough animation.

Now you'll run through the entire slide show to see how all of the animation effects, transitions, video clip, and so on will appear.

To view the entire slide show:

1. Go to **Slide 1**, and then on the status bar click the **Slide Show** button 🖳. The slide show starts with Slide 1 "wiping right" onto the screen and playing the sound clip. These are the special effects you added to Slide 1.

2. While still in Slide 1, click the **sound** icon 🔊. This demonstrates that, even though you've set the sound clip to play automatically when the slide starts, you can also play the sound clip anytime while Slide 1 appears on screen.

3. Click the left mouse button or press the **spacebar** to move to Slide 2, and then press the **spacebar** as needed to advance through the animation of the bulleted list, until the last bulleted item dims (changes to purple text).

4. Press the **spacebar** to continue through the slide show until the title of **Slide 4** ("Delivery") appears on the screen, and then click the left mouse button or press the **spacebar** three more times to display the three bulleted items. The sound clip of applause automatically plays just after the third item appears.

5. Advance to **Slide 5** ("Making the Right Move"), click the left mouse button or press the **spacebar** until all the bulleted items have appeared and dimmed on the screen. The movie then runs automatically in full-screen view.

6. Advance to **Slide 6** ("Base Wholesale Prices"), the slide with the pink tissue paper textured background. This slide has no animation, except for the slide transition.

7. Advance to **Slide 7** ("Volume Discounts"). The column chart slowly and automatically teeters back and forth for three seconds.

8. Press the **spacebar** three more times to finish the slide show and return to Normal view.

9. Save the presentation using the default filename.

Sophie now wants to practice her presentation, including marking slides with the pointer pen.

Marking Slides During a Slide Show

During a slide show, you can mark the slides to emphasize a point using the pointer pen. The **pen** is a mouse pointer that allows you to draw lines on the screen during a slide show. For example, you might use it to underline a word or phrase that you want to emphasize, or to circle a graphic that you want to point out. PowerPoint gives you the option of three pen types: Ballpoint Pen (draws thin, usually blue lines), Felt Tip Pen (draws thicker, usually red lines), and Highlighter (draws thick, usually yellow, transparent lines). You can change the ink color of any of the pens you select. You can also select the Eraser tool to remove pen lines that you've already drawn.

After you go through a presentation and mark it, PowerPoint gives you the choice of keeping the markings or discarding them. Now you'll show Sophie how to use the pointer pen.

To use the pen during a slide show:

1. Go to **Slide 7** and start the slide show. The graph appears and then teeters.

2. Move the mouse until you see the mouse pointer. The pointer appears on the screen, but it will disappear again if you don't move the mouse for a couple seconds.

3. Right-click anywhere on the screen, point to **Pointer Options** on the shortcut menu, and then click **Felt Tip Pen**. You can use the Pointer Options shortcut menu to select the type of pen, the ink color, and other options. After you have selected the Felt Tip Pen, the mouse pointer becomes a small, red dot. By clicking and dragging the pen on the screen, you can draw lines.

4. Click the left mouse button, and then drag to draw a circle around the second column (the one that represents 8% discount) to draw attention to it. See Figure 3-31.

Slide 7 in Slide Show view with felt-tip pen ink mark ◄ Figure 3-31

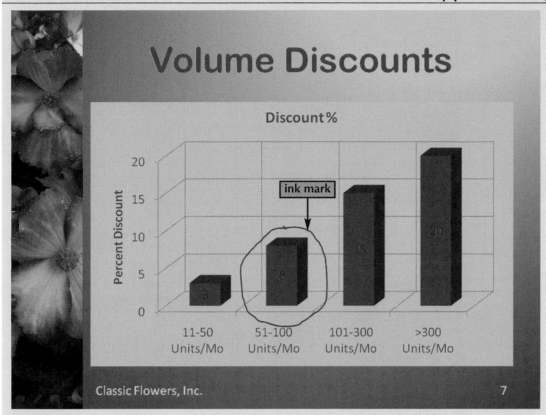

5. Press the **spacebar** to move to **Slide 8**. Note that you can't click the left mouse button to proceed through the slide show while a pointer pen is selected. Also note that the Felt Tip Pen is still active when you change slides, so you can now draw on Slide 8.

6. Click and drag to underline Sophie De Graff's name on the organization chart.

7. Right-click anywhere on the slide, point to **Pointer Options** on the shortcut menu, and then click **Arrow**. The mouse pointer changes back to the ordinary arrow pointer. Now you can click the mouse button to advance the slide show.

8. Click the left mouse button to terminate the slide show and display a blank screen, and then click the left mouse button again to return to Normal view. A dialog box opens asking if you want to keep your ink annotations. You don't want to save the marks with your presentation.

9. Click the **Discard** button.

As you can see, the pointer pen is a powerful tool for highlighting and pointing out information during a slide show.

Hiding Slides

Sophie tells you that some slides aren't appropriate for all prospective clients. For example, if she is giving the presentation to a manager of a small floral shop, she doesn't want to show the manager the volume discounts. In that case, she can temporarily hide that slide so it won't even show up during the presentation. She asks you to show her how to hide a slide.

To hide and unhide a slide:

▶ 1. Go to **Slide 7**, if necessary. This is the slide you want to hide.

▶ 2. Click the **Slide Show** tab on the Ribbon.

▶ 3. In the Set Up group, click the **Hide Slide** button. The button is selected and PowerPoint marks the slide number in the Slides tab so that you know that the slide will be hidden during the slide show. See Figure 3-32. Now you'll see your slides in Slide Show view.

Figure 3-32 ▶ **Slide 7 after hiding slide**

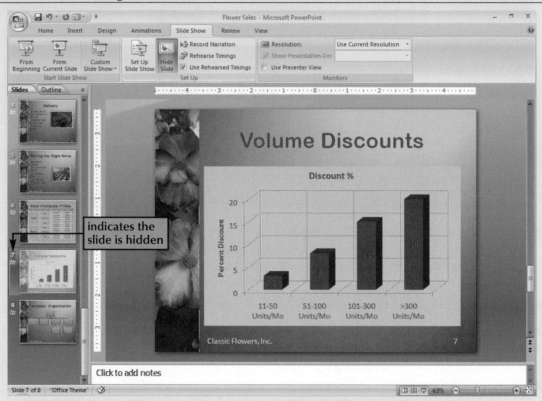

▶ 4. Go to **Slide 6**, and then on the status bar click the **Slide Show** button 🖵. Slide 6 appears in Slide Show view.

▶ 5. Press the **spacebar** or click the left mouse button. Slide 8 ("Company Organization") appears on screen. The slide show skipped Slide 7 ("Volume Discounts") as you intended.

▶ 6. Press the **Esc** key to end the slide show.

Now that you've seen how to hide a slide, you should go back and "unhide" it so it will be available for Sophie's presentation to the board of directors.

To unhide a slide:

▶ **1.** In Normal view, go to **Slide 7**.

▶ **2.** In the Set Up group on the Slide Show tab, click the **Hide Slide** button again. This toggles the Hide Slide effect off for Slide 7. The hidden slide icon disappears from the Slides tab.

▶ **3.** Go to **Slide 6**, switch to Slide Show view, and then press the **spacebar** to view Slide 7, verifying that it does indeed show up in the slide show now.

▶ **4.** Return to Normal view, and then save your presentation using the default filename.

▶ **5.** Submit the presentation in electronic or printed form as requested by your instructor.

Sophie is confident that her presentation will go smoothly, providing the needed information to her audiences in an engaging manner. Your final tasks are to help her prepare the materials to run not only on her computer, but also on the computers in the rooms where she'll give her presentations.

Preparing the Presentation to Run on Another Computer

Sophie will present the electronic (on-screen) slide show to store and floral department managers in conference rooms, classrooms, and other locations that might or might not have PowerPoint installed on their computers. She knows that she doesn't need Power-Point installed because she can use **PowerPoint Viewer**, a separate program that you can install and use on any computer that runs Windows to show your PowerPoint presentation. Sophie can't modify any of the slides using the PowerPoint Viewer, and some of the special effects might not work with the Viewer, but she could at least give the complete presentation.

To prepare the presentation to run on any computer, you can use the **Package for CD** feature to create a CD or a folder that you can store on portable media, such as a USB flash drive, that contains a copy of the presentation and PowerPoint Viewer. Sophie can then use this CD or flash drive to install the Viewer and run the presentation file.

Because each computer that runs Windows can have different fonts installed, you can save the presentation with the fonts embedded. With embedded fonts, the presentation will always have the desired fonts, even if they are not installed on the computer where you present the slide show. Be aware, however, that embedding fonts increases the size of the presentation file, so if you plan to embed fonts, make sure the final file size of the packaged presentation will still fit on the CD or flash drive.

Before completing the following steps, consult with your instructor. You'll need a computer with a CD or DVD writer (often called a CD or DVD "burner") and a blank, unused, writable CD or DVD, or you'll need a flash drive with at least 20 MB of free space.

The following steps show you how to complete the process using a flash drive, but the process works almost the same using a CD or DVD. If you create a CD or DVD, insert the blank disc in the computer drive before you start the steps.

To package the presentation to a folder:

▶ **1.** Click the **Office Button** 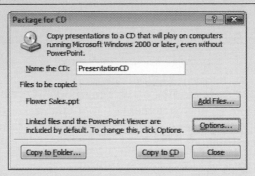, point to **Publish**, and then click **Package for CD**. The Package for CD dialog box opens. See Figure 3-33. First, you'll make sure the fonts will be embedded in the packaged presentation.

   Trouble? If PowerPoint displays a message warning you about updating to compatible file formats, click the OK button.

Figure 3-33 Package for CD dialog box

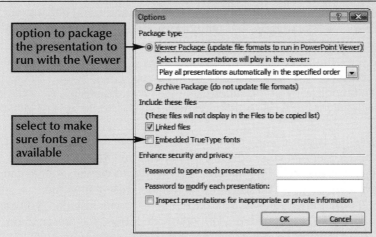

▶ **2.** Click the **Options** button. The Options dialog box opens. See Figure 3-34.

Figure 3-34 Options dialog box for creating a Package for CD

option to package the presentation to run with the Viewer

select to make sure fonts are available

▶ **3.** If necessary, click the **Embedded TrueType fonts** check box to select it. This ensures that the computer on which you run the slide show will have the necessary fonts.

▶ **4.** Click the **OK** button. The Options dialog box closes and the Package for CD dialog box is visible again.

▶ **5.** Click the **Copy to Folder** button. The Copy to Folder dialog box opens.

   Trouble? If you are copying your presentation to a CD or DVD, click Cancel to close this dialog box, click the Copy to CD button, and then skip to Step 8.

▶ **6.** Click the **Browse** button and navigate to your flash drive or to the **Tutorial.03\Tutorial** folder, and then click the **Select** button. You won't change the default name for the folder, PresentationCD.

▶ **7.** Click the **OK** button. A dialog box opens asking if you want to include linked files in your package.

8. Click the **Yes** button. Another dialog box opens briefly as PowerPoint copies all the necessary files to the PresentationCD folder or disc, including the file Flower Sales, any needed TrueType fonts, and PowerPoint Viewer.

   Trouble? If a dialog box appears warning you that the movie file couldn't be processed, click the OK button. PowerPoint will display only a still photo in place of the movie when you show the presentation with the PowerPoint Viewer.

9. Click the **Close** button in the Package for CD dialog box.

You should test the packaged presentation to make sure it works.

To run the PowerPoint presentation from a folder:

1. If you packaged the presentation to a USB flash drive, insert the flash drive into an available USB port on your computer. The Removable Disk dialog box opens.

   Trouble? If the Removable Disk dialog box doesn't appear, use Explorer to navigate to the flash drive, and then proceed with Step 3.

   Trouble? If you packaged the presentation to the Tutorial.03\Tutorial folder, open an Explorer window, and then skip to Step 3.

   Trouble? If you packaged the presentation on a CD or DVD, insert the CD or DVD into the drive, and then skip to Step 5.

2. Click the **Open folder to view files** button in the dialog box, and then click the **OK** button. An Explorer window opens.

3. Navigate in the window to the **PresentationCD** folder on the flash drive or in the Tutorial.03\Tutorial folder, and then double-click the folder to open it.

4. Double-click the file **PPTVIEW**. This is the PowerPoint Viewer.

   A dialog box opens with only one file visible, Flower Sales.

   Trouble? If a dialog box opens asking if you want to run this file, click the Run button.

   Trouble? If a dialog box opens containing the PowerPoint Viewer license agreement, read through the agreement, and then click the Accept button.

5. Double-click **Flower Sales**. The slide show starts.

6. Advance through the presentation by clicking the left mouse button or pressing the **spacebar** or the → key.

   Trouble? If, after the movie plays in Slide 5, you cannot proceed to the next slide by pressing the spacebar or the → key, move the mouse until the mouse pointer appears, and then click the left mouse button.

   Trouble? If the presentation doesn't work exactly as you prepared it, don't worry. Some features don't translate to the packaged presentation exactly.

7. After the blank screen appears at the end of the presentation, click the left mouse button or press the **spacebar** to end the presentation. The PowerPoint Viewer dialog box appears again.

8. Close the Microsoft Office PowerPoint Viewer dialog box, and then close the Explorer window.

Now Sophie can show her presentation on any computer, even if that computer does not have PowerPoint installed.

Delivering a Presentation with Two Monitors (Podium Mode)

Sophie knows she will deliver her presentation in lecture halls with large projection screens and wants to take advantage of a special PowerPoint feature: delivering a presentation with two monitors. This is sometimes called **podium mode** because it involves one monitor at the podium that only the presenter can see and another monitor (such as a projection screen) that the audience can see. For example, in properly equipped lecture halls, Sophie will connect her laptop computer to the video projector, set up her laptop for multiple monitors, set up PowerPoint to run on multiple monitors, and then use podium mode to give her presentation.

In podium mode, the presenter and the audience see the normal Slide Show view on the second monitor, and the presenter also sees a special PowerPoint window, called **Presenter View**, on the first (podium) monitor. In the Presenter View window, you can do the following:

- View thumbnails of the presentation slides. The thumbnails help you see the next slides before you display them and see previous slides. You can click any thumbnail to jump to that slide in your presentation. This is especially valuable while answering questions when you might need to jump back to a previous slide.
- See the speaker's notes in large, readable type so you can easily read the notes and use them as a script for your presentation.
- Blank out the screen at any time during a presentation. This allows you to stop and answer questions, take a break in the middle of the presentation, or pause for group discussion in the middle of a presentation without the distraction of the PowerPoint presentation on the projection screen.
- See (in large type) the time of day, time elapsed since starting your presentation, and pen options (so you can switch the mouse pointer to a pen without having to right-click on the screen viewed by the audience).

Sophie asks you to prepare her laptop computer for podium mode.

Note: These steps assume that you have a laptop computer and a separate monitor. If you do not have this equipment, read through the next set of steps without executing them.

To turn on multiple-monitor support:

Tip

You can also turn on Podium mode and access the Display Settings dialog box by clicking the Slide Show tab, and then, in the Monitors group, clicking the Use Presenter View check box.

1. With your laptop computer turned off, connect a second monitor to the external monitor port.

2. Turn on the second monitor and your laptop computer.

3. After Windows is started on your laptop, right-click the Windows desktop, and then click **Personalize** on the shortcut menu.

4. In the Personalization window, click the **Display Settings** link. The Display Settings dialog box opens. See Figure 3-35.

Display Settings for setting up for two-monitor presentation ◀ Figure 3-35

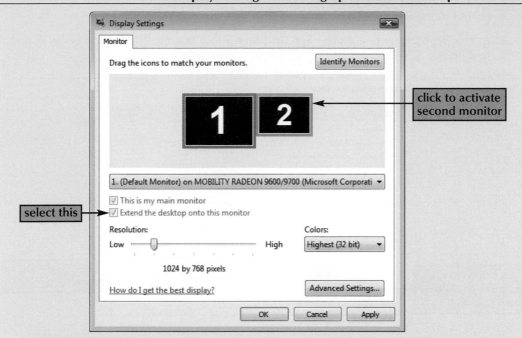

5. Click the arrow of the drop-down menu box below the monitor icons, and then click the option that corresponds to the video card on your computer that supports multiple monitors.

Trouble? If none of the options listed in the Display list include the phrase "(Multiple Monitors)", it probably means that your laptop doesn't support an external monitor, in which case you won't be able to complete these steps. Click the Cancel button, and then read, but do not perform, the rest of these steps.

6. Make a note of the resolution of the laptop monitor, and then click the **monitor 2** thumbnail in the Monitor tab of the dialog box, as indicated in Figure 3-35.

7. Click the **Extend the desktop onto this monitor** check box, if necessary, to make sure it's selected.

8. If necessary, drag the **Resolution** slider, if allowed to do so, until the resolution is the same as on your laptop.

Trouble? If you can't adjust the resolution of the second monitor, just leave it as is and continue these steps. The two-monitor system will probably still work properly.

9. Click the **OK** button.

10. If Windows warns you that your desktop has been reconfigured and tells you that it will revert to the old configuration automatically in a certain number of seconds, click the **Yes** button to accept the changes.

Trouble? If both monitors are not displaying the desktop properly, repeat the preceding steps, as necessary, but try a different resolution for the second monitor in Step 8.

Now that the desktop appears on both monitors, you're ready to set up podium mode in PowerPoint and show your presentation with two monitors.

To set up a slide show for podium mode:

▶ **1.** With the Flower Sales presentation open on the laptop, click the **Slide Show** tab on the Ribbon, if necessary.

▶ **2.** In the Set Up group, click the **Set Up Slide Show** button. The Set Up Show dialog box opens. See Figure 3-36.

Figure 3-36 Set Up Show for using podium view

▶ **3.** In the Multiple monitors section of the dialog box, click the **Display slide show on arrow**, and then, if necessary, click **Monitor 2 Default Monitor** or **Monitor 2 Plug and Play Monitor**, whichever of these two phrases appears in the menu. If you followed the steps in the previous set of steps, Monitor 1 is your laptop; monitor 2 is the external monitor.

▶ **4.** Click the **Show Presenter View** check box. This tells PowerPoint that you want to see the podium-view window.

▶ **5.** Click the **OK** button to close the dialog box.

Now you're ready to use podium mode to deliver the presentation.

To give a slide show in podium mode:

▶ **1.** In the Start Slide Show group, click the **From Beginning** button. Slide 1 of your presentation appears on monitor 2 in normal Slide Show view, and on monitor 1 (the laptop) in the PowerPoint Presenter View window. See Figure 3-37. Look over this figure so you understand the features of Presenter View.

Podium view during a slide show ◀ **Figure** 3-37

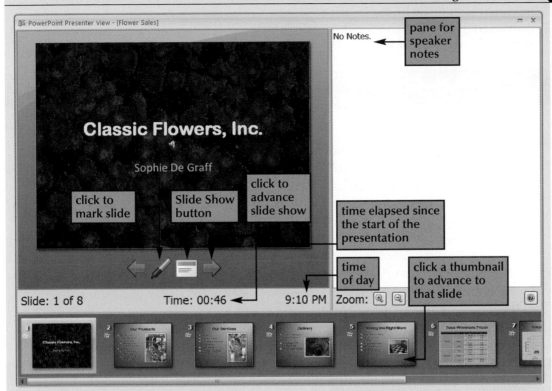

Trouble? If your laptop shows the slide and the other monitor displays the Presenter View window, close the Presenter View window, which automatically terminates the presentation in the other monitor, and then repeat the previous set of steps, but change the monitors in Step 3.

2. In the Presenter View window, click the large blue right arrow button to advance to Slide 2. In Presenter View, you can't click the left mouse button to advance the presentation, but you can use the spacebar and the arrow keys on your laptop keyboard, or you can click the thumbnails at the bottom of the Presenter View window. Slide 2 appears in the Presenter View window and on the second monitor.

3. Click the **Slide 5** thumbnail at the bottom of the Presenter View window. Slide 5 appears on both monitors.

4. Display the animated lists in Slide 5, and then continue on to **Slide 6**.

5. Click the **Pointer Options** button 🖊, select one of the pens, and then underline the title on the slide in the Presenter View window.

6. Note that you can use your mouse to draw on either the slide in Slide Show view on monitor 2 or on the slide in the slide pane in Presenter View.

7. When you have finished, click the **Slide Show** button in the Presenter View window, and then click **End Show**.

8. In the dialog box that opens asking if you want to save your annotations, click the **Discard** button.

9. Close the presentation.

You have completed Sophie's presentation. Sophie believes that the graphics, sound, and special effects for the on-screen slide show will help her audience stay focused on her presentation. She is pleased to be prepared with a packaged presentation containing the PowerPoint Viewer and with the option of giving the presentation in podium mode. She thanks you for your help.

Review | **Session 3.2 Quick Check**

1. What is a video clip?
2. Describe how you insert a chart into a slide.
3. What is an organization chart?
4. How do you insert an organization chart into a slide?
5. Define the following terms:
   a. transition effect
   b. animation effect
   c. sound effect
   d. pointer pen
   e. podium mode
6. Describe how you add a transition effect to a slide.
7. What is the PowerPoint Viewer?

Review | **Tutorial Summary**

In this tutorial, you learned how to insert slides from another presentation and how to create a theme by creating custom theme colors and backgrounds and by changing the font typeface and font color. You also learned how to add a background image, apply graphics and sound in the form of digital images, video clips, and audio clips, and add a textured background. You also learned how to create a chart (graph) and an organization chart, and how to apply special effects such as slide transitions and animations. You learned how to use the pointer pen to mark slides during a slide show, to hide a slide, and to prepare the presentation to run on another computer. Finally, you learned how to run the slide show with two monitors (podium mode).

Key Terms

active cell	Office theme	progressive disclosure
animation	organization chart	special effect
cell	Package for CD	spreadsheet
chart	pen	theme colors
digital movie	podium mode	transition
gradient fill	PowerPoint Viewer	video clip
graph	Presenter View	

| Practice | **Review Assignments** |

Practice the skills you learned in the tutorial using the same case scenario.

Data Files needed for the Review Assignments: Farm.avi, HotSprings.pptx, HSProposal.pptx, Knock.wav

The chief horticulturalist for Classic Flowers, Inc., Kathleen Bahlmann, recently became aware that a particular farm in southern Georgia is for sale. The farm is special because it has a natural hot spring on its premises. The farm owner has set up a system to use water from the hot spring to heat his barns during the winter. Now that the farm is for sale, Kathleen sees this as an opportunity to improve the profitability of Classic Flowers by purchasing the farm, converting the barns to greenhouses, and using the water from the hot spring to heat the greenhouses. This has the potential of saving millions of dollars on heating expenses over the next several years. Kathleen wants to present her idea to the board of directors of Classic Flowers, and she has asked you to help her create the PowerPoint presentation. She has already created a couple of PowerPoint presentation files; one contains a title slide with some elements that she wants to use for a design theme, and the other contains some of the text that she wants in the final presentation.

1. Open the file **HSProposal**, located in the Tutorial.03\Review folder included with the Data Files, change the subtitle from "Kathleen Bahlmann" to your name, and then save the file as **Hot Springs Proposal** in the same Tutorial.03\Review folder.

2. Modify the current theme colors, which are the Flower theme colors that you created earlier in this tutorial by changing the Text/Background – Dark 1 color from dark green to dark purple and changing the Text/Background – Light 2 from light yellow to white. For the Text/Background – Dark 1 color, pick the dark purple that appears on the Standard tab of the Colors dialog box on the far-right corner of the hexagonal palette of color tiles. For the Text/Background – Light 2 color, use the pure white, large, hexagonal tile near the lower-left corner of the dialog box, to the left of the double row of grayscale tiles. Save the new color set using the name **HotSprings**.

3. In Slide Master view, change the background color of the Office Theme Slide Master to "Dark Purple, Text 1," which is the dark purple color you set for Text/Background Dark 1. (*Hint*: Open the Format Background dialog box, and then, with the Solid fill option button selected, click the Color button.) Apply this dark purple color to all the slides.

4. Change the background style to Style 12, which is a gradient from dark purple in the upper-left corner of the background to lighter purple in the lower-right corner.

5. In the Office Theme Slide Master, do the following:
   a. Change the title text to white.
   b. Change the color of the first-level bulleted-list text to Lavender, Text 1.
   c. Change the second-level bulleted-list text color to the lightest yellow color available in the palette.
   d. Change the third-level bulleted-list text color to white.
   e. Change the first-level bullet to a picture of a yellow-gold square.
   f. Change the second-level bullet to a picture of a smaller green and pale green square.

6. In the Title Slide Layout master, change the subtitle text color to Yellow, Accent 5.

7. Save the presentation using the default filename, and then save it as a new Office theme to the Tutorial.03\Review folder using the filename **Flower2**.

8. Close the PowerPoint presentation file, but leave PowerPoint running.

9. Start a new, blank PowerPoint presentation, and then change its design theme to Flower2.

10. Insert the slide from the file **Hot Springs Proposal**, and then delete the extra (blank) title slide, leaving only one title slide.

11. Insert Slides 2 through 7 (that is, all but the first slide) from the file **HotSprings**, located in the **Tutorial.03\Review** folder.

12. To Slide 1, apply the slide transition Comb Horizontal in the Stripes and Bars section, and then change the slide-transition speed to Medium.

13. Add the sound effect Whoosh to the slide transition, and then apply the transition for Slide 1 to all the slides.

14. In Slide 2, change the animation so that the bulleted list uses progressive disclosure with dimming. Use the Animate button to set the animation to the Fade effect, and then use the Custom Animation task pane to set the dimming color to dark green.

15. In Slide 3, select the two text boxes (but not the slide title) and apply the custom animation Zoom, located in the Moderate section of the Add Entrance Effect dialog box.

16. In Slide 4, insert a chart using the 3-D Clustered Column style.

17. In the Excel spreadsheet for the PowerPoint chart, do the following:

    a. Change cell B1 to **Heating Costs (in millions)**.

    b. Change cell C1 to **Profits (in millions)**.

    c. Delete the column with Series 3.

    d. Change Category 1 through Category 4 (cell A2 through cell A5) to the years **2006** through **2009**, and then add **2010** in cell A6.

    e. In cells B2 through B6 (below Heating Costs), replace the current cell contents with **1.8**, **2.2**, **2.7**, **3.3**, **4.1**. Format these cells as Currency by clicking the Accounting Number Format button in the Number group. Decrease the decimal to one place by clicking the Decrease Decimal button in the Number group.

    f. In cells C2 through C6 (below Profits), replace the current cell contents with **3.2**, **3.1**, **2.9**, **2.7**, **2.5**. On the Home tab in the Excel window, click the Number button, and then click the Accounting Number Format button to format these numbers as currency.

18. In Slide 5, click in the bulleted list text box, click the Home tab, in the Paragraph group, click the Convert to SmartArt Graphic button, and then click the Organization Chart graphic in the gallery.

19. After "Tom Briggs" in the top box, press the Enter key, and then type **Farm Manager**. Similarly, add the title **Greenhouse Manager** to the three second-level boxes. Don't add titles to the three subordinate boxes below Alice Abernathy.

20. Change the layout of the organization chart to Hierarchy, and then change the color of the organization chart to Dark 2 Outline (green).

21. In Slide 6, add the movie **Farm** located in the Tutorial.03\Review folder. Set it to start When Clicked.

22. In Slide 7, insert the sound clip **Knock**, located in the Tutorial.03\Review folder. Set it to start Automatically.

23. Add the Zoom custom animation entrance effect to each of the two text items in Slide 7, and then set the Start option to After Previous so that they play one after another. Drag the Knock sound in the animation pane so it is second in the list.

24. Hide Slide 5.

25. Save the presentation using the filename **Hot Springs Proposal**, so that it replaces the current file of that name in the Tutorial.03\Review folder. Run the slide show, making sure you click the movie in Slide 6 to play it. Use the Felt Tip Pen tool to underline the title in Slide 7. Discard this annotation.

26. Delete the custom color set HotSprings.

27. Package the presentation for a CD, either to a CD or DVD, a USB flash drive, or to the Tutorial.03\Review folder. Name the CD or the folder **Packaged Hot Springs**. If you get an error that PowerPoint can't package the file Farm.avi, continue anyway.

28. Insert the CD or open an Explorer window and navigate to the location of the packaged presentation, start the PowerPoint Viewer, and then run the packaged presentation. Close the PowerPoint Viewer dialog box and the Explorer window when you are finished.

29. Submit the final presentation and the packaged presentation in printed or electronic form, as directed by your instructor.

| Apply | **Case Problem 1** |

Apply the skills you learned to create a presentation for an eBay store.

Data Files needed for this Case Problem: CompCase.avi, eBayCase.pptx, JustInCase.pptx, PhoneCase.jpg

Just in Case, an eBay Store Jergen Oleson is a small-electronics aficionado. He had the latest in electronic gadgets—MP3 player, cell phone, palm computer, laptop, GPS receiver, digital camera, and so forth. But he was always frustrated in trying to find proper cases for these items. He was surprised, in fact, by the dearth of companies that sold cases for electronic gadgets. So he decided to start his own company, which he called Just in Case, and to sell his products through his own eBay store. He now asks you to help him create a theme for his PowerPoint presentations and to start creating a presentation that he will give to potential manufacturers of his cases. Do the following:

1. Open the presentation file **JustInCase**, located in the Tutorial.03\Case1 folder included with the Data Files. This is a file with the Just in Case logo placed on three of the slide masters and with modifications to the size, location, and text justification of some of the placeholders. You'll continue creating the Office theme file from here.

2. Create a new set of theme colors using the colors shown in Figure 3-38. Save the theme colors using the name **JustInCase**.

Figure 3-38

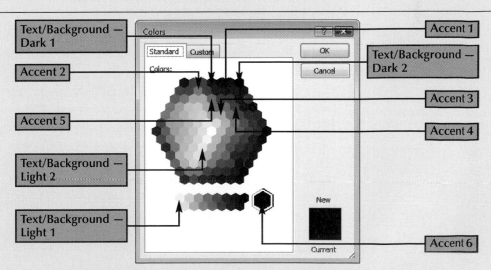

3. Apply the background style Style 4 (solid dark blue, the Text/Background – Dark 1 color).

4. In the Office Theme Slide Master, do the following:
   a. Change the title font to Arial Black.
   b. Change the body text font to Times New Roman.
   c. Change the first-level bullet to a filled square bullet with the Light Yellow, Text 2 theme color.
   d. Change the second-level bullet to a filled round bullet with the Light Blue, Accent 3 theme color.
   e. Change the third-level bullet to a white, hollow, round bullet.
   f. Change the second-level text color to the Light Yellow, Text 2 theme color.
5. Save the presentation as an Office Theme file to the Tutorial.03\Case1 folder using the filename **Just in Case**. Close the file without saving it.
6. Open a new, blank presentation and apply the Just in Case theme. Delete the Justin-Case theme color set.
7. On the title page, insert the title **Case Manufacturing and Order Fulfillment Services**. Insert your name as the subtitle.
8. Save the presentation in the Tutorial.03\Case1 folder using the filename **Case Manufacturing**.
9. Insert into this presentation file all seven slides from the file **eBayCase**, located in the Tutorial.03\Case1 folder.
10. In Slide 2, change the layout to Two Content, insert the picture **PhoneCase** from the Tutorial.03\Case1 folder, and then apply the picture style Reflected Rounded Rectangle.
11. In Slide 3, insert the movie **CompCase**, so that it plays when clicked during a slide show, and then apply the picture style Reflected Rounded Rectangle.
12. In Slide 6, insert a chart as follows:
   a. Insert the Line with Markers chart, in the Line section in the Insert Chart dialog box.
   b. Change "Category 1" through "Category 4" to **2010**, **2011**, **2012**, and **2013** to represent the years.
   c. Change "Series 1" to **Sales (in $Thousands)** and "Series 2" to **Profits (in $Thousands)**.
   d. In the Sales column (cells B2 through B5), insert the values **850**, **1000**, **1100**, **1250**.
   e. In the Profits column (cells C2 through C5), insert the values **80**, **180**, **280**, **400**.
   f. Delete column D.
13. Change the Chart Style to Style 45 (located on the bottom row, fifth column of the Design gallery).
14. In Slide 7, insert an organization chart. Change the Layouts style to Hierarchy, and then change the colors to Colorful Range – Accent Colors 3 to 4. Add the following text to the chart, adding and deleting boxes as needed:
   a. First-level box: **Fulfillment Manager**
   b. Second-level boxes: **Inventory Manager**, **Shipping Manager**, and **Accounts Manager**.
   c. Third-level boxes under Shipping Manager: **Processing Manager** and **Mail Manager**.
15. In Slide 8, add the Purple mesh textured background.
16. In Slides 2, 4, and 5, animate the bulleted lists using the Dissolve In entrance animation. Set the dim color to light blue-green.
17. In Slide 2, animate the picture to enter the screen using the Fly In entrance effect.

18. To all the slides, apply the slide transition Fade Smoothly, and then set the transition speed to Slow.

19. Go through the presentation in Slide Show view. Using the red felt-tip pointer pen, draw a rough circle around "Fulfillment Manager" on Slide 7. When you finish the slide show, save the ink marking.

20. Save the presentation using the default name.

21. Submit the presentation in printed or electronic format, as directed by your instructor.

Challenge	**Case Problem 2**

Go beyond the skills you've learned to create a self-running presentation for a photographer.

Data Files needed for this Case Problem: Wedding01.jpg through Wedding10.jpg

Ultimate Videos   Sharah-Renae Wabbinton has a home business of taking pictures or scanning photos for special occasions—primarily graduations, weddings, family reunions, and religious events—and preparing "videos" using PowerPoint. Her products aren't true videos, but rather self-running, animated, PowerPoint presentations created using the Photo Album feature. She gives you a copy of 10 photographs from a recent wedding, and has asked you to prepare not only a PowerPoint presentation using those photos but also a custom Office theme that she can use with other "videos." Do the following:

1. Start a new, blank presentation (using the Office theme).

⊕ **EXPLORE**

2. Change the background style to a gradient fill, with the preset colors design called Nightfall. Apply this background to all slides. (*Hint*: Use the Preset colors button arrow in the Format Background dialog box.)

⊕ **EXPLORE**

3. In the Office Theme Slide Master, change all the text placeholders to white text, and then draw a rectangle that is the same shape and almost the same size as the entire slide, so that a white border appears between the rectangle and the outer edges of the slide approximately one-quarter of an inch from the edge of the slides. (*Hint*: Use the rectangle Shape tool to draw the rectangle so that it completely covers the slide of the Slide Master, and then, while holding down the Alt key, drag the resize handles to slightly reduce the size of the rectangle on all four sides.)

⊕ **EXPLORE**

4. Set the Shape Fill of the rectangle to No Fill, and set the Shape Outline to a white, 3-point line.

⊕ **EXPLORE**

5. With the Slide Master still in the slide pane, set the slide transition to Random Transition. (*Hint*: Random Transition is the last transition in the Transition gallery.)

⊕ **EXPLORE**

6. Set up the slide show to advance automatically from one slide to the next, with about 5 seconds on each slide. (*Hint*: With the Slide Master still in the slide pane, on the Animations tab in the Transition to This Slide group, deselect the On Mouse Click check box, and then select the Automatically After check box. Change the Automatically After time from 00:00 to **00:05**.)

7. In Normal view, save the presentation as an Office theme titled **Wedding** in the Tutorial.03\Case2 folder included with the Data Files.

8. Close the current presentation without saving it, and then start a new, blank presentation.

⊕ **EXPLORE**

9. In the Illustrations group on the Insert tab, use the Photo Album button to insert all 10 photographs, **Wedding01** through **Wedding10**, located in the Tutorial.03\Case2 folder. (*Hint*: In the Photo Album dialog box, click the File/Disk button, navigate to the folder containing the pictures, select all the pictures, and then click the Insert button.)

⊕ **EXPLORE** 10. While still viewing the Photo Album dialog box, in the Album Layout section, set the Picture layout to 1 picture (meaning, 1 picture per slide). Set the Frame shape to Simple Frame, White. Apply the theme to the Wedding theme you created and saved in the Tutorial.03\Case2 folder. Click the Create button at the bottom of the Photo Album dialog box to create the photo album. (*Hint*: If you already closed the Photo Album dialog box, click the Photo Album button arrow, and then click Edit Photo Album.)

11. In Slide 1, change the title to **Curtis and Cassandra**, and change the name in the subtitle to your name.

12. In Slides 2 through 11, apply a different Entrance animation effect to each photograph. Use only animations in the Exciting group in the Add Entrance Effect dialog box. Test each animation to make sure it works well.

13. For each picture animation, change the Start setting to With Previous, and then change the Speed to Medium.

⊕ **EXPLORE** 14. Set up the presentation to loop automatically, so that it automatically starts over when it reaches the end. (*Hint*: On the Slide Show tab, in the Set Up group, click the Set Up Slide Show button, and then click the Loop continuously until 'Esc' check box.)

15. Start the slide show and make sure that it runs on its own and continues to run until you press the Esc key.

16. Save the presentation as **Wedding Video** in the Tutorial.03\Case2 folder.

17. If your instructor asks you to do so, print the slide show as a handout with 6 slides per page.

| Create | **Case Problem 3** |

Use the skills you learned to create a custom theme and presentation for a cartography company.

Data Files needed for this Case Problem: MntMap.jpg, MntPlateau1.jpg, MntPlateau2.jpg

Cartography Research Systems   Barrett Worthington is founder and president of Cartography Research Systems (CRS), a company that maps geological formations and nearby areas. Sample geological areas include glaciers, caves, canyons, river beds, and wilderness sites. CRS clients mostly are energy and mineral exploration companies, but they also include the National Parks Service and land developers.

Barrett has asked you to create and save a design theme that his company can use for their presentations to their clients. He then asks you to help him prepare a portion of a presentation to one of his clients, Eckstein Energy. Do the following:

1. Create a new set of theme colors as shown in Figure 3-39. Your colors don't have to be exactly the same as those shown in the figure. Just try to select each theme color as close as you can. Save the theme colors as **CRScolors**.

Figure 3-39

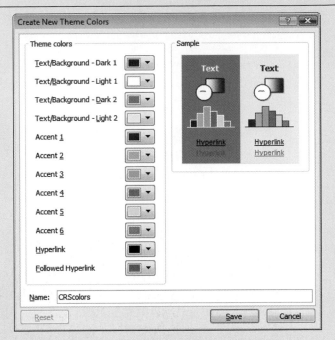

⊕ EXPLORE

2. Use the slide masters to apply the background style, font attributes (titles light yellow, bold), bullets, and title border shown in Figure 3-40. (*Hint*: To create the title border, use the Shape Outline button in the Shape Styles group on the Format tab to add the border, and change the color and thickness—called the weight—of the line. If you're not sure of a particular color, just pick any theme color that is close. Similarly, just get the line thickness (weight) as close as you can to the title border in Figure 3-40.)

Figure 3-40

3. Use the slide masters to add progressive disclosure (without dimming) to the bulleted lists and content placeholders. Use the Fly In (from bottom) entrance animation. Modify the animation so that the second- and third-level bulleted items enter the screen separately during a slide show. Refer to Figure 3-40. (*Hint*: To apply the custom animation to all content, not just bulleted lists, apply it to the content placeholder on the Slide Master.)

4. Save the file as an Office theme in your Tutorial.03\Case3 folder using the filename **CRStheme**, and then close the presentation without saving changes.

5. Start a new PowerPoint presentation, and then apply the theme you created, CRStheme. Delete the CRScolors theme color set.

6. Add content to the new presentation, as shown in Figure 3-41. Refer to the following as you add the content:

Figure 3-41

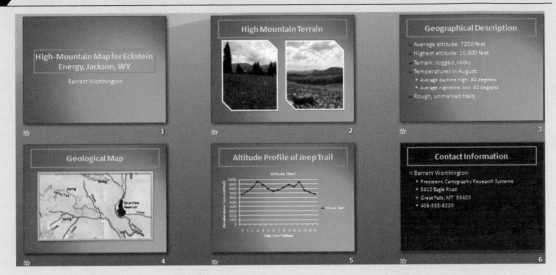

a. In Slide 1, add the title shown, but use your own name for the subtitle.

b. In Slide 2, insert the photos **MntPlateau1** and **MntPlateau2**, and then apply the picture style called Snip Diagonal Corner, White.

c. In Slide 3, type the title and bulleted list, as shown in Figure 3-41.

d. In Slide 4, insert the picture **MntMap**, and then apply the picture style called Metal Frame.

e. In Slide 6, after you enter the information, apply the textured background called Walnut.

EXPLORE

7. In Slide 5, create an elevation chart using the Line type chart format called Line with Markers. Delete all the data from the spreadsheet. (*Hint*: Press the Ctrl+A keys to select all, and then press the Delete key.) Enter the data shown in this table, where the upper-left (empty) cell is cell A1, the label "Altitude (feet)" is cell B1, and so forth:

	Altitude (feet)		Altitude (feet)
0	6800	8	8200
1	7400	9	8800
2	8200	10	8400
3	9500	11	9400
4	8800	12	7600
5	8000	13	7200
6	7400	14	6800
7	7700		

⊕ **EXPLORE**

8. Select the data for the chart in Slide 5. (*Hint*: Select the chart placeholder, and then, in the Data group on the Design tab, click the Select Data button. Drag the pointer over all the cells that you entered into the spreadsheet, and then click the OK button in the Select Data Source dialog box.)

9. Add axis titles to the horizontal and vertical axes, as shown in Figure 3-41. Along the primary horizontal (X) axis, the text is "Miles from Trailhead," and along the primary vertical (Y) axis, the text is "Elevation above Sea Level (feet)."

10. In Slide 4, insert, rotate, and then color the text boxes that label the reservoir, springs, creeks, and trails, as shown.

11. Animate all the text boxes using the Appear entrance effect. (*Hint*: First apply the animation to the "Sliver Flats Reservoir" text box, and then select all the "Creek" text boxes and apply the animation to all of them at once. Then select all the "Spring" text boxes and apply the animation effect to all of them at once, and then finally select the two "trail" text boxes and apply the effect to them.)

⊕ **EXPLORE**

12. To each of the four groups of animations, apply the sound effect Click. (*Hint*: For each of the animation groups, click the arrow to the right of the text box number in the Custom Animation task pane, click Effect Options, and then on the Effect tab, set the Sound to Click.)

13. Test the slide in Slide Show view to make sure that, after the slide appears, you have to click once to have the map "fly in" to the slide, then click four more times to display each of the four groups of text boxes, which appear with a clicking sound. If necessary, edit the text boxes and animation so they work as described.

14. Save the presentation in the Tutorial.03\Case3 folder using the filename **High-Mnt Map**.

15. Submit the presentation in electronic or printed form, as requested by your instructor.

| Create | **Case Problem 4** |

Use the skills you learned to create a presentation about a collection for a volunteer group.

There are no Data Files needed for this Case Problem.

Cabot Collectibles   Cabot Collectibles is a group of volunteer collectors who create PowerPoint presentations about personal collections. They make these presentations available to anyone who wants to present information on collectibles to schools, churches, civic organizations, clubs, and so forth. They rely on collectors to prepare the PowerPoint presentations. Your task is the following:

1. Select a type of collectible: stamps, coins, foreign currency, baseball cards, jewelry, comic books, artwork, rocks, dolls, figurines, chess sets, or almost anything else.

2. Plan your presentation so your audience learns basic information about your chosen collectible and sees pictures, with descriptions, of sample items from the collection.

3. Acquire pictures of sample items. You can take the pictures yourself with a digital camera, take the pictures with a film camera and scan the photographs, scan flat items directly (stamps, bills, cards, book covers, and so forth), or get pictures from the Web.

4. Gather information about the items depicted in your graphics. You might want to include some of the following: name of item, age of item, origin (purchase location or place of manufacture), date of purchase, dimensions, and special characteristics (handmade, natural dyes, first edition, and so forth).

5. Create a custom theme appropriate for your presentation. In selecting theme fonts and theme colors, take into account the nature of the collection and the common colors found in the graphics that you're going to include. Your theme should include the following:

   a. Custom theme colors

   b. At least one graphic—logo, picture, ready-made shape (rectangle, circle, triangle, and so forth), or textured background

   c. A custom set of bullets; include a picture bullet for the first-level bulleted items

   d. Progressive disclosure, with dimming, of the bulleted lists

6. Create a new presentation based on your custom theme.

7. Include a title slide, at least two slides with bulleted lists, and at least six slides with pictures of collectibles.

8. Apply slide transitions to your slide presentation.

9. Animate at least one graphic.

⊕ EXPLORE 10. If you have access to a microphone on your computer, create at least one sound clip and insert it in your presentation. Keep the recording shorter than 3 seconds. For example, record your voice saying a hard-to-pronounce noun or a foreign word associated with a collectible item, or record a sound effect, like a knock on the door, a bell, or a whistle. (*Hint*: Use the Sound Recorder installed with Windows. Click the Start button, point to All Programs, click Accessories, and then click Sound Recorder. With your microphone ready, click the Record button. When you're finished recording, click the Stop button.)

⊕ EXPLORE 11. If you have access to a digital camera with video capture and have the technical know-how, create a video shorter than 5 seconds of one of your collectibles or of someone admiring your collectibles. Insert the video into one of the slides of your presentation.

12. Save the presentation in the Tutorial.03\Case4 folder using the filename **Collection**.

13. Save the theme in the Tutorial.03\Case4 folder using the filename **Collectible**.

14. Submit your presentation in electronic or printed form, as requested by your instructor.

Research | Internet Assignments

Go to the Web to find information you can use to create presentations.

The purpose of the Internet Assignments is to challenge you to find information on the Internet that you can use to work effectively with this software. The actual assignments are updated and maintained on the Course Technology Web site. Log on to the Internet and use your Web browser to go to the Student Online Companion for New Perspectives Office 2007 at **www.course.com/np/office2007**. Then navigate to the Internet Assignments for this tutorial.

Assess | SAM Assessment and Training

If you have a SAM user profile, you may have access to hands-on instruction, practice, and assessment of the skills covered in this tutorial. Log in to your SAM account (**http://sam2007.course.com**) to launch any assigned training activities or exams that relate to the skills covered in this tutorial.

Review | Quick Check Answers

Session 3.1

1. In the Slides group on the Home tab, click the New Slide button arrow, click Reuse Slides, browse to the location of the presentation with the slide you want to insert, and then click the slide thumbnails of the desired slides.
2. Theme colors are the set of matching colors that makes up the background, fonts, and other elements of the presentation.
3. In creating a custom theme, you might want to change the following elements: background style, fonts, font sizes, font colors, bullets, and background graphics.
4. Gradient fill is a type of shading in which one color blends into another or varies from one shade to another.
5. Click the Office Button, click Save As to open the Save As dialog box, click the Save as type arrow, click Office Theme, navigate to the desired location, type a filename, and then click the Save button.
6. In the Background group on the Design tab, click the Background Styles button arrow, click Format Background, click the picture or texture fill option button, click the Texture button arrow, and then click the desired texture.

Session 3.2

1. A video clip is an animated picture file, usually with the filename extension .avi.

2. Change the slide layout to a different content layout (if necessary), click the Chart button in the content placeholder, select the type of chart, edit the spreadsheet, and then change other chart options as desired.

3. An organization chart is a diagram of boxes, connected with lines, showing the hierarchy of positions within an organization.

4. Change the slide layout to a different content layout (if necessary), click the Insert SmartArt Graphic button in the content placeholder, select a Hierarchy graphic (usually Organization Chart or Hierarchy), click the OK button, type text into the boxes, and then add and remove organization chart boxes as desired.

5. a. **Transition effect**: A method of moving one slide off the screen and bringing another slide onto the screen during a slide show

   b. **Animation effect**: A special visual or audio effect applied to an object (such as graphics or bulleted text)

   c. **Sound effect**: A sound that takes place during a slide show

   d. **Pointer pen**: A PowerPoint mouse pointer that allows you to draw lines on the screen during a slide show

   e. **Podium mode**: A slide show mode involving two monitors, one that's usually at a podium and that only the presenter can see, and another one (such as a projection screen) that the audience can see

6. With the desired slide in the slide pane, click the Animations tab, and then, in the Transition to This Slide group, select the desired transition. If desired, modify the transition to include a sound effect or to execute at a faster or slower rate. If desired, click the Apply To All button to apply the same transition to all slides in the presentation.

7. PowerPoint Viewer is a separate program that you can use to give your slide show on any Windows computer.

Objectives

Session 4.1
- Apply a design theme from another presentation
- Import, modify, and export a Word outline
- Import graphics into a presentation
- Copy an object from another presentation
- Embed and modify a table from Word
- Link and modify an Excel chart

Session 4.2
- Create and edit hyperlinks
- Insert text into shapes
- Add action buttons to a presentation
- View a slide show with embedded or linked objects
- Print a presentation as an outline
- Customize handouts
- Publish a presentation as a Web page
- Learn about Windows Meeting Space
- Identify features not supported by previous versions
- Use the Document Inspector

Integrating PowerPoint with Other Programs and Collaborating with Workgroups

Presenting Information for Landon Pharmaceuticals Testing, Inc.

Case | Landon Pharmaceuticals Testing, Inc.

Allysa Byington is director of customer service at Landon Pharmaceuticals Testing (LPT), a company that performs clinical trial testing of medicinal drugs developed by other pharmaceutical companies. Allysa works with the pharmaceutical companies to develop effective testing protocols, and then she prepares presentations on the results of the testing. Allysa asks you to help create an effective Microsoft PowerPoint presentation on the results of a pharmaceutical clinical trial for a client, Pamerleau Biotechnologies of Newton, Massachusetts. Pamerleau has developed a drug, with the code name Asperitol and code number PB0182, for the treatment of autoimmune diseases such as rheumatoid arthritis and lupus.

In this tutorial, you apply a design theme from another presentation, you'll import, modify, and export a Microsoft word outline to and from your presentation, and you'll import pictures into your presentation. You'll also embed and modify a Word table in your presentation and link and modify a Microsoft Excel chart. You'll then create and edit hyperlinks, and add action buttons. Finally, you'll learn how to print the presentation outline, to customize handouts, to publish a presentation on the World Wide Web, and to share your presentation with others over the Internet.

Starting Data Files

Tutorial	Review	Case1	Case2	Case3	Case4
Chart.xlsx	Hospitals.docx	CredUnion.jpg	BirdBlt.jpg	72HrKit.jpg	Wetland1.jpg
Clinical.pptx	Landon.pptx	FLCUChart.xlsx	FlwBlt.jpg	EPR.pptx	Wetland2.jpg
ClinOtl.docx	LPTChart.xlsx	FLCUDes.pptx	WMCchart.xlsx	EPRChart.xlsx	Wetland3.jpg
Demogr.docx	LPTInfo.docx	FLCUOtln.docx	WMCDes.pptx	EPROtl.docx	Wetland4.jpg
Landon.pptx	Patient.jpg	FLCUTbl.docx	WMCOtl.docx	EPRTabl.docx	Weland5.jpg
Pills.jpg	Placebos.jpg	Money.jpg		Flood.jpg	
X-ray.jpg				Wheat.jpg	

Session 4.1

Planning the Presentation

Before you begin to create Allysa's slide show, she discusses with you her plans for the presentation.

- **Purpose of the presentation**: To present an overview of the fund-raising clinical-trial report and assign responsibilities
- **Type of presentation**: Report
- **Audience for the presentation**: Management team of Pamerleau Biotechnologies
- **Audience needs**: An overview of efficacy of their drug in treating arthritis
- **Location of the presentation**: Meeting room at the headquarters of Landon Pharmaceuticals Testing, Inc., and online
- **Format**: On-screen slide show and online Web presentation

With the preceding general plan for the presentation, Allysa prepared the outline of the presentation, as well as some of the key information about the presentation to Pamerleau.

Applying a Design Theme from Another Presentation

You already know how to apply a design theme from a theme file. You can use a similar method to apply a design from any other presentation file. For the clinical-trial presentation, Allysa wants you to use the design theme from an existing presentation she recently prepared for another clinical-trial presentation. You'll apply that design theme now.

To apply a design theme from the Landon presentation:

▶ 1. Open the file **Clinical** from the **Tutorial.04\Tutorial** folder included with your Data Files, and then save the file with the new filename **Clinical Report** to the same folder. The title slide appears on the screen with the name of the presenter, Allysa Byington. The presentation has the Technic design theme applied. Notice that this presentation includes only this one slide. See Figure 4-1. You'll create additional slides later.

Title page of new presentation with Technic theme applied | Figure 4-1

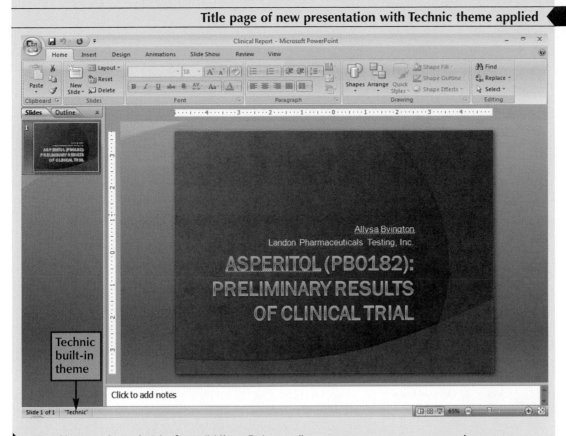

2. Change the subtitle from "Allysa Byington" to your own name, so your instructor can identify you as the author of this presentation.

3. Click the **Design** tab on the Ribbon, and then in the Themes group, click the **More** button. You won't use one of the built-in or custom themes, but rather a slide design already created in another presentation file.

4. Click **Browse for Themes**, and then navigate to the **Tutorial.04\Tutorial** folder included with your Data Files. The dialog box displays all the presentation files within the folder. Now you'll select the presentation Allysa prepared earlier.

5. Click **Landon**, and then click the **Apply** button. The design theme from the presentation Landon is applied to the Clinical Report presentation.

6. Click the **Insert** tab on the Ribbon.

7. In the Text group, click the **Header & Footer** button to display the Header and Footer dialog box, and then click the **Slide number** check box to select it.

8. Click the **Footer** check box to select it, and then type **Landon Pharmaceuticals Testing** in the Footer box.

9. Click the **Apply to All** button. The footer appears on all the slides, including the title slide. See Figure 4-2.

Figure 4-2 **Presentation with new theme from Landon presentation**

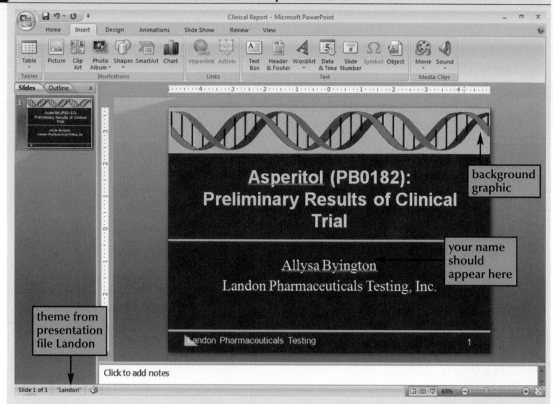

10. Save the file with its new design using the default filename.

In Figure 4-2, you can see some of the design elements that Allysa created in her original presentation, including the color scheme with a solid brown background, yellow title text, white body text, and a background graphic of a DNA double helix.

Now you're ready to add more slides to your presentation. All the slides you'll add exist in some format already; your job will be to integrate files created in other programs into the presentation. First, however, you must understand about importing, embedding, and linking objects.

Using Integration Techniques: Importing, Embedding, and Linking

An **object** is anything in a presentation that you can manipulate as a whole. This includes clip art, photos, and text boxes, as well as other graphics, diagrams, and charts that you've already worked with. In addition, you can insert objects, such as a word-processing document or a spreadsheet chart, that were created in other Office programs. The program in which an object is created is the **source program**; the program into which an object is inserted is the **destination program**.

When you insert objects, you import, embed, or link them. Refer to Figure 4-3 as you read the definitions of each of these following terms.

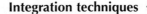

Integration techniques ◀ Figure 4-3

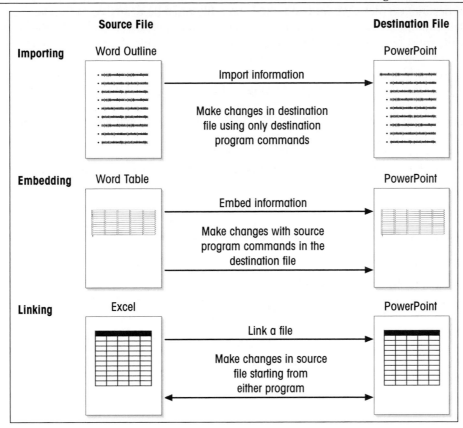

Importing an object means simply copying a file that was created using one program into the file of another program. For example, when you insert graphics and sounds into a presentation, you actually import them. Imported objects become part of the Power-Point presentation. When you import a file, the source program and the destination program don't communicate with each other in any way, as illustrated in Figure 4-3. For example, if you want to modify a graphic (such as change its size or colors) after importing it into PowerPoint, you make these changes in PowerPoint rather than in the graphics program. If you want to access the commands of the source program to modify the object, you need to start the source program and open and modify the file in the source program. The changes will not be reflected in the destination program unless you import the object again.

Embedding is similar to importing but allows a one-way connection to be maintained with the source program, not the source file. For example, if you embed a Word table in a Power-Point presentation and then double-click the table, you will be able to access and use Word commands to edit the table while still in PowerPoint. When you finish editing the embedded table and return to PowerPoint, the changes you made to the table will appear in the object in PowerPoint only; the changes do not appear in the original Word file that you used to create the table. This is because the embedded object is a copy of the original Word file, not the Word file itself. Therefore, if you make subsequent changes to the original Word file using Word, the changes will not be reflected in the embedded Word table in PowerPoint. In other words, an embedded object has no relationship to the original source file, but it does maintain a connection to the source program.

When you **link** an object, you create a connection between the source file and the linked object. You don't place a copy of the source file in the destination file; instead, you place a representation of the actual source file in the destination file. When an object is linked, you can make changes to the source file, and those changes are reflected in the representation of the linked object in the destination file. For the object in the destination file to be updated, the source file must be available to the destination file. For example, when you link an Excel spreadsheet to a PowerPoint slide, the spreadsheet file must be available to the PowerPoint presentation file if you want to edit the file; otherwise, PowerPoint treats the spreadsheet as an embedded file.

You should be aware that not all software allows you to embed or link objects. Only those programs that support **object linking and embedding** (or **OLE**, pronounced oh-LAY) let you embed or link objects from one program to another. Fortunately, sophisticated programs, such as PowerPoint, Word, and Excel, are all OLE-enabled programs and fully support object linking and embedding.

Allysa has created an outline in Word listing the text of many of the slides she wants to include in her presentation. Your next task is to import the Word outline into the presentation.

Importing and Exporting a Word Outline

If your presentation contains quite a bit of text, it might be easier to create the outline of your presentation in Word, so that you can take advantage of the extensive text-editing features available in that program. Fortunately, if you create an outline in a Word document, you don't need to retype it in PowerPoint. You can import it directly into your presentation.

Although you can create handouts in PowerPoint, sometimes you might want to take advantage of Word's formatting commands to make the text easier to read. You might also want to use the presentation of the outline as the outline for a more detailed document. To do this, you can export the outline to a Word document.

First, you'll import an outline into your presentation.

Importing the Word Outline

As you know, when you work in the Outline tab in PowerPoint, each level-one heading (also called Heading 1 or A head) automatically becomes a slide title; each level-two heading (also called Heading 2 or B head) automatically becomes a level-one bulleted paragraph; each level-three heading (also called Heading 3 or C head) automatically becomes a level-two bulleted paragraph, and so forth. Similarly, Word has an Outline view in which you can create outline text that automatically becomes level-one text, level-two text, and so forth, in the Word document. The level-one text becomes a built-in Heading 1 style; level-two text becomes a built-in Heading 2 style, and so forth. So Allysa created a Word document using Outline view (alternatively, she could have simply applied the built-in headings to the outline text). Your next task, then, is to import her outline into PowerPoint.

To import a Word outline:

▶ 1. Click the **Home** tab on the Ribbon, and then, in the Slides group, click the **New Slide button arrow**.

▶ 2. On the menu below the New Slide gallery, click **Slides from Outline**. The Insert Outline dialog box opens.

▶ 3. Navigate to the **Tutorial.04\Tutorial** folder included with your Data Files, click **ClinOtl**, and then click the **Insert** button. The Word outline is inserted as new slides after the current slide in the PowerPoint presentation, with all the level-one text becoming new slide titles. Unfortunately, PowerPoint uses the fonts and text colors of the outline document rather than of the PowerPoint theme. But you can easily fix that.

4. On the status bar, to the left of the Zoom slider, click the **Slide Sorter** button.

5. Click **Slide 2** to select it, press and hold the **Shift** key, and then click **Slide 9** (the last slide) to select all the slides from Slide 2 to 9.

6. In the Slides group, click the **Layout** button, and then click **Title and Content**. The Title and Content layout is applied to the selected slides. Now you need to reset the slides to the default settings from the Slide Master.

7. In the Slides group, click the **Reset** button. The font style and color are "reset" to the design theme. Now, you want to add the footer and page number to the imported slides.

8. Click the **Insert** tab on the Ribbon, and then in the Text group, click the **Header & Footer** button to display the Header and Footer dialog box.

9. Click the **Slide number** check box, click the **Footer** check box, and then click the **Apply to All** button. Now all the slides have a footer and page number.

10. Double-click **Slide 2** to return to Normal view with Slide 2 in the slide pane. See Figure 4-4. The imported Word outline is now in the PowerPoint slides with the proper design theme applied.

Presentation with imported Word outline ◀ **Figure 4-4**

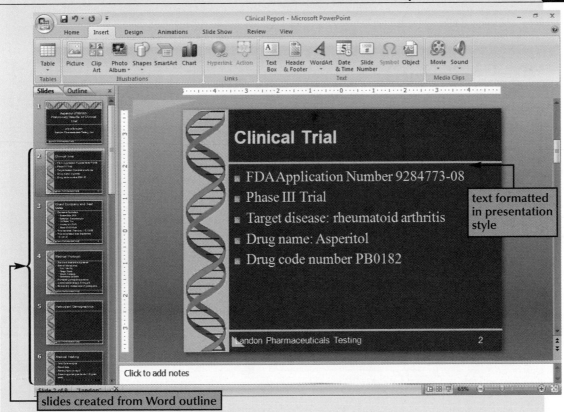

Because you imported the outline, the text is now part of PowerPoint and has no relationship with the Word file ClinOtl. Any changes you make to the PowerPoint text will have no effect on the ClinOtl file.

Exporting the Outline to Word

After looking over the presentation, Allysa wants Slide 9 ("Contents") to become Slide 2, so that her audience gets an overview of the contents of the presentation near the beginning. She then wants you to export the revised text as a Word document so that she can create a written report based on the revised outline. You'll do this now.

To modify the presentation outline in Slide Sorter view:

▸ **1.** Switch to Slide Sorter view.

▸ **2.** Drag the **Slide 9** thumbnail to the right of Slide 1 (and to the left of Slide 2). The Contents slide becomes the new Slide 2. The old Slide 2 ("Clinical Trial") becomes the new Slide 3, the old Slide 3 becomes the new Slide 4, and so forth.

▸ **3.** Double-click **Slide 1** to return to Normal view, and then click the **Outline** tab in the pane on the left so you can see the text of the outline. By changing the order of the slides, you changed the outline. See Figure 4-5.

Figure 4-5 ▸ **Presentation outline after "Contents" slide is moved**

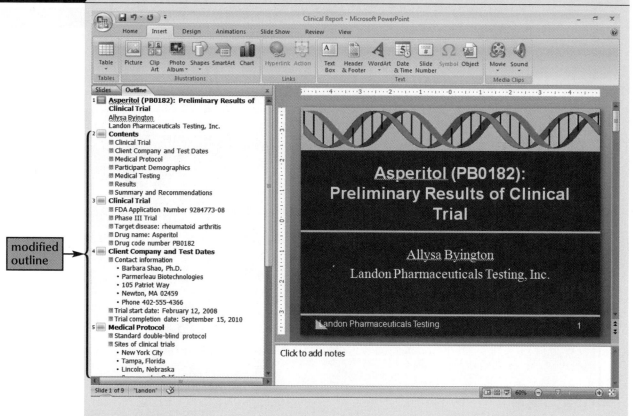

Now you'll export the revised outline to a Word file.

To export the outline to Word:

▸ **1.** Click the **Office Button** 🔘, and then click **Save As**. The Save As dialog box opens.

▸ **2.** Click the **Save as type** arrow, and then click **Outline/RTF**. *RTF* means Rich Text Format (RTF), which is a text format that preserves most formatting and can be read by most word processors.

3. Click the **Save** button. PowerPoint saves the text of the PowerPoint file as an RTF file with the filename **Clinical Report**. The file is saved in your Tutorial.04\Tutorial folder because it is the default folder.

4. Start Microsoft Word 2007, and then open the document **Clinical Report**, located in the **Tutorial.04\Tutorial** folder. As you can see, the text is barely visible because PowerPoint created the RTF file with the same font sizes and colors as in the presentation. You'll now make the text more visible.

5. Press the **Ctrl+A** keys; all the text in the document is selected.

6. Change the font to **Times New Roman**, change the font size to **12**, and then change the font color to **Automatic** (black).

7. Click anywhere to deselect the text. Now you can read the text. See Figure 4-6.

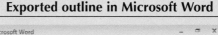
Exported outline in Microsoft Word | Figure 4-6

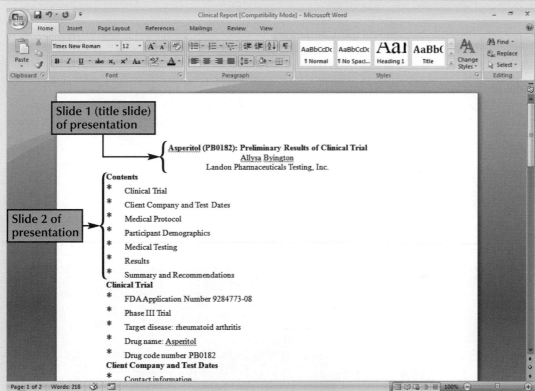

Trouble? If you are unfamiliar with Microsoft Word 2007, skip this and the subsequent steps on modifying and saving the RTF file.

8. Click the **Office Button**, point to **Save As**, and then click **Word Document**. The Save As dialog box opens with Word Document listed in the Save as type box.

9. Click the **Save** button. Word saves the Clinical Report outline as a Word document.

   Trouble? If you are asked about saving the document to the new Word 2007 format, click the OK button to verify that you do indeed want to save the file in Word 2007 format.

10. Exit Word. PowerPoint is the active window again.

Allysa or one of her associates can now reformat the Clinical Report outline using the formatting commands in Word, and then add explanatory text under each heading, as desired.

Now, Allysa wants you to import digital photographs into the presentation. You'll do that now.

Importing Graphics

You already know how to import graphics, as you have inserted digital images and clip art into earlier presentations. Now, to make the Clinical Report presentation more attractive, you'll import digital photographs to illustrate key slides.

To import (insert) graphics into the presentation:

▶ 1. Click the **Slides** tab. The Outline tab is hidden, and the slide thumbnails appear.

▶ 2. Go to **Slide 3** ("Clinical Trial"), and then, if necessary, click the **Home** tab on the Ribbon.

▶ 3. In the Slides group, click the **Layout** button, and then click **Two Content**. Slide 3 changes to the Two Content layout, with the bulleted list on the left and a placeholder on the right, where you will insert a picture.

▶ 4. In the placeholder, click the **Insert Picture from File** button 🖻, navigate to the **Tutorial.04\Tutorial** folder, and then double-click the filename **Pills**. A photo of the asperitol and placebo look-alike pills appears on the slide. See Figure 4-7.

Figure 4-7 ▶ **Slide 3 after importing picture**

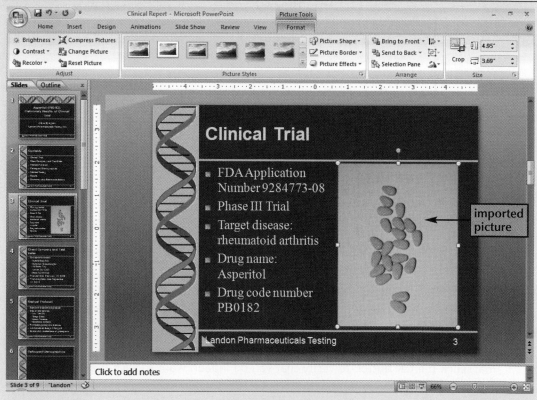

Now Allysa wants you to compress the picture. This will reduce the file size of the presentation, which saves disk space and increases transfer times when she shares the presentation with her colleagues and clients.

To compress pictures in the presentation:

1. With the picture still selected, click the **Format** tab below Picture Tools, if necessary.

2. In the Adjust group, click the **Compress Pictures** button. The Compress Pictures dialog box opens.

3. Click the **Options** button. The Compression Settings dialog box opens.

4. Make sure both check boxes in the Compression options group are selected, so that PowerPoint automatically performs a basic compression when you save the file and deletes cropped areas from the picture, if you happen to perform a crop. (Cropping is the process of trimming the pictures on one or more of its sides.)

5. Click the **OK** button to close the Compression Settings dialog box, and then click the **OK** button again to close the Compress Pictures dialog box. Now PowerPoint will compress all the pictures you import into this presentation.

6. Using the same procedure, apply the Two Content layout to Slide 7, and insert the picture file **X-ray**, located in the **Tutorial.04\Tutorial** folder, into the slide.

7. Save the presentation using the default filename.

You can also import graphics (and other objects) by copying (or cutting) from one presentation and pasting into the current presentation. Allysa wants you to do that now.

Copying an Object from Another Presentation

You'll now do a copy-and-paste operation by copying the Landon Pharmaceuticals Testing (LPT) logo from one file into your Clinical Report.

To copy an object from the Landon presentation:

1. With the Clinical Report presentation still in the PowerPoint window, open the presentation **Landon**, which is located in your **Tutorial.04\Tutorial** folder.

2. In Slide 1 in the Landon presentation, click anywhere in the logo to activate it, and then click the outermost edge to select the entire object. See Figure 4-8.

Figure 4-8 | **Selected logo in Slide 1 of the Landon presentation**

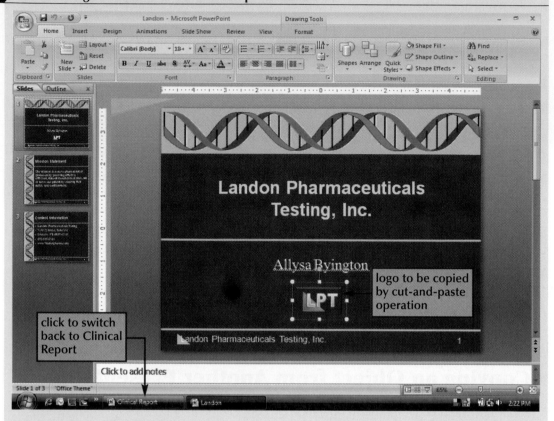

▶ **3.** In the Clipboard group, click the **Copy** button 🖼. The logo is copied to the Clipboard.

▶ **4.** Click the **Clinical Report** button on the taskbar at the bottom of your screen to switch to the Clinical Report presentation.

Trouble? If you don't see the Clinical Report button on the taskbar, you should see a Microsoft Office PowerPoint button. Click it, and then click Clinical Report to make that presentation active.

▶ **5.** In the Clinical Report presentation, go to **Slide 1**, and then in the Clipboard group, click the **Paste** button. The logo appears below your name on the slide, but overlaps the company name.

▶ **6.** Press the **Down Arrow** key three or four times to center the logo between the company name and the yellow line above the footer.

▶ **7.** Click in a blank area of the slide to deselect the pasted object. See Figure 4-9.

Slide 1 with pasted logo centered below company name   Figure 4-9

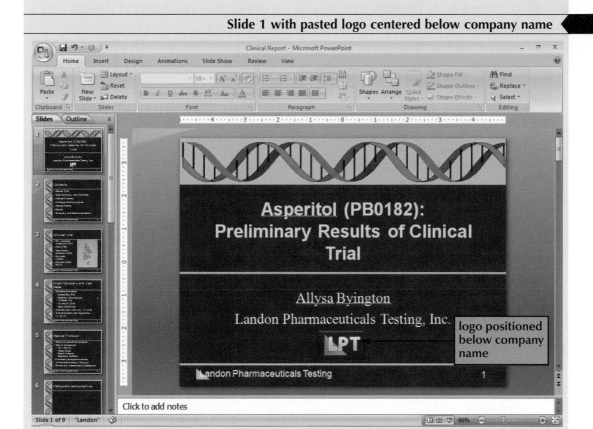

▶ **8.** Save the presentation using the default filename.

▶ **9.** Switch back to the Landon presentation, and then close the file.

The Clinical Report presentation now has the desired design theme, text slides, pictures, and logo. Your next task will be to embed a table into one of the slides in the presentation.

Embedding and Modifying a Word Table

You know how to use PowerPoint commands to create a table in a slide, but what if you've already created a table using Word? You don't have to re-create it in PowerPoint; instead, you can copy the table and place it in a slide. If you embed the table instead of importing it, you can then edit it using Word's table commands.

Alyssa created a table in a Word document that lists the demographics of the participants in the trials. You're going to embed that Word table in a slide. Alyssa created the table with a black font on a white background, so it is legible in a Word document. But as you'll see, it's not legible in the PowerPoint presentation, with its dark background.

To embed a Word file in a presentation:

▶ **1.** Go to **Slide 6**, and then click the **Insert** tab on the Ribbon.

▶ **2.** In the Text group, click the **Object** button. The Insert Object dialog box opens. You can now create a new embedded file or use an existing one. You'll use an existing file.

3. Click the **Create from file** option button, and then click the **Browse** button to open the Browse dialog box.

4. Navigate to the **Tutorial.04\Tutorial** folder included with your Data Files, click the Word filename **Demogr**, and then click the **OK** button. See Figure 4-10.

Figure 4-10 | Insert Object dialog box for embedding Word table

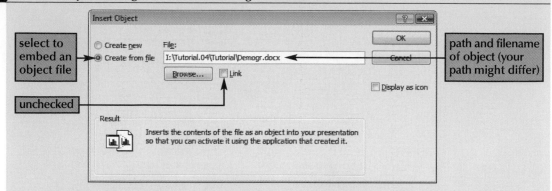

In Figure 4-10, the path and name of the file appear in the File text box. (Note that the path shown on your computer might be different.)

Tip

If you copy and paste the table from Word into PowerPoint, the table will be imported but not embedded in the PowerPoint presentation.

5. Make sure the **Link** check box is not selected, as shown in Figure 4-10, and then click the **OK** button. The embedded table appears in Slide 6.

6. Resize the table by dragging the corner sizing handles so that the table is as large as possible and still fits on the middle of the slide without overlapping background objects. You will have to drag the object border beyond the edges of the slide to make the table as big as possible. See Figure 4-11.

Figure 4-11 | Slide 6 with embedded Word table

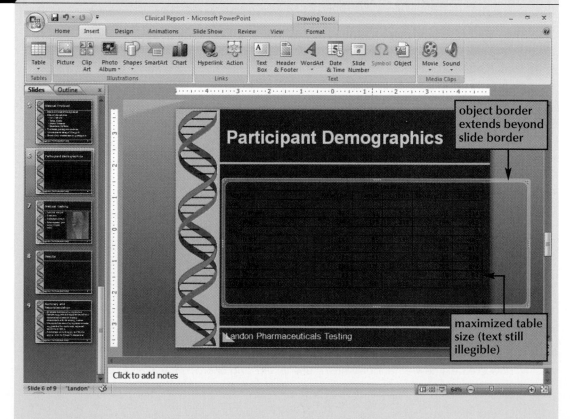

7. Click a blank area of the slide to deselect the table.

8. Save the presentation using the default filename.

Allysa asks you to modify the embedded table by changing the table color scheme and font size. Because you embedded the table, you will use the program that created the object (in this case, Word) to make the changes.

To modify an embedded table:

1. Double-click anywhere in the **table** in Slide 6. The embedded table object becomes active in Word; the Word ruler appears above and to the left of the table, and the Word menu bar and toolbars replace the PowerPoint menu bar and toolbars. See Figure 4-12.

Slide 6 with embedded Word table made active | **Figure 4-12**

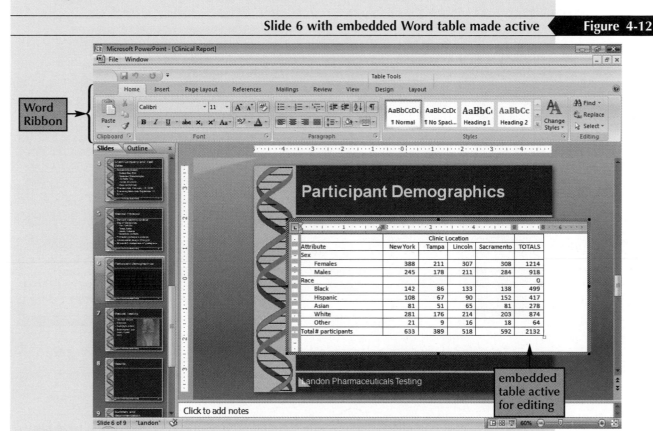

2. Drag the mouse pointer from the upper-left cell to the bottom-right cell to select the entire table, and then, if necessary, click the **Home** tab on the Ribbon.

3. In the Font section, click the **Font button arrow**, and then click **Times New Roman**.

4. Click in the **Font Size** text box, type **13**, and press the **Enter** key. The text of the table is now 13-point Times New Roman.

5. Click the **Font Color button arrow** , and click the white color tile. The font in the Word window seems to disappear, because it is white on a white background.

Trouble? The text will disappear when you change the color to white, because in Word, the background is white. Don't worry about this, because in the PowerPoint presentation, with its dark brown background, the text will show up nicely.

▶ **6.** In the Paragraph group, click the **Borders button arrow** ▦ ▾, and then click **Borders and Shading** at the bottom of the gallery. The Borders and Shading dialog box opens.

▶ **7.** Click the **Color** arrow, click the **Yellow tile** at the bottom of the palette under Standard Colors, and then click the **OK** button.

▶ **8.** Click in a blank area of the slide to exit Word and return to PowerPoint, and then click a blank area again to deselect the table. See Figure 4-13.

Figure 4-13 ▶ **Slide 6 with modified table**

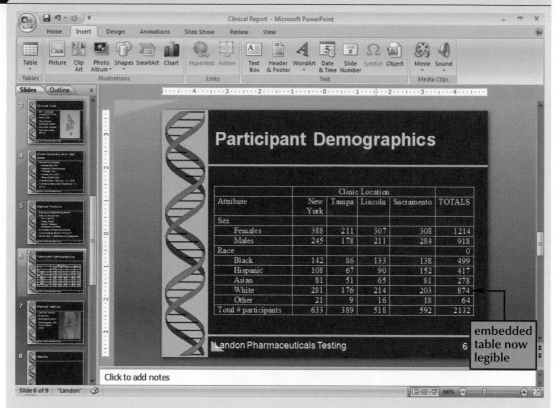

Trouble? If your table doesn't look similar to the one in Figure 4-13, make any adjustments now.

▶ **9.** Save the presentation using the default filename.

You have now completed Slide 6, which contains the embedded object. You have also edited the object using Microsoft Word. Keep in mind that the changes to the object did not change the original table in the Word document because embedding maintains a connection only with the program that was used to create the object, not with the original object itself.

Why would you want to embed rather than import an object into PowerPoint? In the case of a table, you wouldn't, because PowerPoint has all the same table commands as Word, so it's easier to modify the table directly using PowerPoint table commands rather than Word commands. However, sometimes you might want to embed an object because PowerPoint lacks the necessary editing commands. For example, you might want to embed in Power-Point a drawing created using Adobe Illustrator or CorelDRAW. In this case, if you ever wanted to modify the drawing, you'd want Adobe Illustrator or CorelDRAW commands to be available to make the changes.

Next, you'll link an Excel chart to the presentation.

Linking and Modifying an Excel Chart

Now you know how to insert objects into a PowerPoint slide by importing them and by embedding them. What if you needed to include in your presentation data that might change? For example, you might need to include data from an Excel worksheet, but you know that the final numbers won't be available for a while or that the numbers will change over time. In this case, you can link the data. Then, when the source file is updated, you can automatically update the linked object in the destination file so that it reflects the changes made to the source file.

Allysa wants to include a bar graph of the results of the clinical trial of the drug in the Clinical Report presentation. She chooses a bar graph because it emphasizes the effects of the drug-trial participants. The bar graph was created already using Excel, based on data in an Excel workbook, but Allysa anticipates that she will have to modify the work-book after she creates the PowerPoint presentation because some of the trial results were incomplete. Allysa wants any changes made to the workbook to be reflected in the Pow-erPoint file, so rather than retype or import the data into a PowerPoint chart, she asks you to link the Excel workbook to the PowerPoint presentation.

You'll link the Excel graph of income and expenses in Slide 8 in Allysa's presentation now.

To insert a chart linked to an Excel worksheet:

▶ 1. Go to **Slide 8** ("Results"), and then change the slide layout to **Title Only**.

▶ 2. Start Microsoft Office Excel 2007, open the file **Chart** located in the **Tutorial.04\ Tutorial** folder, and then save it as **Clinical Chart** in the same folder. Now you can make changes to the chart without modifying the original document.

▶ 3. Click the edge of the chart to make it active, and then press the **Ctrl+C** keys to copy the chart to the Clipboard.

▶ 4. Switch back to the Clinical Report presentation, and then press the **Ctrl+V** keys to paste the chart into Slide 8.

▶ 5. Drag the corners of the object to resize the chart so it fits within the large blank region of the slide. See Figure 4-14.

Tip

When you copy and paste an object from another program into a PowerPoint presentation, the object is normally imported, not embedded or linked. But Microsoft Office 2007 is set up so that when you copy and paste a chart from Excel into PowerPoint, the chart is automatically linked in PowerPoint to Excel.

Figure 4-14 | **Slide 8 with linked Excel chart**

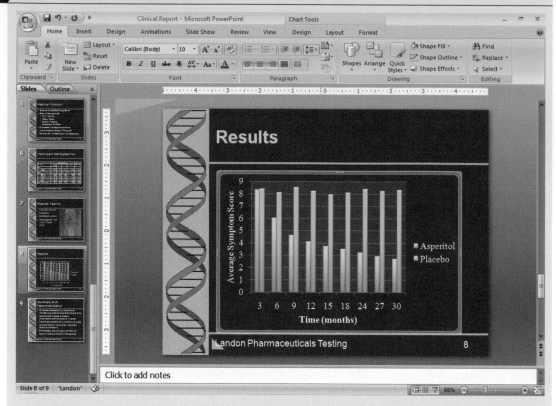

Notice that the linked chart doesn't keep the color theme as it appeared in Excel but rather takes on the color theme of the PowerPoint presentation. Also be aware that, for Excel charts, when you do a copy-and-paste operation, PowerPoint automatically links the file rather than imports or embeds the file.

6. Click outside the chart in a blank area of the slide to deselect the object.

7. Save the presentation using the default filename.

Another method for linking a file to a PowerPoint presentation is to use the Paste Special command in the Clipboard group on the Home tab. You select the object in the source file that you want to link, and then press the Ctrl+C keys in the source program. Next, you switch to the destination file in PowerPoint, and in the Clipboard group on the Home tab, click the Paste button arrow, and then click Paste Special to open the Paste Special dialog box. Click the Paste link option button, and then click the OK button.

After you linked the chart, Allysa received updated information about one of the results in the clinical-trial report. As it turns out, the scientists at Landon estimated that the average symptom score after 30 months would be 2.7, but after all the data was collected, the value was actually 3.1. Allysa asks you to make changes to the Excel worksheet data, which will then be reflected in the chart, both in the Excel and PowerPoint files.

To modify the linked chart:

1. Click anywhere in the **chart** in Slide 8, and then, if necessary, click the **Design** tab on the Ribbon below Chart Tools.

2. In the Data group, click the **Edit Data** button. The screen becomes split in two, with the PowerPoint window on the left and the Excel window on the right.

3. In the Excel window (on the right), click the **Sheet1** tab at the bottom of the window, and then click in cell **B10** (at the bottom of the Asperitol column).

4. Type **3.1**, but don't press the Enter key yet. Look at the chart in the PowerPoint window on the left. Focus on the rightmost yellow bar, which indicates the average symptom score at 30 months.

5. Press the **Enter** key. The rightmost yellow bar in the chart in the PowerPoint window changed.

   Trouble? If you didn't see the change, click the Undo button on the Quick Access Toolbar of Excel, and then, while watching the PowerPoint chart, click the Redo button on the Excel Quick Access Toolbar. Make sure you leave the value at 3.1, not 2.7, in cell B10.

6. In the Excel window, click the **Close** button ☒, and then click the **Yes** button when asked if you want to save the changes to the Excel file. PowerPoint now fills the screen again.

7. On the status bar at the bottom of the PowerPoint window, click the **Slide Show** button ☐ to see how the chart looks in Slide Show view. See Figure 4-15.

Linked and modified chart in Slide Show view | **Figure 4-15**

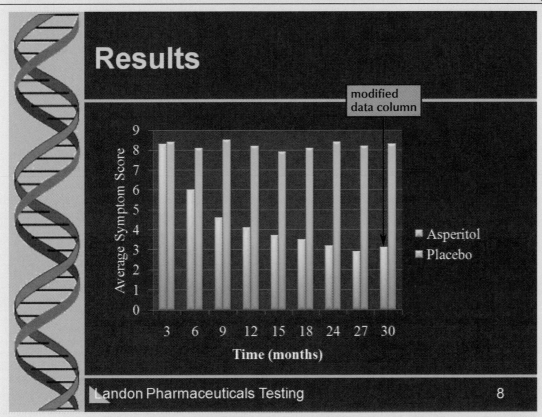

8. Press the **Esc** key to exit Slide Show view and return to Normal view.

9. Save the presentation using the default filename.

You have now linked and edited an Excel chart from PowerPoint. If you decide later to make further changes to the data in the workbook, you can do so either by directly starting Excel and opening Clinic Chart or using the Edit Chart button in PowerPoint. Either way, any changes made to the workbook will be reflected in the linked object in the PowerPoint slide.

Review | **Session 4.1 Quick Check**

1. How does applying a design theme from another presentation differ from applying a design theme from built-in themes?
2. Describe how you use a Word outline to create slides in PowerPoint.
3. Define or describe:
   a. import
   b. embed
   c. link
4. If you modify the source file of a linked object, such as an Excel chart linked to a PowerPoint slide, what happens to the linked object in the PowerPoint slide?
5. If you insert a picture created with scanning software and hardware, is the picture file imported, embedded, or linked?
6. Why would you link an object rather than embed it?

Session 4.2

Creating and Editing Hyperlinks

As you know, a **hyperlink** (or **link**) is a word, phrase, or graphic image that you click to "jump to" (or display) another location, called the **target**. The target of a link can be a location within the same document (presentation), a different document, or a page on the World Wide Web. Graphic hyperlinks are visually indistinguishable from graphics that are not hyperlinks, except when you move the mouse pointer over the link, the pointer changes to 🖑. Text links are usually underlined and are a different color than the rest of the text. After clicking a text link during a slide show, the link changes to another color to reflect the fact that it has been clicked, or **followed**.

Allysa wants to easily move from Slide 2, which lists the presentation contents, to the other slides, because she knows that as her audience asks questions, she'll need to jump around through the slides. Therefore, she asks you to create hyperlinks between each item in Slide 2 and the corresponding slides in the presentation, and then to create hyperlinks from each slide back to Slide 2.

To create a hyperlink to another slide in the presentation:

▶ 1. If you took a break after the last session, open the **Clinical Report** presentation located in the **Tutorial.04\Tutorial** folder included with your Data Files, and then, if necessary, switch to Normal view.

▶ 2. Go to **Slide 2**. First, you'll link the text "Clinical Trial" on Slide 2 to the slide that gives key information about the clinical trial.

▶ 3. In the first bulleted item, select the text **Clinical Trial**.

▶ 4. Click the **Insert** tab on the Ribbon, and then, in the Links group, click the **Hyperlink** button. The Insert Hyperlink dialog box opens. See Figure 4-16.

Insert Hyperlink dialog box ◀ **Figure 4-16**

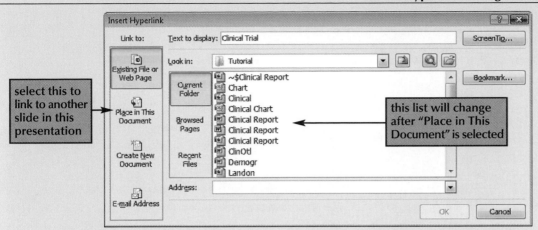

select this to link to another slide in this presentation

this list will change after "Place in This Document" is selected

You need to identify the file or location to which you want to link. In this case, you're going to link to a place in the existing document, so you'll want to select that option in the Link to panel on the left side of the dialog box.

▶ 5. In the Link to panel on the left side of the dialog box, click **Place in This Document**. The dialog box changes to list all of the slides in the presentation.

▶ 6. In the Select a place in this document list, click **3. Clinical Trial**. The Slide preview area on the right side of the dialog box shows Slide 3. This is the slide the text will be linked to. See Figure 4-17.

Insert Hyperlink dialog box after selecting a slide in current document ◀ **Figure 4-17**

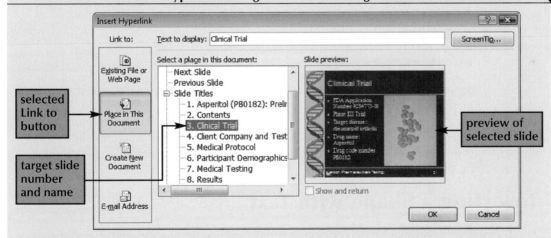

selected Link to button

target slide number and name

preview of selected slide

▶ 7. Click the **OK** button, and then click a blank area of the slide to deselect the text. The text "Clinical Trial" is now a hyperlink, and it is now formatted as green and underlined. (Recall that you can specify the hyperlink color when you set the presentation theme color.)

▶ 8. Repeat this procedure to add hyperlinks for each of the other bulleted items in Slide 2 so that each item is a hyperlink to its corresponding slide. Slide 2 should then look like Figure 4-18.

Figure 4-18 Slide 2 with hyperlinks to other slides in presentation

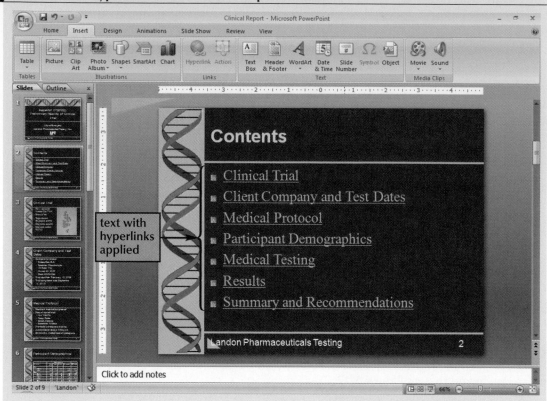

Trouble? If you make a mistake, repeat the procedure. The Edit Hyperlink dialog box will open in place of the Insert Hyperlink dialog box. You can then change the target of the hyperlink.

▶ **9.** Save the presentation.

Now that you have added hyperlinks from the text in Slide 2 to the corresponding slides, you need hyperlinks from all the other slides back to Slide 2. This way, Allysa can easily jump to any desired slide, jump back to the contents on Slide 2, and then jump to another slide. To create a link back to Slide 2, you will insert a shape, insert text into that shape, remove the borders of the shape, and then convert it to a hyperlink back to Slide 2.

Inserting a Shape with Text

You'll create a hyperlinked shape by first inserting and positioning the shape, and then inserting text into the shape.

Slide 3 with Shapes gallery open   Figure 4-19

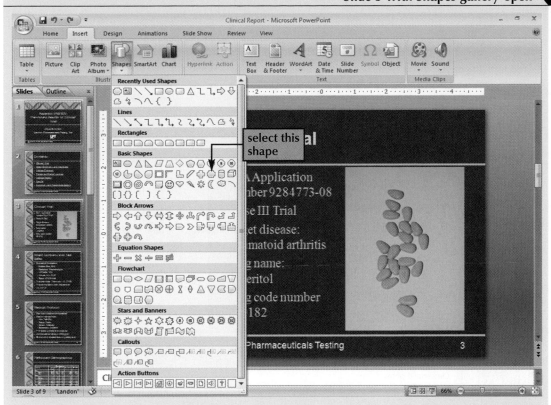

▶ **4.** Move the pointer down between the footer and the slide number near the bottom of the slide.

▶ **5.** Drag the mouse pointer down and to the right to make the shape shown in Figure 4-20. Don't worry about the exact location and size of the shape; you can fix it later.

Figure 4-20 | Slide 3 after plaque shape is inserted

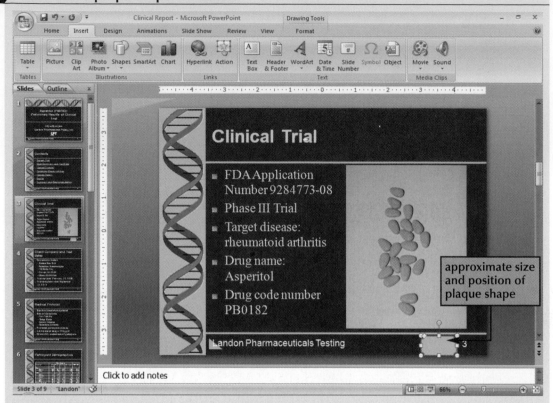

6. With the shape still selected, click the **Format** tab below Drawing Tools on the Ribbon, and then, in the Shape Styles group, click the **More** button.

7. In the Shape Styles gallery, click the **Intense Effect – Dark 1** button located in the first column in the last row in the gallery. The plaque shape changes to a beveled dark brown, similar in color to the background color of the slide but with a subtle gradient fill.

Now that you have the shape to which you'll add a hyperlink, you'll next add text.

To add text to a shape:

1. With the shape still selected on Slide 3, type **Contents**. This will remind Allysa that clicking this shape will jump back to the Contents slide. You might need to adjust the shape size.

2. If necessary, drag the middle sizing handle on the left or right edge of the shape until the shape is big enough to fit the word "Contents" on one line. You might need to make the adjustment two or three times to get the shape just the right size.

3. Deselect the shape. See Figure 4-21.

Slide 3 with completed shape with text and hyperlink | Figure 4-21

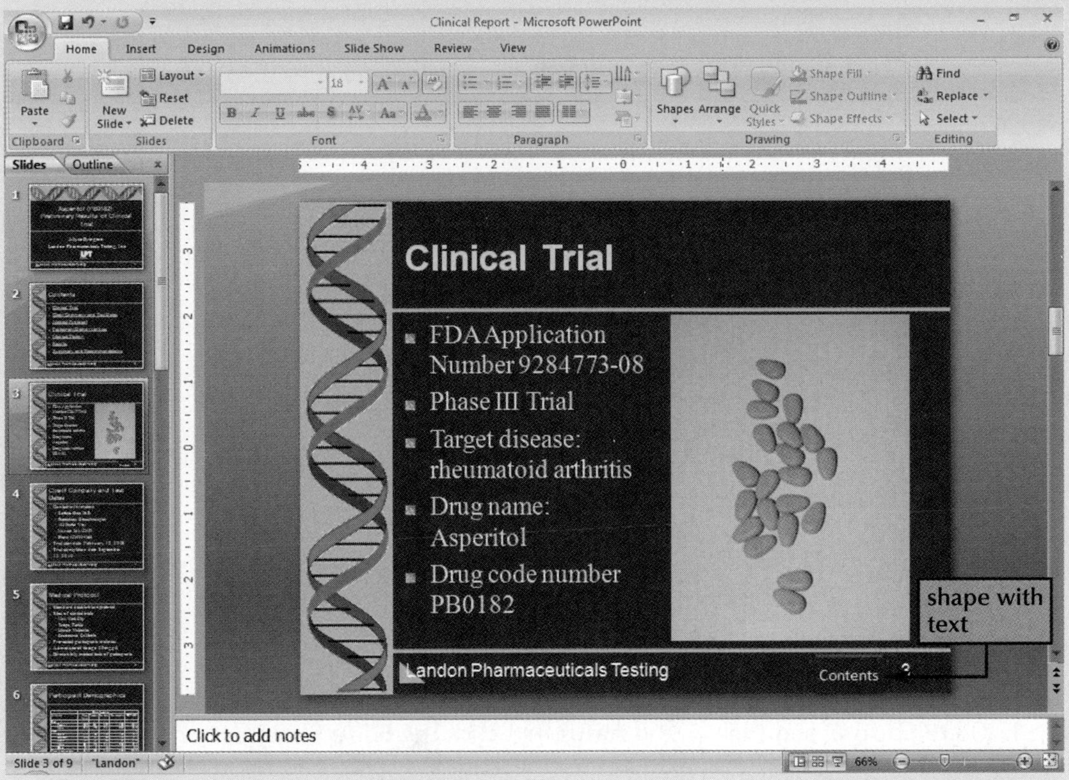

Trouble? If the size and position of the shape in your slide doesn't look like Figure 4-21, make any adjustments now.

You're now ready to make the "Contents" plaque a hyperlink.

To create a hyperlink from the plaque shape to Slide 2:

▶ **1.** Click the edge of the shape to select it.

   Trouble? If you selected the slide number placeholder instead, click in a different location on the shape's edge, for example, on the bottom edge of the Contents plaque.

▶ **2.** Click the **Insert** tab, and then in the Links group, click the **Hyperlink** button. The Insert Hyperlink dialog box opens.

▶ **3.** In the Link to panel on the left side of the dialog box, make sure **Place in This Document** is selected, and then click **2. Contents**. This is the target of the hyperlink.

▶ **4.** Click the **OK** button. The dialog box closes and the shape is formatted as a hyperlink to Slide 2.

   Notice that the entire shape is a hyperlink, not just the text inside the shape, and therefore, the text doesn't change to the green hyperlink color. Shapes and other non-text objects don't change color when they become hyperlinked.

Now you'll copy and paste the hyperlinked Contents shape on the rest of the slides. Because all the links will jump to the same slide, you can copy the shape, its text, and its hyperlink from Slide 3 to the other slides.

To copy the plaque hyperlink to the other slides:

▶ **1.** Make sure the shape is still active, and then press the **Ctrl+C** keys.

▶ **2.** Go to **Slide 4**, and then press the **Ctrl+V** keys. The link text is copied to the same position on Slide 4 as it was on Slide 3. Now you'll verify that the pasted link on Slide 4 has the same target as the original link on Slide 3.

▶ **3.** Right-click the edge of the newly pasted linked shape, and then click **Edit Hyperlink** on the shortcut menu. The Edit Hyperlink dialog box opens.

   Trouble? If you don't see Edit Hyperlink on the shortcut menu, you clicked the text box border instead of the link text. Repeat Step 3, but make sure you right-click the link text.

▶ **4.** In the Select a place in this document list, verify that **2. Contents** is selected, and then click the **Cancel** button.

▶ **5.** Repeat Step 2 to paste the link text to Slides 5 through 9 (that is, all the slides that are targets of the hyperlinks on Slide 2).

▶ **6.** Save the presentation.

With all the items on Slide 2 hyperlinked to the other slides and then back again, you're ready to test the results.

To use hyperlinks to jump to specific slides:

▶ **1.** Go to **Slide 2**, and then on the status bar, click the **Slide Show** button 🖳 . You'll test the hyperlinks in Slide Show view because they aren't active in Normal view.

▶ **2.** Click the **Clinical Trial** hyperlink. PowerPoint displays Slide 3 ("Clinical Trial").

▶ **3.** Click the **Contents** hyperlink on Slide 3. PowerPoint again displays Slide 2. See Figure 4-22. The Clinical Trial link text is now yellow, indicating that the hyperlink was followed.

Slide 2 in Slide Show view with followed hyperlink   Figure 4-22

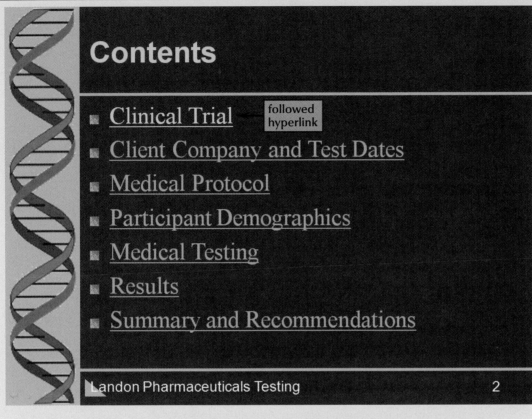

Contents

- Clinical Trial — [followed hyperlink]
- Client Company and Test Dates
- Medical Protocol
- Participant Demographics
- Medical Testing
- Results
- Summary and Recommendations

Landon Pharmaceuticals Testing   2

▶ **4.** Try all the other hyperlinks to make sure they work, and then return to Slide 2 in Normal view.

You have completed the set of hyperlinks within the presentation.

In addition to creating hyperlinks among the slides, you can add action buttons that have essentially the same effect or that can be hyperlinked to another presentation. Allysa wants you to insert an action button that will add a link to another presentation.

Adding Action Buttons

An **action button** is a ready-made shape for which you can easily define a hyperlink to other slides or documents, as well as several other actions. You can use one of the 12 action buttons in PowerPoint, such as Action Button: Home or Action Button: Sound.

Reference Window | **Adding an Action Button as a Link to Another Presentation**

- Click the Insert tab. In the Illustrations group, click the Shapes button.
- Click an action button in the Action Buttons section at the bottom of the menu.
- Click the pointer at the location on the slide where you want the action button to appear.
- In the Action Settings dialog box, click the Hyperlink to option button, click the Hyperlink to list arrow, and then click Other PowerPoint Presentation to open the Hyperlink to Other PowerPoint Presentation dialog box.
- Select the presentation to which you want to jump, and then click the OK button.
- Click the OK button in the Action Settings dialog box.
- Resize and reposition the action button icon as desired.

Allysa wants you to add a link between her presentation and the Landon presentation, which gives the mission statement and contact information of Landon Pharmaceuticals Testing. You'll create a hyperlink to that presentation by adding an action button.

To add an action button to link to another presentation:

1. Go to **Slide 2**, if you're not there already, and then, if necessary, click the **Insert** tab on the Ribbon.

2. In the Illustrations group, click the **Shapes** button. The gallery of shapes appears, with the action buttons at the bottom.

3. Click the **Action Button: Document** button 🔲 located fourth from the right in the bottom row of the gallery. The gallery closes and the pointer changes to ╋.

4. Click to the left of the slide number near the bottom of Slide 2, at about the same location as you placed the hyperlinked plaque shape on the other slides. A large button with a document icon appears on the slide and the Action Settings dialog box opens.

5. In the dialog box, click the **Hyperlink to** option button, click the **Hyperlink to** arrow, scroll down, and then click **Other PowerPoint Presentation**. The Hyperlink to Other PowerPoint Presentation dialog box opens. It is similar to the Open dialog box.

6. Navigate to the **Tutorial.04\Tutorial** folder included with your Data Files, if necessary, click **Landon**, and then click the **OK** button. The Hyperlink to Slide dialog box opens.

7. With **1. Landon Pharmaceuticals Testing, Inc.** selected, click the **OK** button, and then click **OK** in the Actions Settings dialog box.

8. Adjust the size and position of the action button, as shown in Figure 4-23.

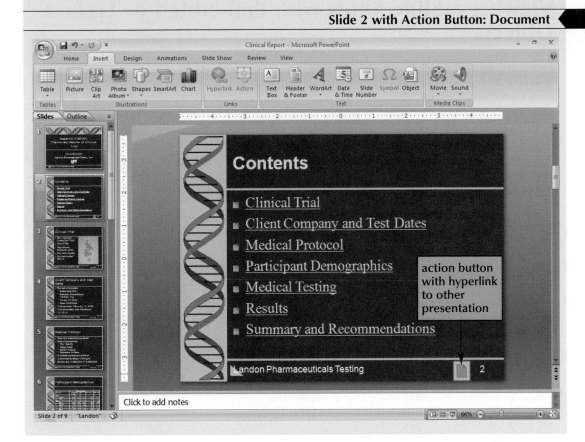

You're now ready to test the action button.

To use the action button to start another presentation:

▶ **1.** Switch to Slide Show view with Slide 2 ("Contents"), on the screen, and then click the **action button**. Slide 1 of the Landon presentation appears on the screen.

▶ **2.** Go through the slides of the Landon presentation until you reach the blank slide at the end, and then press the **spacebar** once more. PowerPoint returns to Slide 2 of the Clinical Report presentation.

▶ **3.** Return to Normal view, and then save the presentation using the default filename.

Tip

To return to the original presentation from a linked presentation, press the Esc key or right-click any slide, and then click End Show on the shortcut menu.

Allysa looks at your work so far and is pleased with your progress. The presentation now includes an imported table from Word, an Excel chart, text links to other slides in the presentation, shapes with hyperlinks back to the Contents slide, and an action button with a link to another presentation.

Viewing a Slide Show with Embedded or Linked Objects

When you present a slide show using a presentation with linked files, those files must be available on a disk so that PowerPoint can access them; and when you embed a file, the source program must be available if you want to edit the embedded object. This is because a copy of the linked file or source program for an embedded file is not included within the PowerPoint file itself; only the path and filename for accessing the linked fileare there. Therefore, you should view the presentation on the system that will be used for running the slide show to make sure it has the necessary files and that the hyperlinks are set up properly. If embedded or linked objects don't work when you run the slide show, you'll have to edit the object path so that PowerPoint can find the objects on your disk.

To view the slide show:

▶ 1. Go to **Slide 1**, and then on the status bar, click the **Slide Show** button 🖳 . Slide 1 appears in Slide Show view.

▶ 2. Click the left mouse button (or press the **spacebar**) to go to Slide 2, and then click the **action button** to jump to the other slide show. Slide 1 of the Landon presentation appears on the screen.

▶ 3. Press the **Esc** key. The Landon slide show ends and Slide 2 of the Clinical Report presentation appears again.

▶ 4. While on Slide 2, test some of the hyperlinks, using the "Contents" hyperlinked shape on each slide to jump back to Slide 2.

▶ 5. After viewing all the slides and testing the hyperlinks, return to Slide 1 in Normal view.

| InSight | **Editing Hyperlinks** |

If you want to copy the presentation file Clinical Report from, for example, your hard drive to your flash drive, you also have to copy the linked files: the presentation file Landon and the Excel file containing the chart. But you'll find that the links to the Landon presentation and to the Excel chart don't work if you try to run the Clinical Report presentation from your jump drive on another computer. This is because the links include the original path and filename to the files on the hard drive of the computer where you created the links. Therefore, you need to update the links. To update an action button link, you right-click the action button, click Edit Hyperlink on the shortcut menu, and then change the path in the Hyperlink to pathname box. To update the link to an Excel chart, you need to click the Office Button, point to Prepare, and then click Edit Links to Files to open the Links dialog box. Then, you can change the path to the source file.

Allysa is pleased with how well the embedded and linked objects work in her slide show. She now asks you to print the slides in several different formats, to meet the needs of her various audiences.

To prepare the presentation to print in grayscale:

1. Click the **Office Button** 🔘, point to **Print**, and then click **Print Preview**.

2. In the Page Setup group on the Print Preview tab, make sure the **Print What** box displays **Slides**.

3. In the Print group, click the **Options** button, point to **Color/Grayscale**, and then click **Grayscale**. The presentation now appears in grayscale.

4. In the Preview group, click the **Next Page** button five times until you get to Slide 6 ("Participant Demographics"). As you can see, the text of the table isn't visible. This is because you changed the text to white so it would be visible on the dark background, but now with a white background, the text is invisible. The only solution that will allow you to print this slide on a black-and-white printer is to change the text back to black. You'll do that now.

5. In the Preview group, click the **Close Print Preview** button, double-click the outer edge of the table on Slide 6, and then drag to select the entire table.

6. In the Font group on the Home tab, click the **Font Color button arrow** 🅰️▾, and then click **Automatic** to change the font to black.

7. Click a blank area of the slide twice, once to deselect the Word interface and a second time to deselect the table completely. Now the black text on a brown background is hard to read, but the text will be visible when you print the slides in grayscale.

Now you're ready to print the presentation in grayscale.

To print the presentation as handouts:

1. Return to Print Preview, and then go to **Slide 6**. See Figure 4-24. As you can see, the text in the table is now visible.

Figure 4-24 **Slide 6 in grayscale Print Preview with modified table**

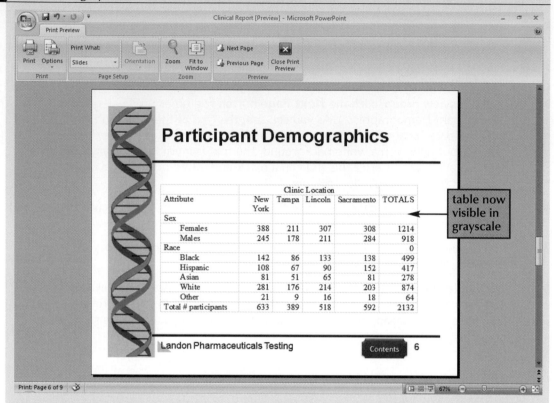

If your instructor asks you to do so, print the presentation as handouts in grayscale.

▶ **2.** In the Page Setup group, click the **Print What arrow**, and then click **Handouts (6 Slides Per Page)**.

▶ **3.** In the Print group, click the **Print** button. The Print dialog box opens.

▶ **4.** Click the **OK** button. The printed presentation should be clear and legible.

▶ **5.** Close the Print Preview window. Now you'll want to undo the change you made to the table text color.

▶ **6.** In the Quick Access Toolbar, click the **Undo** button ![undo]. This restores the color of the text on Slide 6.

Printing the Presentation as an Outline

Now Allysa wants you to see what the presentation will look like if she decides to print it in Outline view.

To print the presentation as an outline:

▶ **1.** Click the **Office Button** ![office button], point to **Print**, and then click **Print Preview**.

▶ **2.** In the Page Setup group, click the **Print What arrow**, and then click **Outline View**. The Print Preview window shows your presentation in Outline view.

▶ **3.** In the Zoom group, click the **Zoom** button. The Zoom dialog box opens.

▶ **4.** Click the **100%** option button, and then click the **OK** button.

▶ **5.** Scroll down until the text of Slide 1 is at the top of the pane and at least part of the text of Slide 5 is visible near the bottom of the screen. See Figure 4-25.

Print Preview of Outline view ◀ **Figure 4-25**

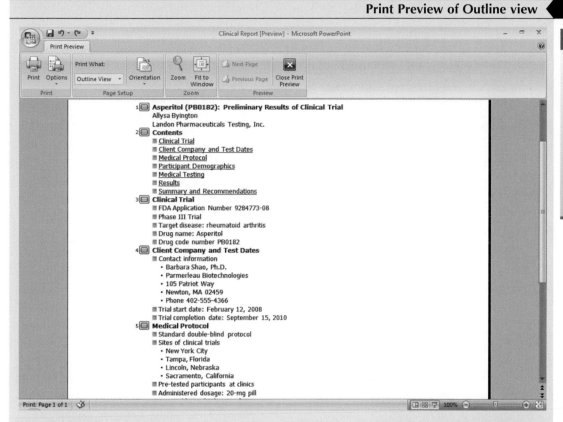

Tip

If all the important information in your presentation is text, an Outline view printout makes an excellent handout for your audience, but if you have important graphics such as charts and tables in your presentation, Outline view is not an appropriate type of handout for your audience.

As you can see, only the text of the presentation appears on the page, and the entire presentation fits on one page. Print the outline if your instructor asks you to do so.

▶ **6.** In the Print group, click the **Print** button to open the Print dialog box, and then click the **OK** button. The outline prints.

▶ **7.** In the Preview group, click the **Close Print Preview** button.

Allysa decides not to copy the Outline view printout for her audience because the outline lacks the important table in Slide 6 and the chart in Slide 8.

Customizing Handouts

Allysa still wants to give her audience handouts, but she doesn't want them to appear like the usual PowerPoint handouts. Therefore, she asks you to customize the Handout Masters.

To customize the Handout Masters:

▶ **1.** Click the **View** tab on the Ribbon, and then in the Presentation Views group, click **Handout Master**. The commands on the Handout Master tab appear.

▶ **2.** In the Placeholders group, click the **Header** check box to deselect it, click the **Date** check box to deselect it, and then make sure the **Footer** and **Page Number** check boxes are selected.

▶ **3.** In the lower-left corner of the Handout Master, click the edge of the Footer place-holder to select it, click the **Home** tab on the Ribbon, and then change the font size to **20** points.

▶ **4.** Similarly, change the font size of the text in the page number placeholder located in the lower-right corner of the Handout Master.

▶ **5.** Click in the Footer placeholder, type **Clinical Report of Asperitol**, and then dese-lect the placeholder.

▶ **6.** Click the **Handout Master** tab.

▶ **7.** In the Background group, click the **Background Styles** button, and then click **Style 2** in the gallery. The gallery closes and the page background changes from white to light tan. You have now modified the Handout Master according to Allysa's specifications. See Figure 4-26.

Figure 4-26 ▶ **Customized Handout Master**

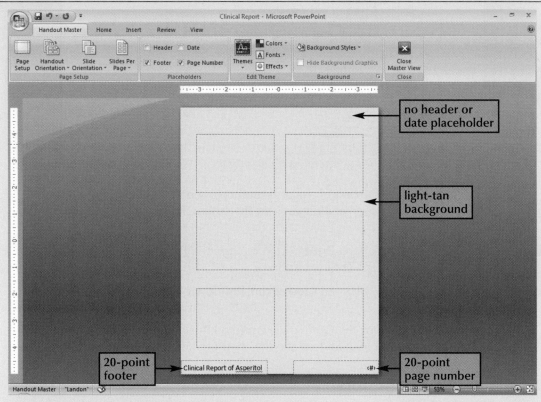

▶ **8.** In the Close group, click the **Close Master View** button, and then save the presentation.

Allysa likes the customized handouts and makes printed color copies of handouts with nine slides per page so that all nine slides of the presentation fit on one page.

Now Allysa wants you to help her prepare the presentation for posting on the Web.

Publishing Presentations on the World Wide Web

As you probably know, the **Internet** is a network of thousands of smaller networks, all joined together electronically as part of a global information-sharing system called the **World Wide Web** (also called simply the **Web**). The Web allows you to find and view electronic documents called **Web pages**. Organizations and individuals make their Web pages available by placing them on a **Web server**, a dedicated network computer with high-capacity hard disks. The Web, then, is a connected network of these Web servers. The location of a particular set of Web pages on a server is called a **Web site**. You can access a particular Web site by specifying its address, also called its **Uniform Resource Locator** (**URL**). To specify URLs and to view Web pages, you use a **Web browser**, a software program that sends requests for Web pages, retrieves them, and then interprets them for display on the computer screen. Two of the most popular browsers are Microsoft Internet Explorer and Mozilla Firefox.

Most Web sites contain a **home page**, a Web page that contains general information about the site. Home pages are like "home base"—they are starting points for online viewers. They usually contain links to the rest of the pages in the Web site.

Publishing a Web page usually means copying files (or saving them) to a Web server so that others can view the Web page. In PowerPoint, you'll use the Save As command to save your presentation as Web pages. When you select the Web pages file type, the Save As dialog box provides options by which you can customize the Web page you are saving.

Normally, you and the organization for which you work would create Web pages using a **Web page editor**, software specifically designed for this purpose, such as Microsoft Expression Web. But sometimes you want to publish a PowerPoint presentation, for example, as a link from the organization's home page. Therefore, Allysa wants you to save the Clinical Report presentation as Web pages so they can be copied onto Landon Pharmaceuticals Testing's Web site. After being placed on the Web site, the presentation will be available to company and client personnel who have access to the Web pages.

To prepare Allysa's PowerPoint presentation (or any presentation) for viewing on the World Wide Web, first you have to convert it to a file format called **HTML**, with the filename extension .htm or .html. HTML stands for **Hypertext Markup Language**, a special software language for describing the format of a Web page so that Web browsers can interpret and display the Web pages. The HTML markings in a file tell the browser how to format the text, graphics, tables, and other objects. Fortunately, you don't have to learn Hypertext Markup Language to create HTML documents; PowerPoint does the work for you. You can easily save any PowerPoint presentation as an HTML document using PowerPoint's Save As command and selecting Web Page or Single File Web Page as the file type. This procedure allows you to create a Web page file (with the filename extension .htm) that includes all the necessary images and controls to produce a professional online presentation.

If you want to edit a resulting HTML document, you'll have to use either a word processor that supports HTML editing (for example, Microsoft Word) or, better still, a dedicated HTML editor (for example, Microsoft Expression Web). PowerPoint doesn't support direct editing of HTML documents. You can, of course, make editing changes in PowerPoint and then save the results again as a Web page.

Publishing the Web Pages

Allysa wants you to save the Clinical Report presentation as a Web page so that she can copy it to the company's Web site. You remember that you added an action button to link to the Landon presentation, so that presentation will need to be saved as a Web page as well. You'll do that first.

To save a presentation as a single file Web page:

▶ **1.** Open the presentation **Landon** from the **Tutorial.04\Tutorial** folder included with your Data Files.

▶ **2.** Click the **Office Button** , and then click **Save As**.

▶ **3.** Click the **Save as type** arrow, and then click **Single File Web Page**. The bottom part of the Save As dialog box now displays options for publishing the Web page. See Figure 4-27.

Figure 4-27 ▶ **Save As dialog box for saving presentation as a single file Web page**

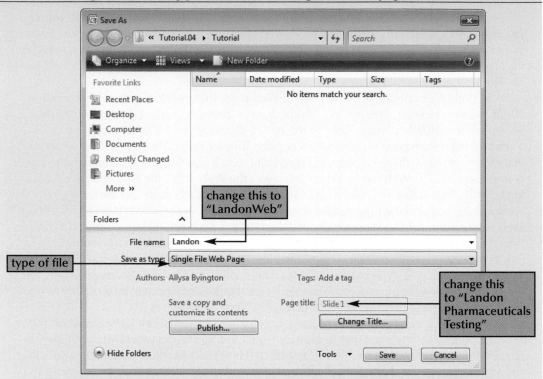

You'll now change the Web page title, which is the title of the page displayed in the title bar of the Web browser.

▶ **4.** Click the **Change Title** button. The Set Page Title dialog box opens.

▶ **5.** If necessary, change the page title to **Landon Pharmaceuticals Testing**, and then click the **OK** button. Now you're ready to publish the Web page.

▶ **6.** In the Save As dialog box, change the File name to **LandonWeb** (no spaces). This ensures that any type of browser can open the file, even browsers that don't accept spaces in the filenames. See Figure 4-28.

Completed Save As dialog box ◀ Figure 4-28

Trouble? If any of the options in your dialog box are different from those in Figure 4-28, make the changes now.

7. Click the **Save** button in the Save As dialog box to save the presentation as a single file Web page in the Tutorial.04\Tutorial folder.

8. Close the LandonWeb presentation without saving changes.

Having saved the Landon presentation as a Web page file named LandonWeb, you now need to fix the hyperlinked action button in the Clinical Report presentation so that its target is the Web page file LandonWeb rather than the PowerPoint presentation file Landon. You need to do this before you save Clinical Report as a Web page because you cannot edit Web page files within PowerPoint.

To edit the hyperlink target and save the presentation as a Web page:

1. With the Clinical Report presentation in the PowerPoint window, go to **Slide 2** in Normal view.

2. Right-click the **action button**, and then click **Edit Hyperlink** on the shortcut menu. The Action Settings dialog box opens with the Mouse Click tab on top. Now you want to change the target file from Landon to the Web page LandonWeb.

3. Click the **Hyperlink to** arrow, and then click **Other File**, if necessary.

4. Navigate to the **Tutorial.04\Tutorial** folder, if necessary, click **LandonWeb**, and then click the **OK** button.

5. Click the **OK** button in the Action Settings dialog box. Now you're ready to save Clinical Report as a Web page.

▶ 6. Using the procedure previously described, save the Clinical Report presentation as a single file Web page with the page title **Clinical Report of Asperitol** and the filename **ClinicalReportWeb** (without spaces).

Now that you saved the presentation as a Web page file, you're ready to see how it looks in a Web browser.

Viewing a Presentation in a Web Browser

It's always a good idea to see exactly what the presentation looks like in a browser before you actually publish it to a Web server. Use your Windows Explorer to navigate to and open ClinicalReportWeb.

To view the presentation in a Web browser:

▶ 1. Right-click the **Start** button ⊕ in the lower-left corner of your screen, and then click **Explore** on the quick menu.

▶ 2. Navigate to the **Tutorial.04\Tutorial** folder included with your Data Files, and then double-click **ClinicalReportWeb**.

At this point, you might see the message "This presentation contains content that your browser may not be able to show properly. If you would like to proceed anyway, click here."

▶ 3. If the message appears, click the **here** link in the preceding phrase.

If you are using Internet Explorer, you might see a partial display of Slide 1 of ClinicalReportWeb, with the Information bar above it that says "To help protect your security, Internet Explorer has restricted this webpage from running scripts or ActiveX controls that could access your computer. Click here for options." You might also see the Information Bar dialog box. Because you created the content, you don't have to worry about viruses and other dangers, so you can allow it to open.

▶ 4. If the Information Bar dialog box is open, click the **Close** button.

▶ 5. If the Information bar is at the top of the window, click it, click **Allow Blocked Content** on the menu that opens, and then click **Yes** in the dialog box that opens to verify that you do indeed want to use active content.

▶ 6. If necessary, maximize the browser window and close the Favorites or other type of pane in the window. Slide 1 of the presentation appears in the large pane on the right, and the slide titles appear in the Outline pane on the left. See Figure 4-29.

Clinical Report presentation Web page in browser   Figure 4-29

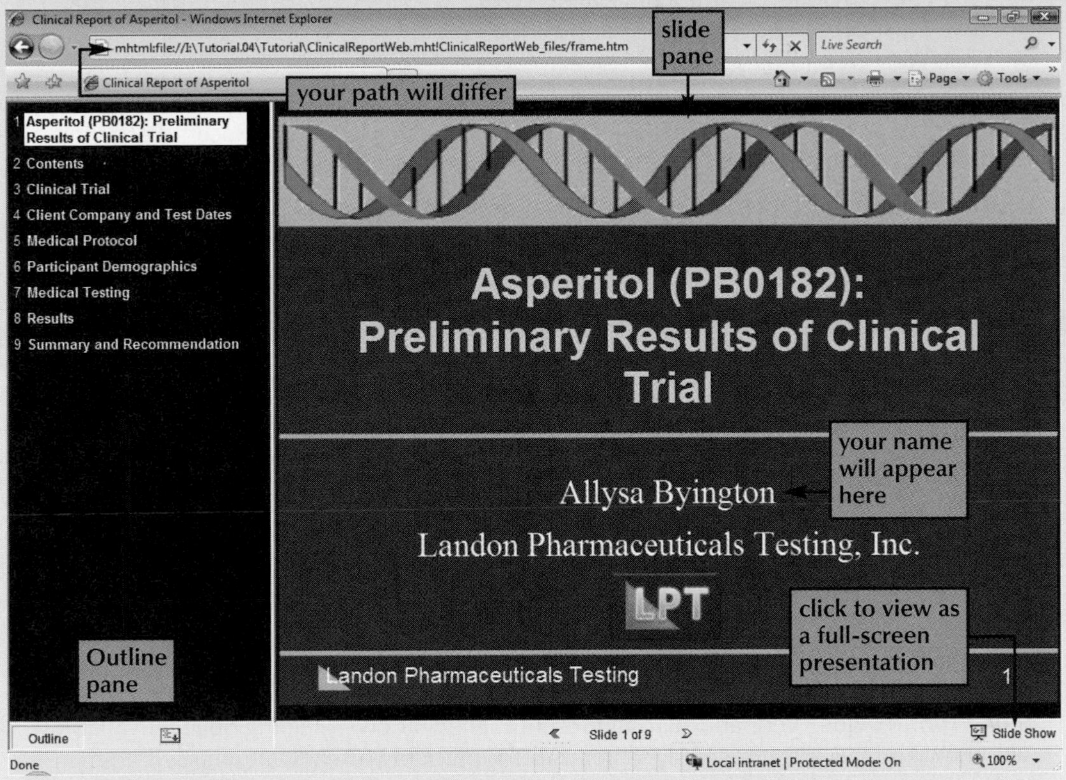

Trouble? If you don't see the outline, click the Outline button at the bottom of the screen.

Now you're ready to browse through the presentation Web page using the navigation controls and the hyperlinks.

To navigate through the presentation in the Web browser:

▶ **1.** On the navigation toolbar at the bottom of the Web page, click the **Next Slide** button ⧩ . The slide pane now displays Slide 2 of the presentation.

▶ **2.** In the Outline pane of the Web page, click **8 Results**. The slide pane now displays Slide 8.

▶ **3.** On the navigation toolbar at the bottom of the Web page, click the **Previous Slide** button ⧸ . Slide 7 ("Medical Testing") appears on the screen. As you can see, the navigation buttons help you easily move one slide forward or backward, whereas the outline hyperlinks allow you to jump from one slide to any other—in any order.

▶ **4.** In the Outline pane, click **2 Contents**, and then click the **action button** on the slide. Slide 1 of the LandonWeb page appears in the browser window, or in a new window of the browser.

Trouble? You'll probably see the same warning messages as before. Repeat the preceding steps until Slide 1 of the LandonWeb page appears.

▶ **5.** Go through the slides of LandonWeb as desired.

▶ **6.** To the left of the Address bar at the top of the browser window, click the **Back** button in the upper-left corner of the browser toolbar as many times as necessary to return to Slide 2 of the ClinicalReportWeb presentation. (In the browser, you can't just press Esc to exit the LandonWeb Web page and return to the ClinicalReportWeb Web page.)

Trouble? If Slide 1 of the LandonWeb presentation stays in your browser window no matter how many times you click the Back button, click the Recent Pages button, and then click the top Clinical Report of Asperitol.

▶ **7.** Look through ClinicalReportWeb as you desire, and then exit your Web browser.

Trouble? If a second instance of Internet Explorer started when you used the action button on Slide 2, close both Internet Explorer windows.

▶ **8.** In the Explorer window, click the **Close** button ![X].

Allysa is pleased with how the presentation looks in the browser and sends the files to the company's technical support person to publish to the Landon Pharmaceuticals Testing Web site. Next, she wants to schedule a specific time to broadcast her presentation over the Internet to get feedback from others.

Sharing and Collaborating with Others

PowerPoint provides various methods for delivering your presentations and collaborating with others, including sending presentations via e-mail, making a presentation available on the World Wide Web, and sharing files through Windows Meeting Space, available with the Windows Vista operating system. You're probably already familiar with e-mail, and you just learned about publishing a presentation as a Web page. This section focuses on holding online meetings and sharing files through Windows Meeting Space.

An **online meeting** is a method of sharing and exchanging information with people at different locations in real time (the actual time during which an event takes place), as if all the participants were together in the same room. To hold an online meeting, you can use **Windows Meeting Space**, a program that manages file sharing and online meetings. It allows participants to write notes or draw sketches on an electronic "whiteboard," send and receive typed messages, share handouts, exchange files, and to log activities that occur during the meeting.

Windows Meeting Space requires that you have the Windows Vista operating system to initiate a meeting and that all attendees likewise have Vista.

Setting Up an Online Meeting with Windows Meeting Space | Reference Window

- To initiate an online meeting, click the Start Button in the lower-left corner of your Vista screen, click All Programs, and then click Windows Meeting Space. The Meeting Space window opens.
- Click Start a new meeting, type a meeting name in the indicated box, type a password in the indicated box, and then click the Create a meeting button (a green circle with a right arrow). The Windows Meeting Space dialog box now has three sections. The large section on the left allows you to share a program or your desktop; the section in the upper right lists the participants and allows you to invite other people to the meeting; and the section in the lower right allows you to add handouts to the meeting.
- To invite participants, click the Invite people icon on the right side of the Meeting Space window. The Invite people dialog box opens. If other people are on your local area network (LAN), their names will appear in the Invite people dialog box. Click the names of those you want to invite. You can also invite anyone else who is running Vista and for whom you have an e-mail address. Click the Invite others button at the bottom of the Invite people dialog box, click Send an invitation in e-mail to open an Outlook e-mail window (you have to be set up to send e-mails in Outlook), type the e-mail address of the invitee, click the Office Button, and then click Send.
- To accept an invitation to the online meeting, open the e-mail invitation, open the attachment to the e-mail, save the attachment to your hard drive, run Windows Meeting Space (as explained previously), open an invitation file, and then select the file you just saved.
- To pass a text note (for typing text messages) or an ink note (for drawing diagrams, equations, and so forth), right-click the attendee to whom you want to send the note, click Note or Ink, type or draw your note, and then click Send.
- To share handouts, which each participant (one at a time) can change and have those changes appear on all participants' handouts, click the Add a handout button in the Handouts section of the Windows Meeting Space dialog box, navigate to the file that you want to share as a handout, and then click the Open button.
- To leave a meeting, click Meeting on the Windows Meeting Space menu bar, and then click Exit.
- To end the online meeting, click Meeting on the menu bar, and then click Exit.

Allysa decides to arrange an online meeting of her presentation for the people in the headquarters of her clients at Parmerleau Biotechnologies. Then, she and her staff give a successful presentation of the clinical-trial report of Asperitol.

Besides holding an online meeting, Allysa wants to prepare the presentation for maximum sharing with others. She asks you to help her identify features of the presentation not supported by previous versions (in case other interested parties haven't upgraded to PowerPoint 2007), to use the Document Inspector to make sure the presentation is in proper order, to use the Information Rights Manager to make sure only those who should view the presentation can view it, and to prepare customized handouts based on the presentation.

Identifying Features Not Supported by Previous Versions

Allysa realizes that some of her clients and colleagues haven't yet upgraded to PowerPoint 2007, so she asks you to check the Clinical Report presentation for features not supported by previous versions. For this purpose, you'll use the Microsoft Office PowerPoint Compatibility Checker.

To check for features not supported by previous versions:

▶ 1. Click the **Office Button** 🔘, point to **Prepare**, and then click **Run Compatibility Checker**. PowerPoint searches your presentation for features that aren't supported by earlier versions of PowerPoint, and then opens the Microsoft Office PowerPoint Compatibility Checker dialog box. See Figure 4-30.

Figure 4-30 ▶ **Compatibility Checker dialog box**

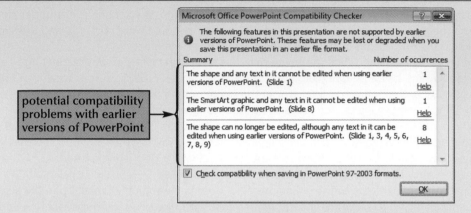

▶ 2. Look over the features in the dialog box. As you can see, some of the Office 2007 features are not compatible with PowerPoint 97–2003 formats, but none of the issues is serious. Most of the incompatible features would probably show up properly; you just wouldn't be able to edit them. You inform Allysa of these incompatibilities so she can decide later if she wants to save the presentation in an early format.

▶ 3. Click the **OK** button. The dialog box closes.

Using the Document Inspector

The **Document Inspector** is a tool you can use to check a presentation for hidden data, such as the author's name and other personal information. Allysa decides that she should check the Clinical Report presentation for hidden data. She asks you to do this now.

To check the document using the Document Inspector:

▶ 1. Click the **Office Button** 🔘, point to **Prepare**, and then click **Inspect Document**. The Document Inspector dialog box opens.

▶ 2. If any of the check boxes in this dialog box are not checked, click them. See Figure 4-31.

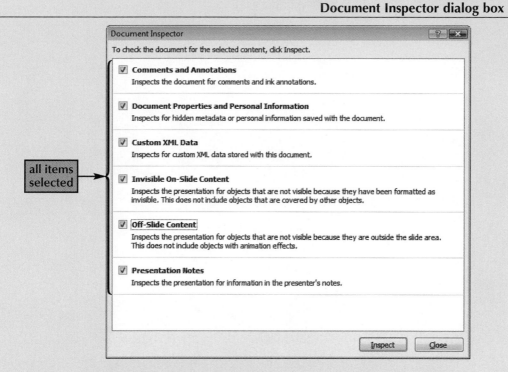

3. Click the **Inspect** button at the bottom of the dialog box. After a moment, the Document Inspector displays the results. Your presentation will probably have no problem items except document properties (which include the author's name) and Publish to Web Page information (which includes the Web page title that you used when you saved the presentation as a single file Web page). Allysa doesn't feel that these pieces of information are private, so she sees no reason to remove them.

4. Look over the various types of items that the Document Inspector checks. For example, if you happen to import, embed, or link an object that extends beyond the edges of a slide, the Off-Slide Content feature would have detected the problem.

5. Click the **Close** button on the dialog box.

6. Switch to Slide Sorter view and adjust the zoom to approximately **85%** so that all nine slides appear at once at maximum size in the slide sorter window. See Figure 4-32.

Figure 4-32   **Completed Clinical Report presentation**

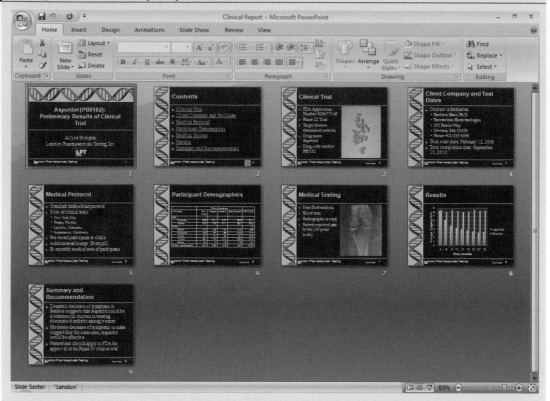

▶ **7.** Submit the file to your instructor in either electronic or printed form as requested, and then close the file.

Marking the Presentation as Final

Before Allysa shares the Clinical Report with others, she wants to make the presentation read-only, which means that others can read but cannot modify the presentation. In PowerPoint, to make a presentation read-only, you use the Mark as Final command, which disables all typing and editing commands. You'll mark Clinical Report as final now.

To mark the presentation as final (read-only):

▶ **1.** Click the **Office Button** , point to **Prepare**, and then click **Mark as Final**. PowerPoint displays a dialog box so you can confirm that you want to mark the presentation as final.

▶ **2.** Click the **OK** button. PowerPoint marks the document, disables typing and editing features, and then saves the document. Another dialog box opens telling you that the document has been marked as final.

▶ **3.** Click the **OK** button.

   Trouble? The dialog box telling you that the document has been marked as final might not appear.

   The Marked as Final icon appears in the status bar.

Managing Information Rights

Now Allysa wants you to use the **Information Rights Manager** (**IRM**), which allows you to specify access permissions to your presentation. This is extremely important for sensitive information such as the results of a clinical trial, where confidentiality is essential but yet you'll be e-mailing the presentation to many people.

To use the IRM, your computer and the computers of those with whom you are going to share sensitive information must have installed Windows Rights Management Services (RMS). This software is automatically installed on all computers that use Windows Vista. However, the IRM comes only with Microsoft Office 2007 Professional Plus or Office 2007 Ultra, so you might not have IRM available.

Using the Information Rights Manager | Reference Window

- Open the presentation that you want to share.
- Click the Office Button, point to Prepare, point to Restrict Permissions (if this doesn't appear on your computer, you can't use the IRM), and then click Do Not Distribute. The Permissions dialog box opens.
- Select the Restrict permission to this document check box, and then select the desired access level that you want for each user to whom you plan to send the presentation. The permission levels are Read (users can only read the presentation but not edit, print, or copy it), Change (users can read, modify, and save the new version of the presentation), or Full Control (users have full rights to do anything the author can do).

Allysa uses the IRM to distribute secure copies of the Clinical Report to colleagues and customers.

Session 4.2 Quick Check | Review

1. What is a hyperlink?
2. What is an action button?
3. How do you save a presentation as a single file Web page?
4. Describe what a presentation looks like in your browser.
5. What appears on the printed page when you print your presentation as an outline?
6. Describe how to hold an online meeting using Windows Meeting Space.
7. What does the Document Inspector reveal?

Review | **Tutorial Summary**

In this tutorial, you learned how to apply a design theme created in one PowerPoint presentation to another presentation, and how to import, modify, and export a Microsoft Word outline to your presentation and import a digital photograph. You learned how to embed and modify a Word table in your presentation and link and modify an Excel chart. You also learned how to create and edit hyperlinks, add action buttons, publish a presentation as a Web page, and securely share your presentation and collaborate with others over the Internet.

Key Terms

action button
destination program
Document Inspector
embed
follow
home page
HTML (Hypertext Markup
   Language)
hyperlink (link)
import

Information Rights
   Manager (IRM)
Internet
link
object
object linking and embed-
   ding (OLE)
online meeting
publish
source program
target

Uniform Resource
   Locator (URL)
Web browser
Web page
Web page editor
Web server
Web site
Windows Meeting Space
World Wide Web (Web)

Practice	Review Assignments

Get hands-on practice of the skills you learned in the tutorial using the same case scenario.

Data Files needed for these Review Assignments: Hospitals.docx, Landon.pptx, LPTChart.xlsx, LPTInfo.docx, Patient.jpg, Placebos.jpg

Allysa not only gives reports to clients of Landon Pharmaceuticals Testing clinical trials but also gives presentations to prospective clients. She now asks you to help prepare an information presentation on Landon Pharmaceuticals Testing. Complete the following:

1. Open a new, blank presentation, and then import the Word outline **LPTInfo** located in the Tutorial.04\Review folder included with your Data Files.
2. Type "Getting to Know Landon Pharmaceuticals Testing" as the title in the title slide, and type your name as the subtitle in the title slide, and then save the presentation to the Tutorial.04\Review folder using the filename **Landon Info**.
3. Apply the design theme from the presentation file **Landon**, located in the Tutorial.04\Review folder.
4. Turn on slide numbering in the Header and Footer dialog box, and set the Footer to **Landon Pharmaceuticals Testing** for all slides, including the title slide.
5. In Slide Sorter view, select all the slides except Slide 1 (title slide), apply the Title and Content layout to all the selected slides, and then reset the slides.
6. Still in Slide Sorter view, select Slides 4 and 5, and then apply the Two Content layout to the selected slides.
7. In Slide 4 in Normal view, import the picture **Patient.jpg**, located in the Tutorial.04\Review folder.
8. In Slide 5, import the picture **Placebos.jpg**, located in the Tutorial.04\Review folder. If necessary, resize the picture so it's as large as possible without covering the background objects.
9. In Slide 8, embed the Word table from the Word file **Hospitals**, located in the Tutorial.04\Review folder.
10. Make the Word program active, change the font size for all the text in the table to 20 points, and then adjust the size of the table by increasing the width of the columns so the table appears as large as possible on the slide.
11. Change the font color in the table to white, click the Design Tab under Table Tools, and then, in the Table Styles group, click the Light List – Accent 6 style. Close the Word Ribbon and return to PowerPoint.
12. Start Excel, open the Excel file **LPTChart**, located in the Tutorial.04\Review folder, and then save it as **Landon Cost Chart** in the same folder.
13. Copy the chart, and then return to the Landon Info presentation (but do not close the Landon Cost Chart workbook). Click the edge of the content placeholder, and then paste the chart onto Slide 9.
14. Display the PowerPoint and the Excel windows side by side, go to Sheet1 in the Excel window, edit the cost per patient in 2006 to $3417, and then save the file and exit Excel. (Resize the chart on Slide 9, if necessary.)
15. Open the **Landon** presentation file, located in the Tutorial.04\Review folder, and then copy the main text box containing the mission statement on Slide 2. Switch to the Landon Info presentation, go to Slide 2, change the layout to Title Only, and then paste the mission statement into the slide.
16. Copy the contact information from Slide 3 of the Landon presentation, go to Slide 10 in the Landon Info presentation, change the layout to Title Only, and then paste the contact information into the slide.

17. In Slide 3, use the bulleted items to create hyperlinks to the corresponding slides in the rest of the presentation.

18. In Slide 3, create a Plaque shape in the lower-right corner of the slide. Add text to the shape with the text **Mission Statement**. Resize the shape so it fits to the left of the slide number and below the yellow horizontal line, and so the text fits inside the shape. Make the shape a hyperlink to Slide 2.

19. In Slide 4, insert the Action Button: Home at the bottom of the slide, between the footer and slide number. Click Slide in the Hyperlink to list, and then select 3. "What We Will Cover".

20. Adjust the size of the action button so that it fits between the yellow line at the bottom of the slide just to the left of the slide number.

21. Change the shape style of the action button to Intense Effect – Accent 6, located in the lower-right corner of the Shape Style gallery.

22. Copy the action button to Slides 5 through 10.

23. View the slide show, test all the links, and then save the presentation using the default filename.

24. Customize the Handout Master so that it displays only the date and the page number, view the presentation in grayscale, make any adjustments necessary so that all the elements are legible, and then, if requested by your instructor, print the presentation as handouts with four slides per page and print the outline.

25. Save the presentation as a single Web page named **LandonInfoWeb** (no spaces), with the page title **Landon Pharmaceuticals Testing Information**. View the Web page in your browser, test the links, and then close your browser.

26. Export the outline to a Rich Text file named **Landon Info Final** in the Tutorial.04\Review folder.

27. Start Word, open the file **Landon Info Final**, located in the Tutorial.04\Review folder, and then change all the text to 12-point, black Times New Roman. Save the document as a Word document using the same file name. Exit Word.

28. Check the presentation for features not supported by earlier versions of PowerPoint, and then inspect the document for hidden data.

29. Submit the completed presentation in printed or electronic form, as requested by your instructor, and then close all open files.

| Apply | **Case Problem 1** |

Apply the skills you learned in this tutorial to create a presentation to recruit new customers for a credit union.

Data Files needed for these Review Assignments: CredUnion.jpg, FLCUChart.xlsx, FLCUDes.pptx, FLCUOtln.docx, FLCUTbl.docx, Money.jpg

Flat Lake Credit Union   Dwayne Harris is the manager of the Flat Lake Credit Union in Safford, Arizona. One of his responsibilities is to give presentations to potential customers about the services and benefits of membership in the credit union. Complete the following:

1. Open a new, blank presentation, type **Services and Benefits of Credit Union Membership** as the title in the title slide, and then type your name as the subtitle in the title slide.

2. Import the Word outline **FLCUOtln**, located in the Tutorial.04\Case1 folder included with your Data Files.

3. Apply the design theme from the presentation file **FLCUDes**, located in the Tutorial.04\Case1 folder.

4. Apply the Title and Content layout to all the slides with bulleted lists. (*Hint*: Switch to Slide Sorter view, select Slides 2 through 7, and in the Slides group on the Home tab, use the Layout button.)

5. With Slides 2 through 7 still selected in Slide Sorter view, reset the selected slides.

6. Save the presentation to the Tutorial.04\Case1 folder using the filename **FLCUServices**.

7. Add the footer **Flat Lake Credit Union**, and display slide numbers. Do not display the footer or the slide numbers on the title slide.

8. In Slide 3, change the slide layout to Two Content and import the picture file **Money.jpg**, with the bulleted list on the left and the picture on the right.

9. In Slide 7, without changing the slide layout, insert the picture **CredUnion.jpg**, and then resize and position it below the bulleted list and above the footer.

10. Add a new Slide 8 to the presentation, type the slide title **Credit Union Branches**, and embed a Word table from the file **FLCUTbl**, located in the Tutorial.04\Case1 folder. Resize the table so it appears as large as possible.

11. Edit the table so that the text is yellow and the borders are white.

12. Add a new Slide 9 with the title **Credit Union Earnings**, change the layout to Title Only, and then link the chart in the Excel worksheet **FLCUChart** (located in your Tutorial.04\Case1 folder) to that slide using a copy-and-paste operation. Resize the chart as large as possible on the slide.

13. Change the Chart Style (in the Design tab) to Style 6 and set the font size of the two axis labels ("Earnings ($Millions)" and "Year") to 28 points.

⊕ EXPLORE 14. Copy Slide 2 from FLCUDes to make it Slide 10 of FLCUServices. (*Hint*: With FLCUDes open, click the miniature of Slide 2 in the Slides tab on the left edge of the PowerPoint window, use the Copy command to copy the slide, and then, in FLCUServices, with Slide 9 as the active slide, paste the new slide.)

15. In Slide 10, insert the Action Button: Home and make it a hyperlink to the first slide in the presentation. (*Hint*: Change the Hyperlink to value to First Slide.) This will allow Dwayne to easily jump from the end to the beginning of the slide show.

⊕ EXPLORE 16. Resize the action button to 0.75 by 0.75 inches. (*Hint*: With the action button selected, click the Format tab below Drawing Tools, and in the Size group, set the desired vertical and horizontal dimensions.)

17. Move the action button to the lower-left corner of the slide, so it's near the bottom of the picture panel of Flat Lake, and then change the Shape Style to Intense Effect – Accent 1 (located on the bottom row, second from the left, in the Shape Style gallery).

18. After completing the slide show, save the presentation using the default filename.

19. View the slide show in Slide Show view and test the action button that you inserted.

20. Submit the completed presentation in printed or electronic form, as requested by your instructor. If you print the presentation in grayscale, hide the background graphics on Slide 1. After printing in grayscale, make sure you unhide the background graphics before you proceed to the next step.

21. Save the presentation as a single file Web page with the filename **FLCUWeb** with the Page title "Services and Benefits of Credit Union Membership."

22. View the Web page in your browser, and then close all open windows.

Challenge | Case Problem 2

Expand the skills you learned in this tutorial to create a presentation for a wildlife management company.

Data Files needed for this Case Problem: BirdBlt.jpg, FlwBlt.jpg, WMCchart.xlsx, WMCDes.pptx, WMCOtl.docx

Wildlife Management Consultants Hillary Trejo of DeForest, Wisconsin, is president of Wildlife Management Consultants (WMC), a small company that contracts with the Wisconsin Division of Natural Resources and the Bureau of Wildlife Management to manage wildlife (plants and animals) in wildlife refuges and state forests. Hillary asks you to help her prepare and publish a presentation on the services offered by WMC. Complete the following:

1. Open the presentation file **WMCDes** located in the Tutorial.04\Case2 folder included with your Data Files. Hillary wants you to modify this file so you can use it in other presentations as a design theme.

2. Switch to Slide Master view, and then click the Office Theme Slide Master at the top of the pane on the left side of the window.

⊕ **EXPLORE** 3. Click the placeholder text of the level-1 (top) bullet, and change the bullet to the picture **BirdBlt** (head of a bird), located in the Tutorial.04\Case2 folder. (*Hint*: Open the Picture Bullet dialog box, click the Import button, navigate to the Tutorial.04\Case2 folder, and then import **BirdBlt**.)

⊕ **EXPLORE** 4. Repeat the procedure in Step 3 to make the second-level bullet the picture **FlwBlt** (flower bullet), and then reduce its size to 80% of normal. (*Hint*: To adjust the size, use the Size feature in the Bullets and Numbering dialog box.)

5. Return to Normal view, save the presentation to the Tutorial.04\Case2 folder using the filename **WMCDesign**, but leave the presentation open as you complete the remaining steps.

6. Open a new, blank presentation, type **Services of Wildlife Management Consultants** in the title placeholder, and then type your name in the subtitle placeholder.

7. Apply the design theme **WMCDesign**, which you saved to the Tutorial.04\Case2 folder.

8. Import the Word outline in the file **WMCOtl**, located in the Tutorial.04\Case2 folder. Reapply the Title and Content layout to all the slides with bulleted lists, and then reset the slides to follow the default design theme.

⊕ **EXPLORE** 9. Insert the current date, the footer **Wildlife Management**, and the slide number on all the slides including the title slide. (*Hint*: To insert the date, use the same dialog box that you use to insert a footer and the slide number.)

10. Save the presentation as **WMCServices** in the Tutorial.04\Case2 folder.

⊕ **EXPLORE** 11. Change the layout of Slide 3 to Two Content, and then into the left content placeholder on Slide 3, import a photograph of one of the animal species listed on the slide. Use the Microsoft online clip art and media service to find this photo. (*Hint*: Make sure your computer is connected to the Internet, and then click the Clip Art button in the content placeholder to open the Clip Art task pane. In the Results should be list, select only Photographs and deselect all the others.)

12. Make each of the bulleted items in Slide 2 a link to the corresponding slide in the presentation.

⊕ **EXPLORE** 13. Format the background image Wilderness (text with overlaid plants and animals) as a hyperlink to Slide 2. (*Hint*: Switch to Slide Master view, click the WMCDesign Slide Master, make the "Wilderness" object a hyperlink to Slide 2, and then return to Normal view.)

⊕ **EXPLORE**   14. In Slide 3, swap the bulleted list in the left content placeholder with the photograph on the right. (*Hint*: Use the Cut and Paste commands to move the bulleted list.) Adjust the size and position of the photograph as desired.

15. In Slide 8, change the layout to Title Only, and then link the Excel chart **WMCchart**, located in the Tutorial.04\Case2 folder. Resize the chart so it fits on the slide.

⊕ **EXPLORE**   16. Change the color of all the text in the chart to white. (*Hint*: Select the entire chart by clicking the outer edge of the object, and then change the font color.)

⊕ **EXPLORE**   17. Change the chart design to Style 45. (*Hint*: Click the Design tab below the Chart Tools, click the Chart Styles More button, and select Style 45 located on the bottom row, fifth column from the right.)

⊕ **EXPLORE**   18. Copy Slide 2 from WMCDesign, to make it Slide 10 of WMCServices. (*Hint*: With WMCDesign open, click the miniature of Slide 2 in the Slides tab on the left edge of the PowerPoint window, copy the slide, and then, in WMCServices, make sure Slide 9 is the active slide, and paste the new slide.)

⊕ **EXPLORE**   19. Customize the Handout Master in the following ways:
   a. Change the font size of the header, date, footer, and page number to 20 points.
   b. Add the footer text **Wildlife Management Consultants**.
   c. Add the header text **WMC Services**.
   d. Increase the width of the footer so the footer text fits all on one line.
   e. Set the background to a light-yellow color. (*Hint*: Click Format Background located at the bottom of the Background Style gallery, set the Fill to Solid fill, and select a light-yellow color from the Colors palette of color tiles.)

20. In Slide Show view, check all the hyperlinks.

21. Check the presentation for features not supported by earlier versions of PowerPoint. Make a note of these features.

22. Save the presentation using the default filename.

23. Export the outline to an RTF file named **WMCServices Outline**. Start Word, and then open the file you created. Reformat the text so that it is 10-point, black Calibri. Go to the end of the document, and add text describing the features of the presentation that are not supported in earlier versions of PowerPoint. Save your changes.

24. Return to the presentation, save it as a single file Web page with the filename **WMCWeb**, and then view the slide show in your browser.

25. Submit the completed presentation in printed (including the custom handouts) or electronic form, as requested by your instructor, and then close all open files.

| Create | **Case Problem 3** |

Create a presentation for a company that sells emergency preparedness products.

Data Files needed for this Case Problem: 72HrKit.jpg, EPR.pptx, EPRChart.xlsx, EPROtl.docx, EPRTabl.docx, Flood.jpg, Wheat.jpg

Emergency Preparedness Resources   Emergency Preparedness Resources (EPR) is a growing business in West Wendover, Nevada. The owner and president of EPR, Parker Salvatore, gives presentations on his company's products at emergency preparedness seminars, conferences, and trade shows. Parker asks you to set up a PowerPoint presentation on his company's products. Create the finished presentation, as shown in Figure 4-33, and then create a Web page of the presentation.

Figure 4-33

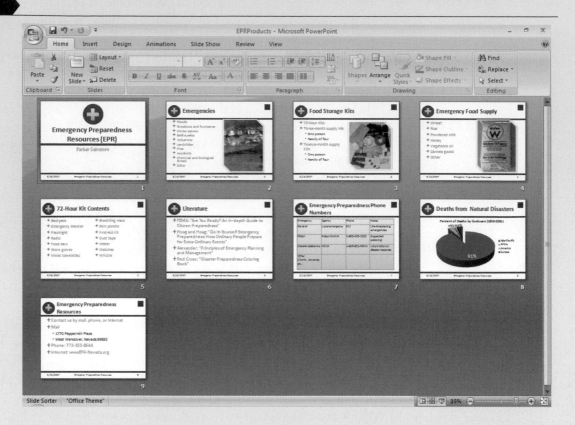

Read all the steps before you start creating your presentation. Not all the necessary steps are included below. You'll have to figure out on your own some necessary steps to complete the assignment.

1. The presentation is created from the **EPR** presentation, located in the Tutorial.04\Case3 folder included with your Data Files. Change the name "Parker Salvatore" on Slide 1 to your name, and save it as **EPRProducts**.

2. The text for the subsequent slides in the presentation comes from the Word outline file **EPROtl**, located in the Tutorial.04\Case3 folder. Adjust the slides with bulleted lists by reapplying the slide layout and then resetting the slides. Make sure the current date, footer, and slide number appear on all the slides.

3. Images that appear in Slides 2 through 4 are **Flood**, **72HrKit**, and **Wheat**, respectively, located in the Tutorial.04\Case3 folder.

4. In Slide 5, because the double-columned bulleted list appears as a single list when you first import the outline, change the slide layout to Two Content and use a cut-and-paste operation to move the last seven bulleted items to a second content placeholder.

5. The table of contact numbers on Slide 7 comes from the file **EPRTabl**, located in the Tutorial.04\Case3 folder. You'll have to modify the table later so that its size, fonts, and borders are legible and attractive, as shown in Figure 4-33. (*Hint*: In EPRTabl, click anywhere in the table, and then click the small button located above the upper-right corner of the table to select the entire table. Use copy and paste to copy the table from the Word document to the PowerPoint presentation.)

6. The pie chart in Slide 8 comes from the Excel file **EPRChart**, located in the Tutorial.04\Case3 folder.

7. The Action Button: Home buttons shown in the upper-right corner of Slide 2 through 9 are hyperlinked to Slide 1.

8. Save your final presentation using the default filename, and then save it as a Web page using the filename **EPRWeb** and the Page title **Emergency Preparedness Resources**.

9. Submit the completed presentation in printed or electronic form, as requested by your instructor, and then close the file.

| Apply | | **Case Problem 4** |

Apply the skills you learned in this tutorial to create a presentation about wetlands.

Data Files needed for this Case Problem: Wetland1.jpg, Wetland2.jpg, Wetland3.jpg, Wetland4.jpg, Wetland5.jpg

Campus Conservation Consortium The Campus Conservation Consortium (CCC) is an organization of college students that gives presentations to other students on conserving America's wetlands. Prepare a presentation to your classmates on information about wetlands. You might choose a topic such as grants and scholarships on wetland conservation, analysis and information about wetlands in a particular state, legislation on wetland conservation, description of wetland types (saltwater habitats, freshwater habitats, and upland habitat), use of wetlands by migratory birds or other animals, information about an organization involved in wetland conservation, conservation plans for private owners of wetlands, or other related topics. Do the following:

⊕ EXPLORE

1. Using Microsoft Word, create an outline of your presentation on wetland conservation. Include at least six titles, which will become slide titles. (Remember to switch to Outline view in Word to type your slide titles, which will be formatted with the Heading 1 style.) Under each title, add information (content) items (formatted in the Heading 2 style), which will become the bulleted lists on each slide. Use books and magazines from your college library, encyclopedia, the Internet, or other sources of information to get the necessary information on wetland conservation. If you haven't covered Microsoft Word in your courses and don't know how to create an outline with heading styles, use the Help feature of Word.

2. Save the Word file using the filename **WetlandOtl** to the Tutorial.04\Case4 folder included with your Data Files.

3. In another Word document, create a table. Your table might list various wetland preserves, their total area, examples of major wildlife in the area, or other information. You might be able to find a table on the Internet from which you can extract the data.

4. Save the Word file with the table using the filename **WetlandTbl** to the Tutorial.04\Case4 folder included with your Data Files.

5. Open a new, blank presentation, and include an appropriate title of your choosing and a subtitle with your name as the presenter.

6. Import the Word outline into PowerPoint.

7. Apply the built-in design theme Flow.

8. Reapply the slide layouts to, and reset, the slide, as needed, so they use the proper font and have the proper format.

9. Embed your table into a slide of your presentation. Resize, reposition, and reformat it as needed to maximize its readability.

10. Include a text box either on the first slide or the last slide acknowledging the sources of your information.

11. Insert at least one action button into your presentation with a link to another slide within your presentation.

12. Include at least two text hyperlinks in your presentation, with links to other slides. The text of the hyperlinks can be bulleted items, text in a table cell, or text boxes.

13. Add graphics and slide transitions to the slide show, as desired. If you want, you can use any of the pictures **Wetland1** through **Wetland5** located in the Tutorial.04\Case4 folder.

14. Save your presentation using the filename **Wetlands**.

15. Save your presentation as a single file Web page, with the Page title **Wetland Conservation** and the filename **WetWeb**.

16. Submit the completed presentation in printed or electronic form, as requested by your instructor, and then close the file.

Research | **Internet Assignments**

Go to the Web to find information you can use to create presentations.

The purpose of the Internet Assignments is to challenge you to find information on the Internet that you can use to work effectively with this software. The actual assignments are updated and maintained on the Course Technology Web site. Log on to the Internet and use your Web browser to go to the Student Online Companion for New Perspectives Office 2007 at **www.course.com/np/office2007**. Then navigate to the Internet Assignments for this tutorial.

Assess | **SAM Assessment and Training**

If you have a SAM user profile, you may have access to hands-on instruction, practice, and assessment of the skills covered in this tutorial. Log in to your SAM account (**http://sam2007.course.com**) to launch any assigned training activities or exams that relate to the skills covered in this tutorial.

Review | **Quick Check Answers**

Session 4.1

1. For a built-in theme, you use the Themes gallery on the Design tab. To use a theme from a presentation file, you use the More button on the Themes group, click Browse for Themes, and navigate to the file with the desired theme.

2. On the Home tab, click the New Slide button arrow, click Slides from Outline, select the Word file with the outline, and then click the Open button.

3. a. Import means to insert a file that was created using one program into another program's file.

   b. Embed means to insert a file so that a connection with the source program is maintained.

   c. Link means to insert a file so that a connection between the source file and the destination file is maintained, and changes made to the source file are reflected in the linked object in the destination file.

4. The object is updated to reflect the changes made to the source file.

5. imported

6. so that modifications you make to the source file are reflected in the destination file

Session 4.2

1. A hyperlink is a word, phrase, or graphic that you click to display an object at another location.
2. An action button is a ready-made shape for which you can easily define hyperlinks to other slides or documents.
3. Click the Office Button, click Save As, set Save as type to Single File Web Page, and then click the Save button.
4. A frame on the left contains an outline of the slides, the slide itself appears in a frame on the right, and navigation buttons appear at the bottom of the slide.
5. The slide numbers, slide titles, and bulleted lists on the slides, but no graphics.
6. To initiate an online meeting, click the Start button in the lower-left corner of your Vista screen, click All Programs, and click Windows Meeting Space. The Meeting Space window opens. To invite participants, click the Invite people icon on the right side of the Meeting Space window. Click the names of those you want to invite or invite anyone else who is running Vista and for whom you have an e-mail address. Open the presentation that you want to broadcast, click Slide Show, point to Online Broadcast, and then click Begin Broadcast.
7. Comments and annotations, document properties and personal information, custom XML data, invisible on-slide content, off-slide content, and presentation notes.

Ending Data Files

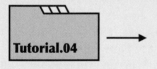

Tutorial.04 → **Tutorial**

Clinical Chart.xlsx
Clinical Report.docx
Clinical Report.pptx
Clinical Report.rtf
ClinicalReportWeb.mht
LandonWeb.mht

Review

Landon Cost
Chart.xlsx
Landon Info
Final.docx
Landon Info Final.rtf
Landon Info.pptx
LandonInfoWeb.mht

Case1

FLCUServices.pptx
FLCUWeb.mht

Case2

WMCDesign.pptx
WMC Services Outline.rtf
WMCServices.pptx
WMCWeb.mht

Case3

EPRProducts.pptx
EPRWeb.mht

Case4

WetlandOtl.docx
Wetlands.pptx
WetlandTbl.docx
WetWeb.mht

Reality Check

Have you been on a trip lately? Perhaps you traveled somewhere for Spring Break, went on a camping trip, traveled home during a semester break, spent a semester studying abroad, or went on tour with a college musical group. Whatever your travel experience, others might be interested in your trip. A good vehicle for sharing your trip with family and friends is a PowerPoint presentation or possibly a Web page created from a Power-Point presentation. In this exercise, you'll use PowerPoint to create a presentation about your travels using the skills and features presented in Tutorials 3 and 4.

Note: Please be sure *not* to include any personal information of a sensitive nature in the documents you create to be submitted to your instructor for this exercise. Later on, you can update the documents with such information for your own personal use.

1. Start a new, blank PowerPoint presentation.
2. Create a new set of theme colors, and save it with an appropriate name.
3. Using your theme colors, create an attractive, tasteful design theme using slide masters. Choose design elements that match your travels. For example, if your trip was a serious culture experience (like a visit to European museums), your design should be conservative, but if your trip was festive (like a trip to a football bowl game), your design could be more exciting. In the appropriate slide masters, use picture bullets for the bulleted lists. Save the file as an Office Theme.
4. Start a new presentation using the theme that you created. Save it with an appropriate name.
5. On Slide 1, type an informative title for your presentation. For example, if you traveled to New York City for an internship, your title could be "My New York City Internship," or if you spent a year with the Peace Corps in Bolivia, your title might be "My Year in the Peace Corps in Bolivia." Add your name as a subtitle.
6. Create at least six slides (not counting the title slide) about your trip. Include things such as the purpose of your trip, information about the places you visited, special experiences during your trip, scenic vistas (described in words and shown in pictures), modes of travel you used (airplane, private vehicle, subway, taxi, and so forth), and recommendations for others who might be thinking of a similar trip.
7. Your presentation should include pictures. You can use pictures that you or your friends took, or you could scan printed photos, postcards, ticket stubs, showbills, or other items from your trip. If necessary, go online to find appropriate pictures for your presentation. Apply styles to your pictures.
8. Add movies and recorded sounds to your presentation if you have any.
9. Add slide transitions and custom animations to your presentation. Add sound effects if they will enhance the presentation. Decide whether you want the animations to start automatically (after the previous item) or if you want to let the user control them with the mouse.
10. Use hyperlinks and action buttons to allow the person viewing the presentation to easily jump to different slides.
11. Apply a picture background to one of your slides, and include appropriate footer information.
12. View your presentation in Slide Show view. Make sure the transitions, animations, sound, movies, and links work as you expected. Save your final presentation.
13. If you want to publish the presentation to a Web server, edit links as necessary, and then save the presentation as a single file Web page. Give the Web page a page title that makes sense.
14. Submit the completed presentation in printed or electronic form, as requested by your instructor, and then close the file.

Objectives

Session 5.1
- Copy a slide to another application
- Copy a slide to another slide as a picture object
- Create and modify a SmartArt diagram
- Apply complex animation and sound effects to a presentation
- Download clip art from Microsoft Office Online
- Manipulate background objects on a slide
- Apply special effects to a text box
- Create a numbered list on a slide

Session 5.2
- Use drawings and diagrams from other applications in a PowerPoint presentation
- Apply callouts to a diagram
- Insert an audio track from a CD into a presentation
- Record a narration
- Set up a self-running presentation
- Create and edit a custom show

Applying Advanced Special Effects in Presentations

Adding Complex Sound, Animation, and Graphics to a Presentation

Case | Mountain Peak Homes

Corrine T. Moritz is a sales agent for Mountain Peak Homes in Billings, Montana. Corrine's main focus is selling lots and the new homes that her company will build on those lots. She also works with the new home owners to help them do the following:

- Choose a home design from Mountain Peak Homes' catalog.
- Customize the home design plans, as desired.
- Select interior and exterior materials, designs, and colors—including cabinets, paint colors, floor coverings, and exterior walls and roof coverings.
- Communicate with the construction supervisors to resolve issues that arise during construction of new homes.

Corrine is preparing a Microsoft PowerPoint presentation for potential and new clients. She asks you to help finish the presentation and to prepare handouts on all phases of the purchasing, financing, and building processes.

In this tutorial, you'll copy a slide to another application and copy and make hyperlinked picture thumbnails on a slide. You'll create, modify, and animate a SmartArt diagram, apply complex animation and sound effects to other objects in your presentation, and create a numbered list. You'll also download clip art and music, insert a CD audio track, and record a narration. Finally, you'll set up a self-running presentation, insert and manipulate graphic objects, and create a custom show.

Starting Data Files

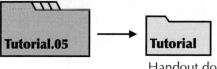

Tutorial.05 →	Tutorial	Review	Case1	Case2	Case3	Case4
	Handout.docx	ColorForm.jpg	Cyclist.jpg	Arches.jpg	Salsa.pptx	(none)
	MPHomes.pptx	MPHColors.pptx	Race.pptx	Camera.jpg		
	PlatMap.jpg		Runner.jpg	DPJ.pptx		
			RunPic.jpg	Falls.jpg		
				MntLake.jpg		
				Tahoe.jpg		
				Trevor.jpg		
				Yosemite.jpg		

Session 5.1

Planning the Presentation

Before creating the presentation, Corrine and you sit down to plan the presentation using the following guidelines:

- **Purpose of the presentation**: To provide information about building a new home through Mountain Peak Homes
- **Type of presentation**: Overview of products and services
- **Audience**: Potential and new clients of Mountain Peak Homes
- **Audience needs**: To understand the process of buying and building a new home
- **Location of the presentation**: Primarily in the model home in the Bella Vista development of Mountain Peak Homes; a room in the model home serves as Corrine's sales office
- **Format**: Electronic slide show for oral and self-running presentations

With this general plan for the presentation, Corrine started to create a presentation by adding text and applying a custom-designed template to the presentation. She also needs a handout about the Bella Vista development in which she's currently a sales agent. She wants you to copy one of the slides to a Microsoft Word document that briefly describes the Bella Vista development. You'll do this first.

Using PowerPoint Slides as Picture Objects

To copy a slide as a picture object, you select the slide in Slide Sorter view or in the Slides tab, and then copy the slide to the Clipboard. The slide is copied as a PowerPoint slide object. You can then switch to another slide in Normal view or open another file and paste the slide and, using Paste Special, paste the slide as a picture object (not a PowerPoint object). If you simply paste the slide into the document, it would become an embedded Microsoft Office PowerPoint Slide Object. Using the Paste Special command and pasting a slide as a picture object doesn't allow you to edit the picture using Power-Point commands, but it does take up much less disk space.

Reference Window | **Copying a Slide as a Picture into Another Program**

- In the Slides tab in Normal view or in the slide pane in Slide Sorter view, select the slide from which you want to make a picture image.
- In the Clipboard group on the Home tab, click the Copy button.
- Switch to the document into which you want the picture object inserted.
- In the Clipboard group on the Home tab, click the Paste button arrow, click Paste Special to open the Paste Special dialog box, click Picture (PNG) or some other picture format, and then click the OK button.

Corrine informs you that Mountain Peak Homes wants to have one-page handouts available at the model home in the Bella Vista development. She already created the handout in Microsoft Word 2007. She wants to include a copy of Slide 2 in the presentation, which contains a picture of the model home in the Bella Vista subdivision. To create the handout, you'll open the presentation that Corrine started, and then copy the slide and paste it as a picture object into the Word document. As you save your work, you'll need to use a hard disk or a USB (flash) drive, not a low-capacity floppy drive, because of the size of the Word and PowerPoint files in this tutorial.

To copy a slide into a Word document:

1. Open the PowerPoint presentation file **MPHomes** from the **Tutorial.05\Tutorial** folder included with your Data Files, and then maximize the PowerPoint window, if necessary. The title page of the Mountain Peak Homes presentation appears in the slide pane.

2. Save the presentation file as **Mountain Peak Homes** to the Tutorial.05\Tutorial folder.

3. Quickly go through the presentation to get an idea of its content and design, and then return to Slide 1 ("Building Your Future with Mountain Peak Homes"). See Figure 5-1. As you can see, the presentation includes a picture of a newly constructed home, with a custom theme (theme colors, background color, fonts, and background graphics) developed by a graphic designer under Corrine's direction.

Slide 1 of Mountain Peak Homes — Figure 5-1

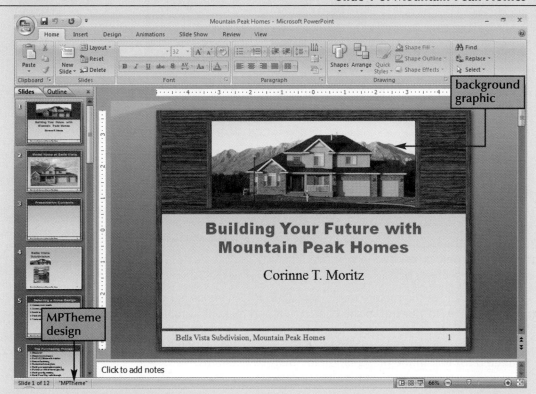

4. In the Slides tab (to the left of the slide pane), click **Slide 2**. Corrine wants you to put a copy of Slide 2 into the Mountain Peak Homes handout.

5. In the Clipboard group on the Home tab, click the **Copy** button. Slide 2 is placed as a picture object on the Clipboard.

6. Start Microsoft Word, open the file **Handout** from the **Tutorial.05\Tutorial** folder included with your Data Files, and save it to the same folder using the filename **Mountain Peak Handout**. The insertion point is at the beginning of the Word document in the blank space above the first line of text.

7. In the Clipboard group on the Home tab, click the **Paste button arrow**, and then click **Paste Special**. The Paste Special dialog box opens.

8. In the As list, click **Picture (PNG)**, if necessary, to select it, and then click the **OK** button. The image of Slide 2 appears at the beginning of the Word document.

▶ **9.** With the picture still selected, in the Paragraph group, click the **Center** button ▤, and then deselect the picture. The picture is centered between the left and right margins on the page. See Figure 5-2.

Figure 5-2 ▶ **Word document with Slide 2 pasted as a picture**

▶ **10.** Save the Mountain Peak Handout file, submit the file to your instructor in either electronic or printed form, as requested, and then exit Microsoft Word.

Having added the picture to the Mountain Peak Homes handout, you can now give the document to Corrine so she can copy it and make it available to her clients at the model home of the Bella Vista subdivision.

Next, you will continue developing Corrine's presentation by changing some of the bulleted list text in the presentation to SmartArt diagrams.

Creating and Modifying SmartArt Diagrams

You're already familiar with SmartArt diagrams, having created a process diagram in Tutorial 2 and an organization chart in Tutorial 3. Here, you'll create a cycle diagram, create another process diagram, learn more about modifying SmartArt diagrams, and later learn how to animate diagrams.

Corrine wants you to create a cycle diagram from the text in Slide 5 of the Mountain Peak Homes presentation.

To create a cycle diagram from existing text:

▶ **1.** In the Mountain Peak Homes presentation, go to **Slide 5**.

▶ **2.** Click anywhere in the bulleted list to make it active.

3. In the Paragraph group on the Home tab, click the **Convert to SmartArt Graphic** button, and then click the **Basic Cycle** layout located in the second row, last column. The bulleted list changes to a cycle diagram. The arrows between the circles are hard to see on the slide background, so you'll modify the diagram by changing its style. You can change the SmartArt layout of any SmartArt diagram by clicking a different style in the Layouts group. You can even change the diagram type; for example, you can change the diagram from a cycle diagram to a process diagram.

4. Click the **SmartArt Tools Design** tab on the Ribbon, if necessary, and then in the SmartArt Styles group, click the **Intense Effect** style located fifth from the left. See Figure 5-3.

Slide 5 with cycle diagram ◄ **Figure 5-3**

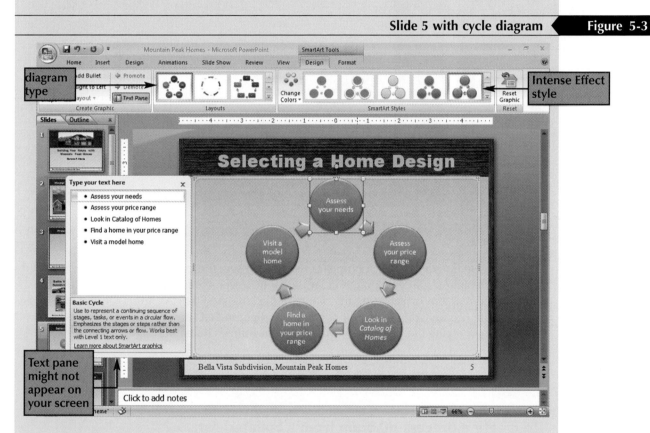

You'll now change the circles into rectangles with beveled edges.

5. With the upper-middle circle selected, click the **SmartArt Tools Format** tab, and then in the Shapes group, click **Change Shape**.

6. In the Basic Shapes section on the menu, click the **Bevel** shape, located in the second row of the Basic Shapes section, last column.

7. Click each of the other circles in turn, and then change its shape to the beveled rectangle.

8. Drag each of the four lower rectangles of the cycle diagram so they are farther apart. Notice that, as you move the cycle diagram text boxes, the arrows between the boxes adjust accordingly.

9. Deselect the diagram, and then compare your screen to Figure 5-4 and make any necessary changes.

Figure 5-4 | Repositioned text boxes in cycle diagram with beveled shape applied

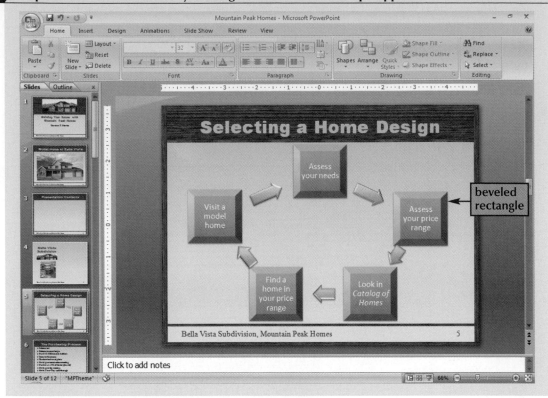

Your cycle diagram is now complete. As you can see, the cycle goes clockwise, the default orientation for cycle diagrams. You can, however, change the orientation (direction) of the diagram by selecting the diagram, clicking the SmartArt Tools Design tab, and then, in the Create Graphic group, clicking the Right to Left button. You can make the same type of change in orientation in process diagrams, charts, and other SmartArt graphics.

Corrine is pleased with the cycle diagram, and now wants you to create a process diagram from the bulleted list on Slide 6.

To create a process diagram from a bulleted list:

▶ 1. Go to **Slide 6**, and then click anywhere in the bulleted list to make it active.

▶ 2. On the Home tab in the Paragraph group, click the **Convert to SmartArt Graphic** button [icon], and then click **More SmartArt Graphics** at the bottom of the gallery. The Choose a SmartArt Graphic dialog box opens.

▶ 3. In the pane on the left side of the dialog box, click **Process**, in the middle of the dialog box, click the **Basic Bending Process** style, located in the fifth row, first column in the gallery, and then click the **OK** button. Again, the arrows are difficult to see on the slide background, so you'll change the diagram style.

▶ **4.** In the SmartArt Styles group on the Design tab, click the **Intense Effect** style, as you did with the cycle diagram previously. See Figure 5-5.

Slide 6 with Intense Effect style applied to the process diagram ◀ Figure 5-5

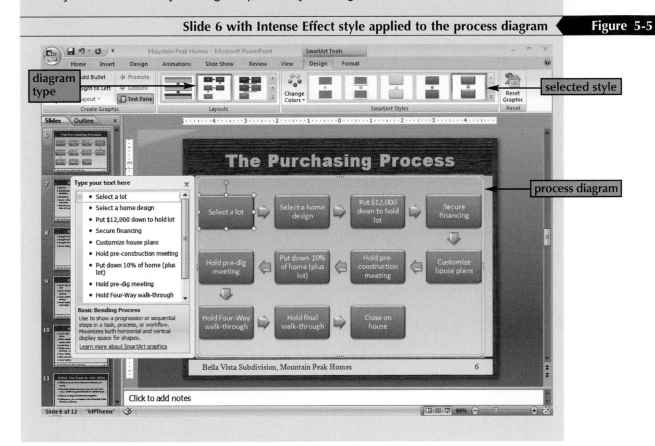

Corrine likes the look of the process diagram that shows the process for purchasing a lot and a home from Mountain Peak Homes. Next, she wants you to apply animation and sound effects to the presentation.

Applying Complex Animation and Sound Effects

Corrine wants you to make the presentation for potential customers as attractive and eye-catching as possible. You decide that one way to achieve this goal is to add complex animation and sound effects to the presentation.

Animating a Process Diagram

You can apply custom animations to any object on a slide, including a SmartArt diagram. Corrine wants the process diagram to be animated by having each text box appear on the slide one at a time, in order. You'll apply the animation now.

To apply an animation and identify the animated items:

▶ **1.** Click the first box ("Select a lot") in the process diagram.

▶ **2.** Click the **Animations** tab, and then in the Animations group, click the **Animate** arrow. Because you are working with a process diagram, the animation effects on the menu have three options.

▶ **3.** In the Wipe section, click **One by one**. PowerPoint automatically animates the diagram by "wiping" each box and the arrow in front of it, one set at a time, onto the slide. Notice that the boxes and arrows wipe from bottom to top, but you want them to wipe in the direction of the process, that is, the top row to wipe left to right, the second row to wipe right to left, and the third line to wipe left to right again. You'll make the changes in the Custom Animation task pane.

▶ **4.** In the Animations group, click the **Custom Animation** button. The Custom Animation task pane opens on the right side of the PowerPoint window and the numbers 1 through 11 appear on the left edge of the slide pane. These numbers correspond to the boxes and arrows in the diagram.

▶ **5.** In the Custom Animation task pane, under Modify: Wipe, click the **Direction** arrow, and then click **From Left**. PowerPoint automatically plays the animation, and the wipe goes from left to right. Although you want the top and bottom rows to animate from the left, you want the middle row to animate from right to left. Before you can make that change, you need to identify the items in the middle row in the list of animated items in the Custom Animation task pane.

▶ **6.** In the Custom Animation task pane, click the **Click to expand contents** arrow ⚡ to expand the contents of the animated objects. See Figure 5-6. In addition to the numbered items, there are unnumbered items in the list.

Figure 5-6 | **Custom animation of process diagram**

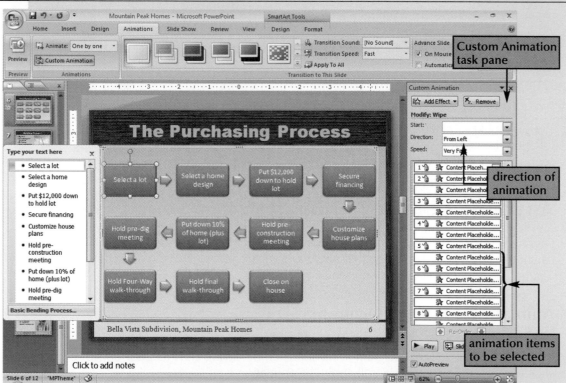

▶ **7.** In the Custom Animation task pane, position the pointer over the first numbered item in the list. The ScreenTip identifies it as the content placeholder that holds "Select a lot."

8. Point to the next two items in the list. The item numbered 2 is the right-pointing arrow to the right of the "Select a lot" box. The unnumbered item below item number 2 is the content placeholder that contains "Select a home design." Remember that items marked with a mouse icon require the user to manually advance the slide show in Slide Show view for the animation to occur. Each numbered item has the mouse icon next to it.

9. Click the item under item number 2 in the list. At the top of the Custom Animation task pane, With Previous appears in the Start box. So, you know that each unnumbered item animates at the same time as the previous item in the list.

When you animate items on a slide, the items are added to the list in the Custom Animation task pane. You can modify the animation for any of the items listed. You'll now change the animation direction to wipe from the right for the objects in the middle row, which are objects numbered 5 through 8 and the arrow object after each of them.

To modify a complex animation:

1. In the list of animated objects in the Custom Animation task pane, point to the item below the number 5 item. This is the "Customize house plans" box in the middle row. You want this box and the rest of the items in the middle row to wipe from right to left.

2. In the Custom Animation task pane, click the item below item number 5, press and hold the **Shift** key, and then click the item below item number 8. Seven animation objects are selected in the list.

3. In the Custom Animation task pane, under Modify: Wipe, click the **Direction** arrow, and then click **From Right**. The wipe for the selected objects now goes from right to left. Now every other row wipes in the opposite direction, which is what you want. Now you want to change the wipe direction of the two arrows that point down in the diagram.

4. Click item number 5, press and hold the **Ctrl** key, and then click item number 9. The two animation objects are selected.

5. At the top of the task pane, click the **Direction** arrow, and then click **From Top**. The wipe for the selected objects goes from top to bottom.

Now, you want to modify the start of each animation so that each object animates automatically *after* the previous item, not after a mouse click.

6. In the Custom Animation task pane, click the first (top) item, press and hold the **Shift** key, and then click the last (bottom) item. All the animation items are selected. See Figure 5-7. With the animation objects still selected, you can change the speed by clicking the Speed arrow in the Custom Animation pane, and selecting the desired speed. Here, you won't change the speed; you'll only change the start settings.

Tip
If you ever want to remove an animation, select the animation item in the Custom Animation task pane, right-click it, and then click Remove.

Figure 5-7 ▶ **Slide 6 with all items selected in the Custom Animation task pane**

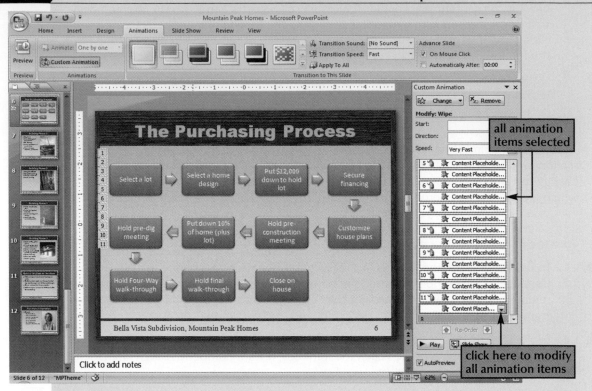

▶ **7.** Click the down arrow next to the bottom object in the list of selected animated objects, and then click **Start After Previous**. This means that, during animation in Slide Show view, each item will not appear on the screen until the previous one has appeared, and that the process will happen automatically, without user intervention.

▶ **8.** On the status bar, click the **Slide Show** button 🖵 . The slide show starts on the current slide. Watch as the diagram appears on the slide one item at a time, in order.

▶ **9.** When the animation has finished, press the **Esc** key. You return to Normal view with the Custom Animation task pane still open.

Trouble? If any of the objects don't animate properly, make the necessary changes in the Custom Animation task pane now.

Now, when you show the presentation, the animation will begin automatically as soon as PowerPoint displays this slide, and the boxes and arrows in the process diagram will appear one at a time in order from first to last.

Next, you'll animate objects in the slide background.

Animating a Background Object

You can animate background objects (objects on the slide masters) similar to how you animated ordinary objects on a slide. To animate a background object, you need to switch to Slide Master view. When you animate an object on a Slide Master, the animation occurs on every slide in the presentation with the corresponding slide layout. The steps for applying a custom animation to an object on a Slide Master are the same as the steps for applying a custom animation to objects on normal slides. You'll add a line to the Title Slide Master, apply animation effects to it, and apply animation effects to other background objects.

To create and animate a background graphic:

1. Click the **View** tab, and then in the Presentation Views group, click the **Slide Master** button.

2. In the pane on the left, click the **Title Slide Layout** master. You'll now insert a line between the title placeholder and the subtitle placeholder.

3. Click the **Insert** tab, and then in the Illustrations group, click **Shapes**.

4. In the Lines section on the menu, click the **Line** button, which is the first (leftmost) button in the row. The mouse pointer changes to $+$.

5. Position the pointer on the left edge of the slide in the slide pane between the title and subtitle placeholders.

6. Press and hold down the **Shift** key, drag the mouse pointer to the right edge of the slide, and then release the **Shift** key. By holding down the Shift key, you make sure the line is exactly horizontal. See Figure 5-8.

Title Slide Layout master with line inserted   Figure 5-8

Trouble? If the line you drew isn't positioned between the title and subtitle text placeholders, as shown in Figure 5-8, drag it there now.

▶ 7. With the line still selected, click the **Drawing Tools Format** tab below, and then in the Shape Styles group, click the **Shape Outline button arrow**. The Shape Outline palette and menu appear.

▶ 8. Point to **Weight**, and then click **6 pt**. The line thickness (weight) changes to 6 points.

▶ 9. In the Shape Styles group, click the **Shape Outline button arrow** again, and then click the **Brown, Accent 2** color tile, located in the top row of the Theme Colors, in the sixth column. See Figure 5-9.

Figure 5-9 ▶ **Title Slide Layout master with modified line**

You've added a brown horizontal line to the Title Slide Master. Now you want the line to appear behind the other graphic objects on the Slide Master. Objects on a slide are arranged in layers. Each object you place on a slide is on top of any other objects on the slide. You can send objects to the back (bottom) of the layers, or you can bring an object to the front (top) of the layers. To arrange the objects in order, you use commands in the Arrange group on the Drawing Tools Format tab.

To send the line to the back of the objects:

▶ 1. Click the line you drew to select it, if necessary.

▶ 2. In the Arrange group on the Drawing Tools Format tab, click the **Send to Back button arrow**. Two commands appear on the Send to Back button menu. If you click the Send to Back command, the selected object moves to the back of all the layers. If you click the Send Backward command, the selected object moves back one layer.

3. Click **Send to Back**. The line is sent to the back of all the objects on the slide. If you look closely, you can now see that the two ends of the lines are behind the vertical wood-grain objects on each side of the slide.

Now you want to animate the line so it flies in from the left.

To animate the background object:

1. With the line still selected, in the Custom Animation task pane, click the **Add Effect** button, point to **Entrance**, click **More Effects**, click **Fly In**, and then click the **OK** button.

2. Change the Direction to **From Left**, and set the animation to **Start After Previous**.

3. Click just above the footer and slide number placeholders to select the **wood-textured bar** located there. This is a graphic object inserted on the Slide Master by the graphic designer who created the presentation.

4. Set the bar to have the Entrance effect **Fly In** with the direction **From Left**. The item appears in the Custom Animation task pane as "Rectangle 9."

5. Set the animation to **Start With Previous**. When you display this slide in Slide Show view, the two objects will automatically fly in from the left simultaneously instead of one after the other. See Figure 5-10.

Title Slide Layout master after adding animation to two objects ◀ **Figure 5-10**

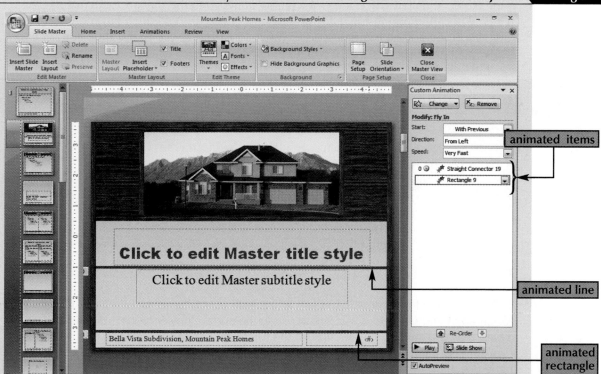

6. Click the **Title and Content Layout** master, select the **wood-textured bar** just above the footer, set the Entrance effect to **Fly In**, set the direction to **From Left**, and set the animation to **Start After Previous** so that the bar flies in after the slide appears on the screen.

7. Repeat the same procedure described in Step 6 for the **Two Content Layout** master.

▶ **8.** Return to Normal view, close the Custom Animation task pane, and save the presentation using the default filename.

You've completed custom animation effects for the process diagram in Slide 6 and for all the slides with the Title Slide layout, Title and Content layout, and Two Content layout.

Next, Corrine wants to add background music and an animated picture to Slide 6. Unfortunately, the clip art installed on your computer doesn't include the desired music and GIF files that you need. Therefore, you decide to download some clip files from the Office Online Web site.

Downloading Clips from Microsoft Office Online

Microsoft provides a Web site called **Microsoft Office Online** that contains many images and sound clips for you to use in your PowerPoint presentations. When you open the Clip Art task pane and use one or more keywords to search for a clip, PowerPoint will search the Microsoft Office Online database of clips, and allow you to insert them into your presentation. Sometimes, however, you want to make a clip available even when you are offline. In that case, you have to download the clip from Microsoft Office Online to your computer hard disk. If, after that, you do a search using the Clip Art task pane while you're offline, PowerPoint can still find and use the clip. If, on the other hand, you do a search using the Clip Art task pane and you are online, PowerPoint might find two copies of the same clip, one on your local computer and one on the Microsoft Office Online Web site.

Corrine wants you to download and insert an animated GIF and background music to Slide 6. An **animated GIF** is a movie clip, identified with the filename extension .gif, which you can import just like any photograph or clip art but which has motion (animation). To add background music, you'll add a sound clip to the slide and set it to replay over and over again until you go to the next slide.

Reference Window | Downloading Clips from Microsoft Office Online

- Display the slide into which you want to insert a picture, motion, or sound clip.
- Click the Insert tab on the Ribbon, and then in the Illustrations group, click the Clip Art button to open the Clip Art task pane.
- Click the "Clip art on Office Online" link at the bottom of the task pane.
- Use the search feature on the Office Online Web page to find the clips that you want, and then click the check box below each clip that you want to download.
- Click the Click to Download button. The clips will be downloaded to your computer and organized in your Microsoft Clip Organizer, which the Clip Art task pane uses when you search for clips.

You'll connect to Microsoft Office Online with your Internet browser and then search for an animated GIF and music file to use in the current presentation. You should be aware that you can search for clips on the Microsoft Office Online Web site from the Clip Art task pane, but using the browser has several advantages. First, the Clip Art task pane doesn't show the motion of the animation clip art, whereas your browser does, so it's easier to tell the difference between a normal clip and an animation clip on the Web page. Second, it is easier to download several clips at once to your computer for later use using a browser. And third, music clips that are MIDI (musical instrument digital interface) files (sound files that play music, not just make sound effects) often don't work by inserting them directly from the Clip Art task pane; you must download them to your computer from the Web page, and then insert them into your presentation. You'll go to the Microsoft Office Online Web site now.

To download an animated GIF from Microsoft Office Online:

▶ **1.** With **Slide 6** in the slide pane, click the **Insert** tab, and then in the Illustrations group, click the **Clip Art** button. The Clip Art task pane opens on the right side of the PowerPoint window.

▶ **2.** Click the **Clip art on Office Online** link near the bottom of the task pane. The Clip Art page of the Microsoft Office Online site appears in your Web browser.

Trouble? If you get an error message telling you that the Internet connection failed, start your browser, and then repeat Steps 1 and 2. Now you'll search the online Microsoft Office Clip Art and Media page for animated GIF and sound files.

▶ **3.** If necessary, click the **Clip Art** tab located just below the Web page title "Microsoft Office Online," and then click in the text box located to the right of the clip-art icon and to the left of the orange Search button.

▶ **4.** Type **construction**, click **Search button arrow**, and click **Animations**. After a moment, Microsoft Office Online displays a group of animations (GIF clip art) that deal with construction.

▶ **5.** Click **Next** at the bottom of the group of GIF clip art to go to Page 2.

▶ **6.** Click the check box below the animation clip of the man laying bricks. He has a red hat, wears green coveralls, and is laying red bricks, as shown in Figure 5-11. Because Microsoft continually updates the Office Online pages, the picture might not be in the same place as in the figure.

Microsoft Office Online Web page after searching for GIF file ◀ **Figure 5-11**

▶ **7.** In the Selection Basket group, click **Download 1 item** in the pane on the left. The Download window appears identifying the number of items you've selected to download and the total download size.

Trouble? If Microsoft displays a Terms of Use screen, click the Accept button. If you now see a Security Warning dialog box, click the Yes button to install the Microsoft Office Template and Media Control, and then click the Continue button after the installation is complete. If you see a window informing you that Microsoft Office Template and Media Control has been installed, click the Continue button.

▶ **8.** Click the **Download Now** button near the bottom of the window. The File Download dialog box opens.

▶ **9.** Click the **Open** button. The Tools - Microsoft Clip Organizer dialog box opens, showing the clip you just downloaded added to the Tools folder in the Downloaded Clips folder. "Tools" in the title bar of the dialog box is the category name of the selected clip.

Trouble? If the Add Clips to Organizer dialog box also opens, click the Now button. Microsoft then organizes the clip art within your Organizer. This might take a few minutes. After the clip art is organized, the Add Clips to Organizer dialog box won't open again when you download clip art.

Trouble? If you get a message warning you that the Web site wants to open Web content using a program on your computer, click the Allow button.

▶ **10.** Close the Tools - Microsoft Clip Organizer dialog box, but leave the browser open to the Microsoft Office Clip Art and Media page.

You've successfully downloaded the desired animated GIF picture into your Organizer. Now you'll download a music clip.

To download a music clip from Microsoft Office Online:

▶ **1.** In the browser window, again click in the search box, type **jazz**, click the **Search button arrow**, and click **Sounds**. Office Online displays all the music clips that fit the description "jazz."

▶ **2.** Click the check box below the sound clip titled **Smooth Jazzy**, which might be the first clip shown in the browser. If you don't see that sound on the first page of clips, continue on to subsequent pages until you see it. See Figure 5-12.

Microsoft Office Online Web page after searching for sound clip | Figure 5-12

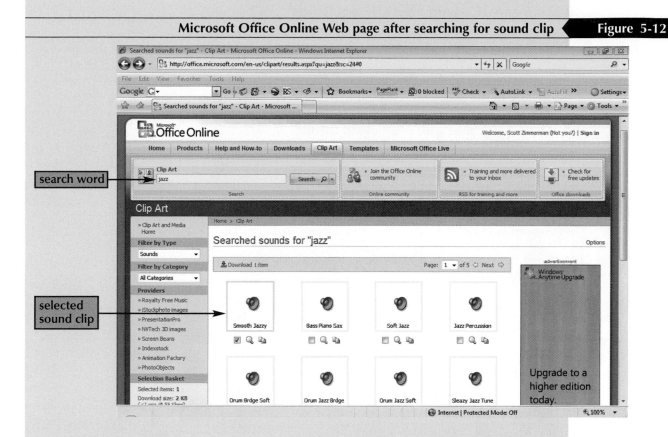

Trouble? If you can't find the Smooth Jazzy sound clip, download a different jazz sound clip.

Trouble? If PowerPoint displays a security warning and asks if you want to install the Microsoft Office on the Web Control, click the Yes button, click the Continue button, and then click the Download Now button.

▶ **3.** Download the sound clip the same way you downloaded the motion clip, and then close the Microsoft Clip Organizer dialog box.

▶ **4.** Exit your Web browser.

Having downloaded an animation (GIF) clip and a sound clip, you're ready to apply them to your PowerPoint presentation.

Applying the Downloaded Motion and Sound Clips

Corrine wants the animated GIF and the background music to "play" while potential clients view the animation that you added to the process diagram on Slide 6. You'll begin by applying the motion clip.

To insert the animated GIF on a slide:

▶ **1.** Make sure Slide 6 is in the slide pane, select any text in the Search for text box of the Clip Art task pane and type **construction**, click the **Results should be** list arrow, click the **All media types** check box, if necessary, to select it, and then click the **Go** button in the task pane. The task pane displays a set of pictures similar to the ones shown in Figure 5-13.

Figure 5-13 ▶ **Clip Art task pane with downloaded GIF file**

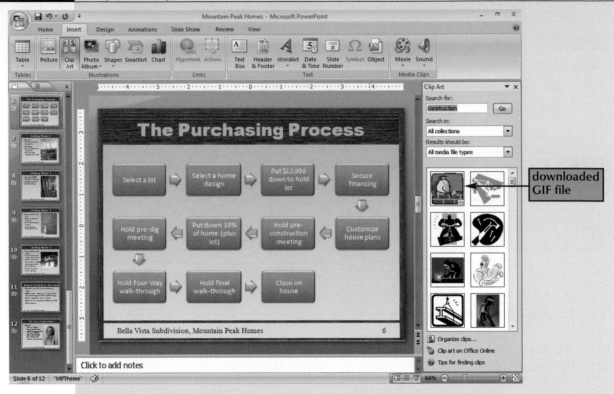

▶ **2.** Click the picture of the man laying bricks (or the picture you downloaded). The picture is inserted into the center of Slide 6.

▶ **3.** Position the image to the right of the last text box, and then deselect the image. See Figure 5-14.

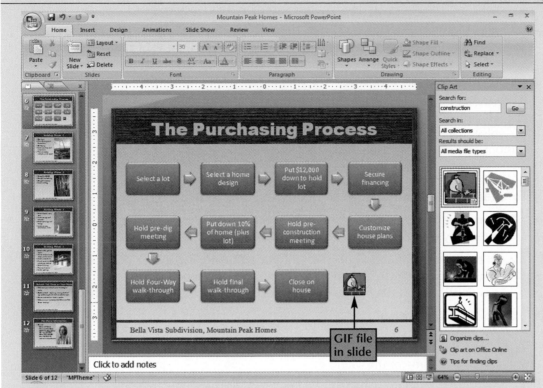

You don't need to do anything special to an animated GIF to make it play continuously in Slide Show view; it does this by default. You'll test it now.

4. On the status bar, click the **Slide Show** button. The slide show starts from the current slide. Slide 6 appears in Slide Show view and the clip of the bricklayer animates automatically, and stays animated, even after the process diagram animation has finished.

5. Press the **Esc** key to end the slide show.

Now you'll insert the sound clip and set it up to play as background music while the slide is on the screen in Slide Show view.

To insert the sound clip as background music:

1. In the task pane, select the text in the **Search for** text box, type **jazz**, and then click the **Go** button. The Clip Art task pane displays one or more clips with the word "jazz" in the title.

2. Scroll to the top of the list of clips in the task pane as necessary until you see the icon for Smooth Jazzy (you might see only "Smooth J. . ."), and then click it. A dialog box opens asking how you want the sound to start in the slide show.

3. Click the **Automatically** button to indicate that you want the sound clip to play as soon as the slide appears on the screen. PowerPoint inserts the sound icon in the middle of the slide.

4. Close the Clip Art task pane.

▶ **5.** Drag the **sound** icon 🔊 to the lower-right corner of the slide, just to the right of the animation clip. You don't really have to move the sound clip icon, because later you'll set the icon so it doesn't appear during a slide show.

▶ **6.** Start the slide show from Slide 6. The animated GIF appears and plays and the diagram animates, but the sound doesn't start until after all of the images in the process diagram appear. Also, the sound clip plays once, and then stops.

Because the sound clip is listed last in the Custom Animation task pane, the sound clip won't play until all the objects appear because the sound clip is the last object. You can solve that problem by moving the sound object to the top of the animation list in the Custom Animation task pane. You'll do that now.

To change the animation order of the sound clip:

▶ **1.** Press the **Esc** key to stop the slide show, close the Clip Art task pane, and then if necessary, click the **Sound Tools Options** tab.

▶ **2.** In the Sound Options group, click the **Hide During Show** check box, and then click the **Loop Until Stopped** check box. Now the sound icon won't appear during a slide show, and the music will play until the slide changes in Slide Show view.

▶ **3.** Click the **Animations** tab, and then in the Animations group, click the **Custom Animation** button. The item at the bottom of the animation list is selected. This is the sound you inserted. The name of the item, j0431058.wav (or something similar), is the name of the sound file.

Trouble? If you downloaded a sound file other than Smooth Jazzy, the filename listed in the animation list will be different.

▶ **4.** In the Custom Animation task pane, if necessary, click the **Click to hide contents** arrow ⭧ to hide the full contents of the process diagram animation, and then drag the sound object animation item to the top of the animation list (above the top Content Placeholder animation box). See Figure 5-15.

Slide 6 with sound clip inserted | Figure 5-15

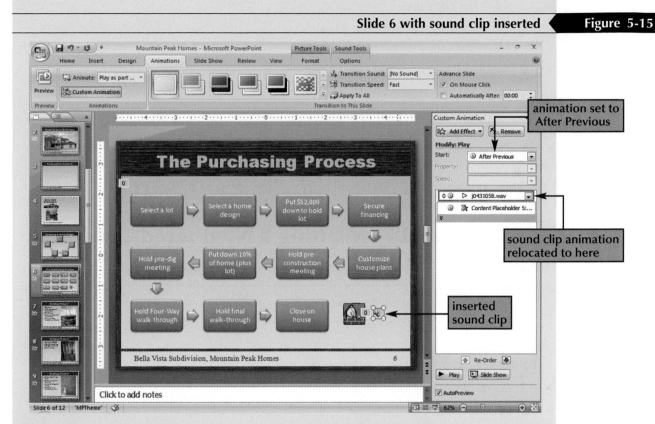

5. In the Custom Animation task pane, click the **j0431058.wav** arrow, and then click **Effect Options**. The Play Sound dialog box opens.

6. In the Start playing section of the dialog box, make sure the **From beginning** option button is selected, and then in the Stop playing section, click the **After current slide** option button. See Figure 5-16. This tells PowerPoint to play the sound until you go to the next slide in Slide Show view.

Play Sound dialog box | Figure 5-16

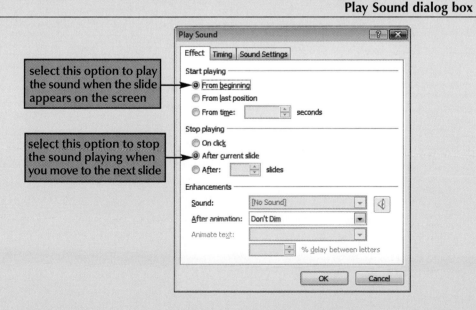

▶ **7.** Click the **OK** button.

▶ **8.** On the status bar, click the **Slide Show** button 🖳. The animation and the background music on Slide 6 play.

▶ **9.** After the animation ends, but while the sound is still playing, press the **Esc** key to return to Normal view.

▶ **10.** If everything worked correctly, save your presentation. If you noticed any problems, fix them, and then save the presentation.

▶ **11.** Close the Custom Animation task pane.

This completes the animation and sound effects for Slide 6.

Creating and Formatting a Numbered List

Corrine now tells you that she wants you to convert the bulleted list in Slide 11 to a **numbered list**, which is a set of numbered text items on a slide, to emphasize that the four items are steps that clients must follow in a particular order. You'll now create and format the numbered list.

To create and format a numbered list:

▶ **1.** Go to **Slide 11**.

▶ **2.** Click anywhere in the bulleted list to make it active, and then click the edge of the bulleted list placeholder to select the entire list.

▶ **3.** If necessary, click the **Home** tab, and then in the Paragraph group, click the **Numbering** button ⬚. You've created a numbered list from a bulleted list. See Figure 5-17.

Slide 11 after changing bulleted list to numbered list | **Figure 5-17**

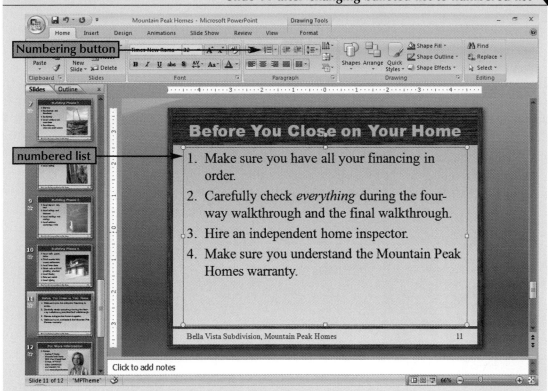

Next, you format the numbered list so that the numbers are colored and larger than the other text.

▶ **4.** In the Paragraph group, click the **Numbering button arrow** ⠿☰⁞, and then click **Bullets and Numbering** to open the Bullets and Numbering dialog box.

▶ **5.** Click the **Color** button ⠿🎨, and then click the **Brown, Accent 2** tile (the sixth tile from the left under Theme Colors).

▶ **6.** Double-click the contents of the **Size** box, type **125**, and then click the **OK** button. Deselect the numbered list. See Figure 5-18.

Figure 5-18 ▶ **Slide 11 with modified numbered list**

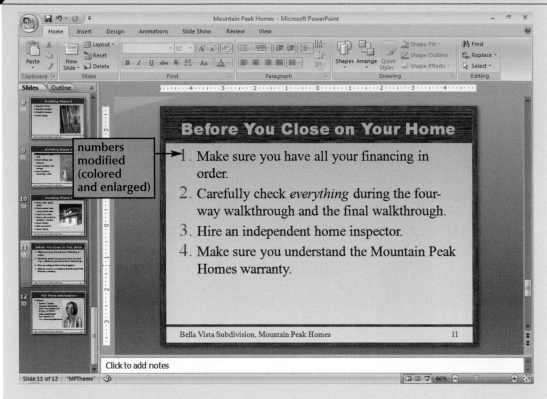

▶ **7.** Save your changes to the presentation.

You've now created and formatted a number list. Corrine is pleased with the progress you've made and has only a few more features that she wants you to add to the presentation.

Review | **Session 5.1 Quick Check**

1. Explain how to insert a PowerPoint slide into another program.

2. True or False: PowerPoint can proceed with animations in a slide even while a sound clip associated with a slide is playing.

3. True or False: If you add several objects to a slide and want to animate them one at a time, they must always animate in the same order in which you added them.

4. If your computer doesn't have a picture, animation, or sound clips that you want, where can you get additional clips?

5. What is a GIF animation clip?

6. Describe how to convert a bulleted list to a numbered list.

Session 5.2

Corrine now wants you to add a graphic showing a plat map of Mountain Peak Homes' Bella Vista subdivision to Slide 4 and add callouts to the illustration. A plat map is a diagram that shows the shape and location of the lots in a housing subdivision. The plat map sometimes includes the dimensions of the lot borders or the total square footage of the lot.

Adding Illustrations and Callouts

She wants the colors of the plat map to match the color scheme of the presentation, and she would like to include graphics on the map to make it more attractive and meaningful. To accomplish this, she obtained the services of her company's architect, who used specialized graphics programs to create the graphical elements in the drawing.

Although PowerPoint has drawing tools, sometimes you need illustrations or diagrams that are more complex than PowerPoint's drawing tools could produce. For those types of illustrations and diagrams, you'd have to use a more sophisticated drawing software package. The more popular high-end drawing software includes Adobe Illustrator and CorelDRAW. Because this type of software is complex and difficult to learn, it's meant primarily for skilled artists and draftspersons. People with moderate artistic ability, however, might also find sophisticated illustration software useful in creating complex drawings.

The architect who created Corrine's plat map used a sophisticated illustration program, colored the various lines and text, and merged a picture of the model home. You'll import this plat map into PowerPoint, resize it, and then label it using PowerPoint drawing tools.

To insert a graphic produced with illustration software:

▶ **1.** If you took a break at the end of the previous session, open the presentation **Mountain Peak Homes** in PowerPoint from the **Tutorial.05\Tutorial** folder included with your Data Files.

▶ **2.** Go to **Slide 4**, click the **Insert** tab, and then in the Illustrations group, click the **Picture** button. The Insert Picture dialog box opens.

▶ **3.** Navigate to the **Tutorial.05\Tutorial** folder, and then double-click **PlatMap**. The graphic appears on Slide 4, covering most of the current text and graphics there.

▶ **4.** Drag the upper-left sizing handle down and to the right until the top of the map is even with the top of the large title text "Bella Vista," and then drag the lower-left resizing handle up and to the right until the bottom of the map is just above the footer.

▶ **5.** Drag the map so that its right edge is just above the slide number, as shown in Figure 5-19.

Figure 5-19 | Slide 4 after inserting the plat map drawing

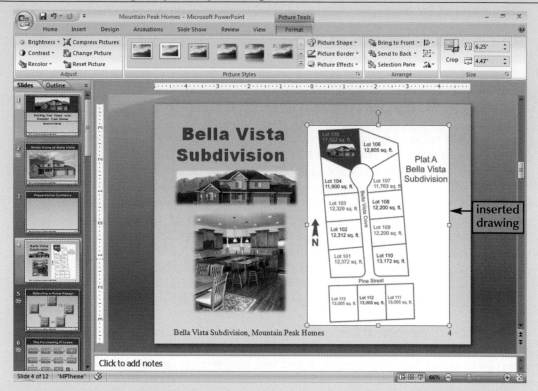

Next, you'll set the white background color of the graphic to transparent, so that the slide background (the light-tan gradient fill) becomes the map background.

▶ **6.** With the graphic still selected, click the **Picture Tools Format** tab, if necessary, and then in the Adjust group, click the **Recolor** button. A gallery opens.

▶ **7.** Click **Set Transparent Color** at the bottom of the Recolor gallery, click anywhere in the white area of the map, and then deselect it. See Figure 5-20.

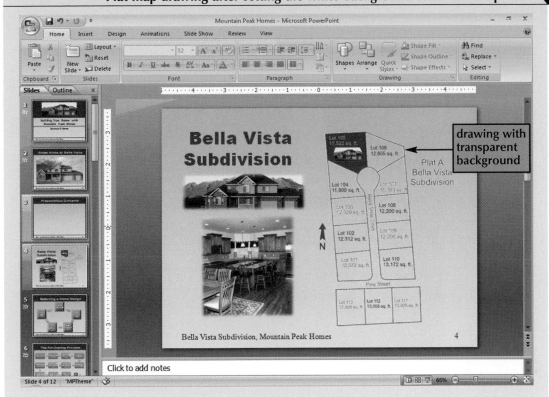

Plat map drawing after setting the white background color to transparent | **Figure 5-20**

For the illustration in Slide 4, you'll create callouts. **Callouts** are labels that include a text box and a line between the text box and the item being labeled.

To add callouts to the illustration:

1. Click the **Insert** tab, and then in the Illustrations group, click the **Shapes** button.

2. In the Callouts section near the bottom of the Shapes menu, click the **Line Callout 1** button located in the first row below Callouts, fifth column.

3. In the map, click above and to the right of the map. A box with a line is inserted at the location you clicked.

4. Type **Model Home**. Notice that you don't need to click in the callout box; you can just start typing when the callout is selected, and the text appears in the box.

5. Click the edge of the callout text box to select the entire object, and then drag the callout so that the square is positioned above the Lot 106 section in the map.

6. Position the mouse pointer over the yellow diamond-shaped adjustment handle at the end of the callout line (the adjustment handle farthest from the callout text box). You can drag the **adjustment handle** of a callout line to change the length and position of the line. The pointer changes to an arrowhead ▷.

7. Drag the adjustment handle until it almost touches the picture of the home in Lot 105, the section of the map with the picture of a home.

8. Drag the adjustment handle at the end nearest the callout text box to the right and down, until it touches the edge of the callout text box, at the same location as the left-center resize handle on the box. See Figure 5-21.

Figure 5-21 | **Slide 4 with callout**

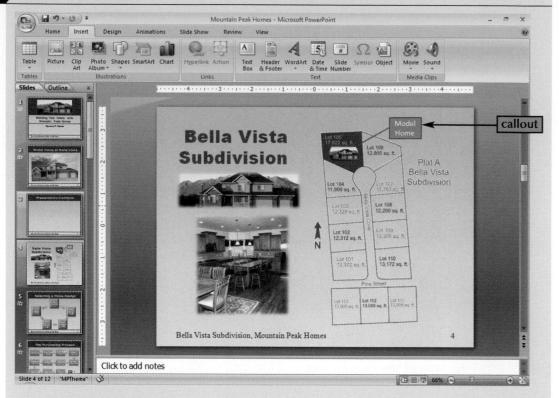

Trouble? If your callout doesn't look like the one shown in Figure 5-21, make the necessary adjustments now.

9. Deselect the callout.

With the callout on the slide, you can modify the callout text box just as you can regular text boxes. You can change the background color, font color, font style, outline color, text box size, and so forth. In the case of the callout on Slide 5, the default text and colors look fine, so you'll leave them as they are.

Applying Special Effects to a Text Box

Corrine now wants you to add a text box to Slide 4. The text box will contain the price range for lots in the Bella Vista subdivision. To make the text box look right on the slide, you'll apply special effects, including changing the fill, border, margins, and text direction.

To insert and apply special effects to a text box:

1. In the Text group on the Insert tab, click the **Text Box** button.

2. Click just below "Plat A Bella Vista Subdivision" on the imported illustration, and then type **Price of lots range from $250,000 to $325,000**. As you can see, the text extends beyond the right edge of the slide. You'll solve the problem by, first, splitting the phrase onto two lines, and second, changing the text direction.

3. Click just to the right of "from" in the text box, press the **Enter** key, and delete the space before "$250,000." Now "Price of lots range from" is on one line, and "$250,000 to $325,000" is on another line. Now you'll change the text direction.

4. Click the edge of the text box to select the entire box, click the **Home** tab if necessary, and then in the Paragraph group, click the **Text Direction** button ⬛. The Text menu that opens shows the various directions that you can arrange the text in the text box.

5. Click **Rotate all text 90°**. The text rotates so it reads from top to bottom.

6. Drag the text box so it is centered under "Subdivision," as shown in Figure 5-22.

Slide 4 with modified text box   Figure 5-22

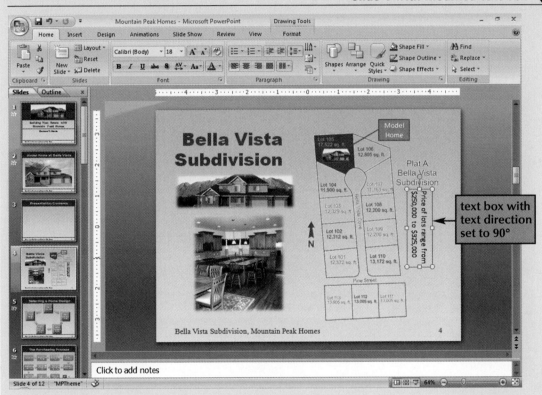

With the text box inserted and the text rotated, you'll now apply other special effects to the text box.

To apply other special effects to the text box:

1. In the Paragraph group, click the **Text Direction** button ⬛ again, and then click **More Options** at the bottom of the menu. The Format Text Effects dialog box opens with Text Box selected in the list on the left. This dialog box provides a wide range of options to modify the text box to your specifications.

2. In the Internal margin section of the dialog box, change all four margins to **0.2"**. As you can see, this increases the size of the text box, leaving a bigger margin around the text.

3. Click the **Close** button in the Format Text Effects dialog box. Now you'll change other features of the text box.

▶ **4.** On the Home tab, in the Drawing group, click the **Shape Fill button arrow**, and then click the **Orange, Accent 1** tile, located in the first row under Theme Colors, fifth column.

▶ **5.** In the Drawing group, click the **Shape Outline button arrow**, point to **Weight**, and then click **1½ pt**.

▶ **6.** Again click the **Shape Outline button arrow**, and then click the **Brown, Accent 2** tile, located in the top row of the Theme Colors, sixth column. Deselect the text box. See Figure 5-23.

Figure 5-23 **Slide 4 with modified text box**

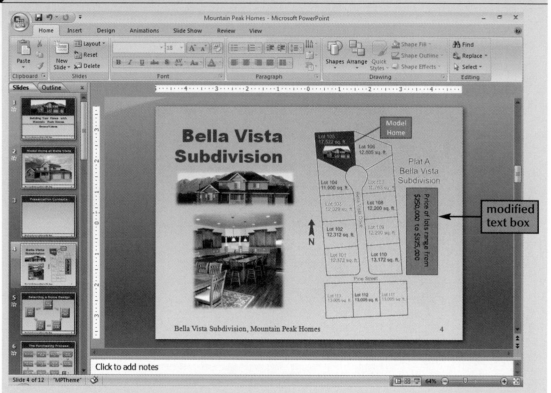

▶ **7.** If the appearance and position of your text box is different from the one shown in Figure 5-23, make any adjustments now.

▶ **8.** Save the presentation using the default filename. Slide 4 is now complete.

In the preceding steps, you used the Format Text Effects dialog box to modify how text appears within a text box. You can also use that dialog box to make other modifications. For example, to put text in columns within a text box, you click Text Box in the left pane of the Format Text Effects dialog box, click the Columns button, and set the desired columns feature. To make the font size of the text automatically increase or decrease as you resize the text box, you can click the Shrink text on overflow option button in the AutoFit section of the dialog box. To change text appearance (fill color, drop shadow and so forth), you can use other features in the Format Text Effects dialog box.

Pasting Slides into Another Slide as Pictures

Next, Corrine wants you to create hyperlinks in Slide 3 to all the subsequent slides in the presentation. But instead of inserting text hyperlinks, she wants you to paste a copy of other slides in the presentation as picture objects to create thumbnails, and then to make each thumbnail a hyperlink to its respective, full-size slides.

Copying a Slide as a Picture Object	Reference Window

- Switch to Slide Sorter view, and then select the slide you want to copy.
- In the Clipboard group on the Home tab, click the Copy button.
- Switch to Normal view, and then go to the slide into which you want to paste the picture of the copied slide.
- In the Clipboard group, click the Paste button arrow, click Paste Special, and then click one of the Picture options in the As list box.
- Click the OK button in the Paste Special dialog box.

The Title Only layout is already applied to Slide 3, so you have a big empty space into which you can insert thumbnails of the nine slides, Slide 4 through Slide 12. But to make it easier to align the thumbnails on the slide, you'll modify the slide grid. A **grid** is an array of dotted vertical and horizontal lines **(gridlines)** that can make positioning objects easier. Usually the gridlines are hidden, but you can make them visible. You can also change the spacing of the dots on the gridlines to make it easier to position small or large objects. Another handy feature of the grid is the **Snap to Grid** option, which is selected by default. With this option selected, objects you place on the slide automatically align with a gridline, even if the gridlines are not visible.

Aligning Objects on a Slide	InSight

PowerPoint provides two ways to align objects precisely. One way is to use gridlines with the Snap to Grid feature. Another is to use the Align button in the Arrange group on the Format tab. You select two or more objects on the slide and then use the Align button to align them along their tops, bottoms, left sides, or right sides. You can also use the Align button to access the Distribute Horizontally or Distribute Vertically feature, which you can use to space three or more objects evenly. If you want to treat several objects as one object (for the purpose of positioning, resizing, aligning, and so forth), you can group the objects together by selecting the objects, and then clicking the Group button in the Arrange group on the Drawing Tools Format tab.

Setting Up Gridlines

Now, you'll display the gridlines to make it easier to align the thumbnails. When you insert a picture into the slide or resize a picture, the edge of the picture "snaps" to an intersection of two gridlines (seen or unseen). PowerPoint doesn't allow the picture to be partway between two gridlines unless you position them while holding down the Alt key and moving the object with the mouse, or while holding down the Ctrl key and moving the object with the keyboard arrow keys. You can change the gridline spacing to suit your needs. You'll do that now.

To view and modify the gridlines:

▶ **1.** Go to **Slide 3**.

▶ **2.** Click the **View** tab on the Ribbon, and then in the Show/Hide group, click the **Gridlines** check box to select it. A grid of dotted lines appears on the slide. The gridlines might be faint, so you might have to look hard to see them.

Each dot in your gridlines might be 1/8 (0.125) or 1/16 (0.083) inch apart.

▶ **3.** Right-click anywhere in the slide pane, and then on the shortcut menu, click **Grid and Guides**.

▶ **4.** In the Grid settings section of the dialog box, click in the **Spacing** text box to select the current setting, and then type **1.4** to change the spacing to 1.4 inches.

▶ **5.** At the top of the dialog box, click the **Snap objects to grid** check box to select it, if necessary. See Figure 5-24.

Figure 5-24 ▶ Grid and Guides dialog box

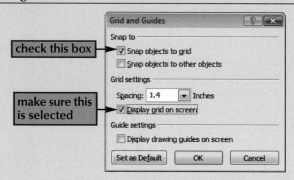

▶ **6.** Click the **OK** button. The space between each dot in the gridlines changed to 1.4 inches.

Now, you're ready to copy and paste the slide pictures into Slide 3. To do this, you first copy each slide to the Clipboard, and then you use Paste Special to paste the slide picture into the slide, similar to the way you copied and pasted a slide into a Word document.

To make thumbnails by copying slides:

▶ **1.** Switch to Slide Sorter view, and then click the **Home** tab on the Ribbon.

▶ **2.** Click **Slide 4** to select it, and then in the Clipboard group, click the **Copy** button.

▶ **3.** Double-click **Slide 3** to switch to Slide 3 in Normal view, in the Clipboard group click the **Paste button arrow**, and then click **Paste Special**. The Paste Special dialog box opens.

▶ **4.** In the As list, click **Picture (PNG)**, and then click the **OK** button. The dialog box closes and Slide 4 is inserted as a picture in Slide 3. See Figure 5-25.

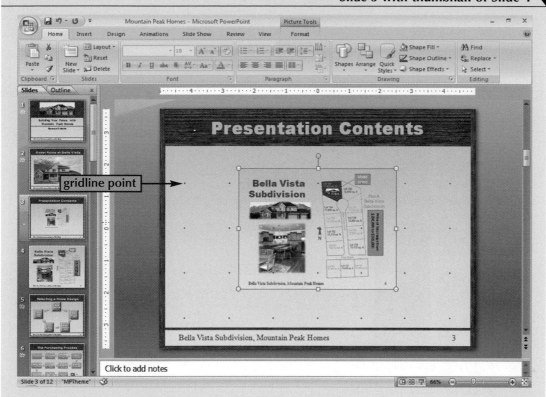

Now, you'll resize and reposition the slide thumbnail.

▶ **5.** With the picture still selected, click the **Picture Tools Format** tab, in the Size group, click the value in the **Shape Width** text box, type **1.6**, and then press the **Enter** key. The picture is now much smaller and appears more like a thumbnail.

▶ **6.** Drag the **thumbnail** so it snaps to the gridline dot near the upper-left corner of the blank area of the slide, as shown in Figure 5-26.

Figure 5-26 Slide 3 with thumbnail resized and repositioned

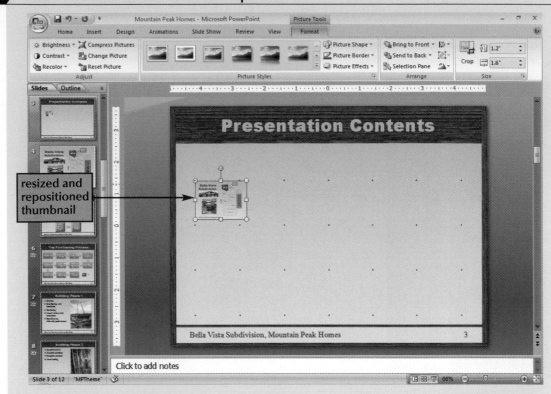

Trouble? If the size and position of the thumbnail of Slide 4 are different from the one shown in Figure 5-26, make sure you've adjusted the picture width (not the height) to 1.6 inches and positioned the slide as shown.

▶ **7.** Repeat Steps 1 through 6 to insert Slides 5 and 6, positioning them to the right of the previous slide, so that the first three thumbnails are in a row.

▶ **8.** Repeat Steps 1 through 6 to insert Slides 7 through 12, and position Slides 7 through 9 in the second row between gridlines, and Slides 10 through 12 in the third row. Compare your screen to Figure 5-27 and make any adjustments necessary.

Slide 3 with all nine thumbnails ◀ **Figure 5-27**

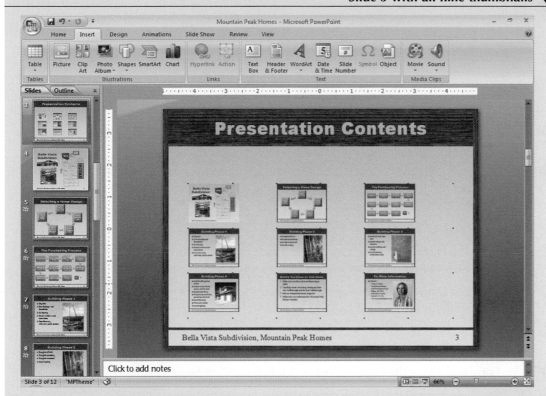

9. Click the **View** tab, and in the Show/Hide group, click the **Gridlines** check box to deselect it. The gridlines are hidden.

10. Right-click a blank area of the slide in the slide pane, on the shortcut menu, click **Grid and Guides** to open the Grid and Guides dialog box, click the **Snap objects to grid** check box to deselect it, and then click the **OK** button. Now, when you try to move other objects on this slide or other slides in your presentation, they won't try to snap to the gridlines.

| **Using the Snap Objects to Grid Feature** | InSight |

Although the Snap objects to grid feature can be helpful, there are times when it is more helpful to turn it off. Always turn off the Snap objects to grid feature if you have set the grid space to a high number and you have finished using the grid to position the desired objects. If you don't, you'll have difficulty moving objects to precise locations on the subsequent slides. You can always turn the Snap objects to grid feature back on if you need it later.

Creating Hyperlinks from the Thumbnails

Now, you'll make the thumbnails hyperlinks to their respective slides in the presentation and insert an action button on the other slides so that they link back to Slide 3.

To create hyperlinks from the thumbnails:

▶ 1. With Slide 3 in the slide pane in Normal view, click the **first thumbnail** (the copy of Slide 4), click the **Insert** tab, and then, in the Links group, click the **Hyperlink** button. The Insert Hyperlink dialog box opens.

▶ 2. In the Link to panel on the left, click **Place in This Document**, in the Select a place in this document list of slides in the middle of the dialog box, click **4. Bella Vista Subdivision**, and then click the **OK** button. Now, when you run the slide show and click the picture of Slide 4 on Slide 3, PowerPoint will jump to Slide 4.

▶ 3. Repeat Steps 1 and 2 to make the pictures of Slides 5 through 12 a hyperlink to their respective slides in the presentation.

▶ 4. Go to **Slide 4**, on the Insert tab in the Illustrations group, click the **Shapes** button, and then in the Action Buttons section on the menu, click the **Action Button: Home** button.

▶ 5. Click anywhere on the slide. The Action Settings dialog box opens.

▶ 6. Click the **Hyperlink to** arrow, click **Slide**, in the Hyperlink to Slide dialog box, click **3. Presentation Contents**, and then click the **OK** button twice.

▶ 7. Click the **Drawing Tools Format** tab, and then in the Size group, adjust the size of the action button to **0.35** by **0.35** inch.

▶ 8. Drag the action button to the lower-right corner of the slide, just to the left of the slide number.

▶ 9. Copy and paste the hyperlinked action button from Slide 4 onto Slides 5–12.

▶ 10. Save your presentation. You'll test the hyperlinks later.

In this example, you used the picture objects of the slides as hyperlinks to the actual slides in the presentation, but you can design any PowerPoint slide and use it as a picture of any type on any other slide, or in any other Windows program. You can also save any or all of the slides in a presentation as picture files (in GIF, JPEG, PNG, TIF, BMP, or WMF file format) by displaying the desired slide in the slide pane in Normal view, clicking the Office Button, clicking Save As, and then selecting one of the picture formats as the file type. PowerPoint then gives you the option of saving just the current slide as a picture or saving the entire presentation as a set of pictures.

| InSight | **Using PowerPoint to Create Illustrations** |

Because PowerPoint allows you to save slides as picture files, you can use PowerPoint as an illustration program for drawing diagrams, making graphs, creating images with text on photographs, and producing other types of graphics. PowerPoint is actually a good choice for an illustration program for people who are already familiar with PowerPoint but who don't have the time or inclination to learn a sophisticated illustration program like Adobe Illustrator or CorelDRAW. Be aware, however, that dedicated illustration programs have dozens of special features to help users prepare professional illustrations, features that PowerPoint just can't match.

The slides of your presentation are now complete. Your final set of tasks involves helping Corrine set up the presentation to run on its own, so that visitors to the model home in the Bella Vista subdivision will be able to watch the presentation regardless of whether Corrine is there. You'll begin by setting up background music for the For More Information slide (Slide 12), the one with the thumbnail hyperlinks.

Playing a CD Audio Track on a Slide

Just as you can play a music clip on a slide, you can also play a CD audio track on a slide. The difference is that the music clip becomes part of the presentation file, whereas with a CD audio track, only the information identifying which track that will play and when it plays is saved in the presentation file. You still have to insert the CD into your computer CD player during the slide show.

Corrine wants you to set up the presentation so that CD music plays while Slide 12 ("For More Information") is on the screen in Slide Show view. You'll do that now.

To play a CD audio track on a slide:

1. Go to **Slide 12**.

2. Insert a music CD into the CD drive that has a track you want to play in the background of Slide 12.

   Trouble? If you don't have a music CD, continue with the steps using 1 as the track number in Steps 6 and 7.

3. Click the **Insert** tab, and then in the Media Clips group, click the **Sound button arrow**.

4. Click **Play CD Audio Track**. The Insert CD Audio dialog box opens.

5. In the Play options section of the dialog box, click the **Loop until stopped** check box, and in the Display options section, click the **Hide sound icon during slide show** check box to select both check boxes.

6. In the Clip selection section of the dialog box, change the value in the **Start at track** box to the track number of the song you want to play. You can play two or more consecutive tracks, but in this case, you want to play only one track.

7. Click the **End at track** box, and then type the same track number that you typed in the Start at track box. See Figure 5-28.

Insert CD Audio dialog box   Figure 5-28

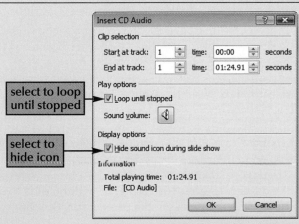

8. Click the **OK** button. The Insert CD Audio dialog box closes and another dialog box opens asking how you want the sound to start in the slide show.

9. Click the **Automatically** button. The dialog box closes and a CD icon is inserted in the middle of the slide.

▶ **10.** Drag the **CD** icon 🎵 from the middle of the slide to just above the slide number in the lower-right corner.

Reference Window | **Playing a CD Track While Showing a Slide**

- Click the Insert tab on the Ribbon, and then in the Media Clips group, click the Sound button arrow.
- Click Play CD Audio Track.
- Select the starting and ending track in the Clip selection section of the dialog box, and specify other options, as desired.
- Click the OK button.
- Place a music CD into your computer's CD-ROM or DVD drive before you run the slide show to play the selected track during the slide show.

Your slide is ready to play a CD music track. Now you just have to make sure your music CD is inserted into the drive whenever you start the slide show. If the CD is not inserted when you run the slide show, the music simply will be omitted. Note that the CD icon is not linked to the specific CD that was in the CD drive when you set the options. The track number you specified will play from any CD.

Recording a Narration

Having set up a CD track to play on Slide 12, you're ready to add narration to the slides to help potential clients understand how to run the slide show.

Reference Window | **Recording a Narration**

- In Normal view, go to the slide where you want to start recording a narration.
- Click the Slide Show tab on the Ribbon, and then in the Set Up group, click Record Narration.
- Click the Set Microphone Level button, position the microphone where you want it while you record the slide show narration, read the text shown in quotes in the dialog box, and then click the OK button.
- Leave the Link narrations in check box unselected if you want to save the narration with the presentation; select it if you want to save the narration in another file that is linked to the presentation file.
- Click the OK button.
- Speak into the microphone to record the narration for the current slide.
- Press the spacebar to go to the next slide (if desired), record the narration for that slide, and then continue, as desired, to other slides.
- After completing the narrations, press the Esc key to end the slide show.
- Click the Save button to save the timing of the presentation, or click the Don't Save button to save only the narration.

Corrine told you that she would use the PowerPoint presentation not only for oral presentations, but also as a self-running presentation. A **self-running presentation** runs without human interruption, but it can accept human intervention to advance to another slide or return to a previous one. Corrine wants to set up the self-running presentation on a computer at the model home in the Bella Vista subdivision. Visitors to the model home can go through the presentation on their own. So that the visitors will know how to navigate through the presentation, Corrine suggests that you add narration to the slides. Before you record narration for a presentation, you should always write a brief script for each slide so you won't hesitate while recording. This tutorial assumes that you've already done that, and you're ready to record the narration.

To set the recording options for a narration:

1. Make sure your computer is equipped with a microphone.

   Trouble? If your system doesn't have a microphone, find a computer that does, connect a microphone to your computer, or check with your instructor or technical support person. If you cannot connect a microphone to your computer, read the following steps but do not execute them.

2. Go to **Slide 1**, click the **Slide Show** tab, and then in the Set Up group, click the **Record Narration** button. The Record Narration dialog box opens.

3. Click the **Set Microphone Level** button. The Microphone Check dialog box opens.

4. Position the microphone where you want it while you record the narration, and then read aloud the text between quotation marks in the dialog box. PowerPoint automatically adjusts the microphone level for you.

5. Click the **OK** button in the Microphone Check dialog box. The Microphone Check dialog box closes.

6. Click the **Change Quality** button. The Sound Selection dialog box opens.

7. Click the **Name** arrow, click **Telephone Quality**, and then click the **OK** button. This format gives a sufficiently high quality of recording without taking up excessive disk space as CD or radio quality formats do.

8. Make sure the **Link narrations in** check box is not selected, so that the recorded sound file is saved within the presentation rather than in a separate file linked to the presentation.

When you click the OK button to close the Record Narration dialog box, PowerPoint automatically starts the slide show. Be prepared to start talking as soon as each slide appears, without waiting for the animation to finish. If you want to comment on each bullet as it appears, time your narration to coincide with the animations.

To record the narration for the presentation:

1. Click the **OK** button in the Record Narration dialog box. PowerPoint automatically starts the slide show.

2. As soon as the slide appears, speak the following into the microphone, using a clear and steady voice: "**Welcome to the Bella Vista subdivision of Mountain Peak Homes. This is a self-running presentation, so just watch the show and read the information on the slides. The presentation will advance automatically from one slide to the next.**"

▶ 3. Press the **spacebar** to go to Slide 2, and then immediately say into the microphone, **"You're currently in the model home at Bella Vista. Please feel free to walk through the home on your own."**

▶ 4. Press the **spacebar** again to go to Slide 3, and then immediately say into the microphone, **"This is the Presentation Contents slide, or Home slide. To jump directly to another location in the slide show, click one of the miniature slides on the screen."**

▶ 5. Press the **spacebar** to go to Slide 4, and then immediately say into the microphone, **"After looking over this slide, or any subsequent slide, click the Home button in the lower-right corner to return to the Presentation Contents slide, or just wait for the presentation to advance to the next slide on its own."**

▶ 6. Press the **spacebar** to go to the next slide, and then immediately press the **Esc** key to halt the recording before going to the next slide. PowerPoint displays a message asking if you want to save the timing that you set for each slide when you recorded your narration. You don't want the slide show to advance on its own, so you won't save the timing.

▶ 7. Click the **Don't Save** button. You've now recorded a narration for your slide show. PowerPoint places a sound icon 🔊 on each of the slides for which you have recorded a narration.

▶ 8. Go to **Slide 1**, and then run the slide show to test your narration, manually advancing the slide show after listening to your narration and watching the animations until you get to Slide 3, and then press the **Esc** key after listening to your narration for Slide 3.

   Trouble? If the narration has mistakes, return to Normal view, click the sound icon in the lower-right corner of the slide, press the Delete key, and then rerecord the narration for that slide. Note that to save a narration of a particular slide, you must advance to the next slide, or the narration won't be saved. After rerecording your narration, repeat Steps 7 and 8.

▶ 9. Save the presentation.

You've now recorded the narration using the Record Narration feature in the Set Up group on the Slide Show tab.

InSight	**Changing the Resolution**

You might notice a feature called Resolution, located in the Monitors group on the Slide Show tab. The box next to Resolution is usually set to "Use Current Resolution," which means that in Slide Show view, PowerPoint uses the current resolution setting of the monitor on which the presentation is being shown. Sometimes, however, that resolution is too low or too high. For example, you might need to increase the resolution if you are showing high-definition pictures, or reduce the resolution if the current resolution causes distortions because of incorrect aspect ratios of objects on the screen. To change the resolution used during a slide show, you would click the Resolution arrow, and then click the desired resolution.

Next, you'll set up the presentation to be self-running.

Setting Up a Self-Running Presentation

Now, Corrine wants you to set up the presentation to be self-running, so that it automatically advances from one slide to another without intervention, and then after the last slide, it loops back to the first slide and runs again. A self-running presentation includes one or more of the following:

- **Automatic timing**: This feature tells PowerPoint to display slides for a certain amount of time before moving to the next slide.
- **Hyperlinks**: These allow users to speed up or change the order of viewing. You can set up a slide show so that, if users don't use the hyperlinks, the slide show will proceed automatically.
- **Narration**: This gives the users more information or instructions for overriding the automatic timing.
- **Kiosk browsing**: This feature tells PowerPoint that, when the slide show reaches the last slide, the presentation should start over again at the beginning.

Looking at this list of items typically involved in a self-running presentation, you've already added hyperlinks and narration. The only items left to add are automatic slide timing and kiosk browsing. You'll manually set the timing next.

Setting the Slide Timing Manually

You can set the slide timing manually or you can rehearse the presentation and save the timing from your rehearsal. You'll set the timing manually.

To set the slide timing:

▶ 1. On the status bar, click the **Slide Sorter** button 🖫 to switch to Slide Sorter view, and then select all the slides.

▶ 2. Click the **Animations** tab, and then in the Transition to This Slide group, click the **Dissolve** transition style, located sixth from the left in the visible row of the Transition gallery.

▶ 3. In the Transition to This Slide group, click the **Automatically After** check box to select it.

▶ 4. With all the slides still selected, click the current value in the **Automatically After** box, type **00:05** to set the slide timing to five seconds, and then press the **Enter** key. The transition effect and manual timing are applied to all of the slides, and the time appears below each slide in Slide Sorter view. See Figure 5-29.

Figure 5-29 ▶ **Completed presentation with timing set manually**

5. Click **Slide 1** to make it the current slide and to deselect all the other slides, and then on the status bar, click the **Slide Show** button 🖵. Watch as the slide show advances through the first several slides. Notice that when a slide has an animation, the slide show advances as soon as the animation finishes because the animations take longer than five seconds.

6. Press the **Esc** key, and then save the presentation.

The manual timing you set is not helpful because the viewer does not have enough time to read all the information on the slide after the last item animates. Instead, you'll rehearse the slide show and record the slide timing.

Rehearsing and Recording the Slide Timing

You can rehearse a slide show and have PowerPoint keep track of the time you spend on each slide as you rehearse the presentation. You can then save those times for the self-running slide show. You'll rehearse the slide show now.

Get ready to read and look over each slide in the presentation, listening to any narration, watching animations, and reading the text. Take the amount of time that you think a student or teacher would take to view each slide or bulleted item. You'll use the spacebar to advance from one slide to the next, according to your desired timing of each item. Don't use the hyperlinks. You should move along at a speed for moderately slow readers. Keep in mind that if you move too slowly, your viewers will become bored or wonder if the slide show is working properly; if you move too quickly, viewers will not have enough time to read and absorb the information on each slide.

To determine the timing of slides for a self-running slide show:

1. Click **Slide 1** in Slide Sorter view, if necessary, and then click the **Slide Show** tab.

2. In the Set Up group, click the **Rehearse Timings** button. PowerPoint automatically starts the slide show, and the Rehearsal dialog box appears on the screen in the upper-left corner.

3. Leave Slide 1 on the screen until the narration you recorded finishes playing, and then press the **spacebar**. Slide 2 appears on the screen.

4. Continue through the slide show using the guidelines discussed in the paragraph that precedes this set of steps. If you need to stop the rehearsal, click the **Pause** button ⏸ on the Rehearsal toolbar to pause the timer; click it again to start the timer again. If you think you've spent too long on a slide, click the **Repeat** button ↻ on the Rehearsal toolbar to restart the timer for the current slide. After you press the spacebar to set the timing for Slide 12 (the last slide), a black screen appears and a dialog box asks if you want to save the timing.

5. Click the **Yes** button. PowerPoint saves the timing and returns you to Slide Sorter view with Slide 1 selected. The rehearsed time appears below each slide thumbnail. See Figure 5-30.

Slides after recording slide timing **Figure 5-30**

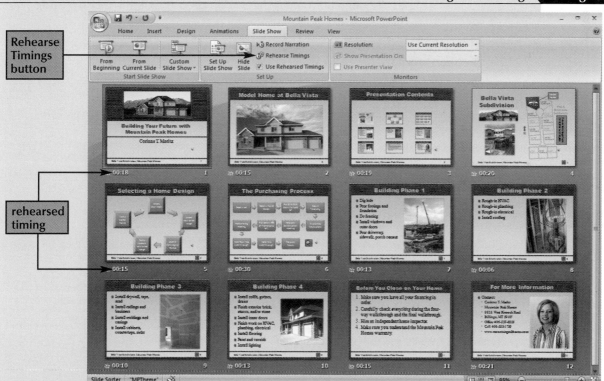

6. Click the **Animations** tab. In the Transition to This Slide group, the exact timing for the selected slide appears in the Automatically After box.

7. Run the slide show to check the animation and timing. If you feel that a slide stays on the screen for too much or too little time, stop the slide show, click the slide to select it in Slide Sorter view, and then change the time in the Automatically After box.

> **Trouble?** If the times you selected are significantly different from those shown in Figure 5-30, you might want to adjust them because you might have selected times that were too short or too long.
>
> **8.** Close the task pane, return to Normal view, and then save the presentation.

If you wanted to remove slide timing and transitions, you would select the Automatically After check box and click the No Transition button in the Transition to This Slide group on the Animations tab.

Applying Kiosk Browsing

The browse-at-a-kiosk feature in PowerPoint allows you to set up a presentation to continually start over. It also disables the spacebar and left mouse-click functions to advance through the slide show. A viewer can, however, click hyperlinks on the screen, including action buttons. You can also still press the Esc key to end the slide show. Now, you'll set up the Mountain Peak Homes presentation for kiosk browsing.

To set up the presentation for browsing at a kiosk:

1. Click the **Slide Show** tab, and then in the Set Up group, click the **Set Up Slide Show** button. The Set Up Show dialog box opens.

2. In the Show type section of the dialog box, click the **Browsed at a kiosk (full screen)** option button. See Figure 5-31.

Figure 5-31 ▸ **Set Up Show dialog box**

Tip

You can show the presentation without the recorded narration by selecting the Show without narration check box in the Set Up Show dialog box.

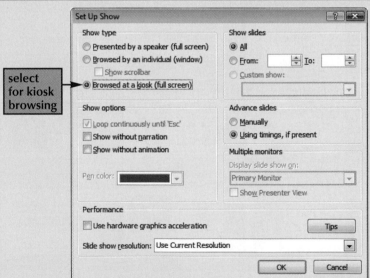

3. Click the **OK** button, and then save the presentation.

With the slide show set for kiosk browsing, when you run the slide show, it will continue to run until someone presses the **Esc** key. Now you'll test the slide show.

To test the self-running slide show:

1. Go to **Slide 11**, and then on the status bar, click the **Slide Show** button 🖵. Watch as the slide show progresses to Slide 12, which is the final slide in the presentation, and then automatically starts over with Slide 1.

2. Watch as much of the presentation as you want, and then press the **Esc** key to end the slide show.

Creating and Editing a Custom Show

After Corrine used the Mountain Peak Homes presentation for several weeks at the Bella Vista model home, she decided that not all the slides were applicable to presentations. Specifically, she felt that Slide 11 ("Before You Close on Your Home") was not something that concerns potential clients at this point in the decision-making process. She also felt that Slide 6 ("The Purchasing Process") should come before Slide 5 ("Selecting a Home Design"). However, Corrine doesn't want to delete Slide 11 or move Slide 6, just in case she later wants to use the presentation as it is now. Therefore, Corrine asks you to create a custom show that leaves out Slide 11 and shows Slide 6 before Slide 5. A **custom show** is a presentation in which selected slides are left out of the presentation or the order of slides is changed without actually deleting or moving slides within the PowerPoint file. You'll create a custom show now.

To create and run a custom show:

1. On the Slide Show tab, in the Start Slide Show group, click the **Custom Slide Show** button, and then click **Custom Shows**. The Custom Shows dialog box opens. You'll begin by creating and naming a new custom show.

2. Click the **New** button. The Define Custom Show dialog box opens.

3. In the Slide show name box, type **Alternate Presentation**. Next, you'll select the slides that you want to keep in the custom show.

4. In the Slides in presentation box on the left, click **1. Building Your Future**, press and hold the **Shift** key, and then click **10. Building Phase 4**. Slides 1 through 10 are selected.

5. Press and hold the **Ctrl** key, and then click **12. For More Information**. Now, all but Slide 11 are selected.

6. Click the **Add** button. The selected slides on the left are added to the Slides in custom show list box on the right.

7. In the Slides in custom show list box, click **6. The Purchasing Process**, and then click the **up arrow** 🔼 located to the right of the Slides in custom show list box. Slide 6 moves up above what was Slide 5. See Figure 5-32.

Figure 5-32   **Define Custom Show dialog box**

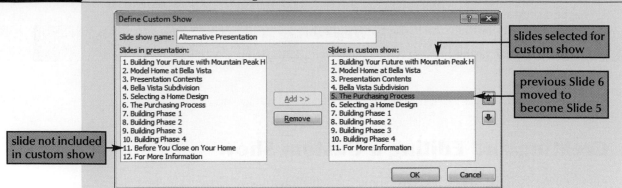

8. Click the **OK** button. The custom show you just created is added to the Custom shows list box in the Custom Shows dialog box. Now, with the Custom Show dialog box open, you can give a presentation using the custom show.

9. Click the **Show** button to switch to Slide Show view, and then go through the custom presentation. Notice that the slides appear in the order you set in the Slides in custom show list box in the Define Custom Show dialog box, and that this order is different from the original presentation.

10. Press the **Esc** key to end the presentation.

11. Save the presentation.

From now on, when Corrine wants to give a presentation of the custom show, she clicks the Slide Show tab, clicks the Custom Slide Show button, and clicks Alternate Presentation (the name you gave for the custom show). If Corrine decides to include additional slides, remove slides, or change the order of the slides in the custom show, she can modify the custom show she created. She would open the Custom Show dialog box, click the name of the custom show in the Custom shows list, and then click the Edit button in the dialog box to open the Define Custom Show dialog box.

Now, Corrine wants you to print the presentation not as a handout but as full-sized slides so that clients can easily read the information on the slides.

To print the slides full-sized:

1. If your instructor directs you to print full-sized slides, click the **Office Button** , and then click **Print**. The Print dialog box opens.

2. If necessary, click the **Print what** arrow, and then click **Slides**.

3. If you do not have access to a color printer, click the **Color/grayscale** arrow, and then click **Pure Black and White**.

4. Click the **Frame slides** check box to add a black border around each slide.

5. Click the **OK** button. The presentation prints on 12 sheets of paper as full-sized slides.

6. Submit the completed presentation in printed or electronic form, as requested by your instructor, and then close the presentation, but do not exit PowerPoint.

Corrine thanks you for your help in preparing the presentation, which helps her generate many new customers for Mountain Peak Homes.

Session 5.2 Quick Check | Review

1. What is a callout?
2. What is the purpose of a gridline?
3. If you use the PowerPoint feature to rehearse slide timing and you make a mistake in the timing, how can you fix the mistake without redoing the entire slide show rehearsal?
4. Why might you want to use illustration software to make a diagram or illustration, instead of the PowerPoint drawing tools?
5. How do you end a slide show running at a kiosk?
6. What are changes to a presentation that you can make to create a custom show?
7. How can a person viewing a presentation in kiosk-browsing mode advance from one slide to another?

Tutorial Summary | Review

In this tutorial, you learned how to use PowerPoint slides in other applications by copying a slide into a Word document. You also learned how to apply special effects and animation to SmartArt diagrams; to create, modify, and animate background objects; and to download motion (animation) and sound clips. You learned how to create a numbered list, add illustrations and callouts to your presentation, and apply special effects to text boxes. You learned how to make thumbnails of slides and paste them in another slide as pictures, and then to create hyperlinks from the thumbnails; how to insert a CD audio track into a slide; and how to record a narration as part of a presentation. Finally, you also learned how to set up and run a self-running presentation and how to create a custom show.

Key Terms

adjustment handles	grid	narration
animated GIF	gridlines	numbered list
automatic timing	kiosk browsing	self-running presentation
callout	Microsoft Office Online	Snap to Grid
custom show		

Practice	**Review Assignments**

Data Files needed for these Review Assignments: ColorForm.jpg, MPHColors.pptx

After the success of the self-running presentation at the model home in the Bella Vista subdivision, Corrine thinks it would be a good idea to set up a kiosk in the lobby of the Mountain Peak Homes design center in Billings. She asks you to design a presentation to help new customers of Mountain Peak Homes in choosing designs and colors of interior and exterior features for their new Mountain Peak home. Do the following:

1. Open the presentation **MPHColors** from the Tutorial.05\Review folder included with your Data Files, and then save it to the same folder as **MPH Design Colors**.
2. In Slide 1, change the name in the subtitle from "Corrine T. Moritz" to your name.
3. Also in Slide 1, add the animated clip art of a construction worker on a ladder applying red paint to a wall. This is available from the Clip Art page on Microsoft Office Online. Position the animated GIF so that it is centered below the subtitle (your name).
4. Also in Slide 1, search for and insert the sound clip "Mozart" (use the search word "classical" and search only for sound clips), which you can find in the Clip Art page on Microsoft Office Online. Set up the sound clip to play as soon as the slide appears in Slide Show view and repeats until the slide no longer appears onscreen, and hide the sound icon during the slide show.
5. Go to Slide 3, convert the bulleted list to a Vertical Bending Process diagram to show the flow of the steps taken when choosing interior and exterior designs and colors. Set the SmartArt Style to Polished.
6. Add custom animation to the process diagram text boxes so they wipe onto the slide one item at a time, and then modify the animation so that the objects wipe from the appropriate direction and in the order of the process flow. Set the speed of the animation to slow, and set the animation to begin soon after the slide appears in a slide show.
7. Change the bulleted list in Slide 4 to a numbered list, change the numbers to a dark brown color, and decrease the font size of the number to 85% of normal.
8. Go to Slide 5, and then insert the image **ColorForm**, located in the Tutorial.05\Review folder included with your Data Files. This is a picture of part of the Design and Color Form; it was created using a program to capture a picture of an Excel spreadsheet displayed on a screen.
9. Using the Size group on the Picture Tools Format tab, adjust the width of the Color-Form picture to 8 inches, and then center the picture in the blank space on Slide 5.
10. Add the following callouts to the picture (adjust the size of the text box to fit the text properly, if necessary):
    a. **Start your selection with kitchen cabinets** with a line pointing to the word "Cabinets"
    b. **See catalogs for proper model numbers** with a line pointing to "RP4E16" (to the right of Door Edge & Panel)
    c. **Be sure to get correct upgrade cost** with a line pointing to "$575" (the upgrade for Door Edge & Panel)
11. Animate the three callouts so that they fly in slowly from the bottom one after another, without any viewer intervention. Set the animation so that the text moves with the text box of each callout.
12. In the empty content placeholder in Slide 6, insert a clip art photograph of a home under construction. Use the search word "construction" in the Microsoft Office Online Web page. Select the photo of the house with wood framing, glass windows installed, and a blue sky and mountain peak in the background.

13. In Slide 2, insert thumbnails of the subsequent four slides in the presentation, adjust their size to 3 inches in width, and then make the thumbnails hyperlinks to their respective slides. To help align the thumbnails, use the Gridlines and Snap to Grid features.

14. Add Back or Previous (hyperlinked to the previous slide), Forward or Next (hyperlinked to the next slide), and Home (hyperlinked to Slide 2) action buttons to all of the slides, except the Back or Previous action button on the first slide should hyperlink to the last slide, and the Forward or Next action button on the last slide should hyperlink to the first slide. Set the size of the action buttons to 0.35 by 0.35 inch. Position them in a row at the bottom of each slide between the footer and the slide number.

15. Record the narration for Slide 2: "Welcome to the Mountain Peak Homes Design and Color Center."

16. Add an audio CD track to Slide 3. Choose any desired track from your CD collection. If you don't have any audio CDs, set the track to track 1. Hide the CD icon during slide shows. Set the CD track to start to play before the process diagram animation and to continue to play until the slide ends.

17. Record timing for the slides so that when the slide show runs on its own, each slide is on the screen an appropriate amount of time. Your timing should be about 14 seconds for each slide without a bulleted list and about 20 seconds for those with a bulleted list.

18. Edit the timing of Slide 1 so it stays on the screen for 10 seconds, and then edit the timing of the last slide so it stays on the screen for 12 seconds.

19. Set up the presentation as a self-running slide show (for kiosk browsing).

20. Create a custom show called Brief Version using only Slides 1, 3, 4, and 6, and then reorder the custom show slides so that the "Making Your Selections" slide is the last slide.

21. Run the slide show and then save the presentation using the default filename.

22. Submit the completed presentation in printed or electronic form, as requested by your instructor, and then close all open files.

| Apply | | **Case Problem 1** |

Apply information you used in the tutorial to create a presentation on an athletic event-management company.

Data Files needed for this Case Problem: Cyclist.jpg, Race.pptx, Runner.jpg, RunPic.jpg

Rat Race, Inc. Lauren Jenkins of Oceanside, California, recognized many years ago the growth potential of fitness events like marathons (26.2-mile races), cycling centuries (100-mile or 100-kilometer rides), and triathlons (swim-bike-run races). She, therefore, started her own company, Rat Race, Inc., to manage such events. She and her eight full-time employees manage races and athletic events sponsored by local government and charitable agencies, as well as by commercial enterprises. For example, Lauren and her coworkers do all the coordination, logistics, monitoring, and computerized timing for the annual Oceanside Marathon, Escondido Half Marathon, Escondido Triathlon, and San Diego County Cycling Festival (which includes mountain-bike races as well as road races). Lauren asks you to help her put together a PowerPoint presentation that she wants to give to city and county recreation departments and to tourism departments to propose fitness and athletic events for Rat Race, Inc. to manage. She also wants the presentation set up for kiosk browsing, so that she can let the presentation run on its own at recreation trade shows and event expositions. Do the following:

1. Open the file **Race** from the Tutorial.05\Case1 folder included with your Data Files, replace the current name in the subtitle with your name, and then save the file to the same folder as **Race Proposal**.

2. Insert the footer "Rat Race, Inc.," and turn on slide numbering.

3. In Slide 1, insert an animated GIF file of a runner breaking the tape at the finish line of a race. The file is located on Microsoft Office Online. Use the search phrase "finish line," and set the media type to Animations. Position the graphic above the slide title and centered between the left and right edges of the slide.

4. In Slide 2, insert the picture file **Cyclist**, located in the Tutorial.05\Case1 folder. Place the graphic to the right of the bulleted list. Change the slide layout as necessary to make the text and picture fit properly.

5. Set the picture style to Drop Shadow Rectangle, and then change the size of the Cyclist picture to a height of 3.5 inches.

6. Also in Slide 2, insert the picture file **RunPic**. Adjust its height to 3.5 inches, and set its Picture Style to Drop Shadow Rectangle.

✛ EXPLORE

7. Move the two pictures so they are side by side, with the cyclist on the left, and then select both pictures and align the pictures along their tops. (*Hint*: Click one picture, press and hold the Shift key, and then click the second picture so that both are selected, and then use the Align button in the Arrange group on the Format tab.)

8. In Slide 3, insert the drawing of a runner, which is the picture file **Runner**, located in the Tutorial.05\Case1 folder.

9. To the drawing in Slide 3, add the following callouts and change their Shape Styles to Colored Outline – Dark 1:

   a. **Bib Number** pointing to the runner's bib number (215).

   b. **Timing Chip** pointing to the blue disk with the yellow strap on the runner's right ankle.

   c. **T Shirt** pointing to the runner's T shirt.

10. Animate the callouts so that they appear in the slide one at a time during the slide show in the order you added them. Use the Appear entrance effect. Modify the animation effects so that the callouts appear one after another on a click of the mouse.

11. In Slide 4, change the bulleted list to a numbered list.

12. In Slide 5, change the bulleted list to a cycle diagram, set the Layout to Block Cycle, change the color to Color Fill – Accent 2, and then set the SmartArt Style to Moderate Effect.

13. Set the animation of the cycle diagram to Fade (One by one), and set the first item in the animation to start immediately when the slide appears.

14. Also in Slide 5, insert a sound clip of any music of your choice from Microsoft Office Online. Set it to play automatically as soon as the slide appears in Slide Show view (so the music starts before the cycle diagram animates), set it to play continuously until the slide ends, and then set the sound icon to be hidden when the slide show is running.

15. Using Fly In by 1st Level Paragraph, animate all of the slides with bulleted or numbered lists so that the lists use progressive disclosure. On Slide 3, make sure the progressive disclosure animation occurs before the animation of the callouts. (*Hint*: Set the animation on each slide, not on the slide masters; otherwise, you'll change the animation that you've already set up in the slide with the cycle diagram and other slides.)

16. Record timing for the slides so that when the slide show runs on its own, each slide is on the screen an appropriate amount of time.

17. Set up the presentation as a self-running slide show (for kiosk browsing).

18. Carefully go through the presentation to make sure all the animations, sounds, and graphics appear as they should, and correct any problems.

19. Save your presentation using the default filename.

20. Submit the completed presentation in printed or electronic form, as requested by your instructor, and then close all open files.

| Create | **Case Problem 2** |

Create a new presentation about a digital photography Web site.

Data Files needed for this Case Problem: Arches.jpg, Camera.jpg, DPJ.pptx, Falls.jpg, MntLake.jpg, Tahoe.jpg, Trevor.jpg, Yosemite.jpg

Digital Photo Journal Trevor Jackson of Charleston, West Virginia, started an online company called Digital Photo Journal (DPJ). Trevor's Web site features the following:

- Photoblogs, in which DPJ members share photographs and their thoughts on photography
- Reviews of digital cameras
- Tutorials on digital photography and image editing software
- Users' forum for exchange of ideas
- Advertisements for digital photographic equipment, software, and services

Trevor has asked you to help him create a presentation on DPJ. He'll use the presentation to describe DPJ to potential site members (who pay a small annual fee) and to potential advertisers, who are his main source of revenue. Your task is to prepare a PowerPoint presentation that includes graphics and information using the five JPEG photos located in the Tutorial.05\Case2 folder included with your Data Files. The eight slides in your presentation should look like the slides in Figure 5-33.

Figure 5-33

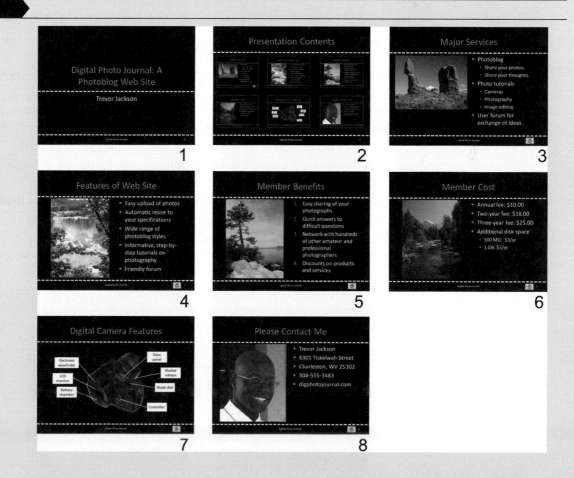

The following information will help you create the slide show. Read all the steps before you start creating your presentation. You will have to do more than just these steps to complete the assignment to make your presentation look like Figure 5-33.

1. The presentation is created from **DPJ**, located in the Tutorial.05\Case2 folder included with your Data Files. Change the subtitle name in the subtitle placeholder on Slide 1 to your name, and then save the file as **Photo Journal** to the same folder.

2. The presentation uses the built-in color theme called Grayscale.

3. In the slide masters, the title text is set to Gray-25%, Accent 2; the level-1 bullet style is set to a filled square with the same color; and the level-2 bullet is set to a filled round with the same color.

⊕ EXPLORE

4. On the Title Slide layout, insert a horizontal white line between the title and subtitle placeholders. Change the line weight (thickness) to 4½ points, and change its style to the Square Dot style of dashes. (*Hint*: Use the Shape Outline button in the Shape Styles group on the Format tab to modify the line.)

5. Animate the white horizontal line on the Title Slide Layout master so that it flies into the slide from the left at a fast speed. Set the animation so that it starts With Previous.

6. Copy the animated line that you just created to the bottom of the slide, just above the footer and slide number placeholders, and then copy it to the Title and Content Layout, the Two Content Layout, and the Title Only Layout masters, so that in all three slides, a copy of the animated line is just below the title placeholder and another copy is just above the footnote placeholder.

7. Slides 3 through 6 contain picturesque digital images. You'll find all these images in the Tutorial.05\Case2 folder.

8. In Slide 7, the picture is the file named **Camera**, located in the Tutorial.05\Case2 folder. Make the image background transparent. The callouts to the camera have the Colored Outline – Accent 6 shape style applied, and the shape outline is white. (*Hint*: Create and format one callout, duplicate it (copy and paste it), edit the text of the new callout, and then move the callout to the new location.)

9. In Slide 8, the picture is the file **Trevor**, located in the Tutorial.05\Case2 folder.

10. Slide 2, which you should create as your last slide, includes thumbnails with hyperlinks to Slides 3 through 8. The height of each thumbnail is 2.0 inches, and the picture border of each slide thumbnail is set to white.

11. Each slide, near the slide number, has an action button with a hyperlink to Slide 2.

12. Set the animation of all the bulleted lists to Fade By 1st Level Paragraphs. Be sure that the photo in each slide does not animate.

13. Manually set the timing of Slide 1 to 5 seconds, Slide 2 to 15 seconds, and Slides 3 through 8 to 25 seconds. Do this in preparation for when the slide show runs on its own (in kiosk browsing).

14. Set up the presentation as a self-running slide show (for kiosk browsing).

15. Create a custom show named Short Version using only Slides 1, 3, 4, and 8.

16. Save your presentation, and submit the completed presentation in printed or electronic form, as requested by your instructor, and then close all open files.

Challenge | **Case Problem 3**

Learn new PowerPoint skills as you modify a presentation for a dance school.

Data File needed for this Case Problem: Salsa.pptx

Salsa Dance School   Amanda Cabrillana is director of the Salsa Dance School, a not-for-profit subsidiary of the Studio City department of recreation in West Palm Beach, Florida. She teaches classes for children and adults on the samba, rumba, tango, and other Latin American dances. She asks you to help prepare a presentation for her to use when she visits schools, churches, and civic organizations to tell them about the dance school. Do the following:

1. Open the file **Salsa** located in the Tutorial.05\Case3 folder included with your Data Files, replace the current name in the subtitle with your name, and then save the presentation back to the same folder using the filename **Salsa Dance**.

2. Apply Opulent theme colors.

✦ EXPLORE   3. Set the background style to Gradient fill. You'll now set up the background with two stops, which are phases of the gradient with different colors. (*Hint*: In the Format Background dialog box, click the Gradient fill option button, and then look for "Gradient fill" in the dialog box.) Set the color of Stop 1 to Pink, Text 2, Darker 25%, and make sure its Stop position is set to 0%. Change the Gradient stop from Stop 1 to Stop 2, and set its color to Orange, Accent 3, Darker 25%. Make sure its Stop position is 100%. Now check to see if there are other gradient stops; if there are, select them one at a time, and then click the Remove button to remove each one. When you're done, click the Apply to All button.

4. In the Office Theme Slide Master, change the text color of title and body text to white. Change the first-level bullet to a yellow, round picture bullet that looks like a sunburst.

5. In the Title Slide Layout master, insert an animated GIF file that shows a dancing couple, the woman in a red dress and a man in black slacks. Use the search word "dance." If you do not have access to Microsoft Office Online, insert another animated GIF in its place or skip this step and subsequent related steps.

✦ EXPLORE   6. Position the GIF image just above and centered over the title placeholder. Animate the picture using a circular motion path. (*Hint*: In the Custom Animation task pane, add the Motion Path effect called Circle. You might have to click More Motion Paths to find the circle.)

✦ EXPLORE   7. Set the animation speed to Very Slow. Turn off the Smooth start and Smooth end effects. Set the timing effect to repeat until the end of the slide, and set the animation to Start With Previous. (*Hint*: Click the arrow on the animated item in the task pane, and then click Effect Options.) If you have set up the animation properly, the clip art moves in a clockwise path over the title and subtitle text boxes.

✦ EXPLORE   8. Insert the Salsa Theme sound file from Microsoft Office Online into the Title Slide layout. (*Hint*: Use the search phrase "Latin rhythms" and select sound as the media type.) In the Custom Animation task pane, set the sound clip to Start With Previous, to stop playing after current slide, and to repeat until end of slide. Hide the sound icon during the slide show. (*Hint*: You can set these features in the Play Sound dialog box, accessed by clicking Effects Options on the animation object menu.)

⊕ EXPLORE

9. Copy the animated picture and the sound icon from the Title Slide layout to the Title and Content Layout master slide. Remove the current animation from the picture, and then change the size of the picture to 0.5 inches in height. Position the picture between the lower-left corner of the title placeholder and the upper-left corner of the content placeholder, and then insert a Right motion path to the picture. Click the red arrowhead at the end of the motion path, position the mouse pointer over the white, round resize handle, and while holding down the Shift key, drag the arrowhead until the resize handle is between the lower-right corner of the title placeholder and the upper-right corner of the content placeholder. Set the animation speed to Very Slow. Set the animation to Start With Previous, so that it animates as music is playing.

10. Copy both the animated picture and the sound icon from the Title and Content Layout master to Two Content Layout and the Title Only Layout masters.

11. In the Title and Content Layout master, set the content to the animation Fade By 1st Level Paragraphs (progressive disclosure). Similarly in the Two Content Layout master, set the left content (but not the right) to the same type of animation.

⊕ EXPLORE

12. In Slide 3, change the text box to the WordArt style called Gradient Fill – Accent 1, Outline – White, Glow – Accent 2. Set the Entrance custom animation to the Moderate animation called Color Typewriter, change its speed to very fast, and set it to Start With Previous.

⊕ EXPLORE

13. In Slide 3, below the text box ("The Salsa Dance School"), insert four clip-art photographs of couples dancing. As you insert each one, change its height to 2 inches. The exact location of the pictures isn't important, but the leftmost pictures should be close to the left edge of the slide, and the rightmost pictures should be near the right edge of the slide. Select all four pictures, and in the Arrange group on the Format tab, click the Align button, and then click Align Top. Now, again click the Align button, and then click Distribute Horizontally. The pictures are now aligned along their tops and evenly spaced.

⊕ EXPLORE

14. With all four pictures on Slide 3 still selected, set the entrance animation to fly in from the left, and set them as a group to Start With Previous at a slow speed. If you've set up all the animations on this slide properly, the GIF picture, the text box, and the four photos should all move from left to right at roughly the same speed across the slide.

15. In Slide 4, convert the bulleted list to the Continuous Cycle diagram (a type of cycle diagram). Set the animation to Fade, One by one, and to Start On Click.

16. In Slide 6, change the bulleted list to a numbered list. Set the numbers to the color Gold, Accent 4 and 120% of normal size.

17. Apply the slide transition called Push Right, located in the Push and Cover group on the Slide Transitions gallery. Set the Transition Speed to Medium.

⊕ EXPLORE

18. Show the slide show without animation. (*Hint*: Click the Slide Show tab in the Set Up group, click the Set Up Slide Show button, and then click the Show without animation check box. Use the navigation buttons to advance each slide.) After going through the slide show with that setup, uncheck the Show without animation check box before you save the presentation.

19. Set the timing of Slides 1, 3, and 4 to 12 seconds, and all the others to 20 seconds. Set up the presentation for kiosk browsing.

20. Save your presentation using the default filename, submit the completed presentation in printed or electronic form, as requested by your instructor, and then close all open files.

Research | **Case Problem 4**

Use the Internet to collect information about U.S. foreign trade with China.

There are no Data Files needed for this Case Problem.

U.S. Foreign Trade with China Over the past 35 years, economic trade between the United States and China has accelerated as Sino-American relations have improved. Your assignment is to prepare a presentation on some aspect of foreign trade between the United States and the People's Republic of China (P.R.C.). You can focus on a particular aspect of U.S.-P.R.C. trade, such as technology in general or computers in particular, or you can focus on more general aspects of the overall trade with China or the overall economic impact of improved Sino-American relations. You might want to discuss the historical perspective, current status of trade relations, congressional bills dealing with U.S.-P.R.C. trade, people's attitudes about trade with China, or major products traded between the two countries. Do the following:

1. Connect to the Internet, open your browser, and then search the Web for information using phrases like "foreign trade China," "China normal trade relations," and "China import exports." Include other words to narrow your search, for example, "congress," "technology," or "computers."

2. Based on your initial Internet search, select a topic dealing with U.S. foreign trade with China. Conduct additional searches or do other research as needed to find sufficient information on your topic.

3. Create a descriptive title for the presentation. Be as specific as possible.

4. Include your name, course, section, and school name in the subtitle on the first slide.

5. Prepare at least six slides. Include clip art on at least three slides.

6. Download and use at least one photograph and one animated GIF file from the Microsoft Office Online Web site.

7. Include at least one numbered list.

8. Prepare the presentation to be attractive and eye-catching, as well as informative.

9. In the title slide, set up the presentation to play a CD music track in the background.

10. Create and animate at least one diagram. For example, you might prepare a flow diagram showing a recent Chinese historical timeline or a cycle diagram showing how trade deficits affect the economy.

11. Include a downloaded Chinese music clip to play while the diagram is animating.

12. Apply slide transitions to all the slides and progressive disclosure (animation of bulleted lists) to all slides with a numbered or bulleted list.

13. Prepare an abbreviated custom slide show, and change the order of at least one slide.

14. Set up the presentation to be self-running. You don't need to include action buttons unless you feel they are appropriate. Set up appropriate slide timing.

15. Save the presentation using the filename **US-PRC Trade**.

16. Submit the completed presentation in printed or electronic form, as requested by your instructor, and then close all open files.

Research | **Internet Assignments**

Go to the Web to find information you can use to create presentations.

The purpose of the Internet Assignments is to challenge you to find information on the Internet that you can use to work effectively with this software. The actual assignments are updated and maintained on the Course Technology Web site. Log on to the Internet and use your Web browser to go to the Student Online Companion for New Perspectives Office 2007 at **www.course.com/np/office2007**. Then navigate to the Internet Assignments for this tutorial.

Review | **Quick Check Answers**

Session 5.1

1. From Slide Sorter view, select the slide, copy it, and then use the Paste Special command to paste the slide in another program as a picture file.
2. true
3. False; you can change the order of animation, regardless of the order in which the objects were applied to the slide.
4. from Microsoft Office Online
5. a movie clip, identified with the filename extension .gif, that you can import just like any photograph or clip art but which has motion (animation)
6. Select the entire bulleted list, and then click the Numbering button in the Paragraph group on the Home tab.

Session 5.2

1. a label that includes a text box and a line between the text box and the item being labeled
2. A gridline helps to position and align objects on a slide, because objects "snap" to the gridlines.
3. Select the slide in Slide Sorter view or go to the slide in Normal view, click the Animation tab, and in the Transition to This Slide, change the time in the Automatically After box.
4. because the illustration might be too complex for the simple PowerPoint drawing tools
5. press the Esc key (you cannot click on the slide to open the shortcut menu to end the slide show)
6. You can omit slides or change the order of slides.
7. The person viewing the show can't use the keyboard or mouse to advance unless the slide contains navigation hyperlinks.

Ending Data Files

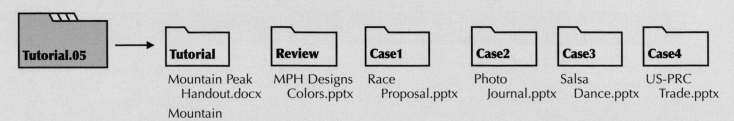

Objectives

Session 6.1
- Create design themes using the slide masters
- Change page setup and character spacing
- Create new slide master with a custom layout
- Make overhead transparencies in black and white (grayscale) and in color
- Prepare a custom photo album using PowerPoint

Session 6.2
- Prepare a multiple-page and single-page poster presentation
- Create a banner
- Insert and review revision comments
- Manipulate text, insert symbols, and use the Format Painter
- Save a presentation file as a PowerPoint Show (PPSX) and as a Portable Document File (PDF)
- Encrypt a presentation file and add a digital signature

Creating Special Types of Presentations

Using PowerPoint to Prepare Transparencies, Photo Albums, Posters, and Banners

Case | Franklin Flyers

Paul Uzzell-Bottemiller is part owner and pilot for Franklin Flyers, an airplane charter company in Hoover, Alabama. Paul and the other owners decided use "Flyers" instead of "Fliers" in the company name to emphasize that their company mission is to fly. The main clients for Franklin Flyers are businesses that need quick, direct flights to major cities in the U.S. These businesses also use Franklin Flyers to travel to vacation spots as part of their business retreats and incentive packages.

Two years ago, Paul made a successful proposal to provide travel services for Mira Vista Software (MVS), a large software-development company in Huntsville, Alabama. Recently, Paul was contacted by the University of Alabama (UA) to be part of a symposium on preparing successful business proposals. UA asked him to lead a classroom discussion, using overhead transparencies, explaining his successful proposal to MVS and to give a poster presentation on the proposal. He asked you to help him prepare the overhead transparencies and the poster presentation.

In this tutorial, you'll create a custom design theme, with custom slide layouts, for overhead transparencies and for a custom photo album. You'll make overhead transparencies, prepare a photo album, and create a poster presentation with a title banner. Finally, you'll save the presentation as a PowerPoint Show (.ppsx) file, as an Adobe Portable Document File (.pdf), and as an encrypted presentation with a digital signature.

Starting Data Files

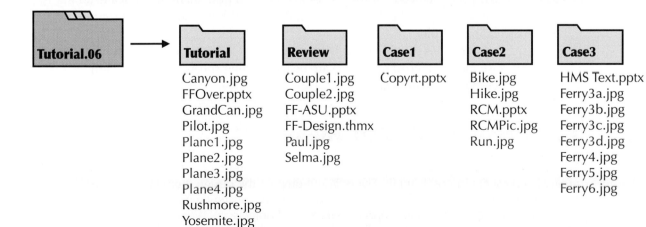

Session 6.1

Creating a Design Theme for Overheads

As you already know, a design theme is a file that contains a color scheme; slide layouts with placeholders for titles, lists, footnotes, and so forth; attributes and colors for the titles, main text, and other text; and the background objects and design for the slides in a presentation. You'll also recall that to make a custom design theme, you prepare a PowerPoint presentation with the desired color scheme, font attributes, and background objects, and then save the file as a design theme, rather than as a normal presentation file. You can then use your custom-designed themes in other presentations.

Paul asked you to prepare design themes for him to use in making his overhead transparencies (transparent sheets containing text that can be projected onto a screen). He knows that overhead transparencies are common media for presentations at professional meetings, so he wants to have design themes to use not only at the upcoming symposium at UA, but at other events as well. Designs that work well for on-screen slide presentations may not work as well for presentations using overhead transparencies. In this tutorial, you'll learn more about the principles and practices of designing themes.

The following are some things you should keep in mind as you prepare the design theme:

- PowerPoint is an excellent vehicle for preparing overhead transparencies. It works better than a word processor because it's specifically designed for preparing presentations, especially those that include graphics as well as text.
- Overhead transparencies offer several advantages over on-screen electronic slide shows. First, many classrooms and lecture halls are equipped with overhead projectors, but not with computer projection systems; some classrooms and lecture halls have both overhead and computer projection systems. Second, overheads are sometimes more reliable than computer projection systems in which incompatibilities are sometimes a problem. Third, overhead projection usually doesn't require the room to be darkened, or at least not as much as with other projection methods, so the audience can more easily take notes and participate in group discussions. And fourth, overhead projection allows the speaker to see the visuals without turning away from the audience, thus maintaining better eye contact.
- The more ink required to print a transparency sheet, the more expensive the sheet is to print, and the longer it takes. So if you have limited resources (some inkjet cartridges are expensive) or limited time (you're in a hurry to print your visuals), use color sparingly. This means that you should generally print black (or dark) text on a white background and limit the number of background objects.
- You can design your overhead transparencies in color and print them in grayscale. So if you aren't sure which type of printer you'll use, don't be afraid to set up the PowerPoint presentation in color.
- Overhead transparencies should normally be printed in portrait orientation, not landscape, because most overhead projectors are better at fitting sheets that are tall and narrow, rather than short and wide.

Preparing the Design Theme

You begin by creating a design theme for overhead transparencies, which Paul will use to create his presentation on Franklin Flyers. You'll prepare the design theme for the overhead transparency with the above concepts in mind. The design theme will include a limited amount of color and appropriate background objects.

Changing the Page Setup and Character Spacing

Overheads are usually in portrait orientation, so you need to change the page orientation to switch from landscape to portrait orientation. You'll also change the page setup to change from onscreen slides to overheads.

Understanding Slide Sizes | InSight

PowerPoint supports many different built-in page (slide) sizes and supports any custom size that you want. The built-in slide sizes include on-screen shows for various monitor sizes and paper sizes, including letter paper, ledger paper, and various European-sized paper. Built-in sizes for 35mm slides, overheads, and banners are also included. PowerPoint 2007 supports on-screen slides of various aspect ratios, from the normal computer monitor (4:3 ratio, which means for every 4 inches in width, the slides are 3 inches in height) to the wide-screen TV-sized monitor (16:10 ratio). Make sure you choose the correct slide size based on how you're going to show or print your PowerPoint presentation.

To change the page setup:

▶ **1.** Open a new, blank PowerPoint presentation in Normal view.

▶ **2.** Click the **Design** tab, and then in the Page Setup group, click the **Page Setup** button. The Page Setup dialog box opens. On-screen Show (4:3) is selected in the Slides sized for box.

▶ **3.** Click the **Slides sized for** arrow, scroll down, and then click **Overhead**.

▶ **4.** In the Slides section under Orientation, click the **Portrait** option button. See Figure 6-1. Notice that the width adjusts to 7.5 inches and the height to 10 inches rather than to 8.5 and 11, respectively. This is because PowerPoint sets the size to the typical printable area on the page, not to the actual size of the transparency film.

Page Setup dialog box with settings for overhead transparencies ◀ Figure 6-1

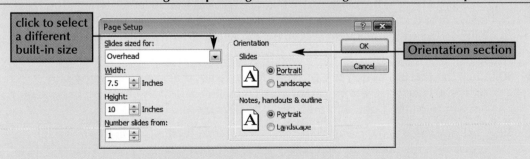

▶ **5.** Click the **OK** button. The title slide in the slide pane changes size and orientation to reflect the changes you made to the page setup.

Your next task is to modify the slide masters. Although you'll keep the default theme colors used in the Office theme, you'll change the theme fonts, font colors, and bullets. You'll also add background objects and create a new, custom slide layout.

In addition, you'll change the character spacing of the title text. **Character spacing** is a feature that allows you to adjust the space between characters in text. For example, you would change the character spacing to tight if you wanted the characters closer together, or you would change the characters to loose if you want the characters farther apart. You'll keep the majority of the background blank (white) to avoid printing excessive ink on the transparency film sheets.

To modify the slide masters:

1. Click the **Design** tab, and then in the themes group, click the Fonts button. The easiest way to change fonts in the entire presentation is to change the theme fonts.

2. Click **Office 2**. The font for the slide titles is still Calibri, but the font for the bulleted list and other text is Cambria. You decide you want the slide titles to be Arial Rounded MT Bold.

3. Click the **View** tab, and then in the Presentation Views group, click the **Slide Master button** to switch to Slide Master view. First, you'll change the theme fonts.

4. In the pane on the left, click the **Office Theme Slide Master** thumbnail, and then in the slide pane, click the edge of the title text placeholder to select it.

5. Click the **Home** tab, change the font to **Arial Rounded MT Bold**, and then change the font color to **Blue, Accent 1**. Next you'll add an outline to the title text placeholder.

6. In the Drawing group, click the **Shape Outline button arrow**, point to **Weight**, and then click **3 pt**.

7. Click the **Shape Outline button arrow** again, and then click the **Dark Blue, Text 2** tile in the first row under Theme Colors. Now you'll change the character spacing.

8. In the Font group, click the **Character Spacing** button ⬛, and then click **Tight**. Now, all the slide titles will have text with tight character spacing.

9. Click anywhere in the placeholder text in the first-level bulleted item, in the Paragraph group, click the **Bullets button arrow** ⬛, and then click Bullets and Numbering on the menu below the bullet gallery. The Bullets and Numbering dialog box opens.

10. Click the **Picture** button to open the Picture Bullet dialog box, click the blue, gradient-filled square with darker blue on the left gradually changing to light-blue and white on the right, and then click the **OK** button.

11. Click anywhere in the placeholder text in the second-level bullet, in the Paragraph group click the **Bullets button arrow** ⬛, and then click the **Filled Square Bullets** style. See Figure 6-2.

Slide master with new formatting ◀ **Figure 6-2**

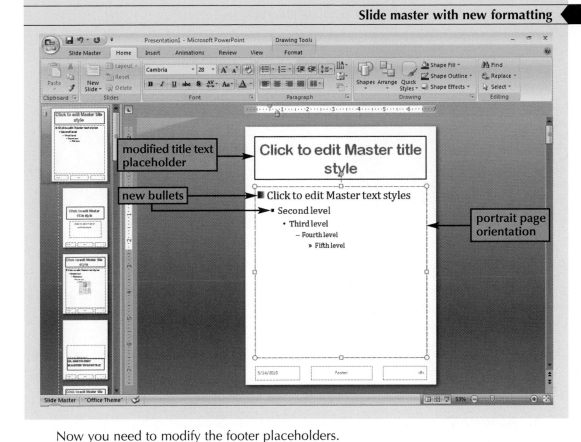

Now you need to modify the footer placeholders.

To modify the footer placeholders:

▶ **1.** Click the edge of the **date** placeholder in the bottom-left corner of the slide layout, press and hold the **Shift** key, and then click the **Footer** placeholder. Both place-holders are selected.

▶ **2.** Change the font of the selected placeholders to **Arial Rounded MT Bold**, the font size to **20** points, and the font color to **Blue, Accent 1**.

▶ **3.** Select the slide number placeholder, and then press the **Delete** key.

▶ **4.** Select the **date** placeholder, press the → key as many times as necessary to move the date placeholder to the position formerly occupied by the slide number placeholder.

▶ **5.** Select the **Footer** placeholder, in the Paragraph group, click the **Align Text Left** button ▤, and then deselect the placeholder. See Figure 6-3.

Figure 6-3 **Slide master with modified footer and date placeholders**

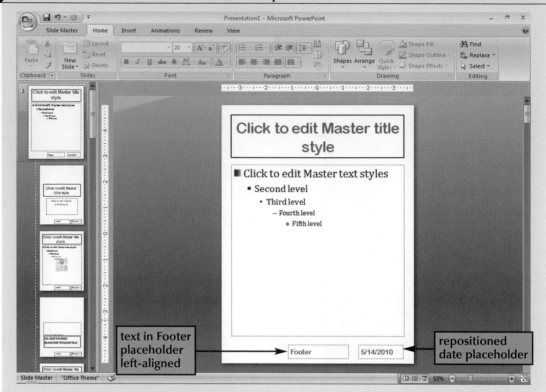

▶ **6.** Delete the slide number placeholder from the Title Slide Layout master and from the Title and Content Layout master.

You've made important progress in designing an appropriate design theme for overhead transparencies. Next, you'll add background objects to the slide masters.

Adding Background Objects to the Slide Masters

To complete your custom design theme, you'll add a logo to the slide masters and a drawn rectangle to the background, behind the title text box. When you draw the rectangle, you'll draw it on top of the title text placeholder, and then you'll send it to the back, behind the title text placeholder. Remember that objects on a slide are layered in an order from front to back, and if you place one object on top of another, you can send either object forward or back.

To add background objects to the slide masters:

▶ **1.** Switch to the Office Theme Slide Master thumbnail, click the **Insert** tab, in the Illustrations group, click **Picture**, navigate to the **Tutorial.06\Tutorial** folder included with your Data Files, click the file **Plane1**, and then click the **Insert** button. A simple picture of a propeller plane appears in the slide pane and the Picture Tools Format tab becomes active on the Ribbon. This picture is designed for Franklin Flyers.

▶ **2.** On the Format tab, in the Size group, select the value in the Shape Width text box, type **0.8**, and then press the **Enter** key.

3. Drag the logo to the lower-left corner of the slide, so its left side is aligned with the left side of the body text placeholder and its bottom is aligned with the bottom of the date and Footer placeholders.

4. Select the footer placeholder, and drag its left-center sizing handle to the left until it almost touches the logo picture. Now you'll insert a yellow rectangle behind the title placeholder.

5. Click the **Insert** tab, in the Illustrations group, click the **Shapes** button, and then, under Rectangles, click the **Rectangle** button.

6. Draw a rectangle from the upper-left corner of the slide to the right edge of the slide between the title and text placeholders, so that the rectangle completely covers the title placeholder.

7. Click the Drawing Tools **Format** tab, in the Shape Styles group, click the **Shape Fill button arrow**, and then click the **Yellow** tile under Standard Colors. You'll remove the border from around the rectangle.

8. In the Shape Styles group, click the **Shape Outline button arrow**, and then click **No Outline**. The outline is removed from around the yellow rectangle. Now you need to send the rectangle behind the title text box.

9. In the Arrange group, click the **Send to Back** button, and then deselect the yellow rectangle. See Figure 6-4.

Slide master with inserted background objects ◄ **Figure 6-4**

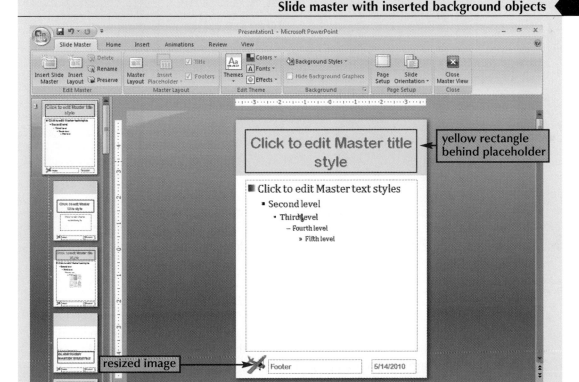

You're almost finished modifying the existing slide master. Now you need to modify the Title Slide Layout master so that the title placeholder and the yellow rectangle fill the top half of the slide.

To modify the Title Slide Layout master:

▶ **1.** In the pane on the left, click the **Title Slide Layout** thumbnail, in the slide pane, select the title text placeholder, change the font size to **60** points, and then drag the top, middle sizing handle on the placeholder up until the top of the place-holder is near the top of the slide.

▶ **2.** Draw another rectangle so that it spans from the bottom of the current yellow rectangle to between the title text placeholder and the subtitle placeholder and from the left to the right edges of the slide.

▶ **3.** Change the outline to **No Outline** and fill the rectangle with **Yellow**, and then send the rectangle to the back. See Figure 6-5.

Figure 6-5 ▶ Title Slide Layout master with added rectangle

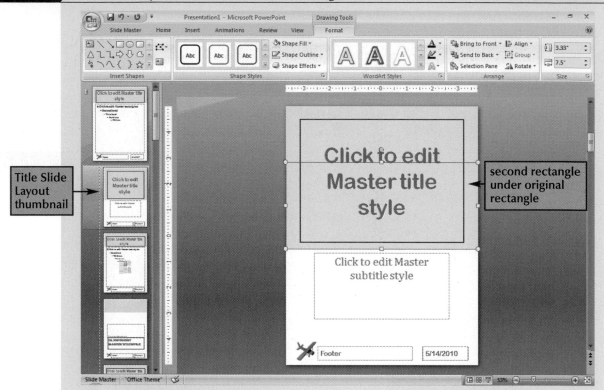

▶ **4.** Deselect the rectangle. The slide layout should look as if it has only one big rectangle.

Next you want to add a footer and the current date to all the slides. You'll open the Header and Footer dialog box to do this. When you click the Date and time check box in the Slide tab of the Header and Footer dialog box, you can choose to update the date and time automatically each time you open or print the presentation, or insert the current date and have it remain fixed at today's date. For notes and handouts, you can click the Notes and Handouts tab to add headers, page numbers, footers, and the date and time to notes pages and handout pages. As you have seen already, you can set all of these options in the masters except the option to have the date update automatically; you can only do that from the Header and Footer dialog box by clicking the Update automatically option button.

To add a footer and the current date to the slide master:

▶ **1.** Click the **Insert** tab, and then in the Text group, click the **Header & Footer** button to display the Header and Footer dialog box.

▶ **2.** Click the **Date and time** check box, and then click the **Fixed** option button. The current date appears in the Fixed box. If you wanted the date to update every time you opened the presentation, you would click the Update automatically option button.

▶ **3.** Click the **Footer** check box, and then in the Footer box, type **Franklin Flyers**.

▶ **4.** Click the **Apply to All** button. The footer and date appear in the slide masters and will also appear on all the slides created in Normal view.

Now you'll check to see if the design works well if the transparency overheads are printed on a black-and-white printer.

To view the transparency overheads in grayscale and save the custom theme:

▶ **1.** Click the **Office Theme Slide Master** thumbnail, click the **View** tab, and then in the Color/Grayscale group, click the **Grayscale** button. The slide is displayed in grayscale and the Grayscale tab appears on the Ribbon. See Figure 6-6.

Slide masters in grayscale view | **Figure 6-6**

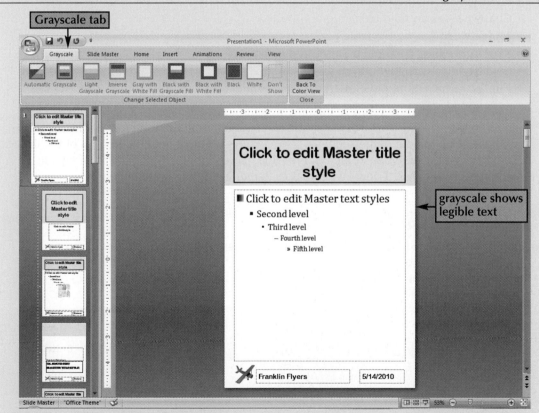

As you can see, the text, bullets, and graphics show up well in grayscale.

▶ **2.** In the Close group, click the **Back to Color View** button.

Now you've completed the slide masters and are ready to save the PowerPoint file as a design theme.

> **3.** Click the **Office Button** ⊙, click **Save As** to open the Save As dialog box, change the Save as type to **Office Theme**, navigate to the **Tutorial.06\Tutorial** folder, type **FF Overhead Theme** as the filename, and then click the **Save** button. The design theme file is saved to your disk.

You created a design theme file for an overhead transparency presentation by changing the page setup to overhead in portrait orientation, and then specifying the overall design and background objects. You also determined that the color scheme and background objects look good if you decide to print the overhead transparencies in grayscale. Next you'll create a new layout for the presentation.

Inserting a Custom Layout

PowerPoint 2007 allows you to modify existing layouts, create and modify new layouts, and even create and modify new slide masters (meaning a group of masters with a similar design). You can change the name of the layout, change the default text in the layout, delete (or keep) footer placeholders (date, footer, and slide number), and insert any of the following types of placeholders:

- **Content**, which can hold a bulleted list, table, chart, SmartArt, picture, clip art, or media (movie)
- **Text**, which can hold bulleted lists or paragraph text
- **Picture**, which can hold photographs or clip-art graphics
- **Chart**, which can hold a chart (graph)
- **Table**, which can hold a table
- **SmartArt**, which can hold a SmartArt diagram
- **Media**, which can hold objects like movies
- **Clip Art**, which can hold clip-art drawings, animation files, and photos

Paul tells you that he wants to include, as part of his overhead presentation, two slides with a special layout. The layout he wants includes a title at the top of the slide, a bulleted list in the middle of the slide, and two pictures (photos) near the bottom of the list but above the footer. None of the built-in slide master is set up for this type of layout; therefore, you'll create a new layout master in the FF Overhead Theme file.

To insert a custom layout:

> **1.** Click the **Slide Master** tab, if necessary, and then in the Edit Master group, click the **Insert Layout** button. The new layout appears at the bottom of the current list of layouts in the pane on the left, and also appears in the slide pane. See Figure 6-7.

Tip

If you want to create a custom layout that doesn't include any of the elements of the current slide master, click the Insert Slide Master button instead of the Insert Layout button on the Slide Master tab. That way, some slides could be based on one design and other slides could based on a different design.

Slide masters with new custom layout ◄ Figure 6-7

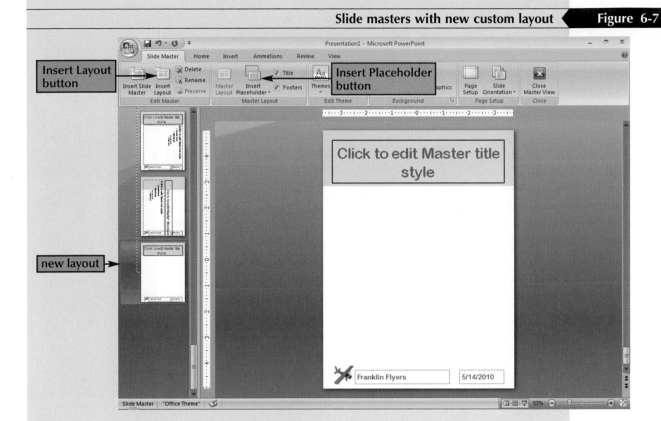

As you can see, the new layout includes many of the elements that you already added to the slide master. You'll add new placeholders now.

▶ **2.** In the Master Layout group, click the **Insert Placeholder button arrow**, and then click **Content**. The mouse pointer changes to ╀.

▶ **3.** Drag the pointer to make a large rectangle under the title placeholder. Don't worry much about its size and position, because you'll adjust it next. A content layout placeholder appears. Note that the layout picked up the custom bullets you defined earlier. Now you'll set the exact dimensions of the new content placeholder.

▶ **4.** Click the Drawing Tools **Format** tab, in the Size group, change the value in the Shape Height box to **4"**, change the value in the Shape Width box to **6.75"**, and then press the **Enter** key. See Figure 6-8.

Figure 6-8 | **Custom layout with inserted Content placeholder**

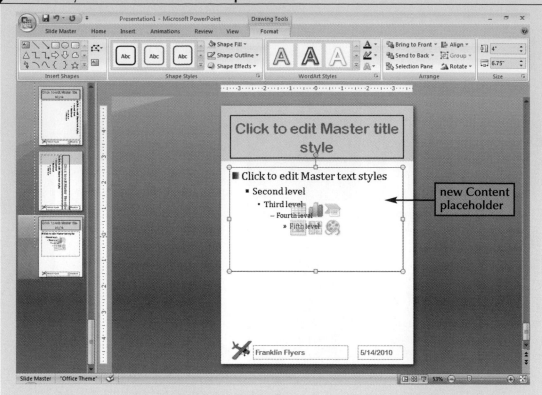

▶ **5.** If necessary, drag the entire placeholder to position it as shown in Figure 6-8.

Now you'll insert two small picture placeholders below the content placeholder.

To insert picture placeholders:

▶ **1.** Click the **Slide Master** tab, in the Master Layout group, click the **Insert Placeholder button arrow**, and then click **Picture**.

▶ **2.** Drag the pointer to draw a rectangle that fits in half of the empty space below the large placeholder.

▶ **3.** Click the Drawing Tools **Format** tab, and then adjust the size of the Picture placeholder to a height of **2.25"** and a width of **3.25"**.

▶ **4.** In the Picture placeholder, click just to the right of the large blue bullet, and then press the **Backspace** key to delete the bullet. Paul prefers that the bullet not appear in the title of this placeholder to emphasize that this placeholder is for a picture, not for a bulleted list.

▶ **5.** Click the edge of the placeholder to select the entire placeholder, and then press the **Ctrl+D** keys. The placeholder is copied and pasted in the slide pane. Pressing the Ctrl+D keys is a shortcut to using the Copy and Paste commands.

▶ **6.** Position the second placeholder to the right of the first one, and then make sure all the placeholders are positioned as shown in Figure 6-9.

Custom layout with new Picture placeholders ◄ Figure 6-9

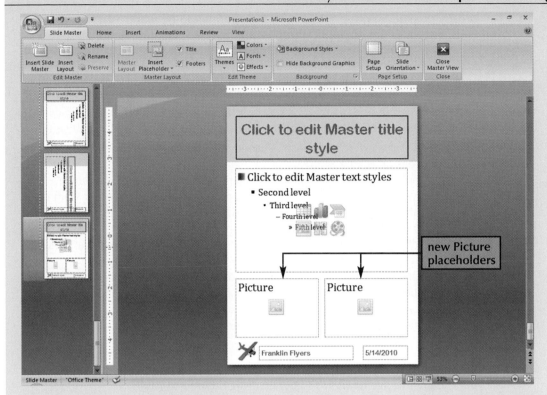

Now you'll give the layout a name.

To name the custom layout:

▸ **1.** In the pane on the left, right-click the thumbnail of the new layout, and then click **Rename Layout** on the shortcut menu. The Rename Layout dialog box opens.

▸ **2.** Type **Title, Content & Two Pictures**, and then click the **Rename** button. Now, when you position the pointer on top of the thumbnail of the custom layout, you'll see the new layout name. This completes the custom design theme.

▸ **3.** Click the **Office Button** 🔘, click **Save As**, change the Save as type to **Office Theme**, and then navigate to the **Tutorial.06\Tutorial** folder. You want to replace the FF Overhead Theme with the current theme.

▸ **4.** Click **FF Overhead Theme**, and then click the **Save** button. A dialog box opens asking if you want to replace the existing file.

▸ **5.** Click the **Yes** button.

▸ **6.** Close the current file, but do not exit PowerPoint, and when asked if you want to save changes to the presentation, click the **No** button. You have already saved all the formatting changes to the theme file.

You asked Paul to check your design theme. He's pleased with the results and instructs you to go ahead and use it to make the overhead transparencies.

Making Overhead Transparencies

Paul has already prepared a presentation with the information he wants you to include in the overheads. He wants you to apply your custom theme to his presentation.

InSight | **Applying a Customized Theme to an Existing Presentation**

When you apply a design theme to an existing presentation, keep in mind that you must often make one or more of the following modifications:

- Change the page setup. PowerPoint doesn't change an existing presentation to the same page setup as the design theme.
- Reset and resize the imported graphics. This is essential if the aspect ratio (relative dimensions of the width and height) of the new design is significantly different from the old design. For example, if your onscreen presentation in landscape orientation changes to portrait orientation, the graphic objects will become distorted.
- Recolor or select different clip art, digital photographs, and other imported graphics so that they match the design theme colors.
- Recolor organization charts, data charts, graphs, and other graphic objects created in PowerPoint as needed so that these objects are visible with the new theme colors.
- Resize text boxes or change font sizes. When the presentation undergoes a font change (in size and style), sometimes the font doesn't fit properly, or the hard returns are in the wrong place.

Now you'll apply the overhead transparency design theme to Paul's presentation—which he already prepared using the default design theme—as well as insert some pictures supplied by Paul.

To apply the overhead transparency design theme to a presentation:

1. Open the presentation file **FFOver**, located in the **Tutorial.06\Tutorial** folder included with your Data Files.

2. In Slide 1, change Paul's name in the subtitle to your name, and then save the presentation in the Tutorial.06\Tutorial folder using the filename **FF Overheads**.

3. Click the **Design** tab on the Ribbon, in the Themes group, click the **More** button, and then click **Browse for Themes**.

4. Navigate to the **Tutorial.06\Tutorial** folder, and double-click **FF Overhead Theme**. The custom theme you created is applied to the presentation.

5. In the Page Setup group on the Design tab, click the **Page Setup** button, click the **Slides sized for** arrow, and then scroll down and click **Overhead**.

6. In the Orientation group, under Slides, click the **Portrait** option button, and then click the **OK** button.

7. Insert the current date (fixed) and the footer **Franklin Flyers** on all the slides. See Figure 6-10.

Presentation with custom theme applied ◀ Figure 6-10

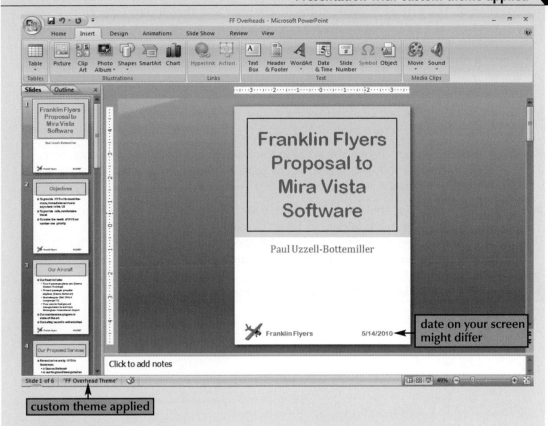

▶ **8.** Save the presentation using the default filename and location.

Paul likes the look of his presentation overheads. He now wants you to apply the custom layout to two of the slides, and add pictures to those slides.

Applying a Custom Layout

You apply a custom layout in the same manner that you apply built-in layouts: You use the Layout button on the Home ribbon. You'll do that now.

To apply a custom layout and insert pictures:

▶ **1.** Go to **Slide 2**, click the **Home** tab, and then, in the Slides group, click the **Layout** button. The FF Overhead Theme gallery of layouts appears.

▶ **2.** Click the **Title, Content & Two Pictures** layout. Two placeholders for adding pictures appear near the bottom of the slide.

▶ 3. Click the **Insert Picture from File** button ▦ in the middle of the left picture placeholder, navigate to the **Tutorial.06\Tutorial** folder, and then double-click **Plane2**. The picture appears in the placeholder and the Picture Tools Format tab becomes the active tab on the Ribbon. As you can see, however, the placeholder doesn't show the entire airplane. The problem is that PowerPoint expands the picture width or height (whichever is smaller) to fit the placeholder, so that the other dimension exceeds the boundaries of the placeholder. You can fix the problem by resetting the picture, and then adjusting its size and position.

▶ 4. With the picture still selected, in the Adjust group on the Picture Tools Format tab, click the **Reset Picture** button. The picture is reset to its original size and shape.

▶ 5. In the Size group, change the value in the Shape Height box to **1.6"**, and then drag the picture so it is centered in the space where the original picture placeholder was located.

▶ 6. In the picture placeholder on the right, insert the picture file **Plane3**, located in the Tutorial.06\Tutorial folder, and then deselect the picture. See Figure 6-11. This picture has an aspect ratio (relative width and height) similar to that of the placeholder, so it doesn't need to be reset and repositioned.

| Figure 6-11 | Slide 2 with custom layout applied and images inserted |

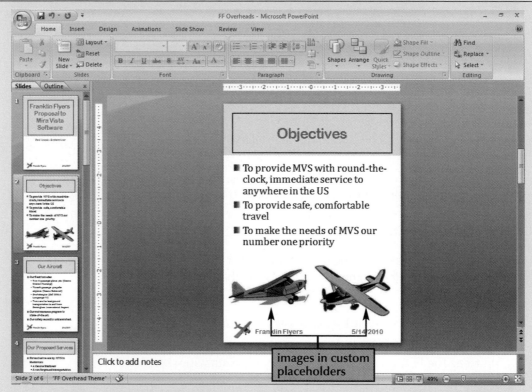

Trouble? If your pictures aren't sized and positioned as shown in Figure 6-11, make any necessary adjustments now.

You'll now repeat the above procedure by adding two pictures to Slide 4.

To apply the custom layout to another slide:

▶ **1.** Go to **Slide 4**, and then change its layout to **Title, Content & Two Pictures**.

▶ **2.** In the picture placeholder on the left, insert the picture file **Pilot**, located in the Tutorial.06\Tutorial folder, and then in the picture placeholder on the right, insert the picture file **Plane4**, located in the same folder.

▶ **3.** On the status bar, click the **Slide Sorter** button 🔲 to view all the slides in the presentation, and then drag the **Zoom slider** all the way to the right to adjust the zoom to 100%. See Figure 6-12.

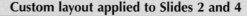
Custom layout applied to Slides 2 and 4 | Figure 6-12

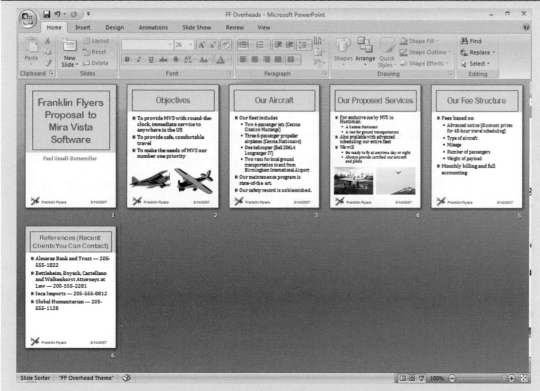

▶ **4.** Carefully look over all the slides to make sure they appear similar to those in Figure 6-12, and then save the presentation.

That completes the overhead transparencies presentation. You're now ready to print the presentation onto transparency masters (film) in color or in black and white.

Printing Overhead Transparencies

Before you print the overheads, you must make sure you purchase and use the right type of transparency film in 8½ × 11-inch sheets. (Check with your instructor before you purchase transparency film. Your instructor will probably just have to print the overheads on regular paper or submit them in electronic format.)

Before you purchase transparency sheets, carefully read the specifications on the package. Make sure the package says that the sheets are designed specifically for your type of printer—laser or inkjet—because the two are not interchangeable. Furthermore, ordinary transparency sheets designed for color felt-tip pens and markers are not acceptable for printers; the film can melt inside the printer, and it doesn't properly hold printer ink.

To print the transparencies:

1. Read the instructions supplied with your transparency film so you know which side of the film is the printable side. (Unless your instructor requires actual transparency film, use regular paper to practice these steps. In fact, your instructor may prefer that you not print anything at all, in which case you should read through these steps but not follow them.)

2. Insert six sheets of transparency film, in the proper orientation for printing on the correct side, into the paper feeder of your printer.

3. Click the **Office Button** , and then click **Print**. The Print dialog box opens.

4. Make sure the Print what box indicates **Slides** (the default).

5. Click the **Color/grayscale** arrow, and then click either **Color** or **Grayscale**, depending on your printer and your preferences.

6. Click the **OK** button to print the overheads.

That completes the overhead transparencies. You can now leave the presentation open, because you'll need it later, or you can close it, and then open it later when you need it.

Preparing a Photo Album Using Custom Layouts

Paul now wants you to create a photo album presentation with pictures of some of the scenic locations where Franklin Flyers have taken clients. He wants to show the photos to potential customers to give them an idea of some of the places to which they, the clients, could fly as part of an incentive package for their employees. Paul has specific ideas as to how he wants the photo album to be formatted.

PowerPoint includes a built-in Photo Album command, which allows you to create a photo album with 1, 2, or 4 pictures per slide, and optionally, with titles and captions. To create this type of photo album, you click the Insert tab, and then, in the Illustrations group, click the Photo Album button. The advantage of this feature is that you can insert a large number of digital photographs all at once into the presentation, without your having to insert each picture individually. The problem, however, with the built-in Photo Album feature is that PowerPoint won't let you customize the slide master layouts, so you can't change the size and position of the text placeholders for the title and caption, which is exactly what Paul wants you to do. Therefore, you'll set up your own custom photo album. It will not, however, work like the built-in Photo Album feature because you'll have to insert the photographs one at a time. This won't be a problem, however, for the short presentation that Paul has in mind.

You'll create a custom layout to create the slides for the photo album. You'll adjust the title text to make it much smaller, so the photos become the focus on the slide. You'll use a WordArt style to format the title text. **WordArt** is a set of text formats with colors, shadows, and other styles collected in a gallery.

To create a photo album with custom layout:

1. Start a new, blank presentation, click the **Design** tab, and in the Background group, click the **Background Styles** button.

2. Click the **Style 4** style (first row, last column). The background changes to solid black.

3. Switch to Slide Master view; in the pane on the left, click the **Title and Content Layout** thumbnail; and then press the **Delete** key. The Title and Content Layout master is deleted, and the Section Header Layout master is selected.

4. Press the **Delete** key nine more times to delete each selected thumbnail. Only the Office Theme Slide Master and the Title Slide Layout thumbnails are left. The Title Slide Layout thumbnail is selected.

5. Press the **Delete** key. The Title Slide Layout is not deleted and remains in the pane on the left. PowerPoint does not allow you to delete the Title Slide Layout master or the Theme Slide Master. You'll now create a new custom layout.

6. In the Edit Master group, click the **Insert Layout** button. A new layout appears.

7. In the slide pane, delete the placeholders for the date, footer, and slide number. Paul doesn't want any of these items on the slides of the photo album.

8. Click the edge of the title text placeholder to select it, click the Drawing Tools **Format** tab, if necessary, and then adjust the Shape Height of the placeholder to **0.5"** and the Shape Width to **5.5"**. The placeholder text is now too big for the size of the placeholder.

9. With the title text placeholder still selected, change the font to **Arial** and the font size to **20** points.

10. Click the Drawing Tools **Format** tab, in the WordArt Styles group, click the **More** button, and then click the **Fill – Accent 1, Metal Bevel, Reflection** style in the lower-right corner of the gallery. After you apply this accent, Paul is concerned that the blue text on a black background might not be sufficiently legible. He asks you to modify the WordArt Style.

11. With the title placeholder still selected, in the WordArt Styles group, click the **More** button, and this time click the **Fill – Accent 1, Inner Shadow – Accent 1** style, located in the second row, fourth column.

12. Click the **Home** tab, and then, in the Paragraph group, click the **Align Text Left** button ▤. The text alignment in the placeholder changes to left.

13. Drag the placeholder so it's near the lower-left corner of the slide, as shown in Figure 6-13.

Figure 6-13 **Custom layout with WordArt title placeholder**

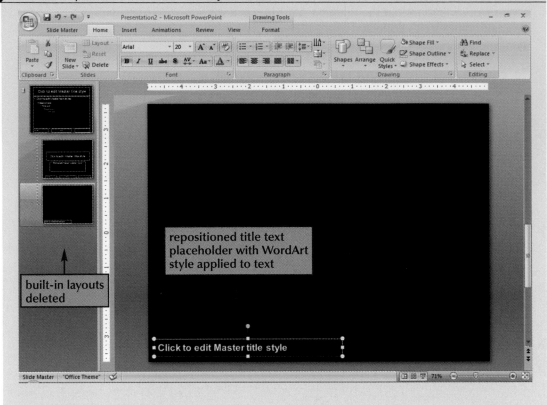

You'll now insert additional placeholders.

To add placeholders to the custom layout:

1. Click the **Slide Master** tab, in the Master Layout group, click the **Insert Placeholder button arrow**, and then click **Text**.

2. Drag the mouse pointer to create a rectangle just to the right of the title placeholder.

3. Change the height of the new text placeholder to **0.5"** and the width to **3.8"**, set the font size to **12** points, and then change the font to **Cambria**.

4. In the new placeholder, click the **bullet** next to the first level of text ("Click to edit Master text styles"). All the text in the placeholder is selected.

5. Press the **Delete** key. All of the text is deleted. Now you want to remove the bullet.

6. Click the **Home** tab, if necessary, and then, in the Paragraph group, click the **Bullets** button to deselect it. All the text and the bullet are removed from the placeholder.

7. Type **Caption**. This is the new placeholder text. Now you want to set the paragraph format so that all lines in the caption are aligned on the left, rather than formatted as a hanging indent, in which all the lines except the first are indented. You'll use the ruler to do this.

8. If the rulers don't appear in your slide pane, click the **View** tab, and then in the Show/Hide group, click the **Ruler** check box to select it.

▶ **9.** With the insertion point in the new text placeholder, on the ruler, drag the little, up-pointing, triangle-shaped marker 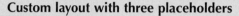 positioned on the .4-inch mark to the left so it's just below the down-pointing triangle indent marker ▽ at the zero mark. The hanging indent in the new text placeholder is removed.

▶ **10.** Press and hold the **Shift** key, click the title placeholder on the left to select both placeholders, click the Drawing Tools **Format** tab, in the Arrange group, click the **Align** button, and then click **Align Bottom**. The placeholder on the right moves down so that the bottom of both placeholders are aligned. (If the placeholders on your screen were already aligned, you will not see a change.)

▶ **11.** Insert a picture placeholder that fills most of the empty space above the title and text placeholders, and then delete the bullet in the new placeholder.

▶ **12.** Deselect the placeholder, compare your screen to Figure 6-14, and then make any adjustments necessary to make your screen match the figure.

Custom layout with three placeholders ◀ **Figure 6-14**

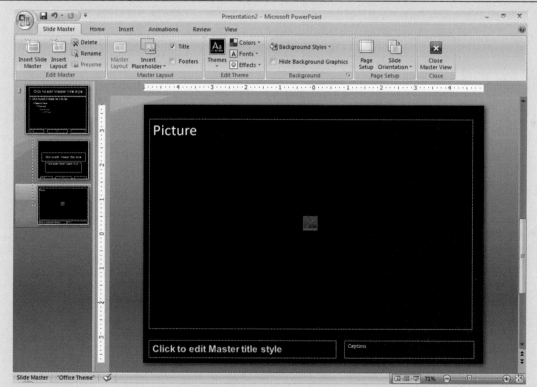

▶ **13.** In the pane on the left, right-click the new layout, click **Rename Layout** on the shortcut menu, type **Photo Album**, and then click the **Rename** button.

▶ **14.** Return to Normal view, and then save the file to the **Tutorial.06\Tutorial** folder using the filename **FF Photos**.

When you create a custom layout, you might want to apply a theme font without actually applying a new design theme. For example, if you want the fonts (but not the design) of the Technic theme, which uses the Franklin Gothin Book font for headings and the Arial font for body text, you would click the Design tab in Normal view. Then in the Themes group, you would click the Fonts button, and then click Technic.

You have now completed the custom photo album layout. Now Paul wants you to start his photo album presentation by adding text to the title slide and then inserting four new slides with pictures, titles, and captions.

To create the custom photo album:

▶ **1.** In the title placeholder, type **Franklin Flyers Flies Everywhere!** (including the exclamation point).

▶ **2.** In the subtitle, type your name.

▶ **3.** Click the **Home** tab, and then in the Slides group, click the **New Slide** button. A new Slide 2 appears in the new photo album slide layout. Normally, when you insert a new slide after a title slide, PowerPoint automatically inserts a slide with the Title and Content layout, but here, because you've deleted the Title and Content layout, PowerPoint uses the Photo Album layout that you created.

▶ **4.** Click the **Insert Picture from File** icon in the picture placeholder, and then double-click **Canyon** in the Tutorial.06\Tutorial folder. The scenic picture of Canyonlands National Park appears on the slide.

▶ **5.** Click in the title placeholder in the lower-left corner of the slide, and then type **Canyonlands National Park**.

▶ **6.** Click in the caption placeholder in the lower-right corner of the slide, type **A view of the canyon near Moab, Utah, capital of the mountain-biking world**, and then deselect the placeholder. See Figure 6-15.

Figure 6-15 ▶ **Slide 2 of photo album presentation**

▶ **7.** Insert a new **Slide 3**, insert the picture file **GrandCan**, type the title **Grand Canyon National Park**, and then type the caption **A view of the Colorado River from the South Rim of the Grand Canyon in Arizona**.

▶ **8.** Insert a new **Slide 4**, insert the picture file **Rushmore**, type the title **Mt. Rushmore National Monument**, and then type the caption **Mt. Rushmore near Rapid City, South Dakota, and near several other national monuments**.

▶ **9.** Insert a new **Slide 5**, insert the picture file **Yosemite**, type the title **Yosemite National Park**, and then type the caption **The popular tourist attraction in northern California**.

▶ **10.** Switch to Slide Sorter view, and increase the zoom to **100%**. Your presentation should now look like the one in Figure 6-16.

Completed photo album presentation | **Figure 6-16**

Zoom slider

▶ **11.** Save the presentation using the default filename, submit the completed presentation in printed or electronic form, as requested by your instructor, and then close the presentation, but do not exit PowerPoint.

Paul is pleased with this photo album presentation and will add more slides with scenic photos of other destinations of Franklin Flyers. He is sure that the presentation will help sell companies on the idea of offering their employees and customers flights to scenic destinations.

Session 6.1 Quick Check | Review

1. List four advantages that overhead transparencies offer over onscreen slide shows.
2. What is meant by character spacing?
3. True or False: It's easy to print overheads in grayscale even when the presentation was designed in color.
4. How would you change presentation slides from landscape to portrait orientation?
5. How do you create a custom layout in the slide masters?
6. How do you insert a picture placeholder in a custom layout?

Session 6.2

Creating a Poster Presentation

A **poster presentation** is generally given at a professional meeting, and the information is formatted as a poster, or in the space of a poster. The poster size is usually about 6×4 feet in landscape orientation. Often the presenters or authors stand by their mounted posters at a designated time and place—during the so-called "poster session" of the conference—to answer questions, pass out business cards, and distribute handouts.

Paul has been invited to give a poster presentation at an upcoming conference on business proposals at the Culverhouse College of Commerce and Business Administration at the University of Alabama. He asks you to help him prepare a PowerPoint poster presentation.

You can format PowerPoint poster presentations in two ways: as a multiple-page poster (with the title slide and each information slide printed on separate sheets of paper) or as a single-page poster with multiple frames (or slides) on one large printout.

A single-page poster has two advantages over a multiple-page poster:

- It's easy to set up. You don't have to bother with different sheets of paper and numerous thumbtacks (you usually need only four to six) to hang and display your poster.
- It looks professional. Usually a service bureau prints the poster on high-gloss paper, which has a photographic-quality appearance.

A multiple-page poster has three advantages over a single-page poster:

- It is less expensive than a single-page poster. A service bureau can charge from $70 to $250 to print a one-page poster, depending on its size and complexity.
- It doesn't take as long to prepare as a single-page poster.
- It is less cumbersome to carry than a large, single-page poster. For example, you can easily slip a multiple-page poster in your briefcase or carry-on luggage, but a large, single-page poster has to be rolled up and stored in a long tube, which is awkward to carry when traveling on an airplane or other mode of transportation.

If you ever need to give a professional presentation at a poster session, check with the session chair for recommendations about which type of presentation to prepare.

Paul asks you to prepare both formats, and then he will choose the one he prefers for his presentation.

Creating a Multiple-Page Poster Presentation

You'll start by preparing a multiple-page poster. Many of the same principles that you learned regarding overhead transparencies apply to poster presentation slides. As a general rule, you'll want dark text on a light background. So for Paul's presentation, you'll use his current overhead transparency presentation and modify it by changing it from portrait to landscape orientation.

To change the page set up to landscape and adjust a background graphic:

1. If you took a break after the previous session, make sure PowerPoint is running, and then open the presentation file **FF Overheads** from the **Tutorial.06\Tutorial** folder.

2. If necessary, on the status bar, click the **Slide Sorter** button 🔲 to switch to Slide Sorter view. You'll now adjust the page setup.

3. Click the **Design** tab, in the Page Setup group, click the **Page Setup** button to open the Page Setup dialog box, click the **Slides sized for** arrow, click **Letter Paper (8.5 × 11 in)**, click the **Landscape** option button, and then click the **OK** button. Now the slides will fit properly on standard-sized paper when you print the individual slides.

   As you can see, especially on Slides 2 and 4, the pictures become distorted. This is because PowerPoint doesn't maintain their aspect ratio, but rather adjusts the aspect ratio of the pictures in the same way it adjusts the aspect ratio of the slides themselves; that is, everything becomes stretched horizontally or crunched vertically. You'll fix that problem now.

4. Switch to Slide Master view, in the left pane, scroll up to the top of the list, and then click the **FF Overhead Theme Slide Master** thumbnail (the large thumbnail at the top of the pane on the left).

5. Click the airplane picture located in the lower-left corner of the slide, click the Picture Tools **Format** tab, and in the Adjust group, click **Reset Picture**. The picture is reset to its original size and aspect ratio.

6. If necessary, adjust the position of the picture so its left edge is aligned with the left edge of the content placeholder and its bottom edge is aligned with the bottom of the footer and date placeholders.

Now you'll need to adjust the pictures in Slides 2 and 4.

To adjust the pictures in Slides 2 and 4:

1. Return to Normal view, and then go to **Slide 2**.

2. Click the picture of the airplane in the lower-left placeholder, reset it, reduce its width to **3.5"**, and then position it between the bulleted list and the footer.

3. Select the picture of the airplane in the lower-right placeholder, reset it, reduce its width to **3.0"**, and position it between the bulleted list and the footer. See Figure 6-17.

Figure 6-17 | Slide 2 in landscape orientation after resizing background and picture objects

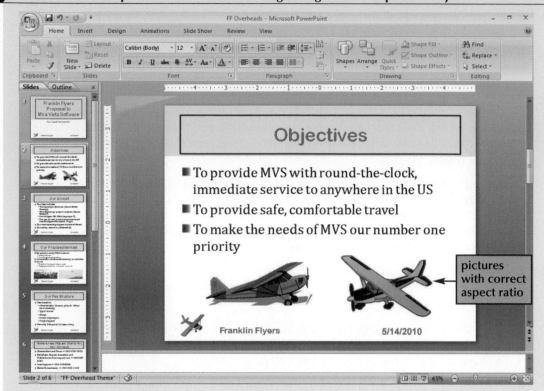

4. Go to **Slide 4**, reset the pictures, reduce their height to **2"**, and position them between the bulleted list and the footer. See Figure 6-18.

Figure 6-18 | Slide 4 after resetting and resizing images

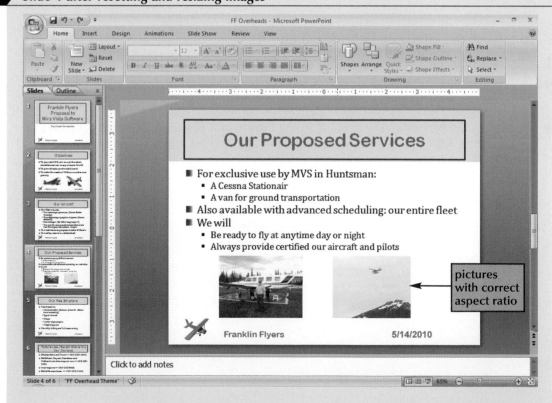

You've almost completed the poster presentation. Normally poster presentations include a large banner with the presentation title rather than a title slide, so you'll delete Slide 1. Before deleting the slide, however, Paul wants you to save the file now in anticipation of a future need to use it as an onscreen (computer) presentation.

▶ 5. Save the presentation as **FF Onscreen** in the Tutorial.06\Tutorial folder. Now you're ready to delete the title slide.

▶ 6. Go to **Slide 1**, click the **Home** tab, if necessary, and then in the Slides group, click the **Delete** button.

▶ 7. Save the presentation as **FF Multi-Page Poster**, also in the **Tutorial.06\Tutorial** folder.

▶ 8. Switch to Slide Sorter view, and then increase the zoom to 100%, if necessary. See Figure 6-19.

Completed multi-page poster presentation   Figure 6-19

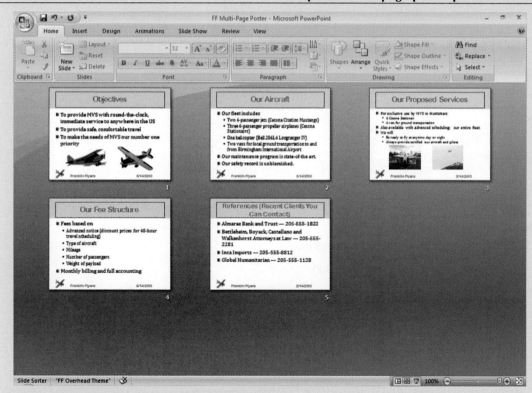

Trouble? If your presentation doesn't look like Figure 6-19, make any adjustments now, and then save the presentation again from Normal view.

▶ 9. Return to Slide 1 in Normal view, and keep the presentation open.

Paul now wants you to create a banner to display the presentation title for the multiple-page poster presentation.

Creating a Banner

Poster presentations need a title so the viewers know the subject of the presentation. You can create a **banner**, which is a large sign or page that typically has dimensions of 4 feet wide by 8½ inches high. Most inkjet printers can print banners from PowerPoint, but some cannot. You'll have to try it on your printer to find out. Even if your printer can't print the banner, you can still design it in PowerPoint and then take the file to a service bureau, which can print large banners as well as large posters. If you want to print your own banners, but your printer and PowerPoint are incompatible in doing it, you'll need access to a specialty printing program that supports banner printing, such as Microsoft Greetings Workshop or Mindscape PrintMaster.

To print banners you also need to buy special banner paper, or you can buy butcher paper and carefully cut it to the desired dimensions.

Reference Window | **Creating a Banner with PowerPoint**

- Start a new presentation, click the Design tab, and in the Page Setup group, click the Page Setup button. The Page Setup dialog box opens.
- Click the Slides sized for list arrow, and then click Banner.
- Set the width and height to the desired dimensions, make sure the slide orientation is set to Landscape, and then click the OK button.
- Adjust the title and subtitle placeholders to the desired size and location on the banner slide.
- Adjust the font size, as desired, so that the title and subtitle text fit well in the banner.
- Type the text, insert graphics, and make other desired modifications and enhancements.
- Save the banner file to your disk, and then print the banner or send the file to a service bureau for printing.

Paul wants you to prepare a banner for his multiple-page poster presentation.

To prepare a banner in PowerPoint:

1. Start a new, blank presentation.

2. Click the **Design** tab, and then in the Page Setup dialog box, click the **Page Setup** button. The Page setup dialog box opens.

3. Click the **Slides sized for** arrow, scroll down the list, and then click **Banner**. The measurements in the Width box change to eight inches and in the Height box to one inch. This is not a large enough banner for your purposes.

4. Change the value in the Width box to **48** inches, and then change the value in the Height box to **11** inches. Notice that the Slide sized for box automatically changed to Custom. See Figure 6-20.

Figure 6-20 ▶ **Page Setup dialog box with custom settings for a banner**

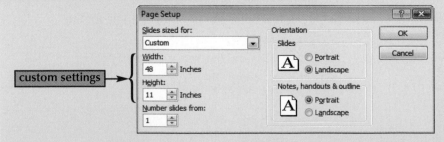

5. Make sure the slide orientation is set to **Landscape**, and then click the **OK** button. The slide in the slide pane reflects the new page setup settings.

6. Click the edge of the title text placeholder to select it, click the Drawing Tools **Format** tab, and then set the dimensions of the text box to a height of **4.8"** and width of **45"**.

7. Drag the title text placeholder up and to the left to center it in the space above the subtitle and between the left and right margins. Now you'll change the font attributes of the title placeholder.

8. Click the **Home** tab, change the font of the title text placeholder to **Arial Rounded MT Bold** (so it matches the font in the titles of the slides), and then change the font color to **Dark Blue, Text 2**.

9. In the Font group, select the value in the **Font Size** button box, type **156**, and then press the **Enter** key. Remember that there are 72 points in one inch, so 156 points is about 2.2 inches in height.

10. Click the edge of the subtitle text box, change the font to **Cambria**, change the font color to **Black, Text 1**, and then change the font size to **113** points (about 1.6 inches high).

11. Drag the subtitle down so that it's centered vertically between the title placeholder and the bottom of the slide. You'll now make sure that the two placeholders are centered on each other.

12. With the subtitle placeholder selected, press and hold the **Shift** key, click the title placeholder so that both placeholders are selected, click the Drawing Tools **Format** tab, if necessary, in the Arrange group, click the **Align** button, and then click **Align Center**. The placeholders shift so they are aligned on their centers. See Figure 6-21.

Placeholders adjusted for banner | Figure 6-21

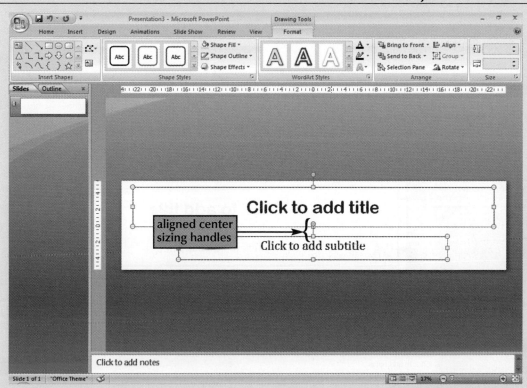

You can see from the sizing handles of the two placeholders that they are aligned. Now, to add interest to the banner, you'll add a box around the banner, and insert the picture of the Franklin Flyers logo.

To finish the banner:

▶ **1.** Click the **Insert** tab, in the Illustrations group, click the **Shapes** button, and then click the **Rectangle** button.

▶ **2.** Drag the pointer to draw a big rectangle so that it covers the entire slide except for approximately a one-inch edge around the slide. Don't worry about getting the exact dimensions and location, as you can adjust those later.

▶ **3.** Click the Drawing Tools **Format** tab, and then adjust the height of the rectangle to **9.5"** and the width to **46"**.

▶ **4.** If necessary, drag the rectangle to center it in the slide.

▶ **5.** In the Shape Styles group, click the **Shape Fill button arrow**, and then click **No Fill**.

▶ **6.** In the Shape Styles group, click the **Shape Outline button arrow**, point to **Weight**, and then click **More Lines**. The Format Shape dialog box opens with Line Style selected in the list on the left.

▶ **7.** Change the value in the width box to **16 pt**, and then click the **Close** button.

▶ **8.** Click the **Insert** tab, in the Illustrations group, click the **Picture** button, and then insert the **Plane1** file located in the Tutorial.06\Tutorial folder.

▶ **9.** Drag the picture to the lower-left corner of the banner, and then deselect the image. Compare your screen to Figure 6-22.

Figure 6-22 ▶ **Completed format for banner**

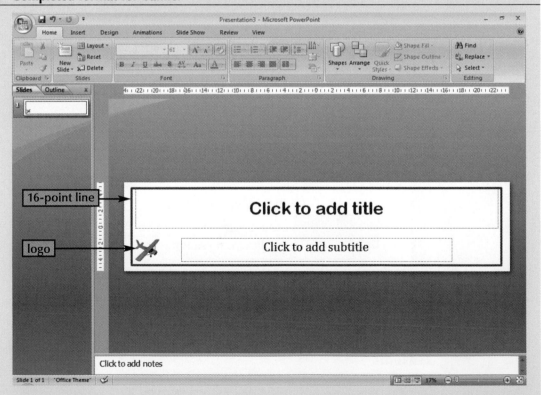

Trouble? If your banner doesn't look like Figure 6-22, make any necessary adjustments now. Pay careful attention to the relative positions of the placeholder and the box around the banner.

You have set up the design for the banner. Now you just need to insert the text.

Using Drag-and-Drop

You've learned how to cut, copy, and paste text and objects using the Cut, Copy, and Paste commands. You can also use a technique called **drag-and-drop** to move selected text. It is similar to dragging a slide to a new position in the Slides or Outline tab or in Slide Sorter view. To drag-and-drop text, you select it, position the pointer on top of the selected text, press and hold the mouse button, and then drag the text to the new location on the slide. You can also copy text using this method. To copy text using drag-and-drop, press and hold the Ctrl key while you are dragging the selected text. You'll add text to the banner now and use drag-and-drop to reposition some of the text.

To add text to the banner and use drag-and-drop to move text:

▶ **1.** Click in the title placeholder, type **Franklin Flyers Mira Vista Proposal**. Paul wants the title to be the same as in his presentation.

▶ **2.** Double-click the word **Proposal**. The word is selected.

▶ **3.** Position the pointer on top of the selected word, press and hold the mouse button, and then drag the selected word to the left until the vertical indicator line is positioned in front of the word "Mira."

▶ **4.** Release the mouse button. "Proposal" now appears between "Flyers" and "Mira." "Proposal" is still selected.

▶ **5.** Press the → key, and then insert the word to and necessary spaces to make the title "Franklin Flyers Proposal to Mira Vista."

▶ **6.** Click in the subtitle placeholder and type your name. See Figure 6-23.

Figure 6-23 ▶ **Completed banner**

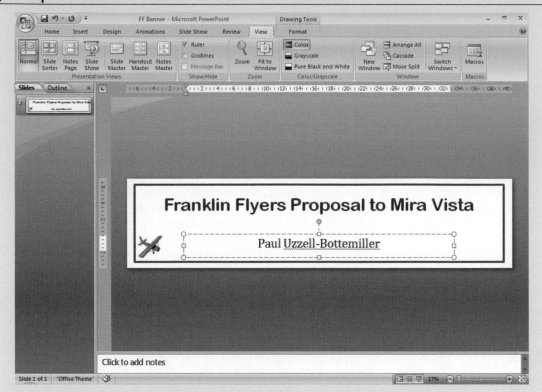

▶ **7.** Save the presentation as **FF Banner** in the Tutorial.06\Tutorial folder.

If you can't print directly from PowerPoint onto banner paper, you must submit the PowerPoint file to a service bureau for printing. (In practice, check with your instructor before you buy banner paper or use a service bureau for printing.)

▶ **8.** Submit the completed banner in printed or electronic form, as requested by your instructor. Keep the presentation open.

Paul can now print the file on the company printer, an Epson 220, which supports banner printing, or he can take this file to a service bureau for printing on a 4-foot wide page. The multiple-page poster presentation, including the title banner, is now complete. Next, you'll create the single-page poster.

Creating a Single-Page Poster

To create a single-page poster, you'll cut and paste all of the individual slides and the banner slide onto one slide. You can then take that one-slide presentation file to a service bureau to print onto a large poster sheet. Now you're ready to create Paul's single-page poster presentation.

To set up a presentation for a single-page poster:

▶ **1.** On the taskbar, click the **FF Multi-Page Poster** button to switch to that presentation, and then save the file to the Tutorial.06\Tutorial folder using the new filename **FF One-Page Poster**. Because all the slide images will end up on one slide, you want to turn off the footer and page number for each individual slide.

2. Click the **Insert** tab, and in the Text group, click the **Header & Footer** button. The Header and Footer dialog box opens with the Slide tab on top.

3. Click the **Date and time** and **Footer** check boxes to deselect them, and then click the **Apply to All** button.

4. Go to **Slide 1**, if necessary, click the **Home** tab, and then in the Slides group, click the **New Slide** button. A new Slide 2 is inserted.

5. In the Slides tab on the left, drag the new **Slide 2** up above Slide 1, and then change the layout to **Blank**. As you can see, a Blank layout does not contain any placeholders, but it does contain the slide background objects. You can easily hide those.

6. Click the **Design** tab, and then in the Background group, click the **Hide Background Graphics** check box to select it. Now the slide is totally blank. Because you'll paste, resize, and position the five slides into the new Slide 1, you'll find it easier if you can view the gridlines.

7. Click the **View** tab, and then in the Show/Hide group, click the **Gridlines** check box. The gridlines appear on the slide.

You're now ready to cut and paste a picture image of the subsequent slides onto Slide 1, similar to how you pasted slides as pictures in Tutorial 5.

To cut and paste images of Slides 2–6 to Slide 1:

1. Switch to Slide Sorter view, click **Slide 2** ("Objectives"), and then press the **Ctrl+X** keys. The slide is removed from the presentation and placed on the Clipboard.

2. Double-click **Slide 1** to switch to Slide 1 in Normal view, click the **Home** tab, in the Clipboard group, click the **Paste button arrow**, and then click **Paste Special**. The Paste Special dialog box opens.

3. In the As list, click **Picture (PNG)**, and then click the **OK** button. The slide picture appears in the middle of Slide 1. Because the slide picture has a white background, it will look better on the single-page poster if it has a border around it.

4. Click the Picture Tools **Format** tab, in the Picture Styles group, click the **Picture Border button arrow**, and then click the **Dark Blue, Text 2** tile. Now the picture has a dark-blue border around it.

5. In the Size group, select the value in the Shape Width box, type **3**, and then press the **Enter** key. The height automatically changes to 2.25 inches.

6. Drag the slide to position it as shown in Figure 6-24. Notice that you are leaving plenty of room at the top for the picture of the banner.

> **Tip**
>
> You can also press the Ctrl+Alt+V keys to open the Paste Special dialog box.

Figure 6-24 > One-page poster slide with first slide picture

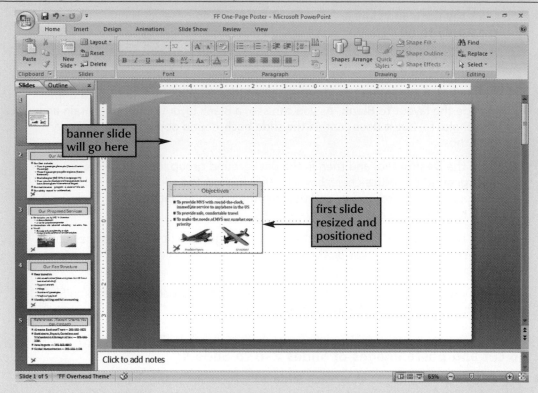

7. Repeat Steps 1 through 5 for the slide that is now Slide 2 ("Our Aircraft"), and then position it *below* the first slide picture. You want the second slide to go below the first, because in poster presentations, viewers read the poster left to right all in one pass, so Slide 3 goes below Slide 2.

8. Repeat Steps 1 through 5 for the next slide, titled "Our Proposed Services", and position it to the right of the first slide picture. You want the third slide to start another column.

9. Repeat Steps 1 through 5 for the last two slides titled "Our Fee Structure" and "References (Recent Clients You Can Contact)", and position them by following the same pattern. See Figure 6-25.

One-page poster presentation with slide pictures ◄ Figure 6-25

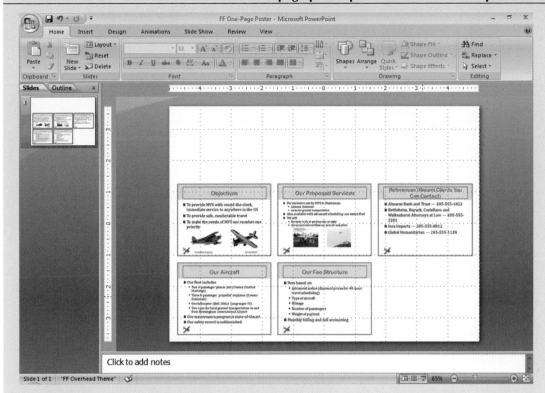

▶ **10.** Save the presentation using the default filename.

To complete the single-page poster, you'll copy the banner to the first slide in the FF One-Page Poster presentation.

To complete the single-page poster:

▶ **1.** On the taskbar, click the **FF Banner** button.

▶ **2.** Switch to Slide Sorter view, and then press the **Ctrl+C** keys to copy the banner to the Clipboard. You want to do a copy-and-paste operation here, not a cut-and-paste operation, because you don't want to delete the banner slide. You can also use the same copy-and-paste operation to copy text in a presentation, just as you can with objects.

▶ **3.** On the taskbar, click the **FF One-Page Poster** button, and then use the Paste Special command to insert the banner as a Picture (PNG) file. The banner is huge compared to the poster slide, but you can easily fix that.

▶ **4.** With the banner still selected, click the Picture Tools **Format** tab, in the Size group, select the value in the **Width** text box, type **8**, and press the **Enter** key. The banner reduces in size to 8 inches and is positioned off the slide to the left.

▶ **5.** Drag the banner to the top of Slide 1 in the presentation, so it is centered in the blank space above the slide pictures, and then deselect the banner picture. See Figure 6-26.

Figure 6-26   **Completed one-page poster presentation**

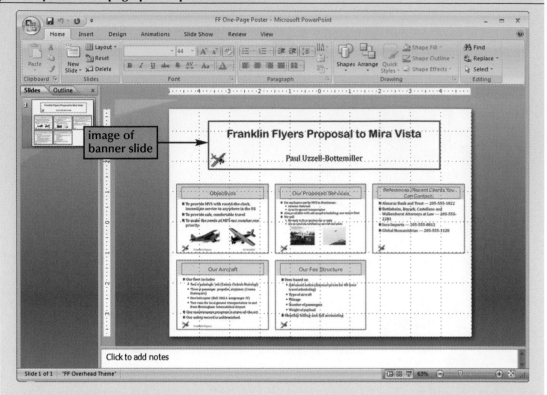

6. Click the **View** tab, and then, in the Show/Hide group, click the **Gridlines** check box to deselect it.

7. Save the presentation, submit the completed presentation in printed (on normal size piece of paper) or electronic form, as requested by your instructor, and then close the open presentations, but do not exit PowerPoint.

You give a copy of both poster presentation files to Paul. He decides he wants to use the single-page poster presentation, so he takes the file to a local service bureau, where he has it printed on a 4-foot sheet of glossy poster paper. The result is clear, easy to read, attractive, and professional.

Reviewing a Presentation with User Comments

Paul wants another Franklin Flyers employee, Barbara Carter, to review his presentation. For that purpose, he sets up a **review cycle**, which is a system for sending out a presentation file for others to review, having them add comments (with questions and suggestions) to the presentation, getting back the copies of the files, and reviewing the comments.

Paul recently found out that he would indeed have opportunities to give his presentation using the onscreen version. Therefore, he decides to send the file FF Onscreen to one of his colleagues, Barbara R. Carter, for review. She will look it over and add comments to the presentation. A **comment** in PowerPoint is the electronic equivalent of an adhesive note that you can "attach" to a slide. You can use comments, for example, to remind yourself to verify information in a report, but comments are most useful when multiple people are reviewing a single presentation. For example, one person might receive a copy of the presentation via e-mail, insert a comment to suggest a revision or to explain a potential problem, and then send the presentation to the next person for additional comments.

Adding Comments to a Presentation

When you insert a comment into a slide, PowerPoint identifies the comment with the name and initials of the person who made the comment and notes the date the comment was inserted. How does PowerPoint know this information? When a person edits and saves a file, PowerPoint also saves the name and initials located in the Popular section of the PowerPoint Options dialog box. You or the computer administrator entered this information during installation of Microsoft Office 2007. You'll change the name and initials to Barbara Carter's information and then insert a comment in the FF Onscreen file.

To specify the user name and initials in PowerPoint:

▶ **1.** Open the file **FF Onscreen**. This is the file you'll edit as if you were Barbara.

▶ **2.** Click the **Office Button** 🔘 , and then click **PowerPoint Options** at the bottom of the menu. The PowerPoint Options dialog box opens with Popular selected in the pane on the left. Notice the name and initials in the Personalize your copy of Microsoft Office section of the PowerPoint options dialog box. When you make changes to this section, the changes apply not only in the current presentation file, but in all Microsoft Office programs installed on your computer.

▶ **3.** Write the name and initials that appear in the User name and Initials boxes. You'll need to return to this dialog box after completing the following steps and replace Barbara's information with the current information.

▶ **4.** Select the name in the User name box, type **Barbara R. Carter**, select the text in the Initials box, and then type **BRC**. See Figure 6-27.

PowerPoint Options dialog box with Popular selected ◀ **Figure 6-27**

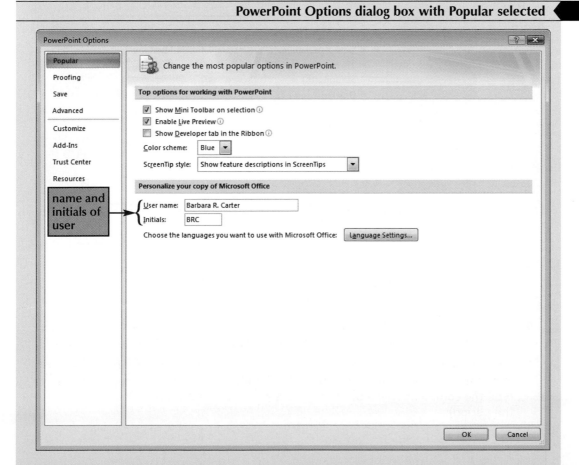

> **5.** Click the **OK** button.

From now on, as you make changes in the presentation and save the results, PowerPoint will save the new version of the file with the name Barbara R. Carter and the initials BRC. Now you'll insert comments as if you were Barbara.

To make revisions and insert comments into the presentation:

> **1.** Go to **Slide 3**, and then click after the second bulleted item on the slide. You'll add a comment about this bulleted item.

> **2.** Click the **Review** tab on the Ribbon, and in the Comments group, click the **New Comment** button. An empty comment box opens with Barbara's name, the current date, and the blinking insertion point in it. A small box containing Barbara's initials followed by the number "1" appears to the left of the comment box, indicating that this is the first comment inserted in the presentation. See Figure 6-28.

Figure 6-28	Slide 3 with inserted comment

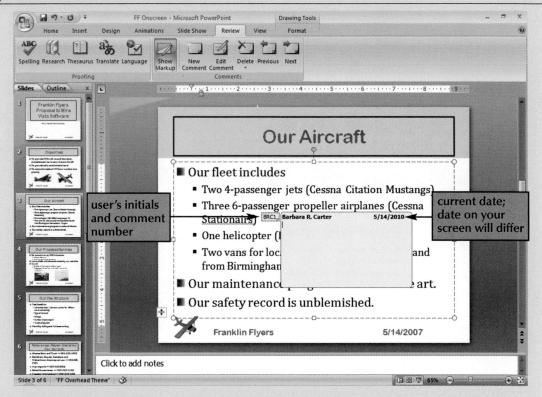

> **3.** With the insertion point in the comment box, type **Move this up to the top of the second-level bullets.** (including the period), and then click anywhere outside the comment. The comment box closes, but leaves a little rectangle labeled with "BRC1."

> **4.** Click the **BRC1** box. The comment box opens with the message that you just typed. You could now click anywhere in the comment to modify the text.

> **5.** Go to **Slide 4**, click the photograph on the right (the small aircraft above the mountain), in the Comments group, click the **New Comment** button, and then type the comment **These photos need a frame around them.** (including the period).

6. Click anywhere outside the comment box to close it. A "BRC2" rectangle appears in the slide.

7. Go to **Slide 6**, click to the right of the phone number for Global Humanitarian in the bulleted list, insert a new comment with the text **Please add Fracasso International. They are high on our service.** (including the periods), and then deselect the comment box. A "BRC3" rectangle appears in the slide. Now you need to change the user information back.

8. Click the **Office Button**, click **PowerPoint Options** at the bottom of the menu, replace Barbara's name and initials in the User name and Initials boxes with the name and initials that were there originally, and then click the **OK** button.

9. Save the presentation using the new filename **FF Onscreen-B** to the Tutorial.06\Tutorial folder.

Sometimes it's easier to review comments when they are printed. You'll do this next.

Printing Comment Pages

In order to print comments in a presentation, you need to make sure the Print comments and ink markup check box in the Print dialog box is selected. This causes any comments in the presentation to print on a separate page. You'll print the comments that Barbara inserted now.

To print a presentation with comments:

1. Click the **Office Button**, and then click **Print**. The Print dialog box opens. You want to print only the slides that contain comments.

2. In the Print range section, click the **Slides** option button, and then type **3,4,6** in the Slides box.

3. Click the **Print what** arrow, click **Handouts**, in the Handouts section, click the **Slides per page** arrow, and then click **3**. Now the three slides will print on a single page.

4. Make sure the **Print comments and ink markup** check box is selected, and then click the **OK** button. PowerPoint prints the slides as three miniatures on a page and prints a separate page with the three comments.

To complete a review cycle, you need to review the comments and then make any changes you feel are necessary to the presentation. You'll do this next.

Reviewing Comments, Editing Text, and Using the Format Painter

To review comments in a presentation, you can scroll through the presentation and click the comment boxes in the slides, or you can click the Next button in the Comments group on the Review tab of the Ribbon. After you read each comment, you can leave the comment in the document or delete it using the Delete button in the Comments group, so the comments don't appear in the final presentation. You can also hide the comments by using the Show Markup button, which is a toggle switch that hides or unhides the comments. If you decide to leave comments in a presentation, they will not appear in the slide show, even if you did not hide the comments in Normal view.

To review the comments and revise the presentation:

▶ 1. Go to **Slide 1**. Usually, when you review a presentation after another person has added comments, you'll want to start at the beginning.

▶ 2. If necessary, click the **Review** tab on the Ribbon, and in the Comments group, click the **Next** button. PowerPoint jumps to Slide 3, the location of Barbara's first comment and opens the comment box. After you read the comment, you delete it so that your final presentation contains no comments or revision markers.

▶ 3. In the Comments group, click the **Delete** button. In this case, Paul decides to delete the comment but to take Barbara's suggestion.

▶ 4. Drag the pointer over all the text of the second subbulleted item, click the **Home** tab, in the Clipboard group, click the **Cut** button ✂ to cut the text and move it to the Clipboard, position the insertion point at the beginning of the first subbulleted item (which begins, "Two 4-passenger jets"), and then, in the Clipboard group, click the **Paste** button. The text is pasted in the new location.

▶ 5. Click the **Review** tab, and then, in the Comments group, click the **Next** button. PowerPoint jumps to Slide 4, and displays the comment on that slide. Leave this comment in the presentation so you have a record that Barbara reviewed it. Paul wants you to take Barbara's suggestions and add a frame to the pictures. You'll use a Picture Style to do that now.

▶ 6. Click the photo on the left (the pilot standing in front of his airplane), click the Picture Tools **Format** tab, and then in the Picture Styles group, click the **Simple Frame, White** style (the first (left-most) style).

Now you want to apply the same frame to the picture on the right, the one with the small aircraft above the mountain. But instead of using the Picture Styles gallery, you'll use the Format Painter. PowerPoint's **Format Painter** is a feature that allows you to select an object (text, graphics, or anything else), copy the formatting to the Clipboard, and then paint (or "paste") the formatting to another object. This feature is especially handy if you have applied several features or attributes to an object and want to use a shortcut to apply all the features to another object.

To use the Format Painter and continue reviewing the comments:

▶ 1. With the picture on the left still selected, click the **Home** tab, in the Clipboard group, click the **Format Painter** button, and then position the pointer over the picture on the right. The pointer changes to ▷▲

▶ 2. Click the picture on the right. The formatting that you applied to the first picture gets applied to the second picture, and the Format Painter is turned off.

▶ 3. Click the **Review** tab, and then, in the Comments group, click the **Next** button. PowerPoint jumps to Slide 6, and displays the "BRC3" comment. You'll leave this comment in the presentation also, but make the suggested change.

▶ 4. Click after the phone number of Global Humanitarian, press the **Enter** key to create a new bulleted item, type **Fracasso International**, and then press the **spacebar**.

Tip

If you need to format several objects using the Format Painter, you can double-click the Format Painter button to toggle it on. It will remain active until you click it again or press the Esc key.

In the other bulleted items, a wide dash appears between the company name and the phone number. This is an em dash, which is a large dash the width of a capital M. You'll insert this next.

Inserting Special Symbols

A **symbol** in PowerPoint is any text character, but usually we think of a symbol as a special character that we can't type from the keyboard, such an alpha (∝) or a greater-than-or-equal sign (≥). In this case, you want to insert an em dash. You can use this method to insert mathematical symbols (such as the multiplication and division signs), typographic symbols (such as a bullet, en dash, em dash, and copyright symbol), and other types of symbols. To insert a symbol, you use the Symbol dialog box. You'll insert the em dash now.

To insert an em dash:

▶ **1.** Click the **Insert** tab, and then in the Text group, click the **Symbol** button. The Symbol dialog box opens.

▶ **2.** If necessary, click the **Font** arrow at the top of the dialog box, and then click **(normal text)**. The Subset box on the right allows you to jump to categories of symbols in the list.

▶ **3.** If necessary, click the **Subset** arrow, scroll down, and then click **General Punctuation**. The list scrolls almost to the bottom, and the hyphen symbol is selected.

▶ **4.** Click the **em dash** symbol. EM DASH appears in the lower-left corner of the dialog box. See Figure 6-29.

Tip

You can also insert an em dash into PowerPoint text by typing the word that precedes the em dash, typing two hyphens (with no spaces on either side or between them), typing the word that follows the em dash, and then pressing the spacebar or typing a punctuation mark. PowerPoint automatically converts the two hyphens into a true em dash.

Symbol dialog box with em-dash symbol selected ◀ **Figure 6-29**

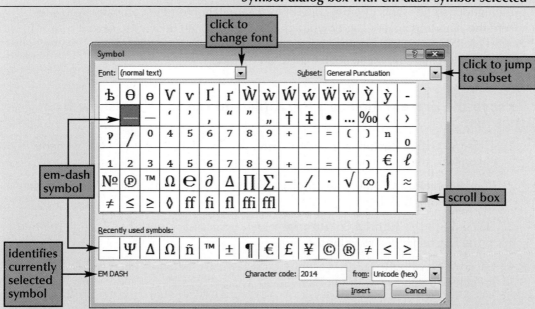

▶ **5.** Click the **Insert** button, and then click the **Close** button. The em dash is inserted into the slide at the insertion point.

▶ **6.** Press the **spacebar**, and then type **205-555-1821**.

▶ 7. Save the presentation using the default filename.

▶ 8. Submit the completed presentation in printed or electronic form, as requested by your instructor.

Now you want to replace the original FF Onscreen presentation with the modified version without the comments.

To delete the comments and save the modified presentation:

▶ 1. Click the **Review** tab, in the Comments group, click the **Delete button arrow**, and then click **Delete All Markup in this Presentation**. A dialog box opens asking if you want to delete all comments and ink annotations in the presentation.

▶ 2. Click the **Yes** button. All the comments in the presentation are deleted.

▶ 3. Click the **Office Button** (🔘), click **Save As**, navigate to the **Tutorial.06\Tutorial** folder, click **FF Onscreen** in the file list, and then click the **Save** button. A dialog box opens asking if you want to replace the existing presentation.

▶ 4. Click the **Yes** button.

Paul sends Barbara an e-mail thanking her for her comments and letting her know of the change you made in the presentation. He will make the same changes in the other versions of the presentation later, so you don't have to worry about it.

Saving a Presentation as PowerPoint Show File

Paul decides that other Franklin Flyers employees would be interested in his onscreen presentation, so he wants to put a copy of the presentation on the company Web site where the other employees can download it and view it. He decides to save it as a **PowerPoint Show (PPSX) file**, which is a file format that opens in Slide Show view when a user double-clicks the filename in an Explorer window.

To save the presentation as a PPSX file and run the slide show from that file:

▶ 1. Click the **Office Button** (🔘), point to **Save As**. The list on the right of the menu changes to display commands for saving the presentation.

▶ 2. Click **PowerPoint Show**. The Save As dialog box opens, with the Save as type set to PowerPoint Show.

▶ 3. Navigate to the **Tutorial.06\Tutorial** folder, if necessary, and then change the text in the File name box to **FF Show**.

▶ 4. Click the **Save** button. The presentation is saved as the type "Microsoft Office PowerPoint Slide Show," with the filename extension ".ppsx."

Now you'll test the PPSX file by starting it from within a folder.

▶ 5. Close the file, but leave PowerPoint running.

▶ 6. Open an Explorer window, and then navigate to the **Tutorial.06\Tutorial** folder. The file FF Show should appear in the list of files.

7. Position the pointer over the filename **FF Show**. A ScreenTip appears identifying the slide type (Microsoft Office PowerPoint Slide Show), the file size (about 143 KB), and the date modified. See Figure 6-30. Your ScreenTip might also show the author (your name or the official user of your PowerPoint program) and the title of the presentation (Franklin Flyers Proposal to Mira Vista Software).

Windows Explorer window with PowerPoint Slide Show file | Figure 6-30

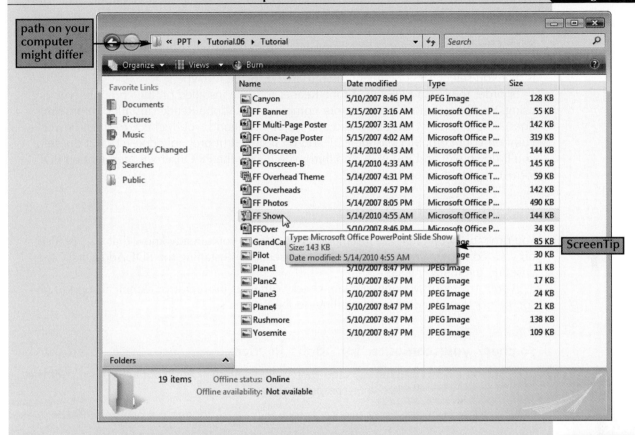

8. Double-click **FF Show**. The presentation opens in PowerPoint in Slide Show view.

9. Go through the slide show as much as you'd like, and then when you're done, press the **Esc** key. The slide show closes.

10. Close the Explorer window.

Tip

If you open a PPSX file from within PowerPoint using the Open command, the file opens in Normal view just as an ordinary presentation file would.

As you can see, when a PPSX slide show ends (at the end of the presentation or when you press the Esc key), the file automatically closes instead of returning to Normal view.

Saving a Presentation as a Portable Document File

Paul decides it would also be a good idea to publish the presentation to the Web site in **Portable Document File (PDF)** format, which is a file format that can be opened on any make or model of computer, as long as the computer has installed the free, downloadable program Adobe Reader. Because most computers have Adobe Reader installed, and any computer connected to the Internet can easily get it installed at no cost, a PDF is an important file format for sharing documents.

In order to create a PDF file from your presentation, you need to use an add-on. An **add-on** is a piece of software that adds to and enhances another program. The PDF add-on for PowerPoint is a piece of software that becomes part of PowerPoint and gives it the facility to publish presentation files in PDF format. The PDF add-on is a free download for registered Microsoft Office users.

The PowerPoint add-on that allows you to publish files in PDF format also allows you to publish a presentation as an **XPS document**, which is a Microsoft electronic paper format that you can view in your Web browser. When you double-click the filename of an XPS document in Windows Explorer, the document opens and shows a faithful reproduction of the Slide Show view of the presentation. You can publish to an XPS document using essentially the same method you use to publish in PDF format; the only exception is that you select XPS document instead of PDF as the file type.

In order to view a PDF file, Adobe Reader must be installed on the computer you are using. You'll now check to see if your computer has Adobe Reader installed (it probably does). If it doesn't, you'll download and install it. Second, you'll check to see if PowerPoint on your computer has the PDF add-on installed (it probably doesn't). If it doesn't, you'll download and install it. And third, you'll save the FF Onscreen presentation PDF format, and then open and read it.

Installing Adobe Reader

You probably won't need to install Adobe Reader. If you already know that it's installed on your computer, you can skip to the next section, "Installing the PDF Add-On." Otherwise, do the following steps.

Note: If you are working in a lab, check with your instructor or technical support person before downloading and installing Adobe Reader.

To check your computer for Adobe Reader:

▶ 1. Click the **Start Button** , and then point to or click **All Programs**. The list of the programs installed on your computer opens.

▶ 2. Scroll through the list of programs to look for an Adobe folder or Adobe Reader.

▶ 3. If you see an Adobe folder, click it. You might see "Adobe Reader" or the number of some other version.

▶ 4. Click outside the program list to deselect (close) it.

If you found Adobe Reader on your computer, skip to the next section, "Installing the PDF Add-On." If you didn't find it, you need to install it.

To install Adobe Reader:

▶ 1. Start your Web browser, and then go to the Web page **www.adobe.com**. This is the home page for the Adobe Web site.

▶ 2. Find and click the **Get Adobe Reader** button. The Adobe Web site checks your computer to determine the operating system that you're using. Be patient; this could take a couple minutes. A Web page opens with information about downloading Adobe Reader. See Figure 6-31. The Web site might look different than the one shown in the figure.

Trouble? If you don't see the Get Adobe Reader button, look for any information you can find on downloading Adobe Reader, and then click the appropriate link or button.

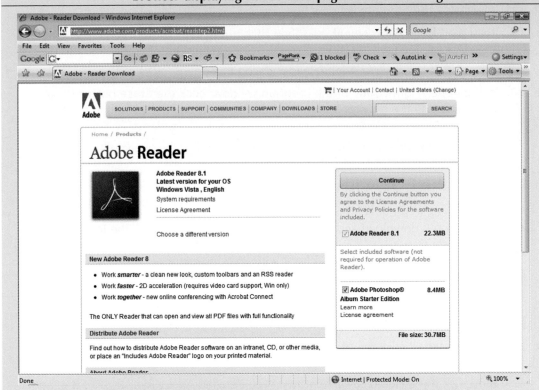

Web sites change frequently, so the exact steps you need to follow to download Adobe Reader might be different from the steps listed here. Read through the rest of the steps first, and then execute them to download the program.

▶ 3. Click the **Continue** or **Download Adobe Reader** button, depending on what appears on your Web page. You'll now probably see a message such as "Your Adobe Reader software download will start automatically."

Trouble? If you get the message that starts "This website wants to install the following add-on: 'Adobe Reader'..." located near the top of your browser, click the message, and then click Install ActiveX Control.

Trouble? If the File Download – Security Warning dialog box opens, click the Run button.

Trouble? If the User Account dialog box opens, click the Continue button.

▶ 4. Watch the dialog box that shows the progress of the download. Again, be patient as the download progresses; it may take several minutes. Other security warning dialog boxes might open, asking if you want to run the software or continue the installation.

▶ 5. Click the **Run** button, the **Continue** button, or the **Next** button for each of the dilalog boxes that appear, as needed.

Trouble? If other types of dialog boxes appear asking for permission or information, follow the instructions as required to continuing installing the software.

▶ 6. If necessary, click the **OK** button after the Abode Reader setup is complete.

▶ 7. If Adobe Reader runs automatically, close the program.

Trouble? If prompted to do so, close Windows Explorer or another program, and click the Retry button. If you have already closed all programs, but a dialog box prompts you that one still needs to be closed, click the Ignore button.

▶ **8.** If necessary, click the **Launch Adobe Reader** check box to select it, and then click the **Finish** button. Adobe Reader starts and the License Agreement opens in a window inside the program window.

▶ **9.** Read the License Agreement, and then click the **Accept** button. Now that you know Adobe Reader is installed correctly, you can close it.

Trouble? If the Beyond Adobe Reader dialog box opens, close it.

▶ **10.** In the upper-right corner of the program window, click the **Close** button ▨, and then close the browser window, if necessary.

Now your computer is set up to read any PDF file, including the one you'll soon create.

Installing the PDF Add-On

First, you'll check to see if you need to download and install the PDF add-on, and then, if necessary, you'll download and install it. You must be connected to the Internet to complete this set of steps.

Note: If you are working in a lab, check with your instructor or technical support person before downloading and installing the add-on.

To download and install the PDF Add-On:

▶ **1.** On the taskbar, click the **Microsoft PowerPoint** button, and then open the file **FF Onscreen**.

Trouble? If you closed PowerPoint when you installed Adobe Reader, start it again.

▶ **2.** Click the **Office Button** 🏠, and then point to **Save As**. The list on the right of the menu changes to display commands for saving the presentation.

▶ **3.** Look for the **PDF or XPS** command, with the subtitle, "Publish a copy of the presentation as a PDF or XPS file." If you see this command, the PDF Add-On has been installed, so skip the rest of these steps and go to the next section, "Publishing the Presentation in PDF Format." If you do not see the PDF or XPS command, the PDF Add-On has not been installed; continue to Step 4.

▶ **4.** In the list on the right side of the menu, click **Find add-ins for other file formats**. The PowerPoint Help window opens displaying the Enable support for other file formats, such as PDF and XPS page.

▶ **5.** Below "What do you want to do?", click the **Install and use the Save as PDF or XPS add-in from Microsoft** link. The window scrolls down to that section.

Trouble? This link might be named Install and use the Publish as PDF or XPS add-in from Microsoft.

▶ **6.** In the first item in the numbered list (of only two items), click the **Microsoft Save as PDF or XPS Add-in for 2007 Microsoft Office programs** link. Your browser starts and the page for that add-in on the Microsoft Download Center Web site opens in the browser window.

▶ **7.** Click the **Continue** button to validate that you are running genuine Microsoft Office.

Trouble? If your browser now gives you a warning that the Web site wants to install an add-on, the Microsoft Download Center will display instructions on how to allow the installation. Click the Information bar in your browser, and then click Install ActiveX Control.

After a few moments, the add-on is ready to install, and the Web page displays the Download button instead of the Continue button.

8. Click the **Download** button. A dialog box opens asking you if you want to run or save this file.

9. Click the **Run** button, and then, if the User Account Control dialog box opens, click the **Continue** button in that dialog box. The download process begins. Another dialog box opens with the license terms.

   Trouble? If the Internet Explorer Add-on Installer – Security Working dialog box opens, click the **Install** button.

10. Read the license terms, click the **check box** at the bottom to accept the Microsoft Software License Terms, and then click the **Continue** button. As the download proceeds, you'll see various messages to inform you of the download status. When the installation is finished, a dialog box opens telling you that the installation is complete.

11. Click the **OK** button.

12. Close your browser window, and then close the PowerPoint Help dialog box.

The PowerPoint program on your computer is now ready and able to publish files in PDF format.

Publishing the Presentation in PDF Format

Now you'll open the FF Onscreen file and publish it to a PDF.

To publish the presentation in PDF format:

1. Open **FF Onscreen** from the Tutorial.06\Tutorial folder.

2. Click the **Office Button** 🔘, point to **Save As**, and then click **PDF or XPS**. The Publish as PDF or XPS dialog box opens with PDF listed in the Save as type box.

3. Navigate to the **Tutorial.06\Tutorial** folder, if necessary.

4. Click in the **File name** text box, and then change the filename to **FF PDF**.

5. Click the **Publish** button. Your presentation is saved in PDF format, and Adobe Reader automatically opens displaying FF PDF in the window. See Figure 6-32.

Figure 6-32 ▶ **PDF document in Adobe Reader**

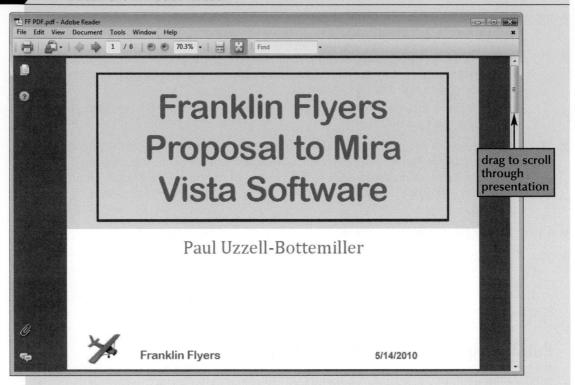

▶ **6.** Drag the scroll box in the vertical scroll bar down to see the entire presentation, one page at a time.

▶ **7.** In the upper-right corner of the window, click the **Close** button [X] to exit the Adobe Reader program.

Paul also wants to distribute his presentation to people outside the company. Before he does this, he wants to save the file as an encrypted file (with a password) and with a digital signature.

Encrypting and Adding a Digital Signature to a Presentation File

PowerPoint provides several features to help you protect your presentation files from unauthorized access or from unauthorized modification. Two of the methods are encryption and digital signature. To **encrypt** a file is to modify the data structure to make the information unreadable to unauthorized people. When you encrypt a PowerPoint presentation, you assign a password to the file. The only way to open the file for reading is by knowing the password.

A **digital signature** is an electronic attachment, not visible within the contents of the document, which verifies the authenticity of the author or the version of the document by comparing the digital signature to a digital certificate. Once a signature is added, the document is in read-only format and can't be modified. When you open a PowerPoint presentation that contains a digital signature that you haven't verified, the Signatures task pane opens to the right of the presentation window, informing you that the document contains an invalid digital signature. You can then click the warning bar and validate the signature, after which other documents with that digital signature will not be flagged as invalid.

When you digitally sign a document, the document is automatically marked as final to protect it from changes. If you remove the Mark as Final status and make any changes to the document, the signature is marked as invalid (because it is no longer the same document the signatory signed).

You'll now encrypt and add a digital signature to the FF Onscreen file.

To encrypt and add a digital signature to the presentation file:

▶ 1. Save the FF Onscreen presentation file as **FF DigSig** to the Tutorial.06\Tutorial folder. You'll first encrypt the file.

▶ 2. Click the **Office Button** 🏢, point to **Prepare**, and then click **Encrypt Document**. The Encrypt Document dialog box opens. Here you'll type a password.

▶ 3. Type **Flyer**, and then click the **OK** button. The dialog box changes to the Confirm Password dialog box.

▶ 4. Type **Flyer** again to verify the password, and then click the **OK** button again. Now, when you save the file, it will be in an encrypted format, so that it can't be opened except by a person knowing the password. (Normally, you would use a stronger password than Flyer, but for the purpose here, you'll keep it simple and easy to remember.) Now you'll add the digital signature to this file.

▶ 5. Click the **Office Button** 🏢, point to **Prepare**, and then click **Add a Digital Signature**.

▶ 6. If a dialog box opens containing an explanation of the purpose and limitations of a digital signature, read the information in the dialog box, and then click the **OK** button. Either the Get a Digital ID dialog box, as shown in Figure 6-33 opens, or the Sign dialog box, as shown in Figure 6-34 opens.

Get a Digital ID dialog box ◀ Figure 6-33

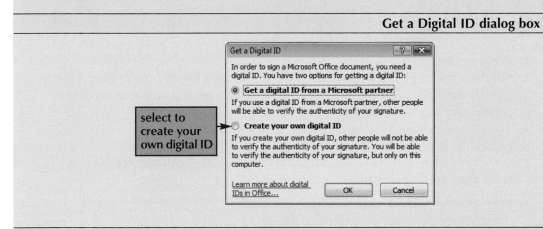

Sign dialog box ◀ Figure 6-34

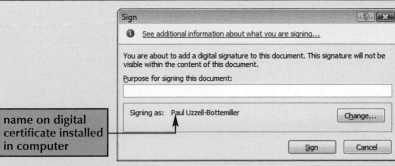

If the Get a Digital ID dialog box opens, that means that there is not a digital certificate stored on the computer you are using. You could click the Create your own digital ID option button and create your own digital certificate, but then others can't verify your digital signature, and you can verify it only on the current computer. Click the Cancel button, and then read but do not execute the rest of the steps in this section.

If the Sign dialog box opens, the insertion point is blinking in the Purpose for signing this document box. The name at the bottom is the name on the certificate issued to or created on this computer.

▶ 7. Type **Authenticate authorship**, and then click the **Sign** button.

▶ 8. If the Signature Confirmation dialog box opens, click the **OK** button. PowerPoint saves the presentation using the default filename and location, and the Signatures task pane opens listing the name on the certificate. An icon 🔏 appears in the status bar identifying the presentation as being signed.

▶ 9. Close the Signatures task pane, and then close the file.

▶ 10. If requested to do so by your instructor, submit the FF DigSig presentation in electronic form.

With the presentation now encrypted and signed, you can no longer edit it or add comments. If you do want to modify it, you have to remove Mark as Final status and invalidate the digital signature. You can also simply remove the signature by clicking the signature list arrow in the Signature pane, and then clicking Remove Signature.

Paul thanks you for all your help in making the presentation and saving it in a wide variety of formats.

Review | Session 6.2 Quick Check

1. What are the general steps required to prepare a banner using PowerPoint?
2. List three instances when you might need to prepare a poster presentation.
3. List one advantage and one disadvantage of a single-page poster over a multiple-page poster.
4. In general terms, explain the review cycle of a presentation file.
5. Define the terms "symbol" and "character spacing."
6. What is the difference between a PowerPoint presentation file (PPTX) and a PowerPoint Slide Show (PPSX) file?
7. What is the advantage of publishing a presentation in PDF format?

Tutorial Summary | Review

In this tutorial, you learned how to create a design theme, with custom layouts and with background objects, for an overhead transparency presentation. You then created and printed the overhead transparencies. You designed a new slide master layout for a photo album, with a slide title and a caption, and you created a short photo album presentation. You also created a multiple-page poster, created and printed a banner, and created a single-page poster. You learned how to insert comments into a presentation and how to review those comments. You also learned how to save a presentation as a Power-Point Show (PPSX) document, as a PDF document, and as an encrypted presentation document with a digital signature.

Key Terms

add-on
banner
character spacing
comment
custom layout
digital signature
drag-and-drop

encrypt
Format Painter
overhead transparency
Portable Document
    File (PDF)
poster presentation
PowerPoint Show
    (PPSX) file

review cycle
symbol
WordArt
XPS document

Get hands-on practice of the skills you learned in the tutorial using the same case scenario.

Data Files needed for these Review Assignments: Couple1.jpg, Couple2.jpg, FF-ASU.pptx, FF-Design.thmx, Paul.jpg, Selma.jpg

After Paul enjoyed success in his presentations at the symposium on proposals at the University of Alabama, he was invited to give a poster presentation at Alabama State University in Montgomery. This time, however, the presentation is part of a conference on successful small businesses in Alabama. He writes the first draft of the text for the presentation and asks you to help get the presentation ready for the conference. Do the following:

1. Open the file **FF-ASU** from the Tutorial.06\Review folder included with your Data Files, in the subtitle text box of Slide 1, replace Paul's name with your name, and then save the file **FF-ASU Conf** to the Tutorial.06\Review folder.
2. Apply the design theme **FF-Design**, which is located in the Tutorial.06\Review folder.
3. Insert the footer "Franklin Flyers," and display the current date so that it is updated automatically.
4. Insert a new layout into the slide masters. Copy the reddish rectangle from any of the other layouts except the Title Layout to the new layout, and then send the object to the back of all the objects.
5. In the new layout, insert a Content placeholder, 4.95 inches in height and 6.75 inches in width. Position the new Content placeholder on the left side of the big blank area in the layout, so its left edge is aligned with the left edge of the title text placeholder.
6. In the new layout, add two new Picture placeholders, set them to 2.0 by 2.0 inches in size, and position them, one above the other, in the space to the right of the Content placeholder. Align the centers of the two Picture placeholders.
7. Rename the new layout "Title, Content & Two Pictures."
8. Switch to Normal view, change the style of the title text to the WordArt style Fill – Background 1, Metal Bevel, and then change the character spacing of the title text on Slide 1 to Loose.
9. Change the layout of Slide 2 to the new Title, Content & Two Pictures layout, and then insert the picture file **Couple1**, located in the Tutorial.06\Review folder, into the upper picture placeholder, and the file **Couple2**, also located in the Tutorial.06\Review folder, into the lower one.
10. Go to Slide 6, apply the Title, Content & Two Pictures layout, and then insert the picture file **Selma**, located in the Tutorial.06\Review folder, in the upper picture placeholder and **Paul**, also located in the Tutorial.06\Review folder, in the lower one.
11. To the picture of Selma on Slide 6, apply the Picture Style called Compound Frame, Black, and then use the Picture Border button arrow in the Picture Styles group on the Picture Tools Format tab to change the color of the frame on Selma's picture to Red, Accent 2.
12. Use the Format Painter to format the other three pictures in the presentation so they have the same frame as the frame on Selma's picture.
13. Change the user name and initials in the PowerPoint Options dialog box to your own name and initials, go to Slide 4, click after the abbreviation "CEO," insert the comment **Paul, use full names on this slide.**, and then change the user name and initials in the PowerPoint Options dialog box back to their originals.

14. In Slide 4, after "Selma," insert a space, and then insert the name "Peña." To find the *n* with a tilde in the Symbol dialog box, change the Font to (normal text) and change the Subset to Latin Extended-A.

15. Copy the last name "Peña" to the Clipboard, and then paste it as the last name for Carlos.

16. After "Gretchen," type a space and the name "Uzell-Bottemiller." Select "Uzell-Bottemiller," press and hold the Ctrl key, and then drag and drop a copy of the name after "Paul."

17. Save the presentation using the current filename, and then, if directed by your instructor, print the slide with the comment on it, along with the comment. Submit the entire presentation in printed or electronic form, as requested by your instructor. Do not close the presentation.

18. Save the presentation as **FF-ASU Overhd** to the Tutorial.06\Review folder, and then modify the presentation from landscape to portrait orientation and size it for Overheads, as if you were going to use the presentation for printing overhead transparencies.

19. Reset the background object (the plane logo) to its original aspect ratio, and then recolor it using the Dark Variation called Accent color 2 Dark. Reposition the logo in the lower-left corner of the slide master.

20. Modify the Title, Content & Two Pictures custom layout so the two picture placeholders are 2 by 2 inches and positioned above the content placeholder. Adjust and position the three placeholders to make the layout master attractive.

21. Switch to Normal view, reset slides 2 and 6 if necessary, save your changes to the presentation using the current filename, and then submit the presentation in printed or electronic form, as requested by your instructor. Do not close the presentation.

22. Save the file as a design theme to the Tutorial.06\Review folder using the filename **FF OverDes**.

23. Save the file in PDF format to the Tutorial.06\Review folder using the filename **FF-ASU PDF**.

24. Save the presentation again as a PowerPoint Show to the Tutorial.06\Review folder using the filename **FF-ASU Show**.

25. Submit the completed overhead presentation in printed or electronic form, as requested by your instructor, and then close the file.

26. Create a new, blank presentation, and then apply the **FF OverDes** theme. Change the slide dimension to 36 inches wide by 8 inches high. In the slide masters, delete all the background objects except the rectangle at the top, and delete the footer, date, and slide number placeholders. In the title slide, type **Franklin Flyers: An Overview** as the title and your name as the subtitle. Save the presentation as **FF-ASU Banner**.

27. Create a new, blank presentation, and then create a one-page poster presentation using the slide from the FF-ASU Banner presentation on the top of the slide and the Brief History and Management slides from the FF-ASU Overheads presentation below the banner. Save the presentation as **FF-ASU One-Page**.

28. Save the file as **FF-ASU Encrypt**, encrypt the file using the password **FF-ASU**, and then, if a digital certificate is installed on your computer, add a digital signature to the presentation with **Authentication of authorship** as the purpose for the signature.

29. Submit the file to your instructor, in printed or electronic form as instructed.

Apply		Case Problem 1

Apply the skills you learned in this tutorial to create a presentation for a small publishing company.

Data File needed for this Case Problem: Copyrt.pptx

Ziff-Cronin Press Amiya Khashan, copyright officer for Ziff-Cronin Press, a small publishing company in St. Louis, Missouri, was recently invited to give a presentation to professors and students at Southern Missouri State University. Her presentation will be on copyright issues for students and professors, an important topic for academic work at the university level. She isn't sure if she will use a computer projector, an overhead projector, or a poster, so she asked you to help her create a version of her presentation for all of those things. Do the following:

1. Create a design theme for overhead transparencies using the following guidelines:
   a. Apply the built-in design theme titled Median.
   b. In the Title Slide Layout master, delete the footer and slide number placeholders, which are located at the top of the slide.
   c. Search for clip art using the search term "writing." Restrict the search to photographs. (If you are not connected to the Internet and cannot search for clips on Microsoft Office Online, you might not find any pieces of clip art that meet this criteria. In that case, expand the search to all types of clip art, and then change the search term to "books." Use any clip art you can find.) Position the clip art you choose above the title placeholder, near the upper-right corner of the slide. Resize it so it is an appropriate size.
   d. In the Median Slide Master layout, delete the slide number placeholder and the orange rectangle located to the left of the blue bar below the title placeholder. Insert a text box in its place, and then insert the copyright symbol, ©, in the text box. (The copyright symbol is located in the Latin-1 subset of the normal text.) Modify the font size of the symbol to 40 points and the font color to Orange, Accent 2.
   e. Copy the copyright symbol from the Median Slide Master layout to the Title Slide Layout master, change the font size of the pasted symbol on the Title Slide Layout master to 80 points, and then position it just to the left of the title placeholder.
2. Insert a new layout, and name it **Content & Three Clips**. Insert a content placeholder similar in size and location to the left placeholder in the Two Content Layout. To the right of the content layout, insert three clip-art layouts, one that is the same width 4.5 inches wide, but 2.5 inches in height. Position it to the right of the content placeholder and aligned to the tops of the two placeholders. Now insert the other two clip-art placeholders, each of which is 2.4 inches in height and 2.0 inches wide, and position them side by side below the large picture placeholder. (*Hint*: Once you create one clip-art placeholder, you can copy and paste it to create the second one.)
3. Save the modified design theme as an Office Theme with the filename **Copyrt-Design** in the Tutorial.06\Case1 folder, and then close the file without saving it.
4. Open the presentation file **Copyrt** located in the Tutorial.06\Case1 folder, apply the design theme Copyrt-Design, replace "Amiya Kashan" with your name, and then save the file in the Tutorial.06\Case1 folder using the filename **Copyrt Onscreen**.
5. Using the Header and Footer dialog box, insert the date and time to be updated automatically and the footer with the text "Copyright Principles." Apply these to all the slides.

6. In Slide 2, apply the new layout Content & Three Clips. In each of the three picture placeholders, include a clip-art photograph from Microsoft Office Online. The pictures should deal with "writing," "composing," or something related. You should match the aspect ratio of the picture to that of the placeholder, as best you can. (If you don't have access to Microsoft Office Online, do the best you can with the clip art installed on your computer.)

7. Select one of the pictures, apply the Picture Style called Simple Frame, White, and change the border color to Ice Blue, Accent 1.

⊕ **EXPLORE**

8. Apply the Offset Left picture effect from the Shadow gallery in the Picture Effects gallery.

9. Use the Format Painter to apply the same formatting effects to the other two pictures in Slide 2.

10. Also in Slide 2, select the title placeholder, which contains "What is copyright?" and change its character spacing to Very Loose.

11. Save the presentation using the default filename and location, and then submit it to your instructor in printed or electronic form, as requested. Do not close the presentation.

12. Save the file in PDF format, using the filename **Copyrt PDF**, in the Tutorial.06\Case1 folder. Submit this to your instructor in the requested format as well.

13. Modify the presentation from landscape to portrait orientation and size it for Overheads.

14. Change the background object on the title slide to its original aspect ratio. Reposition the copyright symbol, if necessary.

15. In the Content & Three Clips custom layout, change all the placeholders in size and position so that the Content placeholder is above the three clip placeholders. Use your own judgment to make sure the placeholders lead to attractive, undistorted pictures in Slide 2.

16. Change the background style for the title slide layout to plain white.

17. Reapply the modified Content & Three Clips layout to Slide 2, and then adjust the size of the clip art if necessary.

18. Save the presentation as **Copyrt Ovrhd** in the Tutorial.06\Case1 folder, submit it to your instructor in printed or electronic form, and then close the file.

19. Create a banner, 40 inches by 8 inches, based on the title slide layout of Copyrt-Design theme, with the title "What You Need to Know About Copyright," and your name as the subtitle.

20. In the slide master, remove the photograph in the background, and change the background style to plain white. Change the font size of the title text placeholder to 115 points and the subtitle placeholder to 34 points. Delete the footer and date placeholders from the title slide master.

21. Resize the title text and subtitle placeholders so they stretch across the width of the slide (leaving space for the copyright symbol to the left of the title text placeholder) and reposition them attractively on the slide. (Notice that you need to resize and reposition the colored rectangle behind the subtitle as well.) Adjust the size and position of the placeholders and the copyright symbol.

22. Save the banner to the Tutorial.06\Case1 folder using the filename **Copyrt Banner**, and then submit the completed presentation files in printed or electronic form, as requested by your instructor. Close all open files.

Challenge | **Case Problem 2**

Learn new PowerPoint skills as you modify a presentation for a medical device company.

Data Files needed for this Case Problem: Bike.jpg, Hike.jpg, RCM.pptx, RCMPic.jpg, Run.jpg

Risinger Cardio Monitoring, Inc. Vanita Risinger is the owner of Risinger Cardio Monitoring, Inc. (RCM), a company in Telluride, Colorado, that sells sports and medical heart-rate monitors and related devices. Vanita spends much of her time talking to coaches, physical therapists, cardiologists, and other health professionals who prescribe heart-rate monitors for their athletes or patients. However, Vanita decided to rent space and set up a booth at the 2010 Sports and Fitness Expo held in conjunction with the Boston Marathon. Her exposition booth will display not only RCM products designed for professional and recreational athletes, but also include a one-page poster presentation giving information about her company. She has asked you to help prepare the PowerPoint presentation. Do the following:

1. Open the file **RCM** from the Tutorial.06\Case2 folder, change the name in the subtitle of Slide 1 to your name, and save the file back to the same folder as **RCM Poster**.
2. Apply the Urban built-in design theme.
3. In Slide 2, change the slide layout to Two Content, and into the content placeholder on the right, insert the picture **RCMPic** from Tutorial.06\Case2 folder.
4. In Slide Master view, insert a new layout, rename it to **Three Columns**, and insert three, side-by-side, equal-sized, evenly spaced, text placeholders. (*Hint*: Make each placeholder 4.5 inches in height and 2.8 inches in width.)

⊕ EXPLORE 5. Go to Slide 3, apply the Three Columns layout, and then divide the items of the bulleted list among the three text placeholders by dragging and dropping the bottom seven bulleted items into the last column, and then the new bottom seven bulleted items into the middle column.

6. In Slide 3, in the last bulleted item, delete "plus/minus" and insert the mathematical symbol for plus/minus, so that the bullet item reads "Off-pace (±) differential."
7. In Slide 4, apply the WordArt style called Gradient Fill – Accent 6, Inner Shadow to the title text. Center the WordArt text in the title placeholder.

⊕ EXPLORE 8. To the title in Slide 4, apply the Text Effect called Perspective Above, located in the 3-D Rotation group of the Text Effects gallery. (*Hint*: Use the Text Effects button in the WordArt Styles group on the Drawing Tools Format tab.)

⊕ EXPLORE 9. To the title in Slide 4, apply the Shape Fill color Gray-25%, Background 2. (*Hint*: Use the Shape Fill button in the Shape Styles group on the Drawing Tools Format tab.)

⊕ EXPLORE 10. Finally, to the title in Slide 4, change the title placeholder to have rounded corners. (*Hint*: In the Insert Shapes group on the Drawing Tools Format tab, click the Edit Shape button, point to Change shape, and click the Rounded Rectangle button.)

11. Use the Format Painter to apply all the same formatting to the title placeholder in Slide 5 as you did in Slide 4. If the Format Painter doesn't apply all the features, apply those separately. (*Hint*: Only one feature doesn't get applied by the Format Painter.)

⊕ EXPLORE 12. In Slide 5, insert the picture **Run** into cell A2 (to the left of "Running" in B2), the picture **Bike** into cell A3 (to the left of "Cycling" in B3), and the picture **Hike** in cell A3 (to the left of "Hiking" in A4). (*Hint*: You can't use the Insert Picture command that you're familiar with. Instead, click the Table Tools Design tab; in the Table Styles group, click the Shading button arrow, and then click Picture.)

⊕ EXPLORE 13. Change the dimensions of the cells A2, A3, and A4, so that the pictures in those cells have a proper aspect ratio. (*Hint*: With the table selected, drag the bottom center of the table, where four little dots appear, downward to expand the row heights. Click just above the A column to select the entire column, and then in the Cell Size group on the Table Tools Layout tab, click the down arrow in the Table Column Width text box to reduce the width. As you click, watch the pictures in the cells until they look about right.)

14. Drag the table so it's centered in the blank area of the slide below the slide title.

15. Save the presentation using its default filename (RCM Poster) and location (Tutorial.06\Case2).

16. Save the presentation in PDF format to the Tutorial.06\Case2 folder, using the file-name **RCM PDF**.

17. Save the presentation as a PowerPoint Show (PPSX) file into the same folder, using the filename **RCM Show**.

⊕ EXPLORE 18. Create a 36-inch-by-8-inch banner by modifying the current presentation. Include the picture from Slide 2. (*Hint*: Use a cut-and-paste operation to copy the figure in Slide 2 to Slide 1. Delete all the slides except Slide 1. Change the Page Setup for a banner.)

19. In the banner, move the placeholders to the right to leave room on the left for the picture; reset and then resize the picture, and then move the picture to the left of the text. The picture should now span the dark gray and the white portions of the banner. Change the white in the picture to transparent.

20. Save the banner as a PowerPoint presentation file using the filename **RCM Banner**.

21. Submit the completed files in printed or electronic form, as requested by your instructor, and then close all open files.

| Create | **Case Problem 3** |

Create a new presentation about a ferry boat manufacturing company.

Data Files needed for this Case Problem: Ferry3a.jpg, Ferry3b.jpg, Ferry3c.jpg, Ferry3d.jpg, Ferry4.jpg, Ferry5.jpg, Ferry6.jpg, HMS Text.pptx

Hunsaker Marine Services (HMS) Seymour Zaccari is marketing manager for Hunsaker Marine Services (HMS) in Vancouver, British Columbia. His company manufactures and services ferry boats. As part of his marketing effort, Seymour is giving a presentation at the International Waterway Transportation Exposition being held in Sydney, Australia. He will make several types of presentations for the exposition, with the aid of his co-workers. He has asked you to help him prepare an overhead presentation that gives an overview of his company. The presentation you'll prepare appears in Figure 6-35.

Figure 6-35

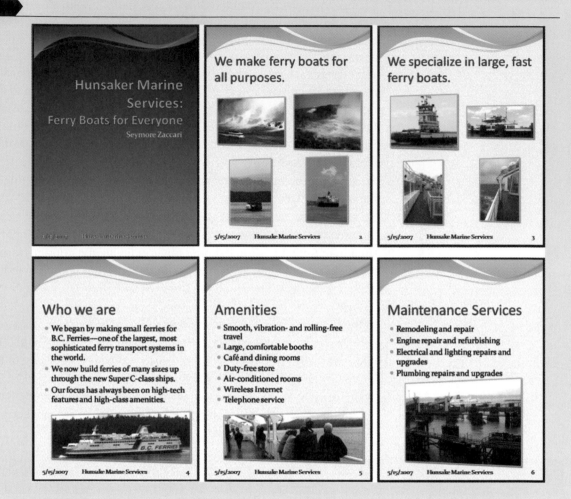

The following information will help you create the slide show. Read all the steps before you start creating your presentation. You'll have to do more than just these steps to complete the assignment to make your presentation look like Figure 6-35.

1. The presentation text is found in the file **HMS Text**, located in the Tutorial.06\Case3 folder included with your Data Files. In slide 1, change the subtitle to your name.

2. The design theme is the built-in theme called Flow.

3. The footer placeholder on the slide master is 4.2 inches wide.

4. The theme has two custom layouts, one called Four Contents and the other called Content Over Picture. The dimensions of the placeholders in your presentation should be close to those shown in Figure 6-35, but they don't need to be exact.

5. The date, footer, and slide number text are included on all slides, including the first one.

6. Slide 2 has the Four Contents layout applied, and then the photo in each of the content placeholders came from the clip art on Office Online. The picture style Simple Frame, Black was applied to one picture; the color of the picture border was then changed to Turquoise, Accent 3; the Picture Effects from the 3-D Rotation gallery is Perspective Left. The Format Painter was then used to copy the picture format to the other three pictures.

7. Slide 3 also has the Four Contents layout applied. The four photos in the slide are files **Ferry3a** through **Ferry3d** located in the Tutorial.06\Case3 folder included with your Data Files. They have the same attributes as the pictures in Slide 2.

8. Slide 4 has the Content Over Picture layout applied. The first bulleted item in the slide includes an em-dash symbol (which is just a hyphen in HMS Text, so you'll have to change it). The photo at the bottom of the slide is **Ferry4** from the Tutorial.06\Case3 folder. The picture at the bottom has the same attributes as the pictures on Slides 2 and 3.

9. Slide 5 has the same layout and format as Slide 4, except that the picture is **Ferry5**.

10. Slide 6 also has the same layout and format as Slide 4, except that the picture, **Ferry6**, was reset to its original aspect ratio and then enlarged.

11. Save the presentation as **HMS Overheads** in the Tutorial.06\Case3 folder.

12. Save the presentation in PDF format using the filename **HMS PDF** in the Tutorial.06\Case3 folder.

13. Save the presentation as a PowerPoint Slide Show file, using the filename **HMS Show**.

14. Make an attractive banner that matches the design of the presentation, and save the banner using the filename **HMS Banner** in the Tutorial.06\Case3 folder.

15. Open the **HMS Overheads** presentation file, and then save it as **HMS Encrypt**. Encrypt the file with the password **Ferry**, add a digital signature (if it is installed on your computer), and then save the file as **HMS Encrypt**. Encrpyt the file with the password Ferry, and a digital signature (if it installed on your computer), and then close the file.

16. Submit the completed presentation in printed or electronic form, as requested by your instructor, and then close all open files.

| Research | **Case Problem 4** |

Use the Internet and other resources to collect information about funding a startup company.

There are no Data Files needed for this Case Problem.

Venture Capital Funding of Startup Companies Entrepreneurs usually have to work hard to find funding for their ideas. How do they get funding? To whom do they pitch their ideas? What kind of information has to be included in a proposal to get venture capital? To answer these questions, you might want to start with the description of "venture capital," "startup company," and "entrepreneur" in Wikipedia, and then look up these topics using Google and other search engines on the Internet. Your task is to prepare a presentation for your classmates or for young entrepreneurs on how to get funding to start a company based on new ideas or inventions. Do the following:

1. Do the necessary research to gather information on venture capital funding of startup companies for your presentation. You can keep your presentation general, you can discuss a specific type of company, or you can discuss a case history of a specific company and its pursuit for funds. You might want to talk to a successful entrepreneur, or talk to an instructor in the business school at your college or university on entrepreneurship. (Most universities have classes on the subject.)

2. Start a new PowerPoint presentation, apply an appropriate built-in or custom design theme, and then change the page setup to portrait, overhead format.

3. Create at least one custom layout, and apply that layout to at least two slides using that custom layout.

4. Insert one or more background objects into the slide master. The objects can be built-in shapes or pictures, or a combination of both.

5. In Slide 1, include a descriptive name for your presentation, your name, course, section, and school name.

6. Prepare at least six other slides of information.

7. Include at least three graphics (photographs that you have taken, photo clip art, or other) in your presentation.

8. Include a least one title placeholder or text box that is formatted with WordArt, and has special Text Effects applied to it.

9. Insert at least one special symbol in your presentation. Examples of common special symbols for this type of presentation include the em dash, the greater-than-or-equal sign, the symbol for British pound or Japanese yen, and the symbols for fractions like ½ or ¾. If you insert a number with a minus sign, use an en dash or a true minus sign symbol, not a hyphen.

10. Save your presentation using the filename **Venture**.

11. Exchange (via e-mail or USB flash drive) your presentation with one of your fellow students, and insert at least two comments to the other person's presentation and get at least two comments on yours. Review the comments the other student inserted in your presentation. Don't delete the comments, but make any desired or necessary revisions based on the comments.

12. Save the final version of your presentation, with the comments, using the default filename.

13. Save another copy of your presentation encrypted with the password **Venture** and with a digital signature (if a digital signature is installed on your computer), using the filename **Venture Encrypt**.

14. Save another copy of your presentation in PDF format using the filename **Venture PDF**.

15. Submit the completed presentation in printed or electronic form, as requested by your instructor, and then close all open files.

Research | **Internet Assignments**

Go to the Web to find information you can use to create presentations.

The purpose of the Internet Assignments is to challenge you to find information on the Internet that you can use to work effectively with this software. The actual assignments are updated and maintained on the Course Technology Web site. Log on to the Internet and use your Web browser to go to the Student Online Companion for New Perspectives Office 2007 at **www.course.com/np/office2007**. Then navigate to the Internet Assignments for this tutorial.

Assess | **SAM Assessment and Training**

If you have a SAM user profile, you may have access to hands-on instruction, practice, and assessment of the skills covered in this tutorial. Log in to your SAM account (**http://sam2007.course.com**) to launch any assigned training activities or exams that relate to the skills covered in this tutorial.

Review | **Quick Check Answers**

Session 6.1

1. Advantages: (a) The room can stay lighter, (b) you can more easily face the audience, (c) most classrooms and conference rooms come equipped with overhead projectors, and (d) overhead projectors tend to be more reliable.
2. a feature that allows you to adjust the space between characters in text
3. True.
4. In the Page Setup group on the Design tab, click the Page Setup button, and in the Orientation section of the Page Setup dialog box, click Portrait option button.
5. In Slide Master view, in the Edit Master group, click the Insert Layout button, and then insert placeholders, as desired.
6. In Slide Master view, in the Master Layout group, click the Insert Placeholder button, and then click Picture.

Session 6.2

1. In the Page Setup dialog box, set up the page for banners, and then if desired, change the page width and height (which changes the page setup to Custom).
2. professional meetings, academic meetings, and informal meetings
3. Advantages: easy to set up, looks professional. Disadvantages: expensive, takes longer to prepare, cumbersome to carry
4. Complete the presentation, e-mail it to a reviewer, have the reviewer add comments and send it back to you, open the reviewed presentation, click the Review button, and move from one comment to the other, making edits as needed.
5. A symbol is any text character, but usually we think of a symbol as a special character that we can't type from the keyboard. Character spacing is a feature that allows you to adjust the space between characters in text.
6. A PPTX usually opens in Normal view or Slide Sorter view, and usually allows the person who opens it to edit it. A PPSX file, when you open it, immediately goes into Slide Show view, and when you stop the slide show, it closes out of PowerPoint.
7. PDF form allows anyone who has the Adobe Reader to view the presentation without opening or even having PowerPoint installed.

Ending Data Files

Tutorial

FF Banner.pptx
FF DigSig.ppts
FF Multi-Page
Poster.pptx
FF One-Page
Poster.pptx
FF Onscreen.pptx
FF Overhead Theme.thmx
FF Overheads.pptx

Review

FF OverDes.thmx
FF-ASU Banner.pptx
FF-ASU Conf.pptx
FF-ASU Encrypt.pptx
FF-ASU One-Page.pptx
FF-ASU Overhd.pptx
FF-ASU PDF.pdf
FF-ASU Show.ppsx

Case1

Copyrt Banner.pptx
Copyrt Onscreen.pptx
Copyrt Ovrhd.pptx
Copyrt PDF.pdf
Copyrt-Design.thmx

Case2

RCM Banner.pptx
RCM PDF.pdf
RCM Poster.pptx
RCM Show.ppsx

Case3

HMS Banner.pptx
HMS Encrypt.pptx
HMS Overheads.pptx
HMS PDF.pdf
HMS Show.ppsx

Case4

Venture.pptx
Venture
Encrypt.pptx
Venture PDF.pdf

Reality Check

If you're like many students, you have participated in an internship, a mentored research project, a senior project (sometimes called a capstone project), an honors thesis, or a similar type of experience. Many of these types of experiences require a formal presentation as part of the requirement. For example, some colleges and universities hold conferences on undergraduate research at which students present their research or creative works. Most honors students have to give a presentation on and defend their thesis in front of a faculty committee. In this exercise, you'll use PowerPoint to create a presentation that will contain information of your choice, using the PowerPoint skills and features presented in Tutorials 1 through 6.

Note: Please be sure *not* to include any personal information of a sensitive nature in the documents you create to be submitted to your instructor for this exercise. Later on, you can update the documents with such information for your own personal use.

1. Visit members of your department or talk to your mentor to see various presentations by other students or faculty so that you know the standards and customs of presentation in your discipline.
2. Start a new PowerPoint presentation using the theme of your choice.
3. Create a new set of theme colors, and give it an appropriate name.
4. Using your theme colors, create an attractive, tasteful design theme using slide masters. If you need to create slides with special formats, create one or more custom layouts. Save the file as an Office Theme using an appropriate filename.
5. Start a new presentation and apply the ProfTheme.
6. On Slide 1, give an informative title to your presentation. For example, if you did a research project in art history, you should use a specific, detailed title such as "The Influence of the Friendship and Rivalry between Picasso and Matisse on the Development of 21st Century Modern Art." Include not only your name, but your department and your mentor's name in the subtitle.
7. Create at least six slides (not counting the title slide) with information about your project. Include at least one slide on each of the introduction, methodologies, results, discussion, and summary, if applicable to your project.
8. Include at least four graphics or tables. Sample graphics might include pictures of your experimental setup, graphs of trends, and a picture of your research group. Sample tables may include data gathered or computer-generated statistics.
9. Apply an attractive style and custom animations to your graphical objects.
10. Apply slide transitions to all the slides in the presentation.
11. Apply a picture background to at least one of your slides.
12. Include a footer and a slide number on each slide except the first (title) slide if you're using an onscreen presentation.
13. Send your presentation to your mentor or to a fellow student, and ask that person to insert comments with suggestions and questions. Review the comments, edit the presentation based on the comments, and then delete the comments.
14. Prepare a one-page or a multiple-page poster, if your presentation is a poster presentation.
15. Save the presentation with an appropriate name.

16. Save the presentation first in PDF format, then in PowerPoint Slide Show format, and finally encrypted (with a password) and with a digital signature.

17. Submit the completed presentations in printed or electronic form, as requested by your instructor, and then close the file.

18. Give the presentation to your class or at some other venue, as the opportunity presents itself.

Creating a Presentation About Automobile Dealerships

Case | George Clark Auto Group

George Clark owns a chain of automobile dealerships, the George Clark Auto Group, in Lubbock, Texas. He sells most types of vehicles—passenger cars, trucks, sport utility vehicles, and so forth—and most makes of vehicles, both foreign and domestic. He asks you to prepare a self-running (kiosk) presentation for his dealerships. Complete the following:

1. Select a make of automobile, any make (or model) that you desire, and do necessary research on that make. You probably want to choose a make with which you are most familiar. You might want to check print or online advertisement for automobiles and for automobile dealerships. You might even want to visit a dealership and to take pictures.

2. Complete a Purpose and Outcome Worksheet for your presentation.

3. Complete an Audience Analysis Worksheet for your presentation. Keep in mind that your audience will be prospective automobile buyers.

4. Complete a Situation and Media Assessment Worksheet for your presentation. Keep in mind that the situation will be a self-running presentation in an automobile dealership.

5. Using the information you glean from your research, prepare the text portion of a PowerPoint presentation with at least six slides, including the title slide (with any title you want, but with your name in the subtitle), contents slide, introduction slide, and a contact information slide. The contact information is George Clark, 1010 Texas Avenue, Lubbock, Texas 79457, 806-555-7757, www.georgeclarkcars.com.

6. Complete a Focus and Organization Worksheet to determine an appropriate organizational pattern for your presentation, and organize the text in your presentation accordingly.

7. Create an advance organizer or overview (as part of the introduction slide) for your presentation.

8. Change the title text on the title slide using WordArt.

9. In the Contents slide, create hyperlinks from each of the items to the subsequent slides in the presentation, and include a Home action button on all the other slides with a hyperlink back to the contents slide.

Objectives

- Complete a Purpose and Outcomes Worksheet
- Complete an Audience Analysis Worksheet
- Complete a Situation and Media Assessment Worksheet
- Complete a Focus and Organization Worksheet
- Create an advance organizer for your presentation
- Add WordArt
- Create hyperlinks to slides
- Create action buttons
- Insert pictures and clip art and apply picture styles
- Insert a background object
- Animate bulleted lists with progressive disclosure
- Add slide transitions
- Add animation effects with sounds
- Create a chart or diagram
- Rehearse slide timings
- Set up the presentation to be self-running and continuous

Starting Data Files

There are no starting Data Files needed for this Additional Case.

10. Include at least one picture or clip art image on each slide. You can obtain your graphics by taking digital photographs, downloading pictures from Web sites, scanning pictures from catalogues or brochures from a local auto dealership, or downloading graphics from the Microsoft Office Online website.

11. To each of your photographs, apply an appropriate Picture Style.

12. Design the presentation with attractive theme colors, insert at least one appropriate background object, and use attractive and legible font styles, colors, and sizes.

13. Set up the bulleted lists for progressive disclosure.

14. Add appropriate slide transitions and slide animation effects with built-in sounds to your presentation.

15. Include at least one graph or diagram in your presentation. For example, you might have a chart showing the number of cars (of a particular make and model) sold over the past few years, or a process diagram showing the procedure for purchasing an automobile.

16. Rehearse the timing of the slides to set the automatic timing for each slide.

17. Make the presentation a self-running, looping presentation.

18. Save the presentation using the filename Clark Autos in the AddCases folder provided with your Data Files.

19. Submit this completed presentation and all the other completed presentations in printed or electronic form, as requested by your instructor.

Ending Data Files

AddCases

Clark Autos.pptx

Objectives

- Complete a Purpose and Outcomes Worksheet
- Complete an Audience Analysis Worksheet
- Complete a Situation and Media Assessment Worksheet
- Complete a Focus and Organization Worksheet
- Create an advance organizer for your presentation
- Create a Presentation Delivery Worksheet
- Create hyperlinks to slides
- Create action buttons
- Insert pictures and apply picture styles
- Modify bullet styles
- Animate bulleted lists with progressive disclosure
- Add slide transitions
- Add animation effects with sounds
- Create a SmartArt diagram
- Save the presentation as a single-file Web page
- Save the presentation as a theme
- Save the presentation as a PowerPoint Show
- Set up the presentation to be self-running and continuous

Creating a Presentation About Family History

Case | Woodall Genealogy Services

Glenda Woodall is the sole owner and proprietor of the online genealogy company called Woodall Genealogy Services and her Web site called www. woodallgeneaologyservices.com. Glenda is a professional genealogist who helps people research their family history and who provides information and advice on her Web page. She asks you to help her create a PowerPoint presentation about genealogy. She want to give the presentation at genealogy seminars and to potential subscribers to her Web site, so you'll create both an onscreen and a Web version of your presentation. Do the following:

1. Search the Internet of consult books in your library about genealogy. Pick a particular topic that interests you. You topic might be an broad overview of the field of genealogy or an overview of such aspects of genealogy as research, software, databases (for example, census records) or Web sites, or you might want to review a specific software product or Web site. You might want to visit a branch of the local genealogical society or talk to a genealogist to get ideas.

2. Complete a Purpose and Outcome Worksheet for your presentation.

3. Complete an Audience Analysis Worksheet for your presentation. Keep in mind that your audience will be current or prospective genealogists.

4. Complete a Situation and Media Assessment Worksheet for your presentation. Keep in mind that the situation will be an onscreen presentation to be given in homes, libraries, churches, and classrooms.

5. Using the information you glean from your research, prepare the text portion of a PowerPoint presentation with at least six slides, including the title slide (with any title you want but with your name in the subtitle), contents slide, introduction slide, and contact information slide. The contact information is Glenda Woodall, Woodall Genealogy Services, 9190 Dorrance Street, Providence, RI 02903, 401-555-4217.

6. Complete a Focus and Organization Worksheet to determine an appropriate organizational pattern for your presentation, and organize the text in your presentation accordingly.

Starting Data Files

There are no starting Data Files needed for this Additional Case.

7. Create an advance organizer or overview (as part of the introduction slide) for your presentation.

8. Using the Presentation Delivery Worksheet, decide on an appropriate presentation style.

9. In the Contents slide, create hyperlinks from each of the items to the subsequent slides in the presentation.

10. Include a Home action button, a Previous action button, and a Next action button on all the other slides with appropriate hyperlinks.

11. Include at least three photographs in your presentation. You can obtain your graphics by taking digital photographs, downloading pictures from Web sites, scanning pictures from your own family history or from someone else's, or downloading graphics from the Microsoft Office Online website.

12. To each of your photographs, apply an appropriate Picture Style.

13. Design the presentation with an attractive theme colors, apply appropriate background objects (at least one), and use attractive and legible font styles, font colors, and font sizes. Use your creativity to give your presentation the look and feel of something old or historical, maybe adjusting your pictures to a sepia or brown color.

14. Select picture bullets for the bulleted lists and set them up lists for progressive disclosure.

15. Add appropriate slide transitions and slide animation effects with built-in sounds to your presentation.

16. Include at least one SmartArt diagram in your presentation. For example, you might include an organization chart of the local genealogical society or club, or a process diagram showing how to search for ancestors.

17. Save the presentation using the filename Genealogy.

18. Save the presentation as a single-file Web page, using the filename GenWeb.

19. Save the presentation as a design theme, using the filename GenDesign.

20. Save the presentation as a PowerPoint Show file (PPSX), with the filename GenShow.

21. Submit this completed presentation and all the other completed presentations in printed or electronic form, as requested by your instructor.

Ending Data Files

AddCases

GenDesign.thmx
Genelogy.pptx
GenShow.ppsx
GenWeb.mht

Glossary/Index

Note: Boldface entries include definitions.

Task Reference

TASK	PAGE #	RECOMMENDED METHOD
Action button, add	PPT 186	*See* Reference Window: Adding an Action Button as a Link to Another Presentation
Animation, apply	PPT 129	*See* Reference Window: Applying an Animation
Background, set style of	PPT 98	Click Design tab, click Background Styles button, click desired style (or click Format Background and create a custom background)
Background, set to picture	PPT 99	Click Design tab, click Background Styles button, click desired style (or click Format Background and create a custom background)
Background, textured, apply to slide	PPT 107	*See* Reference Window: Applying a Textured Background
Banner, create	PPT 300	*See* Reference Window: Creating a Banner with PowerPoint
Bitmapped image, insert on slide	PPT 51	*See* Reference Window: Inserting a Bitmapped Image on a Slide
Bullets, change style	PPT 102	Click next to bullet (or select bulleted text box), click Home tab, click Bullets button arrow, click desired bullet style
Bullets, change to picture	PPT 102	Click next to bullet (or select bulleted text box), click Home tab, click Bullets button arrow, click Bullets and Numbering, click Picture button, click the desired picture, click OK, click OK
Callout, add	PPT 243	Click Insert tab, click Shapes button in Illustrations group, click icon in Callouts section, click pointer where you want callout, drag adjustment handles and callout text box to position callout
CD, play during slide show	PPT 254	*See* Reference Window: Playing a CD Track While Showing a Slide
Character spacing, set	PPT 276	Select text, click Character Spacing button in Font group on Home tab, click desired character spacing
Chart, create	PPT 113	*See* Reference Window: Creating a Chart (Graph)
Clip art, insert	PPT 46	*See* Reference Window: Inserting Clip Art on a Slide
Clip art, recolor	PPT 50	Click clip art image, click Format tab, click Recolor button in Adjust group, click desired color
Clip art, resize	PPT 48	Click clip art, drag sizing handle
Clips, download from Microsoft Office Online	PPT 230	*See* Reference Window: Downloading Clips from Microsoft Office Online
Comment, add	PPT 310	Click Review tab, position insertion point where you want comment, click New Comment in Comments group, type comment
Comments, review	PPT 312	Click Review tab, click Next button in Comments group, read comment, click Delete button or Next button in Comments group
Compressed files, extract	FM 18	Right-click compressed folder, click Extract All, select location, click Extract
Compressed folder, create	FM 17	Right-click a blank area of a folder window, point to New, click Compressed (zipped) Folder
Custom Layout, insert	PPT 282	Click View tab, click Slide Master button, click Insert Layout button in Edit Master group, click Insert Placeholder in Master Layout group, select type of placeholder, draw placeholder on new layout
Custom show, create	PPT 261	Click Slide Show tab, click Custom Slide Show button, click Custom Shows, click New, type name of custom show in Slide show name box, select desired slides, click Add, use up or down arrow to change order of slides, click OK

TASK	PAGE #	RECOMMENDED METHOD
Cycle Diagram, create	PPT 220	Type the items as bulleted list, click anywhere in the list, click Convert to SmartArt Graphic in the Paragraph group on the Home tab, click More SmartArt Graphics, click Cycle in left pane, click a cycle diagram icon in gallery, click OK
Diagram, convert item to	PPT 68–69	In Paragraph group on Home tab, click [icon], click More SmartArt Graphics, click diagram type, click diagram icon, click OK
Digital signature, add	PPT 321	Click [icon], point to Prepare, click Add a Digital Signature, click OK if necessary, type purpose for signing, click OK
Document, inspect	PPT 200	Click [icon], point to Prepare, click Inspect Document, click Inspect, read inspection report, click Close
File, close	OFF 21	Click [icon], click Close
File, copy	FM 14	*See* Reference Window: Copying a File or Folder
File, delete	FM 16	Right-click the file, click Delete
File, move	FM 12	*See* Reference Window: Moving a File or Folder
File, open	OFF 22	*See* Reference Window: Opening an Existing File or Creating a New File
File, print	OFF 27	*See* Reference Window: Printing a File
File, rename	FM 16	Right-click the file, click Rename, type the new name, press Enter
File, save	OFF 18	*See* Reference Window: Saving a File
File, switch between open	OFF 5	Click the taskbar button for the file you want to make active
Files, compress	FM 17	Drag files into a compressed folder
Folder or drive contents, view in Windows Explorer	FM 7–8	Click [icon]
Folder, copy	FM 14	*See* Reference Window: Copying a File or Folder
Folder, create	FM 11	*See* Reference Window: Creating a Folder
Folder, move	FM 12	*See* Reference Window: Moving a File or Folder
Folder, rename	FM 16	Right-click the folder, click Rename, type the new name, press Enter
Font, change	PPT 101	Select text or text holder, click Home tab, click Font button arrow, click desired font style, click Font Size button arrow, click desired size, click Font Color button arrow, click desired color
Font color, modify	PPT 57	Right-click edge of text box, click [icon] on Mini toolbar, click color
Footer, create	PPT 62	Click Insert tab, click Header & Footer button in Text group, select Footer, click in Footer text box, type text, click Apply to All
Format Painter, format objects with	PPT 312	Click object whose format you want to transfer to another object, click Format Painter button in Clipboard group on Home tab, click object you want to format
Graph, create	PPT 113	*See* Chart, create
Grayscale, preview presentation in	PPT 29	Click [icon], point to Print, click Print Preview, on the Print Preview tab, click Options button in Print group, point to Color/Grayscale, click Grayscale
Gridlines, set up	PPT 248	Click View tab, click Gridlines check box in Show/Hide group, right-click in slide pane, click Grid and Guides, click in the Spacing text box, type desired grid spacing, select other options as desired, click OK
Handouts, customize	PPT 191–192	Click View tab, click Handout Master, edit handout master slide, click Close Master View button

TASK	PAGE #	RECOMMENDED METHOD
Handouts, print	PPT 30	Click (icon), point to Print, click Print Preview, on the Print Preview tab, click Print What arrow in Page Setup group, click Handouts (4 Slides Per Page), click Print button
Help task pane, use	OFF 24	*See* Reference Window: Getting Help
Hyperlink, create	PPT 178	Select the object to which you want to apply the hyperlink, click Insert tab, click Hyperlink button in Links group, select the target of the hyperlink, click OK
Information rights, manage	PPT 203	*See* Reference Window: Using the Information Rights Manager
Kiosk browsing, apply	PPT 260	Click Slide Show tab, click Set Up Slide Show button in Set Up group, click Browsed at a kiosk (full screen) option button, click OK
Layout, slide, change	PPT 47	In Slides group on Home tab, click Layout, click a layout
Master, slide or title, modify	PPT 53	*See* Reference Window: Modifying Slide Masters
Movie, insert	PPT 111	*See* Reference Window: Inserting a Movie into a Presentation
Narration, record	PPT 254	*See* Reference Window: Recording a Narration
Notes, create	PPT 27	Click in the Notes pane, type text
Notes, print	PPT 30	Click (icon), point to Print, click Print Preview, on the Print Preview tab, click Print What arrow in Page Setup group, click Notes Pages, click Print
Numbered list, create	PPT 238	Select bulleted list placeholder, click Numbering button in Paragraph group on Home tab
Numbering, slide	PPT 62	Click Insert tab, click Header & Footer button in Text group, click Slide number
Object, copy from another presentation	PPT 169–170	Open another presentation, select object(s), click the Copy button in the Clipboard group, return to first presentation, click the Paste button in the Clipboard group
Object, custom animate	PPT 229	Select object, click Animations tab, click Custom Animation in the Animations group, click Add Effect in Custom Animation task pane, point to the type of animation, select animation effect, adjust animation options
Object (file), embed	PPT 171–172	Click Insert tab, click Object button in Text group, click Create from file option button, click Browse button, navigate to folder with file, click filename, click OK, click OK
Object (file), link	PPT 175	Click Insert tab, click Object button in Text group, click Create from file option button, click Browse button, navigate to folder with file, click file name, click OK, click Link check box, click OK
Object, resize	PPT 48	Click object, drag sizing handle
Object, rotate	PPT 73	Click object to select it, drag rotate handle with ↻
Office program, start	OFF 3	*See* Reference Window: Starting Office Programs
Online meeting, set up	PPT 199	*See* Reference Window: Setting Up an Online Meeting with Windows Meeting Space
Organization chart, create	PPT 123	*See* Reference Window: Creating an Organization Chart
Outline, export to RTF	PPT 166–167	Click (icon), click Save As, click Save as type arrow, click Outline/RTF, click Save button
Outline, import from Word document	PPT 164	Click Home tab, in the Slides group, click New Slide button arrow, click Slides from Outline, navigate to Word file, click Insert

TASK	PAGE #	RECOMMENDED METHOD
Outline, print	PPT 190	Click ⬚, point to Print, click Print Preview, click Print What arrow, click Outline View, click Print button
Outline text, demote	PPT 22	Click Outline tab, click paragraph, in Paragraph group on Home tab, click ⬚
Outline text, promote	PPT 22	Click Outline tab, click paragraph, in Paragraph group on Home tab click ⬚
Overheads, set presentation for	PPT 275	Click Design tab, click Page Setup button in Page Setup group, click Slides sized for arrow, click Overhead, click OK
PDF, save presentation as	PPT 319	Click ⬚, point to Save As, click PDF or XPS, navigate to desired folder, give file desired name, click Save
Picture, copy from slide	PPT 218	*See* Reference Window: Copying a Slide as a Picture into Another Program
Picture, insert (import)	PPT 168	Click Home tab, click Layout button in Slides group, click desired content layout, click Insert Picture from File button in content placeholder, navigate to picture file, click picture file, click Insert
Picture object, copy slide as	PPT 247	*See* Reference Window: Copying a Slide as a Picture Object
Picture style, modify	PPT 49	Click image, click Format tab, click thumbnail in Picture Styles group
Portrait, set page orientation to	PPT 275	Click Design tab, click Page Setup button in Page Setup group, click Portrait option button in Slides section, click OK
PowerPoint, exit	PPT 31	Click ⬚
PowerPoint Show (PPSX) file, create	PPT 314	Click ⬚, point to Save As, click PowerPoint Show, navigate to desired folder, give file desired name, click Save
PowerPoint, start	PPT 2	Click ⬚, click All Programs, click Microsoft Office, click Microsoft Office PowerPoint 2007
Presentation, close	PPT 8	Click ⬚, click Close
Presentation, create	PPT 43	*See* Reference Window: Creating a New Presentation
Presentation file, encrypt	PPT 321	Click ⬚, point to Prepare, click Encrypt Document, type password, type password again, click OK
Presentation, mark as final	PPT 202	Click ⬚, point to Prepare, click Mark as Final, click OK, click OK
Presentation, open	PPT 3	Click ⬚, click Open, navigate to folder, click filename, click Open
Presentation, print	PPT 30	Click ⬚, point to Print, click Print Preview, on the Print Preview tab, click Print in Print group, select options, click OK
Process Diagram, create	PPT 222	Type items as a bulleted list, click anywhere in the list, click Convert to SmartArt Graphic in Paragraph group on the Home tab, click More SmartArt Graphics, click Process in left pane, click a process diagram icon in gallery
Program, Office, exit	OFF 28	Click ⬚ on the title bar
Programs, Office, open	OFF 3	*See* Reference Window: Starting Office Programs
Programs, switch between open	OFF 5	Click the taskbar button for the program you want to make active
Progressive disclosure	PPT 129	*See* Animation, apply
Resolution, set for slide show	PPT 256	Click Slide Show tab, click Resolution in Monitors group, click desired resolution
Ruler, view (or hide)	PPT 60	Click View tab, click Ruler in Show/Hide group

TASK	PAGE #	RECOMMENDED METHOD
Shape, create	PPT 71, PPT 180	Click Insert tab, click Shapes button in Illustrations group, click desired shape, drag ╋ in slide
Slide, add new	PPT 20	In Slides group on Home tab, click New Slide button
Slide, delete	PPT 17	*See* Reference Window: Deleting Slides
Slide, go to next	PPT 4	Click ⬍
Slide, hide or unhide	PPT 138	Go to slide you want to hide, click Slide Show tab, click Hide Slide button
Slide, insert from another presentation	PPT 91	*See* Reference Window: Inserting Slides from Another Presentation
Slides, mark during slide show	PPT 136	In Slide Show view, move mouse to activate pointer, right-click screen, point to Pointer Options, click desired pen type, drag pen to mark slide
Slide, move	PPT 23	Click ⊞, drag slide to new position
Slide Master, modify	PPT 53	*See* Reference Window: Modifying Slide Masters
Slide Show, deliver on two monitors (podium mode)	PPT 142	Plug second monitor into computer, set up computer to run both monitors, click Slide Show tab, click Set Up Slide Show button, click Display slide show on arrow, click whichever monitor you want to display slide show, click Show Presenter View check box, click OK, run slide show
Slide Show, view	PPT 5	Click 🖳
Slide Sorter View, switch to	PPT 5	Click ⊞
Slide timing, rehearse	PPT 259	Switch to Slide Sorter view, click Slide Show tab, click Rehearse Timings button in Set Up group, go through slide show at desired pace, click Yes
Slide timing, set up manually	PPT 257	Switch to Slide Sorter view, click Animations tab, select one or more slides, click Automatically After check box, set the Automatically after time, repeat for all slides
Slide transitions, add	PPT 127	*See* Reference Window: Adding Slide Transitions
SmartArt diagram, animate	PPT 223	Select diagram, click Animations tab, click Animate list arrow in Animations group, click an animation type
SmartArt diagram, change orientation	PPT 222	Select diagram, click SmartArt Tools Design tab, click Right to Left button in Create Graphic group
Sound clip, insert	PPT 109	*See* Reference Window: Inserting a Sound into a Presentation
Sound clips, download and apply	PPT 230	*See* Clips, download from Microsoft Office Online
Speaker Notes, create	PPT 27	Click in the Notes Pane, type text
Spelling, check in presentation	PPT 25	Click Review tab, click Spelling in Proofing group
Symbol, insert	PPT 313	Click Insert tab, click Symbol button in Text group, select desired symbol, click Insert, click Close
Tab stop, add	PPT 60	Select text box, click View tab, click Ruler in Show/Hide group, click tab stop button, click location on ruler
Tab stop, move	PPT 60	Select text box, click View tab, click Ruler in Show/Hide group, drag tab stop to new location on ruler
Table, change style in PowerPoint	PPT 65–66	Click table, click Design tab, click table option in Table Style Options group, click style in Table Styles group
Table, create in PowerPoint	PPT 63	*See* Reference Window: Inserting a Table
Text box, add	PPT 72	Click Insert tab, click Text Box button in Text group, click ↓ in slide, type text
Text box, move	PPT 73	Click text box, drag edge (not sizing handle) of text box

TASK	PAGE #	RECOMMENDED METHOD
Text direction, set in text box	PPT 244	Select text box, click Text Direction button in Paragraph group on Home tab, select desired direction
Text effects, apply to text box	PPT 245	Select text box, click Align Text button in Paragraph group on Home tab, click More Options, select the type of text options from the left pane of the Format Text Effects dialog box, adjust options in the right pane, Click OK
Text, insert into a shape	PPT 180–181	Insert a shape (*see* Shape, insert), with shape selected, type text
Theme, apply to presentation	PPT 45	*See* Reference Window: Applying a Different Theme
Theme, create a custom	PPT 94	*See* Reference Window: Creating and Saving a Custom Theme
Theme colors, create	PPT 95	Click Design tab, click Colors button in Themes group, click Create New Theme Colors, click item button, click More Colors (as desired), select color, click OK, name theme color set, click Save
Theme colors, delete	PPT 98	Click Design tab, click Colors button, right-click theme color set, click Delete
Theme fonts, change	PPT 276	Click Design tab, click Fonts button in Themes group, click desired theme fonts
Thesaurus, use in PowerPoint	PPT 26	Click Review tab, click Thesaurus button in Proofing group
Transparent color, set in graphic	PPT 241	Select graphic, click Picture Tools Format tab, click Recolor button in Adjust group, click Set Transparent Color, and then click desired color in graphic
Transitions, slide, add	PPT 127	*See* Slide transitions, add
Web page, publish a presentation to	PPT 194	Click 🗐, click Save As, click Save as type arrow, click Single File Web Page, change options as desired, click Save button
Window, close	OFF 6	Click �－✕ or click ✕
Window, maximize	OFF 7	Click ▭ or click ▭
Window, minimize	OFF 7	Click ▭ or click —
Window, restore	OFF 7	Click ▱ or click ▱
Windows Explorer, start	FM 7	Click 🏁, click All Programs, click Accessories, click Windows Explorer
WordArt, apply to text	PPT 291	Select text, click Drawing Tools Format tab, click More button in WordArt Styles group, click desired WordArt style, modify WordArt with Text Fill, Text Outline, or Text Effects buttons in WordArt Styles group
Workspace, zoom	OFF 8	*See* Reference Window: Zooming the Workspace